Praise for the Reformation Commentary on Scripture

"Protestant reformers were fundamentally exegetes as much as theologians, yet (except for figures like Luther and Calvin) their commentaries and sermons have been neglected because these writings are not available in modern editions or languages. That makes this new series of Reformation Commentary on Scripture most welcome as a way to provide access to some of the wealth of biblical exposition of the sixteenth and seventeenth centuries. The editor's introduction explains the nature of the sources and the selection process; the intended audience of modern pastors and students of the Bible has led to a focus on theological and practical comments. Although it will be of use to students of the Reformation, this series is far from being an esoteric study of largely forgotten voices; this collection of reforming comments, comprehending every verse and provided with topical headings, will serve contemporary pastors and preachers very well."

Elsie Anne McKee, *Retired Archibald Alexander Professor of Reformation Studies and the History of Worship, Princeton Theological Seminary*

"This series provides an excellent introduction to the history of biblical exegesis in the Reformation period. The introductions are accurate, clear and informative, and the passages intelligently chosen to give the reader a good idea of methods deployed and issues at stake. It puts precritical exegesis in its context and so presents it in its correct light. Highly recommended as reference book, course book and general reading for students and all interested lay and clerical readers."

Irena Backus, *Professeure Ordinaire, Institut d'histoire de la Réformation, Université de Genève*†

"The Reformation Commentary on Scripture is a major publishing event—for those with historical interest in the founding convictions of Protestantism, but even more for those who care about understanding the Bible. As with IVP Academic's earlier Ancient Christian Commentary on Scripture, this effort brings flesh and blood to 'the communion of saints' by letting believers of our day look over the shoulders of giants from the past. By connecting the past with the present, and by doing so with the Bible at the center, the editors of this series perform a great service for the church. The series deserves the widest possible support."

Mark A. Noll, *Professor Emeritus, University of Notre Dame*

"For those who preach and teach Scripture in the church, the Reformation Commentary on Scripture is a significant publishing event. Pastors and other church leaders will find delightful surprises, challenging enigmas and edifying insights in this series, as many Reformational voices are newly translated into English. The lively conversation in these pages can ignite today's pastoral imagination for fresh and faithful expositions of Scripture."

J. Todd Billings, *Gordon H. Girod Research Professor of Reformed Theology, Western Theological Seminary*

"The reformers discerned rightly what the church desperately needed in the sixteenth century—the bold proclamation of the Word based on careful study of the sacred Scriptures. We need not only to hear that same call again for our own day but also to learn from the Reformation how to do it. This commentary series is a godsend!"

Richard J. Mouw, *President Emeritus and Senior Professor of Faith and Public Life, Fuller Theological Seminary*

"Like the Ancient Christian Commentary on Scripture, the Reformation Commentary on Scripture does a masterful job of offering excellent selections from well-known and not-so-well-known exegetes. The editor's introductory survey is, by itself, worth the price of the book. It is easy to forget that there were more hands, hearts and minds involved in the Reformation than Luther and Calvin. Furthermore, encounters even with these figures are often limited to familiar quotes on familiar topics. However, the Reformation Commentary helps us to recognize the breadth and depth of exegetical interests and skill that fueled and continue to fuel faithful meditation on God's Word. I heartily recommend this series as a tremendous resource not only for ministry but for personal edification."

Michael S. Horton, *J. Gresham Machen Professor of Systematic Theology and Apologetics, Westminster Seminary, California*

"The Reformation was ignited by a fresh reading of Scripture. In this series of commentaries, we contemporary interpreters are allowed to feel some of the excitement, surprise and wonder of our spiritual forebears. Luther, Calvin and their fellow revolutionaries were masterful interpreters of the Word. Now, in this remarkable series, some of our very best Reformation scholars open up the riches of the Reformation's reading of the Scripture."

William H. Willimon, *Professor of the Practice of Christian Ministry, Duke Divinity School*

"The Reformation Scripture principle set the entirety of Christian life and thought under the governance of the divine Word, and pressed the church to renew its exegetical labors. This series promises to place before the contemporary church the fruit of those labors, and so to exemplify life under the Word."

John Webster, *Professor of Divinity, University of St. Andrews*†

"Since Gerhard Ebeling's pioneering work on Luther's exegesis seventy years ago, the history of biblical interpretation has occupied many Reformation scholars and become a vital part of study of the period. The Reformation Commentary on Scripture provides fresh materials for students of Reformation-era biblical interpretation and for twenty-first-century preachers to mine the rich stores of insights from leading reformers of the sixteenth century into both the text of Scripture itself and its application in sixteenth-century contexts. This series will strengthen our understanding of the period of the Reformation and enable us to apply its insights to our own days and its challenges to the church."

Robert Kolb, *Professor Emeritus, Concordia Theological Seminary*

"The multivolume Ancient Christian Commentary on Scripture is a valuable resource for those who wish to know how the Fathers interpreted a passage of Scripture but who lack the time or the opportunity to search through the many individual works. This new Reformation Commentary on Scripture will do the same for the reformers and is to be warmly welcomed. It will provide much easier access to the exegetical treasures of the Reformation and will hopefully encourage readers to go back to some of the original works themselves."

Anthony N. S. Lane, *Professor of Historical Doctrine, Lecturer in Doctrine, London School of Theology*

"This volume of the RCS project is an invaluable source for pastors and the historically/biblically interested that provides unparalleled access not only to commentaries of the leading Protestant reformers but also to a host of nowadays unknown commentaters on Galatians and Ephesians. The RCS is sure to enhance and enliven contemporary exegesis. With its wide scope, the collection will enrich our understanding of the variety of Reformation thought and biblical exegesis."

Sigrun Haude, *Associate Professor of Reformation and Early Modern European History, University of Cincinnati*

"This grand project sets before scholars, pastors, teachers, students and growing Christians an experience that can only be likened to stumbling into a group Bible study only to discover that your fellow participants include some of the most significant Christians of the Reformation and post-Reformation (for that matter, of any) era. Here the Word of God is explained in a variety of accents: German, Swiss, French, Dutch, English, Scottish and more. Each one vibrates with a thrilling sense of the living nature of God's Word and its power to transform individuals, churches and even whole communities. Here is a series to anticipate, enjoy and treasure."

Sinclair Ferguson, *Professor of Systematic Theology, Reformed Theological Seminary*

"I strongly endorse the Reformation Commentary on Scripture. Introducing how the Bible was interpreted during the age of the Reformation, these volumes will not only renew contemporary preaching, but they will also help us understand more fully how reading and meditating on Scripture can, in fact, change our lives!"

Lois Malcolm, *Professor and Olin and Amanda Fjelstad Registad Chair for Systematic Theology, Luther Seminary*

"Discerning the true significance of movements in theology requires acquaintance with their biblical exegesis. This is supremely so with the Reformation, which was essentially a biblical revival. The Reformation Commentary on Scripture will fill a yawning gap, just as the Ancient Christian Commentary did before it, and the first volume gets the series off to a fine start, whetting the appetite for more. Most heartily do I welcome and commend this long overdue project."

J. I. Packer, *Board of Governors' Professor of Theology, Regent College*†

"There is no telling the benefits to emerge from the publication of this magnificent Reformation Commentary on Scripture series! Now exegetical and theological treasures from Reformation era commentators will be at our fingertips, providing new insights from old sources to give light for the present and future. This series is a gift to scholars and to the church; a wonderful resource to enhance our study of the written Word of God for generations to come!"

Donald K. McKim, *Executive Editor of Theology and Reference, Westminster John Knox Press*

"Why was this not done before? The publication of the Reformation Commentary on Scripture should be greeted with enthusiasm by every believing Christian—but especially by those who will preach and teach the Word of God. This commentary series brings the very best of the Reformation heritage to the task of exegesis and exposition, and each volume in this series represents a veritable feast that takes us back to the sixteenth century to enrich the preaching and teaching of God's Word in our own time."

R. Albert Mohler Jr., *President, The Southern Baptist Theological Seminary*

"Today more than ever, the Christian past is the church's future. InterVarsity Press has already brought the voice of the ancients to our ears. Now, in the Reformation Commentary on Scripture, we hear a timely word from the first Protestants as well."

Bryan Litfin, *Moody Publishers*

"I am delighted to see the Reformation Commentary on Scripture. The editors of this series have done us all a service by gleaning from these rich fields of biblical reflection. May God use this new life for these old words to give him glory and to build his church."

Mark Dever, *Senior Pastor, Capitol Hill Baptist Church, and President of 9Marks Ministries*

"Monumental and magisterial, the Reformation Commentary on Scripture, edited by Timothy George, is a remarkably bold and visionary undertaking. Bringing together a wealth of resources, these volumes will provide historians, theologians, biblical scholars, pastors and students with a fresh look at the exegetical insights of those who shaped and influenced the sixteenth-century Reformation. With this marvelous publication, InterVarsity Press has reached yet another plateau of excellence. We pray that this superb series will be used of God to strengthen both church and academy."

David S. Dockery, *President of the International Alliance for Christian Education*

"Detached from her roots, the church cannot reach the world as God intends. While every generation must steward the scriptural insights God grants it, only arrogance or ignorance causes leaders to ignore the contributions of those faithful leaders before us. The Reformation Commentary on Scripture roots our thought in great insights of faithful leaders of the Reformation to further biblical preaching and teaching in this generation."

Bryan Chapell, *President Emeritus, Covenant Theological Seminary*

"After reading several volumes of the Reformation Commentary on Scripture, I exclaimed, 'Hey, this is just what the doctor ordered—I mean Doctor Martinus Lutherus!' The church of today bearing his name needs a strong dose of the medicine this doctor prescribed for the ailing church of the sixteenth century. The reforming fire of Christ-centered preaching that Luther ignited is the only hope to reclaim the impact of the gospel to keep the Reformation going, not for its own sake but to further the renewal of the worldwide church of Christ today. This series of commentaries will equip preachers to step into their pulpits with confidence in the same living Word that inspired the witness of Luther and Calvin and many other lesser-known reformers."

Carl E. Braaten, *Cofounder of the Center for Catholic and Evangelical Theology*

"As a pastor, how does one cultivate a knowledge of the history of interpretation? That's where IVP's Reformation Commentary on Scripture and its forerunner, the Ancient Christian Commentary on Scripture, come in. They do an excellent job in helping pastors become more aware of the history of exegesis for the benefit of their congregations. Every pastor should have access to a set of each."

Carl R. Trueman, *Professor of Biblical and Religious Studies, Grove City College*

Reformation Commentary on Scripture

Old Testament
Xa

Isaiah 1–39

Edited by
Jeff Fisher

General Editor
Timothy George

Associate General Editor
Scott M. Manetsch

IVP Academic
An imprint of InterVarsity Press
Downers Grove, Illinois

InterVarsity Press
P.O. Box 1400 | Downers Grove, IL 60515-1426
ivpress.com | email@ivpress.com

InterVarsity Press® is the publishing division of InterVarsity Christian Fellowship/USA®. For more information, visit intervarsity.org.

Cover design: Cindy Kiple
Interior design: Daniel van Loon

ISBN 978-0-8308-2960-6 (print) | ISBN 978-0-8308-4174-5 (digital)

Printed in the United States of America ♾

Library of Congress Cataloging-in-Publication Data
Names: Fisher, Jeff, PhD, editor.
Title: Isaiah 1-39 / edited by Jeff Fisher.
Other titles: Isaiah 1-39 (Fisher)
Description: Downers Grove, IL : IVP Academic, [2024] | Series: Reformation commentary on scripture. Old Testament ; 10 | Includes bibliographical references and index.
Identifiers: LCCN 2023048904 (print) | LCCN 2023048905 (ebook) | ISBN 9780830829606 (hardcover) | ISBN 9780830841745 (ebook)
Subjects: LCSH: Bible. Isaiah, I-XXXIX–Commentaries.
Classification: LCC BS1515.53 .I635 2024 (print) | LCC BS1515.53 (ebook) | DDC 224/.107–dc23/eng/20231129
LC record available at https://lccn.loc.gov/2023048904
LC ebook record available at https://lccn.loc.gov/2023048905

30 29 28 27 26 25 24 | 12 11 10 9 8 7 6 5 4 3 2 1

Reformation Commentary on Scripture
Project Staff

Project and Associate Managing Editor
Zachary Gordon

Executive Editor
Elissa Schauer

Copyeditor
Claire VanderVelde Brubaker

Assistant Project Editor
Travis Ables

Editorial and Research Assistants
David J. Hooper
Alberto I. Bonilla-Giovanetti

Assistants to the General Editors
Evan Musgraves
Bryan Just
Christopher Gow

Design
Cindy Kiple

Proofreader
Michael LeFebvre

InterVarsity Press

President and Publisher
Terumi Echols

Divisional Vice President, Editorial
Cindy Bunch

Associate Publisher and Academic Editorial Director
Jon Boyd

Divisional Vice President, Operations, and Chief of Staff
Benjamin M. McCoy

CONTENTS

ACKNOWLEDGMENTS

A massive project like these volumes in the Reformation Commentary on Scripture series does not happen apart from the support, encouragement, and collaboration of so many people. While daunting and overwhelming at times, the close and careful reading of Isaiah with the Reformers has propelled me to know, understand, and love the words of Scripture with so much more depth and wonder. My hope is that others may receive even a portion of that benefit from using this volume. I truly value works like these that bring some of the treasures of history to the present-day church. So the first group of people I want to thank are the pastors across the campuses of our church in Grand Rapids, Michigan: Joy Bonnema, Andrea Bult, Brad Knetsch, and Ericka Williams. Perhaps the most encouraging actions by others in this entire process were the simple inquiries by these pastors and others about what I was discovering and especially what insights could be used for upcoming sermons. Though I want these volumes to further academic research in Reformation studies and the history of biblical interpretation, my goal is, above all, to help pastors and teachers of the church be strengthened in the Word so they may be edified and serve their people well.

Without those in various academic fields, I could not do this work or even have recognized its value. In the field of Reformation studies, my gratitude especially goes to Bruce Gordon, Amy Nelson Burnett, Mickey Mattox, Yudha Thianto, Jeff Tyler, Todd Hains, and Sujin Pak for their own works in this area, but also their collegiality and interest in my scholarly projects. I am also grateful for Old Testament scholars, such as Andy Abernathy, Amanda Benckhuysen, John Oswalt, and Willem Van Gemeren, who helped guide me in the questions people are asking today, which are sometimes addressed but can often be expanded by the insights of the Reformers. And thanks, of course, goes to my former colleagues in theology and ministry at Kuyper College: Dan Kroeze, Lisa Hoogeboom, Brian Telzerow, and Richelle White. Their friendship, teaching, and support throughout the years aided my growth as a professor and scholar in countless ways.

For this particular project, I must also express appreciation to Timothy George and the IVP Academic staff, many whose names I do not even know. The significant work required behind the scenes makes these volumes shine in ways that I alone could not do. I especially need to thank David McNutt and Zach Gordon for the consistent assistance along the way from each of them and their diligence to keep this project moving to its completion. The most important person, though, for my involvement with the RCS and my vocational calling as a whole is Scott Manetsch. There is too much to say about his role than can be expressed here. For me, Scott is not just the associate editor of this series, he is the professor who inspired my interest in both church history and in being a great teacher for the church. After learning under him during my MDiv days at Trinity Evangelical Divinity School, I returned there a decade later to pursue my PhD and benefited from his mentoring and supervision as my doctoral adviser. No one has shaped me as a professor and scholar more than Dr. Manetsch.

I want to convey my thanks to my colaborers at The Foundry, Branson Parler and Sarah Behm. Together we took the leap by faith to start this new venture of making biblical and theological training more widely accessible to churches and church leaders. I definitely could not have completed this first volume without the space and time granted to me, even amid all the many other responsibilities that go into launching a new ministry of learning and leadership.

And finally and most importantly, I am extremely grateful for my wife, Wendy, and our two sons, Trey and Chase. Their patience with me as I often toiled through all the pieces of the process has been a gift. The vision for our family echoes what is anticipated in the promise from Isaiah 54:13: "All your children shall be taught by the Lord, and great shall be the *shalom* of your children." May these readings of the prophet Isaiah help foster the Lord's teaching and the true peace that comes from it.

ABBREVIATIONS

ACCS	Ancient Christian Commentary on Scripture. 29 vols. Edited by T. C. Oden. Downers Grove, IL: InterVarsity Press, 1998–2009.
CO	*Ioannis Calvini Opera Quae Supersunt Omnia*. 59 vols. Corpus Reformatorum 29–88. Edited by G. Baum, E. Cunitz, and E. Reuss. Berlin: C. A. Schwetschke, 1863–1900. Digital copy online at https://archive-ouverte.unige.ch/unige:650.
CR	*Corpus Reformatorum*. Edited by C. G. Bretsjchneider. Halle, 1834–1860.
CRR	Classics of the Radical Reformation. 12 vols. Scottdale, PA: Herald Press, 1973–.
CTS	Calvin Translation Society edition of Calvin's commentaries. 46 vols. Edinburgh, 1843–1855.
LCL	Loeb Classical Library. Cambridge, MA: Harvard University Press, 1911–. Digital copy online at www.loebclassics.com.
LW	Luther's Works [American edition]. 82 vols. planned. St. Louis: Concordia; Philadelphia: Fortress, 1955–1986, 2009–.
MO	*Philippi Melanthonis Opera Quae Supersunt Omnia*. 28 vols. Corpus Reformatorum 1–28. Edited by C. G. Bretschneider. 1834–1860. Digital copy online at books.google.com and archive.org.
NPNF	*A Select Library of the Nicene and Post-Nicene Fathers of the Christian Church*. 28 vols. in two series. Edited by Philip Schaff et al. Buffalo, NY: Christian Literature, 1887–1894. Available online at www.ccel.org.
PG	*Patrologiae cursus completus*. Series Graeca. 166 vols. Edited by J.-P. Migne. Paris: Migne, 1857–1886.
PL	*Patrologiae cursus completus*. Series Latina. 221 vols. Edited by J.-P. Migne. Paris: Migne, 1844–1864.
r, v	Some early books are numbered not by page but by folio (leaf). Front and back sides (pages) of a numbered folio are indicated by *recto* (r) and *verso* (v) respectively.
WA	*D. Martin Luthers Werke: Kritische Gesamtausgabe*. 73 vols. Weimar: Hermann Böhlaus Nachfolger, 1883–2009. Digital copies online at archive.org.
ZSW	*Huldreich Zwinglis Sämtliche Werke*. 21 vols. Corpus Reformatorum vols. 88-108. Edited by E. Egli et al. Leipzig / Zurich: Heinsius / Theologischer Verlag Zurich, 1905-2013.

A GUIDE TO USING THIS COMMENTARY

Several features have been incorporated into the design of this commentary. The following comments are intended to assist readers in making full use of this volume.

Pericopes of Scripture

The scriptural text has been divided into pericopes, or passages, usually several verses in length. Each of these pericopes is given a heading, which appears at the beginning of the pericope. For example, the first section in this commentary is Isaiah 1:1-9, "A Vision Regarding Unrepentance." This heading is followed by the Scripture passage quoted in the English Standard Version (ESV). The Scripture passage is provided for the convenience of readers, but it is also in keeping with Reformation-era commentaries, which often followed the patristic and medieval commentary tradition, in which the citations of the reformers were arranged according to the text of Scripture.

Overviews

Following each pericope of text is an overview of the Reformation authors' comments on that pericope. The format of this overview varies among the volumes of this series, depending on the requirements of the specific book(s) of Scripture. The function of the overview is to identify succinctly the key exegetical, theological, and pastoral concerns of the Reformation writers arising from the pericope, providing the reader with an orientation to Reformation-era approaches and emphases. It tracks a reasonably cohesive thread of argument among reformers' comments, even though they are derived from diverse sources and generations. Thus, the summaries do not proceed chronologically or by verse sequence. Rather, they seek to rehearse the overall course of the reformers' comments on that pericope.

We do not assume that the commentators themselves anticipated or expressed a formally received cohesive argument but rather that the various arguments tend to flow in a plausible, recognizable pattern. Modern readers can thus glimpse aspects of continuity in the flow of diverse exegetical traditions representing various generations and geographical locations.

Topical Headings

An abundance of varied Reformation-era comment is available for each pericope. For this reason we have broken the pericopes into two levels. First is the verse with its topical heading.

The reformers' comments are then focused on aspects of each verse, with topical headings summarizing the essence of the individual comment by evoking a key phrase, metaphor, or idea. This feature provides a bridge by which modern readers can enter into the heart of the Reformation-era comment.

Identifying the Reformation Authors, Texts, and Events

Following the topical heading of each section of comment, the name of the Reformation commentator is given. An English translation (where needed) of the reformer's comment is then provided. This is immediately followed by the title of the original work rendered in English.

Readers who wish to pursue a deeper investigation of the reformers' works cited in this commentary will find full bibliographic detail for each Reformation title provided in the bibliography at the back of the volume. Information on English translations (where available) and standard original-language editions and critical editions of the works cited is found in the bibliography. The Biographical Sketches section provides brief overviews of the life and work of each commentator, and each confession or collaborative work, appearing in the present volume (as well as in any previous volumes). Finally, a Timeline of the Reformation offers broader context for people, places, and events relevant to the commentators and their works.

Footnotes and Back Matter

To aid the reader in exploring the background and texts in further detail, this commentary utilizes footnotes. The use and content of footnotes may vary among the volumes in this series. Where footnotes appear, a footnote number directs the reader to a note at the bottom of the page, where one will find annotations (clarifications or biblical cross references), information on English translations (where available) or standard original-language editions of the work cited.

Where original-language texts have remained untranslated into English, we provide new translations. Where there is any serious ambiguity or textual problem in the selection, we have tried to reflect the best available textual tradition. Wherever current English translations are already well rendered, they are utilized, but where necessary they are stylistically updated. A single asterisk (*) indicates that a previous English translation has been updated to modern English or amended for easier reading. We have standardized spellings and made grammatical variables uniform so that our English references will not reflect the linguistic oddities of the older English translations. For ease of reading we have in some cases removed superfluous conjunctions.

GENERAL INTRODUCTION

The Reformation Commentary on Scripture (RCS) is a twenty-eight-volume series of exegetical comment covering the entire Bible and gathered from the writings of sixteenth-century preachers, scholars and reformers. The RCS is intended as a sequel to the highly acclaimed Ancient Christian Commentary on Scripture (ACCS), and as such its overall concept, method, format, and audience are similar to the earlier series. Both series are committed to the renewal of the church through careful study and meditative reflection on the Old and New Testaments, the charter documents of Christianity, read in the context of the worshiping, believing community of faith across the centuries. However, the patristic and Reformation eras are separated by nearly a millennium, and the challenges of reading Scripture with the reformers require special attention to their context, resources and assumptions. The purpose of this general introduction is to present an overview of the context and process of biblical interpretation in the age of the Reformation.

Goals

The Reformation Commentary on Scripture seeks to introduce its readers to the depth and richness of exegetical ferment that defined the Reformation era. The RCS has four goals: the enrichment of contemporary biblical interpretation through exposure to Reformation-era biblical exegesis; the renewal of contemporary preaching through exposure to the biblical insights of the Reformation writers; a deeper understanding of the Reformation itself and the breadth of perspectives represented within it; and a recovery of the profound integration of the life of faith and the life of the mind that should characterize Christian scholarship. Each of these goals requires a brief comment.

Renewing contemporary biblical interpretation. During the past half-century, biblical hermeneutics has become a major growth industry in the academic world. One of the consequences of the historical-critical hegemony of biblical studies has been the privileging of contemporary philosophies and ideologies at the expense of a commitment to the Christian church as the primary reading community within which and for which biblical exegesis is done. Reading Scripture with the church fathers and the reformers is a corrective to all such imperialism of the present. One of the greatest skills required for a fruitful interpretation of the Bible is the ability to listen. We rightly emphasize the importance of listening to the voices of contextual theologies today, but in doing so we often marginalize or ignore another crucial context—the community of believing Christians through the centuries. The serious study of Scripture requires more than the latest

Bible translation in one hand and the latest commentary (or niche study Bible) in the other. John L. Thompson has called on Christians today to practice the art of "reading the Bible with the dead."[1] The RCS presents carefully selected comments from the extant commentaries of the Reformation as an encouragement to more in-depth study of this important epoch in the history of biblical interpretation.

Strengthening contemporary preaching. The Protestant reformers identified the public preaching of the Word of God as an indispensible means of grace and a sure sign of the true church. Through the words of the preacher, the living voice of the gospel (*viva vox evangelii*) is heard. Luther famously said that the church is not a "pen house" but a "mouth house."[2] The Reformation in Switzerland began when Huldrych Zwingli entered the pulpit of the Grossmünster in Zurich on January 1, 1519, and began to preach a series of expositional sermons chapter by chapter from the Gospel of Matthew. In the following years he extended this homiletical approach to other books of the Old and New Testaments. Calvin followed a similar pattern in Geneva. Many of the commentaries represented in this series were either originally presented as sermons or were written to support the regular preaching ministry of local church pastors. Luther said that the preacher should be a *bonus textualis*—a good one with a text—well-versed in the Scriptures. Preachers in the Reformation traditions preached not only about the Bible but also from it, and this required more than a passing acquaintance with its contents. Those who have been charged with the office of preaching in the church today can find wisdom and insight—and fresh perspectives—in the sermons of the Reformation and the biblical commentaries read and studied by preachers of the sixteenth century.

Deepening understanding of the Reformation. Some scholars of the sixteenth century prefer to speak of the period they study in the plural, the European Reformations, to indicate that many-diverse impulses for reform were at work in this turbulent age of transition from medieval to modern times.[3] While this point is well taken, the RCS follows the time-honored tradition of using *Reformation* in the singular form to indicate not only a major moment in the history of Christianity in the West but also, as Hans J. Hillerbrand has put it, "an essential cohesiveness in the heterogeneous pursuits of religious reform in the sixteenth century."[4] At the same time, in developing guidelines to assist the volume editors in making judicious selections from the vast amount of commentary material available in this period, we have stressed the multifaceted character of the Reformation across many confessions, theological orientations, and political settings.

Advancing Christian scholarship. By assembling and disseminating numerous voices from such a signal period as the Reformation, the RCS aims to make a significant contribution to the ever-growing stream of Christian scholarship. The post-Enlightenment split between the study of the Bible as an academic discipline and the reading of the Bible as spiritual nurture was foreign

[1]John L. Thompson, *Reading the Bible with the Dead* (Grand Rapids: Eerdmans, 2007).
[2]WA 10,2:48.
[3]See Carter Lindberg, *The European Reformations*, 2nd ed. (Malden, MA: Wiley-Blackwell, 2010).
[4]Hans J. Hillerbrand, *The Division of Christendom* (Louisville, KY: Westminster John Knox, 2007), x. Hillerbrand has also edited the standard reference work in Reformation studies, *OER*. See also Diarmaid MacCulloch, *The Reformation* (New York: Viking, 2003), and Patrick Collinson, *The Reformation: A History* (New York: Random House, 2004).

to the reformers. For them the study of the Bible was transformative at the most basic level of the human person: *coram deo.*

The reformers all repudiated the idea that the Bible could be studied and understood with dispassionate objectivity, as a cold artifact from antiquity. Luther's famous Reformation breakthrough triggered by his laborious study of the Psalms and Paul's letter to the Romans is well known, but the experience of Cambridge scholar Thomas Bilney was perhaps more typical. When Erasmus's critical edition of the Greek New Testament was published in 1516, it was accompanied by a new translation in elegant Latin. Attracted by the classical beauty of Erasmus's Latin, Bilney came across this statement in 1 Timothy 1:15: "Christ Jesus came into the world to save sinners." In the Greek this sentence is described as *pistos ho logos,* which the Vulgate had rendered *fidelis sermo,* "a faithful saying." Erasmus chose a different word for the Greek *pistos—certus,* "sure, certain." When Bilney grasped the meaning of this word applied to the announcement of salvation in Christ, he tells us that "immediately, I felt a marvellous comfort and quietness, insomuch as 'my bruised bones leaped for joy.'"[5]

Luther described the way the Bible was meant to function in the minds and hearts of believers when he reproached himself and others for studying the nativity narrative with such cool unconcern:

> I hate myself because when I see Christ laid in the manger or in the lap of his mother and hear the angels sing, my heart does not leap into flame. With what good reason should we all despise ourselves that we remain so cold when this word is spoken to us, over which everyone should dance and leap and burn for joy! We act as though it were a frigid historical fact that does not smite our hearts, as if someone were merely relating that the sultan has a crown of gold.[6]

It was a core conviction of the Reformation that the careful study and meditative listening to the Scriptures, what the monks called *lectio divina,* could yield transformative results for *all* of life. The value of such a rich commentary, therefore, lies not only in the impressive volume of Reformation-era voices that are presented throughout the course of the series but in the many particular fields for which their respective lives and ministries are relevant. The Reformation is consequential for historical studies, both church as well as secular history. Biblical and theological studies, to say nothing of pastoral and spiritual studies, also stand to benefit and progress immensely from renewed engagement today, as mediated through the RCS, with the reformers of yesteryear.

Perspectives

In setting forth the perspectives and parameters of the RCS, the following considerations have proved helpful.

Chronology. When did the Reformation begin, and how long did it last? In some traditional accounts, the answer was clear: the Reformation began with the posting of Luther's Ninety-five

[5]John Foxe, *The Acts and Monuments of John Foxe: A New and Complete Edition,* 8 vols., ed. Stephen Reed Cattley (London: R. B. Seeley & W. Burnside, 1837), 4:635; quoting Ps 51:8; cited in A. G. Dickens, *The English Reformation,* 2nd ed. (University Park, PA: The Pennsylvannia State University Press, 1991), 102.

[6]WA 49:176-77, quoted in Roland Bainton, "The Bible in the Reformation," in *CHB,* 3:23.

Theses at Wittenberg in 1517 and ended with the death of Calvin in Geneva in 1564. Apart from reducing the Reformation to a largely German event with a side trip to Switzerland, this perspective fails to do justice to the important events that led up to Luther's break with Rome and its many reverberations throughout Europe and beyond. In choosing commentary selections for the RCS, we have adopted the concept of the long sixteenth century, say, from the late 1400s to the mid-seventeenth century. Thus we have included commentary selections from early or pre-Reformation writers such as John Colet and Jacques Lefèvre d'Étaples to seventeenth-century figures such as Henry Ainsworth and Johann Gerhard.

Confession. The RCS concentrates primarily, though not exclusively, on the exegetical writings of the Protestant reformers. While the ACCS provided a compendium of key consensual exegetes of the early Christian centuries, the Catholic/Protestant confessional divide in the sixteenth century tested the very idea of consensus, especially with reference to ecclesiology and soteriology. While many able and worthy exegetes faithful to the Roman Catholic Church were active during this period, this project has chosen to include primarily those figures that represent perspectives within the Protestant Reformation. For this reason we have not included comments on the apocryphal or deuterocanonical writings.

We recognize that "Protestant" and "Catholic" as contradistinctive labels are anachronistic terms for the early decades of the sixteenth century before the hardening of confessional identities surrounding the Council of Trent (1545–1563). Protestant figures such as Philipp Melanchthon, Johannes Oecolampadius and John Calvin were all products of the revival of sacred letters known as biblical humanism. They shared an approach to biblical interpretation that owed much to Desiderius Erasmus and other scholars who remained loyal to the Church of Rome. Careful comparative studies of Protestant and Catholic exegesis in the sixteenth century have shown surprising areas of agreement when the focus was the study of a particular biblical text rather than the standard confessional debates.

At the same time, exegetical differences among the various Protestant groups could become strident and church-dividing. The most famous example of this is the interpretive impasse between Luther and Zwingli over the meaning of "This is my body" (Mt 26:26) in the words of institution. Their disagreement at the Colloquy of Marburg in 1529 had important christological and pastoral implications, as well as social and political consequences. Luther refused fellowship with Zwingli and his party at the end of the colloquy; in no small measure this bitter division led to the separate trajectories pursued by Lutheran and Reformed Protestantism to this day. In Elizabethan England, Puritans and Anglicans agreed that "Holy Scripture containeth all things necessary to salvation: so that whatsoever is not read therein, nor may be proved thereby, is not to be required of any man" (article 6 of the Thirty-Nine Articles of Religion), yet on the basis of their differing interpretations of the Bible they fought bitterly over the structures of the church, the clothing of the clergy and the ways of worship. On the matter of infant baptism, Catholics and Protestants alike agreed on its propriety, though there were various theories as to how a practice not mentioned in the Bible could be justified biblically. The Anabaptists were outliers on this subject. They rejected infant baptism altogether. They appealed to the example of the baptism of Jesus and to his final words as recorded in the Gospel of Matthew (Mt 28:19-20): "Go therefore, and make disciples of all nations, baptizing them in the name of the Father, and of the Son, and of the Holy Spirit, teaching them to observe all that I have commanded you." New Testament Christians, they argued, are to follow not only the commands of Jesus in the Great Commission, but also the exact order in which they were given: evangelize, baptize, catechize.

These and many other differences of interpretation among the various Protestant groups are reflected in their many sermons, commentaries and public disputations. In the RCS, the volume editors' introduction to each volume is intended to help the reader understand the nature and significance of doctrinal conversations and disputes that resulted in particular, and frequently clashing, interpretations. Footnotes throughout the text will be provided to explain obscure references, unusual expressions and other matters that require special comment. Volume editors have chosen comments on the Bible across a wide range of sixteenth-century confessions and schools of interpretation: biblical humanists, Lutheran, Reformed, Anglican, Puritan, and Anabaptist. We have not pursued passages from post-Tridentine Catholic authors or from radical spiritualists and antitrinitarian writers, though sufficient material is available from these sources to justify another series.

Format. The design of the RCS is intended to offer reader-friendly access to these classic texts. The availability of digital resources has given access to a huge residual database of sixteenth-century exegetical comment hitherto available only in major research universities and rare book collections. The RCS has benefited greatly from online databases such as Alexander Street Press's Digital Library of Classical Protestant Texts (DLCPT) and Early English Books Online as well as freely accessible databases like the Post-Reformation Digital Library (prdl.org). Through the help of RCS editorial advisor Herman Selderhuis, we have also had access to the special Reformation collections of the Johannes a Lasco Bibliothek in Emden, Germany. In addition, modern critical editions and translations of Reformation sources have been published over the past generation. Original translations of Reformation sources are given unless an acceptable translation already exists.

Each volume in the RCS will include an introduction by the volume editor placing that portion of the canon within the historical context of the Protestant Reformation and presenting a summary of the theological themes, interpretive issues and reception of the particular book(s). The commentary itself consists of particular pericopes identified by a pericope heading; the biblical text in the English Standard Version (ESV), with significant textual variants registered in the footnotes; an overview of the pericope in which principal exegetical and theological concerns of the Reformation writers are succinctly noted; and excerpts from the Reformation writers identified by name according to the conventions of the *Oxford Encyclopedia of the Reformation*. Each volume will also include a bibliography of sources cited, as well as an appendix of authors and source works.

The Reformation era was a time of verbal as well as physical violence, and this fact has presented a challenge for this project. Without unduly sanitizing the texts, where they contain anti-Semitic, sexist or inordinately polemical rhetoric, we have not felt obliged to parade such comments either. We have noted the abridgement of texts with ellipses and an explanatory footnote.

While this procedure would not be valid in the critical edition of such a text, we have deemed it appropriate in a series whose primary purpose is pastoral and devotional. When translating *homo* or similar terms that refer to the human race as a whole or to individual persons without reference to gender, we have used alternative English expressions to the word *man* (or derivative constructions that formerly were used generically to signify humanity at large), whenever such substitutions can be made without producing an awkward or artificial construction.

As is true in the ACCS, we have made a special effort where possible to include the voices of women, though we acknowledge the difficulty of doing so for the early modern period when for a variety of social and cultural reasons few theological and biblical works were published by women. However, recent scholarship has focused on a number of female leaders whose literary remains show us how they understood and interpreted the Bible. Women who made significant contributions to the Reformation include Marguerite d'Angoulême, sister of King Francis I, who supported French reformist evangelicals including Calvin and who published a religious poem influenced by Luther's theology, *The Mirror of the Sinful Soul*; Argula von Grumbach, a Bavarian noblewoman who defended the teachings of Luther and Melanchthon before the theologians of the University of Ingolstadt; Katharina Schütz Zell, the wife of a former priest, Matthias Zell, and a remarkable reformer in her own right—she conducted funerals, compiled hymnbooks, defended the downtrodden, and published a defense of clerical marriage as well as composing works of consolation on divine comfort and pleas for the toleration of Anabaptists and Catholics alike; and Anne Askew, a Protestant martyr put to death in 1546 after demonstrating remarkable biblical prowess in her examinations by church officials. Other echoes of faithful women in the age of the Reformation are found in their letters, translations, poems, hymns, court depositions, and martyr records.

Lay culture, learned culture. In recent decades, much attention has been given to what is called "reforming from below," that is, the expressions of religious beliefs and churchly life that characterized the popular culture of the majority of the population in the era of the Reformation. Social historians have taught us to examine the diverse pieties of townspeople and city folk, of rural religion and village life, the emergence of lay theologies, and the experiences of women in the religious tumults of Reformation Europe.[7] Formal commentaries by their nature are artifacts of learned culture. Almost all of them were written in Latin, the lingua franca of learned discourse well past the age of the Reformation. Biblical commentaries were certainly not the primary means by which the Protestant Reformation spread so rapidly across wide sectors of sixteenth-century society. Small pamphlets and broadsheets, later called *Flugschriften* ("flying writings"), with their graphic woodcuts and cartoon-like depictions of Reformation personalities and events, became the means of choice for mass communication in the early age of printing. Sermons and works of devotion were also printed with appealing visual aids. Luther's early writings were often accompanied by drawings and sketches from Lucas Cranach and other artists. This was done "above all for the sake of children and simple folk," as Luther

[7]See Peter Matheson, ed., *Reformation Christianity* (Minneapolis: Fortress, 2007).

put it, "who are more easily moved by pictures and images to recall divine history than through mere words or doctrines."[8]

We should be cautious, however, in drawing too sharp a distinction between learned and lay culture in this period. The phenomenon of preaching was a kind of verbal bridge between scholars at their desks and the thousands of illiterate or semiliterate listeners whose views were shaped by the results of Reformation exegesis. According to contemporary witness, more than one thousand people were crowding into Geneva to hear Calvin expound the Scriptures every day.[9] An example of how learned theological works by Reformation scholars were received across divisions of class and social status comes from Lazare Drilhon, an apothecary of Toulon. He was accused of heresy in May 1545 when a cache of prohibited books was found hidden in his garden shed. In addition to devotional works, the French New Testament and a copy of Calvin's Genevan liturgy, there was found a series of biblical commentaries, translated from the Latin into French: Martin Bucer's on Matthew, François Lambert's on the Apocalypse and one by Oecolampadius on 1 John.[10] Biblical exegesis in the sixteenth century was not limited to the kind of full-length commentaries found in Drilhon's shed. Citations from the Bible and expositions of its meaning permeate the extant literature of sermons, letters, court depositions, doctrinal treatises, records of public disputations and even last wills and testaments. While most of the selections in the RCS will be drawn from formal commentary literature, other sources of biblical reflection will also be considered.

Historical Context

The medieval legacy. On October 18, 1512, the degree *Doctor in Biblia* was conferred on Martin Luther, and he began his career as a professor in the University of Wittenberg. As is well known, Luther was also a monk who had taken solemn vows in the Augustinian Order of Hermits at Erfurt. These two settings—the university and the monastery—both deeply rooted in the Middle Ages, form the background not only for Luther's personal vocation as a reformer but also for the history of the biblical commentary in the age of the Reformation. Since the time of the Venerable Bede (d. 735), sometimes called "the last of the Fathers," serious study of the Bible had taken place primarily in the context of cloistered monasteries. The Rule of St. Benedict brought together *lectio* and *meditatio*, the knowledge of letters and the life of prayer. The liturgy was the medium through which the daily reading of the Bible, especially the Psalms, and the sayings of the church fathers came together in the spiritual formation of the monks.[11] Essential to this understanding was a belief in the unity of the people of God throughout time as well as space, and an awareness that life in this world was a preparation for the beatific vision in the next.

[8]Martin Luther, "Personal Prayer Book," LW 43:42-43* (WA 10,2:458); quoted in R. W. Scribner, *For the Sake of Simple Folk: Popular Propaganda for the German Reformation* (Cambridge: Cambridge University Press, 1981), xi.

[9]Letter of De Beaulieu to Guillaume Farel (1561) in *Theodor Beza nach handschriftlichen und anderen gleichzeitigen Quellen*, ed. J. W. Baum (Leipzig: Weidmann, 1851), 2:92.

[10]Francis Higman, "A Heretic's Library: The Drilhon Inventory" (1545), in Francis Higman, *Lire et Découvire: la circulation des idées au temps de la Réforme* (Geneva: Droz, 1998), 65-85.

[11]See the classic study by Jean Leclercq, *The Love of Learning and the Desire for God* (New York: Fordham University Press, 1961).

The source of theology was the study of the sacred page *(sacra pagina)*; its object was the accumulation of knowledge not for its own sake but for the obtaining of eternal life. For these monks, the Bible had God for its author, salvation for its end and unadulterated truth for its matter, though they would not have expressed it in such an Aristotelian way. The medieval method of interpreting the Bible owed much to Augustine's *On Christian Doctrine*. In addition to setting forth a series of rules (drawn from an earlier work by Tyconius), Augustine stressed the importance of distinguishing the literal and spiritual or allegorical senses of Scripture. While the literal sense was not disparaged, the allegorical was valued because it enabled the believer to obtain spiritual benefit from the obscure places in the Bible, especially in the Old Testament. For Augustine, as for the monks who followed him, the goal of scriptural exegesis was freighted with eschatological meaning; its purpose was to induce faith, hope, and love and so to advance in one's pilgrimage toward that city with foundations (see Heb 11:10).

Building on the work of Augustine and other church fathers going back to Origen, medieval exegetes came to understand Scripture as possessed of four possible meanings, the famous *quadriga*. The literal meaning was retained, of course, but the spiritual meaning was now subdivided into three senses: the allegorical, the moral, and the anagogical. Medieval exegetes often referred to the four meanings of Scripture in a popular rhyme:

> The letter shows us what God and our fathers did;
> The allegory shows us where our faith is hid;
> The moral meaning gives us rules of daily life;
> The anagogy shows us where we end our strife.[12]

In this schema, the three spiritual meanings of the text correspond to the three theological virtues: faith (allegory), hope (anagogy), and love (the moral meaning). It should be noted that this way of approaching the Bible assumed a high doctrine of scriptural inspiration: the multiple meanings inherent in the text had been placed there by the Holy Spirit for the benefit of the people of God. The biblical justification for this method went back to the apostle Paul, who had used the words *allegory* and *type* when applying Old Testament events to believers in Christ (Gal 4:21-31; 1 Cor 10:1-11). The problem with this approach was knowing how to relate each of the four senses to one another and how to prevent Scripture from becoming a nose of wax turned this way and that by various interpreters. As G. R. Evans explains, "Any interpretation which could be put upon the text and was in keeping with the faith and edifying, had the warrant of God himself, for no human reader had the ingenuity to find more than God had put there."[13]

With the rise of the universities in the eleventh century, theology and the study of Scripture moved from the cloister into the classroom. Scripture and the Fathers were still important, but they came to function more as footnotes to the theological questions debated in the schools and brought together in an impressive systematic way in works such as Peter Lombard's *Books of Sentences* (the standard theology textbook of the Middle Ages) and the great scholastic *summae* of the thirteenth

[12]Robert M. Grant, *A Short History of the Interpretation of the Bible* (New York: Macmillan, 1963), 119. A translation of the well-known Latin quatrain: *Littera gesta docet/Quid credas allegoria/Moralis quid agas/Quo tendas anagogia.*

[13]G. R. Evans, *The Language and Logic of the Bible: The Road to Reformation* (Cambridge: Cambridge University Press, 1985), 42.

century. Indispensible to the study of the Bible in the later Middle Ages was the *Glossa ordinaria*, a collection of exegetical opinions by the church fathers and other commentators. Heiko Oberman summarized the transition from devotion to dialectic this way: "When, due to the scientific revolution of the twelfth century, Scripture became the *object* of study rather than the *subject* through which God speaks to the student, the difference between the two modes of speaking was investigated in terms of the texts themselves rather than in their relation to the recipients."[14] It was possible, of course, to be both a scholastic theologian and a master of the spiritual life. Meister Eckhart, for example, wrote commentaries on the Old Testament in Latin and works of mystical theology in German, reflecting what had come to be seen as a division of labor between the two.

An increasing focus on the text of Scripture led to a revival of interest in its literal sense. The two key figures in this development were Thomas Aquinas (d. 1274) and Nicholas of Lyra (d. 1340). Thomas is best remembered for his *Summa Theologiae*, but he was also a prolific commentator on the Bible. Thomas did not abandon the multiple senses of Scripture but declared that all the senses were founded on one—the literal—and this sense eclipsed allegory as the basis of sacred doctrine. Nicholas of Lyra was a Franciscan scholar who made use of the Hebrew text of the Old Testament and quoted liberally from works of Jewish scholars, especially the learned French rabbi Salomon Rashi (d. 1105). After Aquinas, Lyra was the strongest defender of the literal, historical meaning of Scripture as the primary basis of theological disputation. His *Postilla*, as his notes were called—the abbreviated form of *post illa verba textus*, meaning "after these words from Scripture"—were widely circulated in the late Middle Ages and became the first biblical commentary to be printed in the fifteenth century. More than any other commentator from the period of high scholasticism, Lyra and his work were greatly valued by the early reformers. According to an old Latin pun, *Nisi Lyra lyrasset, Lutherus non saltasset*, "If Lyra had not played his lyre, Luther would not have danced."[15] While Luther was never an uncritical disciple of any teacher, he did praise Lyra as a good Hebraist and quoted him more than one hundred times in his lectures on Genesis, where he declared, "I prefer him to almost all other interpreters of Scripture."[16]

Sacred philology. The sixteenth century has been called a golden age of biblical interpretation, and it is a fact that the age of the Reformation witnessed an explosion of commentary writing unparalleled in the history of the Christian church. Kenneth Hagen has cataloged forty-five commentaries on Hebrews between 1516 (Erasmus) and 1598 (Beza).[17] During the sixteenth century, more than seventy new commentaries on Romans were published, five of them by Melanchthon alone, and nearly one hundred commentaries on the Bible's prayer book, the Psalms.[18] There were two developments in the fifteenth century that presaged this development and without which it

[14]Heiko Oberman, *Forerunners of the Reformation* (Philadelphia: Fortress, 1966), 284.

[15]Nicholas of Lyra, *The Postilla of Nicolas of Lyra on the Song of Songs*, trans. and ed. James George Kiecker (Milwaukee: Marquette University Press, 1998), 19.

[16]LW 2:164 (WA 42:377).

[17]Kenneth Hagen, *Hebrews Commenting from Erasmus to Bèze, 1516–1598* (Tübingen: Mohr, 1981).

[18]R. Gerald Hobbs, "Biblical Commentaries," *OER* 1:167-71. See in general David C. Steinmetz, ed., *The Bible in the Sixteenth Century* (Durham: Duke University Press, 1990).

could not have taken place: the invention of printing and the rediscovery of a vast store of ancient learning hitherto unknown or unavailable to scholars in the West.

It is now commonplace to say that what the computer has become in our generation, the printing press was to the world of Erasmus, Luther, and other leaders of the Reformation. Johannes Gutenberg, a goldsmith by trade, developed a metal alloy suitable for type and a machine that would allow printed characters to be cast with relative ease, placed in even lines of composition and then manipulated again and again, making possible the mass production of an unbelievable number of texts. In 1455, the Gutenberg Bible, the masterpiece of the typographical revolution, was published at Mainz in double columns in gothic type. Forty-seven copies of the beautiful Gutenberg Bible are still extant, each consisting of more than one thousand colorfully illuminated and impeccably printed pages. What began at Gutenberg's print shop in Mainz on the Rhine River soon spread, like McDonald's or Starbucks in our day, into every nook and cranny of the known world. Printing presses sprang up in Rome (1464), Venice (1469), Paris (1470), the Netherlands (1471), Switzerland (1472), Spain (1474), England (1476), Sweden (1483), and Constantinople (1490). By 1500, these and other presses across Europe had published some twenty-seven thousand titles, most of them in Latin. Erasmus once compared himself with an obscure preacher whose sermons were heard by only a few people in one or two churches while his books were read in every country in the world. Erasmus was not known for his humility, but in this case he was simply telling the truth.[19]

The Italian humanist Lorenzo Valla (d. 1457) died in the early dawn of the age of printing, but his critical and philological studies would be taken up by others who believed that genuine reform in church and society could come about only by returning to the wellsprings of ancient learning and wisdom—*ad fontes,* "back to the sources!" Valla is best remembered for undermining a major claim made by defenders of the papacy when he proved by philological research that the so-called Donation of Constantine, which had bolstered papal assertions of temporal sovereignty, was a forgery. But it was Valla's *Collatio Novi Testamenti* of 1444 that would have such a great effect on the renewal of biblical studies in the next century. Erasmus discovered the manuscript of this work while rummaging through an old library in Belgium and published it at Paris in 1505. In the preface to his edition of Valla, Erasmus gave the rationale that would guide his own labors in textual criticism. Just as Jerome had translated the Latin Vulgate from older versions and copies of the Scriptures in his day, so now Jerome's own text must be subjected to careful scrutiny and correction. Erasmus would be *Hieronymus redivivus,* a new Jerome come back to life to advance the cause of sacred philology. The restoration of the Scriptures and the writings of the church fathers would usher in what Erasmus believed would be a golden age of peace and learning. In 1516, the Basel publisher Froben brought out Erasmus's *Novum Instrumentum,* the first published edition of the Greek New Testament. Erasmus's Greek New Testament would go through five editions in his lifetime, each one with new emendations to the text and a growing section of annotations that expanded to include not only technical notes about the text but also theological comment. The influence of Erasmus's Greek New

[19]E. Harris Harbison, *The Christian Scholar in the Age of the Reformation* (New York: Charles Scribner's Sons, 1956), 80.

Testament was enormous. It formed the basis for Robert Estienne's *Novum Testamentum Graece* of 1550, which in turn was used to establish the Greek *Textus Receptus* for a number of late Reformation translations including the King James Version of 1611.

For all his expertise in Greek, Erasmus was a poor student of Hebrew and only published commentaries on several of the psalms. However, the renaissance of Hebrew letters was part of the wider program of biblical humanism as reflected in the establishment of trilingual colleges devoted to the study of Hebrew, Greek and Latin (the three languages written on the *titulus* of Jesus' cross [Jn 19:20]) at Alcalá in Spain, Wittenberg in Germany, Louvain in Belgium, and Paris in France. While it is true that some medieval commentators, especially Nicholas of Lyra, had been informed by the study of Hebrew and rabbinics in their biblical work, it was the publication of Johannes Reuchlin's *De rudimentis hebraicis* (1506), a combined grammar and dictionary, that led to the recovery of *veritas Hebraica*, as Jerome had referred to the true voice of the Hebrew Scriptures. The pursuit of Hebrew studies was carried forward in the Reformation by two great scholars, Konrad Pellikan and Sebastian Münster. Pellikan was a former Franciscan friar who embraced the Protestant cause and played a major role in the Zurich reformation. He had published a Hebrew grammar even prior to Reuchlin and produced a commentary on nearly the entire Bible that appeared in seven volumes between 1532 and 1539. Münster was Pellikan's student and taught Hebrew at the University of Heidelberg before taking up a similar position in Basel. Like his mentor, Münster was a great collector of Hebraica and published a series of excellent grammars, dictionaries and rabbinic texts. Münster did for the Hebrew Old Testament what Erasmus had done for the Greek New Testament. His *Hebraica Biblia* offered a fresh Latin translation of the Old Testament with annotations from medieval rabbinic exegesis.

Luther first learned Hebrew with Reuchlin's grammar in hand but took advantage of other published resources, such as the four-volume Hebrew Bible published at Venice by Daniel Bomberg in 1516 to 1517. He also gathered his own circle of Hebrew experts, his *sanhedrin* he called it, who helped him with his German translation of the Old Testament. We do not know where William Tyndale learned Hebrew, though perhaps it was in Worms, where there was a thriving rabbinical school during his stay there. In any event, he had sufficiently mastered the language to bring out a freshly translated Pentateuch that was published at Antwerp in 1530. By the time the English separatist scholar Henry Ainsworth published his prolix commentaries on the Pentateuch in 1616, the knowledge of Hebrew, as well as Greek, was taken for granted by every serious scholar of the Bible. In the preface to his commentary on Genesis, Ainsworth explained that "the literal sense of Moses's Hebrew (which is the tongue wherein he wrote the law), is the ground of all interpretation, and that language hath figures and properties of speech, different from ours: These therefore in the first place are to be opened that the natural meaning of the Scripture, being known, the mysteries of godliness therein implied, may be better discerned."[20]

The restoration of the biblical text in the original languages made possible the revival of scriptural exposition reflected in the floodtide of sermon literature and commentary work. Of even

[20]Henry Ainsworth, *Annotations upon the First Book of Moses Called Genesis* (Amsterdam, 1616), preface (unpaginated).

more far-reaching import was the steady stream of vernacular Bibles in the sixteenth century. In the introduction to his 1516 edition of the New Testament, Erasmus had expressed his desire that the Scriptures be translated into all languages so that "the lowliest women" could read the Gospels and the Pauline epistles and "the farmer sing some portion of them at the plow, the weaver hum some parts of them to the movement of his shuttle, the traveler lighten the weariness of the journey with stories of this kind."[21] Like Erasmus, Tyndale wanted the Bible to be available in the language of the common people. He once said to a learned divine that if God spared his life he would cause the boy who drives the plow to know more of the Scriptures than he did![22] The project of allowing the Bible to speak in the language of the mother in the house, the children in the street and the cheesemonger in the marketplace was met with stiff opposition by certain Catholic polemists such as Johann Eck, Luther's antagonist at the Leipzig Debate of 1519. In his *Enchiridion* (1525), Eck derided the "inky theologians" whose translations paraded the Bible before "the untutored crowd" and subjected it to the judgment of "laymen and crazy old women."[23] In fact, some fourteen German Bibles had already been published prior to Luther's September Testament of 1522, which he translated from Erasmus's Greek New Testament in less than three months' time while sequestered in the Wartburg. Luther's German New Testament became the first best-seller in the world, appearing in forty-three distinct editions between 1522 and 1525 with upward of one hundred thousand copies issued in these three years. It is estimated that 5 percent of the German population may have been literate at this time, but this rate increased as the century wore on due in no small part to the unmitigated success of vernacular Bibles.[24]

Luther's German Bible (inclusive of the Old Testament from 1534) was the most successful venture of its kind, but it was not alone in the field. Hans Denck and Ludwig Hätzer, leaders in the early Anabaptist movement, translated the prophetic books of the Old Testament from Hebrew into German in 1527. This work influenced the Swiss-German Bible of 1531 published by Leo Jud and other pastors in Zurich. Tyndale's influence on the English language rivaled that of Luther on German. At a time when English was regarded as "that obscure and remote dialect of German spoken in an off-shore island," Tyndale, with his remarkable linguistic ability (he was fluent in eight languages), "made a language for England," as his modern editor David Daniell has put it.[25] Tyndale was imprisoned and executed near Brussels in 1536, but the influence of his biblical work among the common people of England was already being felt. There is no reason to doubt the authenticity of John Foxe's recollection of how Tyndale's New Testament was received in England during the 1520s and 1530s:

[21]John C. Olin, *Christian Humanism and the Reformation* (New York: Fordham University Press, 1987), 101.

[22]This famous statement of Tyndale was quoted by John Foxe in his *Acts and Monuments of Matters Happening in the Church* (London, 1563). See Henry Wansbrough, "Tyndale," in *The Bible in the Renaissance*, ed. Richard Griffith (Aldershot, UK: Ashgate, 2001), 124.

[23]John Eck, *Enchiridion of Commonplaces*, trans. Ford Lewis Battles (Grand Rapids: Baker, 1979), 47-49.

[24]The effect of printing on the spread of the Reformation has been much debated. See the classic study by Elizabeth L. Eisenstein, *The Printing Press as an Agent of Change* (Cambridge: Cambridge University Press, 1979). More recent studies include Mark U. Edwards Jr., *Printing, Propaganda and Martin Luther* (Minneapolis: Fortress, 1994), and Andrew Pettegree and Matthew Hall, "The Reformation and the Book: A Reconsideration," *Historical Journal* 47 (2004): 1-24.

[25]David Daniell, *William Tyndale: A Biography* (New Haven: Yale University Press, 1994), 3.

> The fervent zeal of those Christian days seemed much superior to these our days and times; as manifestly may appear by their sitting up all night in reading and hearing; also by their expenses and charges in buying of books in English, of whom some gave five marks, some more, some less, for a book: some gave a load of hay for a few chapters of St. James, or of St. Paul in English.[26]

Calvin helped to revise and contributed three prefaces to the French Bible translated by his cousin Pierre Robert Olivétan and originally published at Neuchâtel in 1535. Clément Marot and Beza provided a fresh translation of the Psalms with each psalm rendered in poetic form and accompanied by monophonic musical settings for congregational singing. The Bay Psalter, the first book printed in America, was an English adaptation of this work. Geneva also provided the provenance of the most influential Italian Bible published by Giovanni Diodati in 1607. The flowering of biblical humanism in vernacular Bibles resulted in new translations in all of the major language groups of Europe: Spanish (1569), Portuguese (1681), Dutch (New Testament, 1523; Old Testament, 1527), Danish (1550), Czech (1579–1593/94), Hungarian (New Testament, 1541; complete Bible, 1590), Polish (1563), Swedish (1541), and even Arabic (1591).[27]

Patterns of Reformation

Once the text of the Bible had been placed in the hands of the people, in cheap and easily available editions, what further need was there of published expositions such as commentaries? Given the Protestant doctrine of the priesthood of all believers, was there any longer a need for learned clergy and their bookish religion? Some radical reformers thought not. Sebastian Franck searched for the true church of the Spirit "scattered among the heathen and the weeds" but could not find it in any of the institutional structures of his time. *Veritas non potest scribi, aut exprimi*, he said, "truth can neither be spoken nor written."[28] Kaspar von Schwenckfeld so emphasized religious inwardness that he suspended external observance of the Lord's Supper and downplayed the readable, audible Scriptures in favor of the Word within. This trajectory would lead to the rise of the Quakers in the next century, but it was pursued neither by the mainline reformers nor by most of the Anabaptists. Article 7 of the Augsburg Confession (1530) declared the one holy Christian church to be "the assembly of all believers among whom the Gospel is purely preached and the holy sacraments are administered according to the Gospel."[29]

Historians of the nineteenth century referred to the material and formal principles of the Reformation. In this construal, the matter at stake was the meaning of the Christian gospel: the liberating insight that helpless sinners are graciously justified by the gift of faith alone, apart from any works or merits of their own, entirely on the basis of Christ's atoning work on the cross. For Luther especially, justification by faith alone became the criterion by which all other doctrines and

[26]Foxe, *Acts and Monuments*, 4:218.

[27]On vernacular translations of the Bible, see *CHB* 3:94-140 and Jaroslav Pelikan, *The Reformation of the Bible/The Bible of the Reformation* (New Haven: Yale University Press, 1996), 41-62.

[28]Sebastian Franck, *280 Paradoxes or Wondrous Sayings*, trans. E. J. Furcha (Lewiston, NY: Edwin Mellen Press, 1986), 10, 212.

[29]BoC 42 (BSLK 61).

practices of the church were to be judged. The cross proves everything, he said at the Heidelberg disputation in 1518. The distinction between law and gospel thus became the primary hermeneutical key that unlocked the true meaning of Scripture.

The formal principle of the Reformation, *sola Scriptura,* was closely bound up with proper distinctions between Scripture and tradition. "Scripture alone," said Luther, "is the true lord and master of all writings and doctrine on earth. If that is not granted, what is Scripture good for? The more we reject it, the more we become satisfied with human books and human teachers."[30] On the basis of this principle, the reformers challenged the structures and institutions of the medieval Catholic Church. Even a simple layperson, they asserted, armed with Scripture should be believed above a pope or a council without it. But, however boldly asserted, the doctrine of the primacy of Scripture did not absolve the reformers from dealing with a host of hermeneutical issues that became matters of contention both between Rome and the Reformation and within each of these two communities: the extent of the biblical canon, the validity of critical study of the Bible, the perspicuity of Scripture and its relation to preaching, and the retention of devotional and liturgical practices such as holy days, incense, the burning of candles, the sprinkling of holy water, church art, and musical instruments. Zwingli, the Puritans, and the radicals dismissed such things as a rubbish heap of ceremonials that amounted to nothing but tomfoolery, while Lutherans and Anglicans retained most of them as consonant with Scripture and valuable aids to worship.

It is important to note that while the mainline reformers differed among themselves on many matters, overwhelmingly they saw themselves as part of the ongoing Catholic tradition, indeed as the legitimate bearers of it. This was seen in numerous ways including their sense of continuity with the church of the preceding centuries; their embrace of the ecumenical orthodoxy of the early church; and their desire to read the Bible in dialogue with the exegetical tradition of the church.

In their biblical commentaries, the reformers of the sixteenth century revealed a close familiarity with the preceding exegetical tradition, and they used it respectfully as well as critically in their own expositions of the sacred text. For them, *sola Scriptura* was not *nuda Scriptura*. Rather, the Scriptures were seen as the book given to the church, gathered and guided by the Holy Spirit. In his restatement of the Vincentian canon, Calvin defined the church as "a society of all the saints, a society which, spread over the whole world, and existing in all ages, and bound together by the one doctrine and the one spirit of Christ, cultivates and observes unity of faith and brotherly concord. With this church we deny that we have any disagreement. Nay, rather, as we revere her as our mother, so we desire to remain in her bosom." Defined thus, the church has a real, albeit relative and circumscribed, authority since, as Calvin admits, "We cannot fly without wings."[31] While the reformers could not agree with the Council of Trent (though some recent Catholic theologians have challenged this interpretation) that Scripture and tradition were two separate and equal sources of divine revelation,

[30]LW 32:11-12* (WA 7:317).
[31]John C. Olin, ed., *John Calvin and Jacopo Sadoleto: A Reformation Debate* (New York: Harper Torchbooks, 1966), 61-62, 77.

they did believe in the coinherence of Scripture and tradition. This conviction shaped the way they read and interpreted the Bible.[32]

Schools of Exegesis

The reformers were passionate about biblical exegesis, but they showed little concern for hermeneutics as a separate field of inquiry. Niels Hemmingsen, a Lutheran theologian in Denmark, did write a treatise, *De methodis* (1555), in which he offered a philosophical and theological framework for the interpretation of Scripture. This was followed by the *Clavis Scripturae Sacrae* (1567) of Matthias Flacius Illyricus, which contains some fifty rules for studying the Bible drawn from Scripture itself.[33] However, hermeneutics as we know it came of age only in the Enlightenment and should not be backloaded into the Reformation. It is also true that the word *commentary* did not mean in the sixteenth century what it means for us today. Erasmus provided both annotations and paraphrases on the New Testament, the former a series of critical notes on the text but also containing points of doctrinal substance, the latter a theological overview and brief exposition. Most of Calvin's commentaries began as sermons or lectures presented in the course of his pastoral ministry. In the dedication to his 1519 study of Galatians, Luther declared that his work was "not so much a commentary as a testimony of my faith in Christ."[34] The exegetical work of the reformers was embodied in a wide variety of forms and genres, and the RCS has worked with this broader concept in setting the guidelines for this compendium.

The Protestant reformers shared in common a number of key interpretive principles such as the priority of the grammatical-historical sense of Scripture and the christological centeredness of the entire Bible, but they also developed a number of distinct approaches and schools of exegesis.[35] For the purposes of the RCS, we note the following key figures and families of interpretation in this period.

Biblical humanism. The key figure is Erasmus, whose importance is hard to exaggerate for Catholic and Protestant exegetes alike. His annotated Greek New Testament and fresh Latin translation challenged the hegemony of the Vulgate tradition and was doubtless a factor in the decision of the Council of Trent to establish the Vulgate edition as authentic and normative. Erasmus believed that the wide distribution of the Scriptures would contribute to personal spiritual renewal and the reform of society. In 1547, the English translation of Erasmus's *Paraphrases* was ordered to be placed in every parish church in England. John Colet first encouraged Erasmus

[32]See Timothy George, "An Evangelical Reflection on Scripture and Tradition," *Pro Ecclesia* 9 (2000): 184-207.

[33]See Kenneth G. Hagen, "'*De Exegetica Methodo*': Niels Hemmingsen's *De Methodis* (1555)," in *The Bible in the Sixteenth Century*, ed. David C. Steinmetz (Durham: Duke University Press, 1990), 181-96.

[34]LW 27:159 (WA 2:449). See Kenneth Hagen, "What Did the Term *Commentarius* Mean to Sixteenth-Century Theologians?" in *Théorie et pratique de l'exégèse*, eds. Irena Backus and Francis M. Higman (Geneva: Droz, 1990), 13-38.

[35]I follow here the sketch of Irena Backus, "Biblical Hermeneutics and Exegesis," *OER* 1:152-58. In this work, Backus confines herself to Continental developments, whereas we have noted the exegetical contribution of the English Reformation as well. For more comprehensive listings of sixteenth-century commentators, see Gerald Bray, *Biblical Interpretation* (Downers Grove, IL: InterVarsity Press, 1996), 165-212; and Richard A. Muller, "Biblical Interpretation in the Sixteenth and Seventeenth Centuries," *DMBI* 22-44.

to learn Greek, though he never took up the language himself. Colet's lectures on Paul's epistles at Oxford are reflected in his commentaries on Romans and 1 Corinthians.

Jacques Lefèvre d'Étaples has been called the "French Erasmus" because of his great learning and support for early reform movements in his native land. He published a major edition of the Psalter, as well as commentaries on the Pauline Epistles (1512), the Gospels (1522), and the General Epistles (1527). Guillaume Farel, the early reformer of Geneva, was a disciple of Lefèvre, and the young Calvin also came within his sphere of influence.

Among pre-Tridentine Catholic reformers, special attention should be given to Thomas de Vio, better known as Cajetan. He is best remembered for confronting Martin Luther on behalf of the pope in 1518, but his biblical commentaries (on nearly every book of the Bible) are virtually free of polemic. Like Erasmus, he dared to criticize the Vulgate on linguistic grounds. His commentary on Romans supported the doctrine of justification by grace applied by faith based on the "alien righteousness" of God in Christ. Jared Wicks sums up Cajetan's significance in this way: "Cajetan's combination of passion for pristine biblical meaning with his fully developed theological horizon of understanding indicates, in an intriguing manner, something of the breadth of possibilities open to Roman Catholics before a more restrictive settlement came to exercise its hold on many Catholic interpreters in the wake of the Council of Trent."[36] Girolamo Seripando, like Cajetan, was a cardinal in the Catholic Church, though he belonged to the Augustinian rather than the Dominican order. He was an outstanding classical scholar and published commentaries on Romans and Galatians. Also important is Jacopo Sadoleto, another cardinal, best known for his 1539 letter to the people of Geneva beseeching them to return to the Church of Rome, to which Calvin replied with a manifesto of his own. Sadoleto published a commentary on Romans in 1535. Bucer once commended Sadoleto's teaching on justification as approximating that of the reformers, while others saw him tilting away from the Augustinian tradition toward Pelagianism.[37]

Luther and the Wittenberg School. It was in the name of the Word of God, and specifically as a doctor of Scripture, that Luther challenged the church of his day and inaugurated the Reformation. Though Luther renounced his monastic vows, he never lost that sense of intimacy with *sacra pagina* he first acquired as a young monk. Luther provided three rules for reading the Bible: prayer, meditation, and struggle *(tentatio)*. His exegetical output was enormous. In the American edition of Luther's works, thirty out of the fifty-five volumes are devoted to his biblical studies, and additional translations are planned. Many of his commentaries originated as sermons or lecture notes presented to his students at the university and to his parishioners at Wittenberg's parish church of St. Mary. Luther referred to Galatians as his bride: "The Epistle to the Galatians is my dear epistle. I have betrothed myself to it. It is my Käthe von Bora."[38] He considered his 1535 commentary on Galatians his greatest exegetical work, although his massive commentary on Genesis

[36]Jared Wicks, "Tommaso de Vio Cajetan (1469-1534)," *DMBI* 283-87, here 286.

[37]See the discussion by Bernard Roussel, "Martin Bucer et Jacques Sadolet: la concorde possible," *Bulletin de la Société de l'histoire de protestantisme français* (1976): 525-50, and T. H. L. Parker, *Commentaries on the Epistle to the Romans, 1532–1542* (Edinburgh: T&T Clark, 1986), 25-34.

[38]WATR 1:69 no. 146; cf. LW 54:20 no. 146. I have followed Rörer's variant on Dietrich's notes.

(eight volumes in LW), which he worked on for ten years (1535–1545), must be considered his crowning work. Luther's principles of biblical interpretation are found in his *Open Letter on Translating* and in the prefaces he wrote to all the books of the Bible.

Philipp Melanchthon was brought to Wittenberg to teach Greek in 1518 and proved to be an able associate to Luther in the reform of the church. A set of his lecture notes on Romans was published without his knowledge in 1522. This was revised and expanded many times until his large commentary of 1556. Melanchthon also commented on other New Testament books including Matthew, John, Galatians, and the Petrine epistles, as well as Proverbs, Daniel, and Ecclesiastes. Though he was well trained in the humanist disciplines, Melanchthon devoted little attention to critical and textual matters in his commentaries. Rather, he followed the primary argument of the biblical writer and gathered from this exposition a series of doctrinal topics for special consideration. This method lay behind Melanchthon's *Loci communes* (1521), the first Protestant theology textbook to be published. Another Wittenberger was Johannes Bugenhagen of Pomerania, a prolific commentator on both the Old and New Testaments. His commentary on the Psalms (1524), translated into German by Bucer, applied Luther's teaching on justification to the Psalter. He also wrote a commentary on Job and annotations on many of the books in the Bible. The Lutheran exegetical tradition was shaped by many other scholar-reformers including Andreas Osiander, Johannes Brenz, Caspar Cruciger, Erasmus Sarcerius, Georg Maior, Jacob Andreae, Nikolaus Selnecker, and Johann Gerhard.

The Strasbourg-Basel tradition. Bucer, the son of a shoemaker in Alsace, became the leader of the Reformation in Strasbourg. A former Dominican, he was early on influenced by Erasmus and continued to share his passion for Christian unity. Bucer was the most ecumenical of the Protestant reformers seeking rapprochement with Catholics on justification and an armistice between Luther and Zwingli in their strife over the Lord's Supper. Bucer also had a decisive influence on Calvin, though the latter characterized his biblical commentaries as longwinded and repetitious.[39] In his exegetical work, Bucer made ample use of patristic and medieval sources, though he criticized the abuse and overuse of allegory as "the most blatant insult to the Holy Spirit."[40] He declared that the purpose of his commentaries was "to help inexperienced brethren [perhaps like the apothecary Drilhon, who owned a French translation of Bucer's *Commentary on Matthew*] to understand each of the words and actions of Christ, and in their proper order as far as possible, and to retain an explanation of them in their natural meaning, so that they will not distort God's Word through age-old aberrations or by inept interpretation, but rather with a faithful comprehension of everything as written by the Spirit of God, they may expound to all the churches in their firm upbuilding in faith and love."[41] In addition to writing commentaries on all four Gospels, Bucer published commentaries on Judges, the Psalms, Zephaniah, Romans, and Ephesians. In the early years of the Reformation, there was a great deal of back and forth between Strasbourg and Basel, and both

[39]CNTC 8:3 (CO 10:404).

[40]*DMBI* 249; P. Scherding and F. Wendel, eds., "Un Traité d'exégèse pratique de Bucer," *Revue d'histoire et de philosophie religieuses* 26 (1946): 32-75, here 56.

[41]Martin Bucer, *Enarrationes perpetuae in sacra quatuor evangelia*, 2nd ed. (Strasbourg: Georg Ulrich Andlanus, 1530), 10r; quoted in D. F. Wright, "Martin Bucer," *DMBI* 290.

were centers of a lively publishing trade. Wolfgang Capito, Bucer's associate at Strasbourg, was a notable Hebraist and composed commentaries on Hosea (1529) and Habakkuk (1527).

At Basel, the great Sebastian Münster defended the use of Jewish sources in the Christian study of the Old Testament and published, in addition to his famous Hebrew grammar, an annotated version of the Gospel of Matthew translated from Greek into Hebrew. Oecolampadius, Basel's chief reformer, had been a proofreader in Froben's publishing house and worked with Erasmus on his Greek New Testament and his critical edition of Jerome. From 1523 he was both a preacher and professor of Holy Scripture at Basel. He defended Zwingli's eucharistic theology at the Colloquy of Marburg and published commentaries on 1 John (1524), Romans (1525), and Haggai–Malachi (1525). Oecolampadius was succeeded by Simon Grynaeus, a classical scholar who taught Greek and supported Bucer's efforts to bring Lutherans and Zwinglians together. More in line with Erasmus was Sebastian Castellio, who came to Basel after his expulsion from Geneva in 1545. He is best remembered for questioning the canonicity of the Song of Songs and for his annotations and French translation of the Bible.

The Zurich group. Biblical exegesis in Zurich was centered on the distinctive institution of the *Prophezei*, which began on June 19, 1525. On five days a week, at seven o'clock in the morning, all of the ministers and theological students in Zurich gathered into the choir of the Grossmünster to engage in a period of intense exegesis and interpretation of Scripture. After Zwingli had opened the meeting with prayer, the text of the day was read in Latin, Greek, and Hebrew, followed by appropriate textual or exegetical comments. One of the ministers then delivered a sermon on the passage in German that was heard by many of Zurich's citizens who stopped by the cathedral on their way to work. This institute for advanced biblical studies had an enormous influence as a model for Reformed academies and seminaries throughout Europe. It was also the seedbed for sermon series in Zurich's churches and the extensive exegetical publications of Zwingli, Leo Jud, Konrad Pellikan, Heinrich Bullinger, Oswald Myconius, and Rudolf Gwalther. Zwingli had memorized in Greek all of the Pauline epistles, and this bore fruit in his powerful expository preaching and biblical exegesis. He took seriously the role of grammar, rhetoric, and historical research in explaining the biblical text. For example, he disagreed with Bucer on the value of the Septuagint, regarding it as a trustworthy witness to a proto-Hebrew version earlier than the Masoretic text.

Zwingli's work was carried forward by his successor Bullinger, one of the most formidable scholars and networkers among the reformers. He composed commentaries on Daniel (1565), the Gospels (1542–1546), the Epistles (1537), Acts (1533), and Revelation (1557). He collaborated with Calvin to produce the *Consensus Tigurinus* (1549), a Reformed accord on the nature of the Lord's Supper, and produced a series of fifty sermons on Christian doctrine, known as *Decades*, which became required reading in Elizabethan England. As the *Antistes* ("overseer") of the Zurich church for forty-four years, Bullinger faced opposition from nascent Anabaptism on the one hand and resurgent Catholicism on the other. The need for a well-trained clergy and scholarly resources, including Scripture commentaries, arose from the fact that the Bible was "difficult or obscure to the unlearned, unskillful, unexercised, and malicious or corrupted wills." While forswearing papal claims to infallibility, Bullinger and other leaders of the magisterial Reformation saw the need for a kind of Protestant magisterium as a check against the tendency to read the Bible in "such sense as everyone shall be persuaded in himself to be most convenient."[42]

Two other commentators can be treated in connection with the Zurich group, though each of them had a wide-ranging ministry across the Reformation fronts. A former Benedictine monk, Wolfgang Musculus, embraced the Reformation in the 1520s and served briefly as the secretary to Bucer in Strasbourg. He shared Bucer's desire for Protestant unity and served for seventeen years (1531–1548) as a pastor and reformer in Augsburg. After a brief time in Zurich, where he came under the influence of Bullinger, Musculus was called to Bern, where he taught the Scriptures and published commentaries on the Psalms, the Decalogue, Genesis, Romans, Isaiah, 1 and 2 Corinthians, Galatians and Ephesians, Philippians, Colossians, 1 and 2 Thessalonians, and 1 Timothy. Drawing on his exegetical writings, Musculus also produced a compendium of Protestant theology that was translated into English in 1563 as *Commonplaces of Christian Religion*.

Peter Martyr Vermigli was a Florentine-born scholar and Augustinian friar who embraced the Reformation and fled to Switzerland in 1542. Over the next twenty years, he would gain an international reputation as a prolific scholar and leading theologian within the Reformed community. He lectured on the Old Testament at Strasbourg, was made regius professor at Oxford, corresponded with the Italian refugee church in Geneva and spent the last years of his life as professor of Hebrew at Zurich. Vermigli published commentaries on 1 Corinthians, Romans, and Judges during his lifetime. His biblical lectures on Genesis, Lamentations, 1 and 2 Samuel, and 1 and 2 Kings were published posthumously. The most influential of his writings was the *Loci communes (Commonplaces)*, a theological compendium drawn from his exegetical writings.

The Genevan reformers. What Zwingli and Bullinger were to Zurich, Calvin and Beza were to Geneva. Calvin has been called "the father of modern biblical scholarship," and his exegetical work is without parallel in the Reformation. Because of the success of his *Institutes of the Christian Religion* Calvin has sometimes been thought of as a man of one book, but he always intended the *Institutes*, which went through eight editions in Latin and five in French during his lifetime, to serve as a guide to the study of the Bible, to show the reader "what he ought especially to seek in Scripture and to what end he ought to relate its contents." Jacob Arminius, who modified several principles of Calvin's theology, recommended his commentaries next to the Bible, for, as he said, Calvin "is incomparable in the interpretation of Scripture."[43] Drawing on his superb knowledge of Greek and Hebrew and his thorough training in humanist rhetoric, Calvin produced commentaries on all of the New Testament books except 2 and 3 John and Revelation. Calvin's Old Testament commentaries originated as sermon and lecture series and include Genesis, Psalms, Hosea, Isaiah, minor prophets, Daniel, Jeremiah and Lamentations, a harmony of the last four books of Moses,

[42]Euan Cameron, *The European Reformation* (Oxford: Oxford University Press, 1991), 120.

[43]Letter to Sebastian Egbert (May 3, 1607), in *Praestantium ac eruditorum virorum epistolae ecclesiasticae et theologicae varii argumenti*, ed. Christiaan Hartsoeker (Amsterdam: Henricus Dendrinus, 1660), 236-37. Quoted in A. M. Hunter, *The Teaching of Calvin* (London: James Clarke, 1950), 20.

Ezekiel 1–20, and Joshua. Calvin sought for brevity and clarity in all of his exegetical work. He emphasized the illumination of the Holy Spirit as essential to a proper understanding of the text. Calvin underscored the continuity between the two Testaments (one covenant in two dispensations) and sought to apply the plain or natural sense of the text to the church of his day. In the preface to his own influential commentary on Romans, Karl Barth described how Calvin worked to recover the mind of Paul and make the apostle's message relevant to his day:

> How energetically Calvin goes to work, first scientifically establishing the text ("what stands there?"), then following along the footsteps of its thought; that is to say, he conducts a discussion with it until the wall between the first and the sixteenth centuries becomes transparent, and until there in the first century Paul speaks and here the man of the sixteenth century hears, until indeed the conversation between document and reader becomes concentrated upon the substance (which must be the same now as then).[44]

Beza was elected moderator of Geneva's Company of Pastors after Calvin's death in 1564 and guided the Genevan Reformation over the next four decades. His annotated Latin translation of the Greek New Testament (1556) and his further revisions of the Greek text established his reputation as the leading textual critic of the sixteenth century after Erasmus. Beza completed the translation of Marot's metrical Psalter, which became a centerpiece of Huguenot piety and Reformed church life. Though known for his polemical writings on grace, free will, and predestination, Beza's work is marked by a strong pastoral orientation and concern for a Scripture-based spirituality.

Robert Estienne (Stephanus) was a printer-scholar who had served the royal household in Paris. After his conversion to Protestantism, in 1550 he moved to Geneva, where he published a series of notable editions and translations of the Bible. He also produced sermons and commentaries on Job, Ecclesiastes, the Song of Songs, Romans and Hebrews, as well as dictionaries, concordances, and a thesaurus of biblical terms. He also published the first editions of the Bible with chapters divided into verses, an innovation that quickly became universally accepted.

The British Reformation. Commentary writing in England and Scotland lagged behind the continental Reformation for several reasons. In 1500, there were only three publishing houses in England compared with more than two hundred on the Continent. A 1408 statute against publishing or reading the Bible in English, stemming from the days of Lollardy, stifled the free flow of ideas, as was seen in the fate of Tyndale. Moreover, the nature of the English Reformation from Henry through Elizabeth provided little stability for the flourishing of biblical scholarship. In the sixteenth century, many "hot-gospel" Protestants in England were edified by the English translations of commentaries and theological writings by the Continental reformers. The influence of Calvin and Beza was felt especially in the Geneva Bible with its "Protestant glosses" of theological notes and references.

During the later Elizabethan and Stuart church, however, the indigenous English commentary came into its own. Both Anglicans and Puritans contributed to this outpouring of biblical studies.

[44]Karl Barth, *Die Römerbrief* (Zurich: TVZ, 1940), 11, translated by T. H. L. Parker as the epigraph to *Calvin's New Testament Commentaries*, 2nd ed. (Louisville, KY: Westminster John Knox, 1993).

The sermons of Lancelot Andrewes and John Donne are replete with exegetical insights based on a close study of the Greek and Hebrew texts. Among the Reformed authors in England, none was more influential than William Perkins, the greatest of the early Puritan theologians, who published commentaries on Galatians, Jude, Revelation, and the Sermon on the Mount (Mt 5–7). John Cotton, one of his students, wrote commentaries on the Song of Songs, Ecclesiastes, and Revelation before departing for New England in 1633. The separatist pastor Henry Ainsworth was an outstanding scholar of Hebrew and wrote major commentaries on the Pentateuch, the Psalms, and the Song of Songs. In Scotland, Robert Rollock, the first principal of Edinburgh University (1585), wrote numerous commentaries including those on the Psalms, Ephesians, Daniel, Romans, 1 and 2 Thessalonians, John, Colossians, and Hebrews. Joseph Mede and Thomas Brightman were leading authorities on Revelation and contributed to the apocalyptic thought of the seventeenth century. Mention should also be made of Archbishop James Ussher, whose *Annals of the Old Testament* was published in 1650. Ussher developed a keen interest in biblical chronology and calculated that the creation of the world had taken place on October 26, 4004 B.C. As late as 1945, the Scofield Reference Bible still retained this date next to Genesis 1:1, but later editions omitted it because of the lack of evidence on which to fix such dates.[45]

Anabaptism. Irena Backus has noted that there was no school of "dissident" exegesis during the Reformation, and the reasons are not hard to find. The radical Reformation was an ill-defined movement that existed on the margins of official church life in the sixteenth century. The denial of infant baptism and the refusal to swear an oath marked radicals as a seditious element in society, and they were persecuted by Protestants and Catholics alike. However, in the RCS we have made an attempt to include some voices of the radical Reformation, especially among the Anabaptists. While the Anabaptists published few commentaries in the sixteenth century, they were avid readers and quoters of the Bible. Numerous exegetical gems can be found in their letters, treatises, martyr acts (especially *The Martyrs' Mirror*), hymns, and histories. They placed a strong emphasis on the memorizing of Scripture and quoted liberally from vernacular translations of the Bible. George H. Williams has noted that "many an Anabaptist theological tract was really a beautiful mosaic of Scripture texts."[46] In general, most Anabaptists accepted the apocryphal books as canonical, contrasted outer word and inner spirit with relative degrees of strictness and saw the New Testament as normative for church life and social ethics (witness their pacifism, nonswearing, emphasis on believers' baptism and congregational discipline).

We have noted the Old Testament translation of Ludwig Hätzer, who became an antitrinitarian, and Hans Denck that they published at Worms in 1527. Denck also wrote a notable commentary on Micah. Conrad Grebel belonged to a Greek reading circle in Zurich and came to his Anabaptist convictions while poring over the text of Erasmus's New Testament. The only Anabaptist leader with university credentials was Balthasar Hubmaier, who was made a doctor of theology (Ingolstadt, 1512) in the same year as Luther. His reflections on the Bible are found in his numerous

[45]*The New Scofield Reference Bible* (New York: Oxford University Press, 1967), vi.
[46]George H. Williams, *The Radical Reformation*, 3rd ed. (Kirksville, MO: Sixteenth Century Journal Publishers, 1992), 1247.

writings, which include the first catechism of the Reformation (1526), a two-part treatise on the freedom of the will and a major work *(On the Sword)* setting forth positive attitudes toward the role of government and the Christian's place in society. Melchior Hoffman was an apocalyptic seer who wrote commentaries on Romans, Revelation, and Daniel 12. He predicted that Christ would return in 1533. More temperate was Pilgram Marpeck, a mining engineer who embraced Anabaptism and traveled widely throughout Switzerland and south Germany, from Strasbourg to Augsburg. His "Admonition of 1542" is the longest published defense of Anabaptist views on baptism and the Lord's Supper. He also wrote many letters that functioned as theological tracts for the congregations he had founded dealing with topics such as the fruits of repentance, the lowliness of Christ, and the unity of the church. Menno Simons, a former Catholic priest, became the most outstanding leader of the Dutch Anabaptist movement. His masterpiece was the *Foundation of Christian Doctrine* published in 1540. His other writings include *Meditation on the Twenty-fifth Psalm* (1537); *A Personal Exegesis of Psalm Twenty-five* modeled on the style of Augustine's *Confessions; Confession of the Triune God* (1550), directed against Adam Pastor, a former disciple of Menno who came to doubt the divinity of Christ; *Meditations and Prayers for Mealtime* (1557); and the *Cross of the Saints* (1554), an exhortation to faithfulness in the face of persecution. Like many other Anabaptists, Menno emphasized the centrality of discipleship *(Nachfolge)* as a deliberate repudiation of the old life and a radical commitment to follow Jesus as Lord.

Reading Scripture with the Reformers

In 1947, Gerhard Ebeling set forth his thesis that the history of the Christian church is the history of the interpretation of Scripture. Since that time, the place of the Bible in the story of the church has been investigated from many angles. A better understanding of the history of exegesis has been aided by new critical editions and scholarly discussions of the primary sources. The *Cambridge History of the Bible*, published in three volumes (1963–1970), remains a standard reference work in the field. The ACCS built on, and itself contributed to, the recovery of patristic biblical wisdom of both East and West. Beryl Smalley's *The Study of the Bible in the Middle Ages* (1940) and Henri de Lubac's *Medieval Exegesis: The Four Senses of Scripture* (1959) are essential reading for understanding the monastic and scholastic settings of commentary work between Augustine and Luther. The Reformation took place during what has been called "le grand siècle de la Bible."[47] Aided by the tools of Renaissance humanism and the dynamic impetus of Reformation theology (including permutations and reactions against it), the sixteenth century produced an unprecedented number of commentaries on every book in the Bible. Drawing from this vast storehouse of exegetical treasures, the RCS allows us to read Scripture along with the reformers. In doing so, it serves as a practical homiletic and devotional guide to some of the greatest masters of biblical interpretation in the history of the church.

The RCS gladly acknowledges its affinity with and dependence on recent scholarly investigations of Reformation-era exegesis. Between 1976 and 1990, three international colloquia on the

[47] J-R. Aarmogathe, ed., *Bible de tous les temps*, 8 vols.; vol. 6, *Le grand siècle de la Bible* (Paris: Beauchesne, 1989).

history of biblical exegesis in the sixteenth century took place in Geneva and in Durham, North Carolina.[48] Among those participating in these three gatherings were a number of scholars who have produced groundbreaking works in the study of biblical interpretation in the Reformation. These include Elsie McKee, Irena Backus, Kenneth Hagen, Scott H. Hendrix, Richard A. Muller, Guy Bedouelle, Gerald Hobbs, John B. Payne, Bernard Roussel, Pierre Fraenkel, and David C. Steinmetz (1936–2015). Among other scholars whose works are indispensible for the study of this field are Heinrich Bornkamm, Jaroslav Pelikan, Heiko A. Oberman, James S. Preus, T. H. L. Parker, David F. Wright, Tony Lane, John L. Thompson, Frank A. James, and Timothy J. Wengert.[49] Among these scholars no one has had a greater influence on the study of Reformation exegesis than David C. Steinmetz. A student of Oberman, he emphasized the importance of understanding the Reformation in medieval perspective. In addition to important studies on Luther and Staupitz, he pioneered the method of comparative exegesis showing both continuity and discontinuity between major Reformation figures and the preceding exegetical traditions (see his *Luther in Context* and *Calvin in Context*). From his base at Duke University, he spawned what might be called a Steinmetz school, a cadre of students and scholars whose work on the Bible in the Reformation era continues to shape the field. Steinmetz served on the RCS Board of Editorial Advisors, and a number of our volume editors pursued doctoral studies under his supervision.

In 1980, Steinmetz published "The Superiority of Pre-critical Exegesis," a seminal essay that not only placed Reformation exegesis in the context of the preceding fifteen centuries of the church's study of the Bible but also challenged certain assumptions underlying the hegemony of historical-critical exegesis of the post-Enlightenment academy.[50] Steinmetz helps us to approach the reformers and other precritical interpreters of the Bible on their own terms as faithful witnesses to the church's apostolic tradition. For them, a specific book or pericope had to be understood within the scope of the consensus of the canon. Thus the reformers, no less than the Fathers and the schoolmen, interpreted the hymn of the Johannine prologue about the preexistent Christ in consonance with the creation narrative of Genesis 1. In the same way, Psalm 22, Isaiah 53, and Daniel 7 are seen as part of an overarching storyline that finds ultimate fulfillment in Jesus Christ. Reading the Bible with the resources of the new learning, the reformers challenged the exegetical conclusions of their medieval predecessors at many points. However, unlike Alexander Campbell in the nineteenth century, their aim was not to "open the New Testament as if mortal man had never seen it before."[51]

[48]Olivier Fatio and Pierre Fraenkel, eds., *Histoire de l'exégèse au XVIe siècle: texts du colloque international tenu à Genève en 1976* (Geneva: Droz, 1978); David C. Steinmetz, ed., *The Bible in the Sixteenth Century* [Second International Colloquy on the History of Biblical Exegesis in the Sixteenth Century] (Durham: Duke University Press, 1990); Irena Backus and Francis M. Higman, eds., *Théorie et pratique de l'exégèse. Actes du troisième colloque international sur l'histoire de l'exégèse biblique au XVIe siècle, Genève, 31 août–2 septembre 1988* (Geneva: Droz, 1990); see also Guy Bedouelle and Bernard Roussel, eds., *Bible de tous les temps*, 8 vols.; vol. 5, *Le temps des Réformes et la Bible* (Paris: Beauchesne, 1989).

[49]For bibliographical references and evaluation of these and other contributors to the scholarly study of Reformation-era exegesis, see Richard A. Muller, "Biblical Interpretation in the Era of the Reformation: The View From the Middle Ages," in *Biblical Interpretation in the Era of the Reformation: Essays Presented to David C. Steinmetz in Honor of His Sixtieth Birthday*, ed. Richard A. Muller and John L. Thompson (Grand Rapids: Eerdmans, 1996), 3-22.

[50]David C. Steinmetz, "The Superiority of Pre-Critical Exegesis," *Theology Today* 37 (1980): 27-38.

[51]Alexander Campbell, *Memoirs of Alexander Campbell*, ed. Robert Richardson (Cincinnati: Standard Publishing Company, 1872), 97.

Rather, they wanted to do their biblical work as part of an interpretive conversation within the family of the people of God. In the reformers' emphatic turn to the literal sense, which prompted their many blasts against the unrestrained use of allegory, their work was an extension of a similar impulse made by Thomas Aquinas and Nicholas of Lyra.

This is not to discount the radically new insights gained by the reformers in their dynamic engagement with the text of Scripture; nor should we dismiss in a reactionary way the light shed on the meaning of the Bible by the scholarly accomplishments of the past two centuries. However, it is to acknowledge that the church's exegetical tradition is an indispensible aid for the proper interpretation of Scripture. And this means, as Richard Muller has said, that "while it is often appropriate to recognize that traditionary readings of the text are erroneous on the grounds offered by the historical-critical method, we ought also to recognize that the conclusions offered by historical-critical exegesis may themselves be quite erroneous on the grounds provided by the exegesis of the patristic, medieval, and reformation periods."[52] The RCS wishes to commend the exegetical work of the Reformation era as a program of retrieval for the sake of renewal—spiritual réssourcement for believers committed to the life of faith today.

George Herbert was an English pastor and poet who reaped the benefits of the renewal of biblical studies in the age of the Reformation. He referred to the Scriptures as a book of infinite sweetness, "a mass of strange delights," a book with secrets to make the life of anyone good. In describing the various means pastors require to be fully furnished in the work of their calling, Herbert provided a rationale for the history of exegesis and for the Reformation Commentary on Scripture:

> The fourth means are commenters and Fathers, who have handled the places controverted, which the parson by no means refuseth. As he doth not so study others as to neglect the grace of God in himself and what the Holy Spirit teacheth him, so doth he assure himself that God in all ages hath had his servants to whom he hath revealed his Truth, as well as to him; and that as one country doth not bear all things that there may be a commerce, so neither hath God opened or will open all to one, that there may be a traffic in knowledge between the servants of God for the planting both of love and humility. Wherefore he hath one comment[ary] at least upon every book of Scripture, and ploughing with this, and his own meditations, he enters into the secrets of God treasured in the holy Scripture.[53]

Timothy George
General Editor

[52]Richard A. Muller and John L. Thompson, "The Significance of Precritical Exegesis: Retrospect and Prospect," in *Biblical Interpretation in the Era of the Reformation: Essays Presented to David C. Steinmetz in Honor of His Sixtieth Birthday*, ed. Richard A. Muller and John L. Thompson (Grand Rapids: Eerdmans, 1996), 342.
[53]George Herbert, *The Complete English Poems* (London: Penguin, 1991), 205.

INTRODUCTION TO ISAIAH 1–39

For centuries the book of Isaiah, with its prophecies about a virgin birth, a servant who dies to bear the punishment of the people, and a son who will reign on David's throne forever, offered Christian (and Jewish) interpreters plenty of reasons for commentary. Among Christian interpreters, the prevalence of passages about the Messiah even led some to refer to Isaiah as "the Fifth Gospel."[1] Like many other biblical books, Isaiah received increased attention during the time of the Reformation. Isaiah in particular ranked high among Old Testament biblical commentaries in the early modern period. These commentaries, like those in the medieval era, took many different forms and names.[2] Interpreters published paraphrases, translations, sermons, annotations, and expositions from their lectures.[3] These commentaries included differing amounts of philological, linguistic, textual, exegetical, theological, and practical comments, with a variety of approaches in style and interpretive assumptions. Very few of these commentaries were first written versions of material like commentaries in the modern sense of the term.

Between 1525 and 1654, Protestant theologians published more than thirty substantial Isaiah commentaries. This, of course, is on top of the considerable number of individual sermons and theological treatises that used portions of Isaiah.[4] The major Protestant commentaries on Isaiah in this timespan tally nearly twenty thousand pages. The majority of these Protestant commentaries exceeded four hundred pages each, with several of them surpassing eight hundred pages.

Reformation Commentaries on Isaiah: Historical Context

These commentaries were intended to clarify the words of Scripture—not replace or displace them. Protestant interpreters engaged primarily with the biblical text but also dialogued with other interpreters—from both the past and the present. The most important medieval exegetes on Isaiah included Origen (third century), Eusebius of Caesarea (c. 325), John Chrysostom

---

[1]For the use of this term, see John F. Sawyer, *The Fifth Gospel: Isaiah in the History of Christianity* (Cambridge: Cambridge University Press, 1996).

[2]For a thorough description of the various types of commentaries in the Reformation era, see Kenneth Hagen, "What Did the Term Commentarius Mean to Sixteenth-Century Theologians?," in *Théorie et pratique de l'exégèse: Actes du troisième colloque international sur l'historie de l'exégèse biblique au XVIe siècle*, ed. Irena Backus and Francis Higman (Geneva: Droz, 1990), 13-38. See also Scott Manetsch, ed., *1 Corinthians*, Reformation Commentary on Scripture New Testament 9a (Downers Grove, IL: InterVarsity Press, 2017), xlvii-lii.

[3]Commentaries based on lectures by professors took various titles, such as *enarrationes*, *explicationes*, or *expositiones*. Commentaries from sermons by preachers received titles such as *postillae*, *conciones*, or *homiliae*.

[4]For example, Luther's sermons on Is 9 were published in 1526 and later translated into English. Likewise, there are hundreds of published sermons on Is 53 alone.

(c. 386), Jerome, (c. 408–410), Cyril of Alexandria (c. 428), Isidore of Seville (c. 600), Thomas Aquinas (c. 1252), and Nicholas of Lyra (1322–1333). Reformation commentators also engaged with the *Glossa Ordinaria*, commonly included in many versions of their Vulgate Bibles. Additionally, for several interpreters of this time, on Old Testament books such as Isaiah, they also engaged with Jewish rabbinic interpreters such as Rabbis David Kimchi, Abraham Ibn Ezra, and Solomon ben Isaac (also known as Rashi). These commentaries—and the sermons and lectures on which they were based—supplied future pastors and theologians with significant content necessary for their academic and ecclesiastical training.

Commentary on Isaiah in the Reformation era comes from all the various traditions that developed during this time period.[5] Not all of them produced actual commentaries, but they certainly exegeted, interpreted, and applied passages from Isaiah in their writings. Among those who did publish commentaries on Isaiah, Johannes Oecolampadius (1482–1531), the reformer of Basel, was the first Protestant to produce a Reformation commentary on Isaiah in 1525, based on his lectures from 1523.[6] This important event launched a renewed interest in the prophet and in the exposition of Old Testament literature. Oecolampadius's teaching on Isaiah gained the attention of Martin Luther, who even sent him words of encouragement while he was lecturing.[7] In his own later published work on Isaiah, Luther noted, "Oecolampadius has translated Isaiah with adequate care," and, "Oecolampadius has sufficiently done good work in the grammar."[8] Not only did Oecolampadius's work pioneer new ways of commenting on Isaiah, but his Isaiah lectures stood as a model for how the prophet would be discussed in the early years of the Reformation.

Apparently, the commentary by Oecolampadius was sufficient enough that it nearly stood alone in the Strasbourg-Basel tradition. In fact, when Ulrich Zwingli explains the reason for his own annotations on Isaiah published in 1529, he states, "I do not want you to suspect me of calling the most learned and most godly commentary of Oecolampadius into doubt."[9] Zwingli praises Oecolampadius's commentary as a "cornucopia" that "truly made clear" the genuine sense of Isaiah.[10] While Zwingli's work was the first in the Zurich tradition, many others taught and preached on Isaiah. Theodor Bibliander (c. 1504–1564) published his "Oration on the Life and Times of

[5]See the General Introduction to this volume, xxxii-xxxviii.

[6]For background on Oecolampadius, see Jeff Fisher, *A Christoscopic Reading of Scripture: Johannes Oecolampadius on Hebrews* (Göttingen: Vandenhoeck & Ruprecht, 2016); Ernst Staehelin, *Das theologische Lebenswerk Oekolampad*, Quellen und Forschungen zur Reformationsgeschichte 21 (Leipzig: Heinsius, 1939).

[7]In a letter to Nicholas Grebel in June 1523, Luther writes, "I am glad indeed that Johannes Oecolampadius is lecturing on Isaiah, though I hear that many are not pleased, but that is the fortune of Christian teaching." He later wrote directly to Oecolampadius, "Certainly we have exceedingly approved of your spirit and this excellent deed. . . . May the Lord strengthen your intention in lecturing on Isaiah, though it was written to me that Erasmus is displeased." See WA 12:56; Ernst Staehelin, ed., *Briefe und Akten zum Leben Oekolampads*, Quellen und Forschungen zur Reformationsgeschichte 10 (Leipzig: Heinsius, 1927; repr., New York: Johnson, 1971), 222-23; Martin Luther, *Luther's Correspondence and Other Contemporary Letters*, ed. Preserved Smith and Charles M. Jacobs (Eugene, OR: Wipf and Stock, 2009), 2:187-189 (no. 589) and 190 (no. 591).

[8]LW 16:4 (WA 31.2:2); WA 25:88. Brooks Schramm notes that Luther made "significant use" of Oecolampadius's Isaiah commentary. See Schramm, "Lectures on Isaiah 53, 1528–1530," in *The Annotated Luther: The Interpretation of Luther*, ed. Euan Cameron (Minneapolis: Fortress, 2017), 6:346.

[9]ZSW 14 / CR 101:88. See also Staehelin, *Briefe und Akten* 19:342 (no. 679).

[10]Zwingli explains, "After those [the LXX and Jerome], Oecolampadius—a man in all respects more fluent than [them] according to the opinion of a multitude—also gave to us Isaiah, truly made clear in his commentary, such that no work at any time by

Isaiah" in 1532, which Bullinger recommended and included a portion of in his own commentary.[11] Konrad Pellikan (1478–1556) composed a relatively short commentary in 1534. In 1557, Wolfgang Musculus (1497–1563) produced the most thorough and substantial commentary on Isaiah, incorporating lexical, philological, grammatical, exegetical, historical, and theological comments. Both Heinrich Bullinger (1504–1575) and Rudolf Gwalther (1519–1586) had their extended sermon series on Isaiah published as commentaries in 1567 and 1583 respectively. Bullinger preached 190 homilies on Isaiah, and Gwalther's volume includes 327 weekday homilies from the 1580s. There is no shortage of material on Isaiah from the Zurich exegetical tradition.

The Lutheran-Wittenberg tradition also saw a significant number of commentaries published on Isaiah. Martin Luther taught on Isaiah from 1527 to 1530. While Luther's lectures were not published more completely until 1914, an edition of his scholia was published in 1532, and in an expanded version in 1534.[12] Lutheran authors produced more than half the Protestant commentaries during this time period. The two earliest Lutheran commentaries were by Veit Dietrich (1506–1549) and Johannes Brenz (1499–1570), published in 1548 and 1550. In 1549, Philipp Melanchthon (1497–1560) began lecturing on Isaiah and sent his early work to Leipzig for publication. However, Melanchthon's posthumously published comments in 1561 only cover the argument of the book and the first four chapters.[13] Among the many Lutheran commentaries published in the late 1560s to the late 1580s, the volumes by Nikolaus Selnecker (1530–1592) in 1569 and Dietrich Schnepff (1525–1586) in 1575 are the most significant. A unique contribution from the Lutherans is the 1584 publication by Philipp Heilbrunner (1546–1616), which provided a series of questions and answers on theological topics drawn from Isaiah similar to the format of a catechism. The majority of this work is quotations from Isaiah organized around thirty-four theological topics.[14]

In the Geneva tradition, of course, the commentary on Isaiah by John Calvin (1509–1564) is and remains the most important. Like Oecolampadius before him, Calvin chose Isaiah as the first Old Testament book on which he lectured. His lectures from 1549 were published in 1551 based on the careful notes taken and developed by Nicolas Des Gallars (Gallasius).[15] The other important work in the Geneva tradition was published posthumously from the work of French Reformed pastor Augustin Marlorat (1506–1562). His 1564 compilation commentary on Isaiah includes excerpts from Oecolampadius, Zwingli, Luther, Pellikan, Calvin, Musculus, and François Vatable interspersed with some of his own exposition. This work is quite important since

anyone has emerged that can be equally called κέρας ἀμαλθείας, that is a cornucopia, that holds to the sense and comparison of the sacred letters" (ZSW 14 / CR 101:87-88).

[11]See Bullinger, *Isaias*, 353r. Bibliander's oratio on Isaiah was held on January 11, 1532, and printed as a reworked version on February 9. See also Bruce Gordon, "'Christo testimonium reddunt omnes scripturae': Theodor Bibliander's Oration on Isaiah (1532) and Commentary on Nahum (1534)," in *Shaping the Bible in the Reformation* (Leiden: Brill, 2012), 107-41.

[12]See LW 16:ix-xi; 17:ix-x, on this background and the discovery of the Lauterbach manuscript, which provides Luther's lectures on Isaiah. Luther announced his teaching on Isaiah in May 1527 and began in July but was interrupted by an outbreak of the plague and later by the Marburg Colloquy.

[13]MO 13:793-806.

[14]See Heilbrunner, *Esaiae Prophetae Vaticinia*, 14-16, for the index of these topics.

[15]CO 36:1.

Marlorat not only selected significant interpreters but also selected what he deemed most important from those significant interpreters. This work was republished in 1610.

Others in the Reformed tradition who produced commentaries on Isaiah include the German Reformed author of the Heidelberg Catechism, Zacharias Ursinus (1534–1583); Italian Reformed Giovanni Diodati (1576–1649); and Abraham Scultetus (1566–1625), a German Reformed professor who had previously been Lutheran. Ursinus's posthumous publication in 1584 only covers the first twenty-two chapters of Isaiah but goes into significant depth with many different approaches to addressing matters raised by the biblical text.[16] Diodati's publication of 1607 provides a seventeen-page outline, which he labels an *Analysis*, of the entire book organized and subdivided into many parts, followed by several brief annotations on each chapter. Scultetus's 1618 volume is unique in that he provides sermon ideas on every chapter of Isaiah.

There are few so-called radical or Anabaptist commentators. Those most closely associated with this group who published comments on Isaiah include Sebastian Castellio (1515–1563) and Martin Cellarius Borrhaus (1499–1564). Castellio's 1551 annotations are part of his larger work on the whole Bible and are typically quite brief. The 1561 commentary on Isaiah by Borrhaus is far more thorough. However, there are also comments in polemical and catechetical writings from figures such as Andreas Bodenstein von Karlstadt (1486–1541), Balthasar Hubmaier (1480/1485–1528), and Menno Simons (c. 1496–1561). Some of these are included in this volume.

While there were not many biblical commentaries published in England during the Reformation era, John Trapp (1601–1699), John Mayer (1583–1664), and William Day (c. 1605–1684) all published Isaiah commentaries in the 1650s. In addition to these works, comments in this volume have been drawn from the *English Annotations* edited by John Downame (c. 1571–1625) and expositions by the bishop of Lincoln, Thomas Cooper (1517?–1594), on the portions of Isaiah that lined up with the Common Prayer readings on Sundays around Advent and Christmas.

Other voices incorporated in this volume include women who, though they did not produce commentaries, produced written works that used excerpts from Isaiah to address issues of their day.[17] This volume features interpretations and applications of Isaiah by Argula von Grumbach (c. 1490–c. 1564) and Katharina Schütz Zell (1497/8–1562) among others.

In addition to the explosion of Protestant commentaries on Isaiah, between 1534 and 1642 Roman Catholic theologians published thirteen significant commentaries on Isaiah. Cardinal (Thomas de Vio) Cajetan was the earliest to publish a volume on Isaiah, although he only completed the first three chapters before his death. Most of these Catholic commentaries were published around the time of the Council of Trent in the late 1550s to mid-1570s.

[16]Urisunus's Isaiah commentary came from lectures he delivered in Neustadt between May 26, 1578, and May 11, 1582. A long illness in 1583 prevented him from completing the lecture. For an analysis of Ursinus's theology and hermeneutical methodology from his lectures on Isaiah, see Boris Wagner-Peterson, *Doctrina schola vitae: Zacharias Ursinus (1534–1583) als Schriftausleger* (Göttingen: Vandenhoeck & Ruprecht, 2013).

[17]See Marion Ann Taylor, ed., *Handbook of Women Interpreters* (Grand Rapids, MI: Baker, 2012).

Table 1. Major Published Commentaries on Isaiah (1523–1654)

Protestant

Author	Type	Pages	Tradition	Year Published
Johannes Oecolampadius (1482–1531)	commentary	619	Reformed (Basel)	1525
Ulrich Zwingli (1484–1531)	commentary	215	Reformed (Zurich)	1529
Martin Luther (1483–1546)	scholia, lecture notes	585	Lutheran	1532, 1534, 1914
Theodor Bibliander (c. 1504–1564)	oration	64	Reformed (Zurich)	1532
Konrad Pellikan (1478–1556)	commentary	160	Reformed (Zurich)	1534
Veit Dietrich (1506–1549)	commentary	575	Lutheran	1548
Johannes Brenz (1499–1570)	commentary	1079	Lutheran	1550, 1555
Sebastian Castellio (1515–1563)	annotations	67	French humanist / radical	1551
John Calvin (1509–1564)	commentary	978	Reformed (Geneva)	1551
Wolfgang Musculus (1497–1563)	commentary	856	Reformed (Zurich)	1557
Philipp Melanchthon (1497–1560)	argument and notes (Is 1–4)	14	Lutheran	1561–1564
Martin (Cellarius) Borrhaus (1499–1564)	commentary	642	German Reformed / radical*	1561
Viktorin Strigel (1524–1569)	oration	40	Lutheran	1564
Augustin Marlorat (c. 1506–1562)	excerpted expositions	530	French Reformed (Geneva)	1564 [1610]
Heinrich Bullinger (1504–1575)	exposited homilies	705	Reformed (Zurich)	1567
Nicolas Selnecker (1530–1592)	commentary	1064	Lutheran	1569, 1579
Andreas Hyperius (1511–1564)	annotations	615	Flemish Lutheran, Reformed	1574
Dietrich Schnepff (1525–1586)	scholia and para-phrases	1005	Lutheran	1575
Lucas Osiander (1534–1604)	brief explanations	454	Lutheran	1578
Johann Wigand (c. 1523–1587)	brief explanations	712	Lutheran	1581
Martin Moller (1547–1606)	sermons and arguments	220	Lutheran	1581
Rudolf Gwalther (1519–1586)	homilies	857	Reformed (Zurich)	1583
Philipp Heilbrunner (1546–1616)	theological topics	587	Lutheran	1584
Zacharias Ursinus (1534–1583)	lectures (Is 1–22)	591	Reformed (German)	1584
Heinrich Möller (1530–1589)	commentary (Is 1–27)	472	Lutheran	1588
Johannes Pappus (1549–1610)	commentary	135	Lutheran	1593
Giovanni Diodati (1576–1649)	annotations	57	Reformed (Italian)	1607, 1648
Daniel Arcularius (c. 1540–1596)	commentary	862	Lutheran	1607
Johannes Piscator (1546–1625)	commentary	502	German Reformed (Arminian)	1612
Tilemann Hesshusius (1527–1588)	commentary	728	Lutheran	1617
Abraham Scultetus (1566–1625)	sermon ideas	391	Lutheran/Reformed	1618
Johannes Förster (1496–1558)	commentary	819	Lutheran	1620

John Trapp (1601–1699)	commentary	218	English Puritan	1650
John Mayer (1583–1664)	commentary	325	English Separatist	1652
William Day (c. 1605–1684)	exposition	537	Anglican	1654

Roman Catholic

Cardinal Cajetan (Thomas de Vio) (1469–1534)	commentary (Is 1–3)	13	Roman Catholic	1534
Adam Sasbout (1516–1563)	commentary	438	Roman Catholic	1558, 1563
Francisco Foreiro (1523–1581)	commentary	478	Portuguese Roman Catholic Dominican	1563, 1565, 1566, 1567
Hector Pinto (1528–1584)	commentary	542	Roman Catholic	1561, 1567, 1572
Léon de Castro (d. 1580/86)	commentary	1021	Spanish Roman Catholic	1570
Miguel de Palacio (c. 1525–1593)	tropological explanations	1086	Roman Catholic	1572
Jerónimo Osório da Fonseca (1506/15–1580	paraphrases	288	Portuguese humanist, Roman Catholic	1579, 1584, 1612
Thaddaeus Guidellus (Perusinus) (1511/15–1605/6)	explanations	856	Augustinian Roman Catholic	1598
Benito Arias Montano (1527–1598)	commentary	1463	Spanish Roman Catholic	1599
Diego Alvarez de Medina (c. 1550–1635)	commentary	1346	Roman Catholic	1599/1602
Hieronymus Oleastri (d. 1563)	commentary	650	Roman Catholic	1622
Cornelius á Lapide (1567–1637)	commentary	412	Flemish Jesuit Roman Catholic	1622

Already in the sixteenth and seventeenth centuries, later interpreters were identifying and recommending the most significant Isaiah commentaries. Nearly a decade before he taught on Isaiah himself, when John Calvin was asked for recommendations on Isaiah, he gave his less favorable opinions about other works on Isaiah before stating, "No one so far has engaged more diligently in this work than Oecolampadius, though he too does not always hit the mark."[18] Even after Calvin's commentary was published, Genevans were still also using Oecolampadius's Isaiah commentary—with it being republished in Geneva in 1558, both as an individual volume and as part of a set on all the prophets (and again in 1577 and 1578).[19]

In an appendix to his 1567 collection of sermons, Heinrich Bullinger identifies several sets of interpreters on Isaiah worth consulting and lists among his Reformation contemporaries Oecolampadius, Zwingli, Pellikan, Bibliander, Musculus, Calvin, and Marlorat for the Reformed, and

[18]John Calvin to Pierre Viret, May 19, 1540 (CO 11:36 [no. 217]).

[19]See Ernst Staehelin, *Oekolampad-Bibliographie* (Basel: Verlag der historischen und antiquarischen Gesellschaft, 1918; repr., Nieuwkoop: B. De Graaf, 1963), 108 (nos. 209.1a, 209.4, 209.5); Heinrich Bullinger to John Calvin, May 22, 1553 (CO 14:534 [no. 1739]).

Luther, Brenz, and Viktorin Strigel for the Lutherans.[20] Bullinger particularly highlights "the most learned and most pious man, professor Johannes Oecolampadius," and affirms the "true commentaries" by Musculus and Calvin.[21] Pellikan also highlights the teaching on Isaiah by Bibliander, Bullinger, and Zwingli.[22] Similarly, in Scultetus's *Sermon Ideas*, the commentaries from sermons by Gwalther, Bullinger, and Brenz are commended, as well as those by Zwingli, Oecolampadius, Calvin, Pellikan, Musculus, Ursinus, Heinrich Möller, and Roman Catholic Francisco Forerius.[23] Lutheran theologian August Pfeiffer also includes a suggestion of Isaiah commentaries in the various editions of his *Hermeneutica Sacra* (published in 1684, 1687, 1698, 1704, and 1726).[24] He lists fellow Lutherans Dietrich Schnepff (1575) and August Varenius (1673), and in later editions Sebastian Schmidt (1693). But he also includes Reformed commentators Oecolampadius and Scultetus, as well as Borrhaus, and Roman Catholics Gabriel Alvarez, Forerius, Hector Pinto, and Leo de Castro. The Protestant interpreters repeatedly mentioned in these recommendations from the sixteenth to early eighteenth centuries include Oecolampadius, Zwingli, Bullinger, Pellikan, Calvin, Musculus, and Brenz.[25] These influential commentaries identified in the prime time of their usage form the core of this volume. They provide insight on the most important topics from the most regarded and likely most used commentaries of the time.

Themes of Isaiah

The themes interpreters identified as most important in Isaiah are frequently found in the prefaces to these commentaries. Commentators used their prefaces to articulate what they identified as the significant passages, elements, and applications from Isaiah. The exposition of Isaiah by Protestant reformers certainly resonated with many of the major emphases of the previous generations. The key themes on Isaiah from the medieval exegetical tradition are best found in works like those by Bernard Smalley, Brevard Childs, and John Sawyer—and substantiated in the volumes by Robert Louis Wilken, Steven McKinion, and Mark Elliott.[26] These scholars demonstrate that Jerome's commentary on Isaiah (c. 408–410) especially shaped the exegetical tradition, with very little new exposition during the late Middle Ages.[27] The works on Isaiah by Cyril of

[20]Bullinger's breakdown also includes Jewish rabbis Abraham Ibn Ezra and David Kimchi, and church fathers Origen, Jerome, Eusebius Pamphili, Didymus, Cyril of Alexandria, John Chrysostom, Hyppolitus, and Bede.

[21]Bullinger, *Isaias*, 354v-r.

[22]Pellikan, *Commentaria Bibliorum*, 3:6r.

[23]See the preface by Balthasar Tilesius in Scultetus, *Idea concionum*, iii.v.

[24]Pfeiffer, *Hermeneutica sacra* (1698), 198; (1687), 196; (1726), 415.

[25]Others mentioned in these lists include Gwalther, Ursinus, Scultetus, Borrhaus, Vatable, Bibliander, Marlorat, Strigel, and Schnepff. Excerpts from and references to their works are included in this volume.

[26]Beryl Smalley, *The Study of the Bible in the Middle Ages*, 3rd ed. (Notre Dame, IN: University of Notre Dame Press, 2007); Brevard S. Childs, *The Struggle to Understand Isaiah as Christian Scripture: A Hermeneutical Study* (Grand Rapids, MI: Eerdmans, 2004); Sawyer, *Fifth Gospel*; John F. A. Sawyer, *Isaiah Through the Centuries* (Hoboken, NJ: Wiley, 2018); Robert Louis Wilken, *Isaiah: Interpreted by Early Christian and Medieval Commentators*, The Church's Bible (Grand Rapids, MI: Eerdmans, 2007); Steven A. McKinion, ed., *Isaiah 1–39*, ACCS 10 (Downers Grove, IL: InterVarsity Press, 2007); Mark W. Elliott, ed., *Isaiah 40–66*, ACCS 11 (Downers Grove, IL: InterVarsity Press, 2007).

[27]For example, see John F. A. Sawyer, "Isaiah," in *Dictionary of Biblical Interpretation*, ed. John H. Hayes (Nashville: Abingdon, 1999), 1:550.

Alexandria, Aquinas, Nicholas of Lyra, Denis the Carthusian, and the *Glossa Ordinaria* all feature Jerome prominently. In the 1530s, Jerome's commentary on Isaiah was published as part of a work that included annotations by Sebastian Münster and David Kimchi.[28]

Medieval exegetes regularly repeated Jerome's statement and perspective that the book of Isaiah was written "not only by a prophet, but by an evangelist, for all the mysteries of Christ and the church are pursued to clarity."[29] The greatest emphases from Isaiah in the exegetical tradition center on the noticeable connections to Christ and the New Testament. Lyra even identifies four reasons why the book of Isaiah should be called a Gospel more than a prophecy.[30] Despite this statement, most of these interpreters still include a section on what prophecy is and how Isaiah indeed proclaimed prophecies.

The themes from Isaiah in the Middle Ages are well summarized in a list of praises for the prophet Isaiah by Denis the Carthusian: Isaiah predicted the mysteries of Christ and the church, was sent to preach good news, was eloquent with words, reached an honorable old age, lived a most holy life, was dependent on God's grace, performed glorious miracles, prophesied in the face of persecution, and died as a martyr.[31] These exegetes maintain that the book of Isaiah—though sometimes obscured by the Septuagint—teaches about the sacraments, the Trinity, and the incarnation, especially the virgin birth; Christ's suffering, death, and resurrection; and the announcement of salvation to all peoples. While they acknowledge that Isaiah addresses the Assyrian defeat and Babylonian captivity, they specify that Isaiah's chief contributions are prophecies regarding the calling of the Gentiles and the coming of Christ. Protestant exegetes continue with much of this tradition throughout their comments on Isaiah. Yet there are also significant ways in which their interpretive approaches, exegetical emphases, and theological conclusions diverge from the exegetical tradition.

A Guide to Reading Isaiah with the Reformers

While messianic themes still found prominence in Reformation writings on Isaiah, Protestant interpreters also stress the biblical passages that epitomize the Reformers' changed views on Scripture, tradition, justification, the Eucharist, and other church practices.[32] The main themes

[28]Münster, *Isaias Propheta*.

[29]Nicholas of Lyra refers to Isaiah as "the Jerusalem Evangelist." See Nicholas of Lyra, *Bibliorum* 4:7. He reiterates, "Isaiah does not seem to defend prophecy, but rather the gospel, since as the same Jerome says in his prologue on the book of Isaiah that he should not so much be called a prophet as an Evangelist" (4:7-8). On some of the reception history of this perspective in the Middle Ages, see Andrew Abernathy, *Discovering Isaiah: Content, Interpretation, Reception* (Grand Rapids, MI: Eerdmans, 2021), 17-18.

[30]Nicholas of Lyra, *Bibliorum*, 4:8. Lyra argues from the principle, material, formal, and efficient reasons why Isaiah could be called an Evangelist and the "book could be designated a Gospel" (4:8).

[31]Denis the Carthusian, *Enarratio in Isaiam*, in *Doctoris Ecstatici Dionysii Cartusiani Opera Omnia* 8 (Monstrolii: M. De Pratis, 1899), 317-19. Denis concludes his opening section on Isaiah by addressing "what is prophecy, about the kinds and positions of a prophet, and what kind of prophecy is more worthy; likewise about the seven rules of understanding the Scriptures, and about the fourfold exposition of Sacred Scripture" (319). Some of the text in this section was previously posted on Jeff Fisher, "Isaiah in the Reformation," Christoscopic: Theological and Ministry Reflections of Jeff Fisher (blog), October 31, 2017, http://christoscopic.net/isaiah-in-the-reformation/.

[32]For additional analysis of Reformation commentaries on Isaiah, see David Steinmetz, "John Calvin on Isaiah 6: A Problem in the History of Exegesis," *Interpretation: A Journal of Bible and Theology* 36, no. 2 (1982): 157; Steinmentz, *Calvin in Context* (New York: Oxford University Press, 2010), 94-95; Peter Opitz, "The Exegetical and Hermeneutical Work of John Oecolampadius, Huldrych Zwingli and John Calvin," in *Hebrew Bible, Old Testament: The History of Its Interpretation*, ed. Magne Sæbø

emphasized by Reformation commentators include a new focus on the office of the prophet, the proper interpretation of Scripture, and how the critiques and comforts spoken by Isaiah apply to their own churches and worship. For the Protestant interpreters, Isaiah was the model prophet who revealed the mysteries of Christ and his church by insisting on the truth of God's Word and rejecting false worship.

The office of prophet. First, while medieval exegetes on Isaiah had expounded on what prophecy is as one of the first matters, a subtle but significant shift among the Reformers was to expound also on the office of a prophet. Marlorat's selection from Calvin's preface includes Calvin's exposition on the responsibilities of a prophet to (1) teach doctrine, (2) call the people to repentance, and (3) trust in God's covenant promises.[33] One of the key themes evident in several of the Protestant commentaries is the role of the pastor or minister to faithfully preach the Word of God. Oecolampadius, for example, espouses that in order to maintain the principle of *sola Scriptura*, there is also the need for "most worthy men faithfully preaching it."[34] Likewise, he insists that they "trust in the fruit" that will come from the Holy Spirit's work through the "the honored reading of the Word."[35] In order for ministers to faithfully preach Scripture and listeners to rightly hear God's Word, the Reformers emphasize that Scripture must be properly interpreted. This major theme incorporates several repeated aspects of hermeneutics among the Protestant interpreters found in their comments on Isaiah.

Scripture alone. At the heart of Reformation exegesis was the insistence on the supremacy of Scripture. Isaiah provided the language and the biblical texts (such as Is 40:8; 55:10-11) for the Reformers to affirm that "the word of the Lord" has ultimate authority—it "stands firm, endures forever, does not return void." They find in Isaiah the call to recover the true meaning of Scripture, which was buried by the teachings and traditions of the church. He was the "prince of prophets" who modeled how to rightly handle the Word of God and faithfully fulfill one's calling to Christ and the church. In many of the prefaces, the interpreter addresses the objection that the prophets, and Isaiah in particular, are full of enigmas and obscure sayings that are hard to understand.[36] Their response is often that this demonstrates exactly why it is so important to learn how the Word should be handled and rightly interpreted and applied.[37]

Original language. Perhaps the most noticeable change in the approach to interpreting Isaiah during the Reformation was the renewed interest in and insistence on understanding the Hebrew language.[38] A startling innovation occurred when Oecolampadius began lecturing in the spring of

(Göttingen: Vandenhoeck & Ruprecht, 2008), 2:407-51; G. Sujin Pak, *The Reformation of Prophecy: Early Modern Interpretations of the Prophet and Old Testament* (New York: Oxford University Press, 2018), especially the last three chapters.

[33]Marlorat, *Esaiae*, iv.v-iv.r. See CTS 13:xxvi-xxxii (CO 36:19). As evident in the comments below, these themes recur among Reformation commentators.

[34]Oecolampadius, *In Iesaiam*, 1r.

[35]Oecolampadius, *In Iesaiam*, 2r.

[36]For example, see Oecolampadius, *In Iesaiam*, 2r; Pellikan, *Commentaria Bibliorum*, 3:1r, 4r. Portions of these are also quoted in Marlorat, *Esaiae*, iii.r.

[37]See CTS 13:xxx; Marlorat, *Esaiae*, iv.r.

[38]See, e.g., Stephen G. Burnett, *Christian Hebraism in the Reformation Era (1500–1660): Authors, Books, and the Transmission of Jewish Learning* (Leiden: Brill, 2012).

1523 on Isaiah using the Hebrew text rather than the Latin Vulgate. The Renaissance humanist return to "the sources" (*ad fontes*) led several Reformation theologians to employ the use of Hebrew in explaining words and phrases, comparing translations with the Latin Vulgate, interacting more thoroughly with Jewish rabbinic interpreters, and providing more precise readings of the biblical text based on the original context. Later interpreters even recommended previous commentaries on Isaiah based on what they viewed as Hebrew accuracy.[39]

For centuries, not only had Jerome's Latin translation been the primary text of the Old Testament, but also the arguments Jerome had raised in the fifth century for the value of his translation had been repeated and passed down. In the sixteenth-century versions of the *Glossa Ordinaria*, the argumentation for the Vulgate's value is included three times.[40] When Oecolampadius began his teaching on Isaiah, he admitted that he had previously assumed Jerome's translation was sufficient but then discovered that in order to be able to discern the mind of the prophet, the Hebrew text had to be used. He rhetorically asked, "Since I was able to drink from the fount, why should I stoop to the stream?"[41] He desired to remain as close as possible to the Hebrew text in his translation and exegesis in order to discern the true meaning of the Bible. Though Protestant exegetes often stated that they did not intend to belittle Jerome or the LXX, this renewed attention to the Hebrew text challenged both the authority of the Vulgate and the Septuagint, and the conclusions that had been derived from them.

The Hebrew text most often used was the *Biblia Rabbinica* of Pratensis and Bomberg (1517/1518), which included textual variants, the Targum of Johnathan, and the commentary by David Kimchi.[42] Several Protestant interpreters produced separate translations (*complanationes*) of the Hebrew text, such as Luther's 1528 German translation, Zwingli's 1529 Latin translation, and George Joye's 1531 English translation. Other Reformers included their own Latin translations as part of their commentaries. In his seventeenth-century commentary, John Trapp refers to Oecolampadius's alternate translation based on the Hebrew more than fifty times.[43] In 1540, Sebastian Münster (1488–1552) published the first edition of his Hebrew Bible (alongside the Vulgate), which also included the commentary by David Kimchi.[44] Reading Hebrew also enabled Christian interpreters to engage directly with rabbinic literature, such as Rashi (eleventh century), Abraham Ibn Ezra (twelfth century), and David Kimchi (thirteenth century), especially to defend interpretations that identified Jesus as the promised Christ in passages such as Isaiah 7; 9; 11; 53; 61.

[39]For example, see Scultetus, *Idea Concionum*, iii.v.

[40]*Glossa Ordinaria*, 3v. Many of Jerome's comments and defense for his translation are included in the main text, the Jerome gloss, and the Brito gloss.

[41]Oecolampadius, *In Iesaiam*, 3r-4v. Oecolampadius explains why he gives a new translation. Marlorat quotes all of Oecolampadius on the importance of Hebrew names and pointing to Christ as type (*Esaiae*, ii-iii).

[42]Pratensis, *Biblia Rabbinica*. Since an edition was published in 1523 by Froben in Basel, it is very likely that Oecolampadius had access to it again. See Thomas Willi, "Der Beitrag des Hebräischen in Basel," *Theologische Zeitschrift* 35, no. 3 (1979): 150.

[43]Trapp, *Commentary or exposition*. Examples are given in the comments below.

[44]A critical edition of Kimchi's Hebrew commentary is available as David Kimchi, *The Commentary of David Kimchi on Isaiah*, ed. Louis Finkelstein (repr., New York: AMS, 1966).

Increased attention to historical background. For the Reformers, proper interpretation of Scripture also required the reader to understand the historical setting of the prophet. Repeatedly, Protestant interpreters denounce the glossing of biblical texts, especially patristic and medieval allegories that ignore or torture the original context. In their prefaces on Isaiah, nearly all of them include a summary (in varying levels of detail) on the biblical background for the history of Isaiah that could be found in Hosea, 1–2 Kings, 2 Chronicles, and Amos.[45] Oecolampadius states that it is necessary "to properly remember the histories of the times in which the prophecies occurred. For unless those are rightly laid as a foundation, whatever is built on top will collapse."[46] Several also include geographical details, genealogical information, and a kind of biographical sketch of Isaiah himself with calculations for the years of Isaiah's service and life.[47]

In continuity with previous interpreters such as Nicholas of Lyra and Thomas Aquinas, the growing interest in the "sense of the letter" led to an increased reluctance to use allegory as a means of explanation. Reformers sought to attain the simple, plain, or genuine sense of the text by considering its historical, grammatical, and literary elements. Though their methods still often included allegory, the Reformers elaborated less and preferred the language of types, figures, and shadows because of the abuse of allegorizing in the Middle Ages. They identify that Isaiah spoke "mysteries" through the Spirit, which requires the interpreter to grasp both the original, historical context and the future promises. Depending on the passage—and the exegetical tradition to which an interpreter belonged—the exposition could jump quite readily to the time of Christ or engage in lengthy explanation about the events during Isaiah's time.

Authorship and organization. With regard to the *history* of the book of Isaiah, typical questions raised by Protestant exegetes included whether Isaiah authored the whole thing and how the various parts of the book fit together. Of course, these premodern exegetes did not subscribe to a Deutero- or Trito-Isaiah, but several of them do recognize that the historical details, the lengthy time frame, and the varied contents indicate that the entire book of Isaiah may not have all been written by the prophet Isaiah and certainly is not recorded or organized chronologically. Marlorat includes sections of the prefaces from Calvin, Luther, and Musculus, who each affirm that it is probable that Isaiah's spoken or written prophecies were collected and gathered together and compiled at various points, which would explain why the discourses are not arranged in a "regular order."[48] Calvin questions whether Isaiah himself or someone else wrote the inscription, for example.

While interpreters vary in how they divide the various parts of the book, most identify a definite shift between Isaiah 39 and Isaiah 40. Oecolampadius organizes the divisions of the book around the kings (Uzziah in Is 1–5, Jotham in Is 6, Ahaz in Is 7–14, Hezekiah in Is 15–39) and then observes, "It is uncertain whether the rest that follows he also preached under King Hezekiah

[45]See Marlorat, *Esaiae*, i.v-iii.r.

[46]Oecolampadius, *In Iesaiam*, 5r.

[47]See Marlorat, *Esaiae*, i.v-i.r. Additional examples can be seen below in the commentary.

[48]Calvin concludes that it is probable the books of the Prophets were compiled (CO 36:24; CTS 13:xxxii; also quoted in Marlorat, *Esaiae*, iv.r).

or under Manasseh," but the remainder of the book of Isaiah prophesies about Cyrus and the liberation from the Babylonian captivity in Isaiah 40–48 and about Christ and the church in Isaiah 49–66.[49] Bullinger, among others, follows this structure and in his opening comments on Isaiah 40 specifies, "The second part of this book now begins, and it is divided into two parts." He particularly notes that the "occasion for this consoling speech [in Is 40] is aimed at and drawn from the end of chapter 39, where we heard that the kings of Judah and all the people would be taken to Babylon."[50] Wolfgang Musculus takes a different approach with a very detailed but rather unique outline that breaks the book into sections of Isaiah 1–12; Isaiah 13–48; and Isaiah 49–66. However, he too acknowledges a significant difference between the history of the Assyrian devastation against Judah in Isaiah 34–39 and the destruction and liberation from Babylon in Isaiah 40.[51] Johannes Brenz goes so far as to say at the beginning of Isaiah 40, "What follows is like a new book of Isaiah."[52]

Zacharias Ursinus later observed that the two main approaches of dividing the book were into six parts according to the sequence of the kings or in two parts based on subject matters. Yet, he points out that even with the thematic approach that sees the first part as a "mix of threats, warnings, exhortations, and promises," Isaiah 1–39 "subdivide[s] into four," and the second part "from the beginning of chapter 40 to the end containing promises and comforts, also subdivides into the two parts previously identified."[53] A likely example of this thematic approach is Strigel, who articulates, "There are two parts to the book of Isaiah. One is containing the historical in thirty-nine chapters, the other part is the prophetic." He clarifies that in the first part of the book, "promises about the Messiah and the calling of the Gentiles are woven in," but it focuses much more on the sieges on Jerusalem and the exile of the ten tribes.[54]

A final example is Abraham Scultetus, who states that Isaiah preached about two major changes among God's people. "He preached about the first in thirty-nine chapters, where he terrified the wicked with the announcement of the attack by the hostile Assyrians but raised up the godly with hope that although the rest of Judah might be devastated, Jerusalem would still be preserved. Then he spoke about the second of these changes in the following chapters." His comments helpfully add the important recognition that Isaiah 40–66 refers to events that Isaiah himself did not live to see, "yet it was by the prophetic spirit that he foresaw what would happen much later." Scultetus reasons that Isaiah "determined that he could not use the rest of his life better than if he left many consoling sermons for the people, which would benefit them during and after the captivity, even after his own death."[55] Brenz adds another significant qualification about the aspects of the second part of Isaiah that were future to Isaiah when he insists that it is

[49]Oecolampadius, *In Iesaiam*, 5v.
[50]Bullinger, *Isaias*, 188v.
[51]Musculus, *In Esaiam*, 7-8; quoted in Marlorat, *Esaiae*, iii.v-iii.r.
[52]Brenz, *Esaias*, 532.
[53]Ursinus, *Iesaiam*, 9.
[54]Strigel, *Oratio De Propheta Esaia*, 39.
[55]Scultetus, *Idea Concionum*, iii.4.

"certainly clear that this part of Isaiah was confirmed with the greatest authority by Christ himself and his apostles."[56] Calvin concludes that the final form the book of Isaiah takes is "a remarkable instance of the providence of God."[57]

The unity of Scripture and the Jesus lens. Another key element of proper interpretation of Isaiah was its relationship to the New Testament. Reformation theologians reemphasize the point found among previous exegetes that Isaiah is quoted among New Testament writers more than any other prophet. While it would be unfair and inaccurate to say that medieval exegetes strongly separated the Old and New Testaments, during the Reformation, a more robust understanding of the unity of Scripture developed, with new approaches to discerning ways Isaiah's prophecies refer to Christ and his kingdom.

Luther and other Lutheran interpreters tend to emphasize a christological reading of Isaiah, identifying many of the prophecies as referring directly to the time of Jesus.[58] In slight contrast, Calvin and other Reformed theologians explain how given prophecies spoke to the original Old Testament people and then how it also points to Christ and the church in the future. Oecolampadius observes that in Luke 4, Christ "taught the way it [Isaiah] ought to be read," with attention first given to the original context but then also identifying how it points to or leads to Christ.[59] Rather than merely allegorizing certain passages, Oecolampadius and others generate explanations that incorporate types, allegories, parables, and illustrations to let the prophet speak to the past, present, and future.

Contemporary application. With regard to their own time period, Protestant interpreters identify that Isaiah spoke clearly and directly against many teachings and practices of the institutional Roman church. While earlier generations had primarily applied passages about idolatry and empty worship to Jews and Muslims, during the sixteenth and seventeenth centuries, Protestant interpretations shifted to primarily applying Isaiah's ridicule and condemnation of idolatry, rejection of God's Word, arrogance, and false practices to Roman Catholics and heretics. They particularly contrast those who rightly learn from and follow the Word of God with those who attempt to follow God with all "their empty prayers, weekly ceremonies, and sacrifices."[60]

Protestant interpreters often make the connection that the root cause of the people's "empty worship" (using the language from Is 29) was that the church leaders of their day were like Israel's leaders of Isaiah's day, who were also like the Pharisees of Jesus' day. Contemporary Roman Catholic lay people had been led astray by the power-hungry, glory-seeking, idolatrous religious leaders just like Israel had been during the time of Isaiah. In contrast, Isaiah and others, such as Hezekiah,

[56]Brenz, *Esaias*, 532.

[57]CTS 13:xxxii; Marlorat, *Esaiae*, iv.r.

[58]For a recent accessible treatment of this, see Abernathy, *Discovering Isaiah*, 42. He notes, "Although Luther attends to the grammar and historical dynamics of Isaiah's time, he often directs his gaze directly to how a passage figuratively speaks of Christ and the church." This approach is also quite apparent in the Lutheran commentators.

[59]Oecolampadius, *In Iesaiam*, 2v. He maintains that both Luke and Jesus were intentional in showing that "the sense of Scripture is disclosed to no one except those who also strive for Christ and to whom Christ reveals himself."

[60]Oecolampadius, *In Iesaiam*, a-3.r-5v. Others who make this point include Brenz, *Esaias*, iiii.r; Pellikan, *Commentaria Bibliorum*, 3:5r; Zwingli (ZSW 14:3 / CR 101); and Melanchthon (MO / CR 13:800).

represent the faithful leaders who do not close their eyes to the Word of God and who endure through troubled times.

Repentance and faith. A final theme of application repeated among these interpreters is the prophetic call to repentance. The Reformers identify that the book of Isaiah especially and repeatedly admonishes people to repentance and is therefore fitting for every time. Like Isaiah himself and the people of his time, Christians of all times need to be purified and abstain from evil desires, sinful ways, and empty trifles. Many exegetes, but especially the Lutherans, not only emphasize the theme of repentance but also seize the opportunity to teach justification by faith alone apart from works based on the passages in Isaiah that speak about righteousness—whether God's righteousness or the righteous life to which his people are called.[61] The corruption in the world and the church around them led these Protestant exegetes to contend that this message from Isaiah on repentance and righteousness needed to be applied in their day.

Reformation theologians insisted that Isaiah needed to be heard again in their day. From this prophetic book, they provide Christ-centered, church-directed, truth-seeking explanations about the revealing and unfolding of God's redemptive plan. The reception history of biblical interpretation in general provides us with a valuable lens where they may have seen things we have not, and it can function as a mirror, where they reflect back to us the assumptions or conclusions that we may have brought to the text.[62] With these Reformation commentators in particular, we can benefit greatly from hearing what they had to say in their pursuit of making known the enduring Word of God through the prophet Isaiah. Oecolampadius's opening commentary on Isaiah 25 represents several recurring themes among Christian interpreters on the first part of this biblical book and fittingly concludes the introduction of this volume:

> As is his custom, the prophet breaks forth into praise and singing when he hears about the glory of the life to come in which the elders reigning with Christ will glorify God and say on that day, "Lord, you are my God. Idols are nothing to us, whatever is in the world is nothing to us. You are the one and only Lord and God; you are sufficient for us, and nothing is a danger to us—even the destruction of the whole world. Since you delight us, the end of the world does not frighten us. It is enough for us that you, God, are glorified. And so we will exalt you, not ourselves or our works, or any creatures, which we consider all as flax. But we will not only glorify you with our heart; we will also confess with our mouth and testify to your name, that is, your renown, with our actions and with joyful and perpetual thanksgiving. This is especially because of your power, since you do marvelous things that exceed the capacity of human understanding—and because of your goodness and truth, since of everything predicted through your prophets, nothing remains undone."[63]

[61]See, e.g., Brenz, *Esaias*, iiii.r, iv.v-v.r.

[62]Abernathy identifies "exegetical pay-off" from the fact that "earlier interpreters may see elements in the texts of Isaiah that we might be overlooking (perhaps due to our current and social locations)," which helps us "ponder how best to read Isaiah as Christian Scripture today" (*Discovering Isaiah*, 21).

[63]Oecolampadius, *In Iesaiam*, 153r.

COMMENTARY ON ISAIAH

Overview: Reformation commentators often begin their commentaries, even those based on sermons, with introductory remarks about the nature of prophecy and the work of prophets. They address the different terms used to refer to prophets and prophecies. They explain how prophetic literature compares to other genres in Scripture. They articulate the differences between the prophecies found in the Old Testament and their fulfillments in the New Testament regarding Jesus, the apostles, and the church. Many of these interpreters addressed the historical context of Isaiah himself, in addition to the book's relevance for the New Testament and the church at their time. To many of them, Isaiah was the most important of the writing prophets—a perspective in continuity with medieval interpreters. Of course, the primary reason they esteemed Isaiah so much was the many passages that could be directly and indirectly connected to Jesus as the promised Messiah. The preliminary comments of these exegetes often included a description of how the book as a whole was organized as well.

Prolegomena: Introduction to Isaiah

Titles for Prophets. Konrad Pellikan: Holy men of God who explained the divine mind that the Spirit breathed and inspired, or who otherwise considered the heavenly will, or who explored and observed the divine will, the Hebrew names *nābîʾim* [prophets]. This was generally translated in Greek with the term *prophētēs* [prophets], which Latin speakers and other foreign peoples used. Moreover, that term in Greek specifically signifies one who declares and speaks something from the divine mind before it happens. From these, along with the common and general use of the term, the view is accepted that prophets to this extent are prescient and are able to predict and announce things in future times. Preface to Isaiah in Commentary on the Bible.[1]

The Definition of a Prophet. Philipp Melanchthon: Therefore the definition of prophet should be considered. A prophet is a person immediately called by God to teach the gospel and give divine testimonies that do not err to certain political bodies. Already at the beginning, you should consider this immense kindness so that you give thanks to God that so many times he renewed the light of doctrine. Argument of Isaiah.[2]

The Principal Meaning of *Prophet*. Zacharias Ursinus: Generally and principally *prophet* signifies the person announcing to the people to whom he is sent whatever was revealed directly to him by God. This may be by dream or divine vision or inspiration or apparitions and conversations with God or angels. He reports this to the people in the name of God. Finally, it signifies having the gift of interpreting and using it in the present to properly apply those oracles of the prophets to the church. . . . The excellence and worth of the prophetic ministry is evident from this. The highest of kindness is communicated by God to humanity—especially the knowledge of God and the divine will. Eternal life depends on

[1]Pellikan, *Commentaria Bibliorum*, 3:2r.
[2]MO 13:794.

such knowledge, as testified by Christ. . . . Further, since it is true that so many of the prophets came after Moses, it is also right to say that they are interpreting the law of Moses. For God arranged that those uttered words be unveiled here in order to confirm, urge, and declare the law handed down by Moses. Now we understand by the term *law*, the entire teaching of Moses in the manner of Scripture, which is the source and foundation of the prophets. Preface to Commentary on Isaiah.[3]

Two Kinds of Prophets. Wolfgang Musculus: The Hebrews call *nābî* what the Greeks call prophet and we call seer. These signify those who speak not from human understanding and will but by the Spirit of God. Moreover, there are two kinds of prophets. One kind is those who predict the future. So the Greeks call them prophets, from *prophēteuō*, that is, "to foretell." And in this sense, we call them seers. The other kind is those who either instruct or warn about present things, comfort or rebuke sinners, or proclaim the mighty works of God. Most join these two kinds of prophesying together, as evident in the writings of the prophets. The apostle later speaks about this . . . where he says, "Follow the way of love, and desire spiritual things, but especially prophecy. For one who speaks in a tongue does not speak to people, but to God. For no one is able to hear when he speaks mysteries by the Spirit. The one who truly prophesies speaks to the people for their upbuilding, encouragement, and consolation." So Paul, the interpreter of the divine will, also called one a prophet even when they did not predict the future. Preface to Commentary on Isaiah.[4]

The Difference Between Prophets, Apostles, and Teachers. Zacharias Ursinus: Second, it is evident from what was said how much the authority of the prophets and apostles differs from the authority of other teachers and ministers in the church. Prophets and apostles, since they have the divine testimonies that were directly taught by God and thus governed by the Holy Spirit, were teaching the church nothing in what they said or wrote except what the Spirit of God had dictated to them. Without exception and uncertainty, everything known that they passed down in the church must be heard. But other teachers with this office, however excellent, do not have these same gifts and testimonies as the prophets and apostles. They are those who should extend, explain, impress, and apply doctrine for the benefit of the church. They are able to err at any time, mixing some human opinion with heavenly truth or not rightly understanding and applying the words of Scripture. For that reason, it is not enough when they teach to know their own ideas, but in addition they must seek whether those ideas are true based on what is said by others. That is, if they agree with the foundation—the rule of the prophetic and apostolic Scripture—their teaching is accepted. But if their ideas disagree with them, they should be rejected. Isaiah teaches this distinction . . . : "To the law and testimony! If they did not speak according to this word, there is no light of dawn in them." Preface to Commentary on Isaiah.[5]

The Humility of the Apostles and Prophets. Menno Simons: Their looks and titles prove that they do not walk in humility of heart before the Lord. They suffer themselves to be greeted as lords and masters, despite the fact that it is forbidden by the mouth of the Lord. Say, kind reader, did you ever hear or read that the holy apostles and prophets were covetous of such high, vain titles as are the learned and the preachers of the world? It is true the term *rabbi* and *master* was applied to the ambitious scribes and Pharisees, but not to the apostles and prophets. For we do not read of Doctor Isaiah, or Master Ezekiel, and of Lords Paul and Peter. No, no! All these who have rightly taught the word of the Lord were in their

[3]Ursinus, *Iesaiam*, 2; citing 1 Cor 12; Jn 17.
[4]Musculus, *In Esaiam*, 2; citing 1 Cor 14:1-3.
[5]Ursinus, *Iesaiam*, 5-6; citing Is 8:20; 1 Cor 3.

time not honored with such high-sounding names. This I write that you may know that such ambitious, proud spirits can never rightly teach you the humble word of the cross. Hearing the Preachers.[6]

The Reason for the Prophets. Philipp Melanchthon: The reasons why and how prophets were sent, from the time all the way back in the beginning of humankind, may be obtained from what God has disclosed and from the promise handed down soon after the fall of the first parents. For these certain and illustrious testimonies he disclosed to humanity are the highest kindnesses of God. They handed down the promise about the mediator, by whom and because of whom humanity would be restored to righteousness and eternal life. . . . And this is the particular reason why prophets are called and sent: so that the testimonies of divine disclosures would be revealed by men who excel, and the doctrine of God would be restored by them, and the promise of the mediator would be repeated and illustrated. Now, we may know what the particular duty of all the prophets is, all the way from Adam. It is for them to reveal the testimonies of divine disclosures so that the promise of the gospel be restored, all doctrine of God be purified, and the church be renewed. Argument of Isaiah.[7]

Two Kinds of Scripture. Johannes Brenz: For there are two kinds of Scriptures on which the church of the Lord is founded. One is the prophetic writings, the other the apostolic writings. "You are fellow citizens," Paul says about the saints, "and the household of God, built on the foundation of the apostles and prophets, with Jesus Christ as the chief cornerstone." Because these writings are confirmed by many great miracles, it is as if the Holy Spirit extends them to us from heaven. All the teaching for our true and perpetual salvation is included in them. And their authority is so great that if an angel from heaven were to announce something else to us, it would be accursed and considered anathema. Preface to Commentary on Isaiah.[8]

The Threefold Distinction of Prophecy. Ulrich Zwingli: And finally because a reminder is entirely necessary, the prophecies about Christ contained in this prophet are sometimes altered so that the genuine sense is entirely something other than what is contained in the commentaries on the Gospels. For prophecies have a threefold distinction. Some are pure prediction, such as, "Behold, the virgin will conceive," and all of chapter 53. And some are sermons that the prophets spoke to the people during their time, and there is nothing else addressed again in the time of Christ. But some occurred both for their very own use and for another. For example, . . . "A voice cries, 'In the wilderness, prepare the way of the Lord.'" The prophet addresses these words to the people at his time so that they prepare everything for the Israelite people returning from the Babylonian captivity. This freeing of slaves, although less well-known than the liberation from Egypt, was a type of the whole world being liberated. So John the Baptist responds to the envoys of the Jews that he is the voice crying out, "Prepare the way of the Lord in the wilderness," that is, he cries out that they must repent. For the Lord arrives in the same way Isaiah previously had when he warned about the coming of Cyrus the liberator. The words of Isaiah there are not properly prediction but a type, and similar to those which John was delivering. Annotations on Isaiah.[9]

Twofold Prophecy. Wolfgang Musculus: Moreover, these utterances are twofold—namely, the prophetic and the evangelical. In the prophetic kind, the mysteries hidden from the ages were foreshadowed with promises and prophecies and were being announced in advance. I propose to

[6]Simons, *Complete Works*, 2:266*.
[7]MO 13:793, 794.
[8]Brenz, *Esaias*, 1; citing Eph 2:19-20.
[9]ZSW 14:94; citing Is 7:14; 40:3.

group together all those oracles of God's promises that were divinely revealed to Adam and the other patriarchs. In the evangelical kind, the truth and fulfillment of these mysteries and prophecies about Christ are announced and made known to the whole world. The former are enigmatic and shadowy figures, enclosed with covers such that it makes sense that the ancients said the writing of prophets was closed. Their closure is opened in the New Testament Scriptures by the Gospel writers and the apostles, as the key ordained for this use. So Christ reveals the sense not only to the apostles and his disciples but to all the elect, all the way to the end of the world. For he is the end of prophecies, the specific scope to which the prophesying of the prophet looked ahead. This is why the knowledge of Christ is that light without which no one will usefully and understandably be able to dwell sufficiently in the prophetic Scriptures. PREFACE TO COMMENTARY ON ISAIAH.[10]

PROPHETIC PREDICTION. ZACHARIAS URSINUS: There are predictions of future things that cannot be foreknown and foretold with this specificity and certainty by anyone unless they are revealed by God. He has that in his power, and the events accurately and in every way correspond to the predictions. This evidence is argued at length. . . . Based on this, therefore, when these testimonies and even this kind of prophetic teaching itself is compared to other religions, it demonstrates that either this is true doctrine from God or it is nothing. PREFACE TO COMMENTARY ON ISAIAH.[11]

THE FIRST AMONG THE PROPHETS. JOHANNES BRENZ: And since after David, no prophet exists besides Isaiah who more seriously, more abundantly, more skillfully, and more clearly explains these things, we think Isaiah has first place among the interpreters of the heavenly and true doctrine of salvation. PREFACE TO COMMENTARY ON ISAIAH.[12]

SIMPLICITY AND BREVITY. ZACHARIAS URSINUS: It is my task to explain the prophet Isaiah to the young men. Isaiah is, so to speak, foremost among those known as the Latter Prophets. This is because he surpasses the rest in the richness of his teaching and in the clarity of his prophecies about Christ. But because the exegesis of the Old Testament is more difficult and this book of prophecy is quite long, I will try to remember both my inadequacy and my obligation. I will emphasize simplicity and brevity as an accommodation to the capacity of these young men. After all, I was called here to train these young men, not ones who stand in need of greater and more finished instruction. PREFACE TO COMMENTARY ON ISAIAH.[13]

ISAIAH'S HEBREW NAME. JOHANNES OECOLAMPADIUS: Quite a few words have been rendered into such a strange and different form that they are foreign and unrecognizable to the Jews themselves, even more so than to us. For if you say "Ezechia" to them, they do not know of whom you speak. But if you pronounce it "Hizkia" or "Jehizkia," you will make sense to them. This practice is of double use to us. We will make ourselves less ridiculous to Jewish scholars, and we will be able, when necessary, to confer with them more conveniently. Now, concerning Isaiah's own name, I know that among our own linguists there once were arguments, with some urging it be written "Isaia" so that its Hebrew origin would be clear, while others, trained in Greek, strongly asserted that it is more correctly written "Esaia." . . . To me it seems that it is most purely said, "Iesaia"—or "Iesaias," if one indeed prefers to inflect it in Latin or Greek. But it is still not displeasing to say "Hesaias" along with the Gospel writers. . . . Further, the very name "Ieschaia" is praiseworthy and of good omen, so to speak. For it has a meaning the same as "salvation of the Lord." For in Hebrew, *yeshu* means "salvation"; *yah* is "the Lord." So then, when the name is heard, you would expect great, pleasing, and saving things in his book, and you will not be disappointed if you persist. The

[10]Musculus, *In Esaiam*, 1.

[11]Ursinus, *Iesaiam*, 4, citing Is 41; 42; 43; 44; 45; 46; 48.

[12]Brenz, *Esaias*, vi.v.

[13]Ursinus, *Iesaiam*, 1.

name is most precious as well, and to be received with reverent eyes for another reason, for the sake of Christ our Lord. For just as the prophet in many respects was a type of him, so also he has been given an affinity in name, something that would appear more readily if you chose "Iesaias" over "Esaias." Preface to Commentary on Isaiah.[14]

The Royal Isaiah. Johannes Brenz: Now it is agreeable at this time to select the prophet Isaiah from these writings. He is included among the greatest ecclesiastical heroes who were ever on this earth. He taught the word of the Lord nearly eighty, or as others think, one hundred years. Let us say a few things about him. We will first speak about his family and when he was born. Then we will show his authority. Afterward we will include some about his kind of teaching. Therefore we receive from what has been interpreted that Isaiah was born about eight hundred years before the birth of Christ our Savior, as is plainly testified by the rule of those kings at the times when Isaiah engaged in his prophetic office. Moreover, he was born from a family that was hardly obscure but most distinguished and royal. For his father was Amos—not the prophet who is included in the list of the Minor Prophets but the one whom the ancestors passed down as the brother of Amaziah, king of Judah. And since Christ descends from the line of Amaziah, who was the uncle of Isaiah, it follows that Isaiah calls Christ his relative. Preface to Commentary on Isaiah.[15]

How to Read the Book. Johannes Oecolampadius: Behold, Christ himself, in reading this book, not only commended it but also taught how it ought to be read, which is going to be demonstrated in this preface. . . . We read that Jesus came to Nazareth, where he was raised, entered the synagogue on the Sabbath day according to his custom, and arose to read. And the book of Isaiah was handed to him, which he unrolled to find the passage in Scripture, "The Spirit of the Lord is upon me, because he has anointed me, he has sent me to preach good news. . . ." Then he rolled up the book to return to the servant and said to them, "Today this Scripture is fulfilled in your hearing." And all the eyes in the synagogue were fixed on him. . . . And if anyone reads it well, they will also learn from it that the glory of Christ is made known and we are admonished. And it is necessary to read the prophet carefully. Or do you think that it is without mysteries that Christ himself unrolls and rolls up the book? Do you think that he rises and reads rashly? Do you think that it is for no reason that he did this on the Sabbath? Therefore, let us learn what seems to us to be the reasons. Christ himself opens the book. For the sense of Scripture is opened to no one except those who seek Christ and to whom Christ reveals himself. For he himself holds the key of David. "He shuts and no one opens; he opens and no one shuts." . . . And in fact, you could say that the Holy Spirit is the doorkeeper, who opens it to no one except those who enter by the gate, which is Christ. Therefore, they waste all their work in vain who seek in the prophets anything other than Christ and the Christian life. That is the way Christ opened and closed the book.

Learn now why he read it on the Sabbath day, for this also pertains to us. For he admonishes us to sanctify the Sabbath as worthy to God, abstaining from servile works, I say, from evil affections: greed, jealousy, empty fear, trifles, delights, and similar things—if indeed we hope to benefit from the reading. Preface to Commentary on Isaiah.[16]

Grammar and History First. Martin Luther: Two things are necessary to explain the prophet. The first is a knowledge of grammar, and this may be regarded as having the greatest weight. The second is more necessary, namely, a knowledge of the historical background, not only as an

[14]Oecolampadius, *In Iesaiam*, 2v-3r; Marlorat, *Esaiae*, iii.
[15]Brenz, *Esaias*, 1.

[16]Oecolampadius, *In Iesaiam*, 2r-v; citing Lk 4:18, 21; Rev 3:7. †A longer portion is quoted in Marlorat, *Esaiae*, i.r-ii.v.

understanding of the events themselves as they are expressed in letters and syllables, but at the same time embracing rhetoric and dialectic, so that the figures of speech and the circumstances may be carefully heeded. Therefore, having command of the grammar in the first place, you must quickly move on to the histories, namely, what those kings under whom Isaiah prophesied did; and these matters must be carefully examined and thoroughly studied. The chief and leading theme of all the prophets is their aim to keep people in eager anticipation of the coming Christ. Lectures on Isaiah.[17]

The Hebrew Language. Johannes Oecolampadius: I am compelled to confess that the mind of the prophet cannot be discerned in many places from the Greek or the Latin. So unless one had the ability to read Hebrew and had consulted the commentaries of the Hebrews, then he certainly would not be prepared to attain it. . . . I gave a new translation, which was not lacking in the Hebrew truth, which in the Old Testament one most especially ought to consider and observe. But I did not, for that reason, disregard what was handed down from Jerome and the Septuagint. Yet since I was able to drink from the fount, why should I to stoop to the stream? And for this reason you will hear in several places what moved me, because I changed several things in my edition. May those who are untrained not entirely believe this was purposeless. Preface to Commentary on Isaiah.[18]

The Appropriate Use of the Hebrew. Francisco Forerius: There are also some other places to be pointed out to the readers, and that especially I did not return to the Hebrew for any reason other than to confirm the old translator. For, as educated people have the habit of doing, he generally expressed not so much the words as the sense. And on this account, one is unfortunately accustomed to hear from those who are too curious and not very learned, and perhaps frequently do not have a good mind. They are those who think they have sufficiently proved what they are saying when they employ the Jews as witnesses, who affirm that the Hebrew words are not often expressed in our old translation. For this reason, I did not judge it useless if rendering something word for word that I would, as far as possible, also show that the Vulgate translator had in countless passages expressed his thoughts very skillfully and well, and that those who accuse him in those same passages depart furthest from the truth. I always affixed myself to the Hebrew words themselves; except when the speech was so unusual that it could in no way be understood in Latin, I retained the Hebraism. I hardly ever changed the order of the words. I did not add any sayings other than, in some passages, a substantive word, as they call it, and relative words, which the Hebrews regularly leave out. I did this more freely for the reason that I wanted to show how much freedom other translators had claimed for themselves, or to say it more accurately, how much recklessness. For if anyone adds some saying in any part of speech, he will by no means interpret Scripture faithfully but will pervert it. Christian reader, you have my view: I want nothing else in my translation, you see, than religion and faith. . . . I have divided the verses almost everywhere with the Hebrews. In some passages, however, I have shown that the divisions or punctuation was done poorly by the Masoretes, or whoever they ultimately were. I often translated the sayings as if they were written with other vowel points than are now read in the Bibles. For the one who applied the points and the divisions performed the duty of an interpreter. Therefore, as he could sometimes be misled, so according to me and many other learned men, those hold no greater weight than the interpretations of the rabbis, especially when I see that among those rabbis themselves, they vary greatly in this matter, and not all in the same way, just like neither the ancient interpreters nor the Chaldean paraphrases

[17]LW 16:3 (WA 31.2:1).

[18]Oecolampadius, *In Iesaiam*, a.4v, 2v-3r; Marlorat, *Esaiae*, ii.v-ii.r.

expressed things in the same voice. Preface to Commentary on Isaiah.[19]

Articles of Faith in Isaiah. Philipp Melanchthon: In the speeches of the prophets, the reasons are explained why the church was subjected to the cross, true and effective consolations are included, and promises are recited and illustrated about the mediator, the forgiveness of sins, the preservation of the church, the presence of God in the church, his hearing us and alleviating punishments in this life to serve the church, and the gift and glory of eternal life when all evil is destroyed entirely. Moreover, it is necessary for every member of the church of God to have a foundation, that is, all the articles of faith. The testimonies of the prophets ought to be sought for each article, and in the writings of Isaiah, the most abundant testimonies exist on all the particular articles. Argument of Isaiah.[20]

Learning Humbly from Isaiah. Johannes Oecolampadius: We read about how that ethnic and unlearned eunuch experienced the wonderful grace of God, since he was dwelling in this prophet so much with a righteous mind. For when he had come to worship in Jerusalem and was returning in his chariot, reading Isaiah, the Spirit said to Philip, "Approach that chariot and join it." . . . Behold how happily the eunuch left, how much treasure reading Isaiah brought him, and ultimately how much joy he brought back to his house, even though at the beginning he was a rudimentary reader. He admitted his ignorance. But he changed from a rudimentary mind to a righteous one, and to a foreigner of arrogance who was not ashamed to learn, nor reluctant to comply. So more plentiful grace also followed. And we, too, will not go away without great fruit if we become eunuchs for the kingdom of heaven, renouncing the pleasures of this world, and if we worship the Lord in the heavenly Jerusalem, asking that his Spirit bring us an apostle—that is, the teaching of the apostles—who, sitting in the chariot of our minds, also reveals hidden things to us that Isaiah preaches about Jesus as the Christ. We, too, would become more learned and happier from that. I think it is clear enough from those few examples how much authority Isaiah has and how it can be usefully read. Preface to Commentary on Isaiah.[21]

The Use of the Prophets After Christ. Wolfgang Musculus: Moreover, it is not that we say, "Therefore after the light of the New Testament, there is no more use for the prophetic Scriptures." There is a different use of them before and after the coming of Christ, because according to the difference of times it is beneficial in one way and another. But in no time should they be judged as useless. Before the coming of Christ, what was being commanded in the books and the future that is promised was given so that the faith of the saints would be directed toward what was promised. It was also so that they would depend on everything contained in these writings and not trust in their own merit of righteousness or external worship. Instead, they were to trust in what was being promised in the divine oracles, so that all the nations of the whole earth would be blessed in them. They were to do this even though they did not clearly understand those mysteries in the same way as we now understand them after his truth began to shine in the world. After the coming of Christ, the oracles of the prophets ought to be read and unrolled, not to impose on them the light of the New Testament Scriptures but to serve our faith by what is reported about Christ to us in the Gospels and the apostolic writings. These are confirmed when compared to the prophetic predictions so that we may understand from them that all the dispensation and doctrine of Christ the Savior was by no means humanly fabricated but divinely determined by God and predicted by the prophets and

[19]Forerius, *Iesaiae*, b.ii.r-v.
[20]MO 13:795.
[21]Oecolampadius, *In Iesaiam*, 2v; citing Acts 8; quoted in Marlorat, *Esaiae*, ii.r.

fulfilled in Christ. This confirmation is of great use to our faith and an exceedingly great necessity. In this way, Christ himself is the goal, as the Gospel writers and the apostles cite the testimonies of the prophets throughout. They confirm that nothing of their own is conveyed, and nothing new and humanly invented proclaimed, but that the time for human salvation to be accomplished has arrived. These trustworthy oracles of the seers predicted those things accordingly much before their times. Preface to Commentary on Isaiah.[22]

The Death of Isaiah. Zacharias Ursinus: Reformed theologians get our knowledge of Isaiah's death from the rabbis. He was killed by Manasseh and cut in two by a saw. Nevertheless, this account survives in Epiphanius's book *On the Death of the Prophets*, as well as in Jerome's commentaries. And this is very much in keeping with Manasseh's wickedness and cruelty as described in the sacred history. I won't mention the other miracles that are told about him by the Jews and recounted in Epiphanius's book. We need only consider his martyrdom, since it confirms Isaiah's teaching more than other arguments, and we learn from his example. In return for his eighty years of labor, the endless slanders and insults he suffered from kings throughout that whole time, from wicked priests, from courtiers and the common people, in return for the prayers and plans he poured out on so many occasions for the salvation of his country, in return for the extraordinary brilliance of his heavenly teaching—and in this he surpassed all the prophets who preceded him—in return for the enormous benefits bestowed on the church in his own generation and indeed all generations until the end of the world, martyrdom is the reward he received from the world, actually from his own people, his close relations, and his own kin. Preface to Commentary on Isaiah.[23]

The Legacy of Isaiah. Johannes Brenz: But although people were ungrateful toward Isaiah, God was nevertheless most gracious toward him, and compensated all his work and all his labor most abundantly. For not only did he preserve him in death and give him the inheritance of a heavenly kingdom, but he also dignified him with such honor many years after his death, such that an angel would announce his words to the virgin when Christ the Son of God was conceived, because the message was the most excellent of all by far and most welcome by all humankind. Preface to Commentary on Isaiah.[24]

Two Parts of the Book. Viktorin Strigel: There are two parts to the book of Isaiah. One is containing the historical in thirty-nine chapters; the other part is the prophetic. This distribution ought to be understood according to the rule, "the announcement is from the leader." For although in the earlier first part, promises about the Messiah and the calling of the Gentiles are woven in, yet Isaiah was a spectator and overseer of those particular matters, which are commemorated in that part. For he saw two sieges of the city of Jerusalem, one when Ahaz was reigning, the other when Hezekiah was reigning. He was also a spectator to the exile of the ten tribes, which happened in the sixth year of the reign of Hezekiah. For in the sixth year of Hezekiah, Samaria was captured and the ten tribes were carried away to Assyria. In the fourteenth year, Sennacherib attacked Jerusalem. Oration on the Prophet Isaiah.[25]

Three Parts to the Book. Martin Luther: But although the larger part of the prophets spoke about the physical kingdom, yet they do (granted, with the most concise words) lead to Christ. Therefore, more ought to be considered in the designs and intentions of the prophets than their words. So, therefore Isaiah says many things about his people and the physical kingdom, in some

[22]Musculus, *In Esaiam*, 1-2.
[23]Ursinus, *Iesaiam*, 9. †See also Melanchthon in MO 13:797.
[24]Brenz, *Esaias*, 4.
[25]Strigel, *Oratio De Propheta Esaia*, 39.

places he condemns sins, in other places he praises righteousness. And it is evident that nearly all the prophecies were directed to the people, but yet at the same time also, he prepares and lifts up the minds of the people to the future kingdom of Christ. . . . But this whole prophecy is best summarized in three parts, namely, the prediction of the future captivity in Babylon, then about the return from that, and third about Christ. Lectures on Isaiah.[26]

The Divisions of the Book. Johannes Oecolampadius:

Under Uzziah, he prophesied all the way to chapter 6.

Under Jotham, he saw the vision in chapter 6.

Under Ahaz, he preached what is from chapter 7 to the end of 14.

Under Hezekiah, from 15 up to chapter 40.

Yet it is uncertain whether the rest that follows he also preached under king Hezekiah or under Manasseh, his successor. Certainly from chapter 40 to 49, he prophesied the history of Cyrus and the liberation from the Babylonian captivity.

From chapter 49 all the way to the end of the book, he clearly and without types preaches about Christ and the church. Preface to Commentary on Isaiah.[27]

The Distribution of the Book. Zacharias Ursinus: Some divide the book into six parts. While some of the earlier interpreters separate it according to the sequence of the kings under whom Isaiah prophesied, two of the more recent interpreters treat it according to the subject matters.

First is from the beginning of the book all the way to the beginning of chapter 6, in which they think the oracles pronounced under Uzziah are contained.

The second is contained in chapter 6, in which the vision portrayed to the prophet under Jotham is described.

The third you have from the beginning of the seventh all the way to the end of the fourteenth chapter, encompassing the speeches under Ahaz.

The fourth, from the beginning of 15 to the end of chapter 39, is what was pronounced under Hezekiah.

The fifth is from the beginning of 40 all the way to the end of 48, which is the promise of liberation of the people from Babylon by Cyrus.

The sixth is from the beginning of 49 all the way to the end of the book, which is about the liberation by the Messiah, that is, about Christ and the church, or his reign.

Others add a division in two parts. The first is all the way to the beginning of chapter 40, containing a mix of threats, warnings, exhortations, and promises, which subdivide into four, as was already said before. And the second is from the beginning of chapter 40 to the end, containing promises and comforts, which also subdivide into the two parts previously identified. Preface to Commentary on Isaiah.[28]

[26]LW 16:3-4, 5 (WA 31.2:2.1-7, 2.31-33).

[27]Oecolampadius, *In Iesaiam*, 5v.

[28]Ursinus, *Iesaiam*, 9.

1:1-9 A Vision Regarding Unrepentance

1 The vision of Isaiah the son of Amoz, which he saw concerning Judah and Jerusalem in the days of Uzziah, Jotham, Ahaz, and Hezekiah, kings of Judah.

2 Hear, O heavens, and give ear, O earth;
for the LORD has spoken:

"Children[a] have I reared and brought up,
they have rebelled against me.

3 The ox knows its owner,
and the donkey its master's crib,

but Israel does not know,
my people do not understand."

4 Ah, sinful nation,
a people laden with iniquity,

offspring of evildoers,
children who deal corruptly!

They have forsaken the LORD,
they have despised the Holy One of Israel,
they are utterly estranged.

5 Why will you still be struck down?
Why will you continue to rebel?

The whole head is sick,
and the whole heart faint.

6 From the sole of the foot even to the head,
there is no soundness in it,

but bruises and sores
and raw wounds;

they are not pressed out or bound up
or softened with oil.

7 Your country lies desolate;
your cities are burned with fire;

in your very presence
foreigners devour your land;
it is desolate, as overthrown by foreigners.

8 And the daughter of Zion is left
like a booth in a vineyard,

like a lodge in a cucumber field,
like a besieged city.

9 If the LORD of hosts
had not left us a few survivors,

we should have been like Sodom,
and become like Gomorrah.

a Or *Sons;* also verse 4

Overview: In the opening chapter, Reformation commentators address some of the same issues as they do in their prefaces. These include the history and background of Isaiah himself, especially the kings identified in the opening verse, and different kinds of prophecies. They introduce the major themes of the book, particularly noting the importance of listening to and obeying God's word, understanding the figures and mysteries of prophecy, and the need for repentance. From this opening chapter, many of these interpreters begin making the connections between the Old Testament people referred to in various ways and the New Testament church. This enables them repeatedly to make direct applications to the time of Jesus and their own times, with a particular emphasis on the smallness of the remnant that remains faithful.

1:1 *The Vision of Isaiah*

The Multiple Times and Audiences of the Prophet's Ministry. Konrad Pellikan: This title is presented first, before all the sermons of Isaiah the prophet in which he faithfully explained the heavenly oracles, as commanded by God, to the kingdom of the tribes of Judah and the inhabitants of the city of Jerusalem. Indeed, they were first directed to the times of Kings Uzziah, Jotham, Ahaz, and Hezekiah. All that Isaiah saw, he prophesied for those times. Second, Isaiah has the most distinguished order of the prophets. He distributed the order of his visions differently from the convention of those others. This is the most erudite and faithful book to be constructed, according to some, as Jerome testifies on this passage. Finally, it is useful to the church of the faithful dispersed throughout the whole earth, who also need exhortations, threats, and examples, just as the Jewish people who sinned by neglecting the Lord's word. So likewise when those in the church continue to sin, they are healed by the same remedies from the word of God. The result is that these sermons of Isaiah equally serve the church gathered from the nations now and always, as they previously did the Jews. Commentary on Isaiah 1:1.[1]

Named Authors. Philipp Melanchthon: The title is the beginning because God does not want books to exist in the church without certain authors; therefore he calls prophets and apostles, and he adorns them with testimonies so that we may know from whom and by whom doctrines are received. Therefore it is necessary for the title to come first. Moreover, the introduction is powerfully great, "Hear, O heavens and earth," because God wants his voice to be heard by every kind of human, and he wants the church to be known in the world. Argument of Isaiah.[2]

Who Is Isaiah? Martin Borrhaus: "Son of Amos." This indeed is not Amos the prophet, who is third among the twelve mentioned, who is not called *ʿāmôṣ* but *ʿāmôs*. Further, it is uncertain from which tribe and which house Isaiah was born. It is old kaballah of the Hebrews that Amoz and Amaziah, king of the Jews, were brothers. And if this is the case, then his royal family brought not a little splendor to Isaiah the prophet, and it would not be surprising that he was more free in his rebuking and more eloquent than others, with his style of speaking considered forceful, full, and impressive. But since this view on the lineage of Isaiah the seer is not proven from the sacred history (and it is not promoted at present), Isaiah was approved by the divine Spirit, not because of his earthly descent and origin but based on the divine oracles, which generate new and heavenly humans in the Messiah, and abolish the old ones. Oracles in Isaiah on 1:1.[3]

Vision as Prophecy. John Calvin: The Hebrew word *ḥazôn* [vision], though it is derived from *ḥazah*, "he saw," and literally is a vision, yet it commonly signifies a prophecy. For when the Scripture makes mention of special visions which were exhibited to the prophets in a symbolical manner, when it was the will of God that some extraordinary event should receive confirmation, in such cases the word *mareh*, "vision," is employed. . . . Thus the inscription of Isaiah recommends to us the teaching of this book, as containing no human reasonings but the oracles of God, in order to convince us that it contains nothing except what was revealed by the Spirit of God. Commentary on Isaiah 1:1.[4]

Hear the Sermon. Johannes Brenz: In this speech, therefore, Isaiah exhorts the inhabitants of the kingdom of Judah and his listeners, the Jerusalemites, to repentance. From the beginning, he blames them for their sins, then he also blames

[1] Pellikan, *Commentaria Bibliorum* 3:A-1; partially quoted in Marlorat, *Esaiae*, 1r.
[2] MO 13:801.

[3] Borrhaus, *In Iesaiae Prophetae Oracula*, 2r.
[4] CTS 13:35-36 (CO 36:27).

their hypocritical and superstitious righteousness. Third, he examines the true fruit of repentance and true good works that God ordered. Finally, when he sees that neither the leaders nor the subordinates were becoming better, either by the preaching of the word of God or by punishments, he promised the revealing of righteousness in the Messiah so that the faithful would indeed be saved while the wicked would perish perpetually. Therefore, let us hear the speech of Isaiah. This is the beginning of his speech where the prophet provokes attention. Commentary on Isaiah 1:1.[5]

Carnal and Spiritual Jerusalem. Johannes Oecolampadius: For these things have been written not only on account of the fleshly but also the spiritual Jerusalem. Isaiah did not write only for his own times but also for ours, which are called "the ends of the ages." He did not write for one race of humanity but for all. This is in the same way that the apostles, when writing an epistle to one church, wanted it to benefit all ages and churches. Under these kings, the prophet was inspired by the Holy Spirit. The studious reader should keep in mind the histories that happened in the times of those kings. Commentary on Isaiah 1:1.[6]

A Call to Repentance like John the Baptist. Ulrich Zwingli: For the sense is: this is the speech that Isaiah had for Judah and Jerusalem, where he charged them with faithlessness and shatters their foreign hopes. Moreover, it should be noted that the Hebrews generally have the custom that when they make mention about the activity of someone, they address only the main and particular points that are said about the activity. This is like when the Evangelists wrote and proclaimed about the blessed Baptist, "Woe to you, you brood of vipers, who showed you the way to flee from the coming wrath?" They were content to mention this mark of prophetic harshness, with the rest of the sharpness and firmness being readily apparent. Without a doubt, the blessed Baptist proclaimed many things to many people before so many people came running to him. But the earlier Evangelists reported only a few things in their accounts. Yet a little later, John delivered the entire sum of the Gospel to be handed down from his preaching. Annotations on Isaiah 1:1.[7]

History as a Foundation Pointing to the Mystery of Christ. Johannes Oecolampadius: Just as it is necessary for those who explain the prophets to have either a faithful interpretation or knowledge of the languages, so, as I said, it was also needed to properly remember the histories of the times in which the prophecies occurred. For unless those are rightly laid as a foundation, whatever is built on top will collapse, and to the extent that they have been handled rightly, the mysteries of allegories can also be happily gathered. Be careful not to despise them entirely, nor unreasonably advance them, for Scripture is unworthy of both. But in order that you may use these more skillfully, know that when the prophets foretold about future things this way, they did not neglect their own times meanwhile. . . . Likewise it often happens that, just as the histories are true in themselves, so also are the mysteries they foreshadow with a certain type—either about Christ or the antichrist. So let the diligent commentator ignore neither. But first let him weave together the history, then also uncover the wrappings of the mysteries, reported by the apostles. And let him show us what the Spirit wants us to either imitate or lift up, aided in doing this by careful comparison of Scriptures. For it cannot be denied that everything that was written "[was] written down for our instruction" . . . not only so we learn but also so that we may receive from it something beneficial; not merely for knowledge, which would be vanity, but also for life. . . . So also in our Isaiah, let us first hear what he said to his own times, and then let us look for

[5] Brenz, *Esaias*, 7.

[6] Oecolampadius, *In Iesaiam*, 4r-5v; Marlorat, *Esaiae*, 2.

[7] ZSW 14:109; citing Mt 3:7.

what is implied for us through those things. Commentary on Isaiah 1:1.[8]

1:2-6 *Rebellion of the Sons*

The Father Calls Them Sons. Dietrich Schnepff: For the first part of the antithesis, he indeed describes the kindness and mercy of the Lord toward his people with three terms. He does this so significantly that it could not be any briefer nor more brilliant. For since he does not call them his servants nor his people but sons, he shows that he is a father toward those who were moved in their soul. Moreover, as nothing is greater than paternal love, so the inclination of his will toward such people could not be expressed with a clearer term than *sons*. Scholia on Isaiah 1:2.[9]

An Allegory of a Father Raising Children. Martin Luther: "They were adopted as children, and indeed they ought to be children, because I showed myself to them as a Father. I not only brought them up, protected them, and increased their number, but I also exalted them, glorified them, and made much of them. I made their name holy. I gave them kings and princes so that there was no other kingdom of this kind on earth." God is good by nature, and he does not cast his kindness in the teeth of those who acknowledge that they have received this from God their Father. On the other hand, he berates the ungodly for their incalculable ingratitude. . . . "But they have rebelled against me." That is, "they have deserted me; they have withdrawn from me; and though exalted by me, they have dropped their excrement into my hand." The world treats us in the same way, no matter how much we have done for it. Whoever wishes to live in the world and desires to imitate God, his Father, should expect from the world the same treatment that God receives. Lectures on Isaiah 1:2.[10]

[8]Oecolampadius, *In Iesaiam*, 5r-6v; citing 1 Cor 10:11; citing the bronze serpent from Num 21 as an example.
[9]Schnepff, *In Esaiae*, 11.
[10]LW 16:7-8 (WA 31.2:4.8-25).

A Heap of Iniquities. Wolfgang Musculus: But the strength of this metaphor ought to be noted, for besides understanding that they were plunged into deep filth in their iniquity, at the same time he charges them, not for erring or for sinning in their thinking (as pliable people have the habit of doing) but rather for having a fixed intention of mind to maintain their stubbornness. It is as if he were saying they were bought by unrighteousness or sold to behave badly. The Jews were sinning and behaving unjustly, but without repentance. And so, also adding to their earlier disgraces, they were accumulating a most serious heap of iniquities on their heads. Commentary on Isaiah 1:4.[11]

Following Human Traditions. Johannes Oecolampadius: Since we sin no less than them when we forsake the word of God and follow human traditions as they did, we who do this are easily convicted of being full of sin. Furthermore, in rebuking one wicked person, the Scripture blames all of them. For all wicked people belong to the one body of antichrist, just as all good persons are members of the body of Christ. And this is precisely why Scripture concludes that we are all under sin, the curse, and slavery, and condemns us as enemies of God and liable to eternal death. Therefore, what God was threatening through the mouth of the prophet to his contemporaries, that was threatened likewise to the later ages through Scripture. Indeed, that rebuke was also serving in the times when Christ was crucified by the Jews, with wickedness raging beyond measure. But it also serves our times, which are no less evil. The wicked in all ages will have their own Sennacheribs, and many are going to die before they migrate from here, just as the Jews were flogged. But generally all who do not return to the voice of God will have far more dreadful sufferings after this life—those that are infernal and eternal. Commentary on Isaiah 1:4.[12]

[11]Musculus, *In Esaiam*, 19, as quoted in Marlorat, *Esaiae*, 4a.
[12]Oecolampadius, *In Iesaiam*, 6v-r.

Pigs Bathing in Mud. Martin Luther: Our Holy One is Christ, who sanctifies us through the word of truth. Yet many attack this true and only sanctification with another sanctity that is counterfeit and false. A pig is led unwillingly to a bath because it thinks this is mud. On the other hand, it is willing to go into mud because it considers this a bath. Thus the wicked sectarians abhor the truth because they are delighted by lies. Lectures on Isaiah 1:3-6.[13]

Underscoring Israel's Obstinacy. Thomas Cooper: From the beginning of the fifth verse to the tenth, he greatly amplifies their wayward stubbornness, declaring that as they could not be won to repentance nor moved to turn to their gracious Lord by consideration of his exceedingly great benefits toward them, neither could they be reclaimed nor at all moved with grievous plagues and punishments. That was the only purpose (as a merciful father) for which he had brought these on them. Rather, by the same plagues, they increased in stubbornness and waxed every day worse than the other. Therefore he says, "To what end should I plague or scourge you with adversity any further seeing your obstinacy, as you will increase in wickedness and still heap sin upon sin and offense upon offense?" Exposition of Old Testament Chapters Read at Common Prayer.[14]

Incurable Unrepentance. Wolfgang Musculus: Therefore it is evident that the prophet demonstrates with an irrefutable argument how incurable Israel's unrepentance is, based on what was happening among them in their present time. For they were behaving just like a wicked boy continuing his malice between beatings. So he shows with clear evidence that they could not be corrected by any blows. Excerpt on Isaiah 1:6.[15]

Unchaste Chastity. Katharina Schütz Zell: However, they do not punish and have never punished the unchaste "chastity" of celibacy, the sin-flowing harlotry of Sodom and Noah's age; but instead they protect it. Indeed, temporal and spiritual authorities have made a covenant together about this to strive powerfully against God. Those who ought to be inclined to all integrity and to give it a helping hand must allow it to be said of them that one has five, six harlots, another seven women in childbed at the same time, and nevertheless a pretty prostitute at home, and many such like things. It is indeed as Isaiah says, "There is no health from the soles of their feet to the head." Apologia for Master Matthew Zell, Her Husband.[16]

1:7-9 *The Devastation of the Land and a Remnant*

Future Destruction. Wolfgang Musculus: So the Lord threatened his people repeatedly that he was going to bring enemies from far away to their land, namely, from Assyria and Babylon, whose language they could not understand. . . . This was to signify that he was going to bring on them enemies who were strangers to all sympathy, and who were all going to be involved in devastating and ruining everything to the point of destruction. So we read about the Assyrians that their heart was prone to not be chastised but was going to be crushed and destroyed, as later. Excerpt on Isaiah 1:7.[17]

Hypocrites as Traitors. Heinrich Bullinger: Then they provoked the Holy One of Israel himself to burning anger by their rebellion. For they contradicted the word of God, they blasphemed God, they persecuted the prophets, they retained idolatry and superstition, they imposed it on others by force—all things that provoke God. Finally, they "defected from the rear." This is why he especially treats them as hypocrites.

[13]LW 16:10 (WA 31.2:6.18-23).
[14]Cooper, *Brief Exposition*, 3r*.
[15]Musculus, *In Esaiam*, 22 as quoted in Marlorat, *Esaiae*, 4r.
[16]Zell, *Katharina Schütz Zell, Church Mother*, 74-75.
[17]Musculus, *In Esaiam*, 22 as quoted in Marlorat, *Esaiae*, 5r; citing Deut 28; Is 49; 10:7.

For just as traitors in an army are civilians who join the ranks, but when there is about to be fighting they defect from the rear and betray the army, so hypocrites imitate piety, but when a crisis comes, they reveal that they are such that they betray ecclesiastical and political matters, defecting from the truth when they should have been especially steadfast. Let each one now likewise apply these things to the customs of his own church and accuse sins equally among the people and the leaders—and all to this end that sins be properly acknowledged, and each one seriously reflect on correction, so that we ourselves do not perish in the end but are saved in Jesus Christ our Lord. Sermons on Isaiah 1:7-8.[18]

Satanic Ingratitude. Johannes Brenz: Ingratitude is entirely a satanic crime. For Satan in the beginning was created by God through his Son and adorned with the highest gifts above all the other angels, but immediately he was ungrateful to God his benefactor. He arrogantly wanted divine majesty for himself and Christ to be overthrown from his seat of majesty, which he is even still attempting and always will be attempting. Then Satan also inspired Adam with ungratefulness when he persuaded him that it was better to believe his word than that of God. And so Adam was ungrateful to God, because he thought God was deceitful and Satan was being truthful. From Adam is derived later ingratitude in all flesh. But those born again in Christ receive the Holy Spirit, in whom they purify the natural human ingratitude. This is why works must be given to us through Christ, so that we flee from ingratitude and not perish eternally together with Satan. Commentary on Isaiah 1:8.[19]

A Small Number of Chosen. John Calvin: The prophet here describes utter destruction; and yet, because God had to deal with his church and his beloved people, that judgment is mitigated by special grace, so that out of the general ruin of the whole nation God rescues his people, whom he justly compares to a very small remnant. . . . This is the reason assigned by Paul, who is the best interpreter of this passage, when, by quoting it, he represses the haughtiness of the Jews, that they may not boast of the mere name, as if it had been enough that they were descended from the fathers; for he reminds them that God could act toward them as he had formerly done toward the fathers, but that through his tender mercies a remnant shall be saved. And why? That the church may not utterly perish; for it is through the favor that he bears toward it that the Lord . . . still reserves some small seed. This statement ought to yield us powerful consolation even in those heaviest calamities in which we are apt to think that it is all over with the church. . . . We also learn from it that we ought not to judge by the largeness of the number, unless we choose to prefer the chaff to the wheat, because the quantity is greater; but we ought to be satisfied with knowing that, though the number of the godly be small, still God acknowledges them as his chosen people. Commentary on Isaiah 1:9.[20]

A Few Saved by God's Mercy. Johannes Brenz: "Unless the Lord," he says, "had left us a few survivors." The Lord saves a few certain ones by his mercy. He does not save them by their own righteousness or wisdom. "In the flood only eight were saved." What about them? Were they really not saved by their own righteousness and prudence? Not at all, but by the mercy of God. For God could also have destroyed them in the flood, if he had been inclined to exercise his severity rather than his compassion. In the burning of Sodom and Gomorrah, Lot was saved with his daughters. Yet they were saved by the mercy of God and not their own merits. In the Babylonian devastation of the city of Jerusalem, some of the Israelites escaped unharmed, but very few, and that by divine benevolence, not by their righteousness. So also in

[18]Bullinger, *Isaias*, 4r.
[19]Brenz, *Esaias*, 10.
[20]CTS 13:52-53 (CO 36:36-37); citing Rom 9:27-29.

the calling of the Gentiles to the knowledge of Christ, and the blinding and rejection of the Jews, some of the Jews were converted to Christ and were saved. Those, too, had merited rejection along with the rest, but God wanted to make a notable remnant among them for the riches of his glory, as Paul says, as vessels of mercy that he prepared in advance for glory. Commentary on Isaiah 1:9.[21]

A Remnant by Election. Martin Borrhaus: God did not reject his people whom he foreknew. So, therefore at this time there was a remnant by the grace of election. When the apostle refers to the preservation of the remnant during Hezekiah's reign, he applies the passage to the remnant who were set free from the power of the spiritual Assyria, the antichrist, at the time the Messiah was presented to the world. The apostles disclosed that the antichrist had begun to construct the errors of his kingdom in their time. And with the veil withdrawn from the Israelites and mystical Jerusalem, we recognize saved remnants also of Gentiles in the church, described as offspring of Abraham's promise—a lost son in the beginning drawn to defection from the gospel at that time. Few, if you consider the entire world, are the survivors vindicated from his tyranny by the ministry of the gospel. Oracles in Isaiah on 1:9.[22]

Warned from Other Cities. Wolfgang Musculus: The prophet does not say the daughter of Zion is besieged or desolated, but the city is besieged or desolated, that is, it was desolated and deserted in the same way as if it had been hostilely besieged. When the chief city is besieged, all the surrounding nearby regions, the district, and the remaining cities have already been conquered. . . . We see in this passage that the city previously most renowned is compared to a cottage in a vineyard with the remains after the harvest. Therefore, the great cities that are also in the nearby regions should also think about what could happen to them if they provoke the Lord by their shameful ways. Excerpts on Isaiah 1:9.[23]

What About the Covenant? Rudolf Gwalther: But so that we may respond to the Jews, it should not be objected, "So God did not forget his covenant, did he?" And then, "He did not abandon his inheritance altogether, did he?" The prophet shows how indulgently they were treating the covenant at this point, even though they deserved to be utterly destroyed. For it says, "Unless the Lord of hosts had left a few survivors. . . ." With these words he totally wants to say this, "So indeed, we have suffered, and we see these heavier things remaining on us—whether the atrocities of our crimes or the power of all the enemies joined together rising up against us with immense cruelty. But it is the goodness of God here that wants a small surviving remnant among us to remain, from whom we are restored. . . ." Therefore, we ought not to lament the severity of God, but rather deplore our stubbornness, which to this point they could not correct with a penalty, nor soften by the leniency of God. Sermons on Isaiah 1:9.[24]

[21]Brenz, *Esaias*, 13-14; citing 1 Pet 3:20; Rom 9.
[22]Borrhaus, *In Iesaiae Prophetae Oracula*, 8.
[23]Musculus, *In Esaiam*, 23 as quoted in Marlorat, *Esaiae*, 6v.
[24]Gwalther, *Isaias*, 5r-v.

1:10-20 FALSE WORSHIP

10Hear the word of the LORD,
you rulers of Sodom!

Give ear to the teaching[a] of our God,
you people of Gomorrah!

11"What to me is the multitude of your sacrifices?
says the LORD;

I have had enough of burnt offerings of rams
and the fat of well-fed beasts;

I do not delight in the blood of bulls,
or of lambs, or of goats.

12"When you come to appear before me,
who has required of you
this trampling of my courts?

13Bring no more vain offerings;
incense is an abomination to me.

New moon and Sabbath and the calling of convocations—
I cannot endure iniquity and solemn assembly.

14Your new moons and your appointed feasts
my soul hates;

they have become a burden to me;
I am weary of bearing them.

15When you spread out your hands,
I will hide my eyes from you;

even though you make many prayers,
I will not listen;

your hands are full of blood.

16Wash yourselves; make yourselves clean;
remove the evil of your deeds from before my eyes;

cease to do evil,
17learn to do good;

seek justice,
correct oppression;

bring justice to the fatherless,
plead the widow's cause.

18"Come now, let us reason[b] together,
says the LORD:

though your sins are like scarlet,
they shall be as white as snow;

though they are red like crimson,
they shall become like wool.

19If you are willing and obedient,
you shall eat the good of the land;

20but if you refuse and rebel,
you shall be eaten by the sword;
for the mouth of the LORD has spoken."

a Or *law* **b** Or *dispute*

Overview: The second part of Isaiah 1 provides the Reformation commentators with the language to address what they saw as false worship and superstitions. They parallel the rituals, sacrifices, and celebrations among the Israelites that God rejected with practices in their own day. Protestant interpreters emphasize the need for true faith and genuine repentance in order for worship to be pleasing to God and for forgiveness to be assured. Commentators frequently address why God was now saying he did not want the very things he previously commanded them to do. This brings up discussion about the relationship between the promises God makes and human responsibility.

1:10-15 *The Hypocrisy of Religious Worship*

GOD WEIGHS THE HEART. KONRAD PELLIKAN: Who was asking for these sacrifices in my temple from such bloody hands? I ask for a heart full of faith and love, not those gifts. I will not be served only in this place, nor with this worship, but "I will be worshiped in spirit and truth" throughout the whole earth. But you think it is great to trample my court and stain it with goat blood, as a way to earn my favor with merely external worship, when nothing pleases me less. . . . The Lord wants the sacrifices of righteousness and a contrite spirit. What is scented of devotion and confidence is fragrant to God. The smoke of ceremonies and incense is a display that is absent of devotion, an abomination, like all hypocrisy. The New Moons had already reached the point of abuse with the worship of the queen of the sky and veneration of the stars, such that honor was being offered to the creation and not to the Creator. The Sabbath was only leisure and a lascivious display of arrogance with all kinds of drunkenness and luxury, not prayer or listening to the word of God. "Throw away your solemn convocations which you assemble for strife and luxury or profit, for they are displeasing and an abomination I cannot bear. It is emptiness. Even your fasting, abstaining, or fast days are iniquities. All your pursuits are displeasing because you are wicked and you bring to me physical things when I want the spiritual. When I ask for your heart, you spread out your hands and those bloodstained things." COMMENTARY ON ISAIAH 1:10-11.[1]

NAUSEA AT SUPERSTITIONS. WOLFGANG MUSCULUS: Here it should be considered how much further the devotion of human superstitions (as they say) plummets than they think. They consider that God is delighted with the multitude of traditions and human inventions; therefore they increase them so immensely that the condition of Christians could be judged more troublesome in this matter than was previously so for the Jews. But here we see that God is so set against them that he gets nausea and disgust from the multitude of even the things he himself had prescribed for the people—on top of those human superstitions they invented. Christ speaks about this. . . . "They worship me in vain, teaching human commandments as doctrine." EXCERPT ON ISAIAH 1:11.[2]

CEREMONIES WITHOUT FAITH. MARTIN BORRHAUS: Because even though God instituted the ceremonies among the Israelites himself, if they are done without faith, he rejected them so much. How much more does he reject the ceremonies which that foolish pastor sets up in the time of the new covenant, represented by the shadow, with the body that of Christ. ORACLES IN ISAIAH ON 1:11.[3]

OUTWARD ORDINANCES ONLY. SEBASTIAN FRANCK: Therefore, I believe that the outward church of Christ, including all its gifts and sacraments, because of the breaking in and laying waste by the antichrist right after the death of the apostles, went up into heaven and lies concealed in the Spirit and in truth. I am thus quite certain that for fourteen hundred years now there has existed no gathered church, nor any sacrament. For this is proven along with experience by the work, outward behavior, and misuse with which antichrist has besmirched and spoiled everything. Yet at the same time, nothing has departed from the truth of baptism, the Supper, the ban, and gathering for worship. Instead, the Spirit has imparted all this in truth to the faithful in whatever lands they be, although, of course, the signs that indicate these are left to the devil since they have been sullied by antichrist. For from the moment when the Sabbath, circumcision, and the commandment concerning the temple and offerings have been cut off, God recognizes them no longer as his ordinances,

[1]Pellikan, *Commentaria Bibliorum*, 3:2v-r; citing Jn 4:24.

[2]Musculus, *In Esaiam*, 30, as quoted in Marlorat, *Esaiae*, 8a; citing Mt 5:9.

[3]Borrhaus, *In Iesaiae Prophetae Oracula*, 9.

although they were hitherto expressly ordained, and says, "What concern are the temple and sacrifices to me? I am full of burnt offerings." A Letter to John Campanus.[4]

Acceptable Sacrifice. William Day: The reason why God abhorred these things and loathed them was not that they were nothing in themselves but because the ones who offered them to God were wicked. Hence it was that, while God accepted the sacrifices of the just, yet the sacrifice of the wicked was an abomination to him. . . . For sacrifice was of that nature, such that God did not at any time accept a person for the sacrifice, but only the sacrifice for the person. Exposition of Isaiah 1:13.[5]

The Rejection of Sacrifices. Martin Luther: What more would one, or could one, offer than himself, all he is and all he has? When the body is yielded a sacrifice, all belonging to the body is yielded also. Therefore, the Old Testament sacrifices, with the priests and all the splendor, have terminated. How does the offering of a penny compare with that of the body? Indeed, such fragmentary patchwork scarcely deserves recognition as a sacrifice when the bodies of Christ and of his followers are offered. Consequently, Isaiah may truly say that in the New Testament such beggarly works are loathsome compared to real and great sacrifices: "He that kills an ox is as he that slays a man; he that sacrifices a lamb, as he that breaks a dog's neck; he that offers an oblation, as he that offers swine's blood; he that burns frankincense, as he that blesses an idol." . . . Similarly, also: "What to me is the multitude of your sacrifices?" says the Lord. "I have had enough of the burnt offerings of rams, and the fat of fed beasts; and I delight not in the blood of bullocks, or of lambs, or of he-goats." . . . Thus, in plain words, Isaiah rejects all other sacrifices in view of this true one. Sermon on First Sunday After Epiphany on Romans 12:1-6.[6]

Why the Institution of Festivals? Heinrich Bullinger: You say, why, then, did God institute festivals, if he so wants to reject them? I respond, it was for the usefulness of the people that God instituted sacrifices, but as sacrificing was abused by making a good thing bad, so also happened to the festivals. God had instituted festivals so that the people would well enjoy sacred leisure by hearing the exposition of the law and the sacred speeches, praying, and religiously enjoying the sacraments. Yet these were neglected. They spent their leisure on shameful things, and they were celebrating the holidays from the devil. Sermons on Isaiah 1:12-15.[7]

Displeasing Worship. Dietrich Schnepff: And the proposition of this whole passage is, "Your worship is displeasing to me." He treats this at length because (as was said) the Hebrews were opposing the prophets—their pursuit and diligence in sacred matters, and it was as if they wanted to contend with the Lord. So later he says, "Come and let us deliver our reason. You want," he says, "to dispute with me, when you oppose me with your sanctity. Do what I command, and then contend with me in judgment." Scholia on Isaiah 1:13-15.[8]

Sabbath Keeping. Rudolf Gwalther: Therefore, their ungratefulness is plainly detestable, who do not even have any regard for the Sabbath and on those days that commemorate the most important kindnesses of Jesus Christ, they spend them all on business. So, what he has done for us hardly ever comes to their minds, or what we owe him in return. And now this is enough said about holidays in general. . . . But when convicted and admonished of any crime by the Word, let us give glory to God and let us confess the failure, and let

[4]Franck, "Letter to Campanus," 149*.
[5]Day, *Exposition*, 7*; citing Prov 15:8.
[6]Luther, *Sermons*, 7:10-11; citing Is 66:3; 1:11.
[7]Bullinger, *Isaias*, 6v.
[8]Schnepff, *In Esaiae*, 18.

us seriously consider his correction. For this is actually to keep the Sabbath spiritually: when we rest from fleshly works and sins and we are intent on those things that pertain to the worship of God. Let one add to these the pursuit of kindness so that when we are rejoicing in the Lord and renewing our exhausted bodies, we also bring joy to those who are overwhelmed with hard poverty, as they indeed cannot rest and rejoice when they are commanded to abstain from the labor of their hands. Moses reminds about this more than once in the law, when he addresses feast days and sacrifices. Sermons on Isaiah 1:13.[9]

The Sabbath Is Not About Us. Andreas Bodenstein von Karlstadt: God is honored when his children become like him, who is our Father. We should regard this foundation alone, and not to our benefit. Just as God is concerned about our benefit and holiness, so we, too, are to be concerned about and seek God's glory, honor, and the benefit of the neighbor, not of ourselves.

When we have eyes only for our own benefit, we defile ourselves and make ourselves unholy, neglecting the reason for the Sabbath. Isaiah understood and declared all this when he said, "I cannot suffer and tolerate your sabbaths or holy days. Your deeds are impure and wicked. Remove from before your eyes your evil thoughts and cease to do evil." According to this, the finding of our soul must cease, and our eyes must directly behold and focus on God and not on what is ours. Regarding the Sabbath and Statutory Holy Days.[10]

Adding Your Own Practices. Martin Luther: "Your." By adding this word, the prophet means that the Jews also established other festivals besides those of Moses, and those additions constantly obscure the first good institution of God. Satan always wants to be God's mimic and ape, but God hates him. Lectures on Isaiah 1:14.[11]

The Spirit of the Sabbath and Feasts. Andreas Bodenstein von Karlstadt: Isaiah testifies to these things. They do not seek what the spirit and will of the law is, because no one plainly searching for the letter and flesh of the precepts actually distinguishes with how much exact care the Lord issued the law of sacrifices through Moses, and with what testimony he instituted the Sabbath and other feasts. Yet he says through Isaiah that the procuring of sacrifices and festivals in name is not the same as the shell of the law, and that he desires one's spirit. The flesh and letter of the law—whether husk, skin, or veil—is a leaf and a skin that we can look at with our eyes and form with our hands as a reed. But the spirit is gathered in the soul alone, and the spirit is not truly in us unless it is engraved on the heart by the divine finger and power. On the Letter or Flesh and the Spirit of the Law.[12]

Unjust Assemblies. Cardinal Cajetan: "Your assemblies are unjust." . . . It appears in the Hebrew original that the festivals of the Lord are called the "callings to holiness," because they were convocations that called the people to holiness. Therefore God alludes to that name when he says, "I will not be able to call the calling of a New Moon, a Sabbath, and the Retention—that is, the solemn assembly that is celebrated on the eighth day from the first day of Tabernacles." Now, the reason why these festivals cannot be called "callings to holiness" is inserted into the saying with the mutilated word, *unjust*. And the sense is, "I will not be able to call a New Moon, a Sabbath, and the Retention, a 'call to holiness,' but to injustice, because they are filled with your unjust minds and works."

"My soul hated your celebrations and your solemn observances." The same thing is signified by celebrations and neomenia, namely, the festival

[9] Gwalther, *Isaias*, 7r-v.
[10] CRR 8:319.
[11] LW 16:17 (WA 31.2:12.6-8).
[12] Karlstadt, *De Legis Litera*, Aii-AiiV.

of a New Moon. Likewise, a soul is attributed to God metaphorically, with attributes like anger. For God speaks to people according to the ways of people. Commentary on Isaiah 1:13-14.[13]

True Prayer by Faith. Martin Borrhaus: Indeed, it stands that the Lord is far from the wicked, but hears the prayers of the righteous. For he does not count the words of prayer, but he weighs the spirit of faith and of love stirred up in the heart of the godly. This relates to what is taught by our Lord Jesus Christ: "But when you pray, do not babble as the foreigners do, who think they are going to be heard for their many words." Oracles in Isaiah on 1:15.[14]

Blood Refers to Adam's Sin. Johannes Brenz: First of all, we will consider what comes from the term *blood*. For in the custom of the Hebrews, not only is murder called "blood" or "bloody," because human blood is shed, and not only are envy and hatred toward people, but all sins are called this, because they are from bloody things, that is, from human nature, and from the bloodline that we have with Adam, are born into, and that cannot be expiated except with blood. . . . Therefore since all humans are smeared with this blood of Adam and evil is poured into them by the blood of Adam, it ought rightly be deduced that by the term *blood* the covenant of Adam that is propagated to all people is expressed. Commentary on Isaiah 1:15.[15]

1:16-20 *Repentance, Forgiveness, and Obedience*

Wash Your Hands. Martin Borrhaus: And he washed us from our sins by his blood. That blood contains the water of the Holy Spirit flowing from the fount of the Messiah, which commends you to God by faith alone when you are sprinkled—not with the blood of sheep, nor the water of purification and cleansing commanded by Moses, nor of a festival, nor New Moons, nor incense, nor any of your ceremonies celebrated by you without his Spirit, which those foreshadowed. Oracles in Isaiah on 1:16.[16]

Washing Hands Is Spiritual. Rudolf Gwalther: And Christ himself testifies to Peter, "Unless I wash you, you will have no share with me." Truly he sprinkles us with the gospel. But it is received by faith, and therefore we are purified by it, as Peter says, evidently looking back to when Christ said that his disciples were clean because of his word. The same faith truly gives birth to the regular pursuit of repentance that the Lord commends to us in footwashing, needing to be washed by him. Therefore, Isaiah forgives the people in his time according to the promise of the Messiah. And what he says to them we think is likewise said to us. Not even the waters of baptism wash from sins, as Peter expressly teaches. Yet, it should not be thought that the prophet speaks about an external means of washing, which corresponds to empty ceremonies. He soon enumerates the effects of those who can be recognized as truly washed. Sermons on Isaiah 1:16.[17]

Pilate and the Pharisees Physically Wash Their Hands. Wolfgang Musculus: When Pilate was going to pronounce the sentence that would be on the blood of Christ, he took water, washed his hands before the people, and said, "I am innocent of the blood of this righteous one; see to it yourselves." . . . He was washing his hands with water, but truly his action was not a washing in innocence and upright judgment. On the contrary, he was still polluting the greater righteous blood he was going to condemn. He was purifying his hands with water, which were making innocent blood impure.

[13]Cajetan, *Tria Priora Isaiae Capita*, 638; citing Lev 23.
[14]Borrhaus, *In Iesaiae Prophetae Oracula*, 10; citing Mt 6:7.
[15]Brenz, *Esaias*, 18-19; citing Rom 5:12 and Hos 6:7.
[16]Borrhaus, *In Iesaiae Prophetae Oracula*, 11.
[17]Gwalther, *Isaias*, 9r; citing Jn 13:8.

The Pharisees and the scribes, according to the tradition of the elders, do not eat bread unless they have first bathed their hands. They observed this tradition so much that they did not hesitate to accuse Christ himself because of it, when his disciples were taking up food with unwashed hands. . . . Great blindness. They want to have the organs of our works cleansed from dirt, which water washes, and at the same time they were retaining their own works and uncleanness of pursuits, which do not cleanse except by true repentance. Commentary on Isaiah 1:16.[18]

Regular Repentance in Remembering Baptism. Johannes Oecolampadius: And the Lord indeed is the one who washes us, but only if we refuse to remain unwashed. For with his precious and pure blood, he cleanses us who are common and unclean. This is why we also pray, "Wash me again from my sins." Here I want us to remember our baptism, that mystery in which the sign is received at the same time. Its perpetual use is good for the soul. For our repentance is also perpetual, and correcting our life's pursuit is perpetual and is to be improved as long as we live. For as long as the old Adam lives in us—the earthly one, also by the name "red and bloody"—we must always be washed, and that thoroughly. And as long as stains and dirt are born in us, it is necessary that we be purified with tears and fervent zeal. We wash ourselves when our evil pursuits or thoughts are removed and when we rest from afflicting others and behaving perversely. Moreover, we make ourselves clean when we learn to bless, for it is not enough to avoid evil unless you also will bless. Commentary on Isaiah 1:16.[19]

Guard Against Sin. Mary Astell: Whoever is in a state of love to God is always on guard against great and manifest sins; if he sins like David or like Saint Peter, he can't be restored but by their solemn, and bitter, and lasting repentance. It matters not whether they be "sins to which our constitution leads us" that overcome us, or whether we "sin against the current of our nature"; this may have more willfulness, but both are "unpardonable" without repentance, which is "ceasing to do evil and learning to do well" and is the conditional clause why "the gospel does not condemn us for every vice." Further, such a proneness to sin as carries us to commit it unwittingly must not be called an infirmity; it is a habitual guilt, arising from many evil actions willfully repeated. The Christian Religion.[20]

Repentance and Forgiveness. Philipp Melanchthon: Now, the whole first chapter is a speech about repentance. He charges them with sins, and especially the worship of idols and false thinking about sacrifices. And weaved into this accusation is the complaint that sins roam rampantly, and only the smallest remnant are thinking rightly and rightly calling on God. This part at the same time testifies that the true church of God is meager, and yet some true remnant remains. Therefore, he says, "Unless God had left behind a seed for us, we would have been like Sodom and Gomorrah." After the accusation, he adds the promise about the forgiveness of sins—a declaration that should be obtained more abundantly from other passages with speeches about the Messiah, which affirm that the forgiveness of sins is given on account of his sacrifice and not on account of other works and sacrifices. Here he speaks only in general about conversion to the true God. Of course what is necessary to grasp from the promise and recognition of the Messiah is this: stop acting perversely.

Moreover, there is a picture illustrated in this part, in which the promise is recited, "Though your sins are like scarlet, they shall be whitened as snow, and though they are red like scarlet, you will

[18]Musculus, *In Esaiam*, 38; Marlorat, *Esaiae*, 9v; citing Mt 27:24; 15.
[19]Oecolampadius, *In Iesaiam*, 15r-v; partially quoted in Marlorat, *Esaiae*, 11.
[20]Astell, *Christian Religion*, 254; citing Charles Hickman, *Fourteen Sermons, Preached at St James in Westminster* (London: James Orme, 1700), 255-56.

be pure as wool." . . . Scarlet signifies the color purple. The same word also signifies worm, since *kokkos baphikē* [seed for dyeing] is a seed produced from a scarlet oak that is changed into a worm,† which they call *skōlēkion* [type of worm]. Therefore the color is scarlet, and they think the term *scharlach* comes from the Greek word *skōlēkion*. But the entire image beautifully corresponds to the Son of God, who is for us the bloody worm who removes our sins. Argument of Isaiah on 1:18.[21]

Forgiveness for Sins and Penalties. Johannes Oecolampadius: Now, at the same time this exhortation provokes us to repentance and confession so that when we confess our sins in faith, he forgives not only the guilt of our sins but also the penalties. For divine mercy has the habit of doing this. . . . "I said, 'I will confess my unrighteousness,' and you forgave the iniquity of my sin." . . . "If we confess our sins, God is merciful and just to forgive us our sins and to cleanse us from all unrighteousness." You see these support our view that if we have accused ourselves before God, nothing prejudges our sins, however great they were, and even if they were many, for he says "sins," not "sin." Even if they are old and serious, "like a red thread, and crimson or purple," he says, they are forgiven in every way, and we will be no less whitened. We are made white as snow or washed wool. Commentary on Isaiah 1:18.[22]

Conditional and Unconditional Promises. Johannes Brenz: These promises must be rightly understood. For great is the difference between the promise about the Messiah and the promise about the kingdom of Canaan. God promised the Messiah from the seed of Abraham without any condition of righteousness or uprightness of the Jews. For he did not want the Messiah to be sent on account of any human merit, but only from his sheer freedom and mercy. But he gave the kingdom of Canaan to the Jews with a condition, if they would uphold the law and pursue piety, then he would want to preserve them in the kingdom against their enemies. But if they would pursue wickedness and cruelty against the law, then he would want to cast them out and hand them over to their enemies again. Commentary on Isaiah 1:18-20.[23]

Not About Free Will. Johannes Oecolampadius: The Pelagians, and even many of the Fathers, misuse this passage to establish "free will." They say, "God says, 'If you are willing and if you are unwilling,'" therefore our election is free. And at this point they drag in the testimony. . . . "Behold, I set before you the way of life and the way of death." . . . We respond to this: If indeed there is contention about the term that we are calling the same thing "desire" and "free will" or *autoexousia* [self-authority], then our response is that the term is not found anywhere in Scripture, and the church does not have the habit of contending: "We allow them to misuse terms. For love is more precious to us than words." For who willingly is unable to sin and to do well? But if the glory and mercy of God is diminished under this pretext, it is better to contradict people than to participate in blasphemy. And that is usually what happens if people determine to rule by their own will, asserting the royal will of our actions. For in this way they make the will free such that we can do good and not do good; we desire and we do not desire; we engage in evil when we want and as much as we want, and again when we want, we do not engage in evil. But we ourselves give this magnificence to God, as he alone is truly free and the only king under whose direction all things are governed—even those that they think are done most freely, even desires. . . . For it is God who works in us to will and to work. Hence also here, when it says, "If you are willing," he is the one who stirs up and works the desire in us. And whatever

[21]CR 13:801. †The LXX of Is 1:18 reads, "*ean de hōsin hōs kokkinon* [and though they be as scarlet]." The Vulgate reads, "et si fuerint rubra quasi vermiculus [and though they were red as a worm]."
[22]Oecolampadius, *In Iesaiam*, 16r; citing Ps 32:5; 1 Jn 1:9.

[23]Brenz, *Esaias*, 25.

that is, it is not from our willing, nor running. Commentary on Isaiah 1:19.[24]

Both Earthly and Heavenly Blessings. Martin Borrhaus: "You shall eat the good of the land." Not the enemies. When exhorting them, he mentioned the promises of good things corresponding to the Old Testament. But under these are signified the heavenly goods, which are gained by faith in the Son Messiah. In regard to this, the divine Spirit shows that both earthly and heavenly blessing fall according to repentance. As the apostle testifies with these words, "Godliness is of value in every way, as it holds promise for the present life and the life to come." Oracles in Isaiah on 1:19-20.[25]

[24]Oecolampadius, *In Iesaiam*, 17r-v; citing Jer 21:8; Sirach 15:17; Deut 30; Phil 2:13; Rom 9:16.

[25]Borrhaus, *In Iesaiae Prophetae Oracula*, 12; citing 1 Tim 4:8.

The Authority of the Lord's Word. Rudolf Gwalther: For Isaiah concludes this passage saying, "For the mouth of the Lord has spoken." And he does not report any other reason that would confirm this pronouncement. For to the one to whom the authority of God seems unworthy, you will bring no other arguments or testimonies, so that one may have faith in what was said. Therefore that is sufficient for us against all who think otherwise. For as the counsel of God remains into eternity, so the same word will also not be changed. And it is noted that concerning the most dangerous condition of the last times and the counsel we must now follow, the eternal Son of God, Jesus Christ, later pronounced, "Heaven and earth will pass away, but my words will not pass away." Sermons on Isaiah 1:20.[26]

[26]Gwalther, *Isaias*, 10v; citing Mt 24:35.

1:21-31 HYPOCRISY AND ITS PENALTIES

21 *How the faithful city*
has become a whore,[a]
she who was full of justice!

Righteousness lodged in her,
but now murderers.

22 *Your silver has become dross,*
your best wine mixed with water.

23 *Your princes are rebels*
and companions of thieves.

Everyone loves a bribe
and runs after gifts.

They do not bring justice to the fatherless,
and the widow's cause does not come
to them.

24 *Therefore the* Lord *declares,*
the Lord *of hosts,*
the Mighty One of Israel:

"Ah, I will get relief from my enemies
and avenge myself on my foes.

25 *I will turn my hand against you*
and will smelt away your dross as with lye
and remove all your alloy.

26 *And I will restore your judges as at the first,*
and your counselors as at the beginning.

Afterward you shall be called the city of
righteousness,
the faithful city."

27 *Zion shall be redeemed by justice,*
and those in her who repent, by righteousness.

28 *But rebels and sinners shall be broken*
together,
and those who forsake the Lord *shall be*
consumed.

29 *For they*[b] *shall be ashamed of the oaks*
that you desired;

and you shall blush for the gardens
that you have chosen.

30 *For you shall be like an oak*
whose leaf withers,
and like a garden without water.

31 *And the strong shall become tinder,*
and his work a spark,

and both of them shall burn together,
with none to quench them.

a Or *become unchaste* **b** Some Hebrew manuscripts *you*

Overview: The first chapter ends with a new complaint about the hypocrisy of the formerly faithful people, with a specific focus on the greed and apathy of the people toward the poor and destitute. The Reformation commentators explain reasons for the severe penalties described, particularly addressing the inextinguishable fire. This section also begins to reveal how much Protestant exegetes continued to repeat or amend allegorical interpretations of ordinary items such as the silver and dross mentioned here.

The Start of a New Pericope. Johannes Oecolampadius: "How it has become." According to the Hebrew, this is the beginning of a new pericope, but it connects well with what was before. God had reproached the Jews with judgment for their shameful actions and had declared his mercy. He had also said what good works he expects from them. Yet now he condemns those convicted with a new complaint. Commentary on Isaiah 1:21.[1]

1:21-23 *The Unfaithful City*

The Faithful City Became an Unfaithful Prostitute. Wolfgang Musculus: He does not simply say, "The faithful city has become a whore," but, "How has the faithful city become a whore?" The twin reasons were their stupor and admiration. One, because this city had not declined slightly but was enormously corrupt and depraved. He expresses that with the metaphor of prostitute and harlot. The other reason was from the comparison of this with what was before. When he thought about the purity and sincerity of earlier Jerusalem and compared that to the present impurity and corruption, he could hardly not be frightened and astounded at such an enormous and ugly transformation.[†] He expresses this comparison with the saying. Commentary on Isaiah 1:21.[2]

The Previously Faithful City. Johannes Oecolampadius: Now, it was called faithful—not on account of the excessive multitude of priests and Levites, not on account of the magnificence of the temple, not on account of the variety of ceremonies, not on account of the solemnity of festivals. These things only showed they were a city more hypocritical than faithful. But on account of faith in God and piety, since there were people there loving and worshiping God above all. Commentary on Isaiah 1:21.[3]

Faith and Judgment for Sale. Cardinal Cajetan: "How have you become a prostitute?" According to the Hebrew, it should be read, "How was the city of the faithful, a city full of justice, into a prostitute?" Following the address to the princes and the people of Judah and Jerusalem in general, the speech descends to deal specifically with the city of Jerusalem. And as what gets addressed insinuates, it deals with the sins in Jerusalem at the coming of the Messiah. The words of the prophet are sorrowful and wondering, "How did it become a prostitute?" For, describing the future as the past, he laments how the faithful city, full of justice, has turned into a prostitute. For the work of a prostitute is to sell the use of her own body for sexual pleasure, and Jerusalem is described as sellable for good pleasure. Indeed, as is clear from the book of Maccabees, the priesthood was for sale, and consequently judgment was for sale. For those buying the priesthood were equal with those who sold the offices. And therefore, the once-faithful city—where what is said is done by faith—was turned into a prostitute. By selling away judgment, the city full of justice was turned into a prostitute, that is, a city for sale, without faith and without judgment. For a prostitute keeps faith with no one, speaks the law to no one. Accordingly, he describes a city corrupt in two political virtues, namely, faith and judgment. Commentary on Isaiah 1:21.[4]

The Chaste Church. John Calvin: By the word *faithful* he alludes, in my view, to the conjugal fidelity that a wife ought to keep for her husband. The signification is undoubtedly more extensive, but when I assess the circumstance of the passage, I do not hesitate to say that *faithful* means "chaste." For immediately afterward he employs another term in contrast with it, calling her a prostitute. While before she was as a wife who honorably cherishes the faithfulness of marriage, now she has turned into a harlot, because she is not ashamed of her shamefulness. The Scriptures frequently call the church the wife of God. That honorable rank Jerusalem held as long as she maintained spiritual modesty and continued in the pure and lawful worship of God; but as soon as she departed from it, she became a prostitute. Commentary on Isaiah 1:21.[5]

---

[1]Oecolampadius, *In Iesaiam*, 18r.
[2]Musculus, *In Esaiam*, 47. [†]See also Gwalther, *Isaias*, 11v.
[3]Oecolampadius, *In Iesaiam*, 18v.
[4]Cajetan, *Tria Priora Isaiae Capita*, 639; citing 2 Maccabees 4.
[5]CTS 13:73* (CO 36:48-49); citing Hos 2:19-20.

Unjust Government Is Unacceptable to God. Balthasar Hubmaier: God will not graciously accept anything from an unjust government. Yes, even if it would make foundations and build into heaven, and move mountains, and distribute all its goods to the poor, as the Spirit of God testifies through Isaiah and speaks to the government. . . .

Observe here, O pious Christian, how severely God accuses the unjust government. Truly, a hard punishment will befall it afterward. God will take revenge on it as his enemies. He will make it like a fir tree without needles and a garden without water, that is, mockery and shame. Its strength will be like stubble and the workman like a little spark of fire; both will burn together, and nobody will extinguish it. These are the words of God.

In this way I admonish all emperors, kings, princes, lords, all governments and rulers, as Moses also commanded his judges, that they hear everybody and do not sentence and condemn anyone uncharged, unheard, yes, even unseen, only on the basis of false witness. For many a person nowadays is being accused of being a heretic and an agitator into whose heart never entered any heresy and discord. But Satan attempts to give the gospel a full blow on the cheek and make it hateful to all the governments. A Brief Apologia.[6]

Heresy and Idolatry. Konrad Pellikan: And without the silver of doctrine, heresies and errors happen. And the wine of faith sustaining the heart is turned into profit and superstitions. And in other human undertakings, everything is likewise corrupted, because the law of God is abolished and the worship of idols was accepted. Commentary on Isaiah 1:22.[7]

Silver and Dross. Wolfgang Musculus: Rabbi David Kimchi explains that according to the letter, this is about fake money, which while it is thought to be silver is dross—the sediment and scum of silver—and about wine diluted by mixing it with water.[†] Some of the more recent among us follow this view. Lyra, following Jerome, understood by silver, the language of teachers; by dross, the false exposition of the law; by wine, the rebuking of sinning done by the teachers; and by water, the relaxing of rebuking. Commentary on Isaiah 1:22.[8]

The Poor and Destitute as Evidence of Greed. Wolfgang Musculus: And they were doing this not only to orphans and widows but also to the remaining destitute, from whom they could not expect any profit. Orphans and widows are mentioned so that it may be discerned in them how great was the foremost of their iniquities, and how greed not only made the judges corrupt but also the people completely inhumane and unmerciful. Accordingly, because the orphans and the widows were alone, they deserved not only the protection of the judges and leaders but also the pity of any people. The one who neglects them and can permit the lust of the reprobate, when they are able to help them in their calamities, is clearly inhumane. And if one should protect them out of duty, they will rightly be considered cruel also. Commentary on Isaiah 1:23.[9]

Thieves Don't Admonish One Another. Balthasar Hubmaier: [Regarding admonition,] in these matters there are two kinds of commandment. The first orders each Christian to admonish his sinning brother according to the order of Christ. The other commands the admonisher, that he must first take the plank out of his own eye in order to be able to see to remove the splinter that is in the eye of his brother.

This is now the true order of Christ, which should be practiced in just this way. But the first commandment is not done away with by the second. For it is better to fulfill one commandment

[6]CRR 5:310-*; citing Deut 1:17.
[7]Pellikan, *Commentaria Bibliorum*, 3:2v.

[8]Musculus, *In Esaiam*, 49. [†]See Kimchi, *Commentary on Isaiah* (1966), 8; Nicholas of Lyra, *Bibliorum*, 26.
[9]Musculus, *In Esaiam*, 52; partially quoted in Marlorat, *Esaiae*, 15.

than to neglect them both. Therefore no one can be excused who would fail to admonish his brother simply because he himself is a sinner, for in this way brotherly admonition would completely collapse. Rather, the greatest sinner of all is obligated to admonish his brother, or else through his silence he makes himself also a participant in the guilt of another.

This is what Isaiah calls being "companions of thieves." David calls it consorting with thieves and partaking with adulterers. I say this for this reason: under the appearance of recognizing that we are all sinners, no one was willing anymore to admonish others, nor to accept admonition, and thus fraternal admonition was completely smothered and turned to ashes. On Fraternal Admonition.[10]

Companions of Thieves. Francisco Forerius: If they do not condemn those who are thieves and rob others, if they are allowed to live when duty demands to punish them, should they not deservedly be called companions and allies of thieves? He seems to persist in this similitude of the sellers who consent to the thefts and receive a portion from them. There are magistrates like this who, when given offerings or great gifts by some people, not only fail to protect and defend orphans and widows but also defraud them and overlook thefts among their allies and great crimes. See, Christian reader, that the prophet connects these things as related vices, like cause and effect. "They pursue bribes and gifts; they do not bring justice to the fatherless. . . ." But "repayments" is a Hebraism, or simply "gifts." For to repay sometimes is to give. But most of the time it indicates reciprocity. This is why what is given to the magistrates is called by this term, because as they take bribes, so they likewise give impunity for crimes and they justify the ungodly for bribes, that is, they absolve them and they move every stone so the case does not fail. Commentary on Isaiah 1:23.[11]

1:24-31 *The Lord Almighty Will Purify the City*

Three Divine Titles. Martin Borrhaus: Three divine titles are read here. The first of them is from "ruler," by which God rules over heaven and earth; this is *ʾādôn* [ruler], which the Paraphrases render *ribôn ʿalma* [eternal sovereign]. The second is derived from the nature and essence of God, that is, *yhwh* [Yahweh], who in himself is the highest nature and from whom everything else exists. The third is derived from the power and strength by which God is going to be deterred by no one, carries out all things by his will, and adorns the righteous with gifts and afflicts the wicked with punishment. This title is *ʾābîr* [mighty]. Oracles in Isaiah on 1:24.[12]

Punishment by Consequence. Zacharias Ursinus: Although God is the fiercest enemy of sinners, and on account of his righteousness does not allow any sin to go unpunished, yet he is far more inclined to do good to us than to punish us. For it is good, and particularly the highest good, that he shared what is his. Therefore he wills in himself our preservation and salvation, but not one's destruction, except by consequence, to the extent it is necessary for the execution of his righteousness. He teaches this when it says, "Ah, I will get relief from my enemies." Therefore, let us turn to him with the certain hope of pardon and salvation. Commentary on Isaiah 1:24.[13]

God as Adversary to the Adversaries. John Calvin: There are various ways indeed of expounding this passage; and I shall not undertake the task of examining all the interpretations and refuting those that I do not approve: it will be enough if we ascertain the true meaning. He does not here speak of Chaldeans or Assyrians, as some imagine, but of Jews, to whom, in the character of a herald, he proclaims war in the name of the Lord. This

[10]CRR 5:380-81*; citing Mt 18:15; 7:4; Lk 6:42; Ps 50:18.
[11]Forerius, *Iesaiae*, 6v.
[12]Borrhaus, *In Iesaiae Prophetae Oracula*, 14.
[13]Ursinus, *Iesaiam*, 56.

threatening sounded harshly in their ears; for they supposed that they were joined in such a confederacy with God, that he was an adversary to their adversaries. He declares, on the other hand, that he is their enemy because he had so often been provoked by their crimes. In this manner we must shake off the slothfulness of hypocrites, who are continually waging war with God, and yet do not hesitate to allege that they enjoy his protection. We need not wonder, therefore, if the prophet sternly pronounces them to be adversaries of God who had broken the covenant and had thus carried on war against him.

And yet, in order to show that he is unwillingly, as it were, constrained to inflict punishment on his people, God utters his threatening with a kind of groan. For as nothing is more agreeable to his nature than to do good, so whenever he is angry with us and treats us harshly, it is certain that our wickedness has compelled him to do so, because we do not allow his goodness to take its free course. More especially, he is disposed to treat his own people with gentleness, and when he sees that there is no longer any room for his forbearance, he takes measures, as it were, in sorrow, for inflicting punishment. Commentary on Isaiah 1:24.[14]

Pure Teaching. Johannes Oecolampadius: For so it says here about the silver, that is, laws that are about public currency and that must be used equally by all, "I will smelt away" to pure, or "as with lye." That is, if the word of the Lord is being taught and is not adulterated with human traditions, it is kept pure. And he compares human traditions with dirt and alloy. Those are dross, which completely conflict with the Word of God, in which there is no sight of piety. But alloy are those that are even good in appearance but teach pharisaical righteousness adorned with rhetorical style. Commentary on Isaiah 1:25.[15]

Purification at Pentecost. Cardinal Cajetan: According to the Hebrew, it has, "And I will make my hand turn back on you, and I will purify, like purifying your dross, and I will cause all your alloy to depart." The turning back of his hand on Jerusalem pertains to something good for them, clearly silver to be purified from dross and the mixture of alloy, but to be purified in the way that purifiers purify. For it alludes to the metaphor spoken earlier, "Your silver was as dross." And God fulfilled this to the letter in giving the Holy Spirit "when the day of Pentecost arrived." For at that time in Jerusalem, he purified the Jewish doctrine from the mixture of dross and alloy and caused the divine speech to be known in its purity. For the Holy Spirit purified the minds of the disciples and the believers among the Jews, as he purifies through purification. Commentary on Isaiah 1:25.[16]

The Church Always Restored. Konrad Pellikan: The church of the faithful is always restored—at least in part—after immense falls by the works of the prophets faithfully handling the word of the Lord. This is what also happened in the times of Hezekiah and Jeremiah, and finally also happened during the time of Christ and the apostles, and no doubt the future shortly thereafter. Of course, the more honest judges of the church are restored, and also the more just senators and councilors are given as leaders by the kindness of God. When it is reformed according to the Word of the Lord, the state of the entire church appears more just, and by faith in God is righteous and more holy toward one's neighbor, and the name by which they are named everywhere is proven by that very fact and the virtue of their works. Commentary on Isaiah 1:26.[17]

Restored Leaders Are the Apostles and Their Preaching. Johannes Brenz: These best ones governed the church of God and counseled for its salvation. For here the speech is not about the external governing and the empire that the kings and princes in Israel administrated

[14]CTS 13:78 (CO 36:52).
[15]Oecolampadius, *In Iesaiam*, 20v.
[16]Cajetan, *Tria Priora Isaiae Capita*, 640; citing Is 1:22; Acts 2:1.
[17]Pellikan, *Commentaria Bibliorum*, 3:2v.

but about the doctrine by which Christ was promised and proclaimed. For these all most diligently and most faithfully preached about Christ. By this preaching, they so counseled for the salvation of the church that however many had faith in this teaching obtained true righteousness and eternal life. Therefore now, similar judges and councilors are promised, whom God is going to raise up at the coming of Christ. These are the apostles, who spread the gospel of Christ in all the world and were established as judges over the twelve tribes of Israel, indeed, over all humankind. Certainly in this way, final judgment is going to be carried out according to the preaching of the apostles, as however many believed their sermon about Christ were saved, and however many did not believe perish eternally. Commentary on Isaiah 1:26.[18]

The Church Needs Political Order. Zacharias Ursinus: Jerusalem, that is, the church, also needs to be reformed and is best established in this life with magistrates, judges, and councilors. Therefore, Christians can govern as magistrates, and Christ also wants his church to produce political order. And the church is not without sins and failures in this life. For otherwise there would be no need for judges. That ought to be observed against the Anabaptists. Commentary on Isaiah 1:26.[19]

The City of Righteousness Is the Reign of Christ. Johannes Brenz: This prophecy is about the reign of Christ, in whom alone true righteousness is exercised and maintained, in whom alone is also true and perpetual happiness. For the kingdoms of this age, although they are instituted divinely, yet because of unconquerable human malice they cannot uphold righteousness and bring true happiness, so they cannot be enduring. This is why God guarantees that when he restores the kingdom of his Christ that he also preserves true righteousness. And it is not subject to change, as with other kingdoms, but remains perpetual. And from the beginning of this part, the Holy Spirit laments about the city of Jerusalem, that is, the Jewish kingdom, because it entirely fell away from great piety, or better, from the rule of the divine law. Commentary on Isaiah 1:26-27.[20]

Vengeance for Sinning Against the Messiah. Cardinal Cajetan: According to the Hebrew it should be read, "And a breaking of rebels and sinners together, and those abandoning the Lord are consumed." A little earlier God had said, "I will get vengeance on my enemies." He only pursues vengeance itself. For it was fair that he first would describe Jerusalem with the future benefits through the Messiah, and later depict the rebellious and sinful part with its punishments. But truly together a breaking of the rebels by the Messiah followed—a breaking of the priests, that is to say, of the senators and of the sinners imitating the elders. And because those who sin against the Messiah are of that source, he therefore adds, "and those abandoning the Lord are consumed." For these things were fulfilled in the destruction of Jerusalem by the Romans, and that is why it is included, "For they shall be confounded by the idols to which they sacrificed. And you will be ashamed because of the enemies you have chosen." Commentary on Isaiah 1:28-29.[21]

Ashamed for Hoping in Idols. Matthew Poole: "They shall be ashamed," not with an ingenuous and penitential shame for the sin but with an involuntary and penal shame for the disappointment of their hopes that they had in their idols. "You desired" after the manner of the heathen. You have consecrated [the oaks] to idolatrous uses so that under them they might worship their idols. . . . "You have chosen" [the gardens] for the place of worship, which is opposed

[18]Brenz, *Esaias*, 34.
[19]Ursinus, *Iesaiam*, 56.
[20]Brenz, *Esaias*, 28.
[21]Cajetan, *Tria Priora Isaiae Capita*, 640; citing Is 1:24.

to the place that God had chosen and appointed for his worship. Annotations on Isaiah 1:29.[22]

Not Producing Righteousness. Wolfgang Musculus: "When you shall be," it says, "like a tree whose leaf falls." Leaves on a tree not only are produced to decorate the tree, but they also serve as much for the flourishing of fruits and their ripening. Where there are no fruits, the tree is not worthy, and it is also destitute of leaves. So, might and power and any other decorations of the city are rightly removed when there is no piety or righteousness, for those serve as fruits. Moreover, those "falling leaves" are the most fitting similarity of all used by our seer. The splendor of might and power, and the kings and priests, is compared to the leaves of trees. Commentary on Isaiah 1:29-30.[23]

Penalty of Fire on the Ungodly. Johannes Oecolampadius: And observe that the prophet closes many of his prophecies with the punishments of the wicked—which he also asserts are perpetual, as in this passage, "There is none to quench them." That is, the worshipers as much as the idols will burn in inextinguishable fire. And who would extinguish it? God? But he was angry. Poor friends? But they were afflicted by them. For Lazarus will not descend to the rich man. Will not an idol? But it has a similar punishment—and they will not at all rescue themselves who themselves are supplying the perpetual fuel for the fire. Therefore cursed is the Origenic dogma that denies the perpetual torment of hell. Commentary on Isaiah 1:31.[24]

Extinguishable and Inextinguishable Fire. Wolfgang Musculus: Fire is twofold, extinguishable and inextinguishable. The inextinguishable fire about which the prophet speaks here is that by which the wicked perish, both here and in the life to come. The extinguishable is that by which the faithful are cleansed in this life when they are chastised and trained by afflictions, and also are tested and refined like gold. Commentary on Isaiah 1:31.[25]

The Fire of Punishment. Cardinal Cajetan: This should be read, "And both will burn together." For he alludes to the comparison given that when a spark is joined to tinder or dirty linen, they burn. And he intends by this that the strong in Jerusalem and its workers will burn together, and there will be no one to extinguish it. This can be understood according to the letter as the evils of the punishment that they incurred by that destruction—and no one will be able to extinguish, because they will never escape from the captivity of the Romans. But if it refers to the punishment of eternal damnation, that is not an error. For the end of the argument corresponds to the end of the book. Commentary on Isaiah 1:31.[26]

---

[22]Poole, *Annotations*, 329*.

[23]Musculus, *In Esaiam*, 64; Marlorat, *Esaiae*, 18.

[24]Oecolampadius, *In Iesaiam*, 22r-v; Marlorat, *Esaiae*, 19.

[25]Musculus, *In Esaiam*, 66.

[26]Cajetan, *Tria Priora Isaiae Capita*, 641; citing and quoting Isaiah 66:24.

2:1-5 FUTURE DAYS ON THE MOUNTAIN

2 The word that Isaiah the son of Amoz saw concerning Judah and Jerusalem.

2 It shall come to pass in the latter days
that the mountain of the house of the LORD
shall be established as the highest of the mountains,
and shall be lifted up above the hills;
and all the nations shall flow to it,
3 and many peoples shall come, and say:
"Come, let us go up to the mountain of the LORD,
to the house of the God of Jacob,
that he may teach us his ways
and that we may walk in his paths."
For out of Zion shall go forth the law,[a]
and the word of the LORD from Jerusalem.
4 He shall judge between the nations,
and shall decide disputes for many peoples;
and they shall beat their swords into plowshares,
and their spears into pruning hooks;
nation shall not lift up sword against nation,
neither shall they learn war anymore.

5 O house of Jacob,
come, let us walk
in the light of the LORD.

a Or teaching

OVERVIEW: Much of the discussion regarding the opening of Isaiah 2 revolves around when these last days are. Most Reformation commentators identify the time directly with the first coming of the Messiah at the time of Jesus. This enables them to teach about the advancement of the gospel during the ministry of Jesus and the later apostles. Many of them draw intertextual connections to equate the church with the language Isaiah uses to describe God's people during his own time. There are several different explanations about how the peace that comes from swords being shaped into plowshares corresponds to the ministry of Jesus.

2:1-3 *Peoples Will Come to the Mountain*

THE GREATER AUTHORITY OF THIS PROPHECY. RUDOLF GWALTHER: Now, a general consolation ought to be sought from this: namely that the stubbornness of the ungodly should not be deceiving to the righteous so long as they persevere in faith in Christ. For this kingdom will stand in the midst of enemies, and his promises will not fail. "For I will not leave you as orphans." "Behold, I am with you to the end of the age. . . ." And for that reason, the authority of this prophecy ought to be greater to us, because by prefixing a specific title, the prophet testifies eloquently that he utters nothing other than what God revealed to him and that many of these same words are repeated in Micah. SERMONS ON ISAIAH 2.[1]

THE LATER DAYS. WOLFGANG MUSCULUS: The Septuagint has *en eschatais hēmerais*, that is, "in the last days," which is how the Latin translation also has it. Others translate, "In the following days," and others, "In later days." In the Hebrew it is באחרית הימים [*bə'aḥărît hayyāmîm*], that is, "in later days." In my judgment, this is simply the same as "after those days." Now, he means the days of God's judgment and the Babylonian captivity,

[1] Gwalther, *Isaias*, 15v; citing Jn 14:18; Mt 28:20.

about which he was frequently prophesying. After those would follow the restoration of Zion, which pertains as much to the purpose of God's plan as the coming of Christ and the kingdom of God. . . . I wanted to give these examples so that we may see how the prophets applied prophecies and adapted them partly to the sad circumstances that were imminent and partly to the happy things that were to come as light after the darkness. So, when they prophesy about the redemption and restoration of Zion that would follow after the Babylonian captivity, at the same time they weave in the glory of Christ's kingdom. And everything at the time of the restoration of Zion and the coming of Christ is encompassed as if in one form. For although there are many differences between the times that preceded the coming of Christ and those that follow after it, nevertheless, so far the restoration of Zion served the glory of the kingdom of Christ. Because when idolatry was despised, faith in the one true God began to spread everywhere among the nations from that time when Zion was freed from the Babylonian captivity and the subsequent rebuilding. Hence, even before the coming of Christ, many of the Gentiles began to worship the one God. But let us return to the words of the prophet. Commentary on Isaiah 2:1-2.[2]

About the Reign of Christ. Dietrich Schnepff: There are many, and indeed not at all fallacious, conjectures that this chapter ought to be understood to be about Christ and his kingdom. For immediately from the beginning, all things that Isaiah prophesied in this passage are said about the future final times. Moreover, as the apostles testify, these are the times of Christ's coming. And the Hebrews themselves even understand that this is about something other than fleshly people, and both this chapter and all the prophecies written in it are about the Messiah in the last days. He adds to this a brilliant testimony of his prophecy about the calling of the Gentiles, who are not going to come armed but most readily to the mountain of the Lord. In addition, it is clear that what Isaiah delivers about the accounts of the kingdom being positioned in allegiance to and in the way of the Lord must certainly be referring to obedience to the gospel. Scholia on Isaiah 2:1-2.[3]

Christ as the Goal of Scripture. Johannes Oecolampadius: First of all, learn the perpetual practice of the prophet. He has the habit that when some prophecy was said that teaches the history of his age, he joins another prophecy that clearly speaks of Christ or the kingdom of Christ, and the church—and so, through the subsequent one, he reveals the type in the earlier prophecy. And it is apparent that when he sees something remarkable that is going to happen in his times—whether happy or troubling—he is pleasantly reminded by the Spirit of a far greater joy that the faithful were going to have at the coming of Christ, or the more serious calamities by which the wicked perish. It is as if he was saying, "That indeed what I say is going to be in our time will certainly happen. But whatever it is, it is only a type of some greater event." So then, let no one suppose that the spirit of the prophets is not subject to them such that they are rashly carried away from one speech to another in the manner of the fanatics. Here you have an example of this. In the first chapter, he had spoken about the salvation of the earthly Jerusalem and the destruction of the ungodly under Hezekiah. Now in this prophecy, the truth of the shadow is the subject, where he explains what that type had wrapped in it—namely that under Christ, the true Hezekiah, we will truly be free. That is the custom of the prophet, and it occurs in many places. For every Scripture looks to Christ as its goal. Commentary on Isaiah 2:1-3.[4]

A Rule About the Last Days. Zacharias Ursinus: Here Kimchi specifies a rule: wherever in Scripture the last days are named, it

[2]Musculus, *In Esaiam*, 67-68; partially quoted in Marlorat, *Esaiae*, 20.

[3]Schnepff, *In Esaiae*, 33.

[4]Oecolampadius, *In Iesaiam*, 22v.

is to be understood about the days of the Messiah, that is, in the last time of the world, which is the coming of the Messiah.[†] And many from among us follow him. Nevertheless, I think that this is to be received cautiously based on the declaration, or restriction, of the circumstances of the passages in which this phrase is used in the Old and New Testaments. COMMENTARY ON ISAIAH 2:2.[5]

A FUTURE VISION OF THE MOUNTAIN FOR CONSOLATION. JOHN CALVIN: The use of this prophecy deserves our attention—namely that Isaiah wanted to bring consolation that would support the hearts of the people in captivity, so that, although no temple would exist, no sacrifices be made, and everything would lay in ruins, still such hope would flourish among the hearts of the godly. And among such devastation and disgraced ruins, they would still hold to this, "The mountain of the Lord is indeed forsaken, but there he will yet have a seat on it; and greater will be the glory of this mountain than that of all others." Therefore, so they would not doubt that this was going to be, the prophet painted a picture here in which they might gaze on the glory of God. For although the mountain was standing, yet there was a polluted loneliness, nearly detestable, after it had lost its beauty when it was deserted by God. Yet the godly ought to look not at those ruins but at this vision. Further, the reason he speaks so magnificently about the exaltation of Mount Zion is sufficiently evident from what follows: because from there the gospel flowed, in which the image of God shines. Other mountains might surpass in height, but because the glory of God excels, it is also necessary that the mountain where it is revealed is preeminent. Therefore, it is not Mount Zion itself that he proclaims but what it is decorated with, which was also going to enlighten the entire world. COMMENTARY ON ISAIAH 2:2.[6]

THE MOUNTAIN OF THE LORD'S TEMPLE IS THE CHURCH. JOHANNES OECOLAMPADIUS: According to the canon of Scripture, it must be taught to us that he sometimes calls the church Jerusalem, sometimes Zion, and also, as he says in this passage, "the mountain of the house of the Lord." For Zion is called this way by *periphrasikōs* [periphrasis]. . . . "You have not come to a mountain that can be touched, and a blazing fire, and darkness and gloom and a tempest, and the sound of a trumpet. But you have come to Mount Zion, and to the city of the living God, the heavenly Jerusalem." . . . Therefore, the church is Jerusalem, and the city of the great king, Jesus Christ. Its citizens are all who truly confess that Christ is God and human, and who pursue him with fervent love as their head and all the inhabitants of that city as members of them and him. Moreover, this is why the church is called Jerusalem and Zion, and by no other name. Soon he says, "For out of Zion shall go forth the law, and the word of the Lord from Jerusalem." Of course, this had to have its origin come from somewhere. So, it took the name from the place where it first gathered when the Holy Spirit was given in Zion to the apostles, and the apostles began to preach. . . . Hence, Jerusalem, that is, the church, as it is often called, was like a desolated city. The prophets and patriarchs prayed for its restoration with remarkable sighs. And we should pray likewise that its walls be rebuilt and that many thousands come to Christ every day. Therefore let us learn what the state of the true church is. COMMENTARY ON ISAIAH 2:2-3.[7]

THE HIGHEST MOUNTAIN IS THE ADVANCE OF THE GOSPEL. RUDOLF GWALTHER: So also salvation is certain and infallible, which depends on that. For since it was established in the eternal decree of God, no one will be able to take it from us or make him angry nor snatch his sheep from the hand of that strong shepherd. Then he says that this mountain "shall be lifted up above the hills." Now, he

---

[5]Ursinus, *Iesaiam*, 58. [†]Kimchi, *The Commentary of David Kimchi on Isaiah*, ed. Louis Finkelstein (repr., New York: AMS, 1966), 11.
[6]CTS 13:92-93* (CO 36:61-62).

[7]Oecolampadius, *In Iesaiam*, 23r-v, 24r; citing Heb 12:18, 22.

understands by this term, "the hills," the kingdoms of the world, which, if they are compared to the kingdom of God, are barely worthy to be called hills or even mounds. Therefore, he teaches that all those ought to be subject to Jesus Christ. And here he composes what he will say below, "The nation and kingdom that will not serve you shall perish." . . . Yet this should not be understood here as an external dominion in the sense that those impostor Roman vicars explain the passage of Isaiah just quoted (for the kingdom of Christ is not of this world). But even with nearly all the kingdoms of the world reluctant and resistant, it will arise through his gospel and stir up churches throughout the whole entire world. SERMONS ON ISAIAH 2:2-3.[8]

ALL NATIONS FLOW TO THE CHURCH. JOHANNES OECOLAMPADIUS: "They will flow to it," it says, to the spiritual Zion, not to the Vatican, not to Palestine or some African mountain. All nations, not only from Europe, not only from Asia, but all those joining themselves together by faith in Christ and mutual love. Oh, how much the joy of the saints would be diminished if so great a number were missing? . . . And it says, "out of Zion," not out of Rome, not out of Constantinople, so that you know not to depart from the Word of God. And where the unadulterated Word of God is, there is the church. But where the Word of God is not, there the church is not. Here the law and the Word of God are the same, but the later word is declared earlier. What is the law? It is not the word of humans but the Word of God. Now, although from the beginning the Holy Spirit was given in the earthly Zion, and from there the preaching of the gospel advanced, yet now the heavenly Jerusalem is also going to be obtained by those who convey nothing besides the apostolic teachings. COMMENTARY ON ISAIAH 2:2-3.[9]

BECOME PURE TO SEE THE MOUNTAIN. DAVID JORIS: You who are competent and chosen, do everything to become pure, to be brought to unity according to the will of God. And then the mountain of the Lord will be established by God at his time, and the city of God will stand as a praise and laud on the earth. See, the beloved shall surely come out into the garden to look at the blossoms of the shrubs and to see the vines bloom and whether the pomegranates are growing. Yes, it will come quickly on those who are found not ready; they will never be found prepared or fit in eternity. THE BUILDING OF THE CHURCH.[10]

BEING SEATED WITH CHRIST. MARTIN BORRHAUS: "Come, let us go up." The apostle explains this "going up" in the letter to the Colossians, "If then you have been raised together with Christ, seek the things that are above, where Christ is, seated at the right hand of God." "At the right hand" is the divine power and majesty, which pertains to this whole nature of things, not in any way defined and bound in place nor in time nor by any elements of the world, so that neither heaven, where Christ dwells, nor his heavenly city, Jerusalem, nor the place of the heavenly throne is bound but extends as far and wide as the majesty of Christ the king extends and is extending. This is why people are called to go up to the heavenly Zion and Jerusalem that the earthly Zion and Jerusalem carries as a type. ORACLES IN ISAIAH ON 2:3.[11]

VIRTUES AND SACRAMENTS AS THE WAY OF THE MOUNTAIN. CARDINAL CAJETAN: "And he will teach us its ways, and we will walk in its paths." Behold, the first action of the mountain is to teach the ways of the mountain itself, that is, the Christian ways, in which one walks for eternal happiness. Now, these ways are the works of virtues, the chief of which is love, and the sacraments of the church. For Christ taught and teaches these things. And the fruit of this doctrine is included, "And we will walk in its paths"; we will progress in the works of virtues; we will receive the sacraments. COMMENTARY ON ISAIAH 2:3.[12]

[8]Gwalther, *Isaias*, 16r; citing Is 60:12.
[9]Oecolampadius, *In Iesaiam*, 24v, 25v.
[10]CRR 7:181; citing Song 6:11; 7:12.
[11]Borrhaus, *In Iesaiae Prophetae Oracula*, 19; citing Col 3:1.
[12]Cajetan, *Tria Priora Isaiae Capita*, 642.

The Word of the Gospel. Konrad Pellikan: For "out of Mount Zion," out of the ancient Israelite church, the law will go forth into the whole earth, pure and converting souls, administering wisdom to the simple and humble. And the gospel of universal and perfect salvation will be spread by the apostles going forth from Jerusalem, like a fountain of salvation, grace, and happiness flowing from the paradise of divine comfort and goodness to the four quarters of the earth. Commentary on Isaiah 2:3.[13]

From Jerusalem on Pentecost. Dietrich Schnepff: The law went out from Sinai but the gospel from Zion, in which the way to eternal salvation is shown to all people. Christ wanted this when, at the end of Luke, he was commanding the apostles to remain in Jerusalem until they would be "clothed with power from on high" and they would receive the Holy Spirit, which happened on the day of Pentecost. Scholia on Isaiah 2:4.[14]

2:4-5 *A Future Time of Peace*

Swords into Plowshares Is like Old to New Testaments. Philipp Melanchthon: What it truly says with "They shall beat their swords into plowshares" indicates the difference between the Old and New Testaments. It is as if he were saying, "In the New Testament, the worldly political powers will not be established as the Jews thought, but the true knowledge of God will be started, as well as righteousness and eternal life, in which there will be perpetual peace and intimacy with God. It will not be a life like this political and mortal life." Argument of Isaiah on 2:4.[15]

The Gospel Pacifies. Thomas Cooper: As the gospel is a doctrine of reconciliation and peacemaking between God and us through Christ Jesus our Savior, so it pacifies and quiets people among themselves also. Those who are the true members of the kingdom of Christ do not strive by fighting and war for their private quarrels but live together in unity, love, and concord. If any do otherwise, it is a great burden to their consciences and an evident note of their imperfection. They show themselves not to have that badge or cognizance whereby the servants and subjects of Christ's kingdom are known. Yet this does not prohibit princes and magistrates from making war for the maintenance of justice and godliness. They have the sword put into their hands by God, whose ministers they are, for the defense of those who are committed to their charge: the widow, the fatherless, and the poor and innocent oppressed. First Sunday in Advent at Evening Prayer.[16]

How Christ's Kingdom Expands. Johannes Brenz: The prophet said that Christ is going to judge the Gentiles and the peoples, that is, he is going to rule from sea to sea; he is going to rule by his gospel over the whole entire earth among all the Gentiles and nations. But now he explains how Christ is going to take up his kingdom and dominion on the earth. For the monarchs who reign among the Gentiles are accustomed to advance their empires with weapons. Darius the Mede and Cyrus the Persian captured the Babylonian kingdom not sleepily and sluggishly but with great and bloodthirsty war. Alexander the Great expanded his empire in Persia and Babylon, indeed in a few years, but with many strong weapons. The Romans made nearly the whole entire earth subject to their empire, but with the most heavy warfare and by the blood of the greatest number of citizens. Therefore, when Christ is going to take his kingdom on the whole earth, how, I ask, will he take it? How will he expand his empire to the ends? This is what the prophet teaches when he says, "They shall beat their swords into plowshares and their spears into pruning hooks." . . . Those who, in the name of Christ, are going to take the kingdom of the whole earth and are going to be made subject to Christ are the Gentiles and the nations. Armies will not march to the Gentiles so

[13]Pellikan, *Commentaria Bibliorum*, 3:3r.
[14]Schnepff, *In Esaiae*, 35; citing Lk 24:49.
[15]CR 13:803.
[16]Cooper, *Brief Exposition*, 8v*.

that they force them to acknowledge Christ with violent hands, nor will they armor their soldiers so that they protect the kingdom of Christ with swords, but they will run quickly to the whole earth unarmed. Commentary on Isaiah 2:4-5.[17]

The Sword of the Spirit and Right Marriage. Menno Simons: They are the children of peace, who have beaten their swords into plowshares and their spears into pruning hooks, and know of no war, and give to Caesar the things that are Caesar's and to God the things that are God's. . . . The sword is the sword of the Spirit, which they hold in a good conscience through the Holy Ghost. Their marriage is that of one man and one woman, according to the ordinance of God. Their kingdom is the kingdom of grace, here in hope, and after this in eternal life. A Fundamental Doctrine from the Word of the Lord, of the New Birth.[18]

This Cannot Be the Pax Romana. Heinrich Bullinger: Therefore, since there is always going to be unfaithful people as long as the world endures, all swords will never be turned into plowshares. At the same time, among the faithful, there will nonetheless be peace and harmony, even if multitudes of wars and riots in the world are going to continue. Therefore, when the Jews object to us about this passage, and they want to prove from it that Christ has not yet come because what we read here has not yet been fulfilled, they abuse this passage. Others explain this to be about the greater peace that we read was at the time of Augustus, after the temple of Janus was finished, when Christ was born in Bethlehem. In reality, though, these things were not fulfilled according to the letter then, since the Roman armies were remaining at their outposts and had not gotten rid of all their swords. Sermons on Isaiah 2:4.[19]

No Need for Christians to Have Weapons. Cardinal Cajetan: It is not the sense of this prophecy that all wars will cease at the coming of the Messiah so that there will be no more weapons of war, as Christ himself made clear in the Gospel when he says, "Nation will raise against nation, and kingdom against kingdom." But the sense of this prophecy is that the people of the Messiah will not acquire, nor spread, nor keep weapons of war. And this is clearly true both from the institution of Christ and from reason: Indeed, from the institution of Christ, because he did not send the apostles armed to acquire the world but as sheep among wolves. And when the disciples asked, "Lord, shall we strike with the sword?" he rebuked, "Put your sword into its sheath. . . ." But as the way to acquire, spread, and preserve Christian people, he instituted evangelical doctrine, the sacraments, and the grace of the Holy Spirit with his perpetual presence. . . . And from reason, because the weapons of war are not by their very nature appointed for the subjection of souls but of bodies, things, and places. And Christian people, in this way, should adhere to Christ by faith, hope, and love, which look to free the soul. And for this reason, the weapons of war do not extend to spreading or preserving Christian people, to the extent that one is Christian. Consequently, the manner by which the nations and people flow together to the Messiah, by which his people will be spread, and by which they will be preserved—clearly without weapons of war—is proclaimed by the prophet in contrast to the Israelites, the people chosen by God for the Promised Land. For they acquired the Promised Land with weapons of war, spread and preserved it by weapons of war. The future people of the Messiah are described as far different, that is to say, they are not going to be acquired, spread, nor preserved by weapons of war. You should not understand from these things that weapons of war are prohibited for Christian princes, because that is to speak about another way of acquiring, spreading, and preserving Christianity, and it is to speak about another way of preserving the republic, according to the right judgments of natural reason, which says that it is sometimes necessary to undertake wars in order to protect the

[17]Brenz, *Esaias*, 44-45, 47.
[18]Simons, *Complete Works*, 1:170-71; citing Is 2:4; Mt 22:21.
[19]Bullinger, *Isaias*, 13v.

republic. For grace does not remove nature but perfects it. Commentary on Isaiah 2:4.[20]

Continuing to Work. Johannes Oecolampadius: How great is the innocence of those who inhabit the city of God, that is, of Christians. They should not think it is enough to abstain from war and robbery, but they should also occupy themselves with honorable ways and devote themselves to blameless labors that not only nurture themselves but also others with them. That is what is insinuated by the phrase "of their savage weapons." . . . "Let the one who was stealing no longer steal, but rather let one labor, doing honest work with one's own hands, so that one may have something to share with anyone in need." . . . "Whoever will not work, let that one not eat." And there is no reason why anyone should be ashamed of this. It was imposed on Adam and on us that we would eat bread by the sweat of our brow. Commentary on Isaiah 2:4.[21]

From All Parts of the World. Dietrich Schnepff: What Isaiah calls "the house of Jacob" is the heavenly kingdom of Christ. But at the same time, it says, they will be eating with Abraham, Isaac, and Jacob, which clearly corresponds with the prophetic saying. For he wants to say, "From all the parts of the entire earth, people will be coming who are going to submit themselves to the gospel of Christ in obedience and come to the church." And after the ascension, when the disciples were sent off to announce the gospel, he said, "Go into all the world and proclaim the gospel to the whole creation." Scholia on Isaiah 2:5.[22]

Christ Is the Light. Johannes Oecolampadius: Yet he does not say here, "Let us go up," since he is speaking to those who were in Jerusalem. Nor does he say, "Let him show us the ways." For the Jew boasts in the Law, he holds Moses in his hands, and he has the Prophets. But he says, "Let us walk in the light." Christ is the light of the world. . . . "Walk while you have the light, so that the darkness does not overtake you. While you have the light, believe in the light, that you may become sons of light. I am the light that has come into the world, so that all who believe in me may not remain in darkness." And you can also understand it this way. At this point all the Jewish things were concealed as figures and shadows and a veil placed on the face of Moses. Commentary on Isaiah 2:5.[23]

Learn the Way of Salvation. Dietrich Schnepff: Come, let us ascend to the church, and that assembly of the blessed whom the Lord wants to gather from the whole world. Let us hear the doctrine of the gospel, and let us learn the way of salvation, which the Lord will disclose in those last days. For he taught us that the only way to the heavenly Father is Christ, who is the way and the door by which we have access and entry to the Father. Therefore may we never turn, either to the right or to the left, from this way, for outside this Christ, there is no salvation and no forgiveness of sins. This will be what I had called the departure of the Gentiles to the city. For one should not suppose that the church will be bound to one place as in our times. But Jerusalem, which we now admire, will extend itself, as it were, to the whole world. For first in this city, the Son of God will perform mighty wonders and preach. There also he is going to release that great work of our redemption. Afterward on that day of Pentecost, which is celebrated among us for the giving of the law, the apostles will be sent by the Holy Spirit to spread the new law and doctrine, and what is much more pleasant and sweet than the old, from the city of Zion to all the parts of the world. So it will happen that the church, now restricted under the Mosaic ceremonies as if it were held tight, will be spread to all the nations, peoples, and Gentiles, who are going to come, as we said, not by roads but by faith and agreement to that doctrine. Paraphrase of Isaiah 2:3-5.[24]

[20]Cajetan, *Tria Priora Isaiae Capita*, 642; citing Lk 21:10; 22:49; Jn 18:11.
[21]Oecolampadius, *In Iesaiam*, 26r; Marlorat, *Esaiae*, 22; citing Eph 4:28; 2 Thess 3:10.
[22]Schnepff, *In Esaiae*, 35; citing Mk 16:15.
[23]Oecolampadius, *In Iesaiam*, 26v; citing Jn 12:35, 46; 2 Cor 3:7-15.
[24]Schnepff, *In Esaiae*, 45.

2:6-22 THE COMING DAY OF JUDGMENT

6For you have rejected your people,
the house of Jacob,

because they are full of things from the east
and of fortune-tellers like the Philistines,
and they strike hands with the children of foreigners.

7Their land is filled with silver and gold,
and there is no end to their treasures;

their land is filled with horses,
and there is no end to their chariots.

8Their land is filled with idols;
they bow down to the work of their hands,
to what their own fingers have made.

9So man is humbled,
and each one is brought low—
do not forgive them!

10Enter into the rock
and hide in the dust

from before the terror of the LORD,
and from the splendor of his majesty.

11The haughty looks of man shall be brought low,
and the lofty pride of men shall be humbled,
and the LORD alone will be exalted in that day.

12For the LORD of hosts has a day
against all that is proud and lofty,
against all that is lifted up—and it shall be brought low;

13against all the cedars of Lebanon,
lofty and lifted up;
and against all the oaks of Bashan;

14against all the lofty mountains,
and against all the uplifted hills;

15against every high tower,
and against every fortified wall;

16against all the ships of Tarshish,
and against all the beautiful craft.

17And the haughtiness of man shall be humbled,
and the lofty pride of men shall be brought low,
and the LORD alone will be exalted in that day.

18And the idols shall utterly pass away.

19And people shall enter the caves of the rocks
and the holes of the ground,[a]

from before the terror of the LORD,
and from the splendor of his majesty,
when he rises to terrify the earth.

20In that day mankind will cast away
their idols of silver and their idols of gold,

which they made for themselves to worship,
to the moles and to the bats,

21to enter the caverns of the rocks
and the clefts of the cliffs,

from before the terror of the LORD,
and from the splendor of his majesty,
when he rises to terrify the earth.

22Stop regarding man
in whose nostrils is breath,
for of what account is he?

a Hebrew *dust*

OVERVIEW: Many commentators identify a new topic at this point, especially those who see this prophecy as a return to addressing the people at the time of Isaiah. Even where this pericope addresses the Old Testament people, several interpreters find a double meaning. The reference to the day of the Lord is viewed as both final judgment and the forthcoming judgment on Judah. The rock to which the people should flee is understood as both the need to flee from impending punishment and as a reference to Christ the rock of salvation. The main theme is that God threatens the punishment of the Jews for their idolatry, for trusting in human strength, and for abusive leadership.

ANOTHER PROPHECY IN ONE SERMON. KONRAD PELLIKAN: It is not without reason that another prophecy is in the context of one speech, whether written or also spoken, following what was written before. He was seeing in the Spirit the calling of the Gentiles to piety. But observing the most wicked Jews in front of him, he exhorted them to turn from idolatry, as if he wanted to say, "O Israelites and descendants of the most holy patriarchs, of whose fame you boast, come now already, and prepare to walk in the light of the Lord, to turn toward his law without quarrel, to abandon the many abominations which the Lord hates, which he seriously forbids, and which he is unable not to punish as you have surpassed the wickedness of the Gentiles, even those you successfully replaced when the Lord destroyed them in your favor." But next the prophet, breaking off the speech, turns it to the Lord, who deserted the wicked on account of the multiplicity of their sins, especially by idolatry, which corrupted the land. COMMENTARY ON ISAIAH 2:6.[1]

2:6-11 *The Lord Rejects Those Filled with Idols*

EVIL RESULTS FROM THE DESERTION OF GOD. HEINRICH BULLINGER: Truly he was exhorting the Jews in vain to walk in the light of the Messiah. For just as the Jews living in the times of Christ spurned Christ and the gospel, so in the times of the prophets, they did not believe the prophecies about Christ, nor did they walk according to the law that God had made known to them. Consequently, therefore, the prophet threatens their end and proclaims that they are going to be severely punished because of their sins. This is what we see fulfilled in the times of Ahaz, . . . and in the times of Manasseh, Jehoiachim, Zedekiah, and the empire of Nero by Vespasian. The beginning of all evil results from the desertion of God. For here he deserted his people, that is, he withdrew his grace from them, and innumerable bad things followed. This is perpetual, as in every time God deserts us; we are soon buried in every kind of evil. Moreover, it ought to be observed that it says God deserts his people (he deserts the incurable in the church, not the true members of the church eternal) without doubt at the time after he has chastised them abundantly. So we truly understand that sometimes even the church itself is abandoned, yet it is never entirely rejected and condemned. SERMONS ON ISAIAH 2:6.[2]

ABANDONED FOR NOT LISTENING TO HIM. JOHANNES BRENZ: For in the same way that the Philistines and other nations at the time when Isaiah lived defended divination, sorcery, and their omens with great pursuit, so during the time Christ spent on the earth the Jews followed the impious doctrine of the Pharisees and scribes with such obstinance that, because of that doctrine, not only did they have contempt for the gospel of the Messiah, but they also crucified the Messiah and cast some of his apostles into exile, and they killed others. This is why they are rightly abandoned by God, because they refused to listen to him whom God had sent forth to be heard. COMMENTARY ON ISAIAH 2:6.[3]

[1]Pellikan, *Commentaria Bibliorum* 3:3v.

[2]Bullinger, *Isaias*, 14r; citing 2 Chron 28.

[3]Brenz, *Esaias*, 50; citing Deut 18.

Using Gold for Luxuries and Idols. Johannes Oecolampadius: Understand the Assyrians and Palestinians as those who were more infamous among other peoples because of their diviners and idols. Therefore, explain it this way, "because the people were filled with idols and diviners more than those from the East." And just as the Philistines were filled with diviners and idols, so also Jerusalem was a kind of metropolis that was also a factory of all wickedness and abomination.[†] . . . Examine the thought here yourselves: he argues that the Jews were addicted to earthly things and neglecting heavenly things, because they placed their hope not in God but in the help of a human arm, and because they abused gold for luxury, equipment for warfare, and were manufacturing idols. Commentary on Isaiah 2:6-8.[4]

Only Thinking About Money. Johannes Brenz: The multitude of gold and silver is not itself what is condemned in this passage, but the wicked pursuit of people who live only so they may overflow with gold and silver. For the prophet does not signify with these words that all the Jews had entirely full chests of gold and silver. For there is always a great number of poor who are accustomed to lacking all things. But he signifies the pursuits of all those who were intent to store up treasures for themselves on this earth. And so, although many were very poor, yet all their thoughts and all their words were filled with gold and silver, that is, they were not thinking about anything else, they were not breathing anything else, they were not speaking about anything else other than about money. Commentary on Isaiah 2:7.[5]

Idolatry as Self-Trust. Dietrich Schnepff: And of course, with regard to an idol, as the same is testified by the apostle, it is nothing in this world; really, it is the idea and the figment of the mind that is rightly called an idol. And this should not only be taken as referring to the trust that people place in images but also the confidence that people have in their own merits. Scholia on Isaiah 2:8.[6]

Trusting in Flesh, Not God. Wolfgang Musculus: Therefore, the charge that the Jews had filled their land with horses and chariots was because they were placing salvation and victory in the strength of the flesh, according to the custom of the nations. It was as if they were best equipped to protect their land if they could resist the enemies with horses and chariots. Meanwhile there is no hope in God, as there must not be any when one maintains trust in the flesh. Commentary on Isaiah 2:7-8.[7]

An Opportunity to Stop Idolatry. Heinrich Bullinger: He implored them so much because he feared that the glory of God would be diminished if all would have been slain or died in the desert. And in the present, when Isaiah was discerning that many were diminishing the glory of God by idolatry, the Spirit cries out with fury, "You are not released unpunished." But sometimes sinners are chastised with punishments and are brought back to the way. So this should not be understood that his people were cursed by the prophet to destruction and perpetual condemnation. Rather, I prefer to follow another sense, in which it is conveyed to them that if they proceed in idolatry this way, the Lord is not going to pardon such an immense sin of their stubborn idolatries. But this is a serious matter for them when, in this age as well as in the age to come, he is going to exact punishment on them. This, too, should be applied to us for admonition, correction, and salvation when caught in a similar sin. Sermons on Isaiah 2:8-9.[8]

The Rock of Salvation. Johannes Brenz: But although what is written in this passage could

[4]Oecolampadius, *In Iesaiam*, 28r, 29r; citing Hos 2. [†]See also Musculus, *In Esaiam*, 79 (misnumbered 97).
[5]Brenz, *Esaias*, 53.
[6]Schnepff, *In Esaiae*, 40.
[7]Musculus, *In Esaiam*, 81.
[8]Bullinger, *Isaias*, 14v-15r.

be understood as the physical penalty of the Jews, nevertheless because the prophet preaches many things about those punishments after the third and fourth chapter, we rightly understand the present text to be about the punishment of the spiritual Jerusalem, that is, their blindness and despair after they had rejected Christ, the true light and salvation. "Enter," it says, "into the rock." That is, "You rejected Jesus Christ, who alone is our salvation and redemption. That is why there is nothing left other than for you to despair about your salvation and for you to perish eternally." For those who lived during wars and were driven into exile do not have a secure place anywhere. They are used to fleeing into earthly rocks and caves. That is the evidence that they are desperate for salvation. . . . This is why, when the prophet exhorts the Jews to flee into the rocks and caves, it signifies that after they were rejected by God and have themselves rejected Christ the Son of God, they are going to completely despair of their salvation. . . . That day about which Isaiah speaks is the time when Christ came into this world and offered himself to God the Father as a sacrifice for our sins and rose again from the dead, and spread his gospel through the apostles to all the whole earth. The Lord Almighty about which Isaiah preaches is Jesus Christ himself, the true and only God. . . . The prophet repeats what he said before about the despair of the Jews with only a changed figure of speech. For before he used the imperative voice, "Enter into the rock." Now he uses the future indicative, "They shall enter into the caves of rocks." Then he repeats the same thing again, and soon also a third time. This is to signify that this speech was not dropped randomly, nor in vain, but that it is most firm and certain. For after the Jews rejected Christ, nothing is more certain, nothing is more firm, than that it is necessary to enter into the caves of the rocks, that is, to despair of their salvation, when the Lord rose to strike the earth, that is, when the judgment of the Lord was revealed against the wicked and unbelieving. COMMENTARY ON ISAIAH 2:10, 19.[9]

THE TWO CHIEF VIRTUES OF THE EARLY CHURCH. CARDINAL CAJETAN: "Enter" or "come" (for the Hebrew expression resonates with either) "into the rock" of fortitude and steadfastness, and "hide" due to the dirt of sins "in the dust" of humility. For these two chief virtues of strength and humility appeared in most frequent use in the primitive church, as is evident from reading the act of the martyrs and prelates of that time. And because their beginning was the fear of the Most High God (for the fear of God is the beginning of wisdom), it is therefore added, "from before the face of the LORD," newly acknowledged, because in another life he repays each one according to his works. But it is added, "and from the splendor of his majesty." It is just as if it said, "and from the beauty of his mind." For the Messiah, whom at the beginning of the chapter he addressed as "Mount Jehovah," now he more clearly addresses in his splendor, that is, the Lord. And the splendor of the Messiah is eternal happiness, seeing that the fortitude and humility of those who come to Christ are predicted to emerge from two heads, namely, from the fear that is the source and from the splendor of Christ's humanity. For when divine judgment is proclaimed, and the blessedness of Christ the man was preached, their souls were kindled to repent of their sins in humility, and they were prepared to imitate Christ in fortitude—even prepared to die for faith in Christ. COMMENTARY ON ISAIAH 2:10.[10]

THE PENALTY IS FEAR. RUDOLF GWALTHER: Now he describes the severity of the punishment from its effects when he commands them to do what he knew they would do out of fear. "Enter into the rock," that is, into the caverns of rock, "and hide in the dust," or caves, "from the fearful presence of the Lord. . . ." The sense of the words here depends on what preceded them. "Now indeed, with too much confidence and immense shamelessness, you openly rush into every crime and promise yourselves perpetual freedom from punishment. But the

[9]Brenz, *Esaias*, 57, 59; citing Is 2:19.

[10]Cajetan, *Tria Priora Isaiae Capita*, 644.

time will come when you will see no hiding place safe enough for you—so much so that you will wish the earth split before you or you would be covered and concealed with rocks, before the fear and terrors which God will send on you in declaring his majesty and power." Sermons on Isaiah 2:10-11.[11]

2:12-22 *The Day God Will Humble Idolaters*

The Double Meaning of That Day. Heinrich Bullinger: But it ought to be known that the day of the Lord is twofold: universal and particular. The universal "day of the Lord" is the day of final judgment in which the Son of God, at the end of the age, will judge all flesh with righteous judgment, weighing each one just as they conducted themselves, whether from faith or against faith. This day is abundantly described in the Holy Scriptures. . . . But since many mortals despise that day of the Lord when the righteousness of God is going to be restored and paid out (if they are warned about it, they say they will accept anything on that day), it is customary in every age, to say the least, that God exercises particular judgments against the atrocities of abominable people. . . . Such a day was the day of the flood, the destruction of Sodom, the disasters against the Egyptians and drowning in the Red Sea, various wars inflicted against the Jews under the judges and kings, especially by Sennacherib, Shalmeneser, and Nebuchadnezzar. Here should be included the wars of the Persians, Alexander and the Alexandrians, the Romans, the Goths, the Saracen Muslims, and the Turks, and what today we still experience in various provinces and kingdoms. God declares his righteousness in this so that the wicked do not suppose that they are always going to get away without punishment, because they act against the Lord. And those individual judgments are a prelude to that great universal judgment. Sermons on Isaiah 2:12.[12]

[11]Gwalther, *Isaias*, 21r.

[12]Bullinger, *Isaias*, 15v; citing 2 Pet 3; Mt 24–25; Rev 19–20; 1 Thess 4; Mal 3–4.

Future Judgment and Present Reign. Dietrich Schnepff: And of course in that final judgment, which Isaiah considers in this passage, it will be fulfilled most fully. When all enemies and even that last one, death, is placed under the feet of the one triumphing, the horrible sentence will be pronounced against the ungodly. Eternal prison with its torture will be decreed. But because at the beginning of the chapter, he shows that this prophecy is not about that day alone when the end is going to be imposed on all humankind, it should also be understood to be about the time when the church is going to be gathered from the Hebrews and the Gentiles. This prophecy is not to be reduced to the interpretation of such adversities but is to be taken as referring to the whole kingdom of Christ. Thus, still, it is rightly applied as an explanation regarding the church and the kingdom that the Lord has in this world.† Scholia on Isaiah 2:12.[13]

Both Physical and Figurative Mountains. Zacharias Ursinus: Some understand the same metaphor or allegory by "mountains and hills" as by "cedars and oaks"—that is, the rich and powerful, and therefore those who swell with arrogance and self-confidence. Yet there can still be a difference that by "cedars and oaks" individual people are understood, and by "mountains and hills" the kingdom itself with the cities, assemblies, magistrates, and their subordinates. For these are sometimes called "mountains and hills" in Scripture. However, some understand these two verses literally without figure, such that the sense is the mountains and the hills in Israel and Judah when Lebanon and the region of Bashan would be devastated by the Babylonians. Each interpretation conveys the words; they also convey many similarities. For in Isaiah 37 the devastation of Lebanon is literally spoken about. In that sense, it is the fulfilling of the oracle. For the cedars of Lebanon, the oaks of Bashan, the mountains, and the high hills of Israel, spoken about both literally and

[13]Schnepff, *In Esaiae*, 44, 45. †See also his paraphrase on 47.

figuratively, were devasted by the Babylonians. Finally, each sense carries the scope of Isaiah, who wishes to repress the arrogance of the Judeans.

The meaning is applied to this scope whether he says, "Even if they are equal, or seem to be, the cedars of Lebanon, the oaks of Bashan, the mountains, and high hills, nevertheless at the breaking in of that day, that is, the judgment of the Lord, they are going to be overthrown." Or, "Lebanon and Bashan, the mountains and hills, and all the surrounding regions in which they trust, are going to be occupied and devastated by the Babylonians." Therefore, there will be no protection for Judah and no hindrance for the Chaldeans when they penetrate a little into Judah and Jerusalem and capture them. Commentary on Isaiah 2:12-14.[14]

Babylon Destroying Judah's Idols. Wolfgang Musculus: Now the prophet speaks about the idols—not those that the Gentiles throughout the earth owned and worshiped at the time. Some understand these words to be about that because it says "against all." Rather, he speaks about the idols that the Jews had in their land, especially in the mountains and the hills . . . , which he mentions above in verse 7, saying, "And the land is filled with idols; they bow down to the work of their hands. . . ." He prophecies what is going to come to those, that they are destroyed completely. And that happened later by the Chaldeans, who plundered them for the gold and silver from which they were forged. Some of our own refer this destruction of idols to the first coming of Christ, supposing that the prophet is speaking at this point about the things to come in the kingdom of Christ. But the following and preceding indicates sufficiently that this pertains to that devastation by the Babylonians, which was imminent at that time. Commentary on Isaiah 2:14-18.[15]

Flee from Images. Andreas Bodenstein von Karlstadt: But God does not want us to call on him when we see images. He wants us to hate them and flee from them. In that day when the Lord is exalted, people will cast away their images and flee from them. . . . From this it follows that images are indeed not books from which we should learn. A Christian, therefore, can understand that pictures should not be called books. Books instruct. But images cannot instruct, as . . . Habakkuk says of a stone idol: "Is it possible that it can teach?" Based on that, it follows, and there is no denying, that images are not books. For if they were books or could teach what books do, then they would have to teach and instruct. On the Removal of Images.[16]

God Awakens to Punish. Wolfgang Musculus: Observe how the word *rises* is attributed to God. This is a human way of speaking. When the king hides and allows things that should be reprimanded to go unpunished, it seems as if he is sleeping. But when at last, the excess of the reprobate, or the iniquity of the enemy, has been enough that he is aroused to execute vengeance and prepares himself to begin vindication, he is said "to rise." In German we say *sich erheben*. With this figure, the prophet speaks about God, who seems to sleep deeply for as long as he does not punish the reprobate. But when he begins to punish, he is awakened to rise. This metaphor of rising is frequently attributed to God in the Psalms. Commentary on Isaiah 2:19.[17]

All Called to Humble Repentance. Cardinal Cajetan: By these four things, namely, trees, mountains, towers, and ships, he intends to express the particular levels of people and the particular places of the entire world. The purpose is that all may be moved to a strong and humble repentance from the fact that the day of the

[14]Ursinus, *Iesaiam*, 88-89.
[15]Musculus, *In Esaiam*, 93; citing Is 2:8; Ezek 6.
[16]Karlstadt, *On the Removal of Images*, 36; citing Is 2:17-18; 31:7; Mic 5:12; Hab 2:19.
[17]Musculus, *In Esaiam*, 94.

Messiah will leave no distinguished place unhumbled under the yoke of faith. And that is said next, "and against all that is seen as beautiful." According to the Hebrew, it has, "and against all the pictures of desire." For the things that are carried on ships are signified as "beautiful" and desirable for decoration. And they are called "pictures" because they appear as if they were wonderful, painted works of art, as we see in tapestries and other ornaments, whether they consist of wool or linen, or silk, or gold. For any ornaments are signified by these, that is, those who use ornaments are going to be humbled under gospel teaching. Commentary on Isaiah 2:16.[18]

Other Forms of Worship Overthrown. Martin Luther: Not only will that which is lofty in matters of state, which he has addressed up to this point, be brought down, but also what is high in the spiritual administration. For the world is divided into these two even among the Gentiles. For no nation has not had gods. In sum, every form of worship, both of the Jews and of the Gentiles, is dung in comparison to the worship of Christ. Therefore all those forms of worship will be changed and overthrown. Moreover, the idol denotes the culture, the religion, the ultimate witness, what people think and have in mind. . . . And now the idols are changed, that is, monks have changed into laypeople, and so on, through the gospel. Even so these spiritual people will, together with their worship, hide themselves in caves. That is, they will confess that everything of theirs, both their righteousness and their religion, are nothing in comparison to the glory of Christ. Lectures on Isaiah 2:18.[19]

How the Messiah Breaks People. Cardinal Cajetan: This verse is a repetition of what was earlier. And it does not differ from it except that the above is a warning and is written in the second person, "Enter into the rock. . . ." But this is written in the third person because the carrying out of the warning is prophesied when it says about the coming of the nations to the Messiah, "And they shall enter into the caves of rocks, and the caverns of dust from before the terror of the Lord, and from the splendor of his majesty, when he rises to shatter the earth." Explain everything as above. But the Messiah rose to shatter the earth when he sent the Holy Spirit and his disciples into the world with a salvific breaking to shatter earthly people from their own affections and opinions, since the word penetrates deeper than any sword. Commentary on Isaiah 2:19.[20]

Repetition Signifies Certainty. Zacharias Ursinus: The frequent repetition of these words about idols signifies the vehemence and the certainty of the prophetic assertions, and the hardness and obstinance of idolaters and hypocrites. No blows of divine threats, whether softened or hardened, are sufficient for them until they are crushed by their execution and outcome. For then what accompanies this follows—the outcome and the punishment for their security and obstinacy, which is the despair that those who want to escape must submit to the threats so they are not overwhelmed with ruin. Commentary on Isaiah 2:20-21.[21]

The Mystery of Humility. Johannes Oecolampadius: The Jews explain that we should not place our hope in any human because they are fragile, as it says both in Jeremiah, "Cursed is the one who makes flesh his strength," and the Psalms, "Put not your trust in princes, in a son of humans, in whom there is no salvation." That meaning is indeed pious, but it misses the mystery. We, too, are admonished not to be ashamed of the humble cross of the gospel and not to despise the humble members of Christ, who in this age are as the refuse of this world that gets thrown away. But let us admire the gifts granted to them by the Lord. Commentary on Isaiah 2:22.[22]

[18]Cajetan, *Tria Priora Isaiae Capita*, 644.
[19]LW 16:37-38* (WA 31.2:27-28).
[20]Cajetan, *Tria Priora Isaiae Capita*, 644-45; citing Is 2:10; Heb 4:12.
[21]Ursinus, *Iesaiam*, 96.
[22]Oecolampadius, *In Iesaiam*, 34r; citing Jer 17:5; Ps 146:3.

3:1–4:1 JUDGMENT AGAINST JERUSALEM AND JUDAH

3 For behold, the LORD God of hosts
is taking away from Jerusalem and from Judah

support and supply,[a]
all support of bread,
and all support of water;

2 the mighty man and the soldier,
the judge and the prophet,
the diviner and the elder,

3 the captain of fifty
and the man of rank,

the counselor and the skillful magician
and the expert in charms.

4 And I will make boys their princes,
and infants[b] *shall rule over them.*

5 And the people will oppress one another,
every one his fellow
and every one his neighbor;

the youth will be insolent to the elder,
and the despised to the honorable.

6 For a man will take hold of his brother
in the house of his father, saying:

"You have a cloak;
you shall be our leader,

and this heap of ruins
shall be under your rule";

7 in that day he will speak out, saying:

"I will not be a healer;[c]
in my house there is neither bread nor cloak;

you shall not make me
leader of the people."

8 For Jerusalem has stumbled,
and Judah has fallen,

because their speech and their deeds are against the LORD,
defying his glorious presence.[d]

9 For the look on their faces bears witness against them;
they proclaim their sin like Sodom;
they do not hide it.

Woe to them!
For they have brought evil on themselves.

10 Tell the righteous that it shall be well with them,
for they shall eat the fruit of their deeds.

11 Woe to the wicked! It shall be ill with him,
for what his hands have dealt out shall be done to him.

12 My people—infants are their oppressors,
and women rule over them.

O my people, your guides mislead you
and they have swallowed up[e] *the course of your paths.*

13 The LORD has taken his place to contend;
he stands to judge peoples.

14 The LORD will enter into judgment
with the elders and princes of his people:

"It is you who have devoured[f] *the vineyard,*
the spoil of the poor is in your houses.

15 What do you mean by crushing my people,
by grinding the face of the poor?"

declares the Lord GOD of hosts.

16 The LORD said:
Because the daughters of Zion are haughty
and walk with outstretched necks,
glancing wantonly with their eyes,

mincing along as they go,
tinkling with their feet,

[17]therefore the Lord will strike with a scab
the heads of the daughters of Zion,
and the LORD will lay bare their
secret parts.

[18]In that day the Lord will take away the finery of
the anklets, the headbands, and the crescents; [19]the
pendants, the bracelets, and the scarves; [20]the
headdresses, the armlets, the sashes, the perfume
boxes, and the amulets; [21]the signet rings and nose
rings; [22]the festal robes, the mantles, the cloaks, and
the handbags; [23]the mirrors, the linen garments, the
turbans, and the veils.

[24]Instead of perfume there will be rottenness;
and instead of a belt, a rope;

and instead of well-set hair, baldness;
and instead of a rich robe, a skirt of
sackcloth;
and branding instead of beauty.

[25]Your men shall fall by the sword
and your mighty men in battle.

[26]And her gates shall lament and mourn;
empty, she shall sit on the ground.

4 *And seven women shall take hold of one man in*
that day, saying, "We will eat our own bread and
wear our own clothes, only let us be called by your
name; take away our reproach."

a Hebrew *staff* **b** Or *caprice* **c** Hebrew *binder of wounds* **d** Hebrew *the eyes of his glory* **e** Or *they have confused* **f** Or *grazed over*; compare Exodus 22:5

OVERVIEW: Reformation interpreters differ on the time frame for the prophecies in Isaiah 3, which then affects how they understand the specific elements of the chapter. Some maintain that the words clearly apply to the time of Jesus, while others explain the various points in Isaiah's history where they correspond. One area of common agreement among the male interpreters is that the references to women and children leading are metaphorical for childish and soft male leaders. The mention of "the righteous ones" provides Reformers with the opportunity to address justification by faith alone. Most connect the frequent comments about the leaders in this passage with leaders in the church rather than being about political leaders.

3:1-7 *Judah and Jerusalem Without True Leadership*

MULTIPLE TIMES OF EVIL LEADERSHIP. ZACHARIAS URSINUS: These evils began to advance and increase under the reign of Manasseh, who began to reign as a twelve-year old boy. It also happened under Hezekiah with the hypocrites and evil counselors who were compelled to conceal their malice, corruption, idolatry. This filled Jerusalem and Judah with the blood of the righteous. And so, for about fifty years, the state of the people was most miserable, certainly during the tyranny of Manasseh and the captivity. But when Manasseh had been restored to the kingdom from the Babylonians and had established the political and ecclesiastical state, upon his death, Amon again disturbed and corrupted everything during the two years he reigned. Then, after that, followed the reformation by Josiah, whose young sons were foolish and ungodly. They especially fulfilled this prophecy of Isaiah in those twenty-two years from the death of Josiah all the way to the captivity. For Isaiah is primarily speaking about those years. . . . For it is clear that this deals with the people who were living at that time and not yet taken from Judah and Jerusalem. . . . And since he was not prophesying about the time of Christ in the preceding chapter, but about the times of the

Babylonians as far as the threats are concerned, this chapter also connects to it, so it is necessary to be understood to be about the same times. At the same time, however, it must be conceded that the time that came before the Babylonian captivity was an image of those times that preceded the Roman captivity. And so by that reasoning the types and examples that are described here could be transferred to the final devastation of Judah in the way that the punishments inflicted on other nations for their ingratitude and contempt of the gospel are rightly applied for the same reasons. Commentary on Isaiah 3:1-3.[1]

Spiritual Bread and Water Strengthen. Johannes Oecolampadius: "One does not live on bread alone, but on every word that proceeds from the mouth of God." Here bread truly strengthens people. By water, the Hebrews understand their traditions. But we understand these waters as what quenches the desire for vices. . . . "In those days living water shall flow out from Jerusalem," that is, spiritual doctrines. . . . "If anyone thirsts, let that one come to me and drink. Whoever believes in me, as the Scriptures say, 'rivers of living water will flow out from within.'" And so one should take "support" to mean the word of God, and "water" to mean the grace of the Spirit, which can also be called sustaining or strengthening. But see, when God takes away himself, how great the gifts he takes away with him, just as in giving himself to us, he delivers all good things to us with him. Commentary on Isaiah 3:1.[2]

Warnings for Our Recovery. Johannes Brenz: Therefore, just as the devastation of their kingdom once began with a famine among the Jews, so also at this time the devastation of the empire among us began with public poverty. Isaiah preached these things to his fellow Jews so that they would not perish but that, by repenting, they might be vindicated from destruction. He preaches these things also to us, so that we would be aroused to repentance and embrace Christ. Then Isaiah adds another punishment: "He is taking away the mighty man and the soldier, the judge and the prophet. . . ." This is both the punishment for wickedness and the evidence of the future desolation of the kingdom, when young men fit for war perish, and when venerable old men, wise judges, learned prophets, righteous diviners, honorable senators, brave princes, wise counselors, industrious craftsmen, and eloquent men are taken away either by death or by some other means, and foolish boys and the effeminate follow in their place as leaders. Commentary on Isaiah 3:1-4.[3]

The Scepter of Judah. Johannes Oecolampadius: In addition, you have here a prophecy that clearly pertains to the time of Christ. For Jacob says . . . , "The scepter shall not depart from Judah, nor the ruler from his loins, until the one who must be sent comes." And you see here it is not the captain of fifty, nor the counselor, nor the old man left behind. In the Babylonian captivity there were still prophets to find and elders and leaders who also brought back the tribe of Judah. From where will it be taken away? From Jerusalem. It will not protect them that Jerusalem is the place especially chosen by God for his worship, which the Jews would hardly hear. And not only Jerusalem but also all Judea was going to be devastated. It is as if he were saying, "Not even in a village or somewhere in some nook of all Judah is something going to remain, but every head is going to be weak and every heart mournful." Commentary on Isaiah 3:1-2.[4]

A Question About Removing Diviners. Cardinal Cajetan: And this is not absent the question, "Why would the removal of the diviners be counted among the punishments on Judah and Jerusalem?" since this kind of removal is a benefit,

[1]Ursinus, *Iesaiam*, 104; citing 2 Kings 23; 24; 25; 2 Chron 36.
[2]Oecolampadius, *In Iesaiam*, 35r; citing Mt 4:4; Zech 14:8; Jn 7:37-38.
[3]Brenz, *Esaias*, 64.
[4]Oecolampadius, *In Iesaiam*, 35r; citing Gen 49:10.

because the diviners are superstitious and their incantations are empty. The answer is that, although this absolutely is a benefit, yet for the Jerusalemites and the Jews who embraced the diviners it was a punishment and is counted among the punishments. And do not understand this as all of them thoroughly removed, but relatively, for the good of Jerusalem and Judah. Many fighting men remained, but not for the good of the city. And understand this similarly regarding the councilors and those mentioned before. Commentary on Isaiah 3:3.[5]

The Destruction of Jerusalem After the Ascension. Dietrich Schnepff: He distributes the rest of the sins according to different persons. For he recounts the offenses of the princes and priests, and soon those of the women. But, as we said, the punishments are also included. Now, the fulfillment of this prophecy is most clearly visible not only in the Holy Bible but also from church histories and Josephus. For these sins flourished among this people when Christ came into this world and also after his ascension. And the calamities that fell on the Hebrews at that time—how Jerusalem was overthrown and the Jewish kingdom was completely destroyed—can be most fully known from the books we have mentioned. Scholia on Isaiah 3:4-5.[6]

Childish Leaders. Johannes Oecolampadius: Therefore, among the disasters in Jerusalem is also this: that their children will be put in charge. This is not about age or innocence but the senses. They are childish in decisions and actions, careless, inexperienced, reckless, and the kind of companions that Rehoboam had, having no affection toward their subordinates. For as we see with boys brought up when their parents and brothers have died, that they ride on a cane, laugh, play, and are silly, so also with foolish princes; they have all the time to play and hunt, to institute feasts, dances, and staged contests, and do many other silly things, even though the poor and their subjects are oppressed and perish. And if those ones come and ask for help, they are ridiculed and despised, and covered with many curses when they are ordered to go away with a heavy cross. Commentary on Isaiah 3:4-5.[7]

The Doubled Evil of Reckless Leaders. Konrad Pellikan: The greatest disaster for citizens is if those put in charge of them are children in the sense that they are inexperienced, reckless, and have no affection or love for their subjects and the many poor and oppressed whom they should assist with their decisions and help. But if, in addition, those who serve as magistrates are treacherous, cunning—either domineering or possessed by a tyrannical mind—and shapeshifters, the evil is doubled. Commentary on Isaiah 3:4-5.[8]

When Women Shall Rule. Argula von Grumbach: Indeed, Paul says . . . , "The women should keep silence" and should not speak in church. But now that I cannot see any man who is up to the task, who is either willing or able to speak, I am constrained by the saying "Whoever confesses me," as I said above. And I claim for myself . . . , "I will send children to be their princes; and women, or those who are womanish, shall rule over them." . . . "Those who err will know knowledge in their spirit, and those who mutter will teach the law."[†] To the University of Ingolstadt.[9]

Metaphor for Weak Male Rulers. Dietrich Schnepff: At the beginning (which he had also written earlier), it says, there are unworthy ones in office and with the name "princes." They are

[5]Cajetan, *Tria Priora Isaiae Capita*, 646 (misnumbered 546).
[6]Schnepff, *In Esaiae*, 49.

[7]Oecolampadius, *In Iesaiam*, 36r.
[8]Pellikan, *Commentaria Bibliorum*, 3:4v.
[9]Von Grumbach, *Argula von Grumbach: A Woman's Voice*, 79; citing 1 Tim 2:12; Is 3:4, 12; 29:24. [†]See also Marion Ann Taylor, ed., *Handbook of Women Interpreters* (Grand Rapids, MI: Baker, 2012), 222-23.

children and women, that is, foolish and effeminate. These two things are the opposite of prudence and courage, the greatest decorations of those established with honor. Yet although they are the most lowly people, nevertheless they disturb the republic and the church with these two great sins. . . . But in their place is going to be given stupid magistrates and those who are hardly boys, the effeminate for the strong, and discord and violent oppression for peace among the citizens. For before the extreme disaster and that most serious siege that will be undertaken by the Romans, the citizens in the middle of the city are going to be slain with mutual wounds. Their age and authority will not be considered, but even the lowliest and the boys will rise up against their elders and those endowed with authority. Scholia on Isaiah 3:4-5.[10]

Children and Childish Kings. Rudolf Gwalther: For children are still inexperienced in imperial matters, weak, delicate, plain, and ignorant of attacking. They pursue nothing other than trifles and games, in which they are generally free from public dangers. Therefore God threatens that he is going to give them such leaders, and the history corresponds to this threat, which tells us that Manasseh succeeded Hezekiah as a boy of twelve years. And even though he lived all the way to the age of sixty-seven (for he reigned fifty-five years), yet he never attained an aged prudence and seriousness. And for that reason by his unruliness and superstition, which ultimately degenerated into cruelty and bloodshed, he exposed himself and the kingdom to be plundered by the Assyrians. He was succeeded by his son Amon, who was in his twenty-second year of age. He indeed followed in the vices of his father, dragged away by juvenile ardor. But he, too, is not an example of repentance. He was so negligent of religion that the book of the law was lost while was reigning. He had Josiah as a son. And although he was a boy, God established him as an example of aged piety and seriousness. But because the people showed themselves unworthy of a king of such character, when he was taken, God gave them children: Jehoahaz, Jehoiakim, Jehoiachin, and Zedekiah, who were more than childish in their levity and rashness and ruined the whole kingdom with their insurmountable negligence and wickedness. Sermons on Isaiah 3:4.[11]

Childish Leaders. William Day: By "children" are meant men who have no more understanding than children on how they ought to govern. "Children are their oppressors." He should have said, "children are their princes," as in verse 4. But because their princes that were placed over them for good did nothing else but oppress them and abuse their power that way, he does not call them (what they were by their positions) "princes," but what they were by the abuse of their positions, "oppressors." But can it be that they are children and yet oppressors? Answer: The prophet calls them children because they were but children with regard to true knowledge and understanding how to manage the positions that they filled; and they were oppressors because they were men of crafty devices, knowing how to fleece and oppress the people, and did that accordingly. And the prophet seems to put these (as it were, contradictory) terms together on purpose in order to show the strange temper of these men—that in one way, they were fools, and yet in another, how crafty and subtle they were. Exposition of Isaiah 3:4-5.[12]

3:8-15 *Judgment Against the Wicked in Jerusalem and Judah*

Numb Faces. Ulrich Zwingli: Moreover, he again used "cutting faces" for a fallen and worried face, as if it were cut with sorrow. He uses the thing for the person. Therefore, we said that the numbness on their faces betrays them, so that those who have appeared with a cheerful face, and with alluring and searching eyes up to this point,

[10]Schnepff, *In Esaiae*, 55, 60.

[11]Gwalther, *Isaias*, 24v-25r.

[12]Day, *Exposition*, 28-29*.

display faces that are filthy and sad, because they are witnesses of suffering and desperation. Annotations on Isaiah 3:9.[13]

The Righteous Will Not Perish. Johannes Brenz: Although the wicked will perish, nevertheless the righteous will not perish. But it should be announced for certain that when they pursue piety, they will also enjoy the reward of piety. This is a necessary speech in a prophecy about future punishment. For when general disaster is foretold because of the wickedness of the people, people are accustomed to think, "What do I do?" . . . But the prophet inserts a consolation for the righteous in this passage and admonishes them to persevere in their pursuit of piety. . . . Now, the salvation of the righteous is from the Lord, and he is their protector in times of tribulation. For us to rightly understand this, it should be seen whom Isaiah calls "the righteous" in this passage. For it is necessary that we rightly understand the term "righteous ones," especially when we are accustomed to deviate from this meaning greatly. For when we ought to be righteous, we consider ourselves unrighteous, but when we ought to be unrighteous, we consider ourselves righteous. What is this saying in the matter? Listen. . . . First, these righteous ones about which Isaiah speaks in this passage are the faithful who clung to faith in the gospel of Christ and pursued the calling of Christ. For he prophesied about the massacre of the Jews that happened to them after Christ's ascension into heaven. That was the time when the gospel was proclaimed by the apostles and others in Jerusalem and in the region of the city. Therefore, those who believed in the gospel are called the righteous ones. Commentary on Isaiah 3:10.[14]

Two Kinds of Righteousness. Johannes Oecolampadius: Now, there are two kinds of righteousness. For there are those who are righteous before people and not before God—the kind that are hypocrites and all who lack faith. These ones are not truly good. But there are others who, having been gifted faith, are indeed righteous before God. These are the ones about whom it is said here that it "shall be well with them, for they shall eat the fruit of their deeds." For it is necessary that good works proceed from faith. Without that juice, it can neither be said that there is good fruit from the tree nor that it is a good tree. Commentary on Isaiah 3:10.[15]

True Repentance. Menno Simons: But if you, by any means, wish to be saved, your earthly, carnal, ungodly life must be reformed. For the Scriptures teach nothing but true repentance and reformation, and present to us admonitions, warnings, reproofs, miracles, examples, ceremonies, and sacraments; and if you do not repent, there is nothing in heaven or on earth that can save you. For without true repentance, we are comforted in vain. The prophet says, "O my people, those who lead you cause you to err, and destroy the course of your paths." . . . We must be born from above, must be changed and renewed in our hearts, transplanted from the unrighteous and evil nature of Adam into the true and good nature of Christ, or we can never be saved by any means, whether human or divine. Wherever true repentance and the new creature are not (I speak of adults), one must be eternally lost; this is incontrovertibly clear. Everyone who does not wish to deceive his soul may confidently rely on this. A Fundamental Doctrine from the Word of the Lord, of the New Birth.[16]

The Lord Rises to Execute Judgment. Rudolf Gwalther: "The Lord stands," it says, "to contend, and has taken his place to judge the peoples. . . ." But judges generally sit and admonish those from the seat of that office, no doubt so that with their minds calmed, they may hear the reasons and speak the law. But here it says that

[13]ZSW 14:141.32-36.

[14]Brenz, *Esaias*, 67-68; citing the examples of Noah, Lot, Jeremiah, and Hezekiah.

[15]Oecolampadius, *In Iesaiam*, 38v.

[16]Simons, *Complete Works* 1:169*.

God had already taken a stand to show that he was ready to execute what he decreed, and at the same time bring help to his people who had been unfairly and cruelly oppressed. Indeed, the faithful frequently ask this, because it sometimes seems to them that he is asleep. Hence those prayers in the Psalms, "Arise, O Lord; save me, my God." Sermons on Isaiah 3:13.[17]

Greater Sin by the Leaders. Philipp Melanchthon: We see now also that as much as the unfortunate and uneducated common people are accused of their vices and offenses, the sins of the princes, the wise, and the learned are far greater. They most audaciously corrupt the doctrine of God and bend religious practices to their desires. They construct idols, and they strengthen errors and a multitude of sins. And they call such counsels "saving wisdom of the homeland." They say that they uphold the nerves of peace and good governing. Argument of Isaiah.[18]

The Final Judgment of the Messiah. Martin Borrhaus: "The Lord stands to judge." The Messiah is the one to whom the Father has given all judgment. But the judgment that Christ the judge executes has its own times and places. For he issued judgment against the Jews when he delivered them into the hands of the Romans, and in later times, he chastised the world with various judgments and vengeances. But in these later times, he is going to strike the whole earth accursed, having disclosed his gospel to all the nations as a witness against the shamelessness of an ungrateful world. He will display his more general judgment through that affliction about which Matthew speaks, and what here our seer and other prophets foretold. Finally, general judgment occurs when the Messiah, surrounded by the angels, will judge the living and the dead. The seer is speaking here about that judgment, we will remind from these passages. . . . For the Messiah, the judge of the universe, whom you despise, will come in judgment against you who are wicked. This sentence is announced to comfort the righteous and to terrify the wicked. Oracles in Isaiah on 3:14.[19]

All Three Types of Judgment. Johannes Oecolampadius: Three times he speaks about judgment with three different terms in Hebrew, and he applies it to three time periods. He previously judged when purging the world with the flood, consuming Sodom with fire, drowning Pharoah in the Red Sea. And now he also judges, administering all things by his wisdom and righteousness. Yet he will also come at the consummation of the world in judgment. The first term for judgment in Hebrew is *rîb*, which literally signifies the action of a case before a judge. The second *ḏîn* is the proclamation of the sentence, so *dan* is said, [meaning] to judge the peoples. Third, *mîšhpāṭ* encompasses the action of judgment and the proclamation of the sentence. And so, in the judgment of God, nothing will be left unpaid. He will not judge alone, but the elders of the people and the princes, namely, the apostles and the patriarchs, will also judge with him. . . . "From now on, you will see the Son of Man seated at the right hand of Power and coming on the clouds of heaven," that is, with the saints. Commentary on Isaiah 3:13-15.[20]

3:16–4:1 *Haughty Women of Zion*

Shameless Excessive Luxury. Johannes Brenz: Women were not adorning themselves in the usual way, modestly and honestly, but they were embellishing themselves from the soles of their feet to their foreheads with such valuable things that they spent their great inheritance, and with such shameless garments that they turn all the eyes of observers to themselves. And they were marching with such arrogance that you would think you were seeing only queens. Now the prophet takes up the labor, perhaps more severely

[17]Gwalther, *Isaias*, 28r; citing Ps 3:7, for example.
[18]CR 13:804.
[19]Borrhaus, *In Iesaiae Prophetae Oracula*, 38.
[20]Oecolampadius, *In Iesaiam*, 39v; citing Mt 26:64.

than one would expect, of enumerating by name the womanly ornamentation from the soles of their feet to the top of their head—not to condemn the honest elegance of women but for other reasons. The first is to signify that, not only does rebuking murders, robberies, and other kinds of crimes that seem to be the most heinous in the eyes of people belong to the ecclesiastical ministry but so does rebuking excessive luxury in clothing and conduct. . . . Then he teaches that, although excessive luxury and adornment of women does not appear to be as cruel a crime as murder or robbery according to human judgment, yet in the judgment of God it is judged so seriously that he punishes and erases a whole nation because of it. And therefore, the seriousness and magnitude of the sins should not be judged according to human opinion but according to the Word of God. For this is what pertains to the duties of women. One is that they ought, as Paul says, to be the keepers of the home. The other is that they ought to walk publicly in modest clothing with respect and chastity, not with braided hair or gold. Commentary on Isaiah 3:16-21.[21]

Tinkling Feet. William Day: "And making a tinkling with their feet." How this tinkling was made with their feet as they went, no one can know for certain, since we are utterly unacquainted with the dressings and fashions of the women of that time. But some conjecture that they wore bells on their feet so that the measure and composure of their steps would be noticed by their tinkling. Others conjecture that these were jewels and pearls in their shoes (and Pliny writes of such in book 9, chap. 35),[†] and that the hitting and striking of these together, as they went mincing along, made this tinkling. Others have other conjectures: but they wore some kind or other of tinkling ornament about their feet. Exposition of Isaiah 3:16-18.[22]

Three Faults of Women. Dietrich Schnepff: Now, it should be noted that the prophet criticizes three things among females: arrogance, haughtiness in marching (to which he immediately adds their punishment when he says the luxury in clothing is going to be taken away), and third, the other delights and weakness of that sex. . . . The prophet assigns their penalties for arrogance: baldness and stripping of their body parts they cannot show modestly. For besides baldness being a sign of grief among the Hebrews, it was also then shameful for females. The apostle wanted them to be covered not only with hair but also with a veil. And the baring of the privates signifies poverty and disgrace. And so with these two terms, the prophet threatens sadness, shameful poverty, and disgrace because of the arrogance with which they were proudly exalting themselves. Scholia on Isaiah 3:16-21.[23]

God Knows and Cares for All Women. Heinrich Bullinger: For there are those who suppose it fitting to explain this to be about the prophetic gravity of women and the vices that infect them—and that these women hardly permit themselves to be persuaded that God cares about their trifles. For that reason, at the beginning of the accusation made against them, the prophet says, "And the Lord said this." Therefore, God knows and cares for all of the women, and he commands the prophets to testify to this in this age. For God has all their thoughts and all their works accounted. And it was not shameful that the male apostles of Christ explain, in addition to the most serious things, the vices and duties of women, too, as was previously cited above from the testimonies of the apostles. So then, no one should suppose that speeches of this sort about women are unworthy in the church of Christ. Further, in this accusation, nowhere do you find those horrible crimes of some: aggressiveness, infanticide, poisioned tongues, and urging men to abominable wickedness. Namely, when these things are among women, who are by

[21]Brenz, *Esaias*, 73; citing 1 Tim 2:9-10.
[22]Day, *Exposition*, 32. [†]See Pliny the Elder, *Natural History* (LCL 353: 9.58).
[23]Schnepff, *In Esaiae*, 55; citing 1 Cor 11:5-6.

nature kind and timid, they are certain omens and portents; therefore he treats the vices that are common to women. Sermons on Isaiah 3:16-23.[24]

Captivity as Shameful Baldness. Konrad Pellikan: Not only will the Lord remove all the ornaments from the head, but he will also replace it with a head of scabs. As the top of the head gets plucked and hairs disappear, so also will those be forced to pull out because of the suffering in the destruction of the city. Finally, he will expose their shameful parts, stripped by their enemies of so much of the clothing they were used to wearing, when they will be taken away naked by their enemies into captivity at the time of Ahaz and Zedekiah. Commentary on Isaiah 3:17.[25]

Discontent with Natural Beauty. Rudolf Gwalther: These are indeed a peculiar decor, but at the same time he admonishes about the submission that God requires from this sex. But for the majority, it happens that when they are not content with their natural beauty, they apply new and sometimes prodigious ornaments on top of the head, which represented either pyramids raised high, or wings spread widely, or even horns. Therefore, rightly he threatens them with baldness. Further, God makes women bald when he either sends enemies who pull out their hair with veils and ribbons or headdresses, or he afflicts them with sicknesses that makes their hair fall out. Christian virgins and matrons should think about these things whenever they might be instigated by a spirit of pride to fashion a new form of superfluous ornaments on their heads, and add dye and skillfuly curled hair. Sermons on Isaiah 3:17-22.[26]

A Picture of Sin's Infection. Zacharias Ursinus: For he describes the greatest poverty and disgrace when he says that not only the costly garments and ornaments that were exceeding the beauty of nature and of persons in material and form are to going to be taken away, but also these things are going to follow: not some mediocrity of habit and fortunes but stink and stench, and the tearing of a belt and sackcloth. He describes the disfiguring of bodies when he predicts the stench, or the filth, the baldness and the burning. The reason for both descriptions is the same. For sins diminish or infect people, unless they are pointed out with a finger in such a way that they can no longer be defended or excused by any reason or pretext. So they despise the warnings of God's wrath, unless the atrocity of evils threatening them is portrayed like something to be contemplated before their eyes. Commentary on Isaiah 3:24.[27]

An Example of Punishment Against Any People from Any Time. Konrad Pellikan: So when the Lord punishes the city with its citizens, men with women, princes with subjects, people with the king, they will experience the most righteous hand of God in their case and at their time—and this will happen not only at the time of Isaiah but in every place, always, and for all persons who cultivate pride in this way. And they will discern that the famous degradation of those vain people is only nobles with pomp, distinguished by no wisdom, honesty, or religion. Commentary on Isaiah 3:24-26.[28]

Three Governing Calamities: Domestic, Civil, Church. Martin Borrhaus: In this oracle is indicated three governments that are institued by God: domestic, civil, and ecclesiastical. Since each one is depraved and vicious, it is going to be affected by disaster. Indeed, the calamity of a domestic government is in the misery of a husband and wife and children. The disaster of the civil is in what is mentioned above, "I will take away judgment from you." The calamity of ecclesastical is discerned from what is written, "I will take away the prophet from you." Oracles in Isaiah on 3:24-26.[29]

[24]Bullinger, *Isaias*, 20r-v.
[25]Pellikan, *Commentaria Bibliorum*, 3:5r.
[26]Gwalther, *Isaias*, 30r.
[27]Ursinus, *Iesaiam*, 120.
[28]Pellikan, *Commentaria Bibliorum*, 3:5v.
[29]Borrhaus, *In Iesaiae Prophetae Oracula*, 41.

A Parable of Rare Men. Johannes Oecolampadius: He speaks to Zion herself, which used to have beloved men, but they were miserably slain by the sword in war. And understand "daughters of Zion" as a parable for Zion. The "mighty men" about which he speaks are the heroes, the soldier, the judge, and the captain of fifty in whom they trusted. The Hebrews explain this to be about the disaster that happened under Ahaz. We view it as one prophecy. For he says, "In that day." Hence, it refers to the prophecy above predicting the subversion of Jerusalem in the times of the Gospels. . . . "Shall take hold of" in this verse shows it is connected to what comes earlier. This passage does not square well as an allegory about Christ and the seven churches. It is simply seven women; that is a significant quantity. A specific number is used for an uncertain one. He wishes to say this one thing: Behold, the wicked women are not content with their marriages. But in the future, the rarity of men will be so great that nearly each one could obtain seven women, because the disaster is going to be so great that the women will be carried into captivity, with only a few surviving men. You have here that it is men who are to raise and clothe women, but in the parable it is said that the women renounce their right. To be called by the name of men over them is nothing other than to be called a husband and thus take away the reproach of those called widows. For barrenness and widowhood were considered a curse. Commentary on Isaiah 3:18–4:1.[30]

Not About the Fine Clothing but the Greed. Dietrich Schnepff: Isaiah thereafter accuses the female sex in the name of pride and luxury, as we have said. And of course most women of that kind sin by indulging in too much for themselves and making effort to attract the world with their appearance or, if they are beautiful, increasing it. Certainly, for either sex, to be clothed and dressed is indeed not condemned in the sacred writings, if it is not too exquisite and it is taken as a condition of a dignified life. For Christ himself speaks about the way Solomon was dressed, and Esther was clothed with royal garments, yet she pleased the Lord. But it is this kind of aspiration and luxury, such as Isaiah describes in this passage, that is rebuked, and which is certainly now the greatest. The Lord could have, if it so pleased him, covered our bodies with all the adornment that is sought with great expense and business. But since it seemed otherwise to him, let us not adorn ourselves with dye and garments but with virtue and piety. Scholia on Isaiah 4:1.[31]

Wives Finding Their Own Food and Clothing. William Day: "We will eat our own bread and wear our own clothes." The husband was to find food and clothing for his wife. . . . Therefore, this man should at least refuse their request and send them off with the concession that he could not find food and clothing for them, so he would not be their husband. They prevent him and tell him that they will not put him to that trouble and charge but will find their own food and their own apparel. Exposition of Isaiah 4:1.[32]

[30]Oecolampadius, *In Iesaiam*, 42v, 43r; excerpts quoted in Marlorat, *Esaiae*, 38.

[31]Schnepff, *In Esaiae*, 59; citing Titus 2; 1 Tim 2; 1 Pet 3.

[32]Day, *Exposition*, 35*; citing Ex 21:10.

4:2-6 The Branch of the Lord

[2]In that day the branch of the Lord *shall be beautiful and glorious, and the fruit of the land shall be the pride and honor of the survivors of Israel. [3]And he who is left in Zion and remains in Jerusalem will be called holy, everyone who has been recorded for life in Jerusalem, [4]when the Lord shall have washed away the filth of the daughters of Zion and cleansed the bloodstains of Jerusalem from its midst by a spirit of judgment and by a spirit of burning.[a] [5]Then the* Lord *will create over the whole site of Mount Zion and over her assemblies a cloud by day, and smoke and the shining of a flaming fire by night; for over all the glory there will be a canopy. [6]There will be a booth for shade by day from the heat, and for a refuge and a shelter from the storm and rain.*

a Or *purging*

Overview: This brief prophecy brings up many of the recurring themes in Isaiah. Interpreters offer differing interpretations about whether the branch refers to Christ himself or to the faithful remnant. Likewise, there are different perspectives on whether this speaks to the remnant returning from Babylon or to the church in the future, particularly at the time of Jesus. Some take the opportunity to explain their approach to multiple fulfillments, allegories, and types. The themes of holiness, cleansing, fire, and smoke lead some exegetes to address the theological topics of sanctification, election, and the nature of the church.

4:2-4 *When the Remnant Will Be Called Holy*

The Remnant Returning from Babylon. Wolfgang Musculus: In this chapter, the prophet prophesies about the remnant returning from Babylon, how holy and brilliant they will be, and how secure in all things by the singular protection of God. . . . Therefore, so they would be comforted, he addresses the joys with the sorrows, and returns to the matter that was above . . . where he had mentioned the future joy and glory of Zion after the return from Babylon. And he repeats that favor toward the righteous so that they do not think they will be cast away entirely from the Lord their God, as Israel was. . . . And so with this metaphorical way of speaking where the seed is compared to the church of God (which is common in the prophets, and in this case), our seer prophesies about this, greatly adapting it. I do not see what prevents it from being understood here that the seed and the fruit of the earth are about the people of God who are going to be restored after the time of captivity. Meanwhile, it cannot be denied that Christ is called "shoot" and "seed" repeatedly. But at the same time, certain things are added. So it may be said that the spirit of the prophet speaks about him, as we read later. Commentary on Isaiah 4:2.[1]

A Prophecy About the Messiah. Dietrich Schnepff: This prophecy seems to go against the prophecy about the patriarch Jacob, who foretold that the scepter would not be removed from Judah until the Shiloh comes, that is, the Messiah. The prophet rightly opposed this apparent discrepancy[†] when he prophesies that in the most deplorable time of the Hebrews, there will be the clearest king Messiah. For the Hebrews also understand this passage to be about the Messiah. Scholia on Isaiah 4:2.[2]

[1]Musculus, *In Esaiam*, 116-18 (mislabeled 142); citing Is 2; 11; excerpts quoted in Marlorat, *Esaiae*, 39.
[2]Schnepff, *In Esaiae*, 63. [†]Schnepff uses the term *antinomy* here for when two apparently contradictory statements can both be reasonable and true.

Multiple Fulfillments of Survivors. Heinrich Bullinger: These things were fulfilled in the times of Hezekiah when the Assyrians (who earlier had devastated the whole kingdom with sword and fire) suffered the heavenly blow under the blessing of the Lord, and people lived in the fullest peace during the entire time of Hezekiah. These were also fulfilled soon after the Babylonian captivity and after the affliction of Antiochus under the Maccabees. But they were most completely fulfilled by Christ in the church and in the life to come. Therefore, they can be applied to all times to the comfort of the afflicted. Sermons on Isaiah 4:2-3.[3]

The Faithful Are the Seed and Branch. Wolfgang Musculus: Thus far we have explained the present prophecy in the historical sense about the remnant of Judah, who, when released from the Babylonian captivity, were touched by the Spirit of the Lord and brought back to the mountain of the house of the Lord and the Promised Land. But since a type of the faithful in Christ was expressed in those things, we will remind the reader about that reality with a few things. . . . This metaphor coincides with the elect, both in the Old and in the New Testaments. As far as they were regenerated by the Spirit and from God, they are rightly called the "seed of the Lord," sprung from him. And the faithful in Christ are called his branches just as he is the true vine. Commentary on Isaiah 4:2-3.[4]

The Mystery of the Incarnation. Johannes Oecolampadius: Often when we speak about the blessedness of the church, a double exposition occurs. The former is about that happiness by which we are blessed with hope and faith in Christ. The latter is about the completion of that happiness. The former is now in the place of history, a type of the future. Therefore, in this paragraph, he teaches the happiness of the church that comes from the joy and glorying in Christ, from holiness and security. Moreover, here Christ is said to be the seed of the Lord and the fruit of the earth. For, as true God, he has God the Father in heaven, which is why it says "seed of the Lord," and as true man, an earthly mother, which is why he is called "fruit of the land." Behold, you have the mystery of the incarnation. . . . Therefore, the sense is: he who is the seed of the Lord and the fruit of the land will be the joy and glory of those who will be liberated then, that is, all the faithful. For the one who does not reject Christ but follows him with their whole heart will be gladdened by the Holy Spirit, and all joy and exultation will be theirs. Commentary on Isaiah 4:2-3.[5]

The Patience and Mercy of God. Heinrich Bullinger: David, the prophet of God and the king chosen by God, testified that God would not always quarrel nor retain his wrath perpetually, but he would for a time exercise his mercy toward those at enmity with him and punish them because of their sins. Isaiah testifies this very thing in the present, inspired by the Lord. Up to this point he has described at much length the divine punishment to be taken against the Jews because of their unrepentance. But now he promises better things, comforting those who, in trials and afflictions, patiently wait for the mercy of the Lord. Sermons on Isaiah 4:2.[6]

The Seed from the Earth Is the Incarnation of Jesus. Johannes Brenz: Now, Isaiah understands by this metaphor of seed and fruit the Messiah or Christ. For here he is said to be "the seed of the Lord," because from his substance he is eternally begotten of God the Father. Then he is said to be "the fruit of the earth," because he received an earthly or human body from the Virgin Mary. So then, he is true God and true human. Therefore in such disasters the Messiah will not die, but he will rise up like pleasing fruit on the earth.

[3]Bullinger, *Isaias*, 21v.
[4]Musculus, *In Esaiam*, 120; citing Jn 15.
[5]Oecolampadius, *In Iesaiam*, 43v.
[6]Bullinger, *Isaias*, 21v.

Not all the Jews will die, but some will be saved, who acknowledge the Messiah, and they will delight in that heavenly happiness. Commentary on Isaiah 4:2.[7]

Time for the Seed to Grow. Martin Borrhaus: Now, the Messiah is called a "seed," which, when it grows, expands immensely through branches, leaves, and fruits, filled with righteousness in heaven and earth and the glory of life. For *ṣemaḥ* literally is "to grow." So in these passages, we understand from our seer at what time this growing seed and its incremental extension is particularly going to be revealed by the revealing of the gospel of salvation. . . . He calls the Messiah "the fruit of the land," partly because he produces the great fruit of righteousness and life on the earth, and partly because Christ, who has a Father in heaven, was conceived by his Spirit and not from human seed, and received a mother on earth, by whom he was born a true man from that birth, so that by the conception of the Holy Spirit, he was declared to truly be the Son of God. Oracles in Isaiah on 4:2.[8]

Multiple Field Metaphors for God's People. Heinrich Bullinger: So by this metaphor the people of God are named the "seed of the Lord," just as they are also the vineyard of the Lord, the branch, and the "fruit of the land." God is the author and the cultivator of his vineyard and plantation. The righteous are the plantation and the seed of God. For they are like fruits or seedlings of the earth, which at springtime, after a sad and hard winter, burst out and grow and bear fruit. Sermons on Isaiah 4:2.[9]

A Seasoned Allegory. Ulrich Zwingli: But when we assert here that the prophet speaks allegorically, I consider it worthwhile to speak about this figure. . . . Therefore, let us first consider that a trope is within an expression, but an allegory is in a speech or a sermon. Then, irony is not without smell, that is, ridicule, jest, misfortune, blame, judgment. But allegory is distinct from all those things. For first when he goes into jest, ridicule, and so on, it is already not allegory but irony. For in my view, irony is salty allegory. Therefore, allegory mentions and commends to us things with a different speech and in other expressions from their own. This is not to ridicule, bite, or judge, that is, to condemn or to injure, but to mention and show, as it were, what needs to be known with another use of words. . . .

Therefore, we see that an allegory is a form of speech that commends to us something other than what appears on the surface, yet in such a way that the truth itself is seen through that appearance of words no differently than a true body is seen in a mirror or through something transparent. This will become more clear with examples. . . . Paul addresses the Ephesian elders, among others, in this way: "Therefore pay attention to yourselves and to all the flock in which the Holy Spirit has made you overseers, to shepherd the church of God." See, he conveys here in the first part a pure allegory! For by "shepherds" and "flock," he means "overseers" and "churches." . . . In the second part, the overseers "to shepherd the church" are still referred to allegorically. But that expression, "the church," shines the light so that even if nothing else were present, you readily understand that this word speaks about the pasture. . . .[†]

In sum, a parable clearly compares; an allegory conceals, not dealing as much in near and clear similarities but with foreign and almost puzzling ones. . . . Briefly, we must unlock the allegories of Scripture with the keys of Scripture. So that no one would take our allegories as the genuine sense, we must remind them that they are seasoning for our time. . . .

Now therefore I return to the words of the prophet. "After this," it says, "the branch of the Lord will rise up happy and large." And the very fruit of the land, which had already been called the "branch of the Lord," will be magnificent and splendid for those Israelites who will survive safe and preserved.

[7] Brenz, *Esaias*, 75.
[8] Borrhaus, *In Iesaiae Prophetae Oracula*, 42, 43.
[9] Bullinger, *Isaias*, 21v.

The obstinance of faithlessness did not drive them away. For the physical lineage of Israel is not typically referred to in the Scriptures as "the fruit of the land." Then he promises this fruit will bring honor to the true Israelites—not to the fruit of the land against the Israelites. Therefore, what other branch is there who will be another fruit than Christ, with his body, the church. Annotations on Isaiah 4:2-3.[10]

Those Recorded Are the Elect of the Church. Dietrich Schnepff: For those who are granted to be in the city are written in the book and the catalog of citizens, and they enjoy all the privileges of the city and its inhabitants. So are Christians recorded in that heavenly city; they are heirs of eternal life. That, too, is what the prophet wanted to say with the other phrase, "everyone who has been recorded for life." For certainly in Scripture, sinners are compared to those who have died, but only Christians live. And not only do they live in this world and enjoy the comforts and spiritual goods, but, as was specified before, they were elected in Christ from the foundation of the world, so they are also going to remain in that eternal city always. For God knows who are his, and no one will snatch the sheep from his hand. . . . From these we see how this passage also provides us with pleasant and necessary teaching on predestination to eternal life. Scholia on Isaiah 4:3-4.[11]

Sanctification and Justification by Faith. Johannes Oecolampadius: Our holiness is in Christ Jesus, on whose account we daily fight with zeal against vices and sins, and so we "sanctify ourselves." And then there is not anything imputed as sin for those saved by faith and love. But if anyone falls, either from faith or from love, that one is already not in the church. But the ungodly, although they are numbered within the church, even if they preside over others by tyranny, they do not belong to the church. For as long as we live in this life, we are sinful and we sin, but we do not always sin unto death. For, knowing that we are holy to the Lord, we abstain from all the things that can pull us away from the Lord. Then from that he afterward applies what is sanctification.

"When the Lord shall have washed away." Again, by "daughters of Zion" and Jerusalem, understand the church. From where, then, is this sanctification—is it really from one's own merits or from the fulfillment of the works of the law? By no means. For the whole world would not wash away even one sin, since we are all sons of wrath. Then from where? Paul responds, by grace and election. Because if it were by works, then it would not be from grace. For that reason the prophet says, "When the Lord washed." He is the one who cleanses those who believe in him, for he justifies them by faith. Commentary on Isaiah 4:3-4.[12]

Different Kinds of Holy. Martin Borrhaus: The Latins call "holy" what is untouched by violence, injury, and defect. But that is not the same reason these are called "holy." For some are holy by their nature, such as God the Father, the Messiah Son, and the Spirit of both, who is called the Holy Spirit. But others are not holy in themselves and their nature but are holy by the Spirit of the Messiah, such as the temple and its elements. . . . To foreshadow that holiness, the law, the tabernacle with its vessels, the priests with their vestments, and the sacrifices themselves are called "holy." These are not holy by nature. But their use was determined by God to prefigure for us those things that were truly holy. So what we read here according to our seer, "he will be called holy," is what will happen in the administration of the new covenant with the revealing of the Messiah, and he declares it with the frequently used expression "holiness." Oracles in Isaiah on 4:3-4.[13]

[10]ZSW 14 / CR 101:148-49, 150, 152; citing Acts 20:28. †Zwingli also cites Jn 10:1 as an example of allegory.
[11]Schnepff, *In Esaiae*, 65; citing Dan 12; Phil 4; Rev 3; 21; Ezek 13.
[12]Oecolampadius, *In Iesaiam*, 44r.
[13]Borrhaus, *In Iesaiae Prophetae Oracula*, 44.

4:5-6 The Lord's Protection of His People

The Spirit of Judgment and the Spirit of Fire. Johannes Oecolampadius: For it is by God alone that sins are washed and forgiven. And when appeased by the blood of his Son, he cleanses them. It does not escape me that there are some who say that Jerusalem and the church will be sanctified by the separation and removal of the ungodly, and this is done with a spirit of judgment and a spirit of fire. . . . Yet the Spirit whom we receive is truly the Spirit of judgment, distinguishing the believing from the unbelieving, and the sons of God from the sons of the world. Moreover, he is the Spirit of zealous heat and the Spirit who makes us hot so one does not permit oneself to be idle. He not only causes one to stand and persevere in adversities (which is denied to the ungodly) but also to enjoy how God so generously behaves toward one. Commentary on Isaiah 4:5.[14]

Multiple Meanings of Smoke and Fire. Dietrich Schnepff: The use of [shade] is also shown in multiple ways. The first is that which kept the enemy away from the camp of the Hebrews; the second is that which covered the tabernacle; and although it is not included, one can easily obtain that from the text: that shade provided in the heat. There was also another use: that column of fire shining at night so that they did not have to move in darkness. The last benefit was that when they were led by the cloud and fire, they knew when and by what means the camp was going to move. Now he shows what cloud it was when he says that it was the glory of the Lord. Indeed, the passage cited about the temple of Solomon explains what he means by the "glory of the Lord," namely, the kind of smoke that would overtake the entire tabernacle and the temple of Solomon during that time. . . . For in the Old Testament, worship was bound to one place. Isaiah says that at the time of the coming of the Messiah, there will be many tabernacles, many future assemblies, all of which that cloud is still going to cover. This is no different from what Christ says, "Where two or three are gathered in my name, there am I among them." Scholia on Isaiah 4:5.[15]

Multiple Meanings of the Clouds. Martin Borrhaus: But what is that cloud? These clouds are the divine ambassadors who sprinkle the teaching of the gospel, which contains the waters of the Holy Spirit, which refreshes our souls in the fire of our life in this day. Further, we know that the vapor of solar light is raised from the waters below by force and condensed into a cloud above, which is dissolved into rain, tempering the heat by its cold. A little later about clouds, "I will command the clouds not to rain." So, it may be that the signs of divine benevolence are also shown in the clouds, just as the rainbow of the covenant stretched in the clouds is proof that the world would not be destroyed by flood again. . . . Further, when we read here that the cloud is going to be created over Zion, it alludes to the pillar of cloud, which . . . went before the Israelites to show them the path. There is a shadow and figure in the Mosaic pillar: in this pillar of the new covenant, which the seer mentions, the things themselves and the reality are observed. Likewise, he alludes to the cloud, which is read about, that filled the Mosaic tabernacle and the temple of Solomon. Oracles in Isaiah on 4:5-6.[16]

God Protects His Church. Johannes Oecolampadius: "For the gates of the dead shall not prevail against it." Since the Lord is present with his people all the way to end of the age, he will save and defend her under his protection. . . . This is the whole church, in all its homes. For the faithful are the house and the temple of the Lord. I say that the whole church will be protected by God in every place and every time, by night and by day, in prosperity and in adversity. And he says this by a

[14]Oecolampadius, *In Iesaiam*, 44v.

[15]Schnepff, *In Esaiae*, 67, 68; citing Ex 14; Num 9; Mt 18:20.

[16]Borrhaus, *In Iesaiae Prophetae Oracula*, 51; citing Is 5:6.

similitude. Just as, in the past, the tabernacle of the covenant that the cloud protected by day and the column of fire guarded by night from their enemies, separating their enemies so they could not overtake the Israelites, and preventing the heat from above from harming them, and illuminating the night (for it was a pillar that warmed and illuminated), so now, too, by divine grace, there will be present in the church a cloud and a pillar, and we will be no less protected than the children of Israel walking through the desert, lacking nothing for forty years. Commentary on Isaiah 4:6.[17]

Fiery Faith. Philipp Melanchthon: It is not enough to hear the promise, but our minds must call on the Son of God with confidence, asking for his governing and defense with fiery faith and waiting for him with certain hope. And by looking to the Son of God, who is our shelter and flaming wall, we conquer our doubts, fears, and sorrows, and we place ourselves before him to be saved, ruled, and protected. And in this faith and hope, may we be constant in our confession and all the duties of our calling. Argument of Isaiah.[18]

[17]Oecolampadius, *In Iesaiam*, 44v-45r; citing Mt 16:18.

[18]CR 13:804.

5:1-7 SONG OF THE VINEYARD

5 Let me sing for my beloved
my love song concerning his vineyard:

My beloved had a vineyard
on a very fertile hill.

[2]He dug it and cleared it of stones,
and planted it with choice vines;

he built a watchtower in the midst of it,
and hewed out a wine vat in it;

and he looked for it to yield grapes,
but it yielded wild grapes.

[3]And now, O inhabitants of Jerusalem
and men of Judah,

judge between me and my vineyard.

[4]What more was there to do for my vineyard,
that I have not done in it?

When I looked for it to yield grapes,
why did it yield wild grapes?

[5]And now I will tell you
what I will do to my vineyard.

I will remove its hedge,
and it shall be devoured;[a]

I will break down its wall,
and it shall be trampled down.

[6]I will make it a waste;
it shall not be pruned or hoed,
and briers and thorns shall grow up;

I will also command the clouds
that they rain no rain upon it.

[7]For the vineyard of the LORD of hosts
is the house of Israel,

and the men of Judah
are his pleasant planting;

and he looked for justice,
but behold, bloodshed;[b]

for righteousness,
but behold, an outcry![c]

a Or *grazed over;* compare Exodus 22:5 **b** The Hebrew words for *justice* and *bloodshed* sound alike **c** The Hebrew words for *righteous* and *outcry* sound alike

OVERVIEW: The first part of Isaiah 5 begins with a song. Several Reformers explain that the song is more like a parable, with many of them commenting on Jesus' parable of the vineyard and the bad fruit of the Pharisees. A few include specific thoughts on how parables such as this one should be interpreted. The commentators give many similar explanations on elements of the parable where the biblical text itself provides the meaning, but they offer a wide variety on many of the other components. They agree, however, that the overall message is God's judgment against his people who were behaving unjustly.

THIS SONG IS NOT MUSICAL. JOHANNES BRENZ: But because he uses a metaphorical or parabolic figure of speaking, he calls this speech a "canticle," not because it is a song like the Davidic psalms but because in the Hebrew custom, something is called a canticle not only when it is set to music but also when it is a figure of speech, that is, proverbial, metaphorical, or parabolic. We have the common custom of saying, "He sings an old ditty," which would be said without figure as, "He recounts an old story or narration." COMMENTARY ON ISAIAH 5:1.[1]

[1]Brenz, *Esaias*, 79.

A Mirror for Repentance. John Calvin: "Now will I sing to my beloved." The subject of this chapter is different from that of the previous one. The prophet wanted to describe the condition of the people of Israel, as it was then, in order that all might recognize their faults, and thus shame and displeasure with oneself would affect them seriously toward a pursuit of repentance. For here, as in a mirror, the people were able to behold the misery of their condition. But otherwise they would have had too much pleasure in their vices, and they were not fairly receiving any warnings. For this reason it was necessary for him to demonstrate clearly their filthiness as if it were a painting. And that it would have greater authority he made use of this preface, since eminent and illustrious things were usually described in verse so they could be repeated in everyone's mouth and that a memorial of them should stand perpetually. In the same way, we see that Moses wrote a song, and many others so that in private and in public, that all these things should resound with these voices. For in this way the teaching becomes more famous than if it had been delivered more simply. It was for this reason that Isaiah composed this song, in order to make their filthiness more visible to the people. And there is no doubt that he handled these with a magnificent and harmonious voice, as poems are also usually composed with the greatest skill. Commentary on Isaiah 5:1.[2]

5:1-4 *The Vineyard Produced Wild Grapes*

A Prominently Placed Vineyard. Dietrich Schnepff: There is no doubt that Isaiah alluded to the placement of Jerusalem, where one part was positioned on the mountain, the other in the plains. And when the prophets speak about the church, they say it is placed on the highest mountain. Similarly also the prophet, when he speaks about the spiritual vineyard, he says that it has been positioned on a lofty place. He clearly means, based on what he said earlier in the first chapter that he "reared and brought up children," that he wants to signify that for no nation has something so great and so remarkable happened. No height of dignity had ever been raised other than this: "There is not," says Moses, "another nation so great that has a god so near to it as the Lord our God is to us whenever we call upon him." But about these things was said above. Scholia on Isaiah 5:1-2.[3]

God the Beloved Friend. Thomas Cooper: The beloved friend that the prophet speaks of in the first verse is God himself. The vineyard is the house of Israel, and the chosen vine is the people of the land that it was planted in, the land of promise flowing with milk and honey. The hedge, or boundary, that he set around it was the providence of God and the defense of his good angels, together with princes, magistrates, and lawmakers, both political and others appointed by him. The stoning was the casting out of the idolatrous Canaanites and other heathen enemies before them. The tower that he built was the name of God and the majesty of his presence among them. The watchmen in the tower were his prophets, which were sent in his name to forewarn his people of all the danger imminent to them, either from God or their worldly enemies. The winepress was sincere and true doctrine according to the law of God with the knowledge of his true worship, which he gave to them alone out of all the nations of the earth. . . . The sweet grapes that God looked for were true faith and worship in God's name, obedience to his holy commandments, a charitable and loving mind toward their neighbors, integrity in government of the commonwealth, and diligent keeping of the laws, punishing of the wicked, and defense of the widow, fatherless, poor, and innocent. Second Sunday in Advent at Morning Prayer.[4]

A Parable of Withheld Rain. Dietrich Schnepff: But that these are to be taken as those times that precede the final devastation, we can

[2]CTS 13:162-63* (CO 36:102).

[3]Schnepff, *In Esaiae*, 74; citing Is 1:2; Deut 4:7.

[4]Cooper, *Brief Exposition*, 12v-13r*.

make a conjecture from the fact that the Lord denies rain to this vineyard in the future. That means the speeches cannot be understood to be about the Babylonian bondage, because they had prophets there, Daniel and Ezekiel among others, and after freedom was restored, Haggai and Zechariah. Finally, Christ himself . . . tells a parable about the abjection and rejection of the Hebrews with the same words that our prophet uses. Scholia on Isaiah 5:1-2.[5]

Infant Baptism Brought Destruction to the Vineyard. Pilgram Marpeck: If, however, baptism had remained steady, according to the command of Christ and the usage of the apostles, and if it had remained unchanged, so that no one had been baptized and accepted into the holy church unless he himself had first confessed his faith, himself denied the devil, committed himself to Christ in baptism, as is proper, and committed and pledged himself to live a new life, surely the whole church would have remained honorable and in a healthy state. But the church departed from God's order and undertook to baptize the unknowing and innocent children, the majority of whom, when they come of age, testify by their deeds that they belong to the devil. Thus, the church, by committing the ignorant and unwilling to Christ, mocked the secret of the covenant, which in actuality takes place between Christ and his believers, and made it into a children's game. Accordingly, God, too, has turned away, left them, and plagued them with worthy and well-deserved punishment. This impure adultery paid little or no attention to the faithfulness of the man he has cast aside, and thus has fulfilled what he promised to the prophet Isaiah. Isaiah spoke of the Lord's having planted a vineyard, which he assumed would bring forth grapes; rather, it brought forth wild grapes and useless fruit. Therefore, the Lord did away with the gate and the walls, and opened the vineyard to wild animals. It has become a desolation and is trodden underfoot. The Admonition of 1542.[6]

A Stoned Wall. Francisco Forerius: Therefore, this is to throw stones into the intended place by hurling them. And when it is in the second conjugation with the accusative noun or pronoun, it seems to have the meaning that I have said. . . . "And he stoned David." So then, I said here it is "to stone," and in the Hebrew custom, these two words can be construed together as "he built and he stoned," that is, "he built with stones," so that you do not understand this as he would make a fence that one could easily climb over, but he built it as a wall, or he enclosed it and stoned it, as if he had placed a hedge of thorns on top of the wall of stones. . . . And let me not be unclear: the verse received in the Vulgate is true, because it is construed with the meaning where the case of the middle preposition *min* ["with"] is removed, as later in chapter 62. For that reason, I have followed another translation in this version. Commentary on Isaiah 5:2.[7]

A Crown of Thorns. John Mayer: "And he built a tower in the midst of it, and a winepress," that is, a temple and an altar, which received the sacrifices brought out of all Israel, as the winepress receives grapes. For wild grapes, Aquila has *pessimos fructus* [worst fruit]. The Septuagint has "thorns," either what they crowned Christ with or the thorns of worldly cares. But the first is to be preferred. Commentary on Isaiah 5:2.[8]

Consider the Works of Wisdom and Understanding. Andreas Bodenstein von Karlstadt: Therefore, God complains through Isaiah that they do not consider his works. . . . And Christ often rebuked his apostles because they did not understand his work or teaching. But they—that is, wisdom and understanding—should be followed not only when you do something but also

[5]Schnepff, *In Esaiae*, 73; citing Mt 21; Lk 20.

[6]CRR 2:215.

[7]Forerius, *Iesaiae*, 21v; citing 2 Sam 16:6; Is 5:5; 62:10.

[8]Mayer, *Commentary upon All the Prophets*, 4:31; citing Ps 80:9.

when you suffer something, so that you know what you are suffering, and why, and for whose honor, and for whose benefit. For that is the characteristic of suffering. As Isaiah says, "Tribulation or worry gives understanding." . . . And Moses says, "God gives you tribulations so that you are ashamed on account of your sins." . . . And Paul says, "Affliction gives birth to patience, but patience brings understanding or experience." . . . For experience is understanding and the perfect work, of which James writes. . . . Without understanding, no work of God is perfect. Without understanding we are like a muzzled horse in which there is no reason. WHETHER ONE SHOULD PROCEED SLOWLY.[9]

ISAIAH'S ROYAL TRAINING. VIKTORIN STRIGEL: Therefore Isaiah, in the fifth chapter, singing the most beautiful song about the vineyard, no doubt identifies Christ as his relative. For the Jews relate that the father of Isaiah was the brother of King Amaziah, from whom Christ was descended according to the flesh. Therefore, this prophet was not only related to Christ the Lord by faith (by which all the godly are made brothers and members of God) but also by blood relationship. And since he was born into a royal family, it is not doubtful at all that he had a course of studies that not only sharpened his language with the practice of speaking but also enriched his eloquence with a tool of greater skill, and with those same skills, he brought together all the honor of virtue with the highest praise of eloquence. ORATION ON THE PROPHET ISAIAH.[10]

THE CHURCH IS THE VINEYARD, AND THE SPIRIT IS THE OIL. WOLFGANG MUSCULUS: And the church is the vineyard of the Lord. "I am the true vine," it says, "and my father is the gardener. And you are my branches." This, too, is a vineyard situated on a lofty and "fatty" hilltop. For those grafted into Christ—in whom is all the "fatness" of heavenly grace—we are called anointed Christians by that oil, the Holy Spirit. . . . And God the Father, the heavenly gardener, hedges his church, surrounding and strengthening it with the word of truth and life, and with the sacraments of the heavenly mysteries, which enclose it like certain walls. This way she is specially consecrated to him and separated from the world. COMMENTARY ON ISAIAH 5:1-4.[11]

THE CHURCH IS GOD'S VINEYARD. MATTHEW POOLE: His church is oft and very fitly called his vineyard because of God's singular respect to it, and care of it, and his delight in it, and his expectation of good fruit from it, and so forth. Hills are places most commodious for vines. ANNOTATIONS ON ISAIAH 5:1.[12]

GOD COMMANDS US TO USE REASON AND JUDGMENT. BALTHASAR HUBMAIER: How seriously all those err who say: "Aye, whatever I do, whether it be good or evil, is the will of God, for we are his lump of clay. He makes of us what he wants." Yes, he has made you a vessel of honor by pouring his holy word into you and has given you the free power and choice to become his child. Since, however, you do not will, you make of yourself out of your own wantonness a vessel of dishonor. Yes, according to his revealed will God also wants to be justified by us. One might say, "Why have you made me thus?" As God himself commands us and says, "Come, I beseech you, and we will reason together," "and you my inhabitant of Jerusalem, and you, man of Judah, judge, I beseech you, between me and my vineyard." David also says to God, "Lord, be merciful to me so that you will be called just in your speaking, when you are judged." Christ also says to the . . . Jews: "Which of you will condemn me of sin?" But Paul writes about the hidden will of God, according to which nobody may say: "Why do you make me thus?" For in this chapter he teaches the killing of the flesh in

[9]Karlstadt, *Whether One Should Proceed Slowly*, 59; citing Is 28; Lev 26:40-46; Rom 5:3-5; Jas 1:4-5.
[10]Strigel, *Oratio De Propheta Esaia*, 4.
[11]Musculus, *In Esaiam*, 122-23; citing Jn 15.
[12]Poole, *Annotations*, 334*; citing Ps 80:10.

order that it not raise itself above God out of its own power. Freedom of the Will, II.[13]

The Purpose for the Parable First. Adam Sasbout: "Now therefore inhabitants. . . ." Before the prophet explains the parable, the judgment of the people is required, so that they are slain by their own sword and conquered by their own testimony. So also the prophet Nathan, who was sent by the Lord to charge David with adultery and be connected to murder, did this by first relating a parable about a sheep. This compelled David to respond. "As the Lord lives," he says, "the man who did this must die." So immediately Nathan added, "You are that man who did this thing!" So also the Lord, in the Gospel, related a parable about two sons, one of whom went, when he had previously refused to go to his father's vineyard, and was later led to repentance. But the other said he was going to go, and yet he did not go. It compelled the Jews to respond that the one who was led to repentance and went to the vineyard did the will of the father. So immediately he added, "Truly I say to you that tax collecters and prostitutes will enter the kingdom of God before you." So also in this same chapter, he related a parable about a father of a family who planted a vineyard, and, going away, he entrusted the care of it to tenants, and when the father sent servants to receive the fruits, they either killed or inflicted abuses on them. It compelled them to confess and bring a verdict against them when they said, "He will badly destroy those evil ones and give the vineyard to others." Consequently he adds to this by saying, "The kingdom of God will be taken from you and given to the Gentiles producing its fruit." Commentary on Isaiah 5:3-4.[14]

Failing the Lord's Expectations. Francisco Forerius: This is a Hebraism, "What is there to do beyond what I have not done?" That is, "What remained to be done that I had not done?" This is the Lord's case; this is a lament. Now, the one who questions like this is certain that there can be no objection against it. But a person could truly say, "What should I have done, my Lord, that I did? Who am I, what sort am I, why am I not bad?" says Augustine.[†] "Or when I expected . . . ," is a specific saying here in Hebrew . . . and it is used for questions that are raised to know the cause of something, that is, "Why? This is why." So, it is a Hebraism, "Why did I expect it to produce grapes, and it produced wild grapes, that is, why did it make wild grapes when I rightly expected grapes?" . . . And when he asks why it produced wild grapes, he knows they have no answer. And indeed, the comment is worthy that we can obtain and bring no excuse, much less respond in every way to the expectations of God, and the expectation of the Lord should be sufficient reason for us to do it. Commentary on Isaiah 5:4.[15]

5:5-7 *The Lord Announces Destruction for the Vineyard*

A Hedge and Wall as Laws. Johannes Brenz: These things correspond to the vineyard. In this way, God cultivated his vineyard, which is the Jewish people. He gave them the kingdom of Canaan. He instituted a politic among his people with his laws, which are like a hedge and a wall. Now, because the public laws are called a hedge or wall, he reminds us as much about the authority as about the usefulness of the law. They distinguish a garden wall from the garden and vines from a vineyard. So laws distinguish politics and kingdoms. A wall and a hedge keep out beasts and thieves from attacking. So laws keep out the evil ones so that they do not disturb public peace. A hedge guards and preserves the garden and the vines so that they are not crushed and trampled by anything. Commentary on Isaiah 5:5.[16]

---

[13]CRR 5:482*; citing Jn 1:12; Is 1:18; Ps 51:1; Jn 8:46; Rom 9:13.
[14]Sasbout, *In Esaiam*, 44; citing 2 Sam 12:1-7; Mt 21:28-43.
[15]Forerius, *Iesaiae*, 22r. [†]Trapp quotes the exact same phrases of Augustine in *Commentary or Exposition*, 25.
[16]Brenz, *Esaias*, 79.

The Lord Renounces His Covenant. Heinrich Bullinger: Therefore, the Lord rejects his covenant and denies helping and defending his people. And with the wall demolished and the divine defense removed, the towers and bulwarks fall, and this happened to even the strongest fortifications of all. Then the vineyard "will be devastated," it says, "it will not be pruned nor hoed." Therefore the servants are taken away with the magistrates, and doctrine, comfort, defense, and all worship is taken away. Therefore horrible devastation follows, it says, "abdication" and "repudiation" of the Jewish people. . . . Thorns and briers will spring up in the vineyard. No good and faithful people will be found, but the treacherous, depraved, and unjust against God and humanity, and they will be like thorns and thornbushes. Likewise the thorns will increase in the uncultivated places. So desolation is signified. And it will not rain on the vineyard. It will be denied all heavenly grace; the wrath of the Lord will remain on the ungrateful and treacherous and rebellious. Moreover, history plainly testifies that all these things happened to the Jewish people, not only in the Babylonian but also the Roman captivity, and experience testifies this happens daily. Sermons on Isaiah 5:5-6.[17]

Disintegrating Christendom Is Like God's Vineyard. Thomas Müntzer: It is known that poor, ailing, disintegrating Christendom can be neither counseled nor aided unless the diligent, untroubled servants of God daily work through the Scriptures, singing, reading, and preaching. But along with that, the head of many a pampered priest will continuously have to suffer great blows or will miss out in his handiwork. But how ought one otherwise to deal with him at a time when Christendom is being so wretchedly devastated by ravenous wolves, as it is written . . . concerning the vineyard of God? And Saint Paul teaches how one should exercise oneself in singing divine praises. For just as in the times of the beloved prophets Isaiah, Jeremiah, Ezekiel, and the others, the whole congregation of the elect of God had become so utterly implicated in the way of idolatry that even God could not help them in the midst of the heathen to the point where they once again recognized his holy name, as it stands written so, no less is it true in the time of our fathers and our time that poor Christendom is even more deeply obdurate and even more, for having the unspeakable resemblance of the divine name with which the devil and his servants adorn themselves. Sermon Before the Princes on Daniel 2.[18]

The End of the Remnant. Francisco Forerius: Now, it would easily be understood when this response of the Jews was given that it was not something they had never experienced before the coming of the Lord, but these things can hardly be understood to be about another devastation than the final one. And therefore also when the prophet had spoken about these in the preceding chapters, and about the small preserved remnant, it now seemed fitting for him to break into a song, which would comprise the whole and explain the beginning, the middle, and the end. For this was the custom of the prophets and the sacred writers. See the books of Judges and Deuteronomy, and we will see this observed again later. . . . When, I ask, was Israel so exposed to the invasions of the enemy that the whole republic was burned and seen in flames? When did the military strength fall like this, and all the strong men of the Jews were crushed? When was the wall of the holy city so broken and demolished? When, I say, other than after the Lord's death? For in the previous captivities, the vineyard was not fully uprooted; vines still remained, and some form of it appeared in part. Commentary on Isaiah 5:5-6.[19]

The Details of a Parable. Konrad Pellikan: This verse is the explanation of the parable,

[17]Bullinger, *Isaias*, 24r.

[18]Müntzer, "Sermon Before the Princes," 49-50; citing Is 5:1-23; Ps 80:9-14; Eph 5:19.

[19]Forerius, *Iesaiae*, 22v.

where the house of Israel is called a vineyard, the Jews, or the men of Judah, his delightful seed. The Lord had expected justice from them but found nothing except wounds and iniquity. He was desiring faithful people but received rebels. He had commanded righteousness to be preserved, and behold, oppression of the poor and the miserable cries of those afflicted with harm cry out to him in heaven. With this brief explanation of the prophet, one may learn that each and every particle of parables is not always sifted out, as if every part of the similitude is examined and corresponds to something. But this example sticks to some principle intention, against interpreters who are too curious. Commentary on Isaiah 5:7.[20]

The Vineyard Is Judah. Dietrich Schnepff: For my vineyard is the Israelites, and especially the kingdom of Judah. For out of the whole earth I chose you as a treasure, and I wanted you to be a garden, which would serve to delight me. Certainly I overlooked nothing that I knew pertained to your defense and decoration. For all the way from the time I led you out of Egypt and kept you safe by that cloud that accompanied you, I was always near to you with my protection, as if you were surrounded with that hedge. I sent preachers, my watchers, who were warning you about all the dangers. I gave attention to your cultivating more pure doctrine, wanting you to be fruitful grapevines. And of course, in the last times I will be that vine, and I will plant others so that they are willing to be branches in me, who bear much fruit. But with this field of mine, they will not respond—during your times or in the future. Rather, instead of virtue and piety, they will produce the wild vines of all vices, blasphemies, and extreme wickedness. Paraphrase of Isaiah 5:7.[21]

Israel and the Church. Johannes Oecolampadius: The vineyard was the people of Israel, which he expelled. The vineyard is also the church, whose branches are in Jesus, the vine. They are never neglected by the Father, the gardener. Moreover, we should see the benefits compared to the first Israel, and at the same time also what will be the same judgment of the just God toward the pseudo-Christians among both groups. The Lord planted the people Israel from the patriarchs Abraham, Isaac, and Jacob, and to save them he brought light with great miracles, gave many commands, sent the wisest prophets to them, promised countless things, and threatened countless things. Commentary on Isaiah 5:7.[22]

The Meaning of Grapes and Wild Grapes. Martin Luther: The Lord had embraced this people as a mother her son. Therefore, he calls it a branch and "pleasant planting," attractive and delightful. This is justice, that the law takes its course, that the innocent are not mistreated, and the criminals do not escape punishment. "Gold and silver make the straightest things crooked." "Power, partiality, and money prevent just verdicts." Righteousness is what imparts benefits and renders good to the deserving. A cry, namely, of those who suffer violence and tyranny, their complaint against tyrants. Here he explains what grapes and wild grapes mean, that is, allegorically. Lectures on Isaiah 5:7.[23]

Justice, Not Ceremonies. Wolfgang Musculus: And observe what he says, "He looked for justice and righteousness." It does not say he looked for circumcision, sacrifices, firstfruits, offerings, legal purifications, and so on, but he looked for justice and righteousness. They were in many ceremonies and lawful acts of worship, as we saw earlier. . . . But that philanthropy of God and love of righteousness required more from what happens among mortals, especially the poor and afflicted, than they thought was obtained from their divine worship. So elsewhere it says, "Learn what this means, 'I desire mercy, not sacrifice.'" . . .

[20]Pellikan, *Commentaria Bibliorum*, 3:6v.
[21]Schnepff, *In Esaiae*, 87.
[22]Oecolampadius, *In Iesaiam*, 47r.
[23]LW 16:60-61 (WA 31.2:42).

But they perpetually neglected those things, as if they did not matter in the sight of God. So today too, we see this happen among those who measure the worship of God by church rituals and meanwhile do not think about justice and righteousness.

Observe also that the verb is "looking for." It does not say, "He required," but "he looked for" justice. The pursuit of justice and righteousness ought to be continuous and undiminished. But the wickedness of human nature is such that this is either interrupted or extinguished. Meanwhile, with what patience there is, God looks for it, so that finally at last, when we repent, righteousness is pursued and is judged rightly. This patience of God ought to invite us to repentance. Commentary on Isaiah 5:7.[24]

Judgment Against the Unjust Society. Johannes Oecolampadius: For God wishes to rescue the destitute and the poor from being oppressed by judges and magistrates. That mercy is the sweetest wine of God. But the people of the Jews and those who despise God's word produce thorns and wild vines, and wine like that from the vineyards of Sodom. For they killed the prophets and the apostles, desiring the master's fruit, and finally the Lord himself, the heir of the vineyard, as Christ explains. . . . For the judgment is against an unjust society. Commentary on Isaiah 5:7.[25]

---

[24]Musculus, *In Esaiam*, 127; citing Is 1; Hos 6:6; Rom 2:4.

[25]Oecolampadius, *In Iesaiam*, 48r; citing Mt 21:33-41.

5:8-30 EXILE FOR DISREGADING THE LORD

[8]*Woe to those who join house to house,*
who add field to field,

until there is no more room,
and you are made to dwell alone
in the midst of the land.

[9]*The* Lord *of hosts has sworn in my hearing:*

"Surely many houses shall be desolate,
large and beautiful houses, without inhabitant.

[10]*For ten acres*[a] *of vineyard shall yield but one bath,*
and a homer of seed shall yield but an ephah."[b]

[11]*Woe to those who rise early in the morning,*
that they may run after strong drink,

who tarry late into the evening
as wine inflames them!

[12]*They have lyre and harp,*
tambourine and flute and wine at their feasts,

but they do not regard the deeds of the Lord,
or see the work of his hands.

[13]*Therefore my people go into exile*
for lack of knowledge;[c]

their honored men go hungry,[d]
and their multitude is parched with thirst.

[14]*Therefore Sheol has enlarged its appetite*
and opened its mouth beyond measure,

and the nobility of Jerusalem[e] *and her multitude will go down,*
her revelers and he who exults in her.

[15]*Man is humbled, and each one is brought low,*
and the eyes of the haughty[f] *are brought low.*

[16]*But the* Lord *of hosts is exalted*[g] *in justice,*
and the Holy God shows himself holy in righteousness.

[17]*Then shall the lambs graze as in their pasture,*
and nomads shall eat among the ruins of the rich.

[18]*Woe to those who draw iniquity with cords of falsehood,*
who draw sin as with cart ropes,

[19]*who say: "Let him be quick,*
let him speed his work
that we may see it;

let the counsel of the Holy One of Israel draw near,
and let it come, that we may know it!"

[20]*Woe to those who call evil good*
and good evil,

who put darkness for light
and light for darkness,

who put bitter for sweet
and sweet for bitter!

[21]*Woe to those who are wise in their own eyes,*
and shrewd in their own sight!

[22]*Woe to those who are heroes at drinking wine,*
and valiant men in mixing strong drink,

[23]*who acquit the guilty for a bribe,*
and deprive the innocent of his right!

[24]*Therefore, as the tongue of fire devours the stubble,*
and as dry grass sinks down in the flame,

so their root will be as rottenness,
and their blossom go up like dust;

for they have rejected the law of the Lord *of hosts,*

and have despised the word of the Holy One
of Israel.

[25]*Therefore the anger of the* Lord *was kindled*
against his people,
and he stretched out his hand against them
and struck them,
and the mountains quaked;

and their corpses were as refuse
in the midst of the streets.

For all this his anger has not turned away,
and his hand is stretched out still.

[26]*He will raise a signal for nations far away,*
and whistle for them from the ends of the earth;

and behold, quickly, speedily they come!

[27]*None is weary, none stumbles,*
none slumbers or sleeps,

not a waistband is loose,
not a sandal strap broken;

[28]*their arrows are sharp,*
all their bows bent,

their horses' hoofs seem like flint,
and their wheels like the whirlwind.

[29]*Their roaring is like a lion,*
like young lions they roar;

they growl and seize their prey;
they carry it off, and none can rescue.

[30]*They will growl over it on that day,*
like the growling of the sea.

And if one looks to the land,
behold, darkness and distress;

and the light is darkened by its clouds.

a Hebrew *ten yoke,* the area ten yoke of oxen can plow in a day **b** A *bath* was about 6 gallons or 22 liters; a *homer* was about 6 bushels or 220 liters; an *ephah* was about 3/5 bushel or 22 liters **c** Or *without their knowledge* **d** Or *die of hunger* **e** Hebrew *her nobility* **f** Hebrew *high* **g** Hebrew *high*

Overview: In the second part of Isaiah 5, Isaiah continues addressing the injustice of the people by issuing a series of woes. The Reformation commentators consistently note that it is not the actions themselves of buying and selling or planting and growing or singing and dancing, but the attitudes and abuses that come from greed and especially contempt for the Lord's word that result in the penalties of exile and desolation. They also explain how the Lord can both be merciful and carry out such severe punishment. There are differing views on when these words are fulfilled, but several of them note that this kind of punishment happened to the Jews by both the Babylonians and later the Romans.

5:8-13 *Woes to the Greedy and Indulgent*

Pursuing Earthly Things Leads to Desolation. Johannes Brenz: For they all were in this, joining houses to houses and fields to fields. If one area was bought, then they thought about another to be acquired, even though the previous one was not yet paid off. Such also are the habits of Christians in this time. They buy, they sell, they join fields with fields, houses with houses, property with properties. So what? Do not those who do such things sin? But it is not the godly who buy two houses, is it? God forbid. One is not condemned for a contract of purchase, if it happened legitimately and righteously. . . . So what is the penalty of this sin? First, the many houses will become deserted, that is, the greed and the pursuit of joining houses results in either pestilence or devastation of the earth. Then, from ten acres of the vineyard the yield is one bottle. . . . That is, the pursuit of joining fields results in barrenness and the scarcity of things. Commentary on Isaiah 5:8.[1]

[1]Brenz, *Esaias*, 83-84.

How Great a Penalty. Wolfgang Musculus: He threatens the barrenness of vineyards and fields, in which it happens that barely a tenth part of the seed is restored to the ground and a thirtieth portion of the usual produce is taken from the vineyards. If you allot three baths of wine to an acre, ten acres will produce thirty baths. But in that barrenness, ten acres was only going to bring forth one bath. So twenty-nine baths would be taken away by the vengeance of God. A core, or a homer, contains ten ephah. If you were given at least three homers of one seed, then also in a typical year, the result would be barely a thirtieth, and as was said, the tenth portion was going to return to the planter of the field. Commentary on Isaiah 5:8-10.[2]

The Penalty of the Tenth. Johannes Oecolampadius: He charges them with three things regarding the buildings: the multitude, the magnitude, and the lavishness. . . . The penalty for those who were joining fields so that they could snatch the fruit of others' farms with their own is also to experience the barrenness of their fields, so that they would not even recover a tenth part of the seed. And ten acres teaches how significantly angry God becomes with those who greedily keep the tithes to be given to the poor and the ministers of God. Commentary on Isaiah 5:10.[3]

The Abuse, Not the Use, of Wine and Music. Heinrich Bullinger: The prophet likewise adds another point, from which it may be gathered that he speaks against excessive use of wine. For he criticizes that they were playing music at their parties, and as if they combined wine and music, they were playing in drunkenness. Indeed, music elsewhere has good use and is not to be condemned universally. But lascivious or unruly music of drunkards is deservedly condemned. Drunks shout and sing obscene and disgraceful songs. In addition, they abuse music to stir up shameful things, especially for teaching degrading dances and dancing. About this, the apostle Paul says, "Do not get drunk with wine, in which is luxury, but be filled with the Spirit, speaking to yourselves with psalms, hymns, and spiritual songs." Sermons on Isaiah 5:11-12.[4]

Drunkenness the Mother of Many Vices. Dietrich Schnepff: It was established by the prophet to recount the sins and vices in order, which he compared above to unripe grapes. And rightly, of course, when he had spoken about the vineyard that did not meet the expectation of the farmer, he especially counts among these sins drunkenness and those vices that come from excessive use of wine and accompany intoxication, as well as the omission of duties, securities, and luxuries. For drunkenness is like a mother of many vices.[†] Scholia on Isaiah 5:11-12.[5]

All Pleasure Without God Is Sin. Andreas Bodenstein von Karlstadt: All pleasure is sin. Soon a person violates this and burns himself with eating and drinking. It would be better for us were we to sprinkle food and drink with ashes than to have our food praised in song; for the nature of our pleasure prevents us from knowing God and his divine works. Therefore Isaiah says, "You have harp, lyre, timbrel, and flute and wine at your feasts, but you do not regard the work of his hands."

It is dangerous to use even the smallest things with pleasure. For, as Christ says, everything one hankers after becomes one's heart and treasure. It turns us into servants and takes possessions as a lord possesses his cattle. Therefore we ought to ask for, seek, take, and enjoy every necessity with fear for the simple reason that we are unworthy of anything good. The Meaning of the Term *Gelassen*.[6]

Exile Is the Fruit of Their Drinking. Wolfgang Musculus: He addresses the

[2]Musculus, *In Esaiam*, 129.
[3]Oecolampadius, *In Iesaiam*, 49r-v.
[4]Bullinger, *Isaias*, 25v; citing Eph 5:18-20.
[5]Schnepff, *In Esaiae*, 80. [†]See also his paraphrase on 84.
[6]CRR 8:139; citing Mt 6:21.

calamities which were going to happen to the people. He attributes these to the corruptions and the inactions of the leaders, because of the luxury, intoxication, drunkenness, and offensive levity of those disdaining the work of the Lord. He introduces God himself saying these things. This adds more weight to the prophecy. "Therefore," he says, that is, "Because the leaders pursuing drunkenness do not respect my work, it happens that everything was corrupted and neglected. For that reason it is going to be that my people, depraved by the vice of those above them, are going to depart into captivity. This is the fruit of their partying. Owed to them are all the disasters that are going to come on my people, whom they ought to have ruled with justice and righteousness and maintained order." Commentary on Isaiah 5:13.[7]

5:14-23 *Death and Woe to the Greedy and Indulgent*

The Number of Carcasses in the Streets. John Trapp: Josephus, Hegesippus, Orosius, and Eusebius tell us fully what havoc was made of men at the last destruction of Jerusalem. With the extreme famine, the fury of the sword, and sickness during the siege, about 600,000 able men perished; or, as others say, 1,100,000—in addition to the 97,000 taken captive. Titus the Roman general, seeing the infinite carcasses of the Jews, cast the unburied outside the walls of the city and was much grieved, and took God to witness that he was not the author of that calamity but that the fault was altogether in those stubborn Jews, who held out the city against him. Exposition on Isaiah 5:14-17.[8]

God's Care for the Grazing Sheep. Konrad Pellikan: Just as the Lord does not allow the arrogant and the proud to provoke him, so also he most mercifully accepts, treats, fosters, comforts, nourishes, and blesses the lambs, that is, the simple, quiet, humble, thankful, kind, and innocent ones. He pursues them as his own with all his benefits, protects them from wolves, refreshes them in the pastures of grace and life, and like those grazing in fertile pastures, they are protected in all things. For the godly, all things work together for good. And they live for the Lord without any hindrance and always progress from good to better until they are filled to satisfaction with the righteousness for which they had hungered. And the fat cattle is presented to the Lord, and with a divine feast of thanks, one is blessed and praised by the Father. Commentary on Isaiah 5:17.[9]

The Poor and Oppressed Will Enjoy Wealth After Judgment. Thomas Cooper: The seventeenth verse is a consolation for the poor and godly who were oppressed by the covetous and wicked drunkards. They shall remain after the plague and take the fruition of the wealth that the wicked were constrained to leave as waste. By sheep and the strangers he means the godly who were left after the punishment of the wicked, who had their houses and land taken from them but were now being restored to them again. Second Sunday in Advent at Morning Prayer.[10]

Mocking the Holy One. Wolfgang Musculus: With the same faithlessness and mockery they were saying this to the seer: "Let him be quick, let him speed his work that we may see it. . . ." By this phrase, "seeing and knowing," they indicate that they are not going to believe unless they had seen and known. . . . And that falsehood also pertains to the contempt when they say, "Let him speed his work." They are refusing to express the name of the Lord with reverence. Then they also add, "Let the counsel of the Holy One of Israel draw near, and let it come," because the prophet had the habit of calling the Lord the Holy One of Israel, as seen earlier. . . . Those scoffers likewise call the Lord this

[7]Musculus, *In Esaiam*, 132; citing Jer 5.
[8]Trapp, *Commentary or Exposition*, 32*.
[9]Pellikan, *Commentaria Bibliorum*, 3:7r.
[10]Cooper, *Brief Exposition*, 14r*.

in mockery. For they did not consider God to be the Holy One of Israel but were ridiculing the prophet who had the habit of calling him the Holy One of Israel. And this mocking corresponds to the idol worshipers who, because they were devoted to the worship of foreign gods, did not support the faith and worship of the one true God and could not bear the ascription to God that calls him the Holy One of Israel. These things would admonish them to worship him alone, who is the one and only God of Israel, and therefore is called the Holy One of Israel. Commentary on Isaiah 5:19.[11]

Human Wisdom. Johannes Oecolampadius: "In all your ways acknowledge him, and he will direct your steps. Be not wise in your own eyes." Therefore he says to them that they "are wise in their own eyes" and not God's—in their own human wisdom, not what is drawn from the Scriptures. Whatever desires of theirs serve them is right, whatever does not serve them is unjust. As long as our mind is not humbled but arrogantly thinks only of itself, so long one cannot be a disciple of Christ. Commentary on Isaiah 5:21.[12]

Order of God's Judgment. Heinrich Bullinger: Now, if you apply these to what the sacred history hands down about Jerusalem and the Jewish people being vanquished by the Assyrians and the Babylonians, and also about the Roman soldiers, you will have the clearest commentary of this prophetic description. For this prophetic prediction was most exactly fulfilled by those things. And to this day, we discern that he proceeds in the same order against his enemies. . . . Truly, to ask the Lord to be merciful and compassionate to us so that he may confer his Spirit on us, who corrects our souls and leads us in the way of the Lord, so that we are not led back on the way by a barbarian solider, derailed by the lusts of the flesh, or altogether destroyed in a severe war. Lord, have mercy on us. Amen. Sermons on Isaiah 5:18-23.[13]

Mixing Drinks. John Mayer: For the last words, by "strong or valiant," is to mix strong drink. Musculus says that mixing is not to be understood as water with wine, which was the usual manner of drinking, but "mixing" is pouring in strong and inebriating liquor, which is the reason mixing is used for pouring. Only he thinks they are hereby charged who give inebriating drink to others, and so indeed it is to be thought. . . . But by mingling, it may also be understood as mingling diverse strong things together, in order to intoxicate others more quickly, as is the manner of some monsters. We could also take it for putting in something to keep one from drunkenness even when the drinking becomes excessive, and so a woe is to them that are not plainly drunken, yet still drink to excess. Commentary on Isaiah 5:22.[14]

Only God Justifies the Ungodly. Heinrich Bullinger: What follows is the seventh wild vine: the corruption of justice and all righteousness by bribes. To "acquit the guilty" is not to make godly or righteous people out of ungodly ones. Only God alone can do that. Rather, it is to pronounce in judgment that the evil case of the ungodly is good, to absolve the ungodly as if they were innocent, and to make a pronouncement as if they were righteous. So, generally this is how the apostle uses this term in the case of justification in Romans and Galatians. For God absolves us from sin and condemnation on account of faith in Christ, and he confers to us the righteousness of Christ, not imputing our sins against us but imputing the righteousness of Christ. This is "to justify" from the apostle. But it is a great sin to tempt justice and righteousness with the favor of bribes. This is seriously prohibited by God in the law . . . and often in other places. And it should be noted that the prophet does not speak about

[11]Musculus, *In Esaiam*, 136; citing Is 1; 10; 12; 17; 23.
[12]Oecolampadius, *In Iesaiam*, 52r; citing Prov 3:6-7; 1 Cor 1.
[13]Bullinger, *Isaias*, 31r.
[14]Mayer, *Commentary upon All the Prophets*, 4:38*; citing Hab 2:14.

tributes simply, which by themselves are not good or evil. The use renders good, the abuse evil. Therefore he speaks about the corruption of tributes. Sermons on Isaiah 5:23.[15]

5:24-30 *Destruction of the Vineyard for Deceit and Immorality*

The Abominable Vineyard. Johannes Oecolampadius: Here at length he recounts the most bitter fruit of the abominable vineyard. That is unrepentance, obvious contempt for divine justice and the prophets, and a sense of rejection, which appear to be sins against the Holy Spirit and unworthy to receive forgiveness. Commentary on Isaiah 5:24.[16]

God Easily Executes His Judgment. Dietrich Schnepff: As a fire consumes stubble and chaff in no time, so are those ones going to perish in a brief time. But in order to teach what is greater, he threatens that they are going to be utterly eradicated. For that reason also, he describes rottenness in the root, dust in the shoots, and decay. For the unharmed root sprouts a shoot, but when the root rots, though the trunk begins to run wild, yet eventually the shoots dry up and disappear into dust. . . . Certainly our prophet compares a kind of fire by which the stubble is consumed in no time. But what is that fire? God, who is a consuming fire, and of course, that wrath that Paul calls the treasure of the wrath of the Lord in Romans, which the unrepentant bring on themselves. Therefore, let us endeavor to extinguish that deadly fire with tears and true repentance. Let us correct our life, strive for virtues, and then behave in such a way that we may commend ourselves to the Lord. Scholia on Isaiah 5:24.[17]

The Seriousness of Punishment for Sin. Johannes Oecolampadius: But if you ask, How could such severe punishments be consistent with the most merciful one? On the contrary, it is said, sin is more serious than the punishments that are inflicted for it. For they refused to hear the law of the Lord, so why would he be merciful to them? It is perpetual, so that the sin is as immense as the one sinned against; and these people did not despise humans but God. They were disobeying not just their own but the Lord of the whole universe. It is the same to reject the law of God and God himself. And they were ridiculing not only the speeches but also his promises that whoever believes in him would not perish, for they said he was a demoniac. Therefore, after the punishments owed for private sins, such as the devastation of fields and houses because of their greed and arrogance, and famine and pestilence because of intoxication, now for the highest sin of faithlessness and unrepentance, the most serious punishment is decreed. For he says that he is going to eradicate the great with the small, the strong with the weak. Commentary on Isaiah 5:24.[18]

All Calls to Repentance. Konrad Pellikan: This ultimate end remains for the ungodly despisers of God's precepts. And here is the end of the first prophetic speech in which Isaiah wants to exhort the Jews to desist from their sins and return to godliness, or face the dread of the most serious punishments. And so he first begins with a tragic exclamation, and then he presents the benefits, destroys their excuses, shows their crimes, adds the punishment, inserts hope about the future in the kingdom of the Messiah, repeatedly rebukes Jewish sluggishness while he predicts the calling of the Gentiles to worship God and their hastening to him with great eagerness. And so he consequently transitions to the reproach of the Jews, rebuking their crimes and again pronouncing the penalty. Then he takes away their confidence in the seed and the promises of God. He shows that they were indeed chosen by God, out of grace, but they will be rejected because of their

[15]Bullinger, *Isaias*, 29r; citing Deut 16.
[16]Oecolampadius, *In Iesaiam*, 51v.
[17]Schnepff, *In Esaiae*, 85-86; citing Rom 2:5.
[18]Oecolampadius, *In Iesaiam*, 53v.

ungratefulness as wicked vineyard workers. He attaches their atrocities as an epilogue. And third, he foretells the vengeance so they would be more careful not to neglect repentance. Commentary on Isaiah 5:24-25.[19]

The Nations Coming Swiftly Is the Plan of God. Wolfgang Musculus: The prophet specifies the calling of the enemies at the beginning, whom the Lord was going to raise up for the purpose of humbling his rebellious people. And they would be expelled from their land. And "he will raise," it says, "a signal for nations." He speaks in a military manner. A soldier is rallied with a raised sign. Where it ought to say, "he will call the nations as a military," he said, "He will raise a signal for the nations." We do not read about any other signal to which the people of Babylon assembled. . . . To express this sense more literally, he says, "And he will whistle for them." To be called with a whistle is not to be called with an open and clear cry but to be called in such a way that only the one who understands is called and rushes. Indeed, by no means did the king of Babylon understand the plan of God, yet at the same time, by his instigation, he was moved to carry out this expedition, even though it was for a different purpose. Commentary on Isaiah 5:26.[20]

Weapons of War Today. Heinrich Bullinger: "All their bows are bent. . . ." By this understand the weapons that are used by soldiers in whatever time. Today rifles are used especially. Arrows and bows lie neglected, except that they are still used by the English, Parthians, and Scythians. In the past, they fought from chariots, as is also clear from history about the ancients. Today, greater bombardments and cannons on a chariot are in use, with warlike lightning. Similarly now, unless their hoofs are hard, horses are not used to serve the military—in fact, they do not firmly hold the iron spur. But a "whirlwind" is violent, swift, and stormy. So that signifies that the armed chariot is going to be quick and horrible. Today, the armed chariot of old is conquered by the chariots with bombardments, from which emanate utterly terrifying thunder and lightning. But the Lord uses these in subduing defiant peoples and ungodly nations. Sermons on Isaiah 5:28.[21]

The Roar Is Ferocious Babylon. Wolfgang Musculus: In this verse, he expresses the ferocity of the Babylonian people. He uses here a similitude of a lion. The lion is most ferocious by nature, with a frightful roar and an attacking and predatory violence that is intolerable. So he gives to that people a ferocious spirit, greedy to prey and violent, and a voice not dissimilar to the roar of a lion, and indeed it is horrifying. Their bodies were thick and robust, with dreadful voices and speech more similar to a roar than the speaking of a human. They were filled with severe wrath and growling, especially among those prowling and preying. The wrath of God was exasperating the ferocious nature, chastising and humiliating his people. . . . "They will growl over it on that day, like the growling of the sea." And this part pertains to the ferocity of the Babylonian nation. He compared them in the preceding verse to the growlings of lions. But to express that this is about the whole entire army joined together in the attack and roar of rushing and invading, he compares it to a sea that is not quiet and peaceful but agitated by a serious storm, and with a horrible sound of gales, it is like it is roaring. So he says, "and it will growl." That is, that nation over them (understand the people of God), in that day, namely, of vengeance and judgment, will be like the growling of the sea. Commentary on Isaiah 5:29-30.[22]

Hear and See the Devastation. Johannes Oecolampadius: "And we may look to the land." You have heard how ferocious are the coming

[19]Pellikan, *Commentaria Bibliorum*, 3:3r.
[20]Musculus, *In Esaiam*, 142-43.
[21]Bullinger, *Isaias*, 30v-31r.
[22]Musculus, *In Esaiam*, 144.

conquerors; hear also how miserable the conquered will be. For they could truly say, "Woe to the conquered." They will not dare look to the heavens for fear of judgment. One will be weary even to consider the dome of the sky because of despair. They will look to the land where they wanted to hide themselves. They will seek help on every side, and nothing but darkness will be there. By darkness, understand tribulation. Even if one looks to the sky, the moon and the light and the stars themselves will be wrapped in darkness. The light, that is, the sun. He wishes to say that the moon has become dark, and the light, that is, the sun, has become dark, since it should be pouring out its rays on you and gladden you. Others explain it as its breadth or its drops. Commentary on Isaiah 5:29-30.[23]

[23]Oecolampadius, *In Iesaiam*, 54v.

Applying the Word. Rudolf Gwalther: But what is as common today as what the prophet charges against the people in his time? Many glory in the profession of evangelical doctrine. They have translated the books of the Bible into all kinds of languages. Many read these in private, and they publicly hear sermons drawn from them. But most do not conform their life and habits to the rule of this doctrine, since they think it does not pertain to them. And if any of the ministers of the word exhort them a little more freely and with more vigor, they expressly reject doing what the gospel demands with no less impudence than those who formerly said to Jeremiah, "The word of the Lord that you have spoken to us in the name of the Lord, we do not accept, but we will do whatever comes out of our mouth." Sermons on Isaiah 5:29-30.[24]

[24]Gwalther, *Isaias*, 40v; citing Jer 44:16-17.

6:1-13 THE CALLING OF ISAIAH

6 In the year that King Uzziah died I saw the Lord sitting upon a throne, high and lifted up; and the train[a] of his robe filled the temple. 2 Above him stood the seraphim. Each had six wings: with two he covered his face, and with two he covered his feet, and with two he flew. 3 And one called to another and said:

“Holy, holy, holy is the LORD of hosts;
the whole earth is full of his glory!”[b]

4 And the foundations of the thresholds shook at the voice of him who called, and the house was filled with smoke. 5 And I said: “Woe is me! For I am lost; for I am a man of unclean lips, and I dwell in the midst of a people of unclean lips; for my eyes have seen the King, the LORD of hosts!”

6 Then one of the seraphim flew to me, having in his hand a burning coal that he had taken with tongs from the altar. 7 And he touched my mouth and said: “Behold, this has touched your lips; your guilt is taken away, and your sin atoned for.”

8 And I heard the voice of the Lord saying, “Whom shall I send, and who will go for us?” Then I said, “Here I am! Send me.” 9 And he said, “Go, and say to this people:

“‘Keep on hearing,[c] but do not understand;
keep on seeing,[d] but do not perceive.’

10 Make the heart of this people dull,[e]
and their ears heavy,
and blind their eyes;

lest they see with their eyes,
and hear with their ears,

and understand with their hearts,
and turn and be healed.”

11 Then I said, “How long, O Lord?”

And he said:

“Until cities lie waste
without inhabitant,

and houses without people,
and the land is a desolate waste,

12 and the LORD removes people far away,
and the forsaken places are many in the midst of the land.

13 And though a tenth remain in it,
it will be burned[f] again,

like a terebinth or an oak,
whose stump remains
when it is felled.”

The holy seed[g] is its stump.

a Or *hem* b Or *may his glory fill the whole earth* c Or *Hear indeed* d Or *see indeed* e Hebrew *fat* f Or *purged* g Or *offspring*

OVERVIEW: The prophetic vision that leads to the calling of Isaiah offered many opportunities for Reformation interpreters to emphasize key themes and address potential problems. Several interpreters address how Isaiah could see the Lord when other passages of Scripture say that no one can see the Lord. Many also connect the New Testament passages to maintain that Isaiah saw the glory of Christ in this vision. Several articulate the doctrine of the Trinity based on the plural wording in God's question. The details of the vision receive differing levels of attention, with some commentators providing allegories of different behaviors that relate to the fringe of God's robe and other symbols. The calling and commissioning of Isaiah, and the expected responses to his ministry, enable these theologians to apply the requirements of the prophetic office to the ministers of their day.

The Book of Jotham. Johannes Oecolampadius: This is the second book, or more accurately booklet. For Uzziah died, and after him Jotham reigned, a sufficiently good king, although he cannot be compared with the best. For he neither removed the high places nor called back the people from idolatry, although he did what was pleasing before the Lord. And indeed he reigned sixteen years. But Isaiah narrates only one vision, which he saw under him, namely, what we explain in this chapter and book. Commentary on Isaiah 6:1.[1]

6:1-2 *Isaiah Sees the Lord in His Glory*

The Prophet Encouraged with a New Vision. John Calvin: This is usually the beginning of the sixth chapter; but some think that it is the beginning of the book itself and that in collecting the prophecies of Isaiah an error was committed. The reason that they assign is that the prophet here declines the office of a teacher, which he would not have refused if he had already discharged it; that he appears to be a mere novice as yet unacquainted with his calling; and besides, that he declares that he has now seen the Lord and that he has not seen him before. But such arguments I consider, as I have already noticed, to be too feeble and unsatisfactory; and I reply that it ought not to be thought strange that he was so completely overpowered by this extraordinary vision as to forget that he was a prophet. For there was no feeling in him that was not overpowered by the presence of God, so that, like one who had lost his senses, he willingly plunged himself in darkness, or rather, like one who despaired of life, he of his own accord chose to die. . . . But why was this vision not shown to him at the beginning? I answer, it was necessary in regard to the time, that he might be more and more confirmed in the discharge of his office. We have an instance of this in the apostles themselves; for at first they were sent out with an injunction not to pass beyond the limits of Judea, but after Christ had risen, he again set them apart in a new and solemn manner, breathed on them, bidding them receive the Holy Ghost, and not only so but, sending his Spirit from heaven in the forms of tongues of fire, invested them with extraordinary power. Thus, on account of the various changes of times and of kings, it was necessary that Isaiah should be encouraged and again attested by a new vision; that he might be excited to perseverance and might afterward proceed with greater cheerfulness in his course; and also that the Jews might perceive his ministry to be supported by heavenly authority.

This appears to me to be a sufficient reason why this vision was not exhibited to him at the very beginning but after he had for some time discharged the office of a teacher. That this was not the beginning of the prophecy is evident enough from the consideration that the preface, which we have already examined, is much better adapted for the commencement and more appropriate than what is contained in this chapter. And every approach having been shut up by the hardhearted obstinacy of the people, it was proper that he should burst forth in this vehement manner. Besides, it is probable that he had long performed the office of a teacher under King Uzziah, who, I think, was dead before this prediction was published. In short, the prophet means that it was not until he had commenced his course that God appeared to him. . . . But so that we do not suppose that the prophet contrived the manner in which he would depict God, we ought to know that he faithfully describes the very form in which God was represented and exhibited to him. It may be questioned whether the prophet was brought into the temple or saw this vision while he was asleep. Though many things are frequently adduced on both sides, which are fitted to leave the matter in doubt, yet it may be conjectured with some probability that even if he had not been within the temple, this vision might have been presented to him, either in his own house or on a field, in the

[1]Oecolampadius, *In Iesaiam*, 55r.

same manner as to other prophets. Commentary on Isaiah 6:1.[2]

The Heavenly King Never Dies. Wolfgang Musculus: See how this vision corresponds to that year in which King Uzziah died, and his throne was vacated. Kings die, and they vacate their thrones when they die. But the heavenly king does not die, nor ever leave his throne empty. But since he is immortal, he reigns eternally. This is why, when an earthly king dies, we are not deprived of a royal office but have a king in heaven, ceaselessly seated on his throne and reigning with justice and righteousness. But the majesty of this is not evident except to faithful and godly people. Commentary on Isaiah 6:1.[3]

The Beginning of the Olympics. Viktorin Strigel: In [Jotham's] second year, the Greek Olympic Games began, as is preserved in the chronicle of Africanus, which exists in the tenth book of *Preparation for the Gospel* by Eusebius, "Before the beginning of the Olympiad, nothing recounted in the Greek histories is certain, but everything is full of confusion and discrepancy."† . . . This chronicle of Africanus ought to be diligently considered so that we may know that the history and doctrine of the church is much older than Greek things. . . . But just as in the second year of Jotham the Greek Olympic Games began, so in the first year when Ahaz was reigning, the seventh Olympic Games were held, when Romulus and Remus began to build Rome. Oration on the Prophet Isaiah.[4]

Isaiah, Mighty Seer, in Days of Old. Martin Luther:

Isaiah, mighty seer, in days of old,
the Lord of all, in Spirit, did behold.
High on a lofty throne, in splendor bright,
with flowing train that filled the temple quite.
Above the throne were stately seraphim,
six wings had they, these messengers of him.
With twain they veiled their faces, as was meet;
with twain in reverent awe they hid their feet,
And with the other twain aloft they soared.
One to the other called and praised the Lord:
"Holy is God, the Lord of Sabaoth!
Holy is God, the Lord of Sabaoth!
Holy is God, the Lord of Sabaoth!
Behold, His glory fills all the earth!"

The beams and lintels trembled at the cry,
and clouds of smoke enwrapped the throne on high.
To Isaiah the Prophet It Happened.[5]

Seeing the Lord with the Eyes of the Mind. Wolfgang Musculus: He did not see him with physical eyes but in a vision of the mind—not in the form of his essence but an assumed appearance, in the way that he appeared to the fathers in the Old Testament. It should not be inquired more curiously whether this vision of the prophet happened when he was awake or sleeping. As he speaks simply, so we simply believe his speaking, as long as we do not insult the divine Majesty. A vision of his essence happens to no one in this life. For he said, "No one shall see me and live." . . . "No one has ever seen God." . . . Perhaps it could be asked how above in verse 1 we explain that "I saw the Lord" is a vision of the mind, not a vision of the eyes, when here he plainly says, "for my eyes have seen the King, the Lord of hosts." But the matter itself teaches that the vision was not with physical eyes but of the mind. Here what was seen were not objects in the body but in the mind. No one may see God with physical eyes unless one is

[2]CTS 13:198-99* (CO 36:124-25); citing Mt 10:5; Jn 20:21-22; Acts 2:3.

[3]Musculus, *In Esaiam*, 147.

[4]Strigel, *Oratio De Propheta Esaia*, 12, 15. †For this quote, see Eusebius, *Praeparatio Evangelica* [Preparation for the Gospel], trans. E. H. Gifford (Oxford: Oxford University Press, 1903), 10.10.487. Julius Africanus composed a work on universal chronology in the third century. The first Olympic Games have historically been dated to 776 BC, and in an earlier chapter, Eusebius identifies the fiftieth year of Uzziah as the first Olympiad. For an accessible English translation see Eusebius, "Chronicle," translated by Andrew Smith, Attalus: Translations, February 26, 2018, http://www.attalus.org/translate/eusebius5.html, which corresponds to Eusebius, *Chronicon Libri Duo*, ed. Alfred Schoene (Berlin: Weidmannos, 1875), 1:120-122.

[5]Luther, "Jessia, dem Propheten, das gescha (1526)."

covered with an assumed figure. Therefore, what he was saying about his eyes—that he saw the Lord—should be considered in the sense that he was experiencing in that vision. He was thinking he saw the Lord with his eyes when everything was still happening in his mind. Yet there is another opinion of some, who, based on the fact that it says, "for my eyes have seen the King, the Lord of hosts," think that is sufficient to indicate that these displays that he remembers were certain kinds of objects to his physical eyes. However, the prior meaning is more satisfactory to me. Commentary on Isaiah 6:1.[6]

Jesus Adapted the Form to Be Seen. Johannes Oecolampadius: So as he does everywhere, Isaiah cries out that he does not announce his own words, but those of the Lord. In this passage, he testifies that he not only heard but also saw the Lord, and that in his glory; and this was how he was ordained to his office. . . . Indeed, this prophecy is not only internal but also external and is presented to the eyes with certain images. For he saw the Lord in the appearance and state of a king and judge, with seraphim surrounding and praising him.[†] Again, as in the first chapter, I opt to treat the Scriptures simply. For the Lord Jesus, who in the fullness of time was made human for us from a woman, had appeared to the patriarchs and the prophets in a form that was expedient and suitable for them. . . . Likewise, it is most evidently testified . . . where it says, "Isaiah said these things when he saw his glory and spoke about it." There it clearly says the glory of Christ was seen by our prophet. Now, they object that no one has ever seen God and that God dwells in inaccessible light. I gladly accept that, and I even say that is true to the extent that God is not reached with either physical or mental eyes. For an exquisite comprehension of him and a direct recognition has happened to no one yet. And God is seen and God is not seen by creatures as he wants to be seen, but the whole is not seen. . . . God is seen in this, so that you will never stop looking to him. And again, a human did not see the face of God, but saw his backside with physical eyes and mental ones. But God takes on an appearance as fits the prophecy. Commentary on Isaiah 6:1.[7]

Christ Portrayed as the Lord God Almighty. Johannes Brenz: Now at the beginning, the majesty of Christ and his kingdom is depicted in this vision. And it should especially be observed above all that you have in this passage clear and irrefutable testimony to the divinity of Christ. For the Evangelist John clearly says . . . that the prophet saw the glory of Christ in this vision. For in quoting the speech of this chapter, "the heart of this people is blind . . . ," he adds, "Isaiah said these things when he saw his glory" (namely, of Christ, for this is what the sermon was about), and it was said about him. Nothing is more certain than that Isaiah affirms that he saw the true Lord God Sabaoth. That is why when the Evangelist testified that Isaiah saw the glory of Christ, he clearly teaches that Christ is the true Lord God Sabaoth. . . . Indeed, Isaiah did not see the essence of God, which no human on this earth is able to see or recognize, but he recognized the majesty of Christ, who is the true Lord God Sabaoth, revealed in the preaching of the gospel and miracles in the world. Commentary on Isaiah 6:1.[8]

Foreshadowing Christ. Dietrich Schnepff: But I saw Christ the Lord, who at this time took on human flesh, seated before the tribunal in human form, with the highest glory and majesty. That throne indeed on which he was sitting was high and exalted, for he is the King of kings and the Lord of lords, to whom all power in heaven and on earth was given. The Jerusalem temple was the footstool for his feet, to which the train of his royal and lengthy garment was flowing. And indeed, as now the ceremonies foreshadow

[6]Musculus, *In Esaiam*, 146, 153; citing Ex 33:20; Jn 1:18.

[7]Oecolampadius, *In Iesaiam*, 55v-56v; citing Jn 12:41. [†]Oecolampadius refers multiple times to Gregory of Nyssa's explanation of seeing the Lord.

[8]Brenz, *Esaias*, 95; citing Jn 12:40-41.

how he is going to dwell with us in his time, he depicted the conversation, as it were, with obscure lines. And he wants us to pray in this temple with the ark (which we call the footstool). So, when he comes, he will teach there, he will perform miracles, and he will show himself merciful to all the faithful. He will confound the parties of the ungodly Pharisees and scribes, and so rightly use this place for his footstool. Paraphrase of Isaiah 6:1-2.[9]

The Fringe of His Robe Is the Humanity of Christ. Johannes Brenz: The robe of the Lord our God is the humanity that the Son of God alone put on as clothing. And when fringes are added to robes, they are a grace of decoration and splendor. So Isaiah seeing the fringes of God's robe fill the temple signifies that Christ was going to illuminate the Jerusalem temple and that region in which this temple was built with his teaching and miracles after he would take on humanity. Commentary on Isaiah 6:1.[10]

Fringe Is Enough to Heal. Heinrich Bullinger: Truly what we hear about the fringes filling the whole court, palace, or temple is not lacking in mystery. For the Lord abundantly pours out gifts on his subjects. In fact, what is the least and last in God is still enough for all the needs, wishes, and desires of everyone in the whole world to be satisfied. Clearly it has so much power and majesty, whose riches no one has explained and whose minutiae surpasses all the resources or faculties of the world. The hemorrhaging woman in the Gospel thought to herself, "If only I grasp the hem of Christ, I will be cured of this incurable disease of mine." And, of course, she was not healed by the hem of the garment, but at the touch of the hem she was healed by the power of Christ, whose strength is so great that if one could imagine anything small, fine, thin, disregarded, and last, this would still be greater, richer, and stronger than the largest, richest, and most powerful of anything in the world. Sermons on Isaiah 6:1.[11]

Only Seeing God's Backside. John Trapp: Oecolampadius says the sense here is that the least part of the divine majesty is greater than the greatest glory of humankind.[†] ... "He has written upon his robe and on his thigh the name King of Kings and Lord of Lords." Here we can see but his backside, his train and line. It is necessary that we see no more, so we may live. Zeuxis, the famous painter, drew on a tablet a fair temple with the doors open and Venus going in, so that the beholders could see only her back and her train, since he could not depict her fair face and frontside. Exposition on Isaiah 6:2.[12]

Indisputable Words of God. Theodor Bibliander: These sacred Scriptures of the Old and New Testaments are a prophetic word, which we "do well by paying attention to it as a lamp set in a dark place," as Peter says. These are the two seraphim perpetually keeping watch before the throne of the Lord of hosts, touching each other with their wings, and shouting to each other in return. These are the certain and indisputable sayings of God, the library of the Holy Spirit, the medication for the soul, the true horn of plenty, the treasure of the wisdom and knowledge of God, the heavenly garden, the healthy, flowery, and pleasant pastures, the most plentiful flock of Christ. From these alone may they draw what concerns God, eternal salvation, and our duty toward our neighbor. Oration on Isaiah the Prince of Prophets.[13]

Incorporeal Seraphim Described. Johannes Oecolampadius: "And with two they were flying." The Hebrew puts this in the singular and third-person future, as if to say, each one was covering and flying. Faces, feet, and wings are

[9]Schnepff, *In Esaiae*, 106.
[10]Brenz, *Esaias*, 96.

[11]Bullinger, *Isaias*, 32r; citing Mk 5:28.
[12]Trapp, *Commentary or Exposition*, 33*; citing 1 Cor 1:25; Rev 19:16. [†]See Oecolampadius, *In Iesaiam*, 57v.
[13]Bibliander, *Oratio*, 25v; citing 2 Pet 2:9.

attributed to angels, although they are incorporeal. But by the face and eyes we understand the cognitive power; by feet, diligent ministry; and by wings in all directions, eager obedience, in the way that poets attribute this to Mercury. Commentary on Isaiah 6:2.[14]

Covering Their Parts. John Mayer: Chrysostom does not differ from Calvin, except that Calvin understands "their covering their feet" as the inability of people on earth to endure the sight of their glory, while he understands it as their being ashamed that God should see the imperfection of their affections (portrayed by their feet) toward him. And to me this view of Chrysostom seems to be best, because if there were many seraphim around God's throne, as doubtless there were thousands, it cannot be conceived how each one with his two wings should cover his face alike, and with two his feet, unless by covering their own faces his face was hid from them and his feet were also not open to theirs, because theirs were covered. And if "covering" be referred to both this way, none of these allegories are impertinent but may well stand together.

By "covering their feet," the Hebrews used to set forth not properly or specifically the feet but the nether parts, which we are ashamed to let be seen—and for this reason are called *pudenda*. This therefore shows that the very angels, which are so glorious, are not without all blemish before the Most High, or at the least, in humility they acknowledge it. How much more then should the holiest among people? Commentary on Isaiah 6:2.[15]

6:3-7 *Isaiah Experiences the Lord's Holiness*

Seraphim Praising the Trinity. Dietrich Schnepff: With their voices they were crying, "You, Lord Jesus Christ, the only begotten Son of God, who is one with the Father and the Holy Spirit, reign and rule over all with your powerful hand, and because of this, you are called the God of armies. You are holy—in fact, you are truly holiness, righteousness, innocence itself—in that most holy triad. You are going to share your righteousness and holiness with all those who believe. You will plead all those things to the Father for humans who are deprived of the glory of God." Paraphrase of Isaiah 6:3.[16]

Better Proofs for the Trinity. John Calvin: The ancients quoted this passage when they wished to prove that there are three persons in one essence of the Godhead. I do not disagree with their opinion; but if I had to contend with heretics, I would rather choose to employ stronger proofs, for they become more obstinate and assume an air of triumph when inconclusive arguments are brought against them. And they might easily and readily maintain that, in this passage, as in other parts of Scripture, the number three denotes perfection. Although, therefore, I have no doubt that the angels here describe one God in three persons (and indeed, it is impossible to praise God without also uttering the praises of the Father, of the Son, and of the Spirit), yet I think that it would be better to employ more conclusive passages, lest, in proving an article of our faith, we should expose ourselves to the scorn of heretics. Commentary on Isaiah 6:3.[17]

Singing the Holy Prayer. Johannes Oecolampadius: "Holy, holy, holy." That angelic hymn that the Greeks call the *trisagiou* without doubt indicates a trinity of persons and a trinity of the divine nature. The angels see this and offer praise, and seeing they are blessed, in which too we are baptized. . . . Certainly it is fitting that God should be praised at all times. But we sing with the church catholic, "Holy Father, Holy Son, Holy Spirit." One holy Lord Sabaoth, that is, of angel armies. Something is holy when there is no

[14]Oecolampadius, *In Iesaiam*, 57v.
[15]Mayer, *Commentary upon All the Prophets*, 4:41.
[16]Schnepff, *In Esaiae*, 106.
[17]CTS 13:201* (CO 36:129).

blemish and it does not contain anything unsatisfied, unclean, profane, or evil. Those who desire to draw near are sanctified by it such that they do not perish and get stoned with the beasts when they dare to approach the holy mountain. And the Lord commanded us to pray this song when he teaches us the petition, "Hallowed be your name." The angels sing, "Holy"; we who confess that we are sinners pray to be sanctified. Commentary on Isaiah 6:3.[18]

Christians Represent a Holy God. Dirk Philips: Consider and take to heart how holy, how upright and blessed, one must live in this evil world and watch for the return of our Lord Jesus Christ, who has given himself for us since he would deliver us from all unrighteousness and cleanse us himself for a people of his own that is zealous after good works, that is intent on heavenly things, that seeks God's kingdom and his righteousness before all things, and considers how all Christians must lead a holy life, since they boast about the holy God and are called saints after him. The Enchiridion.[19]

Smoke from the Fire of God's Wrath. Rudolf Gwalther: Another is added, "And the house was filled with smoke." Clouds and smoke are symbols of the presence of God. In the pillar of cloud he went before Israel when he led them out of Egypt. And the cloud overshadowed the tabernacle anytime God wanted to do something great. And since here only smoke is mentioned, its nature should be considered. Smoke is a vapor arising from fire, and so it is said in the proverb, "Where there is smoke, there is a flame." The same is harmful to the eyes and hinders sight. Therefore, the wrath of God is signified, which was inflamed because of the stubbornness of the Jews. And this was going to be followed with fatal blindness, which brought destruction to the unfortunate, as we will hear later. And of course, those who turned away from the sun of righteousness and were unwilling to walk in the light of truth deserved to perish in that smoke. Sermons on Isaiah 6:4.[20]

The Sign of Smoke. John Calvin: But it may be asked, "Why did God manifest his presence by this sign rather than by any other?" This question may be answered in two ways. First, it was always the will of God to repress the insolence of people, in pushing their inquiries about his majesty beyond what is proper; for on this point almost all people are too rash and daring. They wish to rise above the clouds and to penetrate into the secrets of God, while they do not see what lies at their feet. Hence arises a labyrinth of errors, and when the minds of people have been entangled in it, they adopt false and pretended modes of worship. For when people allow themselves to adopt any false notions about God, there is nothing that they will not venture to attempt against him. It was not without good reason, therefore, that he made use of smoke in order to remind people of their weakness. And yet he did not intend that they should be blind or stupid, that is, that they should have the stupidity and error that the papists disguise under the name of simplicity; but he forbids us to inquire or search beyond what he has revealed to us in his Word. For, as Augustine says, "That is a learned ignorance."† Whenever, therefore, smoke of this kind is mentioned, let us know that it lays a restraint on us from indulging curiosity in our searching into the purpose of God.

Second, this smoke ought to strike terror, as David says when describing an angry and terrible God that "clouds and thick darkness are all around him." . . . This also corresponds well to the present passage. For he pronounces a dreadful judgment, namely, the blinding of the Jews. Others think that it indicated the burning by which he consumed the temple; but the view that I have given is more probable. Commentary on Isaiah 6:4.[21]

[18]Oecolampadius, *In Iesaiam*, 58r.

[19]CRR 6:403; citing Eph 1:4; 1 Pet 1:16; Titus 2:12; Col 3:2; Mt 6:33; Rom 1:7.

[20]Gwalther, *Isaias*, 44r.

[21]CTS 13:206-7* (CO 36:130); citing Ps 97:2. †Calvin most likely refers to refers to Augustine, *Letter* 130.15 (*NPNF*[1] 1:468).

Clean Lips for Ministers of the Word. Wolfgang Musculus: Now, the lips of a prophet should be sacred to the Lord, and purified like gold seven times, and at the same time burning in the Lord's work. Here he acknowledges that there is great uncleanness in his lips. He does not express how he contracted this and what kind it is. There was no need to express that. This was known to him and the Lord, to whom there is no need for specifying any faults. . . . The ministers of the Word have the finest example here that they should ceaselessly consider. Their lips are sanctified according to the doctrine of truth. The purity of lips should be threefold for the minister of the Word, that is, to teach things that are true and useful, to teach without hypocrisy, without sinister affection, from the heart, only with respect to the divine will, and to not revere the powerful and despise or neglect the common and dejected but, without favoritism and fear, teach what should be taught, rebuking what should be rebuked. This triple purity belongs to the lips of the prophets, apostles, evangelists, and teachers. Commentary on Isaiah 6:5.[22]

Polluted Praise. Johannes Oecolampadius: Behold, as Isaiah saw such great glory of the judge, both to him and to the creatures, he also recognized that the angels themselves do not carry the glory of God, but in covering their faces they acknowledge their uncleanness (if they are compared to God). And nonetheless they are ready to serve us, to sing glory to God, and then by their ministry, the thresholds of the temple that smoke was filling were shaken. Then he could not be pleased with himself but lowered himself below them all and said, "Woe is me." . . . But he wants to say, "Woe is me; while everything is praising God, I am more ruined and more unworthy than one who could or should praise God." For he wants this, what follows, "I have polluted lips," that is, I am too polluted to praise God. . . . And even to speak about God rightly does not lack danger. So he does not say, "Woe is me, because I am silent," but because I am more unworthy than one who is to speak. For the silence of the prophet itself was due to humility, a familiar vice that should be given praise. Commentary on Isaiah 6:5.[23]

No Glory Based on Works. Martin Luther: They cannot and dare not glory before God on account of their works, merits, and sanctity. But they must, if they would know themselves rightly and stand before God, condemn themselves and their manner of life; so that here no saint has ever been able to stand on this foundation, neither in the Old nor in the New Testaments. . . . In like manner the prophet Isaiah, . . . when he stands before God and sees his glory, confesses that he is unclean and must be comforted by an angel that his sins are forgiven him. . . . And Jeremiah, when he prayed before God and gloried in opposing his persecutors . . . : "Lord, you know: That which came out of my lips was before your face." Here he is holy and happy; and yet soon after he turns and says, "Be not a terror unto me; you are my refuge in the day of evil." Likewise, . . . "Oh, Lord, correct me, but with measure," that is, with grace; "not in your anger, lest you bring me to nothing." Where is here the pious and holy person with whom the Lord is never angry? The Sermon of Christ on Truly Good Works.[24]

Isaiah's Fear of Judgment. Matthew Poole: I am a great sinner, in many other ways but particularly by my lips, which being in a special manner consecrated to God by my prophetic office should have been entirely devoted to him. But alas! My speeches, either to God in prayer or from God in preaching or prophesying to the people, have been mixed and defiled with so much irreverence, dullness, distraction of thoughts and affections, carnal fear, and many other infirmities that I dread the thoughts of appearing before the judgment seat

[22]Musculus, *In Esaiam*, 152.

[23]Oecolampadius, *In Iesaiam*, 59r.

[24]Luther, *Sermons* 5:34-35; citing Jer 17:16-17; 10:24.

that I see erected in this place. Annotations on Isaiah 6:5.[25]

The Signs of the Coal. Konrad Pellikan: Indeed, it is of the Lord alone to put up with sins, but the displaying of signs belongs to the ministers of God, through whom the Lord consoles, raises, and comforts his own. The coal, or fire, signifies the zealous speech of the Lord, the fervent desire to bless the faithful, and the word of rebuke to burn up the vices of the nation, which are brought down not by natural strength but by the blessing of the divine office. Of course, the words of God, the illuminating of souls, and the hot charity of faith from the altar of the Lord are received by the Holy Spirit, who gives all things according to his will, but yet not to all. . . . Like a sacrament, the angel, the minister of God, touches the lips of the prophet with a coal, while at the same time the grace of God pardons the sins of the lips, and the divine Spirit saturates the mind to receive the word of the Lord and to preach it magnanimously to kings and nations. Commentary on Isaiah 6:6.[26]

A Visible Sign for Confirmation. John Calvin: We see how God condescends to meet the weakness of human sense. He puts the tongs into the hand of a seraph, that by means of it he may take a coal from the altar and apply it to the prophet's mouth. This was, no doubt, done in a vision. But by the aid of the outward sign God assisted the prophet's understanding. There is no reason to believe that the coal possessed any virtue, as superstitious persons imagine that in the magical arts there is some hidden power. Nothing of this sort is to be found here; for it is God alone who can cleanse our pollution, in whatever part it exists.

Here the angel administered the cleansing but was not the author of it; so that we must not ascribe to another what belongs to God alone. This is expressly stated by the angel himself, who claims nothing as his own but, bringing forward the sacred pledge that he had received from God, laid it as a sacrament on the lips of the prophet. It is not as if he could not be cleansed without the coal but because the visible sign was useful for the confirmation and proof of the fact. And such is the use of sacraments, to strengthen us in proportion to our ignorance; for we are not angels, which can behold the mysteries of God without any assistance, and therefore he raises us to himself by gradual advances. Commentary on Isaiah 6:7.[27]

Twofold Propitiation. Johannes Oecolampadius: This power is so great that your sins are erased and you are made clean from the sins that you have contracted from the contagion of others and from the iniquity of believing too little in God. Since he had said that sin was twofold, so also he says that the propitiation is twofold. For the word of God cleanses us from all sins by faith. Commentary on Isaiah 6:7.[28]

6:8-13 *Isaiah Sent by the Lord*

Called by God. Menno Simons: Yes, it was with this sending and calling that all the prophets, apostles, and servants of God came forth. They did not assume the honor to themselves, as do the preachers of this world; but like Aaron, they were called by God or, as has been said, by the spotless church. They were brought by the Spirit of God, with pious hearts, into his service; they had always esteemed themselves unfit to serve the people of God or stand forth in such a high and responsible station. . . . Isaiah was confounded because he was to preach the word of the Lord. He lamented that he was of unclean lips until the angel purged them with a coal from off the holy altar. . . . All who are not sent by God, nor by an irreproachable Christian church that conforms to the regulations of Christ and the apostles, are not called, as was said above. Such are not called by the Holy Ghost; by

[25]Poole, *Annotations*, 338*.
[26]Pellikan, *Commentaria Bibliorum*, 3:9r.
[27]CTS 13:210* (CO 36:132-33).
[28]Oecolampadius, *In Iesaiam*, 60v.

the pure, unfeigned love of God and their brethren; and with a correct knowledge and zeal for the divine word. But they enter on it with a temporal, sensual life, seeking human favor, praise, money, and profit. They will never gather fruit in the vineyard of the Lord, though they may be learned in language, eloquent and esteemed as great and excellent men. But all that they attempt is lost labor. They will rise too early or go out too late; their calling is powerless, their service is vain, their labor without fruit; yes, it is nothing but sowing by the way and beating against the wind; for no one can serve in this high and holy office comformably to God's will except those whom the Lord of the vineyard has made worthy and fit by the spirit of his grace. Sending Preachers.[29]

Cleansing Before Ministering. Adam Sasbout: "Behold I, send me." Now, that the prophet offers himself further for service is not out of rashness or arrogance but out of zeal and love. Gregory . . . also diligently observed that the prophet did not offer himself to the ministry before he had his lips cleansed with the coal from the altar.[†] From this fact we are taught that we should not dare to undertake sacred ministries, such as the office of preaching and the like, unless we have previously been cleansed. And since it is difficult to recognize when we are cleansed, therefore we decline these more thoughtfully. For the prophet did not dare to cry out with the seraphim, "Holy, holy, holy," because of his polluted lips. But when he sensed that he was cleansed, he even offered himself to preach. Augustine . . . treats this question of whether anyone with a free conscience could undertake such an office and ends that we should not undertake it unless necessity prevails.[†] Commentary on Isaiah 6:8.[30]

The Prophet as Learner First. Johannes Oecolampadius: Pay attention here to your office, you who serve as a preacher. For it is necessary that you—with Isaiah—show yourself first as a learner, then a teacher, and that you be among those who have seen God, which Scripture calls *theodidaktous* [taught by God]. Commentary on Isaiah 6.[31]

The Plurality of Persons. Konrad Pellikan: "Who will go for us?" This familiar expression about God is not without reason to have a plural number. It is like at the institution of the creation of humanity, where the divine plurality was revealed, and like in the name *ʾĕlōhîm*,[†] and does not come from human opinion. Except that the divine plurality applies to only one topic, that is, the persons (for no other term was more suitable to the saints). It does not apply to his deity or nature. Commentary on Isaiah 6:8.[32]

Unity and Distinction in God. Heinrich Bullinger: Now, it should be observed presently that the unity of God in his essence and the distinction of persons is affirmed. For he says, "Whom shall I send?" and then, "But who will go for us?" With these words, the persons are identified, as the unity is signified by the previous words. In addition, we hear clearly in this passage that God is seen by the prophet, but according to John 12 it is said about the Son, and in Acts 28 about the Holy Spirit. Sermons on Isaiah 6:8.[33]

Isaiah's Response to the Triune Voice. English Annotations: The voice of God the Father, speaking to the Son, . . . and the Holy Ghost [see similarly in Gen 1, 3, and 11]. "Here am I" in Hebrew is "Behold me," or "Lo, I." . . . "Send me." His readiness in offering himself to be employed by God, contrary to that backwardness of some others. Annotations on Isaiah 6:8.[34]

[29]Simons, *Complete Works* 1:55; also citing Moses, Jeremiah, Peter, Paul, and Matthias as examples.

[30]Sasbout, *In Esaiam*, 56-57. [†]See Gregory, "The Book of Pastoral Rule," *NPNF*[2] 12:586; Augustine, *NPNF*[1] 2:413-14.

[31]Oecolampadius, *In Iesaiam*, 56v.

[32]Pellikan, *Commentaria Bibliorum* 3:9r. [†]The Hebrew term *elohim* can refer to "gods" in the plural or "God" in the singular.

[33]Bullinger, *Isaias*, 34v; citing Jn 12; Acts 28.

[34]Downame, ed., *English Annotations*, 5v*; citing Jn 12:41; Acts 26:25; Gen 1:26; 3:22; 11:7; 22:1; Is 58:9; Ex 3:11; 4:10; Jer 1:6.

This People Is Not My People. Wolfgang Musculus: "Say to this people," it says. He does not say, "Say to *my* people," but emphatically, "Say to *this* people." These words breathe anger and bring together the vision and the command. The Lord was incensed with his people and was thinking about the retribution of the reprobate. This is why he speaks about them as if they were foreign when he says, "Say to this people." They had alienated themselves from him, and that is why they are deservedly considered to be strangers. Commentary on Isaiah 6:9.[35]

The Order of Obtaining Salvation. Wolfgang Musculus: The order of obtaining salvation is beautifully expressed. When the word of the Lord is sent to sinners, it is required that first they have ears to hear and eyes to see. So Christ cried out, "Let the one who has ears to hear, hear." Then it is necessary that what is heard and seen, they understand in their heart. And the understanding of the heart is faith. The one who believes understands. Unless you believed, says the prophet, you will not understand. Third, conversion is required, that is, to the Lord. This is the repentance that Christ requires when he says, "Repent and believe the gospel." Healing follows conversion. Healing is through the forgiveness of sins, and liberation from the bondage of sin and even death. Commentary on Isaiah 6:9-10.[36]

Seeing, Hearing, and Understanding. Johannes Oecolampadius: So we will also explain this simply. But how God wills sin and has hate for it at the same time, the smallness of our intellect cannot comprehend. It is certain that he condemns and blinds no one apart from his righteousness and saves no one without mercy. We are convinced that we are inexcusably evil; God appears remarkably just. For to hear what is to be heard and to see what is to be seen and to have an understanding heart does not happen without divine kindness. But meanwhile, to want to be ignorant, and to be unwilling to understand, and to be envious of one's own salvation, how does that not lack blame? And there are three things here by which we are brought to knowledge: sight, by which the visible works and miracles of God are displayed to us; ears that are given to hear the word of God; and finally the heart, so that the light of nature and conscience may not be extinguished. All these things do not benefit the ungodly, for they resist the Holy Spirit, as we have said. And as long as they resist believing, they cannot be saved, and by resisting and despising such kindness they deserve to be aggravated by such sins. Hence John says, "They could not believe." Commentary on Isaiah 6:9-10.[37]

Hardness Against Christ's Ministry. Martin Luther: We do not here wish anxiously to torture ourselves regarding the secret will of God but only to set forth those matters concerning the mood of God and of his preachers. For God is justly angry with the stubborn who please themselves and have no desire to learn to know themselves and deny themselves. It is to them that this must be said with displeasure, "Hear and hear, but do not understand . . . ," and they must at last be abandoned. The prophet's words, "Make the heart fat, heavy, shut . . . ," mean that by his preaching the prophet would insult them and inflame them to greater hardness. The Evangelists cite this passage in various ways. One cites it in the indicative, another in the imperative; one in the past tense, another in the future; but it does not make any difference. These words can still be explained in an impersonal way, and the meaning briefly is this, that there exists a righteousness different from that of which the Jews boasted, that is to say, not an external but an internal one. But that the Jews would not hear this shows that this is the time when Christ preached and also performed many miracles. The words and deeds of Christ were against the Jews, and they were so embittered

[35]Musculus, *In Esaiam*, 157.
[36]Musculus, *In Esaiam*, 159; citing Mt 1:15; Mk 4:9.
[37]Oecolampadius, *In Iesaiam*, 62v; citing Jn 12:39.

against him that they would not have received him, even if he had created a new heaven and a new earth, simply because he condemned their works. Lectures on Isaiah 6:9-10.[38]

Little Effect from Faithful Teaching. John Calvin: This shows still more clearly how necessary the vision was, that Isaiah might not all at once fail in his course. It was a grievous stumbling block that he must endure such obstinacy and rebellion in the people of God, and that not only for a year or two but for more than sixty years. On this account he needed to be fortified, that he might be like a brazen wall against such stubbornness. The Lord therefore merely forewarns Isaiah that he will have to do with obstinate people, on whom he will produce little effect, but that so unusual an occurrence must not lead him to take offense and lose courage or yield to the rebellion of people. Rather, he must proceed with unshaken firmness and rise superior to temptations of this nature. For God gives him due warning beforehand as to the result, as if he had said, "You will indeed teach without any good effect; but do not regret your teaching, for I enjoin it on you; and do not refrain from teaching, because it yields no advantage; only obey me, and leave to my disposal all the consequences of your labors. I give you all this information in good time, that the event may not terrify you, as if it had been strange and unexpected." Besides, he is commanded openly to reprove their blind obstinacy, as if he purposely taunted them. . . .

This contains a most useful doctrine, which will be of perpetual use in the church of God; for all who shall labor faithfully in the ministry of the Word will be laid under the necessity of meeting with the same result. We, too, have experienced it more than we could have wished; but it has been shared by all the servants of Christ, and therefore we ought to endure it with greater patience, though it is a very grievous stumbling block to those who serve God with a pure conscience. Not only does it give great offense, but Satan powerfully excites his followers to raise a dislike of instruction on the pretense of its being not merely useless but even injurious, that it renders people more obstinate and leads to their destruction. At the present day, those who have no other reproach to bring against the doctrine of the gospel maintain that the only effect produced by the preaching of it has been that the world has become worse.

But whatever may be the result, still God assures us that our services are acceptable to him, because we obey his command; and although our labor appear to be fruitless, and people rush forward to their destruction and become more rebellious, we must continue; for we do nothing at our own suggestion and ought to be satisfied with having the approval of God. We ought indeed to be deeply grieved when success does not accompany our efforts; and we ought to pray to God to give efficacy to his Word. A part of the blame we ought even to lay on ourselves, when the fruits are so scanty; and yet we must not abandon our office or throw away our weapons. The truth must always be heard from our lips, even though there be no ears to receive it and though the world have neither sight nor feeling; for it is enough for us that we labor faithfully for the glory of God and that our services are acceptable to him, and the sound of our voice is not ineffectual when it renders the world without excuse. Commentary on Isaiah 6:9-10.[39]

Truth to Be Spread. Katharina Schütz Zell: For they have spread such lies in all the land! So to be fair, the truth also ought to be spread in every land to disgrace them so that their judgment may therefore be the more heavy and they may become the more hardened. Christ says, "If I had not come and spoken with them, they would have had no sin. But now they have no excuse." And the prophet Isaiah says . . . , "Close your eyes and stop up your ears and blind your heart, that you may not see with the eyes nor hear

[38]LW 16:74-75 (WA 31.2:52).

[39]CTS 13:214-15* (CO 36:135-36).

with the ears, nor understand with the heart, and come that I should make you whole." And God says to Pharaoh, "Even for this have I raised you up, because I want to show my might in you." Apologia for Master Matthew Zell, Her Husband.[40]

The Exile to Babylon Fulfills These Predictions. Heinrich Bullinger: But if any of those surviving from the extreme calamities remain, they will be carried off into captivity, and indeed they will be deported far away into the most remote land, to the nations whose language the captives do not understand. Nor will captivity be dissolved easily. For there will be great and lasting desolation. And this is what other prophets also predicted was going to happen. Further, if you look at the histories of the Jewish people, a remarkable light will arise for us. In fact, Tiglath-pileser, the king of Assyria, at the beginning of the war he inflicted on the ten tribes, also devastated the cities of Galilee in a horrible manner, partly by killing the inhabitants and partly by carrying them off to the East. . . . Then Nebuchadnezzar senior, the father of the great Nebuchadnezzar, carried off Manasseh into captivity and also defeated and devasted Judah. . . . All Judah, along with the city of Jerusalem, was devastated in a miserable way by the junior Nebuchadnezzar. The kings Joachim, Jeconiah, and Zedekiah were carried off into exile, with more groups of people from every rank. The city of Jerusalem was burned, and the land lay devastated and unkempt. What here is predicted by the prophet is fulfilled to the word. But all of those things were most fully completed not many years after the ascension of the Lord into heaven. Sermons on Isaiah 6:11-13.[41]

Foreshadowing the Destruction by Rome. Martin Borrhaus: For if you consider the Babylonian exile, there is discerned a certain shadow of the devastation and exile that is announced here before the ten tribes are carried away to the Medes. But if you look at the later times when the Messiah is presented and rejected, it is also truly predicted here what fully corresponds to the Israelites falling by the Roman destroyer.

"And what is abandoned will be increased." The Hebrew has, "There will be vast desolation in the midst of the land." It will be deserted from people, partly massacred by the sword, partly destroyed by famine, partly carried into exile. This desolation in it is still not to be viewed without mystical reasoning. For just as the mystical Jerusalem, the mystical temple, and the mystical land is desolated and mystical Israel is sent into exile, so also in the other Jerusalem (which is the church of the elect), in the other temple (which we are, miserably profaned by the antichrist), and in the other inheritance, the kingdom of God, one may see its desolation and devastation. But we will address this more in its place. . . . Again, it signifies that the land is going to be ravaged. For what before was devastated by the Assyrians he prophesies will happen again by the Babylonians when the temple and Jerusalem is burned and the people carried off into exile, and in the later times by the Romans, with a remnant preserved. Oracles in Isaiah on 6:11-12.[42]

The Lord Sends Them to Captivity. Wolfgang Musculus: "And the Lord has removed people. . . ." He speaks of the captivity of those who were to be carried off to Babylon. It does not simply say, "And he thrust out," but, "And he removed," to suggest that they would be carried away into a distant land, far from this land that they had received from him and inhabited by the ungrateful and rebellious. Nor does it say, "They were removed," but, "And the Lord removed people." He forewarns the future defeat, devastation, desolation, and captivity that will be the work of

[40]Zell, *Katharina Schütz Zell, Church Mother*, 68; citing Jn 15:22; Is 6:10; Ex 9:16.
[41]Bullinger, *Isaias*, 36r; citing 2 Kings 15; 2 Chron 33.
[42]Borrhaus, *In Iesaiae Prophetae Oracula*, 86-87.

divine vengeance. Commentary on Isaiah 6:12-13.[43]

Ten Kings Until the Exile. Johannes Oecolampadius: "And still ten in it." The Hebrews explain that there will still be ten kings until the destruction of Jerusalem by the Babylonians, namely, Jotham, Ahaz, Hezekiah, Manasseh, Amon, Josiah, Jehoahaz, Jehoiachin, Jehoiakim, and Zedekiah, after whom the land was made desolate. Commentary on Isaiah 6:13.[44]

The Holy Seed. John Calvin: He shows what is that substance, that it consists of a small number of the godly, whom he calls "the holy seed." For he means the elect, who would be preserved by the free mercy of God and thus would survive the captivity. That banishment might be regarded as a cleansing of the church, by which the Lord took away the ungodly. And when they had been cut off, he gathered a people, small in number but truly consecrated to himself. Some commentators consider this phrase to refer to Christ, but that interpretation seems too stretched, and it will be more consistent to apply it to all the godly, for the holy seed is the substance of the church. Commentary on Isaiah 6:13.[45]

A Tenth Return like the Healed Lepers. Wolfgang Musculus: The Lord shares his intention in this verse to limit the future defeat and devastation, with a remnant of the godly remaining. "Until," it says, "there is still a tenth in it," that is, the land, "and it is converted."[†] He specified a certain number for an uncertain one. He signifies that a small number of the godly are going to survive with respect to those who were going to perish. He says that they are going to return to him when it is said, "and is converted." This passage reminds that few are chosen, even among those counted in the church and the people of God. And at the time of Christ, the same was shown with the number of ten lepers, when only one of the ten who were healed returned and gave glory to the Lord and Savior. Commentary on Isaiah 6:11-13.[46]

[43]Musculus, *In Esaiam*, 160.

[44]Oecolampadius, *In Iesaiam*, 63r.

[45]CTS 13:225 (CO 36:142).

[46]Musculus, *In Esaiam*, 160. [†]The Vulgate of Is 6:13 begins, "Et adhuc in ea decimatio, et convertetur [And until a tenth are in it, and it is converted]."

7:1-25 THE SIGN OF IMMANUEL

7 In the days of Ahaz the son of Jotham, son of Uzziah, king of Judah, Rezin the king of Syria and Pekah the son of Remaliah the king of Israel came up to Jerusalem to wage war against it, but could not yet mount an attack against it. 2When the house of David was told, "Syria is in league with[a] Ephraim," the heart of Ahaz[b] and the heart of his people shook as the trees of the forest shake before the wind.

3And the LORD said to Isaiah, "Go out to meet Ahaz, you and Shear-jashub[c] your son, at the end of the conduit of the upper pool on the highway to the Washer's Field. 4And say to him, 'Be careful, be quiet, do not fear, and do not let your heart be faint because of these two smoldering stumps of firebrands, at the fierce anger of Rezin and Syria and the son of Remaliah. 5Because Syria, with Ephraim and the son of Remaliah, has devised evil against you, saying, 6"Let us go up against Judah and terrify it, and let us conquer it[d] for ourselves, and set up the son of Tabeel as king in the midst of it," 7thus says the Lord GOD:

"'It shall not stand,
and it shall not come to pass.

8For the head of Syria is Damascus,
and the head of Damascus is Rezin.

And within sixty-five years
Ephraim will be shattered from being a people.

9And the head of Ephraim is Samaria,
and the head of Samaria is the son of
Remaliah.

If you[e] are not firm in faith,
you will not be firm at all.'"

10Again the LORD spoke to Ahaz: 11"Ask a sign of the LORD your[f] God; let it be deep as Sheol or high as heaven." 12But Ahaz said, "I will not ask, and I will not put the LORD to the test." 13And he[g] said, "Hear then, O house of David! Is it too little for you to weary men, that you weary my God also? 14Therefore the Lord himself will give you a sign. Behold, the virgin shall conceive and bear a son, and shall call his name Immanuel.[h] 15He shall eat curds and honey when he knows how to refuse the evil and choose the good. 16For before the boy knows how to refuse the evil and choose the good, the land whose two kings you dread will be deserted. 17The LORD will bring upon you and upon your people and upon your father's house such days as have not come since the day that Ephraim departed from Judah—the king of Assyria!"

18In that day the LORD will whistle for the fly that is at the end of the streams of Egypt, and for the bee that is in the land of Assyria. 19And they will all come and settle in the steep ravines, and in the clefts of the rocks, and on all the thornbushes, and on all the pastures.[i]

20In that day the Lord will shave with a razor that is hired beyond the River[j]—with the king of Assyria—the head and the hair of the feet, and it will sweep away the beard also.

21In that day a man will keep alive a young cow and two sheep, 22and because of the abundance of milk that they give, he will eat curds, for everyone who is left in the land will eat curds and honey.

23In that day every place where there used to be a thousand vines, worth a thousand shekels[k] of silver, will become briers and thorns. 24With bow and arrows a man will come there, for all the land will be briers and thorns. 25And as for all the hills that used to be hoed with a hoe, you will not come there for fear of briers and thorns, but they will become a place where cattle are let loose and where sheep tread.

a Hebrew *Syria has rested upon* **b** Hebrew *his heart* **c** *Shear-jashub* means *A remnant shall return* **d** Hebrew *let us split it open* **e** The Hebrew for *you* is plural in verses 9, 13, 14 **f** The Hebrew for *you* and *your* is singular in verses 11, 16, 17 **g** That is, Isaiah **h** *Immanuel* means *God is with us* **i** Or *watering holes*, or *brambles* **j** That is, the Euphrates **k** A *shekel* was about 2/5 ounce or 11 grams

Overview: The most familiar part of this passage is the prophecy about the young woman who will give birth to a child to be named Immanuel. Reformation commentators not only deal with questions about the meaning of the words and names of the children mentioned but also seem compelled to address how Isaiah's having a wife and son does not make him less virtuous. The comments on this passage also give evidence of the degree to which several interpreters went to calculate how the length of the kings' reigns added up to fit with Isaiah's statement that Ephraim would not exist within sixty-five years. The wickedness of King Ahaz as demonstrated by his hypocrisy and false humility gets particular attention because of how they see similar attitudes in their own day. The final part of the chapter portrays the consequences that will happen when the Lord brings Assyria against his people.

Setting of the Prophecy. Wolfgang Musculus: Two kings ascended against Ahaz, the ungodly king of Judah who walked in the ways of the kings of Israel and the nations. The first was Rezin of Syria and the second was Pekah of Israel. And they struck Judah with a great blow, so that the king of Israel slaughtered 120,000 men and carried off 200,000 women and infants to Samaria, along with a great plunder. This was the first war those two kings brought against Ahaz. . . . This had begun at the time of the death of Jotham, the father of Ahaz. . . . The seer does not go back to that in the present chapter. Later, they ascended a second time. . . . What is described here by the prophet refers to that, namely that the Lord refused to deliver Judah into the hands of those two kings, and that was the reason he sent Isaiah to King Ahaz for his grace to comfort him. The sign of Immanuel, the one to be born from a maiden, is added to it. And those things that would later happen under King Hezekiah are predicted. Commentary on Isaiah 7.[1]

Ahaz Unlike His Ancestors. Heinrich Bullinger: For the sacred history brings the greatest light to the reading of the prophets. Without it, the reading of the prophets would be completely blind. Therefore, Ahaz degenerated thoroughly from religion and from the customs of the fathers and his ancestors Jotham and Uzziah, and especially the godliness of David. For he did not walk, as Scripture says, in the law of the Lord, but in the ways and ungodliness of the kings of Israel. Indeed, he built up altars, shrines, and idols, and sacrificed to foreign gods, entirely filling the places of the kingdom with superstitions and idol mania. Sermons on Isaiah 7.[2]

7:1-9 *A Prophecy for Ahaz About the Defeat of Kings*

Not Able to Win because God Ordains. Wolfgang Musculus: But again here it is fulfilled, "A person proposes, God ordains." They were kings, but at the same time they were also humans. They had indeed been victors, but victory was not in their hand. Those strong and victorious ones attacked a weakened kingdom. But it is not the weakness of the inferior part that is the reason why it is defeated and oppressed, nor does the strength and multitude of the powerful bring success in victory, but these are completely situated in the hand of the Lord of armies. When he wanted it, Judah was conquered while its entire strength still existed. On the other hand, when he did not want them to be completely crushed, it could not be accomplished, even though they were weakened. Because it had to happen, not because the warring and once-victorious kings were striving, but because the Lord willed it. . . . To this pertains what he says, "And the house of David was told," that is, King Ahaz, who was of the house of David. And when it says, "he led Syria," that is, the king of Syria. And Ephraim is namely the king of the ten tribes of Israel, which was called Ephraim because the seat

[1] Musculus, *In Esaiam*, 161; citing 2 Chron 28; 2 Kings 15–16.

[2] Bullinger, *Isaias*, 37v.

of the kingdom was in that tribe. The sense is that it was reported to King Ahaz that Rezin, king of Syria, had led his forces to Pekah, king of Israel, and these two were ascending against him with combined strength. . . . "And the Lord said to Isaiah." Consequently, it was already explained by whom it stood that the two kings of Syria and Israel could not plunder Jerusalem. The reason for this is attributed to the Lord, because he rendered their decision void and showed that to the king through the prophet Isaiah. Commentary on Isaiah 7:1-3.[3]

The History of Kings First. Martin Luther: To understand the prophet, one must first of all meditate well on the histories. Jotham was godly; Ahaz, his son, was the most ungodly of all. Under Jotham, Isaiah was silent awhile. He began to prophesy again under Ahaz, who instituted many kinds of idolatry and with a pursuit of piety, because he was pressed all around with the worst kind of evils, which he wanted to oppose. Let him be an example to all people in the world so that they may see what faith in God can accomplish, and on the contrary how works themselves avail nothing before him, if one has confidence in them. Ahaz certainly did not adore trees but a divinity, only it was not the right worship. Idolatry is to believe in anything other than God alone. The Christian religion is to believe in the mercy and goodness of God on account of Christ. This is pure and simple; everything else is idolatry, even if it uses the name of the true God as a pretext. There are as many idols as there are sects. Because of the many new installations for the worship of God, Ahaz was proclaimed as the most holy king by the false prophets; David was nothing to him. The crowd goes after the external form. And the holier and more zealous anyone is in a strange faith, the more destructive and deplorable he is. Lectures on Isaiah 7:1.[4]

David's Oil to Shine Until Christ. Heinrich Bullinger: Further, when it seemed that this would extend to the ruin of the house of David and even to the overthrowing of God's promises, God himself opposes those kings in their boldest attempts. And indeed God promised to the house of David that there will always be oil from him that shines forth all the way to Christ on the throne of his kingdom. Therefore, on account of him and his truth, God is already near in desperate situations and sends a prophet to comfort the king along with the people who had already despaired in soul. Sermons on Isaiah 7:2.[5]

The Seed of the Serpent Attacking. Johannes Brenz: Here it ought to be considered that this is not new but an old hatred of Satan against the church of God. It was said previously to Satan, "The seed of the woman will crush your head, and you will strike his heel." This is why, when Satan knows his power is crushed by Christ, who is that seed of the woman, he cannot be kept any less from attacking all those people who he finds are in Christ. And so he afflicted the patriarchs with many evils and always devised their destruction, since he saw that Christ was going to come from their family and even found Christ in them by faith. Commentary on Isaiah 7:2.[6]

Enemies Under the Rule of God. Heinrich Bullinger: Hence we learn that the enemies of humans, whether visible or invisible, can never do as much as they want. For God governs humanity and he rules by his providence. And indeed it seems to me that the singular compassion of God should be observed here. For he does not repay Ahaz according to his ungodliness, but from his mercy he preserves and frees those already struggling in extreme distress. That he can do today too. That is also what should be desired by us in our wishes and indeed [we should] be most passionate about. Certainly God most

[3]Musculus, *In Esaiam*, 163, 165.
[4]LW 16:78* (WA 31.2:54).
[5]Bullinger, *Isaias*, 37v.
[6]Brenz, *Esaias*, 104; citing Gen 3:15.

often is moved by nothing of ours, whether merit or demerit, but, led by his own compassion, he saves people from innumerable evils. Therefore let no one despair. Sermons on Isaiah 7:1-3.[7]

The Reason for Isaiah's Son's Name. Johannes Oecolampadius: Then God instructed Isaiah that he and his son, Shear-jashub, should go to the king, so that every word would stand by the testimony of two or three. Some say this was the natural son of Isaiah, and that is why this refers to when the Jews would return from the Babylonian captivity after seventy years.[†] To me the surname of Shear, that is, "remained," seems to have been taken from that severe defeat when 120,000 perished. And while others died, those trusting in God were saved. It is more that Ahaz is admonished by this. The Septuagint does not specify this as a surname but has *ho kataleiphtheis Iasoub*, "Jashub remained." The Paraphrases say "son" is a disciple, and "remained" is about those who did not sin, or those who turned away from sinning. Indeed, disciples were called "sons of prophets." Commentary on Isaiah 7:3.[8]

Isaiah's Having a Wife and Son Does Not Make Him Less Virtuous. Wolfgang Musculus: Isaiah therefore had a wife, since a son is given to him. And Chrysostom remarks about the prophets near the end of *Homily* 56 on Matthew, saying, "All the prophets had wives and households, such as Isaiah and Ezekiel and that most excellent Moses, and this was not a hindrance to their virtue."[†] He seemed to note these things against the stupidity of some who think that Isaiah was *agamou* [unmarried] and a virgin. I know that some people have embraced the opinion of the Targum that explains that this passage is not about an actual son but about a disciple of the prophet.[‡] Following the simplicity of the letter, we explain that this is about a son, who had Shear-jashub imposed as his name by a prophetic spirit. This was so that he would admonish them all not only in words but also in the name of his son, that even if the number of the sons of Israel was like the sand of the sea, a remnant would still be converted, as later. Commentary on Isaiah 7:3.[9]

Kings Are Smoking Stumps. Wolfgang Musculus: "Because of these two," it says, "smoldering stumps of firebrands." He refers to those despicable ones whom Ahaz feared with a waning figure when he calls them "smoldering stumps." And they are not flaming but smoking, and smoking not in the way that they could soon burst into flames like smoke from a fire. But like logs consumed all the way to stumps, they do nothing other than give off smoke from what little remains of the fire, and they are quickly going to go out. So he calls these two kings of Syria and Israel two smoldering stumps. . . . We will observe in this passage how, with an elegant analogy, the Holy Spirit calls those kings "firebrands," by whom vengeance had been taken on the people of the Jews. The firebrand serves the fire by consuming what is thrown onto it and to this extent is a servant of the fire. But at the same time he does this, he himself is also consumed by the burning. So are the ungodly, whose malice and strength the Lord uses to correct his own. While they rage, afflict, and devastate, they destroy both others and themselves. The coal, by which gold is purified, is reduced to ashes by the burning; but the gold is cleansed. Commentary on Isaiah 7:4.[10]

The Limits of Other Kingdoms. Konrad Pellikan: With certainty, the Lord promised that he was going to destroy the plans of those kings so that their kingdoms would be restrained within their limits. The confidence of the ungodly is foolish. They are not going to inhabit new cities, but they are also not going to expire for a long time, as the prophet Amos had also already predicted

[7]Bullinger, *Isaias*, 38r.
[8]Oecolampadius, *In Iesaiam*, 65v. [†]See also Bullinger, *Isaias*, 38v.
[9]Musculus, *In Esaiam*, 165; citing Is 10:20-21. [†]Chrysostom, *Homily* 55.8 (*NPNF*[1] 10:344); [‡]*The Targum of Isaiah*, ed. and trans. J. F. Stenning (Oxford: Clarendon Press, 1949), 23-24.
[10]Musculus, *In Esaiam*, 165.

before, that both kingdoms were going to be destroyed, both Syria and Samaria. From this prophecy, sixty-five years were to be counted until the end of their kingdoms, namely, until the sixth year of Hezekiah. That is when the kingdom of Israel would come to an end, with that already happening to Syria before then. At that time, the kingdom of Ephraim was irreparably destroyed, and the people dispersed into exile, so that it should not be named among the peoples but be considered like slaves oppressed and dispersed all over. Commentary on Isaiah 7:4-8.[11]

Calculating Sixty-Five Years. Heinrich Bullinger: Isaiah distinctly expresses and says, "Yet within sixty-five years Ephraim will be shattered from being a people." That is the same as if he had said, "Within a brief time the ten tribes will be destroyed, and a remnant will be led into captivity." It is only a matter of time before Jerusalem and the kingdom of Judah are going to be occupied. But interpreters vary on the computation of sixty-five years. It is certain those years cannot be obtained from the reign of Ahaz to the oppression of the Israelites. For if we grant that these things were said in the third year of Ahaz, there would remain thirteen years of his reign (which he reigned sixteen years). If you add six years to this from the reign of Hezekiah, who succeeded Ahaz (for in the sixth year of Hezekiah, the ten tribes were carried off and devastated), you will have no more than nineteen years. Therefore here they turn to the prophecy of Amos, who prophesied in chapter 5 that the Israelites would be carried off into captivity beyond Damascus, which is said to have been in the twenty-fifth year of Azariah or Uzziah, who reigned fifty-two years (others place it in year twenty-seven). This gives twenty-seven years to this calculation of ours. Sixteen from Jotham, the same for Ahaz, and six from Hezekiah makes sixty-five years in total.[†] Others compute differently. And the most famous is the computation of Johannes Functius in his *Chronology*, which has the greatest likelihood. In addition, there are those who suppose that what the Lord actually did here is like what is said to have happened before the flood, when, on account of the depravity of humans, the number of years was reduced, which he had allowed for, based on their repentance. So indeed, here, too, the best part of the years was taken away, because of the extreme corruption of the Israelite kingdom. But if we do not, as is commonly said, hit the mark in every detail with our explanation on these computations, certainly nothing is lost from the doctrine of our true faith and salvation. Sermons on Isaiah 7:8.[12]

The Long Ministry of Isaiah. Philipp Melanchthon: And they calculate a number from when Amos was chosen at the beginning of his preaching, which is recited in the seventh chapter in these words of Isaiah, "Within sixty-five years Ephraim will cease to be a people." Moreover, it is established that Samaria was destroyed in the sixth year of Hezekiah, king of Judah. From that, when we calculate back the sixty-five years, we arrive at the twenty-fourth year of King Uzziah (which is the time when Amos prophesied) to get the number they record for when he began, as will be discussed most abundantly on that passage. . . . Therefore, [Isaiah's ministry] is more than eighty years under the reigns of Jotham, Ahaz, and Hezekiah, and he was a witness of the enormous calamities to Israel and Judah, and he maintained the church with his voice and guided the people with much counsel. Argument of Isaiah.[13]

Exhortation to Trust. Konrad Pellikan: Consequently, with the consolation finished, the prophet turns to exhorting the king to believe the divine promises. Otherwise, it says, if you will not believe the word of the Lord and persist in your unbelief, you will also certainly not remain firm,

[11]Pellikan, *Commentaria Bibliorum*, 3:10r.

[12]Bullinger, *Isaias* 39v. [†]See also Musculus, *In Esaiam*, 168-69, who cites the explanations of Kimchi and the Targum.

[13]CR 13:795-96.

but by not believing the Lord you will be deprived of his help and protection. For nothing offends the goodness of God to the same degree as when we do not dare or want to trust in him and depend on other things. Commentary on Isaiah 7:9.[14]

A Penalty for Refusing Faith. Dietrich Schnepff: I do not report these things from my own fabricated ingenuity but from the commands given to me by the Lord. If you refuse to have faith in him, you will not have rest in your souls, nor will you be able to have success in any of your affairs. For ungodliness and rejecting faith in the Lord earns the most severe judgment and penalty from the Lord. Paraphrase of Isaiah 7:9.[15]

7:10-17 *The Sign of Immanuel*

Imitators of Ahaz Pretend to Be Humble. Heinrich Bullinger: But Ahaz has many imitators in our time. For while it is said that the gospel is believed and that all things should be reformed according to the rule of God's Word, some wise men of this age think that another reason must be followed. "For if we wish to restore all things to the Word of God itself, then there would be serious quarrels and wars. So then, God should not be tempted, but certain things should be established according to the rule of the Word of God, and other things retained in the favor of those who are powerful and can wage war. Then they could be appeased and their favor retained. If we are going to proceed in the way of reforming all things and say that God will be with us and protect us, we are tempting God rather than wisely conducting our affairs." Others, when they hear that it is impressed on them from the Gospel, "Ask and you will receive; whatever you ask in my name, truly I say to you, will be given to you," they shout out, "The Lord must not be tempted in such a way that, without intercessors, we might burst into the presence of a terrifying God; rather, let us bring with us the heavenly saints of God, who commend us miserable sinners and our cause to God." But they also sin with Ahaz, and fake humility in their sin, and because they do not want to tempt the Lord or to burst (as is commonly said) boldly and unwashed into his presence, even though God invites them and commands them to do what they themselves will not do, they also desire what is ungodliness to be seen as godly. Sermons on Isaiah 7:10-12.[16]

Ahaz's Hypocritical Response of Refusing to Ask for a Sign. Martin Borrhaus: This interpretation is simple. This is why those who interpret the words of the prophet in this way thus redeem the failure, "If you do not believe my prediction, ask for a sign," as it follows, "Ask for a sign yourself." But every work is mocked by you all, for among you where there is evidently no faith, you do not believe. Others take it this way, "If you do not have faith in my oracle, then I ask, what happens?" From this, of course, it happens that because you are not faithful, faith in the divine covenant is violated at the same time. These two interpretations are sufficiently simple. . . . The wicked king considers the law, but without the law of which Moses in Deuteronomy says, "You shall not tempt the Lord your God." For he interpreted this falsely against its meaning. In fact, they tempt God who are not content with the divine promise on which the one faith depends, and prescribe to God the manner, place, and time by which he brings help. But those who ask for a sign do not tempt him when it is offered by him,† as he offered it to Ahaz himself through the prophet. . . . In addition, those who reject the protections that are provided and rashly seek what is missing, tempt the Lord as Ahaz did. He refuses the help of God expressed by Isaiah in the oracle and demanded the missing help of the Assyrians, contrary to the reason of the divine covenant. But in this way those who conceal treachery in their heart while presenting themselves with dejection and humility

[14] Pellikan, *Commentaria Bibliorum*, 3:10r.
[15] Schnepff, *In Esaiae*, 129.
[16] Bullinger, *Isaias*, 40v; citing Jn 14:13.

from their mouth by which they confess that they revere God, are hypocrites. These are the ones who are dejected when it is not necessary, but when the matter demands dejection, they are arrogant. Oracles in Isaiah on 7:10-12.[17]

Accepting Signs from God. John Calvin: Do we tempt God when we accept what he offers to us? Certainly not. Ahaz therefore speaks falsehood when he pretends that he refuses the sign, because he is unwilling to tempt God; for there can be nothing fitter or more excellent than to obey God, and indeed it is the highest virtue to ask nothing beyond the word of God. And yet if God chooses to add anything to his word, it ought not to be regarded as a virtue to reject this addition as superfluous. It is no small insult conveyed to God when his goodness is despised in such a manner as if his actions toward us were of no advantage, and as if he did not know sufficiently what was especially necessary for us.... For example, the Lord offers to us in the gospel whatever things are necessary for salvation. For when he brings us into a state of fellowship with Christ, the sum of all blessings is truly contained in him. What, then, is the use of baptism and the Lord's Supper? Must they be regarded as superfluous? Not at all; for anyone who shall actually and without flattery acknowledge one's weakness, of which all from the least to the greatest are conscious, will gladly avail oneself of those aids for his support. We ought indeed to grieve and lament that the sacred truth of God needs assistance on account of the defect of our flesh; but since we cannot all at once remove this defect, anyone who, according to one's capacity, shall believe the word will immediately render full obedience to God. Let us therefore learn to embrace the signs along with the word, since it is not in human power to separate them. Because Ahaz refused the sign offered, it produces both stubbornness and ingratitude.... Now, there are two kinds of signs; for some are extraordinary and may be called "portents," such as that which the prophet will soon discuss and that which, we will later see, was offered to Hezekiah. But some are ordinary and in daily use among believers, such as baptism and the Lord's Supper, which contain no miracle that can be perceived as much by the eyes or any human sense. For what the Lord miraculously accomplishes by his Spirit through those is hidden, but in those that are extraordinary, the miracle itself is seen. Such is also the end and use of all signs; for as Gideon was confirmed by an astonishing portent, so we are confirmed by baptism and the Lord's Supper, though our eyes behold no miracle. Commentary on Isaiah 7:12.[18]

Try the Patience of God. Johannes Brenz: You have a hypocrite. First, then, consider the nature and customs of hypocrites, that, although they are the most ungodly before God, they want to be seen as godly and the most compliant to God. Then, observe that God does not regard the external appearance of one's work but faith and obedience. Ahaz was instituting many sacred things that appeared pious and religious. But there was none in Ahaz, neither faith nor obedience. He did not believe anything of the divine promise about the seed of Abraham and of David, that is, of Christ, because he was hoping that he was going to obtain the forgiveness of sins by his own merits and would preserve the kingdom by human strength. He did not obey God, because while those sacred things that the word of God established remained, he was establishing and pursuing things that he himself had devised. But where there is neither faith nor obedience, what respect could there be for good works and sacred things before God? Finally, what Ahaz pretended about tempting God indeed is truly drawn from the law of God, that God is not to be tempted. But when God commands to either ask for a miracle or receive danger, it is not temptation of God but

[17]Borrhaus, *In Iesaiae Prophetae Oracula*, 91-92; citing Deut 6:16. †Borrhaus cites the example of Gideon positively.

[18]CTS 13:241-42* (CO 36:151-52); citing Is 38:7.

obedience owed to God.† Commentary on Isaiah 7:13.[19]

The Remarkable Mystery of the Sign. Johannes Oecolampadius: By this sign all the fathers were hoping they would be saved. Thus the promise was made to Eve that her seed would crush the head of the serpent. But it was necessary that he ask for a sign that was greater than what is either in heaven or on earth and was clearly transcending the order of nature, namely that remarkable virginal birth. But see how the habit of the prophet also fits this passage. He has the habit of including a prophecy about Christ or his kingdom after the history of his own time. And so he seems to digress in this passage. And because Ahaz refuses to receive the sign, he declares the remarkable mystery. . . . First, he says, "Behold," so as not to signify a common miracle but an excellent sign, worthy of God. And what kind of miracle would it be if a girl conceives from a man? For that happens daily. Now, if they want to keep a miracle with this view, it is that the prophet predicted a firstborn son and affirmed that something uncertain and in the future would be certain. For she could have also given birth to a female. What could be more absurd than this? For no one would rightly call this a sign, if someone successfully guesses what happens in the future. Commentary on Isaiah 7:13-14.[20]

A Mother Naming a Son. John Calvin: The word is in the feminine case in Hebrew. For as to those who read it in the masculine gender, I do not know from where they get that. The copies that we use certainly do not differ. Because if you refer this to the mother, it certainly expresses something different from the ordinary custom. We know that to the father is always assigned the right of giving a name to a child; for it is a sign of the power and authority of fathers over children, and the same authority does not belong to women. But here it is conveyed to the mother; and therefore it follows that he is conceived by the mother in such a manner as not to have a father on earth, otherwise the prophet would pervert the ordinary custom of Scripture, which ascribes this office to men only. Yet it ought to be observed that the name was not given to Christ at the suggestion of his mother, and in such a case it would have had no weight; but the prophet means that, in publishing the name, the virgin will occupy the place of a herald, because there will be no earthly father to perform that office. Commentary on Isaiah 7:14.[21]

The Relevance of the Promised Virgin Birth. John Mayer: The word rendered "a virgin" is by all expositors, except the Septuagint of old, rendered a "young woman" (says Jerome). But it signifies a young one hidden or kept close from the view of men, by the care of her parents. Neither is the word used in any place to set forth a young woman without this addition, "hidden." Moreover, it is absurd to render it this way, since it is no sign or wonder for a young woman to bring forth a son, but it is for a virgin. And in the Punic tongue, which comes from the Hebrew, *alma* always signifies a virgin. The blessed virgin Mary giving birth, then, is what is prophesied here, although it may seem impertinent to the present purpose, as happening many hundreds of years after, and the destruction of those two kingdoms, Syria and Israel, was then at hand. But it is inserted *per raptum Propheticum* [by prophetic rapture], as is usual among the prophets. A spiritual rapture is sometimes brought in, to which the Spirit suddenly carries them, and then they return to that of which they were speaking before. But how is it pertinent to the thing at hand to foretell of the birth of Jesus, when a sign should be given of their deliverance from those two kings? Sasbout answers well, that this sign is not unaptly now given because of the similitude between the deliverance by Jesus and that presently promised.† For as they

[19]Brenz, *Esaias*, 110. †Brenz cites the example of Gideon asking for a sign as not tempting God.

[20]Oecolampadius, *In Iesaiam*, 68v-69r.

[21]CTS 13:248* (CO 36:157).

were unworthy to be saved from those two kings, and yet God out of his mere mercy promised it, so both they and all people are most unworthy of salvation by Jesus, yet God out of his grace and mercy promises this also. COMMENTARY ON ISAIAH 7:14.[22]

"VIRGIN" AND "YOUNG WOMAN" ARE SYNONYMS. BALTHASAR HUBMAIER: That the Jews want to make a "young woman" of this "maid" or "virgin" changes nothing, for Eve is after all also called a "woman" by the Scriptures throughout her virginity. Besides, the Jews have to grant that such a birth was to be a sign from God. But when a young wife bears a child, this is not a sign but the ordinary course of nature. APOLOGIA.[23]

THERE SHOULD BE MORE VIRGINS. JOHN DONNE: That this mother in our text was a virgin is a peculiar, a singular sign, given as such by God, never done but then; and it is a singular testimony how acceptable to God the state of virginity is. He does not dishonor physic that magnifies health, nor does he dishonor marriage that praises virginity: let them embrace that state who can, and certainly many more might do it than do, if they would try whether they could or not. ON THE NATIVITY.[24]

A COVENANT PROMISE OF THE REDEEMER. JOHN CALVIN: But all writers, both Greek and Latin, are too much at their ease in handling this passage; for, as if there were no difficulty in it, they merely assert that Christ is here promised from the Virgin Mary. Now, there is no small difficulty in the objection that the Jews bring against us, that Christ is here mentioned without any sufficient reason; for thus they argue and demand that the scope of the passage be examined. . . . King Ahaz having rejected the sign that God had offered to him, the prophet reminds him of the foundation of the covenant, which even the ungodly did not venture openly to reject. The Messiah must be born; and this was expected by all, because the salvation of the whole nation depended on it. The prophet, therefore, after having expressed his indignation against the king, again argues in this manner: "By rejecting the promise, you would endeavor to overturn the decree of God; but it shall remain inviolable, and your treachery and ingratitude will not hinder God from being continually the deliverer of his people; for he will at length raise up his Messiah."

To make these things more plain, we must attend to the custom of the prophets, who, in establishing special promises, lay down this as the foundation, that God will send a redeemer. On this general foundation God everywhere builds all the special promises that he makes to his people; and certainly everyone who expects aid and assistance from him must be convinced of his fatherly love. COMMENTARY ON ISAIAH 7:14.[25]

GOD WITH US. JOHN DONNE: Immanuel is God with us; it is not we with God: God seeks us, comes to us before we to him, and it is God with us, in that notion, in the last part of the word *El,* which is *Deus fortis,* the powerful God, not only in infirmity, as when he died in our nature, but as he is, *Deus fortis,* able and ready to assist and deliver us in all encumbrances; so he is with us; and with us until the end of the world, in his word and in the sacraments. For though I may not say, as some have said, that by the word of consecration in the administration of the sacrament Christ is so infallibly produced that it as if he had never been incarnate before, yet at the pronouncing of those words of consecration, he must necessarily be incarnate then, yet I may say that God is as effectually present with every worthy receiver to the extent that he is not more effectually present with the saints in heaven. ON THE NATIVITY.[26]

---

[22]Mayer, *Commentary upon All the Prophets* 4:50. †See Sasbout, *In Esaiam,* 63-64.
[23]CRR 5:537; citing Gen 3.
[24]Donne, *Works* 1:35.
[25]CTS 13:245-46* (CO 36:155-56).
[26]Donne, *Works,* 1:38*.

THE SIGN CONFIRMS THE DAVIDIC PROMISE AHAZ SHOULD HAVE TRUSTED. HEINRICH BULLINGER: What in the present is shown to Ahaz is the sign of the conception and birth from an untouched virgin. Besides that, it is remarkable and foreign and outside the course of nature, where women conceive and give birth from the union with men; it also confirms the promise that Ahaz was told, that he, along with the city of Jerusalem and the whole kingdom, would be freed from the immense fury of the two kings, and that the kingdom of David would remain untouched, when meanwhile those two kingdoms of the two kings were going to be utterly destroyed, along with the kings themselves. But this sign does not only serve Ahaz and the house of Judah but also the whole world. SERMONS ON ISAIAH 7:14-17.[27]

PREACHING ABOUT CHRIST. JOHANNES BRENZ: But consider with me that Isaiah preached these things about Christ and his mother not only for the people of his time but also for the entire church of all later times. And here is the sense of this sermon. "You, house of David, do not want to ask for a sign of your freedom. Behold, the Lord himself, who promised a perpetual kingdom to David and his seed, will preserve the kingdom of Judah at this time, and most certainly will fulfill that promise that guaranteed he would give a son to David, who would reign forever. As a sign of this, to understand this promise a little more clearly, this son will not be born of a woman corrupted by her husband but of a virgin." COMMENTARY ON ISAIAH 7:14.[28]

THE MEANING OF THE HEBREW WORD. WOLFGANG MUSCULUS: "Behold the young woman." The Hebrew is *hinēh hā ʿalmâ*. *ʿAlmâ* sounds like "young woman" or "girl." Several translate it as "one raised in hiding," in the way virgins were usually raised. Indeed, the word *ʿalmâ* is from *ʿālam*, which means "to hide." So the Septuagint translated this *idou hē parthenos*, that is, "Behold a virgin," which is the reading that the interpreter of the Gospel according to Matthew used. . . . † Unbelieving Jews, stubbornly turning away from this mystery of the virgin birth, attempt to use the words from this prophecy in their objection against us.

First, they say the birth of this young woman was promised as a sign of the future liberation against the plan of the two kings, Rezin and Pekiah. But since your Mary gave birth to her son five hundred years later, how could his birth be a sign of this liberation, which happened only a few years later? Then, you say that your Mary conceived and gave birth with untouched virginity. But in the words of the prophet, the expression is not *bətûlâ*, which is "virgin," but *ʿalmâ*, which means "young woman" or "girl," who could be a virgin or married. This is why the prophecy cannot apply to this.

Third, the son of your Mary, neither you nor she call him Immanuel but Jesus. But the prophet says about the *ʿalmâ* that she was not going to call her son Jesus but Immanuel.

Fourth, it is not read about your Jesus that from his birth to the age of understanding that he ate curds and honey, as here is foretold about Immanuel.

Fifth, it cannot pertain to your Jesus what is supplied, "For before that boy knows to refuse evil and choose the good, that land whose two kings you dread will be deserted." For it is clearly implied that the prophet is speaking not about some boy who was going to be born five centuries later but about one whose birth was going to precede the ruin of those kings, Rezin and Pekah, such that during his childhood, before the age of understanding, they would be taken from their land. And so clearly it is established that this prophecy cannot correspond to your Jesus. The Jews make these objections to us. And meanwhile, others explain the present passage to be about Hezekiah, the son of Ahaz, which Rabbi Salomon even refutes, and rightly so. COMMENTARY ON ISAIAH 7:14-17.[29]

[27]Bullinger, *Isaias*, 41v.
[28]Brenz, *Esaias*, 115.
[29]Musculus, *In Esaiam*, 172; citing Mt 1. †His lengthier explanation is on 173-74.

Double Meaning of the Sign. Konrad Pellikan: It is not rare in the sacred Scriptures to intend double meanings of one speech. When, of course, it is truly said about Solomon, "he will be to me a son," it is nevertheless most truly written about the Messiah. The same could be said about Cyrus, David, Isaac, and many others like that. This itself is necessarily admitted by Hebrews as much as by Christians. So in this passage, without doubt, the prophetic spirit wanted to indicate the incarnation, the greatest of God's miracles and signs to humanity, such that the same words of sacred history that are treated would harmonize and serve in every way. The spirit of the Evangelist Matthew, by whom the holy Gospel is written, without doubt saw that it was the most blessed virgin mother of God from whom, without male seed, by the overshadowing of the Holy Spirit, the Messiah, the Lord's Christ, was born. And having been admonished by the Lord through the angel, she should call him by no other name than "Savior of his people from their sins." And he would be seen on earth and conversing with people such that he most truly is called and is Immanuel, that is, God with us. For what else is "the Word became flesh" than God with us? What else is the only healer and Savior of human misery than Immanuel? . . . This is the way the spirit of Matthew and the ancient saints understood this passage, and today all the faithful understand and embrace this sense from it. That sense Ahaz with his accomplices neither could nor should comprehend, as a most ungodly and sacrilegious scoundrel. Nor did the divine Spirit and the holy prophet want to cast the pearl of this mystery before that swine. But at the same time, with those same words, another sense is worthy, and if they did not want him to have uttered useless words, they are nevertheless seasoned with prophetic salt. It is as if he says, "You hope for nothing worthy of the Lord your God, to whom you protest in every way. Yet because of the promises made to David, he will deliver you and his people in this way, and no matter how bad you are, that she who is a virgin today will soon conceive and give birth to a son, who will also have the name Immanuel, as a sign that your impending redemption from these two kingdoms and their kings is near. Since, by his help and grace, he will be with us in such a way that we should fear no people, if the Lord stands with us and for us." Finally, he will hardly approach the time for being weaned from milk to be fed with honey and curds. And the time of adolescence, too, will not be expected, when perfect or sufficient knowledge arrives to distinguish good from evil. That is, while the boy was still soon to be born, before he would reach the age of discretion, that is, after not so many years, the land of each kingdom, both Syria and Ephraim, or Israel, will be displaced from their wicked kings and the unjust people whom you also detest most wickedly. You wish for them to be wiped out with their kings, against whom you implore the help of the king of Assyria, and offer tributes, since no one can conquer or eliminate them without the Lord our God, in whose hand are all the decisions of kingdoms, whose favor you esteem less than the king of the Assyrians, who will be the destroyer of your kingdom in his own time. Commentary on Isaiah 7:14-17.[30]

Two Signs Given. Martin Luther: And he foretells two signs: one hidden, the other clear, which he explains in chapter 8 in a way not much different from Hosea chapter 1. But Isaiah includes both signs. The first one does not apply to Ahaz, because he did not live to see it, but the second one does. But since he now resists the word of God and refuses a sign, how can his faith be strengthened? Therefore, the prophet speaks of a sign to come, which they will strike against, just as the sign of Jonah was given the Jews, and those who refuse to believe will perish. Nevertheless, it is a sign of lifting up and building up and strengthening for those who believe. And this is the summary of this chapter until the end, because he says that this prediction is already in the process of fulfillment in these unbelievers. . . .

[30]Pellikan, *Commentaria Bibliorum*, 3:10r.

Again, since he says that it is a sign of God, it is necessary that this conception and birth be in a manner different from what is commonly and naturally the case. For it would not be a sign if one who today is a virgin would become pregnant after a half-year. Therefore, she has to be both a virgin and with child. . . .

"Because before he knows." That is, you, ungodly, you believe nothing. But because they have such faithlessness, those enemies of yours will indeed perish, yet nevertheless you yourselves will also follow them after not a long time, but before the boy has learned to call it butter and honey. This was said to make the prophecy obscure and a stumbling block for the Jews, who still today do not understand this passage and say that Immanuel is Hezekiah. And yet this sign was given on account of the remnant, that the kingdom of Judah would not be destroyed until Christ came; but it is obscured because of the ungodly. "The Lord will bring upon you." He says, since the faithless reject the present sign, they are unworthy of the future one. Lectures on Isaiah 7:14-17.[31]

Immanuel as a Type of Christ. Wolfgang Musculus: They suppose these things in the passage of our prophet about Almah and her son, Immanuel, are going to be connected to the time of the prophet when this is prophesied. There is a type of the blessed virgin in that young woman, and of Christ, our true Immanuel, in that typological Immanuel who preceded him. But later in its time, we experience that truth fulfilled in Christ. . . . In this sense, there was no need that this girl be a typological virgin, to conceive and give birth as a virgin; nor was it required that her son be the true Immanuel. But it was sufficient that he be a typological Immanuel, as a sign that God wanted his people to not miss being freed. For the truth of the virginal birth of the blessed virgin Mary, and the glory of the true Immanuel, was reserved for Christ the Savior, so that the Evangelist might rightly say that this passage of the prophet was fulfilled in his birth from the virgin Mary. Commentary on Isaiah 7:14.[32]

A Child of Miraculous Promise. Catharina Regina von Greiffenberg: Muster all your powers of amazement, all kinds of rapture, and all sorts of spontaneous transports. You will need them all and still more in receiving this miraculous promise. Something that is divinely inspired will enter into human nature; it will be at once true and unbelievable. The matter will appear as impossible as it is impossible for it not to be done, since it was promised by God.

A virgin (meaning the most chaste of all) will be with child (the angel says), not conceive a child in the natural human manner but be with child even as her virginity and unblemished chastity persist; indeed, she is with child from the Holy Spirit. . . .

Thus chastity is not perchance merely pregnant with holy thoughts, with beautiful conceits of divine praise, or with angelic purities and such things, but with a child that chastity will also bring into the world, for chastity will bear a son, a child that is at once divinely inspired and natural, such a son who has the very Almighty as his eternal father and weakness as his temporal mother, a son, I say, who takes upon himself both natures, a son of the wretched mother as well as of the omnipotent Father, for whom the taking on of weakness serves as the guarantor of omnipotence's realizing therein the ardor of love.

She will bear him too. He will not be an adoptive son, but he will take up human nature itself; not a chosen son, but a born son, through whom we are chosen as God's children. His birth will happen both naturally and through divine inspiration so that natural humans may attain salvation beyond their natural powers. Meditations on the Incarnation of Jesus Christ.[33]

[31]LW 16:84-85 (WA 31.2:59); citing Hos 1; Mt 1:21; 12:39; 16:4.

[32]Musculus, *In Esaiam*, 175.

[33]Greiffenberg, *Meditations*, 268-69.

Against the Perpetual Virginity of Mary. Ulrich Zwingli: On this topic Jerome and Oecolampadius have produced enough that is solid and true. Against the papists who teach the perpetual virginity of the blessed Theotokos,[†] that is, the God-bearer, we will be content to state this that it cannot be proven from the sacred writings but depends on the pronunciation of the church (but understand the Roman, which to this point has been wealthy). Annotations on Isaiah 7:14.[34]

The Humanity and Age of Christ. English Annotations: "He shall eat." Christ, as man, shall be fed, as others ordinarily in their infancy are. Or, this my child . . . shall, for all your vain fears, be plentifully brought up. . . . "That he may know."[†] Until he attain to the years of discretion. Annotations on Isaiah 7:15.[35]

Eating Curds and Honey Means the Humanity of Christ. Johannes Brenz: "He shall eat curds and honey when he knows to refuse the evil and choose the good." This is a description of the humanity of Christ. For curds, or milk and honey, are infant food. And infants are therefore cherished and raised, not to learn gluttony, nor to pursue wickedness and iniquity, but to learn to flee evil, and to do good, to learn to know God, and to pursue the calling of God. This is the chief end of raising children. When, therefore, Isaiah says the son of the virgin is going to eat curds and honey, that he may be cherished and raised in the custom of infants and be instructed in learning the fear of God, he clearly teaches that he is going to assume true humanity as one who grows, as Luke says, in wisdom, stature, and favor with God and people. Accordingly, Isaiah describes Christ in this passage as true God and true human, so that we may know that when God became human, a human also becomes God through faith in Jesus Christ, our true and only Savior. Commentary on Isaiah 7:15-16.[36]

Kings Defeated Before the Boy Is Conceived. Johannes Oecolampadius: To those who would say, "If there will not be any salvation for us until his coming, who from among us will live that long?" he responds, "That sign indeed I give to you, if you would believe in it; salvation will come to you, even by the one not yet born." Hence, it is necessary that he who is not yet born will be great and only when called on delivers us from our enemies. Therefore, before the boy knows to refuse the evil, that is, before he eats curds and honey, before he is born, or conceived, the land of Israel and Damascus, which you detest or abhor, will be relinquished from the presence of the two kings. Commentary on Isaiah 7:15-16.[37]

Old Testament Saints Saved by Christ. Heinrich Bullinger: After this he explains a little more significantly that the Jews were saved on account of Christ. For, he says, before this boy Immanuel was born and reaches the age of discretion, those kings would have long since died and those two kingdoms relinquished from those whom you fear so much right now. For the king of Syria is cut down by Assyria, and the king of Damascus is added to the kingdom of Assyria; so also the king of Israel is cut down, and his kingdom ceased to be a kingdom with his successor Osea and is subdued by the Assyrians. This passage of the prophet is truly memorable and observable. For it is as clear as the shining sun that all the ancients of the first Testament who received blessings from God, and were liberated from evil, and were then saved, received all these things on account of Christ and by Christ. Hence it happens that Christ Jesus is the one and eternal Savior of

[34]ZSW 14 / CR 101:180-81. [†]Zwingli recounts the history of Jerome against Helvidius, who taught against the perpetual virginity. See Jerome, *De Perpetua Virginitate B. Mariae, Adversus Helvidium* (PL 23:183-206 [no. 205-30]).
[35]Downame, ed., *English Annotations*, Aa4v; citing Is 7:3; Job 20:17; Jonah 4:11. [†]Job 20:17 refers to "streams flowing with honey and curds."
[36]Brenz, *Esaias*, 117; citing Lk 2:52.
[37]Oecolampadius, *In Iesaiam*, 69v.

the world, by whose grace and redemption, however many are saved, are saved by faith and will be saved in the future. The Lord Jesus himself testifies this when he says Abraham saw his day and was saved. Sermons on Isaiah 7:17.[38]

Praise the Miracle of God-with-Us! Catharina Regina von Greiffenberg: O Divine Miracle! O heavenly God-with-us! Who shall be against us? Gracious God-with-us! Who shall damn us? Almighty God-with-us! Who shall overpower us? Most wise God-with-us! Who shall deceive or seduce us? Omnipresent God-with-us! Who shall insult us? God, the highest good, the totality with us! What more do we want, could we, should we ask for?

Desire has an aim, but an aim that is endless and boundless. An aim that exceeds all the world and all of nature, an aim that has no other place but the one that surpasses all places and destinations, an aim that is affixed in the one who is wider than eternity. So, we have this aim in the desire we have attained. It is therefore the aim of our salvation. Who can think it, speak it, or describe it? It is greater than one can imagine, for having God-with-us is something that is inconceivable to the angels and above the angels, the next thing to God himself, indeed, in a certain way a supradivine joy. For being God himself is natural and thus an imperative and a necessity; this God-with-us is, however, a sign of grace and love of the highest perfection and thus even more gratifying.

God-with-us is like being united with the greatest conceivable good, like being melded at the point of all salvation, for God cannot exist except in most sublime happiness and bliss. If it is not according to the body, then it is certainly according to the spirit and virtue. If he is with us, then we dwell in the highest everlasting bliss of the soul even in the midst of sadness. This God-with-us ought to draw us to God to the extent that we perceive nothing but God. God ought thereby to be in all our faculties and thoughts, to prevail in all powers and capacities, to reign in all operations and practices, to appear in all desire and appetites. All stirrings ought thereby to be his impetus, and all movements his stimulation.

Because he gave us himself, the sum of the universe, we ought to submit ourselves as nothingness to him in everything, and even if it were but the smallest of the small, indeed, only a shadow of gratitude, give nothing for everything! What less can we do than nothing? And we do not even want to do that! Is it not lamentable that we are so thoroughly iniquitous? For that very reason, arise to gratitude, all you people, we who have God-with-us! Pour out floods of knowledge, rivers of exultation, streams of praising, and floodtides of glory! Let the wellsprings bubble with eternal thanksgiving and pour out great seas of God's glory! Exhale an entire airy element of praise and have no other breath than what can glorify God! May all the blood in you become the fire of love and send an offering of praise up to him. May the body, as the earth of the microcosm, in all its undertakings shoot up growth of gratitude. Meditations on the Incarnation of Jesus Christ.[39]

7:18-25 *The Coming Attack from the Assyrians*

Assyria and Egypt Swarming and Shaving. Dietrich Schnepff: But he calls them the hired razor, either because we use hired and borrowed things more freely or because the Lord has employed the Assyrians for a short time. . . . For the most powerful Assyrian king, in whom you now hope for aid and assistance, will attack you with a very powerful army that will include the Egyptians and other people in the fight. For the Lord will both call and provoke these people, like bees and flies, to come in great numbers and to seize all the places of your kingdom. And they are going to carry away all the princes in the republic, which we can compare to hair on the

[38]Bullinger, *Isaias*, 42r.

[39]Greiffenberg, *Meditations*, 271-72.

head, and all the priests, who are the beard, and all of the common people, who are the hair on feet. Their goods will be removed—not stolen and seized—but separated from them, like a razor hired for that purpose shaved them to the closest and smallest hairs. Certainly at that time, even with the greatest scarcity of everything, if anyone has one cow and two sheep, he will be able to live lavishly, for the scarcity of people will be so great that the fewest things will be sufficient for them to be rich. And such disaster will have made it so that those left will eat honey and curds in abundance, because there will be the fewest who inhabit and tend to the land. SCHOLIA ON ISAIAH 7:18-22.[40]

THE BACKWARDNESS OF CHRISTIANS. JOHN TRAPP: Calvin says that here it is set forth that in no lurking place should any of the Jews be hidden or secure from their enemies, but that they shall range about and rage everywhere throughout the whole land. And because all this is done "at a hiss," Musculus says that the backwardness of Christians is condemned, because they cannot be brought to do as God requires them by the most earnest and long-lasting preaching. EXPOSITION ON ISAIAH 7:18.[41]

THE RAZOR CUTS TO THE ROOT. WOLFGANG MUSCULUS: He explains what the Lord is going to be shaving. "And the head," it says, that is, the hair on the head. And the hair of the feet, he understands what is on the legs and every part of the body below the stomach. "And even the beard will be swept away," it says. He added this phrase to signify that nothing would be left. These things are said metaphorically. He compares Judah, his rebellious and stubborn people, to the body of a man being stripped and deprived to such an extent that not only are his clothes pulled off, but he also is deprived of the natural glory that he has in his hair by shaving off everything, and he is disgraced. So, this was going to happen to the people of Judah by the depriving, stripping, and deforming Assyrians. COMMENTARY ON ISAIAH 7:20.[42]

WHEN IMMANUEL DEFENDS JERUSALEM. MARTIN BORRHAUS: In what day? Later in the eighth chapter, this time is explained where the prophet signifies that with Immanuel standing at Jerusalem, the Assyrian enemies would not prevail. Therefore, the meaning is: when Jerusalem is besieged by Sennacherib, he will be so unable to capture it that he, along with his army, is also going to perish miserably in front of it when Immanuel defends his city. So, we do not refer these things to the times of the king of Babylon because this is in the oracle of Isaiah where he explained that Immanuel is going to save Jerusalem and the remnant of the nation of Judah, when the ten tribes had already been carried off into exile and Judah miserably devastated. But it is certain that nothing was left by the Babylonians, but that everything (not without figures of future events) was destroyed. . . . When Hezekiah was reigning, they were devastated by Assyria. A spiritual blessing is foreshadowed in the remnant who were going to be delivered from the hand of the spiritual Assyrians by the defender Immanuel, the Messiah, in the times of the apostles. We have already mentioned several times what the apostle says about the remnant. ORACLES IN ISAIAH ON 7:20-25.[43]

THE DESOLATION OF THE LAND. ADAM SASBOUT: The sense is that at the time when all the riches of the Jews were carried off to Chaldea, the land of Judah will be so desolate and with such incredible devastation that they will by no means have herds of cattle or flocks of sheep like they used to have, but the rare inhabitant will hardly be able to feed one cow and a few sheep. "And he will eat curds, because of the abundance of

[40]Schnepff, *In Esaiae*, 127, 130-31.
[41]Trapp, *Commentary or Exposition*, 41*.
[42]Musculus, *In Esaiam*, 180.
[43]Borrhaus, *In Iesaiae Prophetae Oracula*, 97.

milk." And this pertains to the warnings in this sense: There will be such a small number of people that everything will be full of grass—even the very streets where otherwise sprouts would be trampled by people's feet will be filled with grass. And therefore there will indeed be a sufficiently great abundance of milk, and what he will do because of so much milk is eat curds, since he will have nothing else to feed on. Now, Lyra explains this much differently,[†] but this seems to be the true sense. . . . At that time, because of the small number of people, there will be such a scarcity of wine in the desert vineyards, because out of fear of the enemy those will not be thought about at all, so that each vine will hardly be bought for silver shekels. For all the land will be reduced to thorns and briers, and there will be such terror of violent swords everywhere that no one dares to visit his own field without a bow and arrows and other weapons. And with the countrysides abandoned, they take refuge in the mountains. And while protected by the difficulty of the terrain there, they could hardly dig out the rough mountains, because they would not have oxen, nor plows, nor plowshares. Therefore, if the rare grower was found anywhere in the mountains, he would still endure a miserable life there. COMMENTARY ON ISAIAH 7:21-25.[44]

[44]Sasbout, *In Esaiam*, 66. [†]See Nicholas of Lyra, *Bibliorum*, 95-96.

8:1-18 THE SIGN OF ISAIAH'S SONS

8 Then the LORD said to me, "Take a large tablet and write on it in common characters,[a] 'Belonging to Maher-shalal-hash-baz.'[b] [2]And I will get reliable witnesses, Uriah the priest and Zechariah the son of Jeberechiah, to attest for me."

[3]And I went to the prophetess, and she conceived and bore a son. Then the LORD said to me, "Call his name Maher-shalal-hash-baz; [4]for before the boy knows how to cry 'My father' or 'My mother,' the wealth of Damascus and the spoil of Samaria will be carried away before the king of Assyria."

[5]The LORD spoke to me again: [6]"Because this people has refused the waters of Shiloah that flow gently, and rejoice over Rezin and the son of Remaliah, [7]therefore, behold, the Lord is bringing up against them the waters of the River,[c] mighty and many, the king of Assyria and all his glory. And it will rise over all its channels and go over all its banks, [8]and it will sweep on into Judah, it will overflow and pass on, reaching even to the neck, and its outspread wings will fill the breadth of your land, O Immanuel."

[9]Be broken,[d] you peoples, and be shattered;[e]
give ear, all you far countries;

strap on your armor and be shattered;
strap on your armor and be shattered.

[10]Take counsel together, but it will come to nothing;
speak a word, but it will not stand,
for God is with us.[f]

[11]For the LORD spoke thus to me with his strong hand upon me, and warned me not to walk in the way of this people, saying: [12]"Do not call conspiracy all that this people calls conspiracy, and do not fear what they fear, nor be in dread. [13]But the LORD of hosts, him you shall honor as holy. Let him be your fear, and let him be your dread. [14]And he will become a sanctuary and a stone of offense and a rock of stumbling to both houses of Israel, a trap and a snare to the inhabitants of Jerusalem. [15]And many shall stumble on it. They shall fall and be broken; they shall be snared and taken."

[16]Bind up the testimony; seal the teaching[g] among my disciples. [17]I will wait for the LORD, who is hiding his face from the house of Jacob, and I will hope in him. [18]Behold, I and the children whom the LORD has given me are signs and portents in Israel from the LORD of hosts, who dwells on Mount Zion.

a Hebrew *with a man's stylus* **b** *Maher-shalal-hash-baz* means *The spoil speeds, the prey hastens* **c** That is, the Euphrates **d** Or *Be evil* **e** Or *dismayed* **f** The Hebrew for *God is with us* is *Immanuel* **g** Or *law*; also verse 20

OVERVIEW: This chapter introduces two more named sons and connects them to the judgments that the Lord will carry out through Assyria. These interpreters debate whether the children are actual biological sons of Isaiah or a way to refer to disciples of the prophet. They also have various perspectives on whether the son named Maher-shalal-hash-baz is the same as Immanuel in the previous chapter. Their answers particularly depend on whether they identify the prophetess as Isaiah's wife, Mary the mother of Jesus in the future, or some other woman. This passage reiterates the theme of trusting in the Lord, with the specific contrast of worrying about conspiracies or making treaties. The references to the Lord as the stone and the rock lead many of these commentators to relate this passage directly to Christ as well as connect it to Immanuel and the covenant promise made to David.

8:1-10 *The Sign of a Child to Be Born*

The Swift Spoiler Is Christ the Strong Man. Johannes Oecolampadius: The prophet's argument in this chapter is the same as that above. For just as there, God promised that he was going to free Ahaz, along with his people, from the fear of Kings Razin and Pekah by calling on Immanuel not yet born, so also here he promises salvation with another name: "Swift Spoiler." And again he threatens the penalty that is going to be exacted on the unbelieving by King Sennacherib and Nebuchadnezzar. He also reports with these histories the uncommon mysteries. For, of course, Christ is addressed with two names, in which we will be able to receive consolation in all adversity, and especially any who are afflicted in conscience. For he is called Immanuel, as was said earlier. And he is "Swift Robber," namely, our defender and redeemer. . . . "If the Son has set us free, you will truly be free." We were sold under sin. . . . "But I am carnal, sold under sin." We were carried away from service to God and oppressed with severe tyranny. He freed us again from that captivity and now made us his servants. And for this reason he is called Swift Spoiler, because when we were the spoils of the devil, he rescued us from slavery to him. . . . † It is said that he is the "stronger one" who takes away the weapons of the "strong one" and distributes the spoils. The weapons of the "strong one" are sin, death, and the curse under which we were held. But by the grace of God, he shattered the weapons and freed us by Christ. Commentary on Isaiah 8:1.[1]

The Promised Seed. Adam Sasbout: How then did he write "with the stylus of humankind," that is, a level stylus, so that anyone can understand it without any difficulty or trouble? To this we say that the prophet did write "with the stylus of humankind," but to those whose tongues were soaked in the saliva of Scripture and who had learned what the gospel is elsewhere. For although the term *gospel* seems to originate from the time of Christ, the reality of the gospel has always been. For we see this immediately . . . where it says, "I will put enmity between you and the woman, between your seed and her seed." For she herself, or according to others, the seed himself, that is, Christ, "will crush your head." This is what the prophet wanted to signify in these words, "Swiftly remove the spoils; quickly plunder." It is as if he were saying, "To this point, the devil has exulted in the world and has been effective on human minds; now he will be cast out. The boy who will be born swiftly removes the spoils, which we are, and they will be plundered quickly; they will no longer endure him reigning." Therefore this speech is about the boy whose name in the previous chapter was called Immanuel. Commentary on Isaiah 8:1[2]

Two Faithful Witnesses Known from Other Scriptures. Johannes Brenz: Uriah the priest and Zachariah son of Berekiah. I have no doubt that this is Uriah, who served in the high priesthood at the time of King Ahaz and the prophet Isaiah. . . . And even though he was a wicked high priest because he carried out the custom of the wicked King Ahaz in destroying the Lord's altar and building the Damascene altar, yet since he was the highest priest and positioned at the highest level of religion, he is suitably and conveniently consulted as a public witness to the divine oracle, which was commanded and publicly presented in writing. But Zechariah, who is a witness along with Uriah, I think was the father of Ahaz's wife, the mother of King Hezekiah. . . . It is written, "The name of Hezekiah's mother was Abijah, daughter of Zechariah." Or he is the Levite from the sons of Asaph. For he is also mentioned in the same passage: "The Levites arose," Scripture says, "from the sons of Asaph: Zechariah, and

[1]Oecolampadius, *In Iesaiam*, 72r-v; citing Jn 8:36; Rom 7:14; Lk 11:22. †Oecolampadius reiterates this argument in his comments on Is 8:8, 10; 9:6-7 (74v, 79v, 81v).

[2]Sasbout, *In Esaiam*, 67-68; citing Gen 3:15.

Matthaniah. . . ." And although only these two, Uriah and Zachariah, are said to have been brought in as witnesses by the prophet—obviously in order to follow the law, "In the mouth of two, every testimony must stand"—yet you should not think that these were the only two there, but rather that in addition to them, several thousand people heard the speech of Isaiah that follows. Commentary on Isaiah 8:2.[3]

The Prophetess Is Mary. Johannes Oecolampadius: The words that the prophet testifies here are what he was made to see in the vision he saw. Beware again here the leaven of the Jews, who say that the prophetess in this passage is the wife of Isaiah. Because if that were so, certainly the term *prophetess* in this passage would not be warranted. For even when they heard the commandments of God on Mount Sinai, they abstained from their wives for three days. And when David was asked to eat the bread of the presence, he required the purity of his servants. And Paul, for the sake of prayer, orders wives to be separated for a certain time. So then, it is not likely that the wife of Isaiah is called the prophetess in this passage. But also disregard the Origenic allegory that makes the prophetess to be the Spirit, moved by the weak argument that in Hebrew *rûaḥ* [spirit] is in the feminine case. But the prophetess is that glorious Virgin Mary, about whom he had spoken in the preceding chapter.[†] And it is right to think there is nothing immodest here; the prophet approached her in a vision to admire the one who is praised, proclaimed, and is called blessed by all peoples. For all generations call her blessed. Commentary on Isaiah 8:3.[4]

Prophecies about the Virgin Mary. Johannes Brenz: For the prophet in this passage does not mean the wife of Isaiah, nor of another prophet, nor of any another woman who was living at that time, but he signifies the blessed virgin Mary, about whom was earlier said, "Behold, the virgin will conceive and give birth to a son. . . ." And he does not mean by "approach" in this passage that he sleeps with the woman, but he means that he prophesies about the virgin, that the Holy Spirit was going to approach her and overshadow her with the power of the Most High, so that she would become pregnant and give birth to Christ the Son of God. For the virgin Mary is called by this name *prophetess* not so much because she composed the prophetical song that says, "My soul magnifies the Lord," in which she was filled with the Holy Spirit in the manner of the prophets, as because the prophets prophesied about Christ, how she would conceive Christ by the Holy Spirit. Commentary on Isaiah 8:3.[5]

Isaiah's Wife. John Trapp: Prophets' wives were anciently called prophetesses; just like bishops' wives (as said by Lapide the Jesuit) were also called bishopesses, presbyters' wives presbyteresses, deacons' wives deaconesses. Jesuits still have their Jesuitesses, as majors their majoresses. Exposition on Isaiah 8:3.[6]

The Mother of Prophecy. Wolfgang Musculus: Who she was is not expressed. It is more simple that we understand this to be about the wife of the prophet. He calls his wife "prophetess," not so much because she was the wife of a prophet as because of the prophecy about the distinguished and unique birth in that name. We do not read about any other prophetesses who flourished in that time; and the honor fits, so we explain that it is about no other than the spouse of the prophet. . . . To me there does not appear any reason why I ought to depart from the simplicity of the letter. Therefore this passage is not about an imaginary birth but a true one; nor do I understand that the seer is

[3]Brenz, *Esaias*, 122; citing 2 Kings 16; 2 Chron 29:1, 13; Deut 19:15.
[4]Oecolampadius, *In Iesaiam*, 73r. [†]See also Pellikan, *Commentaria Bibliorum*, 3:11r-v.

[5]Brenz, *Esaias*, 123.
[6]Trapp, *Commentary or Exposition*, 43*.

speaking about the boy Immanuel, but about another, namely, his own son. Commentary on Isaiah 8:3.[7]

Christ Despoiled Hell. Martin Luther: "Call his name." Thus the second sign corresponds with the words. The people were quickly to become prey. The tablet and the son's name have this meaning. It is Christ, however, who most worthily bears this title by his death, for he despoiled hell. But just as the innocent sons of Hosea are called children of whoredom because of the people committing whoredom, so here Isaiah's son bears his name. However, before the boy could say, "My father, my mother," that is, within a few years, three or four, the king of Assyria came. Lectures on Isaiah 8:3.[8]

Immanuel as a Remnant of Hope. John Calvin: "O Immanuel." It may be asked, Why does the prophet direct his discourse to Christ instead of simply calling the land "God's holy land"? For there can be no doubt that by the name "Immanuel" he means Christ. It might be thought that this expression was used in order to express the disgrace more strongly; for, since Judea not only was set apart to God but in the person of the Mediator had God as the guardian of its safety, it was disgraceful that it should be destroyed by a heathen king. But I rather think that the prophet added this name in order to hold out to good people some remnant of hope and to comfort them in so great a calamity. For when the country was wasted and cruelly torn, they might have lost courage. He therefore means that such desolation would not prevent the coming of the Redeemer of whom he had formerly spoken. As if he had said, "Nevertheless, the land shall be yours, O Immanuel; in it you will have your residence and dwelling." This was therefore added instead of a consolation, in order to indicate that the land, though torn and wasted, belongs to God and not to people. Commentary on Isaiah 8:8.[9]

Nothing Stands Against Immanuel. Johannes Oecolampadius: The prophet, seeing such a great calamity on his own people, says with wonder, "O Immanuel, who is the protector and guardian of the saints, how great is this severity." Its "outspread wings," that is, of the king's armies, filled the whole land. . . . The prophet, though at first terrified by the multitude of enemies, has his mind captured again with a reminder of Immanuel. And he insults the enemies, because they accomplish nothing against the faithful. For although the pharisees and the deceitful who hate the cross of Christ, that is, the kingdom of David, and look to the world perish in temptation, yet the faithful are proven as gold in the furnace of fire. Accordingly he says, "Take counsel together," that is, whatever forces you have prepared, and with whatever weapons you armed yourselves, and with whatever prudence you will act, all will be in vain. The unconquerable truth will stand. Immanuel is promised to us, and no one will be able to harm us. . . . Some have explained that Immanuel in this passage is "God is with us," but others as if he says, "Immanuel is our hope and protection." When the Lord is for us, who is against us? "Neither death, nor life, nor anything in creation will be able to separate us from the love of God." Commentary on Isaiah 8:8-10.[10]

The Double Meaning of Spoiling. Martin Borrhaus: A twofold account of spoiling occurs: one, by which he spoils the king of Samaria and Rezin, the king of the Syrians, through the Assyrian enemies of the kingdom of David; the other by which he plundered the Assyrians and the Israelites and the enemies of the kingdom of David, not by human weapons but by his own, that is, by the angel. A little was already mentioned about this manner of spoiling earlier, and more will be said

[7]Musculus, *In Esaiam*, 185-86.
[8]LW 16:88-89 (WA 31.2:62).
[9]CTS 13:269-70 (CO 36:170).
[10]Oecolampadius, *In Iesaiam*, 74v; citing Rom 8:38.

later too. "Assemble, you peoples, and be conquered." Where two things are to be considered, one is a shadow and figure; the other is the thing itself that is foreshadowed. The figure is in the Israelites and the Syrians waging war against the kingdom of David and his city, Jerusalem, and is seen in Assyria itself being conquered by the angel. But the thing itself that is figured appears at the time when the Israelites and the Gentiles openly profess and declare themselves to be enemies of Christ and his gospel and against his city, that is, against the church of those believing the gospel. In both the Assyrian comings, that is, the power of the antichrist, a small remnant was preserved from his tyranny by faith in Immanuel, Jesus Christ. The spoils are brought by him from the existing heavenly Jerusalem, about which our seer mentions later, "And he will divide the spoils of the strong." Oracles in Isaiah on 8:6-9.[11]

The Lord Will Keep His Promise to David. Konrad Pellikan: For this reason, because the Lord is with us, he will not yet let our kingdom end. Even in your reluctance, he will still keep the promises made to David—not because of our merits (who are sinners) but because he has promised that he will be with us. Therefore he will not abandon us. You will not be able to do anything against his power and truth. Commentary on Isaiah 8:9-10.[12]

8:11-18 *The Lord Is the Rock or the Stumbling Block*

Confronting Conspiracies and Covenants. Johannes Brenz: "This," it says, "is what the Lord spoke to me, and as if taking hold of my hand, he led me away from the customs of the wicked people and taught me that I should not follow their wickedness and unbelief. Therefore I warn you, my listeners, however many embrace the pursuit of godliness, that you should follow my example and not fear the conspiracy of the enemy, nor be intimidated by the shouts of wicked people. For when they have heard the plot and conspiracy of the enemy, they always have it in their mouth, 'conspiracy.' That is, they are terrified beyond measure and, despairing of divine help, they seek human help. For they say, 'Behold, the most powerful kings have conspired against us. Who will defend us from so many evils? Why don't we, too, make a covenant with other kings? Why don't we conspire with the king of the Assyrians, so that we may be saved by the aid of his forces?'" You see, then, that the wicked citizens did not fear the Lord their God, nor call for his help, but only feared the conspiracy and the covenants of their enemies, and they thought about forming covenants with foreign kings, by whose power they would be protected from their enemies. Commentary on Isaiah 8:11-12.[13]

Fear the Holy One. Johannes Oecolampadius: "Do not be frightened by those who kill the body and afterwards have no more they can do, but I will show you who you should fear. Fear him who after he has killed, has the power to cast into hell, certainly I say to you, fear him." Those are diabolical tongues who, from this passage, attempt to remove this treasure of fear from the hearts of the godly, calling it superstition and saying that it is contrary to love. Fear is a particular degree of love, as is said later. . . . But we should fear God, if nothing else beside him is feared. That is, he is not to be encountered and he is not to be worshiped less than is proper. He considers this fear greatly pleasing. Commentary on Isaiah 8:13.[14]

Treating the Lord as Holy. Heinrich Bullinger: So what? He further teaches the faithful what they should do. For so far he showed them what they should not do, that is, what they should avoid. The Lord God Almighty, it says, he

[11]Borrhaus, *In Iesaiae Prophetae Oracula*, 99; citing Is 53:12.
[12]Pellikan, *Commentaria Bibliorum*, 3:11v.
[13]Brenz, *Esaias*, 129.
[14]Oecolampadius, *In Iesaiam*, 75v-76r; citing Lk 12:4-5; Is 34.

is the Holy One. He opposes their teaching of empty hope attached to conspiracies or human covenants. For God to truly be considered holy is to prefer God to all things in the world, acknowledge that he is the most holy one, the truest and most certain helper, to believe in him, to worship him religiously, and to praise and celebrate him as our excellent and only God. Therefore we attribute more to God and his strength than to human covenants and strength. So we pray, "Hallowed be your name." Sermons on Isaiah 8:13.[15]

Snare of Justification by Works. John Mayer: But in speaking of Jerusalem he varies the phrase, saying, "a trap and a snare to the inhabitants of Jerusalem," to denote their ensnaring or being taken unaware by that erroneous opinion of justification by works and not by faith in Christ Jesus alone, as Paul argues . . . , applying the words of this passage. In this way, it appears that, although it was fulfilled long before, yet it was chiefly fulfilled in the time of the gospel, as Oecolampadius well notes.[†] Commentary on Isaiah 8:14.[16]

The Cornerstone of the Church. Leonhard Schiemer: Church or *ekklēsia* is a body of people built on Christ, not the pope, Luther, or the emperor. Paul says, "You are no longer guests and strangers but fellow citizens and members of the household, built on the foundation of the apostles and prophets." For the prophets all had the Spirit of Christ in them. This Christ is the cornerstone rejected by the builders (all preachers). This sign (Christ) will also be contradicted. The Twelve Articles of the Christian Faith.[17]

Signs of Christ. Dietrich Schnepff: He attributes to Christ several epithets, to which he assigns the effects of each in this way:

Christ is
the stone of offense
the rock of stumbling
a snare
a trap

Therefore, the wicked:
will strike against it
will fall and be crushed
will be caught
will be captured.

Scholia on Isaiah 8:14-15.[18]

Keeping Promises in Baptism. Katharina Schütz Zell: Therefore I exhort all Christians, by the promise they made to God in their baptism, not to allow this poison spewer to corrupt them but to choose to remain with the wholesome, life-giving teaching of Christ Jesus, who alone is our wisdom, righteousness, sanctification, and redemption. . . . Indeed, he is the cornerstone of which Isaiah and Peter speak, one who is precious to believers but to unbelievers is a cornerstone of offense and a stone of stumbling. Apologia for Master Matthew Zell, Her Husband.[19]

Christ the Stone and Rock. Johannes Brenz: But now about those we call "respectable." What therefore is Christ to them? "A stone," it says, "of offense, and a rock of stumbling," and of ruin. Even if these are worthy to be commended because they lead a respectable life, true righteousness and salvation do not nevertheless follow. For they do not believe in Jesus Christ but are offended by him; first because he teaches a righteousness other than the law. Therefore they say, "What? If people are justified only by faith, who then is going to devote himself to the work of a respectable life according to God's law?" Then, because Christ was crucified and also sends those who believe in him to the cross and to afflictions, they say, "What? If this true

[15]Bullinger, *Isaias*, 46v.
[16]Mayer, *Commentary upon All the Prophets*, 4:62-63*; citing Rom 9:30-32. [†]See Oecolampadius, *In Iesaiam*, 76r-v.
[17]CRR 12:254; citing Eph 2:19; 1 Pet 1:1; Is 28:16; Ps 118:22; Mt 21:42; 1 Pet 2:6; Lk 2:34.
[18]Schnepff, *In Esaiae*, 140.
[19]Zell, *Katharina Schütz Zell, Church Mother*, 72; citing 1 Cor 1:30.

righteousness were given by faith, why would they be so afflicted and despised in this world?" This is to stumble on Christ and his righteousness. And those who stumble in this way fall, are ruined, and are crushed. For "all who fall," Christ says, "on this stone will be broken and crushed." Righteousness does not follow; it does not attain the law of righteousness. Why not? Because it is not from faith, Paul says, but as if from the works of the law. For they are thrust against the stone of stumbling. . . . For after Isaiah exhorted his listeners that they should not fear the two kings, their enemies, who could not destroy the kingdom of Judah, he said they should instead fear the Lord of hosts, who is Christ, for he is the stone by which their descendants will be so offended and be crushed because of their unbelief that they will lose their earthly and heavenly kingdom. Commentary on Isaiah 8:14-15.[20]

Do Not Fear the Enemies of the Church. Zacharias Ursinus: Therefore, it is our responsibility not to be so terrified at the strength and pomp of the enemies, and the intentions and endeavors against us, but rather, above all things, to see diligently that we have Immanuel standing by our side. And with God appeased and propitiated in Christ, no matter what will happen, we flee to him and depend on him alone in true faith and repentance. Commentary on Isaiah 8:14-15.[21]

Seal Instruction Until the Time of Jesus' Disciples. Martin Borrhaus: Therefore they want a command that the seer, Isaiah, and his disciples (people taught by the Spirit), keep this mystical oracle closed and sealed in their hearts until the time when it pleases God to reveal it to the world, when the books of mysteries are opened, and the veil lifted from the eyes of the Israelites, about which the apostle speaks in his letter to the Corinthians: "Now even to this day when the Old Testament is read, the same veil remains unlifted, because through Christ, the veil is taken away." For this reason, I read that veil here, "Seal the law among my disciples." By the term *law*, the mystical oracles are meant. This interpretation is that the hidden prophecies of the prophets reached their fulfilling and opening in the later times of the revelation of Christ and the antichrist. Another interpretation is that the seer is commanded with his disciples to bind the divine law in their hearts, which they will keep even if others shrink back from keeping it. Finally, there are some who wish to refer these words to Christ and his apostles and those who have received their doctrine, as interpreted by the Epistle to the Hebrews. Without doubt, Christ says, "Although many of the Israelites will fall and stumble because of me, there will still be some who will have faith in me, and will be my disciples. The testimony of my gospel will be bound in them and will be sealed by my Spirit. Inspired by him, they believe in me. They will not fall in despair with the rest." Christ is speaking of them in these words, "It has been given to you to understand the mysteries of the kingdom of heaven." And that is what we read here, "Bind up the testimony and seal the law among my disciples." Oracles in Isaiah on 8:16.[22]

Sons Are Disciples. Heinrich Bullinger: He calls his disciples and those who share in the same faith and hope, "his sons." And the apostle also calls those "sons," according to Galatians and Corinthians, who have been born of God through teaching. Further, so that no one should misinterpret that he called his own sons, or boys, as if they were made boys by his own power, he adds, "whom the Lord gave me." For "no one comes to me," the Lord says in the Gospel, "unless my Father draws them." Sermons on Isaiah 8:18.[23]

The Boys Are Disciples. Martin Borrhaus: Further, those who before were called *limûdîm*, that

[20]Brenz, *Esaias*, 133-34; citing Mt 21:44; citing Rom 3.
[21]Ursinus, *Iesaiam*, 272.
[22]Borrhaus, *In Iesaiae Prophetae Oracula*, 104; citing 2 Cor 3:14; Mt 13:11.
[23]Bullinger, *Isaias*, 47b; citing Jn 6:44.

is, disciples, here they are called *yĕlādîm,* that is, those who are born, or boys. Because those who are taught by the Spirit of the Messiah, understand the mysteries of salvation. They are called "sons of God," since they are born by the same Spirit. "They are born of God," is said about those who later are described as "taught by God." For heavenly doctrine contains the divine seed of regeneration, about which Peter says they "have been born again, not of perishable seed but imperishable, through the living and abiding word of God," into eternity. Oracles in Isaiah on 8:18.[24]

True Believers Are Rare. Johannes Oecolampadius: But at the same time, the scarcity is also shown of those who are good and who are marked by their deeds and keep the law of the Lord. Isaiah remains with the few in Jerusalem who truly seek the Lord with their heart. Likewise few follow Jesus. A great number always stray. For true Christians, if they are compared to others, are so rare, and so belittled that they are considered as "signs and portents," even though we boast to the whole world we are Christians. Commentary on Isaiah 8:18.[25]

Mount Zion as the Lord's Habitation. Wolfgang Musculus: "He who dwells on Mount Zion." The fear of King Ahaz and the people of Judah was due to the unbelief and great reputation of the two kings of Syria and Samaria. They acted as if there was no power in Mount Zion sufficient to resist them, even though they had the Lord of hosts, the inhabitant of Mount Zion, who, with many great proofs, had declared his power from there as a fortress against any enemies for his kingdom and his people. That is why with this saying, he reprimands the astonishing unbelief of his people, among whom it was happening that while the Lord of hosts was dwelling on Mount Zion, they were so cowardly fearing "the two smoldering stumps of firebrands." The kind of saying this is, where it says the Lord dwells on Mount Zion when he is contained neither on earth nor in heaven, has been discussed elsewhere. Commentary on Isaiah 8:18.[26]

---

[24]Borrhaus, *In Iesaiae Prophetae Oracula,* 104; citing 1 Pet 1:23.

[25]Oecolampadius, *In Iesaiam,* 77r.

[26]Musculus, *In Esaiam,* 201; citing Is 7:4.

8:19–9:7 LIGHT TO THE DARKNESS

19 *And when they say to you, "Inquire of the
mediums and the necromancers who chirp and
mutter," should not a people inquire of their
God? Should they inquire of the dead on behalf
of the living?* 20 *To the teaching and to the
testimony! If they will not speak according to this
word, it is because they have no dawn.* 21 *They
will pass through the land,*[a] *greatly distressed
and hungry. And when they are hungry, they
will be enraged and will speak contemptuously
against*[b] *their king and their God, and turn their
faces upward.* 22 *And they will look to the earth,
but behold, distress and darkness, the gloom of
anguish. And they will be thrust into
thick darkness.*

9 [c] *But there will be no gloom for her who was in
anguish. In the former time he brought into
contempt the land of Zebulun and the land of
Naphtali, but in the latter time he has made glorious
the way of the sea, the land beyond the Jordan,
Galilee of the nations.*[d]

2[e] *The people who walked in darkness*
have seen a great light;

those who dwelt in a land of deep darkness,
on them has light shone.

3 *You have multiplied the nation;*
you have increased its joy;
they rejoice before you
as with joy at the harvest,
as they are glad when they divide the spoil.

4 *For the yoke of his burden,*
and the staff for his shoulder,
the rod of his oppressor,
you have broken as on the day of Midian.

5 *For every boot of the tramping warrior in*
battle tumult
and every garment rolled in blood
will be burned as fuel for the fire.

6 *For to us a child is born,*
to us a son is given;

and the government shall be upon[f] *his shoulder,*
and his name shall be called[g]

Wonderful Counselor, Mighty God,
Everlasting Father, Prince of Peace.

7 *Of the increase of his government and of peace*
there will be no end,

on the throne of David and over his kingdom,
to establish it and to uphold it

with justice and with righteousness
from this time forth and forevermore.

The zeal of the Lord of hosts will do this.

a Hebrew *it* b Or *speak contemptuously by* c Ch 8:23 in Hebrew d Or *of the Gentiles* e Ch 9:1 in Hebrew f Or *is upon* g Or *is called*

Overview: Most Reformation interpreters identify this as a distinct passage that still continues to speak about Christ, as in the previous chapters. In fact, at least one interpreter argues that Isaiah recounts Christ himself speaking in part of this passage. They give a significant amount of space to explaining how each of the names and titles correspond to Jesus. For some, this includes exposition about the Trinity and the deity of Christ, especially those who seek to refute Jewish interpretations. A few comment on the intriguing appearance of a final-*mem* (the form of the Hebrew letter *m* only used at the end of words) in the middle of a word that is variously interpreted as referring to the Messiah or Mary. From the beginning of this passage and throughout, the Reformers compare the setting of darkness and the deficiencies of good leaders to their own day. They also recognize that this passage continues the theme that one must trust in God because he alone will set his people free.

8:19–9:1 *Darkness and Gloom*

The Metaphor of Darkness and Gloom. Zacharias Ursinus: The metaphor of darkness and light is stated at the end of chapter 8. The Israelites were walking in darkness, with each kingdom devastated. Israel and Judah were deported into exile. Royal dignity, politics, divinely instituted worship of God, the ministry, and the public voice of heavenly teaching were all removed, and finally all protections of human life, property, and decoration were lost. They were especially buried in the ignorance of God, in idolatry, and various errors, without any true consolation.

They were brought out of this darkness into the light, that is, from captivity and slavery into freedom and happiness—of course, only in part—when Jerusalem was besieged by Sennacherib, and all Judea, which had already been occupied, was freed by the angel that slaughtered his army, and again when, after seventy years of Babylonian captivity, their freedom and land was restored to Judah. But truly this most fully happened when the Messiah was presented in the gospel that was preached and, having fulfilled the office of mediator on earth, ascended to heaven, and when he had sent the Holy Spirit, gathered to himself the eternal church from Jews and Gentiles, and so brought the whole elect Israel out of infernal darkness into the heavenly light. Commentary on Isaiah 8:19-22.[1]

The Historical Nature Is the Time of Hezekiah. Martin Borrhaus: If we follow the thread of history, it is evident from the second book of Chronicles that Hezekiah, prefiguring the Messiah for us, sent ambassadors to the remnant of the ten tribes, to bring them to Jerusalem to celebrate Passover. From the time of Jeroboam, these tribes were following the false worship of calves and so were constantly in darkness. And during the reign of Hezekiah, according to the reckoning of time, the light dawned on them. For the holy king called them to repentance with these words, "Return to the Lord, O people of Israel, to the God of Abraham, Isaac, and Jacob, that he may return to the remnant of you who have escaped from the hand of the kings of the Assyrians." And it is recorded in the same Chronicles that some of the Zebulunites and the remaining tribes came to Jerusalem to worship Jehovah.

Now about the mystical history.[†] With this veil drawn back, the times of the Savior Messiah would come when the spiritual Assyrian was destroying everything among the Israelites, so that a clear light would shine on the remnant of the Israelite people. The apostle declares this in his letter to the Romans with a testimony quoted from our prophet about the beginning of the illumination on the tribe of Zebulun and Galilee. For so it is written in the Gospel of Matthew, which describes to us the beginning of Christ's sermons and miracles, "When Jesus heard that John had been arrested, he withdrew to Galilee, and leaving Nazareth, he went and stayed in Capernaum, which is a maritime city on the borders of Zebulun and Naphtali." Oracles in Isaiah on 8:19-22.[2]

Where the Dead Are. Johannes Brenz: These oracles of spirits are to be avoided. For although it cannot be denied that spirits sometimes raise a disturbance and utter the sound of cursing, yet these spirits are not the souls of dead people. For if anyone "falls asleep in Christ," that soul lives with Christ in heaven and does not wander on the earth. But if anyone died in unbelief, that soul was bound with Satan in the chains of night in Tartarus until the last day of this age. For since the wicked are members of Satan, it is clear that they will also be locked up together with Satan in Tartarus for judgment. That is why it

[1]Ursinus, *Iesaiam*, 299.

[2]Borrhaus, *In Iesaiae Prophetae Oracula*, 108-9. Borrhaus cites 2 Chron 30:6; Rom 9:33; Mt 4:12-13. [†]For similar interpretation, see Oecolampadius, *In Iesaiam*, 79v-80r.

should not be thought that the souls of people walk about the earth after death. Then, what are those disturbing spirits? They are mere ghosts of Satan, and therefore neither are they to be feared, nor should their responses be believed. Commentary on Isaiah 8:19.[3]

Magicians and Diviners of the Dead. Zacharias Ursinus: Magicians and diviners are indeed dead in many ways. They are destitute of true and spiritual life, which consists in the true recognition of God. They are sentenced to the punishments from God, from which they cannot extricate themselves or others with their own counsel. They imagine protection for themselves from demons and dead people (as Saul does . . .), who can neither hear nor help them—whether in idols, which are nothing, or in their superstitions and other lifeless things, which have no ability to foresee or advise. In contrast, people were alive right in front of them. At least those alive in this physical life could know, consult, act, and manage the things of this life, which the dead cannot do. But they, too, should be alive, that is, have right counsels and comforts at hand from the knowledge of God and the divine will. And they wanted to be considered and seen as such. Commentary on Isaiah 8:19.[4]

God Alone Gives Life and Light. Heinrich Bullinger: God alone is living and life-giving, and people who live and are strong with divine wisdom are made alive and enlightened by God. And the Spirit of God confers true wisdom. According to this the holy prophets and apostles spoke. Why then should we consult and listen to these "deceased people," who, although they are living in the flesh and in the world, we know they are dead to God? And they asked the necromantic gods of the Gentiles for answers from the dead. But it is foolish to seek learning from the dead, or truth from liars and the father of lies. Satan, who inspires all the gods, is a liar and the father of lies. But every person is a liar unless that one is enlightened by the Spirit of God and is led into the truth by the Spirit of God. Therefore, let none of us believe in any diviner or even in any mortal person (unless that one brings forth the word of life), so that we only appear to be alive but have yielded to the dead. Sermons on Isaiah 8:20.[5]

Light Enough. John Trapp: Happy was Oecolampadius (an excellent commentator on this prophet), who made good the splendor of his own name, when, in addition to the light he lent to the law and testimonies, he could lay his hand on his breast when he lay dying of the plague and say, "Here's plenty of light obtained from the Scripture."[†] Exposition on Isaiah 8:20.[6]

The Word of the Living God. Johannes Oecolampadius: And since God is the author of life, we safely build on his word. For by his word he created heaven and earth, and none fails. But idols and creatures, how can those help when the majority are dead or useless in themselves? What a foolish exchange! The living God calls us, and we turn to the dead? Whatever you compare to God, they are not as effective as dead people are to the living. Nothing is more effective than the word of God. "For heaven and earth will pass away, but my words will not pass away." Nothing is more empty than lying, and these are from the father of lies. Commentary on Isaiah 8:20.[7]

The Sign of the True Church. Menno Simons: The first sign by which to distinguish the church of Christ is the salutary and unadulterated doctrine of his holy and divine word. God commanded Israel to abide by the doctrine of the law and not to deviate from it, either to the right or to the left. . . . Isaiah admonished them to conform

[3]Brenz, *Esaias*, 140; citing 1 Thess 4:14.
[4]Ursinus, *Iesaiam*, 288; citing 1 Sam 28.

[5]Bullinger, *Isaias*, 48v.
[6]Trapp, *Commentary or Exposition*, 46*. [†]See the letter from Simon Grynaeus to Wolfgang Capito in March 1534 in Staehelin, *Briefe und Akten*, 19: 734-35 [No. 968].
[7]Oecolampadius, *In Iesaiam*, 78r; citing Mt 24:35.

themselves to the law and its testimony, or they would not receive light. . . . Christ commanded his disciples, saying, "Go into all the world and preach the gospel to every creature," and, "teach them to observe everything I have commanded you." The prophets testify on every hand that they spoke the word of God. "Thus says the Lord of hosts," they say; and, "the mouth of the Lord says"; and again, "thus speaks the Lord God who has led you out of the land of Egypt," and other similar testimonies. The Signs by Which Both Churches May Be Known.[8]

Against Good Ministers. John Trapp: So in Julian the Apostate's time, Jews and Gentiles joined together against Christians: and in our day, papists and Lutherans against Calvinists. How unworthily and impotently do the Lutherans of Suevia rail on that holy man Oecolampadius, whose note it is on this text that these last dangerous times were foretold by Saint Paul. . . . Do not Paul and Isaiah describe the same people? Bullinger observes concerning the Anabaptists of Germany that, while they are at great odds among themselves, they are still all in agreement against godly ministers of the truth, to despise and disparage them to the utmost. Exposition on Isaiah 9:1.[9]

9:2-5 *A Promise of Light for the People in Darkness*

The Siege and Liberation of the City. Wolfgang Musculus: He understands the people walking in darkness and having the shadow of death in their land to be the people of Judah and Jerusalem. Truly darkness and the shadow of death is the siege of the city of Jerusalem, which was about to happen by Sennacherib, the king of the Assyrians, as we will see later in this passage. He spoke about this previously. Now he gives the reason why he would not say that the gloom about which he was prophesying will be such that it partly had happened and partly was still going to come on Israel. Because he says in that gloom we will see a great light, which will shine on those who will dwell as if they were in the shadow of death, surrounded by the most serious siege. By this "great light," truly understand that most illuminating liberation when the heavenly angel was sent to Jerusalem and was going to liberate them from the hand of those besieging it. Commentary on Isaiah 9:2.[10]

Where Christ Would Teach. Johannes Brenz: Here the prophet is the Messiah or Christ our Lord. Therefore, there is no other teaching that brings true salvation to us besides the teaching of Christ. But now again Isaiah follows in the place of Christ and takes up his own speech, no longer reciting the words of Christ but his own words. And he continues on the same subject that Christ had previously taken up to be treated. For since it was said before that the teaching of Christ alone is to be followed, he now proceeds to explain in what region Christ will initially teach his gospel, and what fruit his teaching is going to produce. . . .

For Christ began the preaching of his gospel in that region, performed his first miracles there, and chose his apostles there. He was wandering around (says Matthew) all Galilee, teaching in their synagogues, and preaching the gospel of the kingdom, and curing every disease and every infirmity among the people. Here again, you see how much Isaiah was illuminated by the Spirit, that he not only knew that Christ would come and preach his gospel but also in what region and even in what part of the region he was going to begin preaching his gospel. Where do you think he drew this from, if not from the Holy Spirit himself? Commentary on Isaiah 9:2.[11]

The Shadow of Death for Jerusalem. Heinrich Bullinger: The shadow is attached,

---

[8]Simons, *Complete Works* 2:81*; citing Deut 5:32; Is 8:20; Mt 28:19-20.

[9]Trapp, *Commentary or exposition*, 51; citing 2 Tim 3:1-2.

[10]Musculus, *In Esaiam*, 209; citing 2 Kings 19.

[11]Brenz, *Esaias*, 142-43.

as it were, to the body, and follows the body. So, we are "in the valley of the shadow of death" when it appears to us to see death most immediately imminent. And what else than immediate death could the citizens of Jerusalem have promised themselves when the city, stripped of all protection and aid, was besieged by the Assyrians with such power that you hardly ever read about another city being besieged like—and then to be attacked, captured, and cut down? But oppressed by such gloom of darkness, there suddenly and unexpectedly arose the wonderful light of divine deliverance. Sermons on Isaiah 9:2.[12]

A Prophecy About the Same Young Women. Sebastian Castellio: "Behold, the young maiden was pregnant." While this brings up the beginning of the prophecy, the seer takes us back to that so that we consider the whole of this prophecy. For this should not be understood as Isaiah saying with these words, "the young maiden was pregnant," that he predicted a birth from a virgin, but rather that this whole prophecy begins with "Behold, the young maiden was pregnant." Nor does it matter that Matthew calls her a virgin and not a young maiden. For either he wrote in Hebrew (as Sophronius passes down in his *Life*)[†] or in Greek (for I can confirm neither), and he followed the Greek translator of this word, which is "virgin." And he did not do this ineptly when he used the words about the true Emmanuel, whom Isaiah had foretold—not with a word but in reality and in thought—would be born of a virgin. Annotations on Isaiah 9:3.[13]

God Does Not Liberate by Human Strength. Heinrich Bullinger: And although indeed all this is clear, he further illustrates it by including the history from the seventh chapter of the book of Judges. "As in the days of Midian" is when the Midianites were oppressing God's people in the same way the Assyrians were now. Then he truly delivered them, not by human strength and with the Jewish people equipped for battle, but by the singular grace and power of God, by which the enemies were slain by mutual wounds when they set against each other and were crushed with fear at the sound of the trumpets. For so now the Assyrians die at the walls of Jerusalem, by the hand of the angel of God, not by the weapons of the scattered and oppressed Jews. Accordingly, the faithful, glorying in the psalm, most rightly sing, "They trust in horses and chariots, but we will trust in the name of the Lord of hosts." Sermons on Isaiah 9:4.[14]

Christ Delivers from Tyranny. Zacharias Ursinus: Just as the people of God, through Gideon and other leaders, were delivered from the tyranny of enemies, not by their own merit or strength but by divine mercy and power, so also Christ delivered us, not by our own merits but by his merit and power, from the devil, sin, death, hell, and the world. Their plans and efforts were remarkably demolished and destroyed by his. But those things that seek to destroy us promote our salvation. Commentary on Isaiah 9:4.[15]

Christ Broke the Yoke in Fulfilling the Law. Johannes Oecolampadius: Our consciences were burdened with the heaviest burdens of sins; but Christ relieved us, who says, "Come to me, all you who labor and are burdened, and I will give you rest. Take my yoke upon you; for my yoke is easy, and the burden is sweet." We now know that through the blood of Christ, the Father has been satisfied for us, and that the punishments of a thousand hells due to our sins have been dismissed in the merit of Christ. And likewise, the burden of the law, which contains precepts, ceremonies, and judgments, was pressing, and it pressed so much that Peter himself said to the apostles that neither they nor their fathers could bear it—not only because most of the laws regarding ceremonies and judgments were intolerable but also

[12]Bullinger, *Isaias*, 50r.

[13]Castellio, *Adnotationes*, 67. [†]Sophronius was the patriarch of Jerusalem from 634–638 and wrote *The Life of the Evangelist Matthew*, a portion of which can be found in PG 127:139-40.

[14]Bullinger, *Isaias*, 50v; citing Judg 7:22; Ps 20:7.

[15]Ursinus, *Iesaiam*, 310.

because the precepts themselves in the Decalogue demand the affection and everything that is in a person. They were more burdensome than our weakness could bear. . . .

The breaking of the yoke, however, is not that the precepts are not required for us to keep in the future, but that the merit of faith in Christ is so much that former sins are not imputed, since Christ made satisfaction for these, and whatever we did not fulfill (since we fulfilled nothing), Christ fulfilled. COMMENTARY ON ISAIAH 9:4-5.[16]

9:6-7 *Titles of the Promised Child*

THE SAME CHILD PROMISED. JOHANNES OECOLAMPADIUS: He again established the promise with an unusual sign, that of a child born, who . . . was born from a virgin, and he calls Immanuel, and . . . he was born from a prophetess and is called Swift Spoiler. Now simply it says, "He is born and given to us." And see now the twofold nature signified by the twofold name, humanity in the child, divinity in the Son. Certainly he cites many names at the same time, by which our hope is confirmed. And he speaks in the past tense so that there may be more certainty about the prophecy. . . . And just as above he assigned the names Immanuel and Swift Spoiler, so also now, in order for us not to distrust his promises, he numerates these names by which the feebleness of our faith may be helped. For he not only is called such, but he also is such and has always been. COMMENTARY ON ISAIAH 9:6.[17]

UPON THE SHOULDER. ADAM SASBOUT: "And he became a ruler. . . ." This is a phrase of Scripture taken from the custom of the Jews by which this boy is signified to become a ruler—whether an emperor or a king. It is as if he says, "That boy who will be born will be a king and emperor." This phrase seems to have been taken from those who carried staffs on their shoulders, which were signs to the Jews indicating power and authority. So, in the preceding words, "the staff for his shoulder, you have broken," that is, his power and rule. And among the Romans, flags were preferred to signify public power and authority. And at the time of Paul, this was indicated by the sword. . . . "The judge does not bear the sword without reason." We have a similar phrase . . . : "And I will bestow the key of the house of David on his shoulder." There not only is power and possession signified, but also the power of rule is at hand and ready so that he may carry out whatever he wills. Two things are signified by this phrase in Scripture: sometimes it is the power of ruling, but sometimes something at hand is said to be either "on the shoulder" or "upon the shoulder." . . . "And he who judges, let him write the charge so that I may carry it on my shoulder." That is, "so that I may carry it around and so that it may be a handbook and a manual for me." COMMENTARY ON ISAIAH 9:6.[18]

CONSTANT TEACHING ABOUT CHRIST. HEINRICH BULLINGER: Therefore Christ is described graphically by much prosopography[†] from Isaiah, and it is shown who he is, how great he is, why such things are attributed to him, what the heavenly Father will give to us in him, and what kind of future reign his is. . . . Yet here he repeats again the teaching about Christ, so that he may teach us by his example that the teaching about Christ, in whom alone is salvation and from whom all good things flow in this world, must be emphasized and repeated constantly in front of the church. SERMONS ON ISAIAH 9:6-7.[19]

THE PROPHETS AGREE ABOUT CHRIST. MENNO SIMONS: Again, with this our confession, foundation, and belief, all the prophets who have spoken of Christ, the Son of God, through the Holy Spirit, agree. . . . Observe, Isaiah says, "Behold,

[16]Oecolampadius, *In Iesaiam*, 81r; citing Mt 11:30; Jn 8; Gal 5; Rom 8; 1 Cor 15.
[17]Oecolampadius, *In Iesaiam*, 81v-82r; citing Is 7:14; 8:1.
[18]Sasbout, *In Esaiam*, 77; citing Is 9:4; Rom 13:4; Is 22:22; Job 31:35-36.
[19]Bullinger, *Isaias* 51v; citing Is 7–8. [†]By the term *prosopography*, Bullinger refers to a compilation of individual characteristics.

a virgin shall conceive and bear a son, and shall call his name Immanuel," which signifies God with us. . . . He further says, "Unto us a child is born, unto us a son is given." A Clear and Incontrovertible Confession and Demonstration.[20]

Christ Given for Us. Johannes Oecolampadius: Great emphasis is on the phrase "to us." There are many who believe that Christ was born—but not for them. They admit that he is Savior—but they do not dare to profess to be his. This is not surprising, because they are not in him but rely on their own works. Commentary on Isaiah 9:6.[21]

Coeternal with the Father. Zacharias Ursinus: Therefore, the Son is from Mighty God, who is also himself Mighty God. Moreover, there is no God but one. Therefore, he is coeternal and *homoousios*[†] with the Father. And he is able to accomplish the plans he gives us and to prosper us with blessed success and outcome. "You have overcome them, because he who is in you is greater than he who is in the world." . . . He speaks here, then, of the same Son who in chapters 7 and 8 he calls Immanuel. Commentary on Isaiah 9:6.[22]

Contrast with Leaders of the Day. Johannes Brenz: The second title is "Counselor." And this epitaph is an antithesis against the earthly rulers. For they are not able to give counsel to all their people in their business, but they need counselors for themselves. They have many "consulters" who assist them in the administration of their rule. And yet neither their rulers nor their counselors are able to give that counsel to the people that results in true happiness. But the Messiah himself is the Counselor; he does not need the counsel of other humans, but he alone suffices to give counsel, and that is going to result in heavenly goods. Moreover, the counsel of the Messiah is his gospel, that whoever follows pursues true life. . . . Briefly, if you seek counsel, how do you obtain true riches, true virtue, true power, true glory, true and eternal life? You cannot be more certain nor more right than to find it in the Messiah and his gospel. Commentary on Isaiah 9:6.[23]

Christ the Conquering Hero. Martin Borrhaus: This strong name of "Hero" is wonderfully comforting to those who, strengthened by faith, know that they are under the signs of a military leader who is God, the Redeemer and Savior, whom no power can resist. Likewise, he is the hero who, with heroic strength, has conquered every opposing power and will display the vanquished in triumph. Abraham, Isaac, Jacob, Joseph, Moses, Joshua, Gideon, David, Hezekiah, the prophets and apostles, and holy martyrs were heroes endowed with the spirit of the royal priesthood. But none of them displayed the strength that Christ Jesus has displayed, so that he himself can say, "I have conquered the world, and with it conquered, I hold the seat at the right hand of God, from where I rule over all that is contained in heaven and earth." Oracles in Isaiah on 9:6.[24]

A Jewish Attempt at Names. Johannes Oecolampadius: The Hebrews corrupt the sense when they read this as, "And he will call his name," so they can explain it as, "Wonderful Counselor, Mighty God, Father of Future Ages called him the Prince of Peace." But this is clear deceit. For almost every other place they translate *yîqrāʾ* impersonally with "will be called," or they understand only one "he will call" as in . . . , "You will be called the city of righteousness." We say all those titles should be attributed to Christ. Commentary on Isaiah 9:6.[25]

Christ's Office as Father of the Church. Zacharias Ursinus: This title and the following pertain to his office. He is called "Eternal Father," not

[20]Simons, *Complete Works* 2:152; citing Is 7:14; Mt 1:23.
[21]Oecolampadius, *In Iesaiam*, 81v-82r; citing Titus 3.
[22]Ursinus, *Iesaiam*, 304; citing 1 Jn 4:4. [†]*Homoousios* is the orthodox term in the Trinitarian debates from the 4th century that means "same essence" and was often rendered as *consubstantial* in Latin.
[23]Brenz, *Esaias*, 152-53.
[24]Borrhaus, *In Iesaiae Prophetae Oracula*, 117.
[25]Oecolampadius, *In Iesaiam*, 82r; citing Is 1:26.

only because he is eternal but particularly because he is the producer and giver of eternal life. . . . So just as he is "Eternal Father," so he will have eternal sons, whose father he will never cease to be. But Christ is called "father," not of God, as the Father of Christ is God the Father, of course, the first person of the Godhead. But together with his father, he is said to be the father of his church, that is, put in charge over us by God, as the firstborn son of the father's house, regenerating us by the Holy Spirit and sharing with us the paternal inheritance. For that reason, the faithful are also named his brothers and his sons. Commentary on Isaiah 9:6.[26]

The True Son Who Takes the Burden. Pilgram Marpeck: By the will of the Father, he was born of a virgin from the generation of the fathers. He was born the true Son of God, full of grace and truth and according to the Spirit. He is the eternal Word and the only born Son of the Father. He is filled with every counsel and knowledge, wisdom, understanding, and perception of the Father's will. As announced . . . : "For unto us a child is born, a son is given, and the kingship will be upon his shoulder." As Samuel told the people of Israel when, like the Gentiles, they desired a king, the kings of this world rest their kingship as a heavy burden on the shoulders of the people. Such a king had the right to expect that his kingship should rest on the shoulders of the people, that they should bear the burden of the king. However, this king, the Lord Jesus Christ, has liberated his people from their eternal burden; he has put it on his own shoulders and fastened it to the cross.

Can we conceive of a more glorious kingdom, priesthood, kingship, or king? Isaiah further says that his name is Wonderful Counselor, the Mighty God, the Everlasting Father, the Prince of Peace. His kingdom shall have no end, and peace will be multiplied. This child has been given to us by the Father with all his treasures and gifts, and he will be the acceptable new year. Concerning the Lowliness of Christ.[27]

Possible Heresies. Wolfgang Musculus: One should beware not to take this inscription as referring to the person of the Father in divinity so that we fall into the heresy of the Patripassians, Sabellians, Noetians, and others like those, who maintain only one person in the divinity and therefore deny the faith and confession of the Holy Triad. Here Christ is called "Eternal Father," not because he is the father in divinity but because he was given to us from God the Father as a father in whom and through whom we are regenerated, obtain adoption as sons, and are made partakers of eternal life. In this sense, he is rightly called our father, by whom we are redeemed and brought into life. But he is called "Eternal Father," so that it is not implied that his fatherly grace is for one age, since it is intended for all ages, enduring from the beginning all the way to the end of the world. "Wonderful," indeed, is this child, who is proclaimed to us as eternal. Wonderful man, who is here called "Mighty God." Wonderful son, who was given to us as a father. Commentary on Isaiah 9:6.[28]

The Affection and Judgment of a Father. Johannes Brenz: First, therefore, he is called father, not in his person in the divine nature, for thus he is the Son, not the Father. But he is called father in affection. For he always has a fatherly affection toward his people, and this affection does not change into eternity. . . . "Can a mother forget her infant that she should not have pity on the child of her womb? Even though she forgets, I will not forget you." . . . "The mountains will be shaken and the hills tremble, but my mercy will not depart from you, and my covenant of peace will not be moved." Why, then, do we confess as an article of faith that he is the judge of the living and the dead? Is it not the judge's duty to punish criminals? Will not Christ condemn the wicked to eternal punishment? Is this fatherly affection?

I answer: Christ always maintains the fatherly affection in what pertains to himself. And he will come at the Last Judgment to judge the living and

[26]Ursinus, *Iesaiam*, 305.

[27]CRR 2:431; citing 2 Sam 8:11-18; Lk 4:19.

[28]Musculus, *In Esaiam*, 126-27.

the dead with this affection. But what pertains to people, not all recognize this affection in Christ; not all receive Christ by faith. For those who believe in him, Christ is an eternal father and never a cruel judge. He defends them not only in this life and in death but also before the tribunal of God so that they may have eternal salvation. But those who do not believe in him, who do not acknowledge him by faith, these do not receive the fruit of his fatherly affection but are judged and perish because of their own wickedness. Commentary on Isaiah 9:6.[29]

Justification by the Prince of Peace. Martin Borrhaus: Christ is the author of every peace, through the spirit of peace, of which the foundation is justification. The apostle speaks about this with these words, "Being justified by faith, we have peace with God." But through whom do we have peace? Through Jesus Christ. For it follows in the epistle, "Through our Lord Jesus Christ." And so our prophet, taught by the Spirit of God, calls him the Prince of Peace. He brought forth this peace in the world when he finished the battle against the enemies of sin, death, and hell. From that victory, the children of God understand how attractive is the peace that the prophet here identifies Christ Jesus as the author of. And the angels celebrated at his birth with these words, "Glory to God in the highest, and on earth peace, goodwill to people." Oracles in Isaiah on 9:6-7.[30]

The Spiritual, Eternal Davidic Kingdom. Heinrich Bullinger: Therefore, Christ arises from the lineage, according to the flesh, of David. Therefore he sits on the throne of his father, to which you cling. This promise was stated to David by Nathan . . . and is explained and applied to Christ the Lord by the angel Gabriel. . . . Indeed, Christ did not sit on the earthly throne of David, which was held by Herod, an Idumaean and a Gentile, when the Lord was born. But the ancient promise refers rather to spiritual things, in which Christ the King is exceptional. This throne was somewhat disturbed and weakened until Christ was born. Therefore, Isaiah rightly says that he is going to administer and establish the kingdom, and indeed with justice and righteousness, that is, in the most equitable way and most perfect manner of all. For the kingdom of Christ is the church—in which Christ reigns by the Spirit and the Word, and governs all things most rightly and best. Sermons on Isaiah 9:7.[31]

Christ Rules with the Father. Dietrich Schnepff: And of course, as with the other things the Holy Spirit attributes to Christ in this chapter that are most certain and most true, so also those things that are said about his power and magnificence are most certain. For, together with the Father, he governs, sustains, and directs all things. For whatever the Father has done, the Son likewise does these things too. Then all our salvation rests on his shoulders. Scholia on Isaiah 9:7.[32]

Mystery of the Final-*Mem*. Johannes Oecolampadius: The form of the Hebrew *lĕmarbēh* is translated "to increase," is a term referring to government, as indicated by its use of a *tsere* [Hebrew vowel ē]. And you will find something rare in this word, that does not occur in all Scripture, that is, a final-*mem* [the form of the Hebrew letter *m* used only at the end of a word], that is, a closed *mem* in the middle of the word.[†] This is not supposed to be placed there unless it is at the end of a word. The mystery of this, I believe, is that the kingdom of Christ was previously inserted into the kingdom of the Jews. Some among us suppose it indicates the perpetual virginity of Mary. Commentary on Isaiah 9:7.[33]

[29]Brenz, *Esaias*, 154 (misnumbered 145); citing Is 49:15; 54:10.
[30]Borrhaus, *In Iesaiae Prophetae Oracula*, 118; citing Rom 5:1; Lk 2:14.
[31]Bullinger, *Isaias*, 52v; citing 2 Sam 7; Lk 1.
[32]Schnepff, *In Esaiae*, 163; citing Jn 5 to support his argument that the Son does what the Father does.
[33]Oecolampadius, *In Iesaiam*, 83r. [†]The Hebrew text has *lĕmarbēh* with a final *mem* as the second character. This phenomenon is most likely dittography, since the previous word ends with *lm*. See also Musculus, *In Esaiam*, 217-18 (217, misnumbered 127).

The Name of God. Adam Sasbout: Dionysius the Carthusian in his commentary on this passage notes that among the Hebrews the name is tetragrammaton or ineffable, but that is false.† For the Hebrews in this passage have *ʾel*, "El," which according to Moses [Maimonides] the Egyptian . . . does not correspond only to God but also to angels and people worthy of admiration. So it does not seem one can effectively obtain from this passage that Christ is God against the impertinent. Commentary on Isaiah 9:7.[34]

Zeal Is Love for His People. Wolfgang Musculus: "The zeal of the Lord of hosts will do this." It does not simply say "the Lord," but the "zeal of the Lord," and he adds "of hosts," will do this. This says more than if he had said "the power" or "wisdom" or "goodness" of the Lord will do it. For the zeal of the Lord is compared in such a way that it includes all these things. Great is the strength of a husband who is zealous for his wife. How much more do we think that the Lord is zealous for the church and his people? It signifies that the Lord has the same affection toward his people as a husband toward his wife, whom, though he may seem to be repudiating for a time, yet, when struck with marital zeal, he eventually claims from the mockery of suitors. Commentary on Isaiah 9:7.[35]

The Conclusion of the Speech on the King. Johannes Brenz: This is the conclusion of this speech that has been described from the beginning of the seventh chapter. The reason we rightly understand this as the conclusion is that the situation of this speech will be repeated. The king and the remaining leaders from the family of David were vehemently afraid that their offspring would assuredly be expelled from the kingdom of Judah. For the enemies, the king of Israel and the king of Syria, were threatening that the family of David was going to be erased, and another king in Judah would be instituted. And they were very powerful kings. That is why the leaders of the kingdom of Judah were despairing about the salvation of their family.

But the prophet rebukes their excessive trifling and comforts them with promises about Christ. For it cannot happen, when Christ is promised to be from the family of David and will sit on the throne of David in the city of Jerusalem and he had not yet come, that the enemies would be able to erase the family of David to the extent that he would not rule over the kingdom of Judah. Indeed, it is entirely going to be that Christ comes and receives the throne and kingdom of David. The zeal of God will make that happen. It is not from human merit; it is not by human power, but it is the zeal of God. Commentary on Isaiah 9:7.[36]

Everlasting Life the Greatest Article of Faith. Martin Luther: There will be that abundance of peace and a reign for eternity, which denotes the resurrection of the dead. David ruled on earth, and his kingdom was no different from others except that it was divinely established over the people of God, and yet the people were mere mortals. Therefore David's reign over the Jews was physical, but at last Christ has begun the spiritual reign over the people, which will last forever. So there will be a resurrection of the dead. Christ is indeed a king different from David, and the government of his kingdom is different, and yet it is a reign over the same people. To believe in life everlasting is the last and greatest article. However, Christ prepares, establishes, and strengthens this kingdom in the world through the Word and faith, and he does this in a hidden way. Lectures on Isaiah 9:7.[37]

---

[34]Sasbout, *In Esaiam*, 77-78. †See Denis the Carthusian, *Enarratio in Isaiam*, in *Doctoris Ecstatici Dionysii Cartusiani Opera Omnia* 8 (Monstrolii: M. De Pratis, 1899), 403; Maimonides, *Guide for the Perplexed*, trans. M. Friedländer (London: Routledge & Kegan Paul, 1904), 14-15. Moses Maimonides was a twelfth-century Hispanic Jewish scholar.
[35]Musculus, *In Esaiam*, 220.
[36]Brenz, *Esaias*, 158-59.
[37]LW 16:101-102 (WA 31.2:72).

9:8–10:34 Judgment Against Israel and Assyria

8 *The Lord has sent a word against Jacob,*
and it will fall on Israel;

9 *and all the people will know,*
Ephraim and the inhabitants of Samaria,

who say in pride and in arrogance of heart:

10 *"The bricks have fallen,*
but we will build with dressed stones;

the sycamores have been cut down,
but we will put cedars in their place."

11 *But the Lord raises the adversaries of Rezin against him,*
and stirs up his enemies.

12 *The Syrians on the east and the Philistines on the west*
devour Israel with open mouth.

For all this his anger has not turned away,
and his hand is stretched out still.

13 *The people did not turn to him who struck them,*
nor inquire of the Lord of hosts.

14 *So the Lord cut off from Israel head and tail,*
palm branch and reed in one day—

15 *the elder and honored man is the head,*
and the prophet who teaches lies is the tail;

16 *for those who guide this people have been leading them astray,*
and those who are guided by them are swallowed up.

17 *Therefore the Lord does not rejoice over their young men,*
and has no compassion on their fatherless and widows;

for everyone is godless and an evildoer,
and every mouth speaks folly.[a]

For all this his anger has not turned away,
and his hand is stretched out still.

18 *For wickedness burns like a fire;*
it consumes briers and thorns;

it kindles the thickets of the forest,
and they roll upward in a column of smoke.

19 *Through the wrath of the Lord of hosts*
the land is scorched,

and the people are like fuel for the fire;
no one spares another.

20 *They slice meat on the right, but are still hungry,*
and they devour on the left, but are not satisfied;

each devours the flesh of his own arm,

21 *Manasseh devours Ephraim, and Ephraim devours Manasseh;*
together they are against Judah.

For all this his anger has not turned away,
and his hand is stretched out still.

10 *Woe to those who decree iniquitous decrees,*
and the writers who keep writing oppression,

2 *to turn aside the needy from justice*
and to rob the poor of my people of their right,

that widows may be their spoil,
and that they may make the fatherless their prey!

3 *What will you do on the day of punishment,*
in the ruin that will come from afar?

To whom will you flee for help,
and where will you leave your wealth?

4 Nothing remains but to crouch among the
prisoners
or fall among the slain.

For all this his anger has not turned away,
and his hand is stretched out still.

5 Woe to Assyria, the rod of my anger;
the staff in their hands is my fury!

6 Against a godless nation I send him,
and against the people of my wrath I
command him,

to take spoil and seize plunder,
and to tread them down like the mire of the
streets.

7 But he does not so intend,
and his heart does not so think;

but it is in his heart to destroy,
and to cut off nations not a few;

8 for he says:

"Are not my commanders all kings?

9 Is not Calno like Carchemish?
Is not Hamath like Arpad?
Is not Samaria like Damascus?

10 As my hand has reached to the kingdoms of
the idols,
whose carved images were greater than
those of Jerusalem and Samaria,

11 shall I not do to Jerusalem and her idols
as I have done to Samaria and her images?"

12 When the Lord has finished all his work on
Mount Zion and on Jerusalem, he[b] will punish the
speech[c] of the arrogant heart of the king of Assyria
and the boastful look in his eyes. 13 For he says:

"By the strength of my hand I have done it,
and by my wisdom, for I have
understanding;

I remove the boundaries of peoples,
and plunder their treasures;
like a bull I bring down those who sit on
thrones.

14 My hand has found like a nest
the wealth of the peoples;

and as one gathers eggs that have been forsaken,
so I have gathered all the earth;

and there was none that moved a wing
or opened the mouth or chirped."

15 Shall the axe boast over him who hews with it,
or the saw magnify itself against him who
wields it?

As if a rod should wield him who lifts it,
or as if a staff should lift him who is not
wood!

16 Therefore the Lord GOD of hosts
will send wasting sickness among his stout
warriors,

and under his glory a burning will be kindled,
like the burning of fire.

17 The light of Israel will become a fire,
and his Holy One a flame,

and it will burn and devour
his thorns and briers in one day.

18 The glory of his forest and of his fruitful land
the LORD will destroy, both soul and body,
and it will be as when a sick man wastes away.

19 The remnant of the trees of his forest will be so
few
that a child can write them down.

20 In that day the remnant of Israel and the survivors
of the house of Jacob will no more lean on him who
struck them, but will lean on the LORD, the Holy One
of Israel, in truth. 21 A remnant will return, the
remnant of Jacob, to the mighty God. 22 For though your
people Israel be as the sand of the sea, only a remnant
of them will return. Destruction is decreed, overflowing
with righteousness. 23 For the Lord GOD of hosts will
make a full end, as decreed, in the midst of all the earth.

[24]Therefore thus says the Lord God of hosts: "O
my people, who dwell in Zion, be not afraid of the
Assyrians when they strike with the rod and lift up
their staff against you as the Egyptians did. [25]For in a
very little while my fury will come to an end, and my
anger will be directed to their destruction. [26]And the
Lord of hosts will wield against them a whip, as
when he struck Midian at the rock of Oreb. And his
staff will be over the sea, and he will lift it as he did in
Egypt. [27]And in that day his burden will depart from
your shoulder, and his yoke from your neck; and the
yoke will be broken because of the fat."[d]

[28]He has come to Aiath;

he has passed through Migron;
at Michmash he stores his baggage;

[29]they have crossed over the pass;
at Geba they lodge for the night;

Ramah trembles;
Gibeah of Saul has fled.

[30]Cry aloud, O daughter of Gallim!
Give attention, O Laishah!
O poor Anathoth!

[31]Madmenah is in flight;
the inhabitants of Gebim flee for safety.

[32]This very day he will halt at Nob;
he will shake his fist
at the mount of the daughter of Zion,
the hill of Jerusalem.

[33]Behold, the Lord God of hosts
will lop the boughs with terrifying power;

the great in height will be hewn down,
and the lofty will be brought low.

[34]He will cut down the thickets of the forest
with an axe,
and Lebanon will fall by the Majestic One.

a Or *speaks disgraceful things* **b** Hebrew *I* **c** 10:12 Hebrew *fruit* **d** 10:27 The meaning of the Hebrew is uncertain

Overview: A new prophecy begins in the middle of Isaiah 9, directed at the tribes of Israel and then Assyria. The commentators note the various parallel names of Jacob, Israel, Ephraim, and Samaria that are used to distinguish them from the people of Judah. They explain that the Lord is still angry with the people of Israel because they continue to behave arrogantly. But the people of Judah should learn from the errors of Israel. This is one of the reasons Isaiah delivers these prophecies about other peoples in the hearing of Judah. The Reformers emphasize that Judah and Jerusalem are not spared because of their own merit but because of God's promises. They also identify God's providence over all things as particularly demonstrated in his use of wicked people such as Assyria to judge and discipline his own people.

A New Prophecy. Johannes Oecolampadius: This is a new prophecy against the ten tribes of Israel, even though in the title of the book he says these are prophecies toward Judah and Jerusalem. Yet here he prophesies against the ten tribes and against Assyria so that the people of Judah either are warned from their penalty or so that they see the mercy of God for justly punishing the cruelty of the enemies of Judah. The primary reason I obtain is that because Judah was following the example of the sins of the Israelites, they could not imagine the penalty of foreigners was also theirs. Commentary on Isaiah 9:8.[1]

Recalling Previous Prophecy. Rudolf Gwalther: Therefore, the sense of the words is, "God has likewise sent his word to the Israelites even though they have made an open departure from him, and that word fell on them," that is, it had its effect, and it, too, will be certain thereafter.

[1]Oecolampadius, *In Iesaiam*, 83v-84r.

In this way, he recalls to the mind of all the admonitions and prophecies by which God sought salvation from the beginning of their kingdom. Indeed, when Jeroboam made golden calves and instituted new worship at Bethel, a certain prophet was sent there from the land of Judah, who also pronounced punishments and confirmed his warnings with a remarkable miracle displayed to the king himself, and then with the uncommon example of his death. Sermons on Isaiah 9:8.[2]

God the Avenger. Wolfgang Musculus: Now he mentions this for the fourth time. It signifies that this will surely not be the end of evils, even after some were killed and some abducted into captivity. But in that captivity, God will be the avenger of his people.† Commentary on Isaiah 9:8.[3]

9:8-12 *The Lord's Anger at Israel's Pride*

The Names of Israel. Wolfgang Musculus: It has "all the people of Ephraim and the inhabitants of Samaria." This was not said in the way that this should narrowly refer to the tribe of Ephraim and the city of Samaria. For this message was sent to the whole kingdom and to the people of the ten tribes. But he specifically mentions Ephraim and Samaria because that kingdom was in the tribe of Ephraim, and Samaria was its capital city.† So, he specified the royal tribe and city for all the people of that kingdom. And this was done not without reason. For both the tribe of Ephraim and the city of Samaria were especially guilty of defection, by which the ten tribes had defected from the Lord their God, so that it was not unmerited that the message of future vengeance was sent to both of them. Commentary on Isaiah 9:8-9.[4]

[2]Gwalther, *Isaias*, 69r; citing the account in 2 Kings 13.

[3]Musculus, *In Esaiam*, 232. †See Oecolampadius, *In Iesaiam*, 86r: "He now recounts this for the fourth time. It signifies that this would not indeed be the end of the evils, even after some were killed and others were taken into captivity. But even in the captivity itself, God would be the avenger against the rebels of this people."

[4]Musculus, *In Esaiam*, 222. †See also Oecolampadius, *In Iesaiam*, 84v.

Rebuild Better and Stronger. Konrad Pellikan: It is as if they were saying, "Our enemies destroyed our cities when they were built of bricks. We will rebuild them much stronger, and in the future we will defend ourselves better; we will ignore the grace of the Lord. Our enemies have cut down the houses built with smaller sticks, so we will replace them with houses of cedar. And then we will live more happily, without being hindered by the words of the prophets. For, armed with the most powerful allies of Syria and Egypt, we will easily defend ourselves from Assyria." Commentary on Isaiah 9:10.[5]

God's Hand Still Upraised. Johannes Oecolampadius: He portrays God as having an angry attitude, as if his face were burning with anger and fury, and he were stretching out his hand to strike. And since even with this punishment, the people are not corrected, nor is God any more appeased, he stirs up the present scourges to convert us and to be signs of his divine mercy. Meanwhile those things are neglected such that the people become much more obstinate toward later punishments, and the later punishments become signs of more severe wrath. These are, of course, the insertion of a spirit of spinning and seducing prophets, vast cruelty, and all unmercifulness. And they do not realize the wrath of the Lord due to such unrepentance and foolishness.† Commentary on Isaiah 9:12-16.[6]

The Wrath of God Not Appeased. Wolfgang Musculus: But because the prophet knew the Israelites were incurable, he repeats the inserted verse, "For all this, his anger has not turned away. . . ." And of course, it is clear that even in the destruction of Samaria itself and the deportation of the surviving remnant to Assyria, the wrath of God was not extinguished. For some of the Israelites, or certainly very few, returned to their own country when Cyrus gave the Jews the

[5]Pellikan, *Commentaria Bibliorum* 3:13v.

[6]Oecolampadius, *In Iesaiam*, 85r. †See also 88r.

opportunity to return. And to this day, the unhappy remnant of that race wander over nearly the whole world.

Although, after so many disasters and calamities of so many ages, the wrath of God cannot be appeased, it appears that eventually those who continue in their sins without repenting will remain tormented with eternal sufferings of the torments of hell. Those, therefore, who think that their sins can be expiated by long-lasting sickness or by temporal punishments are greatly mistaken. Commentary on Isaiah 9:12.[7]

Denying Perverted Judgments. Thomas Müntzer: I have demonstrated to the princes from Scripture that they should employ the sword [to punish evildoers] so that no insurrection may develop. In short, transgression of divine law must be punished. And neither the mighty nor the lowly can escape it. . . . Then right away, along comes Father Pussyfoot [Luther], oh, that docile fellow! And he says that I want to make a rebellion, which he supposedly interpreted from my letter to the journeyman miners. He talks about one part of the letter and stays silent about the most decisive part, namely, how I proclaimed before the princes that the entire community has the power of the sword, just as it also has the keys of remitting sin. . . . So, according to good old customary law, the people must also be present if one of them is to be rightfully judged according to the law of God. . . . And why? If the authorities seek to render a perverted judgment, . . . the Christians present should deny this judgment as wrong and not tolerate it, for God demands an account of innocent blood. . . . It is the greatest monstrosity on earth that no one wants to defend the plight of the needy. A Highly Provoked Defense.[8]

[7]Musculus, *In Esaiam*, 226.

[8]Müntzer, "Highly Provoked Defense," 80; citing Num 25:4; 15:35; Is 10:1-4; Ps 79:10; Dan 7:27; Rev 6:15-17; Rom 13:1; 1 Kings 8:7.

9:13–10:4 *The Lord's Anger at Injustice*

Cut Off Head and Tail—Rulers and False Prophets. Rudolf Gwalther: But what threat does the prophet bring against each rank? He says, "The Lord will cut off the head and tail on the same day." He sets this judgment in opposition to the persuasion that people use to deceived themselves. The elite think that they are sacrosanct, that no one dares to touch them. And as a result, they promise themselves that they will not be punished. On the other hand, false teachers, if they take such people as their allies, think that they have quite good prospects and furthermore fear no one. The prophet therefore says that the Lord will be an enemy to each rank, since he has decided to cut off both prophets and rulers. Therefore, all the ministers of the churches must be mindful of such people so that they don't curry favor with the wicked and profane but instead are loyal to Christ. He entrusted to their care that flock that he purchased for himself with his own precious blood. Sermons on Isaiah 9:13-14.[9]

Israel Compared to a Beast. Wolfgang Musculus: He compares Israel to a tailed beast, not without a bite, when he portrays not only a head but also a tail. By a monstrous metamorphosis, that people had changed from the figure of a human into the figure of a beast—if you do not consider the parts of the human body but the perversion of their ways. . . . Humans figured as beasts are all wicked, malicious, reprobate, carnal, blind in mind, envious, lustful, drunk, greedy, weak, angry, caustic, bloodthristy. . . . This is likewise what is felt about the people. There they showed neither godliness toward God, nor humanity toward their kindred of the same nature, nor purity of life toward themselves, but rather they became wicked toward God, inhumane and unjust toward neighbors, and with beastlike manners toward themselves. I ask, what else can that be called but a beast? . . .

[9]Gwalther, *Isaias*, 70v.

The prophet saw this utterly monstrous metamorphosis in Israel, and therefore attributed to them a tail, a part that is not human but of a beast. So, we say to a biting man, "You are a dog; see how you have a tail." Consequently, he threatens that it will soon happen that the Lord is going to mutilate that monstrous beast and will cut off the extremities, the head, the tail, and the legs. . . . It is not unusal for this prophet of ours to call false prophets shameless, insatiable dogs who do not know how to bark. Commentary on Isaiah 9:14-16.[10]

Crimes That Most Offend God. Rudolf Gwalther: But what are those crimes that especially separate us from God? Here the prophet is thinking of three. First, he says that God will not have mercy because all people are liars. This is because they professed true knowledge of God, faith in him and his worship, even though they did not know him, trust him, nor worship that same God. Instead they were totally hostile to him in their hearts. The prophet places them in the first rank because this is the source of all wickedness. Soon he adds a second vice that wicked crimes produce. Hypocrites refrain from evil only at that moment when they think that it cannot be hidden. But if some opportunity frees them from this fear, then there is nothing so wicked and depraved that they don't dare to do it. Therefore Christ rightly attributes to them malice as well as rank theft and says that on the inside they boil over with these crimes.

The prophet added a third crime: "Every mouth speaks disgraceful things." Under this category he includes the ludicrous things people say about God and his Word, the sort that David attributed to some in the Psalms. Such people say, "God does not see; the God of Jacob does not understand." Add to these whatever things such people say to their neighbor, filthy and disgraceful words that incite shameful thoughts in their hearts and corrupt good character. But if one applies these words to the morals of our generation, all these vices become widespread. Sermons on Isaiah 9:16-17.[11]

How Fire Consumes. Johannes Oecolampadius: For just as the fire first consumes thin and dry materials, such as flax, stubble, and other very dry things, and then proceeds from those to thicker and moister ones, going after thorns and briers and then to other green and moist things, such that it burns up the whole forest and the density of smoke obscures the ground, so also the fire of wickedness. It starts from small beginnings and, as Paul speaks about heresy, creeps like a cancer. It is eventually most troublesome. . . . With this example, the whole forest is soon set on fire. Understand, by the dense forest, the multitude of the people. For just as many trees make a forest, so many humans constitute a people. Such a destructive thing is an analogy of evil. Sodom was burning with this kind of fire before they were destroyed by heavenly flames. So also the wicked who forsake the word of the Lord foster the fire of accursed concupiscence in their hearts, from which hell itself will spring forth. The false prophets among us set this on fire. . . .

He explains how wickedness blazes. For the land is obscured, that is, the whole people are enveloped in darkness and the smoke of their errors. They have become the material by which the fire of wickedness is kindled and thus the "fuel for the fire." Without doubt, this is from the anger of the Lord, who hands them over in the reprobate sense, because the word of the Lord is neglected. Commentary on Isaiah 9:18-19.[12]

Increasing Unhappiness from Internal Sins. Konrad Pellikan: This is a speech taken up on the ways of predatory animals, who turn in all directions, cruel and starved, to fill their gluttony. At the same time, the wicked will also consume themselves with civil discord and

[10]Musculus, *In Esaiam*, 225-26; citing Is 56:10-11.

[11]Gwalther, *Isaias*, 71r.

[12]Oecolampadius, *In Iesaiam*, 86v.

internal hate, while tyranny is embraced by many wicked among the people, and the pursuit of factions are inflamed such that this one favors this king and another the other. So the unhappiness of the people increases every day, and kingdoms are shaken; regions and cities are devastated. This is all because of the sins of people, which God does not spare but punishes. Commentary on Isaiah 9:20.[13]

Unjust and Oppressive Laws. Dietrich Schnepff: There is another specific vice that, no less than the ones previously mentioned, invites God's anger. It is when the magistrates write heavy laws for those beneath them. And when those judgments should be a refuge for the poor and wretched, they not only lay heavy burdens on orphans, wards, and widows, but they also rob and plunder them. Is there any situation so significant as this that would hasten the destruction of the entire Israelite system of power? So then, when the Lord rises up to punish, what will you do? What plans will you hatch when you see a foreign enemy coming? Where will you find help and allies? What use, then, will all your expensive equipment be, the things you now boast in? At that time whom will you blame other than yourselves, when some are led away to slavery but others fall by the enemy's sword? For certainly I would not have punished you, if your many outrageous crimes had not demanded this severe response from me. But these blows will not end until all your power is ruined. Paraphrase of Isaiah 10:1-4.[14]

10:5-19 *Judgment Against Assyria for Arrogance*

Unyieldedness Is Vainglory. Andreas Bodenstein von Karlstadt: Observe what God punishes in [Isaiah], and you will soon understand that Assyria sinned in saying, "In my strength I toppled the princes and nations." And again, "My hand found the might of the nations as one finds a nest." And again, "I gathered them in as one gathers eggs." And again, "In wisdom I reflected. . . ." These are the thoughts and words of Assyria that were against God and for which God punished Assyria, saying that honor and glory are the prerogative of lofty eyes and supercilious hearts.

We find similar material in Isaiah that says words such as *I*, *my*, and the like derive from vainglory. And since everyone says that vainglory is a mortal sin and unyieldedness a common occurrence, it has to be admitted that our daily sin is a mortal sin and that unyieldedness is not an unimportant pock or sin.

I say this so that we look the more seriously to our daily, yes, sinful and momentary life and know that our life is full of mortal sin. For all unyieldedness merits hellfire. Your vainglory pulled you down to hell. Tell me now whether Christ's teaching that he addressed to everyone does not serve as well as this, namely, "Any who intend to follow me must deny themselves and daily carry their cross and follow me." If we wish to be Christians who follow the Lord Jesus Christ, we must deny ourselves, that is, surrender and lose or reject our ego or self, otherwise we cannot follow Christ or be Christians, since we can neither love nor believe God. The Meaning of the Term *Gelassen*.[15]

The Rod of God's Anger. Konrad Pellikan: He foretells and threatens that the king of the kingdom of the Assyrians will come. This kingdom, under many kings, had executed the Lord's judgment against the kingdom of Syria and Samaria. But, with an unjust will and by cruel effort, the king also wanted to destroy Jerusalem along with the kingdom of Judah. For this purpose, he led a very large army against Hezekiah in the fourteenth year of his reign. But an angel struck the army, and the king retreated to Assyria in disarray with only a very few survivors.

[13]Pellikan, *Commentaria Bibliorum*, 3:14r.
[14]Schnepff, *In Esaiae*, 175.
[15]CRR 8:167*; citing Is 2; 5; Ezek 28–29; Is 42:14; Lk 9:23.

Here we learn that wicked men do not live without consequence in this world and they are not useless to the Lord. And so they are not "wicked" to that same Lord, no matter how bad they are to one another and in and of themselves. The king and the kingdom of the Assyrians are a rod of discipline in the hand of the Lord that he uses to correct his disobedient sons. He uses it to train his leadership and to express the severity of his judgment against lawbreakers. Such people, however wickedly they conspire and act against Israel, nevertheless their hand is also guided in every respect by the will of the Lord. He clearly turns to his own use their wicked intention, directing it to the execution of his anger, that is, his just judgment. Yet at the same time the wicked cannot excuse the depravity of their own heart. They cruelly sin and lie in wait to murder and steal from others. COMMENTARY ON ISAIAH 10:5-7.[16]

THE ROD AS DISCIPLINE. JOHANNES BRENZ: And he says: "Assyria has been divinely raised up to afflict them." But God has not permitted him to destroy the kingdom of Judah. Instead, this happens so that Judah most wickedly perishes on its own. I will say more about this subject later. For now, because we encounter it first in this passage, the prophet explains that God has raised up Assyria, King Sennacherib, to afflict the leaders and citizens of the kingdom of Judah. "He is the rod of my anger," he says, "and of my fury." He is a rod in his hands. "Against a godless," or hypocritical, "nation I send him. . . ."

For although the inhabitants of the kingdom of Judah had the true practices of God and were restored through the righteous King Hezekiah when those wicked practices were abolished, nevertheless their character was totally corrupted. They did not repent from the heart but cared more for their stomach than righteousness. Therefore God subjected them to affliction through Assyria, not, however, to destroy them utterly. And so he permitted Assyria to lay waste their whole territory, so the citizens of the kingdom were overwhelmed with the greatest fear for their safety, as the story of Hezekiah relates. . . .

Therefore, when the Holy Spirit, in meting out God's punishment, uses the term *rod*, it is not difficult to understand that the punishment that hits God's people is not destruction. It is instead discipline. God uses it to rule his people and keep them in their duty. We should say the same thing about the "staff of discipline." It is indeed sometimes used to strike those who have gone astray. But it is more properly used to support them. Similarly, then, the punishments that are sent on God's people are more for their help than their harm. COMMENTARY ON ISAIAH 10:5-6.[17]

THE LORD USES THE WICKED. DIETRICH SCHNEPFF: But besides the general point, another doctrine, no less than superior, elegant, and noteworthy, is related to us in this passage, concerning primary and secondary causes. For sometimes the will of God and secondary causes harmonize with regard to their end—as when he accomplishes what he wills through the saints. They often differ from one another with the method for the end, even though the Lord uses them in his service—as the Lord punishes many peoples through Assyria, including the Israelites. And this end is purposed by the Lord to set an example of severity that others should dread.

But Assyria, although it is the Lord's minister and servant in this case, seeks something else, namely, the extension of its empire, glory, and the like. For the prophet says, "But he does not so intend; and his heart does not so think. . . ." Judas does not consider the salvation of humanity when he betrays the Lord with a kiss. But the Lord, working through him, makes good use of his evil will, as Augustine says.† In the same way, he makes good use of the efforts of the devil and of all the

[16]Pellikan, *Commentaria Bibliorum*, 3:14r.

[17]Brenz, *Esaias*, 169, 170-71.

wicked, for the glory of his name and the salvation of his church. Scholia on Isaiah 10:6-7.[18]

The Providence of God over All. Johannes Oecolampadius: Further, we can clearly see here how divine providence uses the service of the wicked as organs, indeed for the benefit of the faithful but also for their own disgrace and destruction, so that nothing is outside the governing of divine providence. Do not be astonished. For good as well as evil are workshops in which God does his work, even with the devil and the antichrist himself. . . . And so Sennacherib and the antichrist are God's instruments. And what they do, they do by the secret command of God. For otherwise there is no power over the good by demons and the wicked. Moreover, knowing that our adversaries are the rod of God, let us not grumble, but let us make use of his patient discipline. Commentary on Isaiah 10:7.[19]

The Punishment of Assyria for Pride. Konrad Pellikan: The expansion of Assyria should not be credited to the king's rule. Nor should whatever had happened in his victories over the nations be ascribed to his wisdom or valor. These are not accomplished by the arm of humankind but by God's decision. The plundering of treasuries too that the wicked store up for the future, and the toppling of tyrants and noble robbers who dwell in the most fortified and secure fortresses, who attribute these accomplishments to their own strength, these well deserve to lose everything and succumb to their enemies. Such were the boasts of the Assyrian king, Sennacherib, as well as the tyrants of the Chaldean kingdom who succeeded him. Commentary on Isaiah 10:7.[20]

Jerusalem Compared to Captured Kingdoms. Wolfgang Musculus: He deduces from the successes of his previous victories a presumption in his proud heart against the city of Jerusalem. And he makes a comparison of the kingdoms that he captured to the fortunes of the Jewish kingdom, extolling the strength of those above the weakness of this one. The sense is, "As I captured those kingdoms, so I will capture Jerusalem, too, in fact, more easily than those." . . . This was the boasting and presumption of this king that would happen at the time when he had captured Samaria and launched the expedition against Jerusalem, as history itself testifies. We will have a greater opportunity to speak about this. Commentary on Isaiah 10:8-11.[21]

Jerusalem Spared by the Lord. Dietrich Schnepff: "Jerusalem is still prosperous. Yet how will it be difficult for me to capture it, when I have conquered all the other cities? But what shall I say about the people, when I am superior to and more powerful than the gods themselves? When the divinities of those kingdoms that they acquired with my weapons could not defend them, how shall the God of the Hebrews be able to rescue his people from my hand?" Such is the presumption of this wicked king; such his arrogance. "But when I, the Lord, unleash the work of my reproof (I use those kings like iron rods for the correction of my people), then that king," as will be explained later, "will face the consequence for his arrogant and proud heart, and his contempt." Scholia on Isaiah 10:10-12.[22]

God Waits with Perfect Patience. Wolfgang Musculus: "And this will happen," it says, "when the Lord will finish all his work." He is indicating the time and full completion of his coming vengeance. Divine justice does not act with recklessness, because it does not carry anything from the weakness of mind and impulsive emotions. But it does all things with moderation. And because it mixes in deserved punishments, it is

[18]Schnepff, *In Esaiae*, 181. †See Augustine, *The Writings Against the Manichaeans, and Against the Donatists*, 22.83 (*NPNF*[1] 4:305)

[19]Oecolampadius, *In Iesaiam*, 88v, 89r.

[20]Pellikan, *Commentaria Bibliorum*, 3:14v.

[21]Musculus, *In Esaiam*, 237; citing Is 36–37.

[22]Schnepff, *In Esaiae*, 192.

slow and deliberate to anger. Yet, this delay is not due to neglect, nor does it go beyond the proper limits of accomplishing its ends. Instead, this delay awaits patiently and wisely for the most opportune moment in the given circumstances. Therefore here the prophet correctly does not say "And it will happen, finally, at some time, and the Lord will finish all his work." God's patience has awaited for the completion of its task. Commentary on Isaiah 10:12.[23]

The True Church Spared by Repentance and Prayer. Zacharias Ursinus: Those who do not just profess but offer true worship to the true God are defended by God. For Samaria was perishing and boasting about their worship of Jehovah but corrupting it with their idolatry. Jerusalem was saved by the repentance and prayers of Hezekiah, Isaiah, and others. Therefore, Assyria was mistaken, thinking that they would do to Jerusalem as they had done to Samaria. And often the wicked and tyrants are mistaken in this way and are defeated and destroyed by a great multitude of profane and hypocritical things, yet they cannot attack and destroy the true church, however small and weak it may be. Therefore, when we see hypocrites perish, if we want to escape their fortune and the threats of tyrants, let us imitate the examples of Hezekiah and Isaiah. Commentary on Isaiah 10:12-13.[24]

The Absurdity of Boasting in Oneself. Rudolf Gwalther: "Shall the axe boast over the one who hews with it? Shall the saw magnify itself . . . ?" He uses similes to show more clearly the absurdity of the matter. He names four instruments that are in frequent use among people: the ax and the saw, which are used to do certain work, and the rod and staff, which are generally used to beat slaves or disobedient children. Now, the sense of the words is this: Who will not say that it is a very absurd thing and like an omen, if an ax or a piece of iron should boast of the work done against the workman who used these as organs and instruments? Or if the rod is proud against the one who carries it or lifts it up to strike? Or if the staff forgets that it is a tree devoid of life and senses, will it claim some glory for itself against him who holds it in his hand? But what else does the tyrant Sennacherib do, who, when he is the rod of the Lord's wrath and the staff in his hand, in contempt of the supreme will, but express pride with insults about the conquered nations? Therefore God punishes him suitable to his stupidity.

Although these things are said about the king of the Assyrians, yet in general they teach that all people are the instruments of God and are governed by his hand. For if the most powerful tyrant of that age, who was not only a despiser of the word of God but a professed enemy, was an ax and a saw, or a rod and staff in his hand, and if the hearts of all kings are also in his hand, as Solomon testifies, by what reason can the rest of humanity be excluded that I could say they are autonomous? . . . Therefore, they err exceedingly who acknowledge only a universal providence by him, which does not extend to individual people but permits both these and other individual creatures to be carried according to their own nature or will. Sermons on Isaiah 10:15-16.[25]

Concurrence. Wolfgang Musculus: In the present case, God, the king of Assyria, and the work of God, which was the transfer of several kingdoms, wealth, and peoples to the kingdom of Assyria, were coinciding. Kings were deposed from their seats. Their treasures were plundered. And the people were chastised together with them. And the merits of their wickedness and crimes brought punishments. God, the just judge, who judges the world and flogs the reprobate, had purposed, instituted, and carried out these things. In this work, the king of Assyria was an organ, he was an axe, he was a saw, he was a staff. Certainly the work was not his but God's. Therefore, neither did the

[23]Musculus, *In Esaiam*, 238.
[24]Ursinus, *Iesaiam*, 347.
[25]Gwalther, *Isaias*, 76r; citing Prov 21:1; Jer 18; Rom 9; 2 Tim 2.

glory of the work belong to him but to God alone. COMMENTARY ON ISAIAH 10:16.[26]

HISTORY PROVES THE FOOLISHNESS OF BOASTING. HEINRICH BULLINGER: Let them examine a little history, and it will be evident that God's continual and most just punishment was exacted on the proud and the multitude of those who rested on their own happiness and power. The kings of the Persians, insolent and proud, attacked the Greeks with a very large army. But they were overcome and routed by a small band of soldiers, and finally subdued. The Romans, too, exulting for a long time and reigning most insolently, were at last overthrown, destroyed, and crushed by the Goths, Herulis, and other nations.

But also, Attila the Hun, who used to boast of a million armed men, besides the legionaries serving under him, and that he was the terror of the world, the scourge of God, was slain on the plains of Catalonia. The Turkish emperor Bayezid I was insolent and very impudent about his victories.[†] But when he was conquered by Timur the Scythian, he supplied his back as a stool for the conqueror to get on his horse and learned to taste humiliation. What was it that Tuman Bay II, the Egyptian sultan, used to boast freely and profusely about his riches and victories of the mighty? Truly, the same man, conquered by Selim I, emperor of the Turks, lost his life and kingdom at the same time, and finally, like another Haman, was hanged at the gate by the enemy. It is documented that pride and insolent boasting of fortune never turned out well for anyone or could ever turn out well. SERMONS ON ISAIAH 10:15-16.[27]

LIGHT AND FIRE BY THE HOLY ONE. DIETRICH SCHNEPFF: In this passage we must carefully note that the prophet says the Lord is both light and fire. But he is "the light of Israel" and fire for the Assyrians. When it comes to fire, light is a very pleasing aspect for all living creatures as well as human beings. They are renewed and comforted by that light, and by it they recognize the right way of doing the various things that have to be done. In short, there is no one who could explain the benefits of light any better. So, the Lord is light, life, and illumination to his people. And Christ fittingly refers to himself as the Light of the World. Without him, everything must be engulfed in the darkest shadows, not only of ignorance but also of sorrow and catastrophe.

But on the other hand, as fire burns and devours all things, so the Lord is the consuming fire to the wicked. There are many examples of his severity that testify to this, and they have been recounted elsewhere. Therefore, in the Scripture these two qualities of fire are attributed to God so that we may understand that the one and same God is very merciful to those who believe, and at the same time he is the most fierce judge of the wicked. SCHOLIA ON ISAIAH 10:17.[28]

LIGHT AND FIRE LIKE THE SUN. JOHANNES OECOLAMPADIUS: But the sense is: God, who is light and joy to his people, is fire and flames to his enemies, just as the sun torments some with heat, while to others it is friendly and pleasing light. "Thorns and briers," that is, the rulers and magnates, are those who poke the people like thorns and briers. Those who have more propensity for sinning and are more apt to set fire to others are themselves being set on fire. . . . "And it will be." The prophet continues with how God will be the light and consolation of Israel, just as he was a consuming fire to the Assyrians. For on that day, when the army of Sennacherib will be shaken, the Jews who remain and have escaped will not follow Ahaz's example to seek help from the Syrians, their most unfaithful allies. For when they should have helped them, they began to persecute them. From that time and afterward, they will flee for safety to the one who is the light and Holy One of Israel

[26]Musculus, *In Esaiam*, 242.

[27]Bullinger, *Isaias*, 59v. †Legends about Timur's humiliation of Bayezid are in *Asiae Europaeque elegantissima descriptio* by Pope Pius II, written in 1450–1460 and published in 1509. Selim's conquering of the Egyptian sultanate happened in 1516–1517.

[28]Schnepff, *In Esaiae*, 185.

and Mighty God. They will not do this with a false heart but one that is true. Commentary on Isaiah 10:17-19.[29]

10:20-34 *The Return of the Faithful Remnant*

Multiple Fulfillments of Those Returning to the Lord. Rudolf Gwalther: These prophecies were partly fulfilled during the reign of Hezekiah, when the example of dreadful divine vengeance exhibited against Sennacherib refreshed the righteous and strengthened their faith. It also terrified many of the Gentiles so that they began to think about God and his people more respectfully, as is evident from the Babylonian embassy that Merodach-Baladan sent to pay respects to Hezekiah. Then more significant events followed, when the kingdom of Judah was destroyed, along with the city, and almost the entire people perished. But the remnants were deported to Babylon, where God's righteousness became known to the whole world. And the worship of him was promoted by King Nebuchadnezzar himself throughout the whole East.

Nevertheless, only a few anticipations and types from these events can be determined that have their later fulfillment in Jesus Christ. Since "his own did not receive him" when he came, God destroyed the ungrateful and stubborn nation of the Jews with a complete annihilation and scattered those miserable persons he had rejected throughout the whole world. Nevertheless, by his unmerited mercy the remnant of the elect were preserved, the apostles, of course, and apostolic men along with them, who believed in their preaching. Sermons on Isaiah 10:20-21.[30]

The Liberation of His People. Ulrich Zwingli: He predicts the freedom of his people. To me, to put it plainly, it seems the liberation from the Babylonian captivity was in every way more humble and smaller than how these prophetic words can be understood. Hence I am persuaded that in more places than to this point was believed, mention is made of the liberation that was accomplished by Christ. For if I recall Roman history as well, there was not a great time before the birth of Christ where Scipio the Asiatic triumphed over Antiochus.[†] So after that time of the Assyrian subjugation, this remnant of people began to depend on God by faith. . . .

So far, it would seem to me that this passage is more august than the prophet speaking about the return from Babylon, but rather about the coming of Christ after the Assyrian kingdom was captured. . . . For then Israel received true solace, after the Assyrian kingdom was conquered by the Romans, when Christ was born. For their liberation was not when Assyria was captured but a long time later. Annotations on Isaiah 10:21-23.[31]

Your People Reduced to a Remnant. Wolfgang Musculus: And in order to influence them as he himself was influenced, the prophet turns the sermon to Israel itself. He does not simply say, "Because though the people of Israel will be . . . ," but, "For though *your* people, O Israel, will be as the sand of the sea. . . ." It is as though he says, "Although I, O Israel, sincerely favor your multitude, still I see that it is absolutely inevitable that this people of yours, from whose multitude you take a portion, because they have turned away from the Lord their God, is reduced to a small number, to just a few particular survivors." And then in the end, because now the majority rejects him, the few are converted to the Lord their God and in truth rely on him. Commentary on Isaiah 10:22.[32]

Cutting Down to a Remnant. Francisco Forerius: There is no doubt, since the first word *klywn* is from the word that signifies both "to

[29]Oecolampadius, *In Iesaiam*, 91v, 92v.
[30]Gwalther, *Isaias*, 78r; citing Jn 1:12.
[31]ZSW 14 / CR 101:210-11. [†]Zwingli is referring to the Roman general Lucius Cornelius Scipio Asiaticus, who is credited with defeating Antiochus III in 189 BC.
[32]Musculus, *In Esaiam*, 246; citing Is 4:3.

consummate" and "to consume," that this can also be translated "consummation" or "consumption"; although Deuteronomy 28 seems to signify it exclusively as "consumption" with "consumption of eyes . . ." [failing eyesight]. And this term is not read anywhere else. But the later word, namely, *hrwṣ*, can be variously received, and certainly is best rendered as an adjective, as the Vulgate has, "abbreviated" or "cut down." There are those who take this as the calamity itself, because God, overflowing with righteousness, both abbreviated the abundance of his people and consumed them. But the construction of this exposition does not favor that view; it does not correspond to what precedes or follows. For if the term *righteousness* is taken in the nominative case, then the plainer sense will be "consumption was abbreviated; righteousness will overflow." But understand by "consumption abbreviated" those few and remaining ones who were preserved from Israel, who were the most holy, as was already said . . . , "All who remain in Zion shall be called holy." Commentary on Isaiah 10:22.[33]

Only a Gentile Remnant Remain True to the Lord. Pilgram Marpeck: As Isaiah said about the Israelites, I say about all so-called Christians, who in their numbers are like the sand of the sea, that only a few (the remainder of the Gentiles) have remained true to the Lord, and only they will be saved. Like the Jews at the time of Christ, the time of the Gentiles is almost over. The fulfillment of their time is at hand. Therefore everything that speaks and teaches against the knowledge of the teaching, word, life, and walk of Christ is falsely acclaimed knowledge; it teaches and persists in sin. Men in Judgment and the Peasant Aristocracy.[34]

Four Consolations of Redirected Wrath. Johannes Oecolampadius: He consoles with four topics. First, because the whip is tolerable. For he says, "he will strike you with a rod," that is, it will not kill you, even though you are beaten. . . .

Second, he consoles by the brevity of time. . . . He consoles, "To a small degree for a short time, I deserted you." . . . "The light momentary affliction is producing for us an eternal weight of glory." Less than a little, changed into a little, or a little from a small amount—that is, "In the shortest amount of time, I will crush him." But now he still acts as my servant and rod to punish human sins. . . .

The third consolation is that the wicked are going to be afflicted more severely than they have afflicted others, and they will fall by the divine hand. The rod fell to the enemies; he should be struck by the whip, a rod harder than the wood of Sethim. . . .

The greatest consolation is the freedom from slavery that would come. For he says that the burden and the yoke, namely that tribute of three hundred talents of silver and thirty talents of gold, is going to be removed. We spoke about this earlier, but here you learn that those who are free in Christ, on account of Christ, with Paul become the servants of all and overcome by their patience. And this is the order of things entirely. Usually the thick necks of oxen are overwhelmed by the hardness of the yoke. Here, the opposite happens, for the yoke is crushed by the neck. Commentary on Isaiah 10:24-27.[35]

The Moderation of Fatherly Discipline. Wolfgang Musculus: He mentions the rod and staff and refers to what he just said above where it says, "Woe to Assyria, the rod of my anger, and my staff in their hands is my wrath." At the same time he warns them that it shall come to pass that they shall be chastised with the rod, because they had departed from his word. Still, he makes known that his chastisement will not at all be what Assyria had conceived in its mind. This is the moderation of fatherly discipline, which does not allow an errant son to go unpunished, and the chastisement does not go beyond the mercy of

[33]Forerius, *Iesaiae*, 46r-v.

[34]CRR 2:468; citing Is 4:3.

[35]Oecolampadius, *In Iesaiam*, 93v-94r; citing Is 54:7; 2 Cor 4:17.

fatherly affection. Commentary on Isaiah 10:24-26.[36]

Learn to Fear God. Johannes Brenz: The Lord desired to demonstrate his mercy to the citizens of Jerusalem through this amazing liberation. He embraced his people with this mercy so that, when they had been warned and stirred up by that mercy, they would strengthen their faith and walk in true righteousness, to attain everlasting liberation. But we must first note in this passage the extent of God's harshness toward sins, so we may truly learn the fear of God. The prophet states that God was offended because of the sins of the citizens. "My wrath," he says, "will consume them, and my anger shall be upon their crimes." And yet these citizens were God's elect people. So you see that God in the meantime is angry at sins and also punishes his elect people for their sins. Commentary on Isaiah 10:25.[37]

The Cut-Down Forest Is the Same as the Rod and Staff. Wolfgang Musculus: But Lebanon was violently cut down by the Assyrians' sword. And the sense here does not differ from the argument for comfort that precedes, nor from what the prophet said earlier. "He shall strike you with his rod, and will raise his own staff over you." For the prophet explains how long the Assyrian staff—indeed, the Lord through them—would strike Judah. It would extend only so far, of course: partly to carry off the people and partly to humiliate those who among that people were more powerful, along with the crowd of reprobates. Then, while laying waste to the region, he would destroy Lebanon, the particular glory of the land of Judea. But he would leave Jerusalem itself unharmed. Commentary on Isaiah 10:34.[38]

A Map of the Approaching Army's Route. Johannes Oecolampadius:

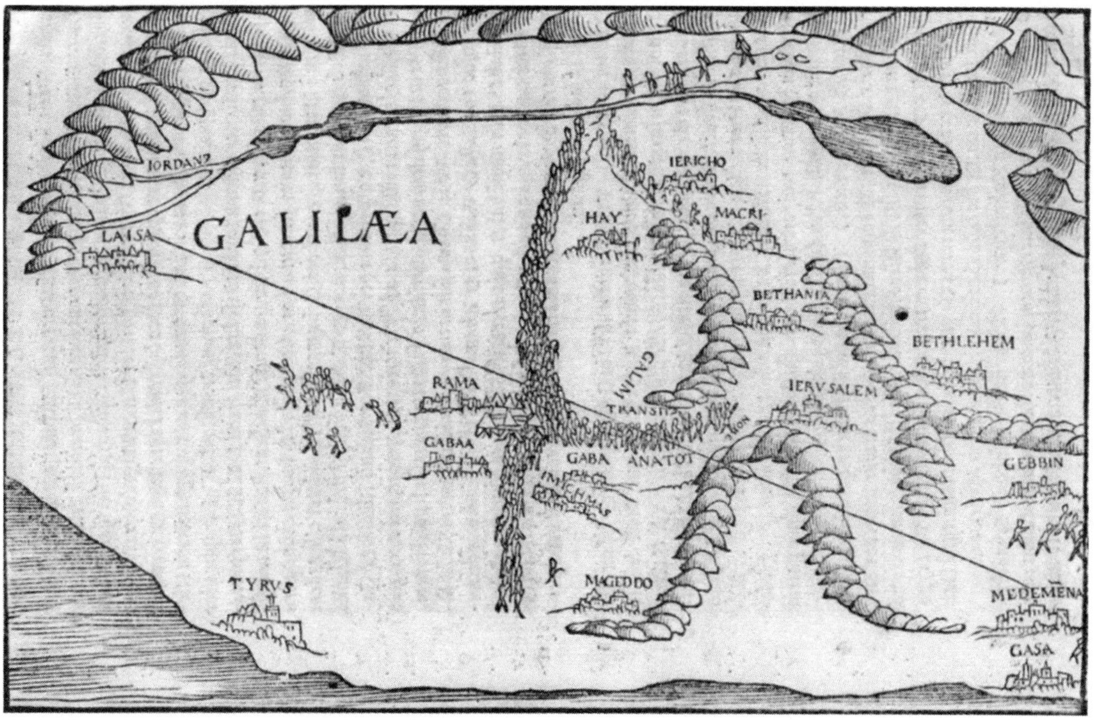

Figure 1. Map of cities threatened by Assyria

[36]Musculus, *In Esaiam*, 248; citing Is 10:5.
[37]Brenz, *Esaias*, 181.
[38]Musculus, *In Esaiam*, 252.

Sennacherib was in the vicinity of Jerusalem,† so they saw the destruction he threatened, but especially from Mount Zion, which is a more prominent hill in Jerusalem. Now see the remarkable power of God that he can extinguish the Assyrians in that land but permits them to approach nearly all the way to the defense walls of Jerusalem, and then finally he destroys them. So he could have also restrained Pharaoh from afflicting Israel, but it was at the Red Sea, when all human help was lacking, that he liberated his people from them. And this is always the way he makes himself most present to his own. Commentary on Isaiah 10:28-32.[39]

A Poetic Call to Faithfulness. Konrad Pellikan: He speaks poetically, however, and with a certain kind of prophetic eloquence, as though depicting the army's equipment as much as the sudden defeat of the wicked. He uses the metaphor of cutting timber in a great forest, without any discrimination of beauty. Instead, he determines that those of loftier stature are now less worth sparing. To summarize, the prophet teaches that the confidence of the righteous depends on the Lord, so that they do not fear the army of their enemy, no matter how large, since they can hope for the Lord's kindness and favor on their behalf. But this happens if they listen to the Lord's prophets, if they delight in the law of the Lord, and if righteousness toward their neighbor and faith in God is preserved. Commentary on Isaiah 10:33-34.[40]

[39]Oecolampadius, *In Iesaiam*, 95v. †The description of the map is on 95r and 96r.

[40]Pellikan, *Commentaria Bibliorum*, 3:15v.

11:1-16 THE SHOOT FROM JESSE

11 *There shall come forth a shoot from the stump of Jesse,*
and a branch from his roots shall bear fruit.

2 *And the Spirit of the LORD shall rest upon him,*
the Spirit of wisdom and understanding,
the Spirit of counsel and might,
the Spirit of knowledge and the fear of the LORD.

3 *And his delight shall be in the fear of the LORD.*

He shall not judge by what his eyes see,
or decide disputes by what his ears hear,

4 *but with righteousness he shall judge the poor,*
and decide with equity for the meek of the earth;

and he shall strike the earth with the rod of his mouth,
and with the breath of his lips he shall kill the wicked.

5 *Righteousness shall be the belt of his waist,*
and faithfulness the belt of his loins.

6 *The wolf shall dwell with the lamb,*
and the leopard shall lie down with the young goat,

and the calf and the lion and the fattened calf together;
and a little child shall lead them.

7 *The cow and the bear shall graze;*
their young shall lie down together;
and the lion shall eat straw like the ox.

8 *The nursing child shall play over the hole of the cobra,*
and the weaned child shall put his hand on the adder's den.

9 *They shall not hurt or destroy*
in all my holy mountain;

for the earth shall be full of the knowledge of the LORD
as the waters cover the sea.

10 *In that day the root of Jesse, who shall stand as a*
signal for the peoples—of him shall the nations
inquire, and his resting place shall be glorious.

11 *In that day the Lord will extend his hand yet a*
second time to recover the remnant that remains of
his people, from Assyria, from Egypt, from Pathros,
from Cush,[a] *from Elam, from Shinar, from Hamath,*
and from the coastlands of the sea.

12 *He will raise a signal for the nations*
and will assemble the banished of Israel,

and gather the dispersed of Judah
from the four corners of the earth.

13 *The jealousy of Ephraim shall depart,*
and those who harass Judah shall be cut off;

Ephraim shall not be jealous of Judah,
and Judah shall not harass Ephraim.

14 *But they shall swoop down on the shoulder of the Philistines in the west,*
and together they shall plunder the people of the east.

They shall put out their hand against Edom and Moab,
and the Ammonites shall obey them.

15 *And the LORD will utterly destroy*[b]
the tongue of the Sea of Egypt,

and will wave his hand over the River[c]
with his scorching breath,[d]

and strike it into seven channels,
and he will lead people across in sandals.

16 *And there will be a highway from Assyria*
for the remnant that remains of his people,

as there was for Israel
when they came up from the land of Egypt.

a Probably *Nubia* **b** Hebrew *devote to destruction* **c** That is, the Euphrates **d** Or *wind*

Overview: This chapter returns to the promise of an ideal king from the line of David. This gives the Reformation interpreters opportunity to draw more parallels to Christ and the righteous qualities of his ministry. Several of them also identify that Isaiah is speaking about the Holy Spirit, who was given to Jesus without measure. The descriptions of the various animals are frequently treated as allegories about how people need to be changed from wild to tame and how different people groups will be reconciled and brought together. These exegetes connect that interpretation to the gathering of the church with the calling of the Gentiles in the second part of the chapter. They recognize that this passage continues the themes of the faithful remnant, the promised Messiah, and the freedom God himself will bring.

11:1-5 *The Spirit upon the Messiah*

Seven Gifts Toward Perfection. Jörg Haugk von Jüchsen: The fear of God is the beginning of wisdom. This is why the prophet in Sirach . . . refers to the holy fear of God as to the root of the tree of wisdom and of life. The trunk, branches, and twigs that grow out of the root of this tree, that is, out of the fear of God, remain forever. They are divine wisdom, understanding, counsel, strength, knowledge, and blessedness. The Sacred Scriptures often communicate these seven degrees toward perfection figuratively or through parables. Thus God shows us his Spirit figuratively through the candelabrum with the seven candlesticks or in John's Revelation through the seven lamps. Proverbs speaks of seven pillars in the house of wisdom, Zechariah refers to seven eyes, Isaiah to seven spirits, to seven degrees or seven gifts of the Spirit. Our spirit must be tested and filtered through seven degrees or stages by the seven gifts of the divine Spirit until the true light, the sun of righteousness, rises in us and illuminates all our darkness. Then we will be encompassed by the clear truth and lifted out of our unbelief. The fear of God is the beginning of wisdom, that is, the root, trunk, and the branches of the whole tree of wisdom and light. From this wisdom sprouts all divine understanding of God in us. It follows that a true Christian life begins in the fear of God and continues in it until the end. A Christian Order of a True Christian.[1]

A Humble Birth. Heinrich Bullinger: Finally, it is shown that the future birth of the Lord would indeed come from the lineage of David, but not with illustrious royal dignity. Just as Jesse was also a Bethlehemite, his small town was indeed an honored city. But he was not a king, nor a leader. Indeed, the ancestors of the blessed virgin Mary who immediately preceded her were not royalty but only citizens. They were, of course, honored on account of the antiquity and nobility of their ancestry, but they were poor and neglected. But all the royal dignity was transferred to Herod and his sons when Christ was born from a virgin in a stable at the city of Bethlehem in Judea. Sermons on Isaiah 11:1.[2]

The Metaphor of Trees. Johannes Brenz: The prophet describes at the end of the previous chapter the destruction of the king of the Assyrians using the metaphor of trees in a forest. "They will be toppled," it says, "the thickets of the forest" and "Lebanon," that is, the lofty trees like the cedars of Lebanon "will fall by the Majestic One." With this metaphor, those trees are understood as the strong and powerful princes of the Assyrian king. Now in this eleventh chapter, keeping the same metaphor of trees at the beginning, Isaiah preaches about Christ and his kingdom. The trees (it says) of the Assyrian kingdom will be cut down, but "a shoot shall come forth from the stump of Jesse," that is, from the family of David, and "a branch from his roots shall bear fruit." This is clearly a prophecy about Christ. Commentary on Isaiah 11:1.[3]

[1]CRR 10:4-5*; citing Ex 25:31-40; Rev 4:5; Prov 9:1; Zech 4:10; Jn 8:12-32; Is 66:5-24; Lk 1; Ps 19; Wis 10.
[2]Bullinger, *Isaias*, 62v.
[3]Brenz, *Esaias*, 183, 199.

Only About Christ. Johannes Oecolampadius: In Christ and in no other this prophecy resounds. And according to his custom, the prophet joins this with what was earlier. So the conjunction *and* is not in vain. For, explaining the reality through a type, it is evident that he says that the boy, Immanuel and Swift Spoiler, not only will aid those trusting in him, but in the future he himself will actually be born from David and, in a while, will deliver a far more glorious triumph over spiritual tyranny than what he now reports about Assyria. Further, he teaches first what kind of king Christ will be in the future, and then also what kind of kingdom his will be in the church. And consider the diligence of the prophet, for he issues omens from the birth itself of Christ. Therefore, he calls Christ a branch and shoot or sprout, as also earlier . . . he was called a delightful shoot, although there it is a different term in the Hebrew. Commentary on Isaiah 11:1.[4]

Tools for Perilous Times. Dirk Philips: The printer made a preface to the booklet and told therein how in these dangerous, perilous times the gifts of the Holy Spirit . . . (namely, wisdom, understanding, counsel, strength, ability, knowledge, and fear of the Lord) are needed by every Christian who has to distinguish various and manifold options and meanings in teaching and faith. The same I acknowledge with the printer, still with such distinction that Isaiah has actually spoken about Jesus Christ, the only born Son of God, [which] his words also announce. . . .

That this prophecy applies entirely to Christ no one who is taught from God can doubt. Even so, no less Christians must also have the same Spirit of the Lord. For while the gifts of the Holy Spirit rest fully on Jesus Christ, . . . the same also comes on all his Christians, and according to measure, first on the ministers through whom he speaks, and his word is in their mouth; and certainly thereafter on all his members who cling to the head, or the same Holy Spirit shares his gifts according to his will. Answer to Sebastian Franck.[5]

A Staff from Jesse's Root. Adam Sasbout: "And a shoot will come forth from the root of Jesse." Here the prophet again in his usual manner transitions to his Immanuel, and this is the sixth transition from the mention of things at that time to the mention of the kingdom of Christ. Yet among Christians, two or three interpret this passage as referring to events at that time, which should be surprising beyond measure, since even the Jews themselves, who have the habit of interpreting and understanding everything according to the letter, refer these things to the Christ.

Now there is an unexpected transition here, because of the particle *and*, which usually notes a connection. "Shoot from the root of Jesse. . . ." These words, *shoot, root, blossom*, are taken figuratively, even by the Jews themselves. And the metaphor seems to be taken from trees that have only been cut down and not completely uprooted. . . . The sense is something like this: from the stump a shoot will be born, and from that shoot later a blossom will be born, that is, from the small remains of the Jewish kingdom, or the Jewish people, which once was indeed a tree but is now only a stump, a girl will be born, and from her Christ will be born. This is how the commentators generally explain the shoot, interpreting it as the Virgin Mary and the blossom as Christ. It is indeed certain that the prophet is speaking about the Christ to be born. But whether it is in this order, that he first has in mind the virgin under the term *shoot* and then Christ under the term *blossom*, that is not so certain.

The word *shoot* actually opposes their explanation that this is a delicate shrub and bush, and so they think it rightly signifies the Virgin Mary. But the Hebrew word does not mean this but rather a staff and rod or a royal scepter. So where it is said . . . , "Jacob took shoots," there is a different word there in

[4]Oecolampadius, *In Iesaiam*, 96v; citing Is 4.

[5]CRR 6:447-48*; citing 2 Thess 2:8.

the Hebrew form in this passage. This is why the sense of this passage here seems to be, "Someone will be born from that root with a royal scepter, or a shepherd's staff." It has such a meaning earlier when it says, "The staff for his shoulder . . . ," that is, the imperial burdens and rule. . . . "A star shall come out of Jacob, and a staff shall rise out of Israel." In that passage again, it is a royal scepter. Commentary on Isaiah 11:1.[6]

Physical Before Spiritual Promises. Martin Luther: This chapter does not seem to cohere with the preceding ones since it discusses a different subject. But the ability to recognize the coherence of the prophets is important. For the prophets did not speak as drunk and raving men, mixing diverse subjects together. But the Holy Spirit is the best rhetorician and logician, and therefore he speaks most clearly.

The first item discussed here is the promise of the spiritual kingdom, which most fittingly follows the prophecy concerning the deliverance of the kingdom of Judah and the restoration of external peace, since this promise speaks of a far nobler deliverance—one that is spiritual. This is the way the prophets usually contemplate the connection between the earthly and the spiritual kingdom, as we do, too, when in our preaching we speak now of faith, now of sight. For this is a proper order, and therefore the prophets, proclaiming either threats or promises with reference to the physical kingdom, in the second place keep the people of the earthly kingdom in a state of expectation for the coming spiritual kingdom. First comes what is physical, and then what is spiritual. . . .

Accordingly, this kingdom will be powerful in goodness and joy, not in weapons. And the protection of the Holy Spirit, who was given to Christ without measure, is certainly strong enough. . . . And here it is plainly indicated that this kingdom will not be physical but spiritual. In that kingdom all affairs will be conducted by the Spirit alone, and the Spirit will be poured out over the whole kingdom. Lectures on Isaiah 11:1-2.[7]

Christ's Humanity Anointed with the Spirit for Us. John Calvin: Some think that this should rather be viewed as referring to Hezekiah; but how groundless that opinion is, we have already shown. For when he was born, David still had a flourishing reputation, and the rank of royalty belonged to his descendants; and Hezekiah was very far from attaining such greatness that is soon described after this. So now we infer that the spiritual kingdom of Christ was formerly promised to the ancient people, because his whole strength, power, and majesty is here made to consist in the gifts of the Spirit. Although Christ was not deficient in gifts of this kind, yet as he took our flesh on himself, it was necessary that he should be enriched with them, that we might afterward be made partakers of all the blessings of which otherwise we are destitute; for as John says, "out of his fullness, we must draw as from a fountain."

"The Spirit of the Lord." We must keep in view what I mentioned a little ago, that this refers to Christ's human nature, because he could not be enriched with the gift and grace of the Father except so far as he became human. Besides, as he came down to us, so he received the gifts of the Spirit, that he might bestow them on us. And this is the anointing from which he receives the name of Christ, which he imparts to us. For why are we called Christians except that he admits us to his fellowship, by distributing to us out of his fullness according to the measure of undeserved liberality? And undoubtedly this passage does not so much teach us what Christ is in himself as what he received from the Father, that he might enrich us with his wealth. Commentary on Isaiah 11:2.[8]

Christ Given the Spirit Without Measure. Konrad Pellikan: The Messiah, to whom

[6]Sasbout, *In Esaiam*, 91-92; citing Gen 30:37; Is 9:4; Num 24:17.

[7]LW 16:117-18 (WA 31.2:83-84); citing Is 61:1; Jn 1:16; Col 2:9; Jn 7:16.

[8]CTS 13:373-74 (CO 36: 235-36); citing Jn 1:16; 7:37-38.

the Spirit was given without measure but to the fullness, will be full of spiritual riches and virtues. From this all the elect should drink. Certainly, the spirit of wisdom, since it is the very word of God by which all things were created, is also the wisdom of God the Father. An example is the intelligence according to which he created all creatures. The spirit of counsel is that by which all things are established and ordered to their end appointed by God—that he should be the firstborn over creation and that he would restore the kingdom to his Father at the consummation of all things.

The spirit of might is that in which we can do all things, and to whom all things are subject, who also overcomes the world and binds the strong one so that he can do no harm. Likewise, the spirit of knowledge and understanding is that by which he told those who believe what he had heard from the Father, not of the vanities of this world but of the knowledge that is from God, which is pure and holy. And the spirit of the fear of the Lord is nothing other than the pursuit of true religion and godliness in God, along with love for neighbor, which the Lord requires for true worship that pleases him and is true religion. These were given to Christ the man, as the head of the church, from whom they will be poured into the souls of the elect through the grace of God and the anointing of the Holy Spirit. Commentary on Isaiah 11:2-3.[9]

Christ the Lampstand. Martin Borrhaus: You should not show favoritism the way those do, who judge by sight. So the eyes of Christ are also given, but those are divine, beholding all things. For in Zechariah, he is called a stone adorned with seven eyes, which are the six spirits just mentioned by our prophet, the seventh being quietness. Just as Christ is also called a lampstand, with seven holy spirits shining as lamps. Nothing deceives or hides from his judgment. The head of the candlestick, the fountain and spring of the light of life, is seen in this. All the saints draw the light of life from it in order to know and judge rightly. Oracles in Isaiah on 11:2-3.[10]

The Strongest Savior. Johannes Brenz: Earlier he calls him Mighty God. Here he says, in him is assigned the "spirit of might." And of course, this praise is most fittingly joined with what was said earlier. Christ is our sweetest and strongest Savior (1) because he is God of armies; (2) because his angel encamped around those who fear him; (3) because he is the victor over the most powerful enemies; (4) because all enemies are a footstool for his feet; (5) because by his gospel, all human arrogance is demolished; (6) thereafter, he will summon all people to his judgment seat on the last day; (7) thus, he is so strong that no one can snatch the sheep from his hand; and (8) finally, in all dangers he is the strength for his own. Commentary on Isaiah 11:2-3.[11]

The Spirit as Fullness in Christ. Heinrich Bullinger: Dr. Johannes Oecolampadius admirably shows here in his commentary that the invention of the scholastics about the seven gifts of the Holy Spirit has no place, since many more are listed by the apostle.[†] Isaiah relates three pairs. He adds "the spirit" to each one to signify that all the fullness is in Christ and that he possesses and administers these things not as extraordinary prerogatives given to a man by God, but he has them himself as true God. Sermons on Isaiah 11:2.[12]

Titles of the Holy Spirit. Johannes Oecolampadius: Where it is said, "the Spirit of the Lord will rest," the Spirit by nature is signified. Thus also the Spirit of God is said to be the Spirit of the Father, the Spirit of the Son, the Spirit of life, and the Spirit of truth. And because Christ received the fullness of the Spirit without measure—and we too receive from his fullness—he

[9]Pellikan, *Commentaria Bibliorum*, 3:16r.

[10]Borrhaus, *In Iesaiae Prophetae Oracula*, 139; citing Zech 3:9.

[11]Brenz, *Esaias*, 199; citing Ps 46.

[12]Bullinger, *Isaias*, 63r. †See Oecolampadius, *In Iesaiam*, 97r.

calls his Spirit the Holy Spirit, saying, "When the Paraclete will come, you will receive the Holy Spirit from me." Truly where it is supplied, "Spirit of wisdom and understanding," . . . it is proper to understand these as gifts and operations through the Spirit. . . . For he is also the Spirit of sanctification, he is the Spirit of faith, he is the Spirit of temperance, the Spirit of promise, the Spirit of delight, the Spirit of humility, the Spirit of discernment, the Spirit of gentleness. Commentary on Isaiah 11:2.[13]

The Smell of Judgment. John Trapp: The Hebrew has, "It shall make him scent or smell."[†] That is, a singular sagacity and sharpness of judgment in smelling out a hypocrite, as Simon Peter did to Simon Magus, who had deceived Philip even to the point that he was baptized. But Peter soon found him out; how much more will Christ? His sharp nose easily discerns and is offended with the stinking breath of the hypocrites' rotten lungs, even though his words were never so scented and perfumed with displays of holiness. Exposition on Isaiah 11:3.[14]

Judge in the Church like Christ. Wolfgang Musculus: This is nothing other than, "He will not judge unjustly," because he will not judge from an opinion brought from another place, nor from the appearance of things, which is most often mistaken, nor from the mouth of another. But he will judge from the most certain knowledge of the truth, which he will have from the Spirit of the Lord. We are here admonished what we should understand about external judgments that are placed before either our eyes or our ears—how uncertain and insufficient they are for this when we judge according to them in matters of godliness and religion. In worldly things, there is less danger. Indeed, sometimes it cannot be otherwise than to make a decision by external judgments. This is not so in spiritual matters. Here, Christ himself does not judge except by the Spirit of the Lord. But what kind are the ecclesiastical judgments—even to the point of shedding blood in them—that are pronounced, when they are based on what was remembered? Commentary on Isaiah 11:3.[15]

The Titles Correspond to the Messiah. Dietrich Schnepff: Because among the other titles, it is attributed to him that he has the spirit of counsel and might. This is why it was written . . . that he is called Counselor and Mighty God. Besides that, he is not going to have a physical and external kingdom but a spiritual one, which is discerned from the fact that it says, "He will overcome by the rod of his mouth," that is, by his word. Scholia on Isaiah 11:4.[16]

Rain from God's Mouth. Argula von Grumbach:

> Show myself a Christian meek
> And turned to you the other cheek;
> But since God's word you seek to hurt
> Strongly I will resist your work
> None of which is of any avail
> The gates of hell will not prevail.
> The words from God's own mouth will rain
> And smite you down; your talent disdain.
> God's very self you have set at naught.
> Pain and shame to his people brought.
> So often I find that Scriptures say:
> One will chase a thousand away.

Johannes of Lanzhut: Attack and Response.[17]

The Rod of Christ's Mouth. Wolfgang Musculus: Yet it is not absurd if you understand by "the rod of his mouth" the scepter of Christ's kingdom. For his gospel is, in place of a scepter,

[13]Oecolampadius, *In Iesaiam*, 97r; citing Jn 15.

[14]Trapp, *Commentary or Exposition*, 56*; citing Acts 8:9-25. [†]The Hebrew text of Is 11:3a reads, "and his smelling is in the fear of the Lord."

[15]Musculus, *In Esaiam*, 257.

[16]Schnepff, *In Esaiae*, 196.

[17]Von Grumbach, *Argula von Grumbach: A Woman's Voice*, 190; citing Is 11:4; 30:17.

containing the power of life and death—life among the elect and those who believe, death among the wicked and unfaithful. Now it does not mention the mouth and lips of Christ to connect this to his person, as if he were speaking about the extent to which his word was pronounced through his person when he was here in the flesh and will be pronounced on the day of judgment when he will say, "Depart, you wicked, into the eternal fire. . . ." The rod of his mouth and the spirit of his lips is also the gospel, insofar as the Holy Spirit, through the apostles and the rest of the ministers of the kingdom of God, convicts the world of sin and is fulfilled—"Whatever you bind on earth will be bound in heaven." Commentary on Isaiah 11:4.[18]

The Belt of Righteousness Is Christ's Blood. Dietrich Schnepff: "And righteousness shall be the belt of his waist." Warriors were once adorned with belts. But the decor of our king and victor is faith and righteousness. For from the beginning all the promises in Christ are yes and amen. What our sweetest Savior promised to the fathers in the Old Testament, he fulfilled them abundantly in the New. And the consistency of those promises is such that the Lord confirmed them with his own blood, and today he feeds and refreshes his people with the same. But what is more beautiful and attractive than to have a belt adorned not with jewels and gold but with innocent blood? This is the decor that our Isaiah describes. . . . "Who is this who comes from Edom, in stained garments. . . ." For Christ, to prove his faithfulness and the consistency of his promises, shed his blood for us and redeemed us by the same. Scholia on Isaiah 11:5.[19]

11:6-9 *The Kingdom of the Messiah*

The Nature of Animals in the Future. Johannes Oecolampadius: The interpretation of the Hebrews who believe beasts will not harm those who are good and righteous at the coming of the Messiah is not to be entirely rejected. For they do not think that the nature of beasts is going to be removed entirely. For their nature is good in itself and was the condition instilled in them by God in the beginning. But they think God, who works out all that will happen, will make it so that neither people nor these things of people would be harmed. Commentary on Isaiah 11:6-7.[20]

Two Kinds of People. Heinrich Bullinger: The prophet foreshadowed these two kinds of people: by tame animals, sheep, goat kids, lambs, cows, and so on; and by fierce and aggressive beasts, insatiable and carnivorous bears, lions. . . .[†] It should be noted from the evangelical teaching of Christ that there are those who are called swine and dogs, before whom he forbids the casting of pearls and holy things. And yet, there will come into the church of Christ those who were formerly infamous for murder, adultery, theft, lewdness, drunkenness, robbery, greed, usury, and other kinds of iniquity, such as in the past Matthew, Zacchaeus, many soldiers, tax collectors, sinners, harlots, and infamous people, such as Paul who was also Saul, drenched in the blood of saints. Sermons on Isaiah 11:6-7.[21]

Regenerated from Wolves to Sheep. Zacharias Ursinus: Christ justifies by his merit those whom he also regenerates and sanctifies by his Spirit. He changes them from wolves and lions to lambs and young goats. Therefore, let us not separate the blessing of justification and regeneration, imagining to take hold of one without the other. Let us also acknowledge that it is his work to change us from wolves into sheep, and let us give thanks for his mercy, for this grace bestowed on us that he made us from enemies into his friends and co-heirs. Commentary on Isaiah 11:6.[22]

[18]Musculus, *In Esaiam*, 257-58; citing Mt 25:41; 18:18.
[19]Schnepff, *In Esaiae*, 202; citing 2 Cor 1:20; Is 63:1.
[20]Oecolampadius, *In Iesaiam*, 98r-v; citing Hos 2; Lev 26; Ezek 5; Mk 1; Acts 28; Lk 10; Mk 16.
[21]Bullinger, *Isaias*, 64v. †See also Musculus, *In Esaiam*, 260.
[22]Ursinus, *Iesaiam*, 385.

Voluntary Obedience to Be Led by Children. Rudolf Gwalther: Then he attributes voluntary obedience to them, as David did, who says that the people of Christ will be willing. Truly he denotes this with these words, "And a little child shall lead them." That is, they will be so manageable and obedient that they will allow themselves to be ruled and led by children. But preachers of the Word are such children who, if you look at the world, have neither power nor authority, and in addition are considered foolish and stupid, as Paul teaches, . . . and what Festus the governor said to him, "Paul, you are insane; much learning has rendered you insane."

They generally object to this with the ministers of Christ, who seem to be more moderate than others. But they utter the same voice of the true shepherd, which the sheep, that is, all the elect, recognize and follow willingly, as they do not consider the person of the minister, but they expend what they owe Christ. So, it can be deduced from this that those who do not want to be ruled by the Word and his servants are by no means among the number of Christ's sheep, but rather they prescribe laws about speaking and being silent. Sermons on Isaiah 11:6.[23]

Allegories of Animals. Martin Luther: "The wolf shall dwell with the lamb." Here is the fruit and effectiveness of that belt and armor—the preaching of faith. These are allegories. It says that then the former tyrants themselves, along with their power, wisdom, and wealth, will lose their feathers and plumes, and with bent necks confess themselves to be sinners, and they will be harmless. And he says the wolf will associate with the lamb, not the lamb with the wolf. The tyrant will become a martyr, the wolf a teacher. The wolves are false teachers. . . . Paul was a wolf before his conversion.

The lambs are Christians. Those who join with them will be wise in spirit. The young goats are, of course, those who were a pure offering according to the law, not those of whom Matthew 25 speaks. They are martyrs. The leopards are persecuting tyrants. This is what the Word of God does—it casts down the proud and lifts up the humble. The calves are the faithful. The lions are the rich. The lion cubs are said to be more ferocious than the adults. That is, those who before submitted to no one now obey the gospel preached to them by the least brother. Although the papists abused their power, nevertheless obedience for Christ's sake was willingly displayed. Thus in the past, prophets directed kings. . . .

The most hostile among people—the ferocious, the wild, the furious, the hateful, the murderous, the untamed—and the meek people of Christ will be joined together through the preaching of the gospel. The church will convert the nations not by force but by the goodness of the Word. The lion will fill himself with straw and stubble, that is, he will become tame and clothe himself with a domestic gentleness, just as the ox will submit to the hand. . . . The little boy will extract snakes with his hand. That is, the preacher will cast out demons by the spoken word where the Holy Spirit is present. Lectures on Isaiah 11:6-9.[24]

Beasts Cannot Harm Believers. Johannes Brenz: This is why, although beasts still retain their ferocity and cruelty, yet because sin is atoned for, they cannot be a curse or cause harm to those who are in Jesus Christ through faith. For if beasts bite us in the body, yet Christ himself, whom we possess by faith, remains unharmed, and our salvation in Christ remains unharmed. If beasts infect us with poison, Christ preserves us with his medicine. If beasts kill us, Christ is our life. And so it was rightly said by the prophet, "They shall not harm and shall not kill in all my mountain." When Ignatius the martyr was condemned to the beasts, he heard the lions roaring and said, "I am the wheat of Christ, being ground by the teeth of beasts, that I may be found as pure bread."[†] Commentary on Isaiah 11:8-9.[25]

[23]Gwalther, *Isaias*, 82-83; citing Ps 110:3; 1 Cor 1; Acts 26:24.

[24]LW 16:122-23 (WA 31.2:86-87); citing Mt 7:15; 25:32.

[25]Brenz, *Esaias*, 190. [†]See Ignatius of Antioch, *To the Romans* 4.2.

A Kingdom of Knowledge. Wolfgang Musculus: This knowledge of the Lord had been extinguished not only among the nations but also in Israel itself for the greater part. And a gross ignorance of this truth had prevailed, under which the ruler of this world, as reigning in darkness, had blinded the minds of mortals and rendered them beastly. Certainly, Christ the Savior, the light of the world, was sent by the Father for this purpose, to enlighten the minds of mortals with the light of the knowledge of God, not only in Judea but throughout the whole earth. He sent the word of his gospel through the apostles into the world, and with them cooperated with the power of his Spirit, so that the knowledge of God would prevail throughout the world. And this is so effectual that not only should there be amazement in religion but also conversion in morals. . . .

We will observe from this passage, first, that the kingdom of Christ is not a kingdom of ignorance but a kingdom of the knowledge of God. Thus the kingdoms of Christ and Satan are distinguished, such that one is of darkness and ignorance, the other of light and the knowledge of God. Then the unique abundance of the knowledge of God belongs to the people of the New Testament. Third, that this breadth of the knowledge of God is not from the law but from the teaching of Christ, that is, the light of the gospel. This is why those who cannot bear the light of the truth of God refuse the teaching of the gospel with their hands and their feet. Commentary on Isaiah 11:9.[26]

11:10-16 *The Messiah Will Gather the Peoples*

Seek the Root of Jesse, Not Others. Martin Borrhaus: They will not inquire of the world, nor the kingdom of the adversary. But, forsaking that, they will inquire of the kingdom of the Messiah and the teaching of the holy gospel. Therefore, he does not say, "They will inquire of Moses, they will inquire of the philosophers, they will inquire of the dark light of human reason shining like the moon in the night." He does not say, "They will inquire of Muhammad, they will inquire of that famous Babylonian prostitute." But he says, "They will inquire of the root of Jesse," the Messiah, that king and ruler of heaven and earth, the Savior of the world, who has written on his forehead, King of kings and Lord of lords. They will inquire of this one who is Wonderful Counselor, Mighty God, Everlasting Father, Prince of Peace. Oracles in Isaiah on 11:10.[27]

The Root of Jesse as a Signal for the Peoples to Gather. Johannes Oecolampadius: What was earlier said more obscurely, he now explains clearly. For in that day, the gospel will be preached and Christ will reign. He who was born from the roots of Jesse and whose condition was more despised from the beginning, he will now be the signal for the peoples, to whom all the peoples will gather, joining themselves to him and pleading with him. And they will gather to the signal, like when those in an army all look to a banner. For he must be heard and his example be respected. The nations will seek him, not idols as before. Commentary on Isaiah 11:10.[28]

A Sign for the Peoples. Adam Sasbout: The metaphor is taken from military signs, from which the Latins call the signs in front. The sense is that this Messiah will be like a flag set up on a hill, on which all will cast their eyes. The idea is the same, but the etymology of the word is different according to the Hebrew and the Latin. For the Latins, what are called "signs" are taken from an image of animals, like an eagle, which were inscribed on a flag. But the etymology for the Hebrews is taken from lifting something on high. For they are lifted on high so they are visible to the whole army. Consequently, in this passage the sign is a raised flag, and displayed in public for every eye. The same word is used . . . : "Make a bronze

[26]Musculus, *In Esaiam*, 261.

[27]Borrhaus, *In Iesaiae Prophetae Oracula*, 142.

[28]Oecolampadius, *In Iesaiam*, 99r.

serpent and place it as a sign." Christ clearly alluded to this word, "Just as Moses lifted up the serpent in the wilderness." Commentary on Isaiah 11:10.[29]

Christ the Root. Martin Luther: We have this declaration. . . . In Hebrew it reads: "And it shall come to pass in that day that the root of Jesse, which stands for an ensign of the people, unto him shall the nations seek; and his resting place shall be glorious." The meaning evidently is that the Gentiles shall possess Christ and he shall reign over them. Paul makes a slight change in the words, following the rendering of the old translators who wrote the Bible in the Greek language. The meaning of the quotation is the same, however.

The "root" of Jesse should not be understood here as "stem" or "tree" in the genealogical sense, as the artist would delineate the "tree" of Jesse, the father of David, with its many branches. That is what we mean when we sing of the blessed virgin, "the stem of Jesse has sprung forth." That would be altogether a forced construction. Christ himself, and none other, is the stem or root. The construction of this passage from Isaiah makes that meaning plain, for it says practically, "The Gentiles shall hope for the stem or root of Jesse, which is to rule the nations." . . . This prophecy cannot be made to refer to the human Jesse or to our blessed virgin. Sermons on Epistle Texts for Advent and Christmas.[30]

The Instrument God Uses to Gather the Church. Zacharias Ursinus: God wants the gospel to be the medium or instrument of the gathering of the church, that is, of calling and conversion to Christ. Consequently, it is to be preached openly and heard in the whole world, and to be known and learned by all people, just as he cries from heaven, "Hear this: Jehovah will raise up a signal to the nations." Therefore, let us also listen carefully, meditate, and strive to preserve and promote the ministry of sound teaching about Christ in all times and places. And let us remember that we are guilty of the most serious crimes and would be inexcusable before the judgment of God if either we had not heard the gospel offered, as is necessary, or in our ungratefulness we deprived ourselves and our posterity of its preaching and light, just as we see has happened to many nations in the past and today.

The gospel calls people, like a military signal, to war against the devil, sin, the world, and various temptations and scandals, and to bear the cross. Moreover, after the unquestionable victory, Christ will dwell with those who fight boldly and share his glory with them, which is yet hidden in this life but afterward will be manifest in the heavenly and eternal life. "His resting place shall be glorious." Commentary on Isaiah 11:10.[31]

The Church Is Christ's Resting Place. Dietrich Schnepff: And he adds, "His resting place shall be in glory," which commonly refers to the grave. For the grave of the Lord, because of the Lord's glorious resurrection, is even celebrated. But I think that the residence, as they commonly say, is to be understood as the residence of this king. "That place," it says, where that prince will stand and reside, "will be glorious." And the resting place of Christ is the church. . . . "This is my resting place forever." Therefore it is understood that the kingdom of Christ, which is his church, would be glorious and magnificent. Scholia on Isaiah 11:10.[32]

Rest After Glorious Victory. Wolfgang Musculus: It seems to me that the tomb is a more humble sense than what would satisfy the spirit of the prophet. The constructing of a tomb and journeying to a monument also happened to such ancient ones. That view would imply that their glory would be equal with Christ, especially if you consider the tomb of the wicked Muhammad. Among more recent ones, others explain this

[29]Sasbout, *In Esaiam*, 96; citing Num 21:8; Jn 3:14.
[30]Luther, *Sermons*, 6:47.
[31]Ursinus, *Iesaiam*, 396.
[32]Schnepff, *In Esaiae*, 204; citing Ps 132:14.

to be about the death of Christ, because one comes to glory through it. Others understand it as his habitation, which is the church, based on the psalm: "This is my resting place forever; here I will dwell, because I have chosen it." Others understand it as that peace and tranquility that exists among the faithful of Christ's kingdom. Kimchi the Jew explains that because war will not be inflicted on him, he will remain in peace and glory.† For all nations will glorify him and serve him.

I say that it seems to me that resting is a sign in warfare after a victory has been won. The glory of this is the glory of victory. This signal of ours, about which the prophet prophesies, conveys victory over the ancient enemy, over sin, death, and the world. Having won the victory, he was transferred to the heavenlies and established in glory. So, the resting of Christ is in glory, and he gloriously defeated the enemy and triumphed over him. Commentary on Isaiah 11:10.[33]

The Reclaimed Remnant. Konrad Pellikan: Indeed, nothing here is said about Jerusalem, the Jewish city, but it is about the holy church, in which the people of the Lord are, and the faithful children of God scattered throughout the world. Christ speaks about this when he was about to die and professes that he would gather them from all nations, kingdoms, and regions of the earth, to Abraham's side, with whom "they will recline." For how and when the Israelites returned from the kingdoms named here to any happiness, they could not show, nor ever will show, unless it is what they can have in Christ, according to the Scriptures, not the flesh. But this should be understood in a sense worthy of God, not as a physical and transitory kingdom among mortals and under mortals but under the reign of the Messiah. Because since it must be eternal, it cannot be physical and therefore not particular to one place, no matter how great—even ten times wider than Judea—for it to be where the living faithful are gathered, much less if they rose from the dead or are only Jews ruling temporarily with their Messiah. Commentary on Isaiah 11:11.[34]

The Second Liberation Is the Calling of the Nations. Dietrich Schnepff: These words seem to have been said about some external leading back of the Hebrews. But since the Hebrews were only brought back from Babylon once, and it is also said here that the Lord is going to liberate them a second time with his mighty hand, it should not be understood as referring to the release of slaves from Babylon. There was not any other external leading back of the Hebrews. Moreover, the ten tribes did not return from Assyria (as is known). Additionally, it is clearly written in this passage that the Hebrews are called from all parts of the world. So this should be understood as either generally about the calling of all the nations—which I especially approve—or about the conversion of the proselytes to Christ, who are written about in Acts, "There were people in Jerusalem from every nation of the world." . . .

When Christ the Lord will do these great things, then that excellent work of true and spiritual liberation will be accomplished. For when the Lord was going to bring them back from the Babylonian captivity—which would happen under Darius Longimanus—he would declare to them the first step of his mercy. Meanwhile, the ten tribes scattered among other nations would not return, nor see their country. But when the Lord "extended his hand a second time," and of course, as a spiritual redemption, the remnants of the people of God, that is, the elect, will return from every place: from Assyria, Egypt, Pathros (which they call Arabian Petra), Ethiopia, Media, Babylon (which we call Shinar), Hamath, which is also Antioch, and then from the most remote places and islands, which today we do not know. But that is going to happen when all the people will walk to

[33]Musculus, *In Esaiam*, 262; citing Ps 132:14; Col 3. †See Kimchi, *Commentary on Isaiah* (1966), 78-79.

[34]Pellikan, *Commentaria Bibliorum*, 3:16v; citing Mt 8:11.

the teaching of the Messiah—not with their feet but with their consent. Scholia on Isaiah 11:11.[35]

Physical and Spiritual Subduing. John Mayer: The Jews think that this is going to be fulfilled in a carnal manner with all their enemies around them eventually being subdued to them by force of arms, as in the time of King David. But because Christ's kingdom is not of this world, they are certainly deceived. The meaning of this is nothing else but spiritual. "They shall swoop down on the Philistines. . . ." By preaching and working miracles for their conversion, those who dwelled on every side of them will be subdued to Christ and brought under the obedience of the gospel, which he intimates by saying, "The children of Ammon shall obey them," that is, obey their teaching, as Jerome says. But Oecolampadius says that this was fulfilled in part when the Jews returning from Babylon prevailed against their old enemies, the Philistines with "flying upon their shoulders" being a phrase to express their subjection to them, and partly fulfilled when by the Spirit we subdue our spiritual enemies, the flesh and the world, by getting mastery over our corruptions.[†]

I prefer the former, and according to it, the Jews preaching the gospel are said to stick out their hand, to intimate their ready obedience to it, so that if the preachers of it simply by pointing with their hand show what they would have them do, they yielded presently without any delay, and became obedient in all things. And accordingly in the time of the apostles, Philip is said to have gone to Azotus . . . and Peter to have been at Joppa, which were both in the country of Idumea, as Strabo says. And in the time of Athanasius and Chrysostom, Adricomius says there were very flourishing churches in Gaza and Ascalon, and other cities of the Philistines. Commentary on Isaiah 11:14.[36]

The Swift Effect of Apostolic Preaching. Francisco Forerius: "And they will fly on shoulders. . . ." These things should be understood as the conversion of the nations by the apostles, who went through all of Palestine and those regions that could be approached by the Mediterranean Sea, that is to say, the whole of Europe, both east and west. And that these things should be understood spiritually, as I said, what follows in verses 15 and 16 proves. For when this verse says that the Jews flew like birds from behind the Palestinians and subjected the Edomites, the Moabites, the Ammonites, and plundered the Eastern peoples, how does what is included in verses 15 and 16 not commemorate victory but the return of the children of Israel from captivity? Therefore, let the Jews understand that this victory is by the word of God and the preaching of the gospel, by which, when the children of God who were dispersed heard it, they came together to the God of Israel, with every hindrance removed.

Do not let the names of Assyria and of the river, namely, the Euphrates, disturb you, as if this were a speech about the return from the Assyrians. For it is not read that the Israelites returned from Assyria, nor are they going to return in any other way than what I just explained, just like from Egypt. For that sea is not going to be dried up again, nor will the Egyptians be suffocated again. If you do not use this method when interpreting in the prophets, it will clearly require you to Judaize throughout.

"They will fly on the shoulders" signifies the speed of preaching and the submission of those who believe. For when a lion or another ferocious beast leaps on the shoulder blades of a cow (as is typical) or another animal, it tears it to pieces without delay. So the disciples of the apostles handed over themselves and all that was theirs to this will, and if it had been necessary, they would willingly have plucked out their eyes, as Paul says. Commentary on Isaiah 11:14-16.[37]

[35]Schnepff, *In Esaiae*, 205, 212; citing Acts 2:5.
[36]Mayer, *Commentary upon All the Prophets*, 4:90; citing Acts 8.
[†]See Oecolampadius, *In Iesaiam*, 100v; Strabo, *Geography* (LCL 241: 16.2.28-29); Christiano Adrichomio, *Theatrum Terrae Sanctae et biblicarum historiarum cum tabulis geographicis aere expressis* (Cologne: Mylius In officina Birckmannica, 1590), 6v.
[37]Forerius, *Iesaiae*, 50r-v; citing Gal 4:15.

The Highway for the Remnant as the New Exodus. Johannes Oecolampadius: The Jews persuade their own that they are going to cross the sea again, as they did in the past when they came out of Egypt, and the sea and the streams dried up. But this refers to a spiritual leading back, by Christ to the kingdom of righteousness, which we threw away in the first Adam. Certainly, by the death of Christ, the way was opened for us, and the spiritual Pharaoh was drowned in the Red Sea, and all the obstacles were removed, even the cruel bars. . . . Just as in the exodus from Egypt, the enemies were destroyed, the sea was passable, and he gave manna from heaven, so also nothing will be lacking for the remnant who are being saved through Jesus Christ, who is the way and the truth. Commentary on Isaiah 11:16.[38]

[38]Oecolampadius, *In Iesaiam*, 100v, 101r.

12:1-6 A Song of Trust in the Holy One

12 *You[a] will say in that day:*

"I will give thanks to you, O Lord,
for though you were angry with me,

your anger turned away,
that you might comfort me.

2 *"Behold, God is my salvation;*
I will trust, and will not be afraid;

for the Lord God[b] is my strength and my song,
and he has become my salvation."

3 *With joy you[c] will draw water from the wells of*
salvation. 4 *And you will say in that day:*

"Give thanks to the Lord,
call upon his name,

make known his deeds among the peoples,
proclaim that his name is exalted.

5 *"Sing praises to the Lord, for he has done*
gloriously;
let this be made known[d] in all the earth.

6 *Shout, and sing for joy, O inhabitant of Zion,*
for great in your[e] midst is the Holy One of
Israel."

a The Hebrew for *you* is singular in verse 1 **b** Hebrew *for Yah, the Lord* **c** The Hebrew for *you* is plural in verses 3, 4 **d** Or *this is made known* **e** The Hebrew for *your* in verse 6 is singular, referring to the *inhabitant of Zion*

Overview: This short chapter recounts praise to God for delivering his people even though he was angry with them. Several Reformation commentators identify this as a song like others found in Scripture. They explain the theological truths they see from this passage related to salvation, forgiveness, and reconciliation to God. Like in many other passages, they frequently identify Christ as the one portrayed. In this case, he is the Holy One of Israel and the one who draws water from the springs. There are differing views on what this water represents, with the most common interpretation being that it is the living water Jesus offers in the Gospel of John.

12:1-3 *A Song of Praise for Deliverance*

Forgiveness and Salvation. Viktorin Strigel: Who among the righteous would ignore this speech of the prophet, repeated in many chapters, about the forgiveness of sins, about the preservation of the church, about the presence of God in the church who listens to us and alleviates the penalties in this life to save the church, and about the giving of eternal life and glory when all evil will be entirely removed? Our prophet adds to these comforts the sweetest thanksgiving song full of prayers with the most ardent affections in chapter 12. "I give you thanks, Lord, because you were angry at me, and when your anger turned away, you comforted me." Oration on the Prophet Isaiah.[1]

Erupting into Song After Victory. Johannes Brenz: Therefore, when the benefits of the kingdom of Christ are greater than what can be adequately explained in human words, and yet we should do it, the prophet then bursts into a song of rejoicing and exhortation. In this he also expresses that he is grateful to God for so many benefits that he identifies are conferred through Christ. In that way he stirs up the whole church of

[1] Strigel, *Oratio De Propheta Esaia*, 30.

Christ to gratitude and to praising the divine kindness. For it is customary, as much in society as in the church of God, that notable victories and other illustrious deeds be celebrated with public songs, and that the memories of those people be commended.

So Moses consecrated the deliverance from Egypt and the escape through the Red Sea with a song. . . . Deborah, too, commended to posterity the victory that she reported about Sisera. . . . There are many such psalms of the godly in the Old Testament, and especially of David. There are also the songs of Zechariah, Mary, and Simeon in the New Testament. And Paul tells us to speak to one another with psalms, hymns, and spiritual songs, by which we are filled with the Spirit and always give thanks to God, evidently not only when we are in the public gathering of church but also when each one is privately carrying out one's business, whether at home or in the country. Commentary on Isaiah 12:1.[2]

Praising God with Song After the Exodus. Wolfgang Musculus: When the prophet, with the eyes of faith and of the Spirit, first considered Israel's amazing restoration—which would occur under Christ, something he prophesied about previously—then in his prophesying, he considers the nearly unbelievable happiness of the remnant who would be restored. He is swept up in this feeling of praise to God and—turning to those who are going to be set free—by apostrophe,[†] begins to address them with his words. And he commands that they must sing of this restoration, obviously referring to the example of Moses. When Israel was led through the Red Sea and Pharaoh with his whole army had been drowned in the waves, Moses was overwhelmed with the greatness of this totally unprecedented salvation and composed a song. He gave this song to the people to glorify their Lord who had freed them, so they would sing it. . . . Later Isaiah would say, "And there will be a highway from Assyria for the remnant that remains of my people, as there was for Israel on the day they came up from the land of Egypt." Commentary on Isaiah 12:1.[3]

Human Righteousness Slaughtered. Martin Luther: Here the prophet describes the true and legitimate worship and sacrifice of the New Testament and sets it up as a certain hidden antithesis against the Old Testament and its sacrifices, which were many and various. But in the New Testament there was a single sacrifice of praise and thanksgiving. So the Lord's Supper is called the Eucharist because we gather to it and we give thanks to God. But the best thanksgiving is that public confession before the world when Christians living in danger confess. The prophet foresaw this future preaching and confession of the gospel, which did not happen in the Old Testament. In the voice of the gospel, God is glorified and preached in Christ. "You will say," namely, in the church, "I will confess."

This is what will happen in preaching. For there is not anything else that should be heard in church other than the voice of praise and the preaching of God's blessings that we have received. And this song fights with all human wisdom and righteousness, which are our works and seeking our own glory rather than giving thanks to God. So to be pleasing to God is simply to confess that we are recipients of his blessings, not givers. Christians confesses that they were condemned and lost and that they have received everything from Christ that belongs to salvation and righteousness, and all their own merits accomplish nothing. This is the fullest and most perfect sacrifice that embraces everything in the Old Testament. There, animals and cattle were slaughtered; in this, our wisdom and righteousness, our pursuits and works. Lectures on Isaiah 12:1.[4]

[2]Brenz, *Esaias*, 195-96; citing Ex 15; Judg 5; Eph 5:19-20.

[3]Musculus, *In Esaiam*, 257; citing Ex 15; Is 11:16. [†]Apostrophe is a literary device by a speaker or writer who directly addresses a person or group who is not actually present.

[4]LW 16:128* (WA 31.2:91).

Sons of Wrath Reconciled. Johannes Oecolampadius. But we were all sons of wrath on account of the sin of Adam. But through Christ, who is the great priest, reconciliation was made in the time of anger, and the enraged face of God, that is, the wrath of God, was turned away. We were carried away into captivity by God's anger toward us, and our minds were afflicted with many penalties. But the Son of God delivers us into true freedom with his blood. Moreover, through the law, we knew we had sinned and were under the wrath of God. And when that could not help us and human things were hopeless, we were helped by the gospel. God humbles sinners by his wrath; he raises up the humble by his grace. In this way, it happens that the wrath of God works together for the good of the righteous. Commentary on Isaiah 12:1-2.[5]

Jesus Is God the Savior with Us. Martin Borrhaus: A commendation of the Messiah, who is to be the Savior of the church, obtained from salvation. This pertains to, "You will give birth to a son and you will call his name Jesus. For he will save his people from their sins." But as an adversary, the Messiah has obliterated the teaching of devils with the knowledge of salvation and its author. So, restored by the light of the gospel, it will raise up this same confession in the church, "Behold, God my Savior," whom above the divine Spirit called "Immanuel" and "Mighty God." And this salvation includes the remission of sins, the gift of the Holy Spirit, the righteousness of God communicated to us through faith in the Son, eternal life, and a hope that does not make us ashamed of the inheritance stored up for us in heaven. It also gives us constant patience in adverse things, with a confidence that we will escape them and that salvation itself is born of the struggle against adversity. Oracles in Isaiah on 12:2.[6]

The Strength of the Lord in Me. Wolfgang Musculus: "For the Lord God is my strength, and he has become my salvation too." Here the prophet adds the reason for his confidence, actually the reason why it says, "I will trust and will not be afraid." This is not something that appears to be sure confidence but is more like recklessness and overconfidence. Rather, the reason given for all these considerations is very strong and sure. He does not say, "Because I am personally brave." No, he says, "Because the Lord is my strength." That is, because the Lord, most powerful of all, protects me, preserves me, strengthens me. On my own I am weakness itself. But he who is the epitome of strength sustains and preserves me in every difficulty. The one who is endowed with this confidence can say with the apostle, "I can do all things through him who strengthens me." Commentary on Isaiah 12:2.[7]

God Is Our Strength. Dietrich Schnepff: Likewise, he is also our strength, because through him we conquer all our enemies. We overcome all our sorrows and tribulations. Finally, he himself has placed our enemies under our feet. The result is that he himself is our song, that is, our glory and peace. So with the prophet we can say, "I will trust and not be afraid, because the Lord is my strength." And we can say with the apostle, "Who shall separate us from the love of God? Not affliction, of course? Not hardship? Not persecution, and so on? But all these things," he says, "we overcome through him who loved us. Because I am persuaded that neither death nor life . . . shall be able to separate us from the love God." Therefore, since all the enormous blessings have obligated us to everlasting gratitude, we owe him unending thanks. But on the other hand, we would be guilty of the greatest wickedness if we wanted to unresponsively bury our memory of these blessings. Scholia on Isaiah 12:2.[8]

Water at the Feast of Tabernacles. The English Annotations: "Draw water." You shall receive abundance of saving grace and sound comfort,

[5]Oecolampadius, *In Iesaiam*, 102r.
[6]Borrhaus, *In Iesaiae Prophetae Oracula*, 150; citing Mt 1:21.
[7]Musculus, *In Esaiam*, 269; citing Phil 1:21.
[8]Schnepff, *In Esaiae*, 216; citing Rom 8:35, 37-38.

as water drawn by full buckets from a wellspring, . . . alluding, as some think, to a solemn ceremony used by the Jews at the Feast of Tabernacles, where their custom was, in the nighttime, with a variety of music and much mirth, to fetch water from the spring of Siloam to the temple in a golden vessel and there pour it on the altar. Annotations on Isaiah 12:3.[9]

Living Water from God Alone. Heinrich Bullinger: And just as the Lord says in the Gospel, "The one who believes in me, streams of living water will flow from within him," so, in what follows here, Isaiah particularly lists or draws out those streams of grace. He shows what the faithful and those pleasing to God use to train themselves. At the same time he instructs us in our duty and that we will truly become pleasing to God if we have trained ourselves in such activities.

First, the faithful and grateful make confession to God. They give thanks to God, I claim, and say that they have received from him alone the gifts within them. For every good thing comes from above, from the Father of lights. Therefore, they must note what sort of doctrine it is by those who command us to thank the Virgin Mary and the company of the saints for benefits we have received, as if they give us such gifts or acquire them for us!

Then, those who are truly grateful call on the name of the Lord, or in the name of God. They do not call on other gods or the saints. Whatever we ask from God in the name of Christ, we receive. So then, let them again be careful what they teach, those who instruct us to pray to the saints. Sermons on Isaiah 12:3.[10]

Waters as Doctrines. William Day: By waters here, the comfortable doctrine of Christ and the spirit of grace are to be understood, which refresh more than any other waters and, as living waters of the best springs, never fail. That is why he says about his, "I would have given you water of life," and, "whoever drinks of it shall never thirst. . . ." And again, "If anyone thirsts, let him come and drink of the water of life freely." Here Calvin understands that this is to partake of doctrines and consolations, which a person comes with joy, when cheerfully and with an earnest desire like a thirsty deer, to the rivers of water. Musculus takes it as the comforts of the Holy Ghost to the troubled soul, which are as waters to the most dry and thirsty, exceedingly refreshing. Exposition of Isaiah 12:3.[11]

Water from the Gospel Ordinances. Matthew Poole: Your thirsty and fainting souls shall be filled with divine graces and comforts, which you may plentifully draw from God in the use of the gospel ordinances, which was often signified by water in both the Old and New Testaments. He seems to allude to the state of Israel in the wilderness where, when they had been tormented with thirst, they were greatly refreshed and delighted with those waters that God so graciously and wonderfully afforded them in that dry and barren land. Annotations on Isaiah 12:3.[12]

The Name of the Savior. Hector Pinto: "You will draw waters in joy from the fountains of the Savior." For "savior" in Hebrew is *hayĕšûʿâ*. The part of speech, *ha*, is the article included in this passage for emphasis. The word *yĕšûʿâ* signifies "savior" and "salvation." And for that reason Pagnini translates it "from the fountains of salvation." And in . . . this prophet, where the same word is in Hebrew, our translators translate it as "in the day of salvation." For Isaiah calls the time of Christ the day of salvation. Although that passage could rightly be translated, "in the time of the Savior." For Christ in the sacred letters is called Savior, safety, and salvation.

To be called Savior indicates his name, Yeshuah. For the angel said to Joseph, the husband of the most holy Mary, . . . "You shall call his name Yeshuah," which the Greek translators put name as *Iēsus* and the Latins as "Jesus." For important

[9]Downame, ed., *English Annotations*, 4B2r*; Jn 4:14; 7:38.
[10]Bullinger, *Isaias*, 67v; citing Jn 7:38.
[11]Day, *Exposition*, 92*.
[12]Poole, *Annotations*, 354*; citing Num 20:11; 21:16-18.

authors state that Saint Matthew wrote his Gospel in Hebrew letters, and Saint Jerome testifies that he observed it written by the Evangelist with his own eyes. And this same name Yeshuah is on the title of the cross that was brought from Jerusalem to Rome and was placed in the temple of the holy cross in Jerusalem, where it is kept today and is displayed, and there I saw it and held it in my hands, although I could not read it completely on account of its old age. Commentary on Isaiah 12.[13]

Joy Follows the Preaching of the Gospel. Martin Luther: After the word of the gospel has been preached and the voice of rejoicing has sounded forth, there follows the discernment of spirits and the distribution of the gifts of the Spirit. . . . "Whoever believes in me, out of his heart will flow rivers of living water." Waters denote the Holy Spirit. . . . In the noonday heat, spring water and running water are the most refreshing. So it is in the scorching heat of sin. The comfort of the Holy Spirit through the word of God is then most sweet. The wells of salvation are the gospel, sermons about Christ in various places, or even the preachers of the gospel. In that day, when the waters will have flowed out to many because the gospel has already been preached, there will follow also in others the praise, that is, the sacrifice that you have. Lectures on Isaiah 12:3.[14]

12:4-6 *A Song Proclaiming the Lord's Name*

The Good Work of Giving Praise. Philipp Heilbrunner: Topic 16. On Good Works. What are some of those good works? . . . VI. Giving thanks and the celebration of the divine name because of the blessings we have received. . . . "And in that day you will say," I confess that you are Lord. . . . And in that day, you will say, "Acknowledge the Lord and call on his name. Make known what he has done among the agreements of their peoples. Remember that his name is exalted." Theological Topics Arranged from the Prophecy of Isaiah.[15]

Remember the Kindnesses of Christ. Johannes Oecolampadius: Never should the extraordinary kindnesses that Christ was born, suffered, and resurrected for our salvation be excised from memory. For God especially requires this one thing from us: namely that, having been saved, we will also be found always eager to be reminded of recent kindnesses in everything. That is what Christ also commended in his Supper when he says, "This do in my memory." Commentary on Isaiah 12:4.[16]

Grounds for Singing. John Calvin: "Sing to the Lord." He continues in his exhortation, showing what is the feeling from which this thanksgiving ought to proceed. For he teaches that it is our duty to proclaim the goodness of God to every nation. We should not exhort and encourage others such that we sit idle at the same time, but it is appropriate to set an example before others, since nothing can be more absurd than to see lazy and slothful people who are exciting others to praise God.

Further, when he declares that God "has done gloriously," he signifies that there is ample grounds for singing. For the Lord does not want his praises to be celebrated for nothing, but he provides the most ample and abundant reason when he frees his people from the most severe bondage. Now, we have said that this song is not limited to a short time but rather to be extended to the whole of Christ's reign. This work therefore is truly glorious, because God sent his Son to reconcile us to himself and to destroy the dominion of death and the devil. If therefore we consider our deliverance as we should, then we will have ample grounds for praising God. Commentary on Isaiah 12:5.[17]

---

[13]Pinto, *In Esaiam*, 137-38; citing Is 49:8; Ps 24; 26; 52; 84; Mt 1:21.
[14]LW 16:130 (WA 31.2:92); citing 1 Cor 12; Jn 7:38; 4:10.
[15]Heilbrunner, *Esaiae Prophetae Vaticinia*, 301-2, 306-7; citing Is 12:5-6; 19:21; 25:1-12; 26:1-21; 38:9-20; 42:10-12; 44:23; 48:20; 49:13; 52:9; 61:10-11; 62:9; 63:7-9 (306-16).
[16]Oecolampadius, *In Iesaiam*, 103r; citing Mk 14:22-25; Lk 22:18-20; 1 Cor 11:23-25.
[17]CTS 13:403* (CO 36:254); citing Jn 3:16-17; Heb 2:14.

The Holy One Is Faithful to His Covenant Promises. Rudolf Gwalther: "Shout and sing for joy, O inhabitant of Zion." It is as though he said, "Although now everything looks very sad, and difficult trials surround you on every side, nevertheless you must not be downcast in heart but rather break forth in shouts of joy and rejoice with all your heart." But he then explains his purpose in this statement: "because great is the Holy One of Israel in your midst." That is, God, who has bound himself to you in covenant and then set you apart as holy to himself, is great and marvelous in your midst, and he will never fail in any of his promises to be with you and save you. But one can make this claim more truly and certainly in the case of the church, which God has purchased for himself with the blood of his only begotten Son, and in which he has established his dwelling place. Therefore, let this be our comfort in every sort of temptation. Sermons on Isaiah 12:6.[18]

Christ Is the Holy One in Our Midst. Wolfgang Musculus: We have also the Holy One of Israel in the midst of heavenly Zion, namely, the church of the saints, according to the promise, "Behold, I will be with you until the end of the age," and, "Where two or three are gathered in my name, there I am in the midst of them." That is also why there is jubilation and singing among us. We explain this prophetic song this way.[†] I think it is sufficiently clear to godly people from what has been said how beautifully this corresponds to the kingdom of Christ, and pertains to the beginnings of it and to the remnants of Israel, as the firstfruits of the faithful. Commentary on Isaiah 12:6.[19]

The Mediator Appears. Hector Pinto: "Exult and praise, O inhabitant of Zion, for great in your midst is the Holy One of Israel." These are words the prophet is speaking to the church. Arise in full voice of praise, and let the catholic church rejoice, which is Zion, that is, you are called a watchtower set on high. Because he is in your midst, that great Christ rules and governs you. He is the sanctifier of Israel.

It is to be noted that the seer did not say, "Because great is the Holy One of Israel in you," but rather, "because great in your midst." It is as if he were saying, "He who will be born small, raised in an obscure country, hidden from the opinion of the ignorant multitude at the dawn of his birth, having rejected human pride, will take the form of a servant and pursue a poor life far removed from the pomp in every age, he is great—the true originator and master of the heavens and the earth. But he will become a man and dwell in your midst to drive away every error, and dispel all the darkness clouded over people's minds by his heavenly teaching and example of holiness and virtue." And he shows the way to the most blessed and eternal home.

Therefore, you see that Christ is found in the midst. For as the sun is positioned in the midst of the planets, and occupies the middle region as the leader and ruler, and the master of the other lights with such remarkable greatness and splendor that it illuminates and fills up nearly everything with its light, so also that "sun of righteousness," Christ our God, willed to appear in the midst of humanity in order to illuminate people's minds entangled with errors and surrounded by darkness. And this is what would be, as we read in the book of Ecclesiasticus, "He was as the morning star in the midst of a cloud." It follows that he stood in the midst as a mediator to reconcile. Commentary on Isaiah 12:6.[20]

Preferring True Joy. Zacharias Ursinus: All true happiness and true joy consists in this—that because God dwells with us, he sanctifies us as his sons. "Because great in your midst is the Holy One of Israel." Therefore, we prefer this joy to all happiness and delights from the world. And we flee from every joy not connected to this, as a destructive plague and poisoned drink. Commentary on Isaiah 12:6.[21]

[18]Gwalther, *Isaias*, 86r; citing Rom 8; 14; Mt 28; 2 Cor 6; Lev 26; Jn 6.

[19]Musculus, *In Esaiam*, 272. [†]See Oecolampadius, *In Iesaiam*, 103r; citing Mt 28:20; 18:20.

[20]Pinto, *In Esaiam*, 136-37; citing Sirach 50:6.

[21]Ursinus, *Iesaiam*, 397.

13:1–14:27 JUDGMENT AGAINST BABYLON

13 *The oracle concerning Babylon which Isaiah the son of Amoz saw.*

2 *On a bare hill raise a signal;*
cry aloud to them;

wave the hand for them to enter
the gates of the nobles.

3 *I myself have commanded my consecrated ones,*
and have summoned my mighty men to execute my anger,
my proudly exulting ones.[a]

4 *The sound of a tumult is on the mountains*
as of a great multitude!

The sound of an uproar of kingdoms,
of nations gathering together!

The LORD *of hosts is mustering*
a host for battle.

5 *They come from a distant land,*
from the end of the heavens,

the LORD *and the weapons of his indignation,*
to destroy the whole land.[b]

6 *Wail, for the day of the* LORD *is near;*
as destruction from the Almighty[c] *it will come!*

7 *Therefore all hands will be feeble,*
and every human heart will melt.

8 *They will be dismayed:*
pangs and agony will seize them;
they will be in anguish like a woman in labor.

They will look aghast at one another;
their faces will be aflame.

9 *Behold, the day of the* LORD *comes,*
cruel, with wrath and fierce anger,

to make the land a desolation
and to destroy its sinners from it.

10 *For the stars of the heavens and their constellations*
will not give their light;

the sun will be dark at its rising,
and the moon will not shed its light.

11 *I will punish the world for its evil,*
and the wicked for their iniquity;

I will put an end to the pomp of the arrogant,
and lay low the pompous pride of the ruthless.

12 *I will make people more rare than fine gold,*
and mankind than the gold of Ophir.

13 *Therefore I will make the heavens tremble,*
and the earth will be shaken out of its place,

at the wrath of the LORD *of hosts*
in the day of his fierce anger.

14 *And like a hunted gazelle,*
or like sheep with none to gather them,

each will turn to his own people,
and each will flee to his own land.

15 *Whoever is found will be thrust through,*
and whoever is caught will fall by the sword.

16 *Their infants will be dashed in pieces*
before their eyes;

their houses will be plundered
and their wives ravished.

17 *Behold, I am stirring up the Medes against them,*
who have no regard for silver
and do not delight in gold.

18 *Their bows will slaughter*[d] *the young men;*
they will have no mercy on the fruit of the womb;
their eyes will not pity children.

[19]*And Babylon, the glory of kingdoms,*
the splendor and pomp of the Chaldeans,

will be like Sodom and Gomorrah
when God overthrew them.

[20]*It will never be inhabited*
or lived in for all generations;

no Arab will pitch his tent there;
no shepherds will make their flocks lie down there.

[21]*But wild animals will lie down there,*
and their houses will be full of howling creatures;

there ostriches[e] will dwell,
and there wild goats will dance.

[22]*Hyenas[f] will cry in its towers,*
and jackals in the pleasant palaces;

its time is close at hand
and its days will not be prolonged.

14 *For the Lord will have compassion on Jacob*
and will again choose Israel, and will set them
in their own land, and sojourners will join them and
will attach themselves to the house of Jacob. [2]*And the*
peoples will take them and bring them to their place,
and the house of Israel will possess them in the Lord's
land as male and female slaves.[g] They will take
captive those who were their captors, and rule over
those who oppressed them.
[3]*When the Lord has given you rest from your*
pain and turmoil and the hard service with which
you were made to serve, [4]*you will take up this taunt*
against the king of Babylon:

"How the oppressor has ceased,
the insolent fury[h] ceased!

[5]*The Lord has broken the staff of the wicked,*
the scepter of rulers,

[6]*that struck the peoples in wrath*
with unceasing blows,

that ruled the nations in anger
with unrelenting persecution.

[7]*The whole earth is at rest and quiet;*
they break forth into singing.

[8]*The cypresses rejoice at you,*
the cedars of Lebanon, saying,

'Since you were laid low,
no woodcutter comes up against us.'

[9]*Sheol beneath is stirred up*
to meet you when you come;

it rouses the shades to greet you,
all who were leaders of the earth;

it raises from their thrones
all who were kings of the nations.

[10]*All of them will answer*
and say to you:

'You too have become as weak as we!
You have become like us!'

[11]*Your pomp is brought down to Sheol,*
the sound of your harps;

maggots are laid as a bed beneath you,
and worms are your covers.

[12]*"How you are fallen from heaven,*
O Day Star, son of Dawn!

How you are cut down to the ground,
you who laid the nations low!

[13]*You said in your heart,*
'I will ascend to heaven;

above the stars of God
I will set my throne on high;

I will sit on the mount of assembly
in the far reaches of the north;[i]

[14]*I will ascend above the heights of the clouds;*
I will make myself like the Most High.'

[15]*But you are brought down to Sheol,*
to the far reaches of the pit.

[16]*Those who see you will stare at you*
and ponder over you:

Is this the man who made the earth tremble,
who shook kingdoms,

17 *who made the world like a desert*
and overthrew its cities,
who did not let his prisoners go home?[i]

18 *All the kings of the nations lie in glory,*
each in his own tomb;[j]

19 *but you are cast out, away from your grave,*
like a loathed branch,

clothed with the slain, those pierced by the sword,
who go down to the stones of the pit,
like a dead body trampled underfoot.

20 *You will not be joined with them in burial,*
because you have destroyed your land,
you have slain your people.

"May the offspring of evildoers
nevermore be named!

21 *Prepare slaughter for his sons*
because of the guilt of their fathers,

lest they rise and possess the earth,
and fill the face of the world with cities."

22 *"I will rise up against them," declares the LORD*
of hosts, "and will cut off from Babylon name and
remnant, descendants and posterity," declares the
LORD. 23 *"And I will make it a possession of the*
hedgehog,[k] *and pools of water, and I will sweep it*
with the broom of destruction," declares the LORD of
hosts.

24 *The LORD of hosts has sworn:*

"As I have planned,
so shall it be,

and as I have purposed,
so shall it stand,

25 *that I will break the Assyrian in my land,*
and on my mountains trample him underfoot;

and his yoke shall depart from them,
and his burden from their shoulder."

26 *This is the purpose that is purposed*
concerning the whole earth,

and this is the hand that is stretched out
over all the nations.

27 *For the LORD of hosts has purposed,*
and who will annul it?

His hand is stretched out,
and who will turn it back?

a Or *those who exult in my majesty* **b** Or *earth*; also verse 9 **c** The Hebrew words for *destruction* and *almighty* sound alike **d** Hebrew *dash in pieces* **e** Or *owls* **f** Or *foxes* **g** Or *servants* **h** Dead Sea Scroll (compare Septuagint, Syriac, Vulgate); the meaning of the word in the Masoretic Text is uncertain **i** Or *in the remote parts of Zaphon* **j** Hebrew *house* **k** Possibly *porcupine, or owl*

OVERVIEW: This passage begins the section of Isaiah that focuses on God's judgments against the nations, starting with Babylon. Many Reformation commentators provide the historical background on Babylon and even suggest other sources in addition to what is found in Scripture. These interpreters insist that God enabled Isaiah to make specific predictions with names and time frames, pointing to later Scripture passages and historical events to show how these prophecies were fulfilled. The frequent themes in this section include the sin of pride among leaders, the justness of God's punishments, the instability of earthly kingdoms, and the need to consider one's own sins in light of God's threats. The references to the day of the Lord and the fall of the morning star lead some to interpret at least portions of this passage as referring to final judgment.

WHY ASSYRIA AND BABYLON? VIKTORIN STRIGEL: But why did Isaiah preach on the changing of the Assyrian and Babylonian kingdoms by name? Because these kingdoms cruelly afflicted the people of God. For Assyria scattered the ten tribes and settled families in other regions. But the Chaldeans, or the Babylonians, carried off the tribe of Judah into exile when Jerusalem was overthrown, which lasted seventy years. Oration on the Prophet Isaiah.[1]

13:1-5 *Oracle Against Babylon*

Where to Read About Babylon. Konrad Pellikan: About the magnitude, glory, and buildings of this incredible city, Quintus Curtius, Strabo, and Herodotus wrote. Its width is said to have been twelve miles. But what is recounted here is in the future. We read about the events in the first year of Cyrus, who with the help of Astyages[†] conquered Babylon. Commentary on Isaiah 13:1.[2]

A Contrast with Christ's Eternal Kingdom. Heinrich Bullinger: There are also other things to be considered by the godly in this matter, especially that the destruction of Babylon is soon subjected to a beautiful description of Christ and his kingdom. . . . For just as the kingdom of Christ is eternal, so all the kingdoms of the world are frail and momentary. So then, although the godly are afflicted for a time in this world, and the wicked exult immersed in pleasures, nevertheless their lots will be reversed, and the afflicted will reign eternally with Christ, but those sons of pleasure will perish in perpetual death with the devil. In addition, when all the kingdoms of the world are ruined, the church alone remains unharmed. And Babylon is a mirror and a type of the world. The apostle John calls Rome "Babylon," the kingdom of the antichrist. Sermons on Isaiah 13:1.[3]

Babylon as a Type. Johannes Oecolampadius: But although, according to the history,[†] these prophecies should not be explained to be about other things—for the prophet also explains that himself when he says, "Behold, I will raise up the Medes against them, who do not seek silver or gold"—yet symbolically the destruction of Babylon also teaches the destruction of the world. . . . But I would not consider the desolation of Babylon after the return of the sons of Israel after all that time to correspond very well here. The history contained in the Sacred Scriptures will be sufficient as a type. Therefore by "Babylon," take it as the kingdom of the world, in which truly there is great confusion and where many are carried off into captivity.

But what if you could also say it is the Roman tyranny, because of how many Christians cannot carry out their legitimate duties properly? Further, just as it was pleasing to the Jews to hear that Babylon was going to be destroyed so they could return to their own country, so also we ought to lift up our heads to the consummation of this age, because in this way, "our redemption draws near." . . . Now let us observe the power and kindness of God in history, who punishes with such severity the enemies of his children, as also was said about Sennacherib. But first Isaiah prophesies against the city of the Babylonians, then against the king. Commentary on Isaiah 13:1-3.[4]

We Ought to Consider Our Own Sin When God Uses Others to Discipline. Zacharias Ursinus: All the calamities of people are burdens imposed on them by God, who alone is the first and supreme author of punishments, to the extent that they are punishments, while people or other creatures are only instruments and servants. "The burden of Babylon." Jehovah and the

[1]Strigel, *Oratio De Propheta Esaia*, 32.
[2]Pellikan, *Commentaria Bibliorum*, 3:17v. [†]Astyages was the last king of the Median Empire, reigning from 585 to 550 BC. According to Herodotus, Cyrus the Great was Astyages's grandson. Most commentators give far more detail and references for where the background on the geography and history of Babylon can be found.
[3]Bullinger, *Isaias*, 68v; citing Is 11–12.
[4]Oecolampadius, *In Iesaiam*, 104r-v; citing Lk 21:28. [†]He recounts various references to Babylon in Ptolemy, Strabo, Tertullian, and Rev 17.

instruments of his wrath are coming. Therefore let us not be angry in vain. Therefore let us not be angry in vain with those who hurt us, but let us look to our own sins, by which we have brought evil on ourselves, and the fatherly hand of God, which chastises us. And reverently and patiently let us submit ourselves to him, not imputing to people or fortunes what happens to us and take God away from governing the world. Let us not fear people more than God, and let us discern the just work of God in punishing or chastising us with the unjust work of evil instruments, whose work is seen to be used by God. Commentary on Isaiah 13:1-3.[5]

God the War Hero. Dietrich Schnepff: And so in fact the prophet portrayed with colorful illustrations those events that preceded the catastrophe and destruction of Babylon. In this passage we must carefully note how accomplished a war hero is the Lord our God. It is no accident that he is called the Lord of hosts. All creatures serve him. When he gave commands to them and enrolled them in his army, immediately they were prepared to obey the Lord completely. Sometimes he uses angels who make war against the wicked, as when he summoned an avenging angel against King Sennacherib. This angel killed many thousands in a single night. Often he sends devils, as we note in the book of Chronicles. A devil, a lying spirit, with the Lord's permission deceived the prophets of Baal so that Ahab suffered the consequences he deserved for his wickedness.

Often he sends wild animals whom he has commanded to attack people. So two bears were enlisted against forty-two children who mocked the prophet Elisha. And Pharaoh's story is well-known. We read that the Lord punished him personally with frogs and other foul pests. Sometimes the Lord had commanded an army of lifeless creatures, as when the sea itself—at the Lord's command—became an enemy of Jonah as he fled. Soon also a whale approached, which swallowed him. Often, the Lord acts through people, as when he sent enemies against his rebellious and disobedient people.

But the Lord typically equips, not only with weapons but also with intent, those whom he wants to be instruments of his wrath. In this passage he says that his soldiers are brave, and they rejoice in the grandeur and glory of the Lord. The same statement is also at the end of chapter 5. Scholia on Isaiah 13:4-5.[6]

13:6-16 *The Day of the Lord Is Near*

A Set Day for Judgment. Rudolf Gwalther: It is also well worth noticing that the time of punishment or destruction is called "the day of the Lord." This is very common in the prophets. Moreover, the Holy Spirit takes up this metaphor from judicial actions or capital cases in which typically fixed days are established for punishing the guilty when their case is decided. Therefore by this expression the prophet teaches that God does not execute his judgments rashly. Instead, he has long since established for the particular peoples his own day on which he intends to avenge and punish their crimes. And this day is approaching when God has sufficiently used their works in his chastising, and they have filled up the measure of their iniquities, as he once said about the Amorites. Therefore they remembered this divine custom, those who misused their prosperity and peace as an untouchable license to do whatever they want. And they should consider then, too, that the day of the Lord is coming with a silent footstep, at the very moment when they least expect it. Sermons on Isaiah 13:6.[7]

How the Day Is Near. The English Annotations: It shall not be long before this judgment is put into execution. . . . It was not until about some two hundred years after this prophecy that Babylon was surprised, sacked, and ruined by Cyrus. But besides that, what may seem long to

[5]Ursinus, *Iesaiam*, 422.

[6]Schnepff, *In Esaiae*, 222.

[7]Gwalther, *Isaias*, 87-88.

humans is short to God. . . . This is what was said by the prophet, as speaking to those in the captivity, for whose comfort and support especially this was delivered and left on record by him. Annotations on Isaiah 13:6.[8]

The Horror of Imminent Punishment. Konrad Pellikan: They will be filled with terror and astounded at the most severe difficulties, such as the twisting of the intestines, which they cannot bear. Because of the pains and panic, they do not know where they are turning. It is also no different from when they are seized in the pains of child-birth, unable to escape, so wherever they turn, they find enemies. As usually happens with tyrants, wherever they turned where they thought they had friends and allies, they found enemies. When they called on them, they were astounded with a confusion of conscience for so many crimes. And with a very confused face, they were shocked by the horror of imminent punishment, which they were forced to recognize they deserved justly from the Lord, or at last, against their will. They thought this way for a long time, during which they could have feared the Lord and reduced their injury. Commentary on Isaiah 13:7-8.[9]

Faces Pale and Aflame. John Trapp: According to Musculus, the prophet alludes here to the face of a blacksmith when it is dark at night and he stands blowing his fire, for his face appears as if it had no blood in it, most faded and pale. Or, as others think, it refers to a frightened person who first looks pale (the blood running to the heart to relieve it), and then later when the blood returns to the outward parts looks red and the color of a flame. Exposition on Isaiah 13:8.[10]

No Visible Star in the Sky. Johannes Oecolampadius: The sense is that they will not be comforted by any consolation, but everything will be against them, because there is no star that will shine for them—not among those in a clear sky, nor those in the rainy sky. They will consider that Suculae, or Hyades,[†] cannot be seen well by day or by night. Of course, by darkness they understand nearly all tribulation. . . . If they do not speak according to these words, there will be no morning light for them. Commentary on Isaiah 13:9-10.[11]

Hyperbole About the Earth Shaking. Wolfgang Musculus: "Therefore I will shake the sky, and the earth will be removed from its place." He says, "Therefore," that is, it is for this reason that I punish the malice on the earth and on the wicked for their iniquities, and stop the arrogance of the proud. And I will throw down the haughtiness of the tyrants and repay the wealthy man for his gold. . . . "I will shake," or as some render it, "I will agitate the sky, and the earth will be removed from its place." Again, the prophet speaks with hyperbolic speech according to human imagination, because to them it seems that heaven and earth are disturbed and agitated when the Lord, in the heat of his anger, exacts punishment on the reprobate and subjects everything to hostile devastation. So the earth is rendered a wasteland, men are slaughtered with the sword, cities are burned, infants are dashed against the rocks, women are raped, and everything generally is given to destruction.

There are some who think that these are not hyperbolic expressions but that they really happened when Babylon was captured. I mean, they think that the heaven was shaken, while the stars, the sun, and the moon withdrew their light, and thunder was heard throughout the world, and lightning appeared. They also think that the earth was moved from its position through earthquakes and tremors. But although it could have been like that, such that those things actually happened, nevertheless it is more natural and likely for us to

[8]Downame, ed., *English Annotations*, 4B2r*; citing Jas 5:8-9; 2 Pet 3:8; Ps 90:4.

[9]Pellikan, *Commentaria Bibliorum*, 3:18r.

[10]Trapp, *Commentary or Exposition*, 62*.

[11]Oecolampadius, *In Iesaiam*, 106r; citing Is 8. [†]The constellation Hyades in Greek has the Latin name Suculae.

hold onto the former interpretation. COMMENTARY ON ISAIAH 13:13.[12]

TWO PURPOSES OF PENALTIES. ZACHARIAS URSINUS: The evils of the wicked and righteous differ in this: the evils on the wicked are punishments that ruin and destroy them. But the evils on the righteous are fatherly chastisements to save them. The Lord comes to bring desolation on the earth and to remove the powerful from it. This great distinction in the nature of calamity should create and maintain within us a distinction of response to hardship. We must not become so afraid, so filled with sorrow and despair, and grumble so much against God like the wicked. Instead, holding onto our sure confidence in divine grace and his presence, we must patiently wait for our freedom. COMMENTARY ON ISAIAH 13:11-13.[13]

FOUR SINS OF BABYLON. MARTIN BORRHAUS: "I will visit" to observe the dishonesty of the wicked. But what is Babylon's dishonesty? First, idolatry comes to mind, which originated in Babylon at the time of the flood, in the worship of Baal. He was described as the son of Nimrod by the Chaldeans and by Berosus.[†] We find that this prophet of ours often blames the Chaldeans for idolatry. The second fault is that pride and haughtiness that raised Babylon up so that she arrogantly despised the God of the Israelites such that her king said, "I will ascend to heaven, and I will raise my throne above the stars of God." . . .

The third crime is charged to Babylon because she was filled with various divinations of sorcerers, fortune-tellers, and astrologists. In the book of Daniel we read that these were assembled by Belshazzar. Now Babylon was so filled with such persons that from that point on diviners of this type were called Chaldeans. The fourth crime was savagery and especially cruelty toward God's people. Our prophet discusses this later on: "I was angry with my people, and I profaned my inheritance, and I gave them over into your hand and you did not show them mercy." These indeed are the faults that are reproved in Babylon of the Chaldeans. ORACLES IN ISAIAH ON 13:11-16.[14]

INFANT DASHING AS FROM THE PSALM. MARTIN BORRHAUS: "Their infants will be dashed." About such slaughter is sung in that psalm: "Blessed are those who repay you with retribution. Blessed is the one who seizes your infants, who dashes them against the rocks." How much more truly blessed will one be judged who, in the midst of this devastation of the kingdom of the antichrist, by the spirit of the preaching of the gospel, has led infants, that is, those brought up on the milk of the errors of the shameful whore of Babylon, to the rock of the Messiah. ORACLES IN ISAIAH ON 13:16.[15]

THE INHUMANITY OF ATTACKING CHILDREN. WOLFGANG MUSCULUS: "Their children," he says, "will not be spared before their eyes." That is, generally speaking, even when they see mothers are in anguish for the safety of their children, when they see the children running to their parents' embrace and pleading for their help, still they will not be moved by any natural pity. But they will slaughter them before their parents' eyes. Even in this one matter, understand the gravity of God's anger against the wickedness and arrogance of Babylon. In order to punish that city, the very feeling of human nature suffers violence and is overturned with insufferable cruelty. Note that he does not simply say, "And they will not spare the children." But, "And before their eyes, they will not spare the children." A person's eye is bent by the sight of human suffering toward pity, and so much so that one may even spare the guilty. When nothing like this happens, it is clear proof of a

[12]Musculus, *In Esaiam*, 279.
[13]Ursinus, *Iesaiam*, 434.
[14]Borrhaus, *In Iesaiae Prophetae Oracula*, 157; citing Is 14:13; 47:6.
[†]Berosus was a writer in the third century BC who published the three-volume *Babyloniaca*, a history of Babylonia.
[15]Borrhaus, *In Iesaiae Prophetae Oracula*, 159; citing Ps 137:9; Rev 19.

hardened and inhumane heart. Commentary on Isaiah 13:16.[16]

Fruit of the Womb. The English Annotations: "The fruit of the womb." The children yet in the womb, either destroying their mothers pregnant with them, or ripping them up in an inhumane manner. Annotations on Isaiah 13:16.[17]

13:17-22 *The Fall of Babylon to the Medes*

Prediction About the Medes and Persians. Zacharias Ursinus: He repeats what he said earlier . . . , "the day of the Lord is near." He names the same day, or time, of the Lord, as it were, for taking and giving punishments to Babylon. There it was explained why the destruction of the wicked is said to be soon even though it is sometimes delayed for several ages, as what Isaiah predicts here. After nearly two hundred years, this eventually begins to be accomplished by Cyrus and then was gradually fulfilled. Only this should be added, that the prophet not so much threatens those in his own time as he threatens with respect to the nearness of the punishments on the Babylonians for the Jewish destruction. That still pertains to a general rule, since the wicked are overwhelmed by punishments when they least expect it, when they flourish in power, prosperity, and peace, and they seem to have conquered all their adversaries, such that they think there is no danger for them to fear either.

For Isaiah does not say that Babylon was going to perish before they would destroy the kingdom of Judah and deport the Jewish people into captivity. On the contrary, they also devastated other kingdoms that were particularly near Judah—the Philistines, the Edomites, the Moabites, the Ammonites, the Egyptians, and so on—and they increased their dominion. That eventually happened several years after the Jewish destruction. Therefore the Jews are said to be punished by the Babylonians first, and then the Babylonians by the Medes and Persians. Commentary on Isaiah 13:17.[18]

The Providence of God and Inspired Scripture. Heinrich Bullinger: It was at that time, even before Babylon would fall, that Isaiah predicted the fall, expressing the name of the Medes, who were going to destroy them. From this we clearly learn not only that all things are governed by divine providence but also that Scripture, inspired by the Holy Spirit, is the very Word of God. For which of the angels, let alone among humans, could have predicted these things with expressed names that Isaiah predicted by the inspiration of God? Let us therefore believe in the written Word of God, in the sacred books of the Bible, and let us not listen to those who ask, "What will make me certain that Scripture is the Word of God?" Sermons on Isaiah 13:17.[19]

Vessels as Instruments for God's Wrath. Martin Borrhaus: Babylon is dealt with by the law of retribution. Babylon had poured out her wrath on Zion and Jerusalem, the city of God. Therefore the divine wrath itself is also proportionate as it is poured out. Jeremiah explains this law of retribution in these words, "'And before your eyes, I will repay Babylon and all the inhabitants of Chaldea for all the evil that they have done in Zion,' says the Lord." Therefore the causes of the divine wrath are extended to Babylon. One is the pride and arrogance of Babylon, in which it exalted itself against the Lord. Another is that it afflicted the nation joined to God by the covenant, with a spirit other than what God intended to afflict it with, as Isaiah recalls earlier about the Assyrian Sennacherib. The same things correspond to our Babylon, as we will demonstrate in their places.

[16]Musculus, *In Esaiam*, 282.

[17]Downame, ed., *English Annotations*, 4B2r*; citing 2 Kings 8:12; 15:16.

[18]Ursinus, *Iesaiam*, 441; citing Is 13:6.

[19]Bullinger, *Isaias*, 71v.

By the Hebrew phrase here, the Medes and the Persians are called "vessels of divine wrath," but for a different reason from when the apostle uses the same manner of speaking to call those destined for hell "vessels of wrath." The apostle calls them this because they were destined for destruction from the foundation of the world; our prophet calls them this because through them God established that he would vent his fury on wicked Babylon. Oracles in Isaiah on 13:17-19.[20]

False Prophets. Menno Simons: Of such a mind are all false prophets and antichrists. That they have on their heads names of blasphemy and crowns like unto gold, by which is meant pride, as may be seen by the Babylonian whore who was arrayed in scarlet color, having a golden cup in her hand, full of abominations and filthiness of her fornication; for she says in her heart, "I sit a queen, and shall see no sorrow." . . . But the Lord cannot tolerate it and says, "Babylon, the glory of kingdoms, the beauty of the Chaldeans' excellency, shall be as when God overthrew Sodom and Gomorrah." . . . Therefore shall her plagues come in one day. . . . And not Babylon alone but also all antichrists, together with their deceit and false writings, shall be destroyed, as Christ says, "Every plant which my heavenly Father has not planted will be uprooted." Testimony Against John Van Leyden.[21]

The Desolation of Babylon. Ulrich Zwingli: Although we do not read that Babylon was reduced to desolation when either Cyrus or Alexander captured it, yet the divine oracles are firm. Therefore, since the history of the East is a little more distant from us, there may have been things that we do not know. And since Babylon continues to thrive today, it could be a new one excised from the old one. Or it could be that it has not yet been overthrown but is going to be overthrown in the future. Unless one believes that, rather than specifically, the prophet spoke in the custom of their language, where they randomly attribute things that are commonly done even if they do not happen in that case. So when they threaten the destruction of a city or a nation, they set before their eyes all kinds of evils they have seen that usually happen when cities were conquered, even if they were not suffered by all in each case, such as the dashing of infants, the cutting of mothers, and that kind of atrocity, which nevertheless were not written about the event itself but belong to an amplification of it. Annotations on Isaiah 13:20-22.[22]

How Babylon Parallels Sodom and Gomorrah. Rudolf Gwalther: The prophets usually use Sodom and Gomorrah as an example when they want to illustrate sudden and irreparable disasters. Isaiah said this with the same meaning previously: "Unless the Lord had left us just a few survivors, we would have become like Sodom and Gomorrah." Jeremiah, too, and Zephaniah, when prophesying about the destruction of the Moabites, referred to the same example.

Although Babylon was not consumed by fire sent from heaven like Sodom and Gomorrah, nevertheless this example is very fitting. For as God previously sent Lot to Sodom so that by his teaching and example they could be called back from destruction, so also Daniel and his companions were led to Babylon and would teach the barbaric and insolent people. In the same way that the residents of Sodom despised Lot, so the authority of Daniel and his associates, even though it counted for something under Nebuchadnezzar and Amel-Marduk, under Belshazzar it became so worthless that he did not even know Daniel's name. Therefore, as Sodom and Gomorrah were burned up in a sudden firestorm when they had finished the previous night in drunkenness and wicked debauchery, so also it was when the Medes and Persians burst suddenly in during the drinking that

[20]Borrhaus, *In Iesaiae Prophetae Oracula*, 155; citing Jer 51:24; Rom 9:22.

[21]Simons, *Complete Works*, 2:430; citing Rev 17:4; 18:7; Is 13:19; Mt 15:13.

[22]ZSW 14 / CR 101:230.30–231.5.

the Babylonians were overwhelmed. Sermons on Isaiah 13:19-20.[23]

No Other Kingdom Is Stable. Heinrich Bullinger: Now follows the destruction of the city itself into perpetual disgrace and everlasting desolation. They were promising to themselves an everlasting kingdom, glory, happiness, and joys that would never end, just as Rome was not afraid to call herself eternal. But the Lord says, "Babylon will not sit, will not rule, nor will it always be inhabited or dwell at the top of the world." It will be dragged down to the bottom of hell. The Lord prophesied in the same way about the new Rome and papism, according to John. . . . Therefore, nothing in the world is stable. Sermons on Isaiah 13:20.[24]

The Final Day for Babylon. Dietrich Schnepff: At the end he adds that this is going to be on the final day. That is, Babylon's final day, which some apply to the time of the Jewish people's captivity. After the Hebrews were led away into captivity, precisely seventy years remained when Belshazzar reigned as king, and the city of Babylon was captured and the kingdom was transferred to the Medes and Persians. Such interpreters follow this position because it was almost two hundred years from the time of the prophet to the storming of Babylon. But I do not think there is a need for such a calculation, since two hundred years—if compared with the expectation of the Babylonians, who convinced themselves that their kingdom was eternal—is not a very long time. Therefore the prophet wants to say that the time of Babylon's destruction would take place in just a few centuries, something they did not believe. But it was going to happen within years, and actually not that many. Scholia on Isaiah 13:20-22.[25]

Know for Certain the Day Decreed. Dietrich Schnepff: I know that these things may seem fabulous to those who admire the magnificence of the city. But it is certain that the day decreed for the Babylonians, that day of devastation, is not many ages away. And when the arrogance of the Babylonians, about which I have spoken, has been cast down and suppressed, the Lord will have mercy on the captives of his people (for our people will be in Chaldea for seventy years of hard servitude), and then they will see and understand that the Lord has not completely cast aside his people but wants them to receive his protection and guardianship. For they shall be returned to their native land, and those who were troublesome to them before, by the king's command, will be forced not only to be companions on the journey but also to be servants and subjects in rebuilding the ruins of the city and the temple. Paraphrase of Isaiah 13:22–14:2.[26]

The Twofold Day of the Lord. Wolfgang Musculus: "And its time is near that it comes, and its days will not be prolonged." What above he said . . . , "Wail, because the day of the Lord is near," he now repeats that. We said there that it says it was near because it would eventually happen after about 250 years. Above he said, "The day of the Lord is near," here, "its time is close, and its day," namely, that of Babylon. The day of the Lord, the day of vengeance, was the day of Babel and the day of destruction. That day was for the Lord to carry out vengeance. It was destined for Babylon to face. So, the day of the Lord is the same also for us. Our day is twofold: of grace for one, of destruction for another. Of grace, by which we are visited for salvation, . . . "now on this day, the things that bring you peace." Of destruction, by which we are visited for perdition. Each is the day of the Lord. Commentary on Isaiah 13:22.[27]

14:1-11 *Return After Babylon's Defeat*

A Type of Future Redemption. Johannes Oecolampadius: "For he will have compassion."

[23]Gwalther, *Isaias*, 90v.
[24]Bullinger, *Isaias*, 72r; citing Rev 18.
[25]Schnepff, *In Esaiae*, 226.
[26]Schnepff, *In Esaiae*, 233.
[27]Musculus, *In Esaiam*, 283; citing Is 13:6; Lk 19:42.

Happy are the righteous and those who await the judgment seat with security and with great cheerfulness, because they know that their full redemption will be manifested and fulfilled in no other way than when Babylon, the city of vanity, is overthrown. For as long as the Babylonian tyrants endure, the Jews are not free. Similarly, as long as it is not yet the consummation of the age, the redemption of the sons of God will not be revealed. . . . "For creation waits in eager expectation" that his happens openly to the sons of God. "For creation was subjected to vanity . . . and creation itself will be freed from servitude to corruption into the freedom of the glory of the sons of God."

So then, both this type and the other things that are spoken about the return of God's people throughout by the prophets, we rightly explain to be about the future blessedness. And learn this, too, at the same time, that as the desolation of Babylon is the salvation of Jacob, so the abolition of the old person is the renewal of the new. For it says, "Although the outward is wasting away, the inward is being renewed." . . . When the Jews were freed from the captivity of Babylon, they found a certain kind of rest in their land and no longer feared the tyranny of the Babylonians. But, we having been justified by faith, have peace with God, and coming to Christ, we find rest for our souls, and we are freed from slavery to sin and the law, so that it can neither accuse nor can it rule. For in Christ is the truest Sabbath found, true freedom, true security, and true joy. But sinners tremble, serve, and toil. In the word of Christ we also recognize that the antichrist has no right over our souls. He falls and perishes in the hearts of all who know his tricks and are now free in spirit, even if for a time they experience his tyranny. COMMENTARY ON ISAIAH 14:1.[28]

THE LIBERATION OF THE HEBREWS AT THE DESTRUCTION OF BABYLON. DIETRICH SCHNEPFF: Now he proposes the second and most important thing that followed the conquest of Babylon: namely, the liberation of the Hebrews. For although these are applied by the majority to chapter 14, yet if we look at the meaning, they are rightly connected with the preceding ones. For the chief cause why the destruction of that monarchy is described is the consolation of the people. The Lord is not going to permit the Babylonians to keep the Jewish people in perpetual captivity but is going to destroy them, so that the people may return free to their own place. So the prophet says, "The Lord will have compassion on Jacob and will again choose Israel." SCHOLIA ON ISAIAH 14:1.[29]

INCOMPLETELY FULFILLED PROPHECY. KONRAD PELLIKAN: The prophecy indeed is about the return from exile to the homeland after Babylon was destroyed, which happened under Zerubbabel, Ezra, and Nehemiah. But as the Jews likewise are forced to admit, this is incompletely sufficient. For the Lord has compassion as much toward Jacob as toward the few returning good Jews, especially the portion of Jews remaining among the nations, even by their own choice. He gave them peace in their land, so that their enemies would not prevail, even though they had continuously attacked those building the temple and the wall of the city, so that the Jews would not have high hopes for this happiness about which is spoken here. So we should not recognize anything other than what Christ the Lord gave his faithful ones.

The king himself, the Messiah, rejoices, chooses, and defends the true Israelites in faith, which includes not only Jacob and Israel but also the nations and foreigners. They rejoice in the Lord, whom they trust alone, so they serve him alone, worship him worthily, and are joined to the true seed and house of Jacob, as if they were kindred brothers and the children of Abraham according to faith, which pleases God and makes them members of one body in Christ. COMMENTARY ON ISAIAH 14:1-2.[30]

[28]Oecolampadius, *In Iesaiam*, 108r, 109r; citing Rom 8:19-21; 2 Cor 4:16.

[29]Schnepff, *In Esaiae*, 227.

[30]Pellikan, *Commentaria Bibliorum*, 3:18v-19r.

The Elect Remnant from Israel. Wolfgang Musculus: He was not going to choose Israel, whom he had already chosen for himself as a people and treasure, and had not yet cast away from him, although he was about to deliver them into captivity for the grace of chastisement. But he was going to choose for himself the remnant, whom he would deliver and bring back to his holy mountain from the midst of Babylon. Therefore, the seer indicated that they would not all return to their land, but only those whom the Lord had chosen from the multitude of his people. So . . . we read of those who went up, whose spirits God raised. Commentary on Isaiah 14:1.[31]

A Parable of the Antichrist. Martin Borrhaus: "You will understand the parable." In the Hebrew language, parables mean allegories, proverbs, pithy maxims, sentences of royal and famous men, and mystical discourses. The mystical discourse fits best here. For under the type of Babylon of the Chaldeans is contained that Babylon in which the Israelites are detained along with the nations, during the time of spiritual desecration. But as for how the spiritual captivity of the Israelites—apart from the external and bodily type—should be understood, this is a topic I have often treated elsewhere.

"How the oppressor ceased." In terms of the metaphor, we are to consider here Nebuchadnezzar and his children Amel-Marduk and Belshazzar. But in terms of the actual substance prefigured by the type and image of the Babylonian tyrant, we are to understand the antichrist, who oppresses the nations of the world beneath the very heavy bondage of his errors. Now our Babylon, by whatever skills she has strengthened her own kingdom for the rulers, kings, and emperors in subjection to her, is revealed in her self-glorification. She haughtily boasts of her power in these words: "I sit like a queen, I am not a widow. I will not see sorrow." In looking toward her, the divine spirit in these last days foresaw that the elect would wondrously say, "How does it happen that the oppressor has ceased?" Oracles in Isaiah on 14:3-4.[32]

Sarcasm at the King's Death. Heinrich Bullinger: The prophet goes on in his song to describe the unhappiness of Belshazzar, the wicked Babylonian king. Through sarcasm he wonderfully rails against the misfortune of the king of the Babylonians. In this, the state of the wicked dead is depicted, that is, what kind of condition is theirs who die in their sins without faith and repentance. It is, moreover, quite often useful to think about these subjects, so that we observe and believe that nothing in this world is stable, perfectly happy, and blessed, as well as what kind of fate awaits all the depraved at the time of their physical death. The comments made here should not be applied to Belshazzar alone but ought to be extended to all those who pass from this life without faith and repentance. Sermons on Isaiah 14:5-8.[33]

The Tyrant's Epitaph. John Trapp: "He that struck the peoples in wrath." This is the tyrant's epitaph: at their death, there is a general joy, as was when the world was well rid of Tiberius, Caligula, Nero, Heliogabalus. . . . When Domitian died, the Senate decreed that his name should be razed, that all his Acts should be rescinded, and his memorial indeed be abolished forever. When Caligula was cut off, his money was all melted by the decree of the Senate, just like King Richard the Third's cognizance, the white boar,[†] was torn from every sign, so that his memory might perish. Exposition on Isaiah 14:5-6.[34]

The Lord Broke the Staff in His Hand. Wolfgang Musculus: Because they pretend that he is surprised, how that powerful exactor ceased, along with his extortion of taxes, they join

[31]Musculus, *In Esaiam*, 284; citing Ezra 1.

[32]Borrhaus, *In Iesaiae Prophetae Oracula*, 163; citing Rev 18.

[33]Bullinger, *Isaias*, 74v.

[34]Trapp, *Commentary or Exposition*, 64. [†]The white boar was the personal badge of Richard III (1452–1485), the king of England from 1483–1485.

in singing, "The Lord has broken the staff of the wicked, the scepter of rulers." As if he were saying, "No one is oppressed by such tyrants, except by the hand of the Lord." The Lord had mercy on the captives and the oppressed; he broke that staff of wicked people and shameless rulers. By staff and scepter, understand a harsh and cruel domination, cruelly treating subjects and captives. The staff of unjust rule is broken when wicked rulers are crushed and all their power is reduced to nothing. . . . As long as he was a minister of the wrath of God and the staff of his indignation, he was not broken. But when the Lord relaxed his anger and indignation (for he is not angry forever), that one was exceedingly proud, and he was indefinitely striking peoples and nations in his fury, and not relaxing anything of his tyrannical rule, it was time for him to be crushed, so that his pride and iniquity would cease and the afflicted people would be brought to rest. Commentary on Isaiah 14:5-8.[35]

The Blasphemy of Belshazzar. Heinrich Bullinger: Moreover, the haughtiness of Belshazzar, who is here charged, was not only arrogant but also wicked and blasphemous. He describes this in hyperbolic terms. We know elsewhere that people sometimes came to such a state of insanity that they claim divine honors for themselves. It is well-known what the two most immoral emperors, Caius and Domitian, once did. But what we review about the ancients, why do we not consider our Roman pontiffs, who do not dread to call themselves vicars of God and persecute all those with iron and fire who do not pay them divine honors? No matter what, it seems that the prophet is speaking here of the wicked and blasphemous pride of Belshazzar, which he exercised against God in that luxurious and last feast of his, which Daniel describes. . . . For his blasphemous boasting was entirely as if he had said it openly, which Isaiah relates here. Sermons on Isaiah 14:11.[36]

Covering for the Corpse. Francisco Forerius: "He cuts down your corpse." This passage clearly proves to others that the learned Hebrews in the past also read this with other points. And the words have not been spoken with the same vocal movements throughout the nations. For who does not see that *hmyt* [sound] can be from the word *mwt*, that is, "died," and in the *hiphil*, "he caused to die, he killed"? And who ignores that *nblh* [harps or empty vessels] signifies a lifeless corpse? There is more about this later. . . . For it is said that the *yod* [Hebrew letter *y*]that it has here can be replaced with a *heh* [Hebrew letter *h*], because it was converted into a *tet* [Hebrew letter *t*], if the rule of grammar were kept everywhere. This is why no one can deservedly flog the Vulgate translator, whose interpretation is not exceedingly violent. For it can be taken as much in the third-person neuter *hiphil*, "your corpse was cut down." And what follows likewise corresponds, for it is an allusion to the custom of burying kings, whose corpses are covered with cloth from animals woven with gold and a great quantity of spices. But for this one, it says, "Maggots are laid as a bed and worms for a covering." Commentary on Isaiah 14:11.[37]

14:12-23 *The Fall of the Arrogant One*

The Fall of the Morning Star. John Mayer: Calvin says this has been ignorantly expounded by some to be the prince of devils, for neither is he ever called, in any other place of Scripture, Lucifer, nor can this be applied to anyone other than the king of Babylon, of whom all things here are spoken.† He is portrayed as Lucifer, the bright morning star, says Musculus, because he sometimes shined in as great glory on the earth as that star in heaven and thought he himself was unalterably set in that high dignity. And he is said to have cast lots on the nations, because he accounted himself lord of all, and as one who had the power to divide by lot the nations

[35]Musculus, *In Esaiam*, 288-89.

[36]Bullinger, *Isaias*, 75v; citing Dan 5.

[37]Forerius, *Iesaiae*, 57r; following the Vulgate; citing Is 26; 14:18-19.

subdued by him among his people like the Lord divided the land of Canaan among his people of Israel in the past. The interpretation understanding the prince of devils by Lucifer, which Calvin rejects, is Origen's, and then Eusebius, Ambrose, Athanasius, and some other ancients held it with him. Some, like Cyprian, understand this to be the antichrist.

But because the whole prophecy is about the proud king of Babylon, it cannot so well be applied to any others than to Nebuchadnezzar, who was for his pride driven from among people to live with the beasts, having before this caused his golden image to be worshiped; and to Belshazzar, the last king of Babylon, who was destroyed by the Medes and Persians after he had reigned a while as his true successor in worldly pomp and pride and contempt for the true God, as evident when he, with his princes and concubines, sat drinking from the precious vessels of the Lord's house the same night that Babylon was taken. And this is the pride of every wicked king, who thinks himself above the condition of humankind, and is lifted up in his heart accordingly. If he prospers and prevails to bring under all nations against whom he wars, he also thinks that he has power as a god in his own hands to establish his throne, and that it shall always so flourish. Commentary on Isaiah 14:12-15.[38]

Lucifer and the Pride of Men. Arcangela Tarabotti: But let us return to Eve, the innocent one who fell for the devil's deceptions. No judicious person would be astonished by her behavior. Rather, let such a person be amazed at Adam, to whom God revealed many profound matters about future happenings such as the flood and the Last Judgment, so that he might be more vigilant in keeping the divine law—all this in addition to taking a rib to shape a sweet companion for him. The male who boasts of his strength should not have fallen but should have withstood that little breeze of ambition; nor should he have given faith to words promising him that he would be like God—words making him similar to haughty Lucifer, who had also claimed for himself the power to become like his Creator.

What brazen audacity of that shameless creature who finds no equal in the history of vainglory because he is the father of pride itself! So puffed up was he that right after his creation he dared to rebel against his maker by relying on his own strength, or rather his nothingness. That is why he lost, with all his descendants, the life of the true light—that is, grace—and remained defiled with the stain of the first sin that, to his greater shame, he committed in paradise. The prophet Isaiah regards him as fallen from his first glory, stripped of all splendor, darkened and stained by the fumes of infernal fire, and breaks out into a mocking but somber taunt. . . .

If Lucifer fell from the greatest heights to the greatest depths because of pride, the same follows for you men, swollen with such conceit and bent on carrying out your perverse determinations. If with Satan you crave greater glory than God's by taking away free will from women, so with Satan may you fall into that horrendous kingdom whose foundations have been laid by pride! If you would not accompany your daughters to wealthy and noble wedding rites with high-ranking and wealthy spouses, as your vainglory requires, then join them at least in more modest marriages. Divide up your estates and wealth among them without preference, for that is the will of God. Do not aim at raising one to the summit of worldly pomp while casting the others down into a chaos of wretchedness and damnation's abyss. Temper the wealth of your sons, and remember that your daughters are also your flesh and blood; do not wish to constrain the feelings that God has left free to all his creatures. Paternal Tyranny.[39]

A Contrast with Descent to the Grave. Johannes Oecolampadius: This is a beautiful contrast, because he who wished to ascend to

[38]Mayer, *Commentary upon All the Prophets*, 4:98*. †See CTS 13:442; Musculus, *In Esaiam*, 293.

[39]Tarabotti, *Paternal Tyranny*, 53-54*.

heaven was dragged down to the bottom of the pit, and he who wished to sit at the north point to be seen by all was cast down to the point of a cistern, that is, into some most despised corner of a cistern. And as he is despised in hell, so also on earth. For he does not dwell in a mausoleum or a pyramid like Cyrus and other kings, but barely a common place in a grave. And he also hears taunts on the earth. . . .

The sense is: other kings rest peacefully in their house, that is, in their graves; but this will not happen to you; instead, you will be thrown out of the grave, not treated with honor but with the utmost indignation, as if one were to dig up a barren and reprobate staff, or the garment of the slain, by which all are repulsed, or to throw out a foul and trampled corpse on to the stones of a cistern, that is, on a grave. For they pass down that when Nebuchadnezzar had spent seven years among the wild beasts, and his son Evil-Merodach had administered the kingdom in the meantime, as soon as he recovered and returned, he threw his son into prison. And when, after his death, the son was called to the throne, fearing that his father might still be alive, he stayed away from the kingdom for a long time, until the corpse of his father was shown from the tombs. Commentary on Isaiah 14:12-15.[40]

The Cruelty of the King Brought Death. Wolfgang Musculus: In my judgment, he did not devastate his whole land, nor did he kill all his people. But because from time to time, inflamed with fury, he lashed out no less against his own people as against foreigners, this is attributed to him by the prophet that he devastated his land and killed his people. Nor is it rare for tyrants to subject entire communities to devastation and extermination in their own kingdoms, and to massacre their own people cruelly. History supplies too many examples, and our own times are not without experience of this cruelty. Commentary on Isaiah 14:16.[41]

[40]Oecolampadius, *In Iesaiam*, 111r.

[41]Musculus, *In Esaiam*, 297.

An Unexpected Grave for Belshazzar. Wolfgang Musculus: The bodies of dead kings are usually preserved so very carefully, with all kinds of spices against stench so that no worms even arise in them. But Belshazzar was denied this honor when he was killed during lavish banqueting while the city was captured by enemies. It seems the prophet predicted this here. There are those who, with Jerome, on "concerning your tomb," or "from your tomb," refer these to Nebuchadnezzar. The Hebrews, as one can see this in the writings of Rabbi David Kimchi, say that Nebuchadnezzar was removed from the tomb by his son Evil-Merodach and thrown to some animals or other to be dismembered.[†]

But I find it more suitable and closer to the truth for us to understand these events as applying to Belshazzar. We know from the book of Daniel that he was killed by his enemies when the city of Babylon was captured. And, as is more likely during the enemy's plundering of that kind, that he was denied an honorable and royal burial but instead tossed in a heap with the bodies of the other slaughtered. Commentary on Isaiah 14:11, 18-19.[42]

Sons Punished for Sins They Followed After Their Forefathers. Johannes Oecolampadius: But Babylon and its kingdom, Nebuchadnezzar and his sons, completely perish. So, God says to Persia, "Prepare slaughter for his sons," that is, there are some of you who kill his sons, "for the iniquity of the fathers," so that the fathers are punished in the sons. But how is this just, you say? For the Lord says through Ezekiel, "As I live, this proverb that is said, shall no more be allowed in Israel, 'The fathers have eaten sour grapes, and the children's teeth are set on edge.' Behold, all souls are mine; as the soul of the father, so also is the soul of the son mine. The soul who sins shall perish itself."

Does this pertain to Israel only and not to Gentiles? But we say that no one entirely perishes

[42]Musculus, *In Esaiam*, 293, 296. [†]Kimchi, *Commentary on Isaiah*, 89.

for the fault of another. For sin is transmitted from the parents to the children, if you speak of that original sin: for, to use the words of Augustine, "although it is foreign by the ownership of the action, yet it is not by the contagion of the offspring."[†] One dare not also deny the same, that the contagion of the fathers and grandfathers descends to the sons and renders them more inclined toward evil. Of course, to not be allowed to assert this, there is certainly a great propensity to sin born in the sons from the habit of parents, for they are accustomed to imitate what they see. So God is not only just but also merciful, who does not allow the children to reach the iniquity of their fathers by hastening their death. This is what he relates about the sons of Nebuchadnezzar when he says, "lest they rise up and possess the earth, and fill the whole earth with enemies." Rulers are the enemies of a homeland, and they fill a homeland with enemies. Commentary on Isaiah 14:20-22.[43]

God Alone Destroys Babylon. Wolfgang Musculus: There are two parts to this oracle. One is a command to the Medes; the other is a threat of God's vengeance. The first is placed before the previous verse, and the second is placed before this present one. The destruction of Babylon is threatened here, to which he himself is going to rise. The judgment of the age seemed impossible, that Babylon would be rendered devastated and desolate. For that reason, so that faith in this prophecy might be produced in godly people, God is brought in this way, when it says, "I will rise up against them."

What is not possible for the whole world is possible—indeed, it is very easy—for God. The prophet signifies that the desolation of Babylon would be such that it would be evident that it was to be attributed not to human strength but to the wrath and vengeance of God, that God himself had risen up to devastate Babylon and had cut down such a powerful and illustrious city. Commentary on Isaiah 14:22-23.[44]

The Certainty of Assyria's Destruction. Konrad Pellikan: As I very accurately prophesy that the kingdom of Babylon must come to an end very shamefully after many years—and there can be no doubt about this (the decision of the Almighty God stands fast; his plan is irrevocable and cannot be changed)—so also no one can doubt that the destruction of the Assyrian kingdom will come to pass in a sure, short time, under King Sennacherib. He is now destroying everything in his tyranny, a man whom you now fear. However, soon in the land of Judah, in the mountains around Jerusalem, I will trample underfoot the one who is obstinately blaspheming my name and seeking to undermine the worship of me. I will redeem my people not only from tribute to him but also from his burdens. Commentary on Isaiah 14:22-23.[45]

When Isaiah Preached the Defeat of Babylon and Assyria. Johannes Brenz: So then, although the sermon that is recorded in this passage is described after the sermon that concerns the destruction of the kingdom of Babylon . . . still it appears that Isaiah delivered this one prior to the previous one about Babylon. This is obvious from the time when it was proclaimed to Hezekiah and to the citizens of Jerusalem that Sennacherib not only was destroying the region of Judah but that he would also attack the city of Jerusalem and overturn the whole kingdom. So, when Sennacherib was preparing his forces and starting the war against the kingdom of Judah, Isaiah was aroused by the spirit of prophecy and ordered his fellow citizens to be of good hope. He also foretold that it would come to pass that, although Sennacherib would bring some calamity on the region, nevertheless he had to leave the city of Jerusalem unharmed

[43]Oecolampadius, *In Iesaiam*, 111v-112r; citing Ezek 18:2-4.
[†]Oecolampadius seems to be referring to Augustine, *Against Julian* 6.10.28, 337.

[44]Musculus, *In Esaiam*, 298.
[45]Pellikan, *Commentaria Bibliorum*, 3:20r.

and to run away in utter disgrace. Commentary on Isaiah 14:22-23.[46]

14:24-27 *God's Plan for Assyria*

God's Plan and Purpose Stand. Zacharias Ursinus: Whatever God desires to accomplish by his divine power will in every way come to pass. But he had absolutely decreed that he would by his own hand bring about the destruction of Babylon. Therefore it was necessary that Babylon perish. He demonstrated the minor premise of this syllogism with a double argument: by divine oath and by example. The latter is like the sign given of the coming liberation from the Babylonians in the liberation from the Assyrians. God will certainly accomplish what he swears to do, because he is truthful and is the most intense vindicator of his own glory. He swore destruction of Babylon. Therefore he earnestly wills to bring it to pass.

But you will learn from the example of the Assyrians that God is the most diligent preserver of his oath and most powerful in keeping it. He swore that he was going to remove their yoke off your shoulders. And he demonstrated this most powerfully. Therefore he will not be less willing and able to accomplish the destruction of Babylon that he swore. But the reason for the outcome in the example is the comparison evident in this passage. This, as in all the comforts of the righteous derived from the examples of divine goodness, truth, power, and anger, is evident and must be carefully noted. Commentary on Isaiah 14:24.[47]

The Plan Refers to Assyria and Babylon, Not Final Judgment. Wolfgang Musculus: What I intend and plan against the king of Assyria—that I will crush and trample him in order to deliver my people—so I intend and plan against all the earth and all the nations, that is, against any of those nations that are trying to oppress my people. This seems to be the plain sense to me, such that there is no need to explain this to be about final judgment. And by saying these things, the prophet builds the faith not only of the righteous people in Israel for the coming destruction of the Assyrians but also of the Babylonians. Commentary on Isaiah 14:25.[48]

God Always Opposes the Wicked. Heinrich Bullinger: Now the prophet applies this example of the Assyrians and the Babylonians, at God's command, to the whole world and every individual age or century. He precisely explains what was God's plan against the Assyrians and Babylon, and what was his vengeance (he understands vengeance as God's hand outstretched against these nations). He also explains what God's plan will be and his vengeance against all the peoples of the world who in their practices resemble the Assyrians and Babylonians. Therefore in this brief sentence, the prophet shows the purpose of discourses like this against the nations, explaining how he applies these lessons to individual men and times, or to cities and kingdoms. He explains that God, because he is forever self-consistent, will always stand opposed to wicked men of every age, just as he is described as acting against the Assyrians and Babylonians. Therefore, we must be very careful about those persons who offend against the Lord, that we not be destroyed with them. Sermons on Isaiah 14:26-27.[49]

God Not Only Foresees but Decrees. Zacharias Ursinus: God not only foresees but also in the eternal plan of his providence has decreed and established what will become of all nations and people, and has determined the beginnings, means, and ends of all things, and governs powerfully and leads them as he sees fit. "As I have intended, so shall it be, as I have decreed, it shall come to pass . . . and this is the plan, the decree over this whole earth, and the hand stretched out over all the nations. . . ." Therefore,

[46]Brenz, *Esaias*, 225; citing Is 12–13.
[47]Ursinus, *Iesaiam*, 474.
[48]Musculus, *In Esaiam*, 300.
[49]Bullinger, *Isaias*, 77v.

having done our duty commanded by him, let us entrust the outcomes to him and not fear that we are permitted to walk by the pleasures of the enemy or the mockery and rashness of fortune, but that good and evil happens to us in the sure and saving design of God. . . .

The counsels and decrees of divine providence are never changed by God himself, nor can they be violated, changed, or hindered by anyone for any reason. And therefore all their outcomes, in their own time, order, and manner, result with unchangeable certainty, whether they be necessary or contingent, with respect to secondary causes: "When Jehovah of hosts determined, who will make it invalid? His hand is stretched out, who will turn it back?" Therefore, in whatever matters the will of God is clear to us, let us not doubt its effect. . . . For he can and does accomplish all that he wills: but he does not accomplish all that he can. Therefore, here the power of God, determined by his will and counsel, is displayed, but his revealed will is confirmed by promise, oath, and example. Commentary on Isaiah 14:26-27.[50]

The Destiny of All Things Belongs to God. Marie Dentière: Is it not in the power of God to do as he pleases, to raise up and to bring down, to exalt and to humble, to elect and to condemn, to save and to damn, to hold back his word and to give it back when it pleases him? Who therefore can take that function away from that great master, since he decreed it and since it is his alone to exercise with power, glory, and honor? Will it be humanity, who is only rot and wickedness, to whom belongs only confusion? Oh, you poor creature!

You should do nothing else but humble yourself and give thanks to that good Father of all mercy for that great gift that he has given you in these times of his holy gospel, letting you see it when so many kings in times past, so many good prophets, wanted to see it but did not see it. They would not have been so ungrateful to receive Jesus and his holy word as we are. So many good people before us would have embraced it, they who only saw in spirit what you see clearly. God may have saved them, not condemning them, as you do, so rashly to be damned, and even if he would condemn them, he would do it in his justice. For if the blind lead the blind, they both fall into the ditch. Epistle to Marguerite de Navarre.[51]

[50]Ursinus, *Iesaiam*, 477.

[51]Dentière, *Epistle to Marguerite of Navarre*, 83; citing Dan 1; Lk 6:39.

14:28–17:14 JUDGMENT AGAINST OTHER NATIONS

28 *In the year that King Ahaz died came this oracle:*

29 *Rejoice not, O Philistia, all of you,*
that the rod that struck you is broken,

for from the serpent's root will come forth an adder,
and its fruit will be a flying fiery serpent.

30 *And the firstborn of the poor will graze,*
and the needy lie down in safety;

but I will kill your root with famine,
and your remnant it will slay.

31 *Wail, O gate; cry out, O city;*
melt in fear, O Philistia, all of you!

For smoke comes out of the north,
and there is no straggler in his ranks.

32 *What will one answer the messengers of the nation?*

"The Lord *has founded Zion,*
and in her the afflicted of his people find refuge."

15 *An oracle concerning Moab.*

Because Ar of Moab is laid waste in a night,
Moab is undone;

because Kir of Moab is laid waste in a night,
Moab is undone.

2 *He has gone up to the temple,*[a] *and to Dibon,*
to the high places[b] *to weep;*

over Nebo and over Medeba
Moab wails.

On every head is baldness;
every beard is shorn;

3 *in the streets they wear sackcloth;*
on the housetops and in the squares
everyone wails and melts in tears.

4 *Heshbon and Elealeh cry out;*
their voice is heard as far as Jahaz;

therefore the armed men of Moab cry aloud;
his soul trembles.

5 *My heart cries out for Moab;*
her fugitives flee to Zoar,
to Eglath-shelishiyah.

For at the ascent of Luhith
they go up weeping;

on the road to Horonaim
they raise a cry of destruction;

6 *the waters of Nimrim*
are a desolation;

the grass is withered, the vegetation fails,
the greenery is no more.

7 *Therefore the abundance they have gained*
and what they have laid up

they carry away
over the Brook of the Willows.

8 *For a cry has gone*
around the land of Moab;

her wailing reaches to Eglaim;
her wailing reaches to Beer-elim.

9 *For the waters of Dibon*[c] *are full of blood;*
for I will bring upon Dibon even more,

a lion for those of Moab who escape,
for the remnant of the land.

16 *Send the lamb to the ruler of the land,*

from Sela, by way of the desert,
to the mount of the daughter of Zion.

2 *Like fleeing birds,*
like a scattered nest,

so are the daughters of Moab
at the fords of the Arnon.

3"Give counsel;
grant justice;

make your shade like night
at the height of noon;

shelter the outcasts;
do not reveal the fugitive;

4let the outcasts of Moab
sojourn among you;

be a shelter to them[d]
from the destroyer.

When the oppressor is no more,
and destruction has ceased,

and he who tramples underfoot has vanished
from the land,

5then a throne will be established in steadfast
love,
and on it will sit in faithfulness
in the tent of David

one who judges and seeks justice
and is swift to do righteousness."

6We have heard of the pride of Moab—
how proud he is!—

of his arrogance, his pride, and his insolence;
in his idle boasting he is not right.

7Therefore let Moab wail for Moab,
let everyone wail.

Mourn, utterly stricken,
for the raisin cakes of Kir-hareseth.

8For the fields of Heshbon languish,
and the vine of Sibmah;

the lords of the nations
have struck down its branches,

which reached to Jazer
and strayed to the desert;

its shoots spread abroad
and passed over the sea.

9Therefore I weep with the weeping of Jazer
for the vine of Sibmah;

I drench you with my tears,
O Heshbon and Elealeh;

for over your summer fruit and your harvest
the shout has ceased.

10And joy and gladness are taken away from
the fruitful field,

and in the vineyards no songs are sung,
no cheers are raised;

no treader treads out wine in the presses;
I have put an end to the shouting.

11Therefore my inner parts moan like a lyre for
Moab,
and my inmost self for Kir-hareseth.

12And when Moab presents himself, when he
wearies himself on the high place, when he comes to
his sanctuary to pray, he will not prevail.
13This is the word that the LORD spoke concerning
Moab in the past. 14But now the LORD has spoken,
saying, "In three years, like the years of a hired worker,
the glory of Moab will be brought into contempt, in
spite of all his great multitude, and those who remain
will be very few and feeble."

17 *An oracle concerning Damascus.*

Behold, Damascus will cease to be a city
and will become a heap of ruins.

2The cities of Aroer are deserted;
they will be for flocks,

which will lie down, and none will make
them afraid.

3The fortress will disappear from Ephraim,
and the kingdom from Damascus;

and the remnant of Syria will be
like the glory of the children of Israel,

declares the LORD of hosts.

[4]And in that day the glory of Jacob will be brought low,
and the fat of his flesh will grow lean.

[5]And it shall be as when the reaper gathers standing grain
and his arm harvests the ears,

and as when one gleans the ears of grain
in the Valley of Rephaim.

[6]Gleanings will be left in it,
as when an olive tree is beaten—

two or three berries
in the top of the highest bough,

four or five
on the branches of a fruit tree,

declares the Lord God of Israel.

[7]In that day man will look to his Maker, and his
eyes will look on the Holy One of Israel. [8]He will not
look to the altars, the work of his hands, and he will
not look on what his own fingers have made, either
the Asherim or the altars of incense.

[9]In that day their strong cities will be like the
deserted places of the wooded heights and the hilltops,
which they deserted because of the children of Israel,
and there will be desolation.

[10]For you have forgotten the God of your salvation
and have not remembered the Rock of your refuge;

therefore, though you plant pleasant plants
and sow the vine-branch of a stranger,

[11]though you make them grow[e] on the day that you plant them,
and make them blossom in the morning that you sow,

yet the harvest will flee away[f]
in a day of grief and incurable pain.

[12]Ah, the thunder of many peoples;
they thunder like the thundering of the sea!

Ah, the roar of nations;
they roar like the roaring of mighty waters!

[13]The nations roar like the roaring of many waters,
but he will rebuke them, and they will flee far away,

chased like chaff on the mountains before the wind
and whirling dust before the storm.

[14]At evening time, behold, terror!
Before morning, they are no more!

This is the portion of those who loot us,
and the lot of those who plunder us.

a Hebrew *the house* **b** Or *temple, even Dibon to the high places* **c** Dead Sea Scroll, Vulgate (compare Syriac); Masoretic Text *Dimon*; twice in this verse **d** Some Hebrew manuscripts, Septuagint, Syriac; Masoretic Text *let my outcasts sojourn among you; as for Moab, be a shelter to them* **e** Or *though you carefully fence them* **f** Or *will be a heap*

Overview: The Reformation commentators recognize that this passage continues issuing judgment against the nations, but several identify that it stands as the beginning of its own part. On this section, many offer backgrounds on the Philistines, Moabites, and the people of Damascus. Yet they also frequently move quickly to explain how these are representative of all the enemies of God's people. In some cases, an interpreter will identify how one or more of these people groups is a type for the Gentiles who will be saved in the future. They also find places in this passages to address what is required to be a good king and how Hezekiah in particular is a type of Christ. The main theme is God's power and authority over all peoples.

The Fourth Part of the Work. Heinrich Bullinger: He prophesies about the calamities of the Philistines and the victory of King Hezekiah and the armies. . . . After the Babylonians, the prophet transitions to the Philistines, the relentless and hostile enemies of God's people, and he again sings his oracles to them. For he details various speeches on the calamities of various peoples. . . . But I said at the beginning of chapter 13 to what end these things are said. . . . They labored with relentless hatred against the people of God. There was not another nation that afflicted the people of God more obstinately and severely than the Philistines, until they were eventually demolished by Nebuchadnezzar. One may see this in the sacred history. Sermons on Isaiah 14:28-32.[1]

Book Four. Johannes Oecolampadius: This verse persuades us to make this the beginning of a new book, in which is narrated either what the prophet saw or what happened when Hezekiah was reigning. For with the death of Ahaz, now Hezekiah succeeds him, the just for the unjust, the religious for the idolater, the holy for the wicked. Commentary on Isaiah 14:28.[2]

14:28-32 *Oracle Against the Philistines*

Against the Philistines. Heinrich Bullinger: And the prophet noted the occasion of this prayer in a few words when he said, "In the year that King Ahaz died, this burden was fulfilled." For the prophet, inspired by the Holy Spirit of God, prophesied against the Philistines that the burden they were under when Uzziah had suppressed them was not going to be relieved at the death of King Ahaz, but that they would be much more oppressed and afflicted by the son of Ahaz, Hezekiah. Sermons on Isaiah 14:28.[3]

Order of Nations Addressed. Johannes Oecolampadius: Do not think that the prophet transitions randomly from one nation to another. For first he predicts about those nearby, namely, the Philistines, who are to the southwest below Jerusalem. Then he proceeds to the Moabites, who are to the east beyond the Dead Sea. After that, he predicts what will happen to the Damascenes, who are to the northeast. In narrating these things, he opposes the Egyptians and the Ethiopians, who are to the south. Commentary on Isaiah 14:28.[4]

Joy at the Tyrant's Death. John Trapp: "In the year that King Ahaz died." A very good riddance from the world. When Tiberius the tyrant died, some of the people offered sacrifices in joy; others, in detestation of him, cried out "Tiberium in Tiberim," [Let Tiberius be thrown into the Tiber]. Think the same for Ahaz, that stigmatical Belialist. Nevertheless, as bad as he was, when the Philistines heard of his death, they hoped to find some advantage against the Jews from it, who are instead encouraged here. Exposition on Isaiah 14:28.[5]

The Deadly Serpent. Heinrich Bullinger: "Because from the serpent's root will be born a *regulus*, and its offspring will be a flying *praester*."[†] Moreover, there is a proverb that means that an evil is exchanged wickedly for another evil or that a more serious evil will replace a lesser one. Serpents or snakes, though they themselves are venomous, nevertheless the poison in them is not as great as that of a *regulus*, which is also called a basilisk. Its sight is said to be deadly. Sermons on Isaiah 14:29.[6]

Hezekiah the Basilisk. Dietrich Schnepff: But that hope of yours is empty, for indeed up to now, Kings Uzziah and Ahaz were formidable to you, and they seemed as if they were a kind of harmful serpents. But their progeny and successor, King Hezekiah, will no longer be a snake to you but will certainly be a basilisk or a flying

[1]Bullinger, *Isaias*, 78v; citing Is 14–21 and 22–36; 13.
[2]Oecolampadius, *In Iesaiam*, 113v.
[3]Bullinger, *Isaias*, 79r.
[4]Oecolampadius, *In Iesaiam*, 113v-114r.
[5]Trapp, *Commentary or Exposition*, 67*.
[6]Bullinger, *Isaias*, 79v. [†]In medieval Europe, the *praester* referred to a magical breed of asp whose steam, coming from its open mouth, was deadly.

dragon. For with just a gaze he will drive you away, and with the fastest speed he will accomplish the greatest military outcomes. He is going to break all your efforts. Paraphrase of Isaiah 14:29.[7]

More Powerful than the Bronze Serpent. Johannes Oecolampadius: In a more remote sense, as I have often said, the things said about Hezekiah are a type that we can also take to be about Christ. The first Adam should have persisted in righteousness to beat the adversary, but since he fell by sinning, Christ was born from him, whose victory is far greater. For certain Hebrews also understand the Messiah by "basilisk." You should not be offended by this name, since it was a serpent that was made into bronze and lifted up by Moses in the desert, and . . . [Hosea] calls him a lioness and the cub of a lion. For the one who is the gentle lamb to the good is also a frightful lion to the evil. And how much more powerful are a fiery *praester*[†] and a basilisk than a serpent. So also the grace through Christ is more powerful than nature. Commentary on Isaiah 14:29-32.[8]

15:1-9 *Oracle Against Moab*

Moabites Mourning Again. Johannes Brenz: Another speech against the Moabites, who inhabited the city of Jerusalem from the east toward the south. Again, who the Moabites were and where they derived their origin is more familiar from Scripture than needs to be mentioned at this point. But the argument of this speech is clearly the same as the previous speech that Isaiah gave against the Philistines. For he prophesied that the Moabites, the enemies of God's people, were going to be in mourning and squalor, and their region was going to be devastated, but the kingdom of God's people was going to remain perpetually. Commentary on Isaiah 15:1.[9]

Shaved Beards. John Trapp: This was commonly done in those times in the Eastern parts as a token of lamentation. . . . When Alexander was mourning for the death of his friend Hephaestion, he not only tore off his own hair but clipped the hair of his horses and mules. He even plucked down the battlements of the walls of the city, too, as Plutarch writes.[†] Oecolampadius says, "What a shame is it, then, for us Christians not to weep over our sins and to bewail our spiritual wounds and wants?" Exposition on Isaiah 15:2.[10]

No Delight in the Destruction of People. Wolfgang Musculus: "My heart cries out to Moab." That is, I foresee such future calamity that I cannot but cry out from my heart to this nation of the Moabites. You see that the soul is inclined to pity the perishing, even the wicked. The prophet does not delight in the destruction of people, no matter how much they are enemies. So [Jeremiah] reads . . . , "Therefore my heart will sound for Moab like a flute, and my heart will sound like a flute for the men of Kir-hareseth." Commentary on Isaiah 15:5.[11]

The Moabites Cry Out. Johannes Oecolampadius: "My heart to Moab." It says they all cry out, "O my heart," which is the sound of suffering. That is, "Woe, how I suffer in all my heart." The prophet does not speak this way as if he were addressing the Moabites, those miserable foes, from his own heart and empathizes with them, as Jerome considered. But the sound is that of the Moabites. Commentary on Isaiah 15:5.[12]

The Destruction of Night Should Instill Fear of the Lord. Konrad Pellikan: Particular cities of this region are here named. Two

[7]Schnepff, *In Esaiae*, 248.
[8]Oecolampadius, *In Iesaiam*, 114r; citing Hos 5:14. [†]In medieval Europe, the *praester* referred to a magical breed of asp whose steam, coming from its open mouth, was deadly.
[9]Brenz, *Esaias*, 233.
[10]Trapp, *Commentary or Exposition*, 68; citing Job 1:20; Ezra 9:3; Ezek 7:18. [†]See Plutarch, *Plutarch's Lives, with an English Translation*, trans. Bernadotte Perrin (Cambridge, MA: Harvard University Press and William Heinemann, 1919), 7; Oecolampadius, *In Iesaiam*, 117v-r.
[11]Musculus, *In Esaiam*, 307; citing Jer 48:36.
[12]Oecolampadius, *In Iesaiam*, 117r.

times these places were sent into exile and destroyed, once by Sennacherib and then by Nebuchadnezzar. Therefore, suddenly and with no one considering it or even fearing it, like a stormy night when danger suddenly becomes more terrifying, he prophesies that Moab is going to be destroyed and in such a way be brought to submission and crushed. So it becomes altogether quiet; it lowers the crest of arrogance in the face of shame and confusion. Even what was the metropolis of the kingdom and the more powerful suffers the same fate. Wickedness, no matter how strong, does not escape the hand of the Lord. When it least expects it, wickedness is overthrown by God's judgment. So then, we must always fear and worship the one who holds the authority to throw both body and soul into Gehenna. Commentary on Isaiah 15:5-9.[13]

16:1-5 *Refuge for Moab*

The Lamb and Ruler. John Mayer: With the verb *send* being plural, it is for the three persons in the Godhead, yet all one. Hugo, Lyra, Adam Sasbout, and Vatable also subscribe to this, who all take it as spoken of Christ;[†] yet as was before said, *ruler* being put opposite to the word *lamb*. But since Hebrew does not have cases, we shall not err whether we render it with the accusative or vocative. Junius was then misled on this by the Hebrews, who in order to avoid that this prophecy touches on Christ refer it to Hezekiah as an exhortation to the Moabites to submit and pay tribute to him as they ought so that he might defend them, for they were never his subjects. Commentary on Isaiah 16:1.[14]

Bring Sacrifices Rather than Send Lambs. Wolfgang Musculus: My opinion is as follows: The prophet exhorts the Moabites not to think that what was done with Judah and Mount Zion was just as they saw it done with the Israelites. But rather, they were to acknowledge the Lord of Mount Zion, whom he here calls "the ruler of the earth," that is, of the whole world, and as a witness to that reality, they would send to Mount Zion a lamb, that is, lambs, not for tribute but as sacrifice,[†] by which they testify that they recognize him as the only and true God, and they ask for the grace of protection from him. . . .

Jerome, whom Lyra follows, explains this verse to be about Christ in this way: "O Moab, take comfort in this: Out of you will come forth an unblemished lamb, who takes away the sins of the world, who shall rule over the world, out of the rock of the desert." That is, from Ruth, who was widowed by the death of her [first] husband, of Boaz gave birth to Obed, and from Obed Jesse, and from Jesse David, and from David Christ. . . . But I do not know whether because of Ruth it is rightly said that Christ was sent from Moab, and that specifically from the rock of the desert. It is not likely to me that the prophet considered this. Commentary on Isaiah 16:1.[15]

Five Conditions of a Good King. Johannes Oecolampadius: You have here five conditions of a good king or judge. First, that he does not invade a kingdom by tyranny, but the throne is prepared for him in grace, that is, he obtains his kingdom or civil office, approved by God and the people. The second is that he presides on the throne not vacating it for other things but acting as king, not an impersonator or hypocrite, who has nothing other than the scepter, crown, and name of king. The third is that he judges all without favoritism nor is corrupted by money.

Fourth, that he does not listen alone and comes to judgments by himself but also seeks judgment, so that when he sees the righteous inflicted with harm, and because of evangelical patience and humility, makes no complaint, nor accuses the one

[13]Pellikan, *Commentaria Bibliorum*, 3:20v; citing Mt 10:28.

[14]Mayer, *Commentary upon All the Prophets*, 4:108*. [†]See Nicholas of Lyra, *Bibliorum*, 175-76.

[15]Musculus, *In Esaiam*, 310. [†]Musculus notes that another possible interpretation is from 2 Kings 3, where the Moabites annually sent lambs to King Ahab as tribute when they should have been sent to Judah. For that view, see Oecolampadius, *In Iesaiam*, 118r; Gwalther, *Isaias*, 99.

afflicted; he himself, by his authority and ordinary office, rescues the weak and destitute, and punishes the one acting unjustly. For this reason, he bears the sword by God. Fifth, that he executes righteousness on time and without delay. The Moabites were unworthy of such a king.

Moreover here, as I have said often, Hezekiah is a type of him who sits on the throne of David . . . teaching truth and is the truth itself, who also received all judgment from the Father. But the Moabites, Sophists, heretics, sons of drunkenness, and those perpetually guilty with the crime of pride and arrogance—in the end they are slow to learn repentance. This is to despise the little flock of Christ and the word of the cross, and how foolishly and wickedly they take pride in their efforts, their free will, and their works. For Christ is the true ruler of the earth, to whom we ought to send ourselves as lambs of living sacrifice and reasonably in all innocence, gentleness, and patience. Commentary on Isaiah 16:1-5.[16]

Christians Employ Exclusion and the Ban, Not the Sword. Anabaptists of Trieste: Concerning the sword we confess the following command of Christ to his own. The sword is an order of God outside the perfection of Christ that punishes evildoers and protects and shelters those who do good. In the law the worldly sword was given to worldly government. In the perfection of Christ the ban and exclusion are used for admonition, change of heart, and conversion of the sinner without killing the body, only with admonition and the command to sin no more. Confession of the Brothers.[17]

16:6-14 *Lament for the Pride of Moab*

Moab's High Place of Prayer. Martin Borrhaus: Up to this point the prophet has described the desert in terms of its strength, its fortifications, and its resources. Now he also describes it as destitute of divine help, which its own god Chemosh could not keep. So the prophet declares that salvation is found in the faith and hope of the God of the Israelites alone. He is the one described a little before under the type of Hezekiah as king, judge, and peacemaker.

The Hebrew word conveys a twofold interpretation. One is that when Moab sees that its fortunes are struggling, he will ascend to the high places and enter into his sanctuary to pray, but that will accomplish nothing. That is, his prayers will be in vain, and he will receive no help from his false god. And this is what Jeremiah says, "the people of Chemosh have perished." The second interpretation is that even though he will wear himself out weeping in the temple of his god, his prayer will be powerless. This is what the *Paraphrastes*† says and some others. Oracles in Isaiah on 16:6-7.[18]

Great Idolatry and Superstition. Konrad Pellikan: Of all those calamities, the not small cause of idolatry is added here, which had also been alleged at the beginning. For the many great and high places in Moab revealed excessive superstition and ignorance of the true God and hatred for the people of Israel who maintained that there was only one God, and others who mocked the gods. The Moabites now call on their own gods to no effect, as they had also worshiped them in vain. These gods give no help in hardships since they are idols and nothing else, neither useful to themselves or any other but worthy of ridicule. Commentary on Isaiah 16:12.[19]

A Three-Year Call to Repentance. Johannes Oecolampadius: Since the people did not respond, neither did the long-suffering God change his mind such that all his glory would be diminished within three years. Moreover, for that reason he calls them "the years of a hired worker," because just as a hired worker does not work

[16]Oecolampadius, *In Iesaiam*, 119r; citing Lk 1.

[17]CRR 10:268-69; citing Wis 2; Rom 13:1-4.

[18]Borrhaus, *In Iesaiae Prophetae Oracula*, 180. †The *Paraphrastes* refers to the Chaldean translations or paraphrases of the Hebrew Bible in the Jewish Targum.

[19]Pellikan, *Commentaria Bibliorum*, 3:22r.

beyond the appointed day, so also God is not going to give a longer truce period and more time for repentance after the three years. And if within three years of this life, which is perhaps not even three months or days, we have not produced the fruit of repentance, we will be ordered to be eradicated as if we were uselessly taking up space. Commentary on Isaiah 16:13-14.[20]

God's Appointed Times. Zacharias Ursinus: This is another circumstance from time. The outcome of which God appoints a certain time and indeed a short one, that is beyond doubt. Here is the argument: since it is beyond doubt that God will not allow himself to know and desire disgracefully, nor the prophet, he categorically and absolutely is not going to name the time of an event, which would not happen at that time. But God says that the destruction of the Moabites will take place after three years. Therefore, there is absolutely no reason to doubt this. And the outcome corresponds to the prophecy, when after three years Moab was devastated and occupied by Shalmaneser.

It is evident from this passage that Isaiah is talking about the war of Shalmaneser, king of Assyria, against Moab. He is the one who captured Samaria and sent Israel into exile. Still, it would not be absurd if anyone wanted at the same time to apply this to the greater catastrophe and slaughter of the Moabites that they suffered from Nebuchadnezzar the Great, the one who brought Judea and all the neighboring regions under Babylonian rule. So then, Jeremiah also uses many phrases from this prophecy of Isaiah, as the Holy Spirit shows that the Moabites would again suffer at the hands of the Babylonians far more bitterly than what Isaiah had previously predicted and what they had suffered under the Assyrians. Commentary on Isaiah 16:13-14.[21]

The Moabites as a Type for Gentiles Saved by the Gospel. Martin Borrhaus: Now, as the prophet here mentioned the remnant that was going to be preserved from the violence and tyranny of the Assyrians, so also in Jeremiah the divine Spirit explains that Nebuchadnezzar drove the Moabites into exile and was going to be avenged in that exile. If one is looking for the type, it is apparent that when the Babylonian captivity of the Jews was finished, then the exile of the Moabites was also completed. But if the thing itself is sketched with a figure, then in what happens in the last times with the revealing of the gospel, we have the beginnings with what happened to the Moabites, that is, the Gentiles. And the Israelites will be set free from the spiritual tyranny of Babylon, which is the kingdom of the son of perdition, through the Messiah, the Savior of the Jews and the Gentiles.

Without any doubt, the mystery foreshadowed in this happened by divine providence so that from the daughters of Lot, that is, from the lineage of the Moabites and Ammonites, the Messiah would be born, who was going to be the Savior of the Gentiles and the Israelites. For it is evident that David is descended from Ruth the Moabite, and that Rehoboam was the son of Naamah the Ammonite, and from there, the Messiah, king of heaven and earth, the ruler and restorer of this whole world, was born. Oracles in Isaiah on 16:13-14.[22]

The Moabites as Counterfeit Friends. Johannes Oecolampadius: These words are sufficient for the description of Moab. Further, in a more flavored† sense, I understand them to be enemies, the same as the Assyrians and Babylonians and Philistines, for they all unanimously conspire against Christ, even though they attack in different ways, some from behind, some from the front, some from the right, some from the left. The Philistines ambush from behind. The Assyrians invade openly. The Moabites pretend to be friends, but they do not keep faith. And the one who is not for Christ will be against Christ. So, for three things in particular Moab is so seriously crushed,

[20]Oecolampadius, *In Iesaiam*, 121r.
[21]Ursinus, *Iesaiam*, 504-5.
[22]Borrhaus, *In Iesaiae Prophetae Oracula*, 181; citing 1 Kings 14:21, 31.

namely, for arrogance, treachery, and inhospitality. COMMENTARY ON ISAIAH 16.[23]

17:1-6 *Oracle Against Damascus*

THREE TIMES AND KINGS. KONRAD PELLIKAN: In these three passages and statements the prophet seems to declare the Lord's decision about three kingdoms: that they are going to be destroyed at almost the same time and by the same enemy. The kingdom of Syria is represented by the name Damascus. The kingdom of the Moabites by the name Aroer, and that of Israel by Samaria. They were all condemned by the same judgment, that their chief cities would be entirely destroyed and that their cities would cease to exist because of the tyranny of the Assyrians as God's just judgment. COMMENTARY ON ISAIAH 17:1-3.[24]

WARNED FOR ALLIANCES. RUDOLF GWALTHER: Now, because the Israelites had made a covenant with the Syrians against the Jews, this prophecy also applies to them, saying, "And the fortress will retreat from Ephraim, and the kingdom from Damascus." Now, by Ephraim, the ten tribes are understood, as said elsewhere. But by the term *fortress* the prophet designates the covenant with Syria, in which they were relying on very strong and invincible protection, and for that reason they were quite arrogantly raging against the kingdom of Judah. So the sense is that it would happen soon that when the kingdom of Damascus was overthrown, at the same time this fortress and hope of the Israelites would collapse. Then the remnants of the Syrians will be as the glory of the sons of Israel.

But the prophet says this sarcastically, to mock the arrogance of both nations. It is as though he were saying, "Now they have joined together in a covenant, and they give one another occasion for boasting. But soon it will be clear what kind of glory is theirs, when they are lumped together in the same destruction and suffer equal disgrace." The sacred history teaches that this is precisely what happened to them. SERMONS ON ISAIAH 17:3.[25]

DAMASCUS NO LONGER A PEOPLE. JOHANNES OECOLAMPADIUS: It was said about their king . . . how he made a covenant with Pekah the son of Remaliah, against Ahaz and the kingdom of Judah. And so then now he describes its destruction. But you say, "How did that city cease to exist, which up until that day was a famous city of the Phoenicians?" Answer the same as you would about Babylon: that the prophecies were said not so much about the stones in the walls as about the people. For that people who were oppressing the Israelites were led into captivity, and other inhabitants were occupying it just like they did Samaria. And not any who inhabited it were those who had troubled that Israel. COMMENTARY ON ISAIAH 17:3.[26]

THE SAME CERTAIN FATE. DIETRICH SCHNEPFF: Therefore when Damascus is conquered, the Israelites will be deprived of their covenant and the kingdom of Syria will cease. And then the condition and the fortune of the Syrians and of the Israelites will be equal. For both will come to the highest desperation of things. Although such a thing can seem to be unbelievable now, yet it is certain. For the Lord, who does not know how to lie, revealed all of that to me, at whose command, as the Lord of armies and all majesty, all things happen and are appointed. PARAPHRASE OF ISAIAH 17:4-6.[27]

17:7-14 *God Has Been Forgotten*

REFORMED WORSHIP UNDER JOSIAH. KONRAD PELLIKAN: Although the status of the kingdom of Judah was reformed under Hezekiah, as it was under Josiah, so that at the time the people began to look to the Lord their God and to despise idols, still this

[23]Oecolampadius, *In Iesaiam*, 116r. †Oecolampadius uses this language of "flavored" to refer to appropriate spiritual meanings.
[24]Pellikan, *Commentaria Bibliorum*, 3:22r.
[25]Gwalther, *Isaias*, 103r.
[26]Oecolampadius, *In Iesaiam*, 121v; citing Is 7.
[27]Schnepff, *In Esaiae*, 279.

reform seemed partial and to last only a short time. In fact, even after the return from Babylon their religion and true worship was thin and weak. But when the gospel was preached by Christ and his apostles, true religion began to appear everywhere. People were converted to their maker, the Creator of all things, and to the Holy One of Israel, the living, true, and only God. For then the whole world began to detest the altars of the idols, the works of their hands intended to be worshiped, the images and statues. And the groves and shrines of Gentile deception were demolished, and they returned to worshiping the one God. Commentary on Isaiah 17:7-9.[28]

Do Not Forget God. Abraham Scultetus: If you forget God, you will not succeed in your efforts. . . . May our households have this as an economic rule. Let the Israelites be an example. With great diligence, they planted vineyards and plantations, but when the time came to gather and store the fruit, they harvested disease instead of grapes and pain instead of oil. Use, "Take care lest you forget the Lord." . . .

The afflictions of the godly yield good things. . . . For they lead to the true God. When others worship idols, as the Israelites do here, they rely on treaties and physical strength. The nature of sincere conversion is expressed. . . . This has two parts:

1. To look back to God his maker (since we are his workmanship . . .), to the Holy One of Israel, who is holy in himself and makes us holy.
2. To testify to that work of repentance itself by abstaining from altars, sacred groves, and images.

Sermon Ideas on Isaiah 17:1-11.[29]

Reaping What Is Sown. Johannes Oecolampadius: But these are caused by those pretending to be pious. And just as he calls new institutions without the word of God "plantings," so also he says they are "sowings." For fruit is usually produced in these two ways. And do not let the difference in terms disturb you. For it is the same as if he had said, "You will plant pleasant plants, and you will plant the vine-branch of a stranger." In this sense, you explain also the following verse as if it says, "With great care you will attend to the planting of what you established and make it blossom, as if you were going to receive fruit that morning. However, as you have sown, so shall you reap. For there will be a harvest of bitter grief and perpetual pain."

Therefore what begins without the word of God requires much labor and ends with punishment. For there cannot be good conscience where the word of God is absent. And where there is a good conscience, there is faith. Where there is no faith, there is sin. Where there is sin, there is toil and burden, and finally, the wages of sin is death. Commentary on Isaiah 17:10-11.[30]

Twofold Idolatry. Johannes Brenz: You will observe this also in Isaiah's sermon, that when he perceives that the Israelites are going to acknowledge Christ, he also says they will return to their maker and will have regard to the Holy One of Israel—which ought to be understood to be about the true God. So he clearly teaches that Christ is the true God, our maker and Creator. Therefore the one truly worships God is the one who worships Christ. So then, it is very clear that neither the Jews (such are the Jews at this time), nor the Turks, nor hypocrites, nor monks, nor papists worship the true God, nor can they call on him even if they boast many things about God. Some of them absolutely deny and despise Christ; others, even if they seem to venerate his name, nevertheless when they persecute his gospel they also persecute Christ himself. So what is more miserable than those who are so far from God that they cannot even call on him?

And we must not simply pass by this point in Isaiah's sermon, that he says that the Israelites are no longer going to look to the altars, the groves, and the shrines that their own hands have made. He teaches

[28]Pellikan, *Commentaria Bibliorum*, 3:22v.
[29]Scultetus, *Idea Concionum*, 236; citing Deut 8:11, 19; Eph 2:10.
[30]Oecolampadius, *In Iesaiam*, 123v-124r.

that idolatry is truly rejected when Christ, the Son of God, is acknowledged by faith. This is because idolatry is twofold. One is open and obvious—when outward idols are made and are worshiped. The other is slender—when a person takes up some work to be done, whether it has been commanded or not by God, and believes that he is meritoriously atoning for his sins by his works, and obtaining eternal life. Here, too, if this one does not fashion an idol for himself with his own hand, he still fashions one in his heart. And even though he does not bow down on his physical knees before his work, he still worships it with the confidence of his heart and sets it up in place of Christ. All hypocrites are such idolaters, not only in Judaism but also in Christianity. Some of them are quite subtle, while others are open and obvious, worshiping the outward images of the dead. Commentary on Isaiah 17:7-9.[31]

Forgetting God Is Lengthy Neglect. Wolfgang Musculus: So he does not simply say, "For you have forgotten the salvation of God and the rock of refuge," but rather, "For you have forgotten the God of *your* salvation, and the rock of *your* refuge." So he chastises them for so shamefully forgetting the blessings they have received. This is to say, you have forgotten your God saves you and is your rock, in which you have been kept safe from your enemies countless times. There is, moreover, the metaphor of a strong rock, not only in this passage but also in many other passages of Scripture, which is used to express faith and the power of divine protection that keeps believers safe, as if one were kept safe in a certain strong and invincible stronghold against the power of the enemy.

That he says "you have forgotten" and likewise "you have not remembered" should not be understood as a kind of brief forgetfulness of God but rather a lengthy neglect of him. This was when Israel abandoned God's law and his house under Jeroboam and began to adhere to the worship of calves, and afterward never put up with being called back to the true worship of their God. The prophet calls this stubborn and exceedingly lengthy neglect of God "forgetfulness." Commentary on Isaiah 17:10.[32]

Nations Raging Against the Messiah. Johannes Oecolampadius: No one does not see that these things are properly said against the Assyrians, but nevertheless they can and ought to be explained as against the enemies of the church and of God. For she always has opponents. For all who rise up against Christ do not spare the church. . . . "Why do the nations rage and the peoples plan in vain? The rulers stand up and the kings take counsel together against the Lord and against his Christ." Commentary on Isaiah 17:12.[33]

Judgment for All the Wicked. Wolfgang Musculus: We will observe from the fact that he does not say, "This will be the portion of the Assyrians," but, "This will be the portion of those who pillage us, and the lot of those who plunder us," how we should—from these specific judgments and chastisements of God against the wicked—deduce some general principles. God is no respecter of persons, but he acts the same toward all of those who behave wickedly, whether they are Assyrians, Babylonians, Romans, Spanish, French, or Germans. And there is nothing to stop us from understanding this statement of the prophet as applying to God's people, who, for their wickedness, God personally handed over into the grip of tyrants to be punished and humiliated. Still, this was their portion, that in the end they would be overturned and destroyed. God punishes and chastises his own people.

Once he has completed this work, he casts the rod of his anger into the fire. This is what happened to the Egyptians, Philistines, Moabites, Ammonites, Syrians, Assyrians, Babylonians, Greeks, and Romans. And we should not doubt that this course of God's judgment will stand firm to the end of the world, in the case of other tyrants as well. Commentary on Isaiah 17:14.[34]

[31]Brenz, *Esaias*, 255.

[32]Musculus, *In Esaiam*, 320.

[33]Oecolampadius, *In Iesaiam*, 124r; citing Ps 2:1.

[34]Musculus, *In Esaiam*, 323.

18:1–20:6 JUDGMENT AGAINST ETHIOPIA AND EGYPT

18 *Ah, land of whirring wings*
that is beyond the rivers of Cush,[a]

2 *which sends ambassadors by the sea,*
in vessels of papyrus on the waters!

Go, you swift messengers,
to a nation tall and smooth,

to a people feared near and far,
a nation mighty and conquering,
whose land the rivers divide.

3 *All you inhabitants of the world,*
you who dwell on the earth,

when a signal is raised on the mountains, look!
When a trumpet is blown, hear!

4 *For thus the LORD said to me:*

"I will quietly look from my dwelling
like clear heat in sunshine,
like a cloud of dew in the heat of harvest."

5 *For before the harvest, when the blossom is over,*
and the flower becomes a ripening grape,

he cuts off the shoots with pruning hooks,
and the spreading branches he lops off and clears away.

6 *They shall all of them be left*
to the birds of prey of the mountains

and to the beasts of the earth.

And the birds of prey will summer on them,
and all the beasts of the earth will winter on them.

7 *At that time tribute will be brought to the LORD of hosts*

from a people tall and smooth,
from a people feared near and far,

a nation mighty and conquering,
whose land the rivers divide,

to Mount Zion, the place of the name of the LORD of hosts.

19 *An oracle concerning Egypt.*

Behold, the LORD is riding on a swift cloud
and comes to Egypt;

and the idols of Egypt will tremble at his presence,
and the heart of the Egyptians will melt within them.

2 *And I will stir up Egyptians against Egyptians,*
and they will fight, each against another
and each against his neighbor,
city against city, kingdom against kingdom;

3 *and the spirit of the Egyptians within them will be emptied out,*
and I will confound[b] *their counsel;*

and they will inquire of the idols and the sorcerers,
and the mediums and the necromancers;

4 *and I will give over the Egyptians*
into the hand of a hard master,

and a fierce king will rule over them,
declares the Lord GOD of hosts.

5 *And the waters of the sea will be dried up,*
and the river will be dry and parched,

6 *and its canals will become foul,*
and the branches of Egypt's Nile will diminish and dry up,
reeds and rushes will rot away.

7 *There will be bare places by the Nile,*
on the brink of the Nile,

and all that is sown by the Nile will be parched,
will be driven away, and will be no more.

8 *The fishermen will mourn and lament,*
all who cast a hook in the Nile;

and they will languish
who spread nets on the water.

9 *The workers in combed flax will be in despair,*
and the weavers of white cotton.

10 *Those who are the pillars of the land will be crushed,*
and all who work for pay will be grieved.

11 *The princes of Zoan are utterly foolish;*
the wisest counselors of Pharaoh give stupid counsel.

How can you say to Pharaoh,
"I am a son of the wise,
a son of ancient kings"?

12 *Where then are your wise men?*
Let them tell you
that they might know what the LORD of hosts has purposed against Egypt.

13 *The princes of Zoan have become fools,*
and the princes of Memphis are deluded;

those who are the cornerstones of her tribes
have made Egypt stagger.

14 *The LORD has mingled within her a spirit of confusion,*

and they will make Egypt stagger in all its deeds,
as a drunken man staggers in his vomit.

15 *And there will be nothing for Egypt*
that head or tail, palm branch or reed, may do.

16 *In that day the Egyptians will be like women,*
and tremble with fear before the hand that the LORD
of hosts shakes over them. 17 *And the land of Judah*
will become a terror to the Egyptians. Everyone to
whom it is mentioned will fear because of the purpose
that the LORD of hosts has purposed against them.
18 *In that day there will be five cities in the land of*
Egypt that speak the language of Canaan and swear
allegiance to the LORD of hosts. One of these will be
called the City of Destruction.[c]
19 *In that day there will be an altar to the LORD in*
the midst of the land of Egypt, and a pillar to the
LORD at its border. 20 *It will be a sign and a witness to*
the LORD of hosts in the land of Egypt. When they
cry to the LORD because of oppressors, he will send
them a savior and defender, and deliver them. 21 *And*
the LORD will make himself known to the Egyptians,
and the Egyptians will know the LORD in that day
and worship with sacrifice and offering, and they will
make vows to the LORD and perform them. 22 *And the*
LORD will strike Egypt, striking and healing, and
they will return to the LORD, and he will listen to
their pleas for mercy and heal them.
23 *In that day there will be a highway from Egypt to*
Assyria, and Assyria will come into Egypt, and Egypt
into Assyria, and the Egyptians will worship with the
Assyrians.
24 *In that day Israel will be the third with Egypt*
and Assyria, a blessing in the midst of the earth,
25 *whom the LORD of hosts has blessed, saying,*
"Blessed be Egypt my people, and Assyria the work of
my hands, and Israel my inheritance."

20 *In the year that the commander in chief, who*
was sent by Sargon the king of Assyria, came
to Ashdod and fought against it and captured it— 2
at that time the LORD spoke by Isaiah the son of
Amoz, saying, "Go, and loose the sackcloth from your
waist and take off your sandals from your feet," and
he did so, walking naked and barefoot.
3 *Then the LORD said, "As my servant Isaiah has*
walked naked and barefoot for three years as a sign and
a portent against Egypt and Cush,[d] 4 *so shall the king of*
Assyria lead away the Egyptian captives and the Cushite
exiles, both the young and the old, naked and barefoot,
with buttocks uncovered, the nakedness of Egypt. 5 *Then*
they shall be dismayed and ashamed because of Cush
their hope and of Egypt their boast. 6 *And the inhabitants*
of this coastland will say in that day, 'Behold, this is what
has happened to those in whom we hoped and to whom
we fled for help to be delivered from the king of Assyria!
And we, how shall we escape?'"

a Probably *Nubia* **b** Or *I will swallow up* **c** Dead Sea Scroll and some other manuscripts *City of the Sun* **d** Probably *Nubia*

Overview: These three chapters form the next part of Isaiah's prophecies of judgment against the nations, with a specific focus on Egypt and Ethiopia. The Reformation interpreters offer multiple theories about the historical events described here. They make connections to the New Testament, such as the Ethiopian eunuch in Acts and where specific phrases in this passage could be applied to the life and ministry of Jesus. The sign of Isaiah walking around naked gets much attention as they seem compelled to explain its legitimacy. In the sermons especially, the descriptions of battle in these chapters are applied to the actual warfare they were seeing in their own time. This passage again reinforces the themes of the remnant, God's providence and interaction in the world, and the calling of the Gentiles. As in many of the previous passages, the Reformers articulate that these judgments reinforce the foolishness of trusting in anything other than God.

18:1-7 *Oracle Against Cush*

New Speeches. Johannes Brenz: This is a new sermon, which some think was spoken against Egypt, and others say against Ethiopia. But because afterward certain sermons against Egypt follow, and here obvious reference is made to Ethiopia, we will conclude that the prophet undertook this sermon against Ethiopia, which is situated below Egypt, as the geographical charts show.

Now, the occasion for this sermon seems to be that after the kingdom of Israel had been devastated by the Assyrians and then the kingdom of Judah was plundered by Sennacherib, it seemed that these events applied to the entire Israelite people who were boasting that they were God's people. This is why the Egyptian Ethiopians, who typically traveled to the land of Israel in ships to engage in commerce, thought that there was no nation more miserable and filled with sorrow than the Israelites. This is because they were so downcast that they could no longer recover their former state and safety. Commentary on Isaiah 18:1.[1]

Various Views on Ethiopia. Wolfgang Musculus: Among the variety of explanations on this, those that refer these to the nation of Ethiopia, to those dwelling at the Arabian border, seem more simple and more right to me, which is the view we think should be upheld. Then I see some relate these things to the time of Christ's kingdom, as if the seer predicts the future so that the true Israelites are gathered from Ethiopia and added to the Lord. And they say this began to happen on the day of Pentecost, when those from all the nations of the whole earth were present who heard the mighty deeds of God celebrated by the apostles. Commentary on Isaiah 18:1.[2]

Where to Learn About Ethiopia. Heinrich Bullinger: For the name of Ethiopia is expressly mentioned in the following chapter. . . . No one is expecting an elaborate dissertation on the Ethiopians. For I leave that to the more learned cosmographers and to the Epitome of Vadian,[†] who knew how much was enough to be compiled about them under the title, "On Ethiopia Under Egypt." The prophet calls that land "shadows of wings," especially for this reason, I think, when considering that Seba, which was later called Meroë, was like an island surrounded by waters and filled with ships whose sails, as it were, overshadowed the region itself. Sermons on Isaiah 18:1.[3]

Twofold Oracle. Zacharias Ursinus: These oracles about the Ethiopians and

[1]Brenz, *Esaias*, 259.
[2]Musculus, *In Esaiam*, 325. Musculus offers multiple theories about historical events regarding Ethiopia. He also gives the example of the Ethiopian eunuch in Acts.
[3]Bullinger, *Isaias*, 88v; citing Is 20. [†]See Joachim Vadian, *Epitome Trium Terrae Parium* (Zurich: Froschauer, 1534), 201-6. Bullinger contributed the letter to the reader in the preface. For the background on Joachim Vadian (1484–1551), see Irena Backus, *Life Writing in Reformation Europe: Lives of Reformers by Friends, Disciples and Foes* (London: Taylor & Francis, 2016), 57-85.

Egyptians have therefore a twofold application. First, their purpose is that the Jews would not place any trust in these nations but wait for God alone to bring the promised defense. Second, that they should not doubt the certainty of the punishments that God threatens for those then considered their enemies: the Syrians, Israelites, Philistines. . . . As if these, aided by Egypt and the Ethiopians, could withstand the Assyrian invasions, and so not be less terrifying to the Jews than before. So then, the prophet shows that they would not, by their own or someone else's power, escape the disasters that had been determined for them by God. Commentary on Isaiah 18.[4]

The Patience of God Before Punishment. Dietrich Schnepff: "I, the Lord, therefore, summon all mortals throughout the world to be spectators of the miseries that these peoples are about to see: and let them do this when the enemies, Assyria and Babylon, will raise a signal on the highest mountains, and blow a trumpet, to lead an army against all these peoples." For I, Isaiah, do not wish to conceal from you anything about the things the Lord has made me more certain. "Although," says the Lord, "those nations deserved a sudden punishment, yet according to my long-suffering and patience, in that high stronghold of mine from where I look on the affairs of all people, I will rest to interpose a time before the execution of my severity. Indeed, I will bestow on them, before that supreme punishment, so much success and the happiness of times that I seem to be to that people what the farmer desires in the ripening of harvest, clearly the heat mixed with rains, and in turn the cloud of dew in the highest heat, by which the ear of grain is as if impregnated." Paraphrase of Isaiah 18:3-4.[5]

The Providence and Interaction of God. Johannes Oecolampadius: "For thus he said." On that account, he says, "I will call on the farthest and all the nations, so that they may learn the counsel and see the work of God, how he will exalt the lowly church and destroy her proud adversaries." "Thus he said." I do not change anything from his words, but as they were said to me, I deliver them to you.

"I will rest and I will see." This especially corresponds to God, who, in the highest happiness and quietness, governs everything by his providence, resting and at the same time providing and assisting with his comforts at the right time. God says, "I will rest," that is, "It will not be labor to me to destroy the wicked," and, "I will see," that is, "I will execute this with the command of my will." That is, quietly from his dwelling. Commentary on Isaiah 18:4.[6]

Three Comparisons of the Preserved Remnant. John Mayer: For they say that the same thing is set forth by three comparisons here: (1) of ears of corn left after a field is reaped, (2) of clusters of grapes left after grape gathering, and (3) two or three olives after olive gathering. And this is allegorically applied by the *Glossa Ordinaria* as setting forth how few shall be saved in comparison to those who will perish. Nilus says that Simeon,[†] a holy man who lived around the year 1000, when asked, "How many should be saved?" and that by the princes of Constantine, answered, not more than one out of ten thousand. So likewise Basil, Chrysostom, and Ephrem.

But Calvin, as well as Junius, based on the former words . . . understands this to be the cutting down of them by the Assyrians, as reapers do corn, and in the end, taking away even the gleanings too.‡ And he says that the comparison . . . serves to set forth another thing for the comfort of the faithful, who, hearing this, might fear that none should be left at all. On the contrary, he says that there will be a few left as a cluster or two of grapes, or two or three olives. Commentary on Isaiah 18:5.[7]

---

[4]Ursinus, *Iesaiam*, 526.

[5]Schnepff, *In Esaiae*, 290.

[6]Oecolampadius, *In Iesaiam*, 126v.

[7]Mayer, *Commentary upon All the Prophets*, 4:112*. [†]See Symeon Metaphrastes, *Christian Novels from the Menologion of Symeon Metaphrastes*, ed. Eustratios Papaïōannou, Dumbarton Oaks

Allegory for Brief Cleansing. Ulrich Zwingli: But see that in this passage only an allegorical pattern is presented, and then the comparison should be left alone. Think: "Thus, I will do this to the whole world, I will cut it down before it is ripe, just as the unripe grapes are pruned for the juice." . . . So the composed story and allegory in this passage signifies enough how God is going to cleanse the world in a short time. Annotations on Isaiah 18:5.[8]

The Calling of the Gentiles. Dietrich Schnepff: Now, two issues can rightly be raised from this passage. First, why does the prophet move so quickly from one subject to the next? And second, what are those gifts that the prophet says are being brought to the Lord's temple? The first should be concluded this way: the prophet is threatening the end for the Gentiles, because the people are miserable, rejected, and as if they are not a people. Nevertheless, at some point it will happen that the Lord will call them to participate in his kingdom and the blessings of heaven. Scholia on Isaiah 18:7.[9]

19:1-15 *Oracle Against Egypt*

The Handing Over of Egypt to Assyria Full of Allegories for Today. Johannes Oecolampadius: "The burden to Mizraim." That is, to Egypt, which is also a figure of this world and human flesh. But let us see first the history. When the land of Israel was devastated by the Assyrians, Tirhakah,[†] king of Ethiopia, armed himself against the Assyrians and Egyptians and soon moved his army against the Egyptians and Assyrians. The devastation is first, but at the end is described the liberation and peace with the Jews. All these are full of allegories. Here one may learn how the wicked are converted: First, the word of God is announced, then the vanity of their idols becomes known. Third, the battle between flesh and spirit emerges. . . .

Learn how the same thing that happened to Egypt is happening today, where the word of God is proclaimed purely, as you will see. Likewise notice that when God permitted us to be struck by spiritual Sennacherib, all strength is in vain, and there is no relief, unless he himself runs to our aid. Commentary on Isaiah 19:1-3.[10]

Swift Clouds in Egypt. John Trapp: Clouds are rarely seen in Egypt where it does not rain, but . . . we read of a cloud that should cover Egypt. By "swift cloud" here, some understand the Virgin Mary, others our Savior's body or his human nature. And they further tell us that as soon as the child Jesus was brought into Egypt, all the idols there fell down, as Dagon did before the ark. Exposition on Isaiah 19:1.[11]

The Allegorical Coming into Egypt. John Mayer: Calvin says it is childish to understand Christ by "the Lord coming to Egypt on a cloud" and, by the "idols being removed," their miraculous falling when Christ was brought into Egypt as an infant, because he did not begin to work any miracles until he came into Cana of Galilee, as is expressly said. . . . "This beginning of miracles Jesus did in Cana." But this reason is insufficient, for he did indeed begin to work miracles in that he was showing himself to be the Messiah. So it cannot be proved from this that God the Father made him known by no miraculous sign before. For the angels coming to Zechariah and to the Virgin Mary was a miracle; and John the Baptist's springing in his mother's belly at Mary's greeting Elizabeth, and the heavens bearing

Medieval Library 45 (Cambridge, MA: Harvard University Press, 2017). This is a collection of 150 lives of saints, which became the standard collection of saints' lives in the later Byzantine period. ‡See CTS 14:42.

[8]ZSW 14 / CR 101:247.18-26; referring to Tarquinis Superbus quote from Livy, *Ab urbe condita* 1.54.7.

[9]Schnepff, *In Esaiae*, 285; citing Rom 12; Hos 2.

[10]Oecolampadius, *In Iesaiam*, 127v. †Oecolampadius refers to Tirhaka as Taraches. In other writings he is referred to as Tarkakah, Tarakos, Tearkos, Tharsikes, and Tarku. See 2 Kings 19:9.

[11]Trapp, *Commentary or Exposition*, 74; citing Ezek 30:18.

of a new star to show the place where he was born, and the heavens opening at his baptism were all miracles.

Yet I do not think that to be the proper meaning of this passage but an allegorical one, and so Cyril, Procopius, Theodor, Augustine, Eusebius, Bernard, and others take it. The literal meaning is that God by the Assyrians should execute his judgments against Egypt for their gross idolatries and that their doing of it was his coming against them. And because they should come irresistibly against them, all their fortifications did nothing to help them withstand. He uses this metaphor of coming on a cloud on high, against which no forts would benefit them, according to Calvin.† Commentary on Isaiah 19:1.[12]

Brother Against Brother in Germany. Wolfgang Musculus: What shall we say here about our own Germany, with the remarkable ways it has torn itself into pieces? Have we not seen Germans to be set against Germans, and that also with the uproars of wars? Does not brother fight with brother, neighbor with neighbor, state with state, principality with principality? And it is not only Germany struggling with this evil, but also any who still remain, all those with the name of Christian in the world, who seem so at war with itself that nothing else is to be expected than that it will in a short time be subjected most seriously to the yoke of tyranny. The devastations of the Turks have prevailed all the way to Hungary, and I will not even mention the evils that threaten the Mediterranean Sea.

Now, if ever, is especially the proper time for Christian magistrates to set aside their mutual quarrels and join together lovingly among themselves, and if any strength remains, to contribute it to the common protection of the Christian world. But the more the most powerful enemy threatens, the more viciously these fight among themselves, and, as it were, they invite such a grave enemy on their own necks. Who does not recognize the most serious wrath of God on us, and really the more certain judgments of our imminent destruction? Commentary on Isaiah 19:2.[13]

Prophetic Application of the Law. Heinrich Bullinger: Now he recounts seven punishments in order, and that from the precepts of the law. . . . For I often repeat that the prophets are interpreters of the divine law, who apply it to time, place, and persons, and show the use of the law. For they are preachers of the eternal God and of the church of God. (1) A plague is the domestic dissension between brothers, and civil war between states and provinces. . . . (2) A plague is the lack of counsel when people are stuck in danger and do not know what to do or where to turn. . . . (3) A plague is the most severe tyranny and the harshest government. . . .

(4) A plague of God is the barrenness of the soil and the famine that follows it, the rarity and scarcity of produce, or the lack of all things. Fertility is from God, and so is sterility and famine. . . . (5) A plague is the unhappy progress of business and the lack of workers that proceeds from the unhappiness in the worker. Egypt had fishers and those who prepared equipment or tools for fishing, and also miners and builders of ramparts, and those who prepared linen and silk. But the Lord did not bless them so they labored in vain. . . .

(6) The prophet continues to recount the plagues with which the Lord struck Egypt. For the sixth plague is the foolishness of rulers, by which they seduce and destroy the whole kingdom when they take up war against Assyria on behalf of the Jews. For what the eye is to the body, that is the king or magistrates to the kingdom or the republic. For when the eyes are blind, the body wanders or trips. . . .

(7) A plague is, and itself severe, of course, when in the danger of war itself and the enemies already rushing, the Lord removes the heart and

[12]Mayer, *Commentary upon All the Prophets*, 4:119*; citing Jn 2:11. †See CTS 14:49.

[13]Musculus, *In Esaiam*, 330.

strength of mind so that the men who are normally strong and bold no longer retain any manliness but are rendered more frightened and timid than women. Sermons on Isaiah 19.[14]

The Nile Dries Up as Metaphor. Johannes Oecolampadius: Jerome understands this as Lake Mariout. You can also understand by the dryness of the Nile that it did not flood, contrary to its custom. But I would prefer you understand this as a parable, and in fact what should be received as allegory does not add after much. For just as there are certain evangelical waters in which the Holy Spirit dives, so are there the murky waters of Egypt, that is, of secular disciplines. Therefore, where the word of God has been heard, that kind of water dries up, for the Holy Spirit cleanses the world from sin and reveals the works of darkness. The reed and rushes spring forth in these waters, but it is empty work, the kind of works of hypocrites that are outwardly green and beautiful, but inwardly empty and fragile. . . .

"The fishermen will mourn." The meaning of this parable is the same as the earlier one. For it follows that where waters dry up, the fishermen also cease to do business, and there is no one to make nets, traps, and spears. There are those working with various cloths who sew certain spots into nets to attract fish. The fishermen will mourn, the workers will be idle, and they will have nowhere to live, dismayed that they are forced to beg. Commentary on Isaiah 19:5-8.[15]

The Secondary Cause of Calamity. Zacharias Ursinus: Therefore, in our perceptions and observations of that kind of disasters and the advantages opposed to them, we must not only focus on secondary causes, or attribute them to the lust of the wicked or of our enemies, or to demonic powers, or to our own hard work. But let us raise our eyes to God, the author of these events, and ponder the cause of these evils, I mean our own sins. We must know that these evils can be lessened when we repent of our sins and call on God, and that he brings good from what seems wicked and inevitable, even in addition to and beyond the normal order of secondary causes. Commentary on Isaiah 19:4-10.[16]

Uses of Reeds and Flags. John Trapp: "The reeds and flags shall wither." These were of great use there. For they made their barks and boats of flags, as well as matts, wheels, baskets. . . . And out of reeds, they made their sails, ropes, paper, and a kind of juice serving them for food. . . . As therefore the palm tree is to the Indians a cornucopia, yielding sundry commodities, so are reeds and flags to the Egyptians. Exposition on Isaiah 19:10[17]

Wise Men Disappear. Wolfgang Musculus: "The officials of Zoan are utterly foolish." The prophet resumes what he said earlier . . . , "And the spirit of Egypt within them will be emptied out, and I will ruin their counsel." And what he expressed there briefly, he now explains more fully. The kingdom of Egypt possessed its own rulers, sages, councilors, and heads of their tribes, that is, prefects, which they called *nomarchas* [nomarchs]. These were famous for their reputation of wisdom and understanding. Nearly all the business of the kingdom was carried out according to their counsels. It was by trust in them that all of Egypt remained secure. All were satisfied in their understanding and skill in governing. Therefore the prophet is describing the future, that all these very men will become very foolish, and the Lord will take away their senses. They will drink in a misleading spirit, be robbed of their ability to give sound advice, and lead all Egypt astray. . . .

At last, it should be observed here the seduction of mind and intoxication of errors that come to

[14]Bullinger, *Isaias*, 91r-v, 92v; citing Deut 28.
[15]Oecolampadius, *In Iesaiam*, 129r-v, 130r.
[16]Ursinus, *Iesaiam*, 539.
[17]Trapp, *Commentary or Exposition*, 75*.

those who depend on the wise and prudent of this world, having rejected the light of God's Word. Clearly, in the end it leads to this: when they perceive that the Lord's hand is against them, they become very timid and terrified like women. And so this happens not only—in keeping with the example of the Egyptians—when they are attacked by the disturbances of war but also, in the end, in whatever kind of serious danger where the inevitability of death is imminent. Because they are deprived of the light of God's knowledge and the strength of faith, they are led astray in all their effort. So when they are subjected to dangers, they have no recourse and possess no courage and fortitude. But instead they are overwhelmed with pitiable anxiety and dread. And here, finally, we will note the outcome of those superstitious works by which people wander wretched and blind throughout their whole life. Commentary on Isaiah 19:11-14.[18]

The Shadow and Figure of Worldly Wisdom. Martin Borrhaus: "They give stupid counsel." The apostle Paul discusses this topic more generally under the shadow and figure of Egyptian wisdom when he says in the letter to the Corinthians, "Has not God made foolish the wisdom of this world?" He says this interpreting the mystical oracle of our prophet that happened during the reign of the heavenly Hezekiah, the Messiah, at the time when the adversary should be conquered by the wisdom of the gospel, and the wisdom of this world was made foolish. . . .

The apostle says about this wisdom, "We preach Christ crucified, the power and wisdom of God, a stumbling block to Jews and folly to Greeks." Yet just as this wisdom is foolishness to the world, so by it the deflated wisdom of the world is ruined, and it ruins those who are inflated by it.[†] Here the wise Egyptians are an example, and with the veil removed, the wise in spiritual Egypt are those in the world who have contempt for the Messiah, the wisdom of God, and his gospel, which is the teaching of true wisdom. Oracles in Isaiah on 19:13.[19]

19:16-25 *Egypt Fears the Lord*

Hearing About Judah Causes Terror. Wolfgang Musculus: This is why there is another explanation that is more suitable, which corresponds to the preceding passage and what is said here and explained about how the Assyrian army devastated the land of Judah before Sennacherib invaded Egypt. This devastation, of course, as is not hard to believe, drove panic and terror into Egypt, since it was a neighboring region. We read about these things. . . . "In the fourteenth year of King Hezekiah, Sennacherib king of Assyria came up against all the fortified cities of Judah and took them. And Hezekiah king of Judah sent messengers to the king of Assyria at Lachish, saying, 'I have sinned; withdraw from me, and whatever you impose on me I will bear.'"

The Egyptians were terrified at this rumor when they heard about Judah. They were not just alarmed for fear of the strength of the Assyrians; they would also experience it a little later. When the prophet says, "And the land of Judah will become a terror to the Egyptians, . . ." this seems to have the sense, "And it will happen to the Egyptians before they are invaded by the Assyrians that they will be overwhelmed with panic because they will hear that the land of Judah has been handed over into the hands of the Assyrians by the Lord." Here it should be observed, the kinds of terrors that overwhelm the hearts of mortals when they hear a rumor of strange and nearby disaster that indicates impending evil. It is like how we say in German, "Nach Bösem ahen kommt selten etwas Gutes" [After sensing evil, something good rarely comes]. Commentary on Isaiah 19:16-18.[20]

[18]Muculus, *In Esaiam*, 334, 336; citing Is 19:3.

[19]Borrhaus, *In Iesaiae Prophetae Oracula*, 191, 192-93; citing 1 Cor 1:20, 23-24. [†]Borrhaus has a play on words with "mundi sapientia infatuata perit, et eos qui ea inflantur perdit."

[20]Musculus, *In Esaiam*, 337; citing 2 Kings 18:13-14.

Other Nations in the Old Testament. Zacharias Ursinus: Although it is more hidden than in the New Testament, still this counsel of God has also been revealed clearly enough in the Old Testament through the prophets for the certainty of our faith. This is because other nations must also be admitted into the kingdom of Messiah who was promised to the Israelites, and in fact not just a few persons from individual nations, as happened formerly before Christ was revealed. At that time, a few were converted to the Jewish religion here and there. But so that the profession of faith in Christ will be public among the peoples, regions, and states, it will still be by that principle that the gospel of Christ be extended from the Jews to those, and the nations are added to the religion proclaimed by the Jews. "In that day there will be five cities in the land of Egypt, speaking by the lip of Canaan." . . .

To be sure there is one God, one Christ, one faith, one salvation, and one catholic church of the Old and New Testament. There is one household of God, having one foundation, builder, and Lord. We must not allow ourselves to be torn away from this unity. We must hold to and consider the agreement of the prophetic and apostolic voice. We must establish our faith and comfort in the antiquity, unity, and certainty of the true and Christian religion, which has remained as one and the same from the beginning of the world to its end. And let us seek out the unity of the church in this agreement, but not in ceremonies or in the decrees of people. Commentary on Isaiah 19:18.[21]

The Fear of God at the Humiliation of His Enemies. Konrad Pellikan: When Assyria was returning from Egypt, they besieged Jerusalem. And when, with an incredible miracle, he had been struck by the angel in accord with the prayers of Hezekiah, all the people nearby were amazed by the great strength of the God of Israel and by the justice displayed, based on the news of the miracle. This was especially true for the Egyptians, who had just been humiliated and experienced the powerlessness and emptiness of their own gods. They not only were thoroughly frightened because of this but also then rejoiced at the destruction of their fiercest enemy. Who would not shudder at the hand of the Lord and not rejoice in the death of a tyrant? Likewise, when one discerns the counsel of the Lord of hosts from the fact that something so horrible happens to the wicked, who would not fear that this also threatens him, if he sins against God? Commentary on Isaiah 19:19-22.[22]

Baptism and Speaking with Tongues. John Trapp: "And they will make vows to the Lord of hosts." They devote themselves to his fear and service, taking a physical oath for that purpose, as in baptism and other holy covenants. Happily, based on this, they might be enabled to speak with tongues, the holy tongue especially, as is most necessary for Christians. Here then we have a description of a true Christian, not such as the Jesuits in their catechism give us: "A Christian is the one who believes whatever the Church of Rome commands to be believed, swearing fealty to her." Exposition on Isaiah 19:21.[23]

Egypt as a Sign of Salvation. Johannes Oecolampadius: "It will be a sign." It will be a most certain sign to Egypt that God is favorable to them, if they do not cry out to idols but to the Lord himself in their troubles, and they would be helped by him. It is significant that he says, "They cry out," because it is with great emotion. For it is not praying with a cold heart. You also see this in the passage of Scripture where he sends us no intercessors. For this is the testimony of God dwelling in us, when "we cry out, 'Abba, Father.'" "He will send a Savior." That is, he will be present to help them. For an angel is not always going to be

[21]Ursinus, *Iesaiam*, 566, 567.

[22]Pellikan, *Commentaria Bibliorum*, 3:24v.

[23]Trapp, *Commentary or Exposition*, 76*.

sent, or anyone else to defend them. But he desires that Christ will be there by his grace, just as he promised he would give whatever we asked the Father in his name. . . .

"And the Lord will strike." This is consistent with the earlier verse. For the Egyptians will restore their vows since they trust in divine mercy. And they were making vows, as is common in tribulations. For although they were afflicted, yet the good ones were consulting and not murmuring against God, certain they were being rebuked by God as loved ones. And they did not imitate the flogged Pharaoh, who became even more hardened when he was rebuked with greater flogs. You also see this in the passage where repentance is given and a return to God without an intercessor. Commentary on Isaiah 19:20-22.[24]

Signs as Figurative Speech. Ulrich Zwingli: There are those who are so uncivil that they either do not understand figurative speech because of ignorance or they disguise it through audacity. Here they grab and hurl the spears of contention, saying this is the altar on which we offer ourselves to Christ. Those do not yet understand that it is precisely at the time he was sacrificed, when he died hanging on the cross and he was being offered, that we attribute this word to us by means of metonymy.† It is like when we say, "Today Christ ascends to heaven or rises from the dead." It is not that he rises or ascends to heaven again but that we renew what happened once by naming it again.

As Saint Augustine argues in a certain letter to Boniface, the altar and the image is the cross of Christ, which is honored not only in Egypt but throughout the whole world.† It is not the wooden one where he breathed his last, but one of salvation, which produced life in us at the moment of his sacrifice and death. That is Christ himself. All languages are full of synecdoche speech.‡ A "cross" refers to what one sacrifices. So, the present allegory is drawn from those altars that were inscribed to the gods positioned near the statues. Annotations on Isaiah 19:19-21.[25]

The Order of Four Steps to Healing. Wolfgang Musculus: Here there are four expressions diligently noted. For in the most beautiful order they are joined together. And these are striking, turning, atoning, and healing. This order has no place among the angels, but has it among every kind of mortals, who by their disobedience render themselves subject to the wrath of God and need to come to their senses, even when forced by plagues. So, it is the custom of God to strike the incompliant and heal the converted. According to the world, a surgeon ought to be cursed who was not only failing to care for the wounded but also was wounding the healthy when he was supposed to care for them. But such is our acquired condition that it is necessary that the Lord do a work that is foreign to himself, by which one arrives at what is truly of God. Commentary on Isaiah 19:22.[26]

Few Converted by the Sign of the Comet. Rudolf Gwalther: For his promise is, "As I live, I do not desire the death of sinners but that one turns from his way and live." Each of those things apply to the ways of our times. The Lord nearly struck the whole earth already with famine for a few years, with the plague, with as many wars as foreign affairs. And now he sets loose new "rods," which a fiery comet† foretells like an unlucky star. But those converted by it are few, and many flee this best Father to return to forbidden mediums. To be sure, they ridicule admonitions from the divine word, they hate exhortations, they wickedly reject rebukes and threats, and they pursue

[24]Oecolampadius, *In Iesaiam*, 133r; citing Rom 8:15.

[25]ZSW 14 / CR 101:251.5-20. Zwingli refers to Augustine, *Letter* 98.9 (*NPNF*[1] 1:409-10). An updated translation can also be found in "Letter 98," in *The Works of Saint Augustine: Letters*, vol. 1, *Letters 1–99*, ed. John E. Rotelle, trans. Roland Teske (Hyde Park, NY: New City Press, 2001), 431-32. †*Metonymy* is a figure of speech when a closely related term or attribute is used to refer to something or someone else. ‡*Synecdoche* is when a part of something is used to refer to the whole.

[26]Musculus, *In Esaiam*, 339; citing Ezek 33:11; 18:23.

mockery with hostile intent. Therefore how surprising is it if, when that one is struck, healing does not follow from these plagues but ruin? SERMONS ON ISAIAH 19:22.[27]

EGYPT AND ASSYRIA ARE THE BLESSED CHURCH. JOHANNES OECOLAMPADIUS: Before Sennacherib was destroyed, Assyria was an adversary to Judah and Egypt. But they entered into an alliance when his army was defeated. But how much happier that "Christ is our peace. He made us both one and he broke down the dividing wall." . . . Our blessings are more excellent than the blessings of the Jews. The blessings conveyed to them were earthly; they are heavenly to us. "Blessed people." And this is the blessing of God, by which those people were formerly blessed.

Now the church, which is from Israel and the Gentiles, is here called Assyria and Egypt. Relate each praise to each: For Egypt is now the inheritance of the Lord, and Israel the spiritual people of God. So he says, "The people who were being despised as not a people are now considered a people." And Assyria, whom God did not deem worthy of being named as his work, he now cherishes as the work of his hand and does not allow them to perish. See how much Egypt, or better yet, the world, will have advanced from the lashes by the word of God. COMMENTARY ON ISAIAH 19:23-25.[28]

ALL PEOPLES GATHERED BY THE GOSPEL. KONRAD PELLIKAN: So, before the slaughter of the Assyrians and the other miracles that happened during the time of Hezekiah, hatred flourished between the Egyptians, Assyrians, and Jews. They easily made peace in their conversion to the true God. Moreover, all peoples of the whole world have been more gathered together through Christ into the communion of the church through the gospel and through faith in Christ. By these three nations neighboring Judea, all the other nations that are brought together in unity and made one in Christian love are symbolized. This was the case until the tyranny of foreign doctrines again split and cut apart the catholic and apostolic church. But when this triple of the Jews, the Egyptians, and the Assyrians was blessed, it was a blessing by the Lord as a blessing of heavenly gifts through Christ.

As a consequence, after this the Jews are not able to boast that they are the only people and worshipers of God, but that all nations have been blessed in the seed of David and Abraham, the promises of God that were fulfilled to the fathers. For he promised that all nations would be blessed, not only the Egyptians. He is the Creator of all peoples, not only of the Assyrians. So, the heirs of the Lord are all those who trust in him and are sons of Abraham by faith, not just the Israelites. COMMENTARY ON ISAIAH 19:23-25.[29]

TRUST IN GOD. HEINRICH BULLINGER: This chapter relates to the two previous chapters, . . . where the prophet said that the Ethiopians and Egyptians would be scattered and slaughtered and in the end most seriously afflicted. Now, this chapter is appended to those comments like a kind of conclusion[†] or summary to be the clearest proof and demonstration of what was earlier. All those things were entirely going to happen to the Ethiopians and Egyptians, as he predicted they would.

And then indeed the Jews, too, stunned by the unexpected disaster of their allies, would abandon their courage, supposing that all this would happen to them and their things. Based on this, too, they should understand that in vain they had placed all their hope for all their protection in the nations, since these could not free them; in fact, they could not even avert the impending evil. These events teach the church to trust in God and to cling to him with true repentance, and place no hope in creatures, in alliances, and other things in which

[27]Gwalther, *Isaias*, 112v-113r. [†]There is a note that this comet was seen in November 1577.

[28]Oecolampadius, *In Iesaiam*, 134r; citing Eph 1:14.

[29]Pellikan, *Commentaria Bibliorum*, 3:25r.

people usually trust. And of course, faith in God is the most important, which is also taught in the books of the New Testament, but it is everywhere urged in the prophets as well. Sermons on Isaiah 19:23-25.[30]

How Faith Shines. Philipp Melanchthon: Then faith shines forth in true calling on God, in contempt for false worship, in the illumination of doctrine, in the counsels of governing, in waiting on divine aid, in forbidding alliances, and in rebuking *polypagmosenē* [busyness], which arises from distrust. Because the kings were wicked and wanted to reinforce their position with merely human wisdom, they scattered in all directions and sought help from the Egyptians at one time, at another time from the Assyrians, though both nations deceived them. Argument of Isaiah.[31]

20:1-6 *Assyria Humiliates Egypt*

Sargon Is Sennacherib. Heinrich Bullinger: At around the same time, it seems Hezekiah entered into a covenant with Ethiopia and Egypt, who perhaps at that time were subject to the same King Tharhak. Sargon is Sennacherib, which all interpreters acknowledge. And it is not new that leaders are called by multiple names. And we judge the conjecture to be persuasive that Sennacherib, the powerful and prudent king, only then decided to attack and capture Azotus, the most protected and coastal city, after he had heard those powerful kings, Hezekiah and Tharhak, entered into or established a covenant to weaken the strength of Sennacherib. Sermons on Isaiah 20:1.[32]

The Name of the Commander. Johannes Brenz: But as it is uncertain that Sennacherib was called Sargon, so it is uncertain that the same one is Thartan, about whom is written in the fourth book of Kings and the twentieth chapter of this Isaiah. For it could be that it is not a proper name but the name of an office in the court of the Assyrian king. That is why we will remain in the middle on this. Truly the city Azotus was assaulted by Thartan, the commander of the Assyrian army. It is one of the five particular cities of the Philistines, otherwise known as Ashdod. Commentary on Isaiah 20:1.[33]

Egypt and Ethiopia as Brothers. Martin Borrhaus: What was forewarned about the Ethiopians and the Egyptians, he repeats in this oracle, preaching that that Egypt and Ethiopia would be attacked in the war with the Assyrians. And why the prophet was commanded to utter this prophecy against the Egyptians and the Ethiopians was partly explained above and will partly be explained later. However, he connects here the Ethiopians with the Egyptians because they were neighbors to each other and brothers descended from their ancestor Ham. Oracles in Isaiah on 20.[34]

The Naked and Shoeless Isaiah as a Type. Johannes Oecolampadius: Naked and shoeless Isaiah is a type of our Christ. For in the same way the prophet, although he had not sinned, was made contemptible to be taught the disgrace of others, so also Christ was made a curse for us, hanging naked and humiliated on the cross, because of our iniquities. He did this so that we would recognize how we are the one going down from Jerusalem to Jericho who has fallen into the hands of the robber and is stripped of the garments of innocence and repentance, which could have covered the shamefulness of our sins. Commentary on Isaiah 20:2-4.[35]

The Mystical Sign of Naked and Barefoot. Martin Borrhaus: Interpreters disagree

[30]Bullinger, *Isaias*, 96v. †The word translated "conclusion" is the term *coronis*, from the Greek *korōnis*, indicating a marking in a text to signify the end of a work or a major section.
[31]MO 13:800.
[32]Bullinger, *Isaias*, 97r.

[33]Brenz, *Esaias*, 278; citing 2 Kings 18:17.
[34]Borrhaus, *In Iesaiae Prophetae Oracula*, 200; citing Gen 6–8.
[35]Oecolampadius, *In Iesaiam*, 135r; citing Lk 10:30-37.

about this passage, with some saying that it actually happened, while others say it was a vision. They say that it is similar to what happened when Hosea was ordered to approach a prostitute in order to produce a child from her, and when Ezekiel was ordered to eat bread that was cooked with human dung. I will leave to your judgment which interpretation you think is the right one. Isaiah, who was the teacher of repentance in these great calamities, is described as wearing a cheap and neglected garment as a symbol of repentance, in the fashion of the prophets. They did not move among the people dressed with finer clothing but more cheaply. . . . † These three years when the prophet walked about naked and without shoes signified the time when Egypt would be overrun by Assyria. We read something similar in Ezekiel: "And Ezekiel will be a sign to you."

"So he will threaten." The mystical meaning of Egypt made barefoot and naked by Assyria is revealed as that stripping and shoe stealing by the spiritual Assyria, the antichrist, against his Egypt. We discussed this above in reference to the Apocalypse of John: he strips and takes shoes, that is, he deprives them of the garments and the "shoes of the gospel" until their privates are exposed. The opposite is discerned about those freed from the tyranny of their Assyria, as the apostle says about them, "Stand, therefore, with your feet fitted with the gospel of peace." In the Apocalypse, John likewise says about them, "Blessed is the one who stays awake and keeps his garments on, that he may not walk around naked and be seen in his shame." ORACLES IN ISAIAH ON 20:2-6.[36]

THE NAKED WALKERS. JOHN TRAPP: The Nudipedales in Moravia might as well claim Isaiah as their founder, like the Carmelites do Elijah. . . . He was not stark naked but stripped as a prisoner; his cloak or upper garment was cast off. EXPOSITION ON ISAIAH 20:2.[37]

THE FOLLY OF TRUSTING EGYPT AND ASSYRIA. WOLFGANG MUSCULUS: Here it is not on account of the Egyptians and Ethiopians that the prophet is to prophesy such things and was ordered to wander with a naked body, by which both the sign and the prediction were plainly ridiculous, but on account of the righteous among the people of God, who should be taught not to place their confidence in Egypt and Ethiopia. That is why the Lord does not say here that this three-year sign and portent is *for* Egypt and Ethiopia but *against* Egypt and Ethiopia. A sign given against is different, and different for a particular nation. This was a sign against the Egyptians and Ethiopians for Judah, that is, it was given for the usefulness and instruction of Judah. That is also why it was appropriate for him to be presented before the eyes of the righteous among the people of God and not of the Egyptians. COMMENTARY ON ISAIAH 20:5-6.[38]

[36]Borrhaus, *In Iesaiae Prophetae Oracula*, 200; citing Ezek 24:24; Eph 6:14-15; Rev 16:15; referring to Elijah, John the Baptist, and Zachariah as also wearing cheaper vestments, unlike those of the monks and others of their day. †See also Brenz, *Esaias*, 278.

[37]Trapp, *Commentary or Exposition*, 78*; citing 1 Sam 19:24; Acts 19:16; Mic 1:8.

[38]Musculus, *In Esaiam*, 344-45.

21:1-17 JUDGMENT AGAINST BABYLON, EDOM, AND ARABIA

21 *The oracle concerning the wilderness of the sea.*

As whirlwinds in the Negeb sweep on,
it comes from the wilderness,
from a terrible land.

2 *A stern vision is told to me;*
the traitor betrays,
and the destroyer destroys.

Go up, O Elam;
lay siege, O Media;

all the sighing she has caused
I bring to an end.

3 *Therefore my loins are filled with anguish;*
pangs have seized me,
like the pangs of a woman in labor;

I am bowed down so that I cannot hear;
I am dismayed so that I cannot see.

4 *My heart staggers; horror has appalled me;*
the twilight I longed for
has been turned for me into trembling.

5 *They prepare the table,*
they spread the rugs,[a]
they eat, they drink.

Arise, O princes;
oil the shield!

6 *For thus the Lord said to me:*

"Go, set a watchman;
let him announce what he sees.

7 *When he sees riders, horsemen in pairs,*
riders on donkeys, riders on camels,

let him listen diligently,
very diligently."

8 *Then he who saw cried out:*[b]

"Upon a watchtower I stand, O Lord,
continually by day,

and at my post I am stationed
whole nights.

9 *And behold, here come riders,*
horsemen in pairs!"

And he answered,
"Fallen, fallen is Babylon;

and all the carved images of her gods
he has shattered to the ground."

10 *O my threshed and winnowed one,*
what I have heard from the Lord *of hosts,*

the God of Israel, I announce to you.

11 *The oracle concerning Dumah.*

One is calling to me from Seir,
"Watchman, what time of the night?
Watchman, what time of the night?"

12 *The watchman says:*

"Morning comes, and also the night.
If you will inquire, inquire;
come back again."

13 *The oracle concerning Arabia.*

In the thickets in Arabia you will lodge,
O caravans of Dedanites.

14 *To the thirsty bring water;*
meet the fugitive with bread,
O inhabitants of the land of Tema.

15 *For they have fled from the swords,*
from the drawn sword,

from the bent bow,
and from the press of battle.

16 *For thus the Lord said to me, "Within a year,*
according to the years of a hired worker, all the glory of
Kedar will come to an end. 17 *And the remainder of the*
archers of the mighty men of the sons of Kedar will be
few, for the Lord, *the God of Israel, has spoken."*

a Or *they set the watchman* **b** Dead Sea Scroll, Syriac; Masoretic Text *Then a lion cried out,* or *Then he cried out like a lion*

Overview: This passage returns to judgment against Babylon, and then the prophet continues to issue judgments against other nations. Reformation interpreters give explanations about the different names for Edom and Arabia along with various interpretations about how these prophecies were fulfilled and to what else these descriptions could apply. One of the key themes they identify in this passage is the certainty of future events prophesied by Isaiah. His role as the watchman and the specific statements he makes about years and kingdoms confirm for them that the Lord speaks through him.

21:1-10 *A Prophecy Against Babylon*

Why More Prophecies Against Babylon. Zacharias Ursinus: More oracles against the Babylonians exist than were issued against other nations. . . . The reason for this repetition is not unclear: it is because the Babylonians harassed the Jews more than any other nation before the time of Christ's advent. And because their power was the greatest, they insulted Jehovah, the God of Israel, and his people as though they had defeated him when his people were conquered. Therefore, God foresaw the extent and force of this scandal, and with manifold comforts desired to comfort the weakness of his elect in order to support and sustain their faith. Thus very often, extensively, and with great pains he promised through his prophets the destruction of the Babylonian Empire and the freeing of his church from its tyranny. . . .

And although some think that Babylon is called a desert because there was a desert situated between it and Judea, yet the more likely reason for this term is that Chaldea, and especially Babylon and Babylonia, would be turned into a desert, including the swamps, in spite of that location being protected by nature with the Euphrates River and the most extensive trenches. . . . "O you who dwell by many waters and rich in treasures." . . . So then, the title itself contains a sort of argument and prophecy that, once the inhabitant of the sea, that is, endowed and rich in streams and trenches, Babylon will become a barren wasteland. In other words, no matter how great her wealth, civilization, influence, and strength, still she shall be reduced to a desert and wasteland. Commentary on Isaiah 21.[1]

A Sweeping Southern Wind. Francisco Forerius: "As whirlwinds." The noun *sûpâ* is from the verb *sûp*, which denotes "to cease" or "to end." That [i.e., *sûpâ*] signifies a whirlwind or a storm that sweeps away everything or is devastating. "From the south," *negeb*, is the meridian, or the southern region, as almost all assert. I would say that it especially signifies the south, or the southwestern wind, which stirs up storms, particularly in Palestine. For it seems to have an affinity with the word *nāgap*, which means "to terrify." Then it is also taken as the region itself, and finally as the dry and barren places, because the southern region of Palestine was wilderness. In this passage I certainly take it as the southern wind itself or the southwestern wind. Like whirlwinds, he says, or storms in the south, that is, blowing southerly winds. . . .

"Restore our captivity like streams in the south," that is, very quickly and with no one stopping it, restore us from captivity. . . . "It comes from the wilderness"—namely, the oracle, for this is a speech about the vision, as he will soon explain. And he compares this revelation, which he has seen on Babylon, to a whirlwind or a storm from the south. So he says this is coming from the wilderness and a terrible land. Commentary on Isaiah 21:1.[2]

The Destroyer Is Destroyed. Rudolf Gwalther: The prophet, moreover, gives the conclusion of his vision, saying, "the traitor betrays; the destroyer destroys," meaning of course that he will come or be sent. But then he says, as if to the Jews dwelling in Babylon, that he is pointing with his finger at her approaching enemy. At the same time he also explains the reason for the coming destruction. It is as if he says: "Up until now the

[1]Ursinus, *Iesaiam*, 577; citing Is 13–14; 21; 47; 48; Jer 50–51.
[2]Forerius, *Iesaiae*, 71r; citing Ps 126:4.

Babylonians, transgressing the bounds of justice and charity, have devastated many lands, afflicted many nations, and have oppressed you, too, for a long time with harsh tyranny. But behold, the hour of reckoning is at hand, when punishments will be given to them. And now new destroyers have come, who will take revenge for the injuries they have inflicted on others." And soon, turning his sermon against them, he declares, "Go up, Persian, lay siege, O Media." So, of course, he implies that God would bring the Persians and the Medes to overthrow Babylon. . . .

Finally, all are repaid with the same measure that they measured out to others. This is seen in the most powerful monarchies. The Assyrians established the first, whose tyranny was described earlier. . . . But then God brought the Babylonians against them as destroyers. When they conquered Nineveh, they transferred the empire to themselves. But then God appointed the Persians and Medes as the destroyers of the Babylonians. Then against them was the Macedonians, who fought among themselves after the death of Alexander. Finally the Romans overthrew them, and the wealth of all Europe and Asia was brought together in Rome itself. Sermons on Isaiah 21:2.[3]

The Wickedness of Belshazzar. Johannes Oecolampadius: "All his sighing." In the Hebrew, this can be expressed actively or passively. Either it means that the sighing that the Babylonians inflicted on others when they were desolating all the land would cease, or that the Medes would not be moved to pity for Babylon, so they would not sigh, as is commanded in Jeremiah, "Do not spare their children." For when the king of the Babylonians saw the handwriting on the wall, all hope and the rule of the Babylonians dissipated, and the torment of the nations ceased. On that very night Babylon was captured, and King Belshazzar was killed. Darius the Mede succeeded him in power. . . . The apostles who are going to storm the world are also consoled so that they do not fear, since he has conquered its tyranny.

"Therefore my loins are filled." These are the words of Belshazzar, king of the Babylonians, which the prophet imitates with a mocking spirit. That king had held a banquet for his leading citizens where he was drinking from the vessels of the temple of Jerusalem. But when he saw the writing on the wall—"mene, tekel, parsin"—he was deeply concerned because of Daniel's interpretation. For as the book of Daniel says the face of the king changed, and his thoughts alarmed him. Commentary on Isaiah 21:2-3.[4]

Mocking the Wicked King. Konrad Pellikan: The words of the prophet are mocking the wicked and ferocious king of Babylon. In the manner of the prophets, he says from the king's perspective, "My loins are filled with great weakness and horrible consternation; I have become totally fragile and too weak to resist my adversaries, seeing that things have changed so much that who I was, commanding over all, now I will surrender to all." . . . Such are the judgments of God against tyrants. This punishment remains for the cruel oppressors of the poor, so the Lord powerfully repays the poor by oppressing those oppressors. Commentary on Isaiah 21:3-4.[5]

Security and Blindness as Part of the Penalty. Zacharias Ursinus: This security and blindness is part of the punishment. This is how God prepares the reprobate for the coming punishment while he renders them unprepared and defenseless to receive the unexpected blows. In this lethargy, they seem to be most blessed, not knowing they are next to be the most miserable of all. Such were the Babylonians when their destruction was near. In contrast, the Jewish captives and slaves were so trained that they were not even allowed to sleep secure at night. With the fall of the Babylonians, God suddenly brought them out

[3]Gwalther, *Isaias*, 115v-116r; citing Is 10.

[4]Oecolampadius, *In Iesaiam*, 136v; citing Jer 13:14; Dan 5.

[5]Pellikan, *Commentaria Bibliorum*, 3:25v.

of prison and the fear of death, and into the freedom and the secure power of returning to their homeland. So, the Lord knows how to rescue the rigtheous from temptation, but the unrigheous he preserves for the day of judgment. Commentary on Isaiah 21:3-4.[6]

Isaiah the Watchman. Dietrich Schnepff: The following words are in some way obscure, because there is not sufficient agreement about who orders the sentries to be set and who are set as guards. Where it is written here, "The Lord said to me, 'Go, and set a watchman,'" some understand the princes and lords of Babylon who placed watchmen and guards on their fortifications and then also watchmen on the highest towers. . . . This is a learned view, but when the prophet says that the Lord told him to appoint a guard, how would we refer that to the princes of Babylon? . . .

Finally, Isaiah concludes this passage with these words, "What I have heard from the Lord of hosts, the God of Israel, I announce to you." Therefore, it is enough that this expressly shows that these words of the Lord are to him, not the prince to his watchmen. . . . And so indeed Babylon will deplore those evils. But since the Babylonians are sleeping about the future when setting watchmen, you, prophet, now many years before, hire a watchful guard who will most diligently recite all the impending dangers so that nothing is hidden from the Babylonians, if only they wanted to pay attention. But when I had placed the watchmen on the highest watchtower (or it all happened in the spirit by a prophetic vision), he saw an immense army approaching, but among the rest he saw two leaders of the army, conspicuous men, one who rode on a mule and the other on a camel. The first was a Mede, the second a Persian. Scholia on Isaiah 20:6-10.[7]

Confirming the Certainty of Future Events. Zacharias Ursinus: Not by his own counsel but by God's command, either he places another prophet as a watchman, for it is customary in Scripture that prophets are called watchmen, . . . or the watchman and the watching guard, who had been shown to him by God, reported from the watchtower, with Isaiah listening. This is nothing other than to make the righteous more certain of the same thing, whether from another prophet or, as it seems, from what was directly revealed to Isaiah himself. For God addressed Isaiah either through the sight of that watchman appearing to him in a vision or through another prophet. God could have shown to Isaiah himself without another watchman the future siege, sudden occupation, and devastation of Babylon after many years. But by appointing a watchman and reporting these things, it was more vivid and expressive of things still far removed from a human perspective and thinking. That way there could then be no conjecture or suspicion. . . .

These things pertain to confirming the certainty of this oracle and the entire prophetic doctrine in the minds of the Jewish people, since what was going to happen would be after nearly two hundred years. He describes not only what was heard but also what was seen and already then shown by God—and that not as if it were future or past, but as if it were now in the present and placed before their eyes. The same applies to what follows about the watchman. . . . Therefore, let us listen attentively and reverently to their voice as the voice of God, and strive to understand it rightly. But above all, the teachers and ministers of the churches, whom God has appointed as guards and watchmen of the people and of his house, should faithfully, sincerely, and completely teach and proclaim in a timely way to the church the will of God, diligently and attentively learned from the prophetic and apostolic writings. Commentary on Isaiah 21:6-8.[8]

The Fall of Babylon to Darius. Konrad Pellikan: It was reported with this sense that

[6]Ursinus, *Iesaiam*, 581; also citing Noah; Mt 25; 2 Pet 2.
[7]Schnepff, *In Esaiae*, 321, 326.
[8]Ursinus, *Iesaiam*, 581-82, 584; citing Is 52; 56, Jer 6; Ezek 3; 33.

Darius, king of the Persians and the Medes, was coming with the two largest armies, who obeyed him like beasts. In addition, the watchman responds to those asking what he was seeing that Babylon will most surely fall, along with all its idols and gods, which would then show that they could do nothing. They had fallen with their worshipers and were crushed. The countless Chaldeans and teachers of all manner of superstition could not help them, since the future had long since been predicted by the prophets of Israel and committed to writing. Commentary on Isaiah 21:9.[9]

The Threshed People Is Babylon. Johannes Oecolampadius: He calls Babylon, not Jerusalem, the threshed and the son of the threshing floor, as Jeremiah says. God was going to thresh them with the army of the Persians and Medes in the same way that grain is threshed. Moreover, the son of the threshing floor is the same as what is going to be tread, of course, the grain and the straw that are threshed. Commentary on Isaiah 21:10.[10]

21:11-17 *Prophecies Against Edom and Arabia*

The Identity of Dumah. John Trapp: The shorter his prophecy is, the harder. The Jews apply this prophecy to Rome. They read for Dumah, Rome. They call the Romans the new Idumaeans, and the pope's kingdom, the wicked kingdom of Edom. Some of them say that Julius Caesar was an Idumaean; others that Aeneas came out of Idumaea into Egypt, from there into Lybia, then to Carthage, then to Italy: and that there he built Alba, out of which sprang Rome. The rise of this fiction seems to have been the destruction of the Jewish state by Titus and his Romans, who because of their cruelty were called Edomites by those Jews. Exposition on Isaiah 21:11.[11]

Perpetual Seeking by the Wicked. Johannes Oecolampadius: And then, "When it dawns in the morning, you will inquire, and you will come back, and you will come," that is, there will be no end to seeking. In fact, in death it will follow that they will always desire the end and never reach it. What others explain in the present, "Inquire, be converted, and come," is more fittingly viewed to be explained in the future tense, because of the sequence, since the first word is future. And it is not rare for our prophet to be in the habit of mentioning the perpetual penalty of the wicked. Commentary on Isaiah 21:12.[12]

A Lack of Faith in God's Providence. Wolfgang Musculus: "Since you inquire, inquire, come back, come." The sense is: although that night has ended, still come back to inquire. The particle *im*, that is, "if," seems to be placed here as "since." So it should be read, "Since you inquire, inquire, come back (understand that they went away), and come, namely, by going back to inquire." The prophet wanted to express the future anxiety of the inhabitants of Dumah, where the guards were shouting at every moment and inquiring about the attempts of their enemies. So, we see an example of those who lack faith in divine providence, and in every kind of crisis they waver anxiously so that they cannot ever reach a calmness of mind, which is the daughter of faith, no matter how much they desire to be secure. Commentary on Isaiah 21:12.[13]

The Fleeing Fugitives of Arabia. Dietrich Schnepff: "A burden against Arabia." The Arabs and the Kedarenes are the same people. Kedar was the son of Ishmael, so part of Arabia takes that name. This illustrates the destruction of this people and its circumstances. . . . Then, not only was their exile harsh (which was a source of greatest sadness to those who, like the Arabs, were wealthy), but also their extreme poverty was

[9]Pellikan, *Commentaria Bibliorum*, 3:26r.
[10]Oecolampadius, *In Iesaiam*, 138r; citing Jer 51:33.
[11]Trapp, *Commentary or Exposition*, 80*.
[12]Oecolampadius, *In Iesaiam*, 138v.
[13]Musculus, *In Esaiam*, 351.

decreed, so that they would have no bread to eat except what the inhabitants of the land of Tema, that is, the southern peoples, provided them out of pity.

And the prophet addresses the reason why, when their homeland was left desolate, they brought themselves into the wildernesses. He says, "because they fear a dangerous enemy." That is what he means by "the bent bow." But who those enemies were is unclear. Jeremiah also contains a prophecy against the Kedarenes. . . . But because the time designated in this passage is brief, what happens between the time of this prophecy and its fulfillment we cannot relate to the Babylonian destruction. And so, I instead apply it to the Assyrians, who practiced their tyranny far and wide. Scholia on Isaiah 21:13-15.[14]

Assyrian Devastation Coming to Kedar. Wolfgang Musculus: "When they fled from the sight of the sword, from the sight of the drawn sword . . ." This signifies that the Kedarenes would be attacked in a severe war and that many of them would be struck down by the hand of the enemy. He alludes to that by mentioning the drawn sword, the drawn bow, and the press of battle. For he speaks of the future conflict when the Assyrians were going to strike that people with sword and bow. A conflict of this kind is a terrible sight and intolerable to those who are too weak to be able to defend themselves. And therefore they see nothing other than imminent death. He understands these things by "fled," when it says, "When they fled from the sight of the sword."

The Kedarenes were proud and glorious. This, no doubt, because warlike men also existed. But the prophet threatened them with a more serious weight of war than anything they would be up to facing in the future. . . . From this passage, it is abundantly clear that this devastation of the Kedarenes does not refer to the Chaldeans but to the Assyrians. For the devastations of the Chaldeans, which came after his death by nearly a hundred years, cannot belong to the time of Isaiah. Commentary on Isaiah 21:15.[15]

The Short Time Displays Certainty. Zacharias Ursinus: For this passage, it is certain that Isaiah is speaking about the disaster that is going to be brought on Arabia by Sennacherib, in Isaiah's time. . . . Jeremiah . . . prophesies about the devastation of that same region by Nebuchadnezzar the Great. No one could specify with certainty when this would happen except God, since the execution of the oracle resided in his power alone. Therefore, because Isaiah boldly and steadfastly made this assertion that it would happen a year after he predicted it, he shows that he is not speaking the word of a human but that of God. Of course he would throw himself into open and deserved mockery and danger if he had not been very resolutely persuaded about what he asserted.

Moreover, if anyone doubted the truth of the matter, the space of a year was a short amount of time. The passage of time showed that Isaiah had spoken according to the mouth of the Lord. . . . He had spoken before it had already been confirmed through the circumstance of time and other divine testimonies that God granted Isaiah. Moreover, that he spoke with certainty about what would happen was evident from all the divine disclosures by which God had here to this point testified to his power and truth. Commentary on Isaiah 21:16-17.[16]

[14]Schnepff, *In Esaiae*, 324-25; citing Is 49.

[15]Musculus, *In Esaiam*, 352.

[16]Ursinus, *Iesaiam*, 599; citing Jer 49.

22:1-25 JUDGMENT IN THE VALLEY OF VISION

22 The oracle concerning the valley of vision.

What do you mean that you have gone up,
all of you, to the housetops,

2 you who are full of shoutings,
tumultuous city, exultant town?

Your slain are not slain with the sword
or dead in battle.

3 All your leaders have fled together;
without the bow they were captured.

All of you who were found were captured,
though they had fled far away.

4 Therefore I said:

"Look away from me;
let me weep bitter tears;

do not labor to comfort me
concerning the destruction of the daughter
of my people."

5 For the Lord GOD of hosts has a day
of tumult and trampling and confusion
in the valley of vision,

a battering down of walls
and a shouting to the mountains.

6 And Elam bore the quiver
with chariots and horsemen,

and Kir uncovered the shield.

7 Your choicest valleys were full of chariots,
and the horsemen took their stand at the
gates.

8 He has taken away the covering of Judah.
In that day you looked to the weapons of the
House of the Forest, 9 and you saw that the breaches of
the city of David were many. You collected the waters
of the lower pool, 10 and you counted the houses of
Jerusalem, and you broke down the houses to fortify
the wall. 11 You made a reservoir between the two
walls for the water of the old pool. But you did not
look to him who did it, or see him who planned it
long ago.

12 In that day the Lord GOD of hosts
called for weeping and mourning,
for baldness and wearing sackcloth;

13 and behold, joy and gladness,
killing oxen and slaughtering sheep,
eating flesh and drinking wine.

"Let us eat and drink,
for tomorrow we die."

14 The LORD of hosts has revealed himself in my
ears:
"Surely this iniquity will not be atoned for you
until you die,"
says the Lord GOD of hosts.

15 Thus says the Lord GOD of hosts, "Come, go to
this steward, to Shebna, who is over the household,
and say to him: 16 What have you to do here, and
whom have you here, that you have cut out here a
tomb for yourself, you who cut out a tomb on the
height and carve a dwelling for yourself in the rock?
17 Behold, the LORD will hurl you away violently, O
you strong man. He will seize firm hold on you 18 and
whirl you around and around, and throw you like a
ball into a wide land. There you shall die, and there
shall be your glorious chariots, you shame of your
master's house. 19 I will thrust you from your office,
and you will be pulled down from your station. 20 In
that day I will call my servant Eliakim the son of
Hilkiah, 21 and I will clothe him with your robe, and
will bind your sash on him, and will commit your
authority to his hand. And he shall be a father to the
inhabitants of Jerusalem and to the house of Judah.
22 And I will place on his shoulder the key of the
house of David. He shall open, and none shall shut;
and he shall shut, and none shall open. 23 And I will
fasten him like a peg in a secure place, and he will

become a throne of honor to his father's house. [24]*And they will hang on him the whole honor of his father's house, the offspring and issue, every small vessel, from the cups to all the flagons.* [25]*In that day, declares the* Lord *of hosts, the peg that was fastened in a secure place will give way, and it will be cut down and fall, and the load that was on it will be cut off, for the* Lord *has spoken."*

Overview: In this chapter, Isaiah turns from prophesying against the other nations to addressing his own people and city. The Reformation interpreters offer reasons why Isaiah refers to Jerusalem as the Valley of Vision. The two parts to this passage address the unfaithful hypocrisy of the people for seeking security in material things and the failure of integrity among the leaders, especially evident in Shebna. In contrast, for these interpreters, Eliakim functions as both a model example of one who is legitimately called to office and a type of Christ. Isaiah's grief that God's people were not looking to the Lord provides these commentators with the opportunity to address true repentance and weeping.

The Valley Between Zion and Moriah. Ulrich Zwingli: This is a paraphrase for the city of Jerusalem. And it is called a valley because of Zion and Moriah. For there cannot be mountains without valleys. And "of vision" is truly either from the same Mount Moriah or from the fame and multitude of prophets who nowhere were more constantly accusing sinners, nor anywhere more audaciously slaughtered. For it is received as a true statement that "it cannot be that a prophet should perish away from Jerusalem." Or the prophet saw these visions that are displayed here from that place. Annotations on Isaiah 22:1.[1]

The Valley of Vision as Seminary of the Prophets. Johannes Oecolampadius: Here Jerusalem is called the Valley of Vision, because the prophet sees a prophetic vision in it. It is also a "seminary of the prophets," as Jerome elegantly calls it.[†] And although it was for the most part situated on the mountain, nevertheless it is called a valley as though it had been cast down by enemies. It is uncertain whether this is to be understood to be about the siege in which Sennacherib harassed them or about the devastation by Nebuchadnezzar. Commentary on Isaiah 22:1.[2]

The Future of Jerusalem. Dietrich Schnepff: Then there is mention of "the covering of Judah," which certainly refers to Jerusalem, since it was the metropolis for the tribes of Judah and Benjamin. In addition, he also mentions the city of David and the lower pool, and specifically the houses of Jerusalem. Finally, it also speaks in this passage about Shebna and Eliakim, who were the courtiers of Hezekiah, as is testified. . . . Based on these inferences, we are certainly taught to take this as a prophecy against Jerusalem. Scholia on Isaiah 22.[3]

Two of the Greatest Crimes. Johannes Brenz: Further, in this speech, Isaiah accuses his fellow citizens of two of the greatest crimes: one is security in prosperous things and contempt for the word of God. The other is unfaithfulness and wickedness in adverse conditions. He says these iniquities are such that they are not forgiven as long as they lived. Commentary on Isaiah 22.[4]

[1]ZSW 14 / CR 101:258.3-9; citing Lk 13:33.

[2]Oecolampadius, *In Iesaiam*, 140r. [†]See Jerome, *Commentaria In Isaiam Prophetam* (PL 24: 201); *St. Jerome: Commentary on Isaiah*, trans. Thomas Scheck; ACW 68 (Mahwah, NJ: The Newman Press, 2015), 366.
[3]Schnepff, *In Esaiae*, 330; citing Is 22:8; 36; 2 Kings 18.
[4]Brenz, *Esaias*, 289.

22:1-4 *Failure of the Leaders in a Time of Crisis*

Defeated Without Battle. Rudolf Gwalther: The sense of the words is: I see what is happening. The streets of the city are strewn with the bodies of the dead, though they were not killed by the sword, nor did they fall in battle. But they were besieged by an enemy; they wasted away partly by famine, partly by disease. Then your princes or military commanders, who should have supplied courage to others, fled just the same from the bow or from fear of the archers. And yet they too did not escape but were intercepted by the enemies and defeated. No indeed, however many were found among you, they all fell at once into the hands of the enemy, even those who seemed to have already gone far enough to have escaped danger. And indeed these things are spoken prophetically about those things that would happen afterward. But the history of the city being besieged and captured by the Babylonians corresponds in everything. Sermons on Isaiah 22:1-4.[5]

Dying from Starvation Within the Walls. Konrad Pellikan: "O city," the prophet says with astonishment and sorrow, full "of tumult, shouting, and disaster." A city that up to this point was always dedicated to God, rejoicing, delightful, filled with people and commotion; a city of exultation and without fear of the Lord. Your citizens will indeed be slaughtered, but not by battle and the weapons of an enemy. They will not dare to go out, nor join their hand in combat because of terrifying fear, but will die of hunger and starvation within the walls of the city. Commentary on Isaiah 22:2.[6]

Cowardly Fleeing Leaders. Wolfgang Musculus: "Your slain are not slain with the sword or dead in battle." The prophet predicts their future cowardice that would strike them so that they would not join in combat with their enemy but instead attempt to escape. The sense is: None of you will fight the enemy with a sword; no one will do battle to defend the city. Therefore none of you will be killed with a sword while fighting like a soldier and as an outcome of war. But how they would be killed he consequently explains when he says, "All your leaders have fled together." Read this as in the future: "They will flee," "They will be captured," "They will be found." This means that the leaders will attempt to flee, and while they are fleeing, part of them would be killed by archers, and part of them would be captured and carried away. Commentary on Isaiah 22:2-3.[7]

The Grieving Heart of Pastors and Preachers. Rudolf Gwalther: Further, as Isaiah amplifies the atrocity of this disaster, he assumes the perspective of a mourner, thus teaching that the grief would be so great that even considering it now would make him shed tears. "Go away," he says, "from me, let me weep bitter tears." That is, let me indulge in the most bitter sorrow and grief. "Do not labor to comfort me over the destruction of the daughter of my people." He calls Jerusalem "daughter" in the Hebrew custom, and in fact they are his own people, among whom he was born and to whom he was given by God as a shepherd and teacher. . . . And the pastors of the churches and the preachers of the Word ought to imitate these examples in order to make known that they can be trusted, because they have a paternal heart according to their faith. Sermons on Isaiah 22:4.[8]

Inconsolable Like Job. Johannes Oecolampadius: But the Lord himself also laments for Jerusalem in the Gospel. Out of excessive sorrow, our prophet even rejects comforters, as Job also did: "Burdensome comforters are you all." But we ourselves should also not lament unless we lament, too, that no comfort is given in the lamentation of

[5]Gwalther, *Isaias*, 120v; citing Jer 39; 52; Lam 4.
[6]Pellikan, *Commentaria Bibliorum*, 3:27v.
[7]Musculus, *In Esaiam*, 354.
[8]Gwalther, *Isaias*, 121r; citing Lk 19; Rom 9.

the church, as the apostle said: "Who is weak, and I am not weak? Who is made to fall, and I am not indignant?" And he wished to become accursed for his brethren according to the flesh and those not yet joined to the church. But today, how would we rightly lament foreign evils we do not yet feel, which I do not call that "weeping"? Commentary on Isaiah 22:4.[9]

22:5-14 *Day of Judgment for Not Depending on the Lord*

Relying on Human Strength. Konrad Pellikan: Divine protection will be dissolved and is removed from Judah and Jerusalem, and it will be like a tent draped over a bed that will tenaciously uphold the habitation of God and as a covering for their sins. But it will be revealed because the temple will be destroyed, and the worship of God with the sacrifices and prayers, the priesthood in which they all trusted and those things they hoped would protect them, will cease. For they will not look so much to the temple of God as "to the weapons of the house of the forest." For their faith in God had failed, contrary to the teaching of all the prophets. And all their hope was in the arm of flesh—in weapons, shields, bows, and instruments of war—not in divine help. . . .

"You collected the waters" in an unusual way, by diverting the water between two walls into trenches or by preparing cement to repair what has collapsed. In short, they will not omit anything in the building of the city, except what above all must not be omitted: to call on the Lord, to commit the effort to him, to implore mercy, and to correct one's way of life. Certainly that is looking with all confidence toward him who had given them the city, who had lavished them with water, who had granted peace, and who had defended it for so long with astonishing miracles. That lesson from David never came to their minds, "Unless the Lord builds the city. . . ." Commentary on Isaiah 22:5-11.[10]

Weapons of God's Word and His Works. John Trapp: These are the best defensive weapons, to which God therefore calls people from his goodness or before he punishes them. He calls them, I say, by his Word and by his works, both ordinary and extraordinary, that his justice may be magnified and every foul mouth stopped. Exposition on Isaiah 22:6-7.[11]

Indulging Instead of Repenting. Martin Luther: "But you did not look to him." O hardened hearts that do not acknowledge their guilt, and when punished do not return to him who is afflicting them but nevertheless soothe themselves by saying, "The temple of the Lord is with us; we are the seed of Abraham; the people of the just and holy God." What they suffer they will more quickly ascribe to the devil than to God, and to the sins of others more readily than to their own. They want to be martyrs without God, and they strut along in their own presumption.

"And the Lord will call," that is, a mournful time will be proclaimed, not one in which you will repent of sins but in which you will mourn over the present disaster. So it happens today also, but such preaching is ridiculed just as it was then. No matter how much sorrowful events were foretold that should have provoked them to weeping, they instead were enjoying and indulging themselves, and so on, and out of contempt for the prophets, they ironically said against them, "Let us eat and drink, for tomorrow we die." Paul cited these words against the Corinthians . . . who similarly were mocking the resurrection of the dead. Lectures on Isaiah 22:11-13.[12]

Reasons for Weeping. Martin Borrhaus: But why did the prophet grieve so much the miserable fall of his city? It wasn't because the city didn't deserve what happened to it, was it? Of course not. For he knew that she deserved this and that they were exiled by God the just judge. So

[9]Oecolampadius, *In Iesaiam*, 140v-141r; citing Job 16:2; 2 Cor 11:29.
[10]Pellikan, *Commentaria Bibliorum*, 3:27r; citing Ps 127:1.
[11]Trapp, *Commentary or Exposition*, 83*.
[12]LW 16:177* (WA 31.2:124-25); citing 1 Cor 15:32.

then, why was he in such grief? It was because this people had once been received into the divine covenant, marked by the law, the oracles, the worship, and the promises of the Messiah. When he saw these marks defiled by the guilt of Jerusalem, and the enemy boasting against it and their God so haughtily that he was not powerful enough to defend his own Israelites, just like Jeremiah complained that those were arrogantly boasting when he said, "Your enemies have opened their mouths against you, hissing and gnashing their teeth. 'We have swallowed her!' they cry. 'This is the day for which we longed; we have it; we see it.'" I say that when the prophet sees these disasters happening among the Jerusalemites, he surrenders himself to so much grief when he, along with the righteous among his people, observes that the holy city is in ruin, and the covenant of God, the glory, the kingdom, the priesthood, worship at the temple, and all the marks that had preceded those are disgraced. Oracles in Isaiah on 22:12.[13]

Symbols of Repentance. Johannes Oecolampadius: These are symbols of repentance, not true repentance. For it is certain that Esau did not obtain forgiveness and that grief and wearing sackcloth and similar things are also found among the false prophets. Hence repentance is not rightly defined by these three parts: contrition, confession, and satisfaction, but consists of the renewal of the person as we put to death the old Adam, and we crucify our members that are on the earth, so that we may rise again to new humanity. Joel says, "Rend your hearts and not your garments." Commentary on Isaiah 22:12.[14]

Assumed Security in Irony. Dietrich Schnepff: "Drinking" here is understood as security. Their disregard is described with these words, "Let us eat and drink, for tomorrow we die." Either these are said ironically with disregard for the prophetic threats in the sense that the prophets predict the fall of a most flourishing city, but those are lightning in a bottle. So, since based on their opinion tomorrow we die, come, let us eat and drink. Or these are really the words of desperately malicious people, who, when they see lethal punishments are approaching and threatening, they turn to drinking and pleasure. Scholia on Isaiah 22:13.[15]

No Forgiveness for Excessive Iniquity. Wolfgang Musculus: "Surely this iniquity will not be atoned for you." This form of swearing is frequent in Scripture. He could have said, "This iniquity will not be atoned for you," but he wanted to utter this in the form of an oath to signify the excess of this iniquity, which is never deserving of pardon. He adds, "until you die." He says nothing other than that this iniquity will never be forgiven for you. It is a common expression that we use when we want to signify that we are never going to forgive, because sin is in us. So we say in German, "I don't want to forgive you for the rest of your life." It cannot be argued here, therefore, that one will be forgiven after death. Commentary on Isaiah 22:14.[16]

22:15-25 *Eliakim to Replace Shebna*

Position of Shebna. Heinrich Bullinger: Shebna was a very powerful leader under Hezekiah in the council of the region around the time of the Assyrian war. It says in the present text *hāsōkēn*, that is, the Sochites. They want one to come from Soche, the city of Egypt, and hence to have been a young man, a stranger or foreign born, which we will soon hear when Isaiah, at God's command, assessed in regard to him. Others interpret this as treasurer. For *sākān* signifies "stored-up treasures." Hence *sākān* is a treasure and the treasurer. Cyril, expounding this passage, says Somnas was a Roman treasurer of a treasury, and the keeper of the money, whether sacred and assigned to the

[13]Borrhaus, *In Iesaiae Prophetae Oracula*, 208; citing Lam 2:16.
[14]Oecolampadius, *In Iesaiam*, 142r; citing Joel 2:13; Is 58.
[15]Schnepff, *In Esaiae*, 332 (misnumbered 352).
[16]Musculus, *In Esaiam*, 362.

temple or the palace is uncertain. Others explain this as an apothecary and the prefect of the market, and others as a chamber servant. I am more inclined toward those who express this as a Sochite. He was the same housemaster, or steward of the house (*hausmeister* or *hofmeister*, who is both the marshal and major of the hall, that is, master of the court), or prefect of the royal residence. In Isaiah 36, this same Shebna here is called a secretary, presumably of the king or the royal chancellor. Sermons on Isaiah 22:15.[17]

Comfort for the Righteous Troubled by Treachery. Rudolf Gwalther: But there were also at the time when Isaiah prophesied these things in the court of King Hezekiah, some untrustworthy counselors, whose leader was Shebna, a foreigner from the city of Sokhna in Egypt. He had risen to the highest honor for his remarkable skills, but he was hated by many and not undeservedly suspected. There is no doubt, therefore, that on the occasion of these various prophecies about the present state of things—with everyone afraid of the Assyrians—when these speeches were delivered, many also complained about the treacherous plans of the young men. But they began to murmur among themselves and to plot against their superiors. So then the prophet takes up a new complaint against Shebna, whom he rebukes bitterly, and predicts that Eliakim, a righteous and faithful man whose advice and work would return things to being better, would replace him who had been ignominiously thrown from his position. And so the point of this action is to comfort the righteous so that they are not troubled by Shebna's pride or despair because of his treachery of mind. Instead, they must remember that God will be the avenger and guardian of his people. Therefore, they should also apply this teaching of his to the comfort of those who labor under similar insolence and tyranny. Sermons on Isaiah 22:15-19.[18]

The Contrast of Shebna and Eliakim. Dietrich Schnepff: In addition, with what was above, the praises for Eliakim, the successor to Shebna with regard to the office, are recounted, most likely as what was lacking in the administration of Shebna. For Eliakim is praised because all the vessels, both small and large, will hang on him, that is, because he cares as much for the poor as the rich. And so Shebna was full of pride; undoubtedly he scorned and neglected the poor. Scholia on Isaiah 22:20-24.[19]

Eliakim Called Legitimately. Martin Borrhaus: "I will call my servant Eliakim." Here are two examples set before us of divine righteousness. One is discerned in the crushing arrogance of the proud, and the other in raising up the humble to honor. And it is clear from these examples which vices are especially to be blamed in arrogant ministers in public offices—whether civil or sacred—and which virtues are to be praised in the good servants. The vices of the wicked were exhibited in Shebna; the virtues will now be exhibited in Eliakim. First, we read here, "I will call." In this phrase, we are reminded that the legitimate minister of God is not one who runs without being sent but one who runs having been called by God—not by the world and not by its ruler, Satan. Eliakim was such a man. But those called by the world are those who lust after honor and money and not the pursuit of magnifying the name of God. . . . Those who are called the other way know that they were honestly and legitimately called, and they approach public office not guided by ambition and greed but by the pursuit of doing good for the republic. Commentary on Isaiah 22:20.[20]

The Servant Eliakim. Johannes Oecolampadius: For here Eliakim did not hear a voice from heaven but was asked by the king, moved by divine counsel. Second, he seeks the things of God, whose servant he is when he serves his neighbor, and is

[17]Bullinger, *Isaias*, 105r-v; citing Is 36:3.
[18]Gwalther, *Isaias*, 123r.
[19]Schnepff, *In Esaiae*, 334.
[20]Borrhaus, *In Iesaiae Prophetae Oracula*, 213.

not a servant of the world, or of empty glory, or of his own affections. So he enters through the door, and here Eliakim is called the servant of God when he says, "I will call my servant." . . . Whatever was said of Eliakim in figure, we find truly and more fully in Christ. Later we read about him, "Behold my servant, whom I uphold, my chosen, in whom my soul delights." He reigned, was clothed with beauty, was clothed with strength, and he girded himself and received all power in heaven and on earth. . . . He has the key, and no one closes what he opens. . . . Further, he is a peg and a protector, on whom we should all cast all anxiety. Commentary on Isaiah 22:20-25.[21]

Eliakim as a Type of Christ. Ulrich Zwingli: But I readily grant that the one mentioned here was a type of Christ. . . . Here in this passage, Eliakim is called the peg to be fastened, because it was going to happen that all will depend on him. It is not too much to say, "in the place of the highest faith." For it is evident among the Hebrews no less than the Romans that the greatest expectations were placed on the prefect of the praetorian guard because he bore all the highest things. Therefore, the highest faith was required here. That is why the Lord promises he was going to install a man worthy of the office. Annotations on Isaiah 22:25.[22]

The Key of David Locks the Gospel to Some. Thomas Müntzer: The gospel and the whole of Scripture are closed to some people. . . . Ezekiel unlocked past events. Christ says . . . that the lawyers will take away the key to this book that is locked. They lock up Scripture and say that God must not speak to people in his own person. But where the seed falls on good ground—that is, in hearts that are full of the fear of God—this is then the paper and parchment on which God does not write with ink but rather writes the true Holy Scripture with his living finger, about which the external Bible truly testifies. And there is no more certain testimony, as the Bible verifies, than the living speech of God, when a father speaks to the son in the hearts of people. All of the elected people can read this Scripture, for they increase their talent. But the damned will surely let God's living voice pass. Their heart is harder than any flint, and it repels the chisel of the master for eternity. The Prague Protest.[23]

The Key to the House of David. Konrad Pellikan: By so diligently describing the good prelate, it is certainly to be believed that he also knew in the Spirit of Christ who would be the prelate and the government, as if by a type. For to place a key on one's shoulder is nothing other than to entrust the faithful care of the entire house of God to the holy prelate so that not just anyone can do whatever they want anywhere and try to teach or act in the Lord's house. But based on his judgment and authority, access to the caring and governing of the church is either opened or is closed, so that no one disturbs, no one contradicts or even interferes with his duty. And even so, he presides and teaches as is legitimately prescribed according to the word of the Lord. Commentary on Isaiah 22:22-23.[24]

The Key of David Opens the Secret of God. Melchior Hoffman: Christ has received this key of David from the Father, who reveals himself through the Spirit of God to his own, [unlocking] the door of grace, which is he himself. . . . On one in whom he opens up the secret of God, none can thereafter close the door. Similarly, for one to whom God closes the door of his word and with that all the knowledge of God that his Spirit could create in one—for that one none can open it, neither in heaven nor on earth, neither in

[21]Oecolampadius, *In Iesaiam*, 144r, 145r; citing Is 42:1; Mt 28:18; Rev 3:7; 1 Pet 5:7.
[22]CR 101:261.22-34.
[23]Müntzer, "Prague Protest," 4; citing Is 29:11; 22:22; Rev 3:7; Lk 11:52; Mt 13:5; 25:14-30.
[24]Pellikan, *Commentaria Bibliorum*, 3:28v.

the sea nor under the earth. Interpretation on Revelation 3:7.[25]

A Peg to Hold Firm. Wolfgang Musculus: The purpose of a peg is that things that are too weak to be able to stand in their own strength are suspended and hung from it. This is why it is necessary that it be firmly fixed—not just in any position whatsoever but secured. For it also needs to be secured from elsewhere, by which it can bear whatever depends on it. That was the future condition of this Eliakim, the overseer of the royal house. He would serve to support all those entrusted to his faith. This is why he had to be fixed, and that in a secure place. The Lord says he would do this. "I will fasten him," it says, "like a peg in a secure place." That is, "I will make him one who is suitable to fulfill his duty. I will give him a faithful and wise heart, and I will cause him to use fixed power, and it becomes so secure that no one can dislodge it." Commentary on Isaiah 22:25.[26]

A Better Peg Given the Keys. Konrad Pellikan: The epilogue is about Shebna being cut down because of his treachery. The Lord will replace him with one far more faithful and esteemed. The peg will be driven out by a better peg. And the conspiracy of the scoundrels will fail, and the city will rest when the Catilinarians† are expelled. This is contrary to what people usually say—that worse things always replace better ones. And not only does this indicate that Shebna is going to be cast aside, but also all those depending on him and propped up by his authority. In summary, we learn from this that a magistrate is to be called by God; is to be a father, not a tyrant; is to look after his sons; and the keys are the symbol of his authority, as is also among the apostles. Commentary on Isaiah 22:24-25.[27]

Shebna or Eliakim as the Removed Peg. Wolfgang Musculus: This verse is explained in two ways. Some interpret it about Eliakim himself, because during his time he too was going to be removed from the place of dignity and power he had received, because of the wickedness of the people. In this sense, we are warned that righteous magistrates are taken away because of the sins of the people. It is easy to give common examples of this in our own time. Others refer this to Shebna to go back to what preceded. And this sense seems to be more likely.

So there are two parts to it. The first, that he was going to be taken and moved from what he thought was a secure place. The place seemed to him to be secure—the power he received from the king. The second part is that all those who depended on him would suffer death and destruction through his downfall. That is what is expressed with "and the load that was on him will be cut off." Commentary on Isaiah 22:25.[28]

[25]Hoffman, *Auslegung der heimlichen Offenbarung Johannis*, f.xr-v [89]; English translation from George Hunston Williams, ed., *Spiritual and Anabaptist Writers: Documents Illustrative of the Radical Reformation* (Philadelphia: Westminster, 1957), 202n41.
[26]Musculus, *In Esaiam*, 366.

[27]Pellikan, *Commentaria Bibliorum* 3:27v-28r. †Pellikan's reference to the Catilinarians alludes to the speeches to the Roman Senate by Marcus Tullius Cicero in 63 BC accusing Lucius Sergius Catilina of leading a conspiracy to overthrow the Roman Senate.
[28]Musculus, *In Esaiam*, 366.

23:1-18 JUDGMENT AGAINST TYRE AND SIDON

23 *The oracle concerning Tyre.*
Wail, O ships of Tarshish,
for Tyre is laid waste, without house or harbor!

From the land of Cyprus[a]
it is revealed to them.

2 *Be still, O inhabitants of the coast;*
the merchants of Sidon, who cross the sea,
have filled you.

3 *And on many waters*
your revenue was the grain of Shihor,
the harvest of the Nile;
you were the merchant of the nations.

4 *Be ashamed, O Sidon, for the sea has spoken,*
the stronghold of the sea, saying:

"I have neither labored nor given birth,
I have neither reared young men
nor brought up young women."

5 *When the report comes to Egypt,*
they will be in anguish[b] *over the report*
about Tyre.

6 *Cross over to Tarshish;*
wail, O inhabitants of the coast!

7 *Is this your exultant city*
whose origin is from days of old,

whose feet carried her
to settle far away?

8 *Who has purposed this*
against Tyre, the bestower of crowns,

whose merchants were princes,
whose traders were the honored of the earth?

9 *The Lord of hosts has purposed it,*
to defile the pompous pride of all glory,[c]
to dishonor all the honored of the earth.

10 *Cross over your land like the Nile,*
O daughter of Tarshish;
there is no restraint anymore.

11 *He has stretched out his hand over the sea;*
he has shaken the kingdoms;

the Lord has given command concerning Canaan
to destroy its strongholds.

12 *And he said:*

"You will no more exult,
O oppressed virgin daughter of Sidon;

arise, cross over to Cyprus,
even there you will have no rest."

13 *Behold the land of the Chaldeans! This is the*
people that was not;[d] *Assyria destined it for wild*
beasts. They erected their siege towers, they stripped
her palaces bare, they made her a ruin.

14 *Wail, O ships of Tarshish,*
for your stronghold is laid waste.

15 *In that day Tyre will be forgotten for seventy years,*
like the days[e] *of one king. At the end of seventy years, it*
will happen to Tyre as in the song of the prostitute:

16 *"Take a harp;*
go about the city,
O forgotten prostitute!

Make sweet melody;
sing many songs,
that you may be remembered."

17 *At the end of seventy years, the Lord will visit Tyre,*
and she will return to her wages and will prostitute
herself with all the kingdoms of the world on the face of
the earth. 18 *Her merchandise and her wages will be holy*
to the Lord. It will not be stored or hoarded, but her
merchandise will supply abundant food and fine clothing
for those who dwell before the Lord.

a Hebrew *Kittim*; also verse 12 **b** Hebrew *they will have labor pains* **c** The Hebrew words for *glory* and *hosts* sound alike **d** Or *that has become nothing* **e** Or *lifetime*

Overview: This chapter concludes Isaiah's oracles of judgments against the nations by addressing Tyre and Sidon. Several themes from the previous chapters are reiterated, such as the justice of God to bring punishment and his previously planned use of foreign nations to carry it out. The specific destruction of markets and businesses compels some to clarify that business itself is not bad, but rather the way the people of Tyre were carrying out their business. This passage also provides the Reformation interpreters with an example of a people who later return to the Lord. Some identify the reference to seventy years with the Babylonian captivity, while others do not. They reinforce, though, that this is another passage that should call God's people to repentance.

23:1-7 *The Collapse of Tyre and Sidon*

A Word to Tyre and Sidon. Johannes Oecolampadius: At the same time, the lust and pride of the Tyrians is punished, and it is shown that nothing is stable in the whole world. Where is Babylon? Where is Memphis? Where is Tanis? Where is Dumah? Where is Moab? And now also Tyre and Sidon are overthrown, so that we may understand, along with them, that nothing under the sun lasts forever and that the world is passing away. But he addresses the neighboring cities as if Tyre had been lamented. . . . Tyre has Tarshish and Cyprus to the north, Egypt to the southwest, and Assyria to the east. The sailors were commanded to weep and howl, because the harbor and the storehouse of Tyre had been devastated, from which they had a great profit. Commentary on Isaiah 23:1-2.[1]

The Antithesis of Joy and Devastation for Tyre. Dietrich Schnepff: Although not all of these antitheses have been expressed, they have nevertheless been presented quite clearly. It ought to be noted that the prophet, when describing that previous happiness, follows those passages that we observe elsewhere in the praise of cities. Scholia on Isaiah 23.[2]

Like the Prodigal Son. Heinrich Bullinger: For at the beginning, he says that Tyre, with its strength, goods, and businesses, is going to be destroyed and entirely laid bare. Then it is going to be restored after seventy years and is going to be saved by Christ, whose virtue is going to surpass the duty of charity. Accordingly, this speech is a remarkable example of divine justice, where the wicked are punished, but also divine mercy. He does not retain his anger forever but shows compassion to those whom he has afflicted. Therefore, imagine Tyre to be the prodigal son whom our Lord Jesus Christ sets before us . . . , as one who certainly was afflicted and miserable at first because of his criminal sins, and divine justice shines on him. Yet he soon received grace from his parent, where again the compassion of God appears. Therefore, let us believe that we also will surely receive grace from the Father of compassion,

Table 2. Joy and devastation in Tyre

1. Before Tyre was a magnificent dwelling.	1. Now there is no house.
2. Tyre was previously a market city.	2. Now all the merchants are ordered to be quiet because there is no more market.
3. To the peoples it was a city and stronghold of the sea.	3. Now it has neither young men nor young women.
4. Once it was hidden from all.	4. Now all are disturbed because of her, especially the Egyptians.
5. It was ancient and had never been conquered.	5. Now it will be conquered and forced to go into exile.
6. Its citizens were kings.	6. Now they are the most despised people.

[1]Oecolampadius, *In Iesaiam*, 146r.
[2]Schnepff, *In Esaiae*, 345.

if we do not imitate the people of Judah, hear these works of God in vain, and regard these divine examples in vain. Sermons on Isaiah 23.[3]

Known for Astronomy and Arithmetic. Martin Borrhaus: The residents of Sidon reportedly were especially prosperous because of their nighttime navigation and their use of arithmetic, both of which had commercial value, and also because of their dockyard and knowledge of astronomy and mathematics. In the same sense that the Egyptians reportedly discovered geometry, these people were challenged by the need to measure their fields since their division was blurred with the flooding of the Nile when the sun passed through its summer signs. And so the literature records that astronomy and arithmetic came to the Greeks from the Phoenicians, as geometry came down to them from the Egyptians.

Now, to illustrate further the destruction of Tyre, the prophet recounts the powerful nations that brought their goods to Tyre. The city was also then deprived of these things along with the disaster and mourning of its neighboring islands. Oracles in Isaiah on 23:2-4.[4]

Business Is Not Bad. Heinrich Bullinger: For business in itself is not bad; in fact, it is necessary that there be farmers, then shepherds of herds, and citizens producing various handcrafts, likewise commerce. Now, there is indeed one commerce of necessary things and another of unnecessary things, which import and increase luxuries and pleasures. Merchants of this kind were excluded from the polity of some republics, and one does not profit from supporting such ones, who ruin poor farmers and stupid citizens. Monopolies, by many names, are the most dangerous and present scourges of the republic. Sermons on Isaiah 23:3.[5]

The Market and Protection Destroyed. Johannes Oecolampadius: For it says, "Be ashamed, Sidon; behold, I destroyed your market and protection, and I became as a woman who is not pregnant nor gives birth nor raises young men and young women." For Tyre gave birth to the most powerful colonies which here are understood by those who are pregnant and giving birth. Commentary on Isaiah 23:4.[6]

No Future for Tyre. Wolfgang Musculus: He calls Tyre "the sea and the stronghold of the sea." For it reigns over the sea. What does it say? "I have neither labored nor given birth; I have neither reared young men nor brought up young women." That is, I was devastated, childless, barren, and empty.

Some explain this to be about the colonies that Tyre produced, as if one were complaining that it, too, is deserted and destitute of all help, and as if no cities that she gave birth to like daughters remain, since it gave birth to not a few, even Carthage itself. That exposition of the reading does not square badly. They read it not in the present but in the preterite. Yet it seems simpler that we read it in the present, and we explain it with the sense that I have assigned: for the preservation of posterity and the public state, first is to be in labor, second is to give birth, third is to nurture, and fourth is to raise up young women. But Tyre was going to be so desolated and devastated that it would be deprived of all these things. The seer signifies that it was entirely going to be devastated and demolished to the extreme, all the way to extermination. Commentary on Isaiah 23:4.[7]

Egypt's Market Also Suffers. Konrad Pellikan: When they hear the rumor of Tyre being ruined, the merchants of Egypt will suffer together with Tyre no differently, not only on account of the mutual commerce of both—for that

[3]Bullinger, *Isaias*, 109r; citing Lk 15.

[4]Borrhaus, *In Iesaiae Prophetae Oracula*, 220; citing Strabo, *Geographica* 16.

[5]Bullinger, *Isaias*, 109r.

[6]Oecolampadius, *In Iesaiam*, 147v; citing Pliny the Elder, *Natural History* 5.19 (LCL 352: 282-283).

[7]Musculus, *In Esaiam*, 370.

is the reason the port there is called Egyptian—but also because they, too, will be afraid of the coming of the Babylonians for them and the devastation exemplified with the city of Tyre. Perhaps also some of the wealth of the Egyptians was ruined in Tyre, as happens when markets are captured and destroyed. Commentary on Isaiah 23:5-7.[8]

23:8-14 *The Lord's Plan Against Tyre*

God's Effective Counsel. Johannes Oecolampadius: It is true that the Lord has decreed this; his counsel is so effective that it cannot be thwarted, no less than necessity itself. Therefore, using the example of the most powerful city of Tyre, the prophet teaches well that nothing is stable in this world. For God humbles the proud of this world. And the overthrowing of so many states is not accidental, as this passage clearly indicates. Commentary on Isaiah 23:8-9.[9]

An Example of God's Providence. Konrad Pellikan: All things are governed by the counsel of the Lord; all things are subject to the providence of God, in which he empties and confounds the things that are exceptional and illustrious, he humbles and debases the proud of the earth, as long as they do not acknowledge the author of their greatness. This is not only said of Tyre but is a general statement and example, because those similar in sin will be punished similarly. The fear of God renders the righteous more secure, as he brings down the proud everywhere, just like in Tyre. Commentary on Isaiah 23:8-9.[10]

The Laughter of the Righteous and the Wicked. Johannes Brenz: If the righteous perish, the wicked laugh. If the wicked perish, the righteous laugh. So, what is the reason that laughter by the wicked is reproved and also divinely punished, yet the laughter of the righteous is judged to be just? Here the source and the end of the laughter must be considered. The source of the laughter of the wicked is impiety, hatred toward God and his gospel. The end is that the glory of God is obscured and his gospel erased for the ruin of the righteous. Since those things are wicked, their laughter is also wicked and most worthy of punishment. Yet the source of the laughter of the righteous is faith, which is invited by the Word of God. The end is that the glory of God is illuminated, and the truth of his promises made evident to the ruin of the wicked. Since those things are righteous, the laughter must also be righteous. Commentary on Isaiah 23:9.[11]

The Virgin Daughter Is Sidon. Wolfgang Musculus: There are those who refer such things to Tyre, because it was as if they were daughters of Sidon, since they were raised by the Sidonians. Truly it is better that, in the same way where we read in Scripture "the virgin daughters of Zion" and "the virgin daughters of Judah," we do not understand that to be about anything other than Zion and Judah themselves, so also here by the "virgin daughters of Sidon," we understand it to be Sidon itself. Commentary on Isaiah 23:10-12.[12]

23:15-18 *Seventy Years*

The Seventy Years a Sign to Judah. Martin Borrhaus: Here, then, we learn first that, just as it was for the people of Judah, so also the exile for the Tyrians was foreshadowed, that each captivity would be seventy years. For we read this about the Jews in Jeremiah, "For thus says the Lord, 'When seventy years have begun to be completed for Babylon, I will visit you.'" So we learn that this prophecy is not about Alexander the Macedonian, to whom Tyre went into exile, but Nebuchadnezzar, as the times indicated are clear from Ezekiel and from the number seventy years

[8]Pellikan, *Commentaria Bibliorum*, 3:28r.
[9]Oecolampadius, *In Iesaiam*, 147r.
[10]Pellikan, *Commentaria Bibliorum*, 3:28r-29v.
[11]Brenz, *Esaias*, 301.
[12]Musculus, *In Esaiam*, 373.

for the Babylonian Empire. Oracles in Isaiah on 23:5.[13]

The Length of a King's Life a Reminder of Mercy. Heinrich Bullinger: He does not keep his anger forever, nor does he eternally retain the memory of the wrong received. . . . These are seventy years of one king, that is, how much and for how long a king or a human is able to live. And the addition of this phrase softens the time of punishment. For it seems that it is not extended indefinitely, because it does not exceed the life of one person. Rather, imagine that you will be under the tyranny of some king for seventy years, because when you hear that the end of tyranny is certain, you endure it more calmly. Yet although you are not brought into that freedom, you do, however, understand that your offspring will experience it. So then, whenever we are forced into adverse circumstances, we do not despair, but we are always of good hope in God's goodness and power. Sermons on Isaiah 23:15.[14]

One Kingdom for Seventy Years. John Mayer: Expositors generally agree about the seventy years as being the time that the Babylonians reigned after this, when no eminent place, such as Jerusalem and Tyre, would be rebuilt out of fear of rebellion and trouble. But in expounding these words, Vatable says that "as the days of one king" may be referred to David, who lived seventy years. Calvin applies this to any person as much as a king, since it is said . . . that one's age is to be seventy years, but here it is said about one king and not one person, because Tyre had a king. I prefer that of Jerome, who understands by one king, one kingdom of the Chaldeans lasting so long that in all that time it triumphed over Tyre as over Jerusalem in ruin. For why David should be meant here, or people indefinitely, especially one well maintained as a king, as Cornelius à Lapide has it, I cannot see.[†]

But why the Chaldean kingdom should be meant, we may see good reason, because although Evil-Merodach reigned after Nebuchadnezzar, and Belshazzar after him before this was fulfilled, yet they were all but as one king, because they were of the same line, in the manner that Scripture thus sets forth any monarch with his issue succeeding him in his kingdom, until the last one is cut off. Commentary on Isaiah 23:15.[15]

Tyre Forgotten for Seventy Years. Johannes Oecolampadius: "And it will be in that day." Now again, they are declared prosperous, for he displays the length of the disasters of Tyre, namely, seventy years, which is how long the Jews were captives in Babylon. And it says seventy years are the days of one king, because those who have reigned for a long time do not reign for more than seventy years, since a life rarely progresses beyond the seventieth year. And so the philosophers in numbers have judged the tenth seventh year to be very dangerous and fatal. After that age, the Psalter promises nothing but toil and pain. . . .

Moreover, the comparison follows: As often happens, lovers do not come to a prostitute and forget her. When, after some time, she sees them passing by, she lures them with a song. So, after seventy years, when Tyre is rebuilt, it will again lure merchants to itself. Moreover, he calls the display of wealth and merchandise, song and lyre, and business truly fornication, because what is most precious to the Tyrians are goods and things that pertain to luxury. Commentary on Isaiah 23:15.[16]

The Figure of a Prostitute for Business. Martin Borrhaus: "As in the song of the prostitute." Isaiah shapes his prophecy with a metaphor obtained from a prostitute. The metaphor is taken in a good sense, not a bad one. For

[13]Borrhaus, *In Iesaiae Prophetae Oracula*, 223; citing Jer 29:10.
[14]Bullinger, *Isaias*, 111r.

[15]Mayer, *Commentary upon All the Prophets*, 4:149*; citing Ps 90:10; Dan 2:39. [†]See Vatable, *Commentarius in Iesaiam*, in *Uratislaviensis Tractationum Theologicarum* (Neustadt, 1589), 2:368; CTS 14:157 (CO 36:394); Musculus, *In Esaiam*, 374; Jerome, *Isaiam* in PL 24:279-280.
[16]Oecolampadius, *In Iesaiam*, 148r-149v.

the restoration that is predicted in this oracle is that of Tyre, which when restored pleases God. This is so she may become a virtuous woman, not displeasing like a shameful prostitute. For so we read later that her business and commerce shall be sacred to the Lord. Therefore this is the principle: with its song of commerce, Tyre will attract merchants to it like prostitutes entice their lovers to their embrace. We read above that the commerce of Tyre was interrupted. But here, "And she will return to her merchants." Here to fornicate is to do business. So Tyre is called a prostitute, since she is not doing business with one merchant but is involved in doing business with many. ORACLES IN ISAIAH ON 23:15-16.[17]

A NEW KIND OF BUSINESS THAT PROSPERS. KONRAD PELLIKAN: The city of Tyre will employ a new kind of business when the worship of the one true God is added. It is going to be named by the apostles and apostolic men, and they are going to offer worthy sacrifices to God, without building an altar or a temple, nor visiting Jerusalem. But with its own wealth, it will help the poor, feed the hungry, and clothe the naked. For this is the true worship of God preached by the prophets and apostles. God is pleased with these sacrifices. With such use, riches are sanctified and increased, when the Lord brings prosperity. He is to be served with this understanding. And we must seek first the kingdom of heaven that temporal things may be added by the Lord, who owns everything. COMMENTARY ON ISAIAH 23:17-18.[18]

RESTORATION REFUTES THE NOVATIANS. JOHANNES OECOLAMPADIUS: Some gather an argument here against the Novatians that pardon should be denied to none who ask for it. For if Tyre was restored after seventy years, how much more if a soul shows repentance over its sins? For the number seventy is sacred to repentance, as seven is also. And so meanwhile, let us consider by Tyre, the soul, which, because of its sins is deprived of spiritual goods and is driven into exile. But through repentance, which is signified by seventy years, it can be restored to a pristine condition, of course, as long it rests from sins and takes sabbath rest from its work. COMMENTARY ON ISAIAH 23:15-18.[19]

[17]Borrhaus, *In Iesaiae Prophetae Oracula*, 223.

[18]Pellikan, *Commentaria Bibliorum*, 3:28v-29r.

[19]Oecolampadius, *In Iesaiam*, 149v.

24:1-23 JUDGMENT ON THE EARTH

24 *Behold, the LORD will empty the earth[a] and make it desolate,*
and he will twist its surface and scatter its inhabitants.

2 *And it shall be, as with the people, so with the priest;*
as with the slave, so with his master;
as with the maid, so with her mistress;

as with the buyer, so with the seller;
as with the lender, so with the borrower;
as with the creditor, so with the debtor.

3 *The earth shall be utterly empty and utterly plundered;*
for the LORD has spoken this word.

4 *The earth mourns and withers;*
the world languishes and withers;
the highest people of the earth languish.

5 *The earth lies defiled*
under its inhabitants;

for they have transgressed the laws,
violated the statutes,
broken the everlasting covenant.

6 *Therefore a curse devours the earth,*
and its inhabitants suffer for their guilt;

therefore the inhabitants of the earth are scorched,
and few men are left.

7 *The wine mourns,*
the vine languishes,
all the merry-hearted sigh.

8 *The mirth of the tambourines is stilled,*
the noise of the jubilant has ceased,
the mirth of the lyre is stilled.

9 *No more do they drink wine with singing;*
strong drink is bitter to those who drink it.

10 *The wasted city is broken down;*
every house is shut up so that none can enter.

11 *There is an outcry in the streets for lack of wine;*
all joy has grown dark;
the gladness of the earth is banished.

12 *Desolation is left in the city;*
the gates are battered into ruins.

13 *For thus it shall be in the midst of the earth among the nations,*

as when an olive tree is beaten,
as at the gleaning when the grape harvest is done.

14 *They lift up their voices, they sing for joy;*
over the majesty of the LORD they shout from the west.[b]

15 *Therefore in the east[c] give glory to the LORD;*
in the coastlands of the sea, give glory to the name of the LORD, the God of Israel.

16 *From the ends of the earth we hear songs of praise,*
of glory to the Righteous One.

But I say, "I waste away,
I waste away. Woe is me!

For the traitors have betrayed,
with betrayal the traitors have betrayed."

17 *Terror and the pit and the snare[d]*
are upon you, O inhabitant of the earth!

18 *He who flees at the sound of the terror*
shall fall into the pit,

and he who climbs out of the pit
shall be caught in the snare.

For the windows of heaven are opened,
and the foundations of the earth tremble.

19The earth is utterly broken,
the earth is split apart,
the earth is violently shaken.

20The earth staggers like a drunken man;
it sways like a hut;

its transgression lies heavy upon it,
and it falls, and will not rise again.

21On that day the LORD will punish
the host of heaven, in heaven,
and the kings of the earth, on the earth.

22They will be gathered together
as prisoners in a pit;

they will be shut up in a prison,
and after many days they will be punished.

23Then the moon will be confounded
and the sun ashamed,

for the LORD of hosts reigns
on Mount Zion and in Jerusalem,

and his glory will be before his elders.

a Or *land;* also throughout this chapter **b** Hebrew *from the sea* **c** Hebrew *in the realm of light,* or *with the fires* **d** The Hebrew words for *terror, pit,* and *snare* sound alike

OVERVIEW: The main theme of judgment continues with this chapter. Some Reformation interpreters see this as judgment on the Hebrew people, while most understand this chapter as an expansion of God's judgment against the whole earth rather than a particular people. In either case, they see this as another occasion to hear about the just judgment of God that will come. Several identify this as God's rejection of the Jewish people because of their rejection of Jesus as the Messiah. Their perspective on the time frame of this prophecy shapes their understanding of the applications regarding the laws and covenant, the liberation, and the signs. This passage gets applied to Judah in Isaiah's time, to Babylon, to the Jews at the time of Jesus, or to the time of the last days of the millennium and final judgment.

DAILY AND UNIVERSAL JUDGMENTS. ULRICH ZWINGLI: It seems this chapter is intended for the whole world, not only as final judgment but also a daily one. It is as if Isaiah proceeded this way: Let no one believe that only the Valley of Vision, Damascus, Tyre, Babylon, and the rest of the peoples then are going to experience bad things from the Lord. Anything can happen to anyone. Therefore, whoever has come in an audacious way, refusing to be alert to divine justice, they will be punished with an equal penalty. Therefore what until now was predicted for specific peoples is predicted for the whole world. Yet here, too, the prophetic fury penetrates, so that he does not allow even the angels to go away unscathed. Therefore it becomes clear in this chapter what I said above: it signifies judgment, whether the day of the Lord, both the daily and the final, for what is said here corresponds to times and ages; sometimes it is about the present, then about the future, then finally about the last of days. ANNOTATIONS ON ISAIAH 24.[1]

THE DEVASTATION OF THE HEBREW PEOPLE, NOT THE WHOLE EARTH. DIETRICH SCHNEPFF: Everyone understands that this chapter contains a threat and threatens a certain land. But to whom these sadnesses are announced is not expressed. And so respectable authors apply these words to what has come before. They think that the prophet Isaiah, as a kind of epilogue, combined together all the nations whom he had previously threatened, and against each of whom he had previously predicted deadly punishment, and now delivers a sad sermon in general to all people. Others

[1]CR 101:266.22-34.

understand this to be about final judgment and the end of the world.

We will provide some sufficiently evident reasons that the prophet is preaching about the rejection of the Hebrews, and the kingdom of Christ in the whole world. If we demonstrate that, then the above positions are not going to hold. At the beginning, there is mention of the priest, which suggests that Isaiah was speaking about his own people, among whom the true priesthood existed. . . . It immediately follows that they transgressed the "everlasting covenant," that is, the covenant with Abraham and the patriarchs, entered into at the beginning. From this, the consequence is no doubt deduced that this chapter should be taken to be about the Hebrew people, who alone were in that covenant (for the Gentiles were strangers to the divine promises). Scholia on Isaiah 24.[2]

24:1-6 *Judgment on the Earth*

The Consummation of All Things by Fire. Johannes Oecolampadius: After the prophet enumerated the destruction of certain cities, as is his custom, he addresses the general desolation of the whole earth. Most of the Hebrews consider this a hyperbolic saying that refers to the captivity of the ten tribes. We easily accept that, as it represents a certain type, but from the phrase of the speech, it is clear that something more serious is being predicted. For he basically says this: "Why do I lament when one city or another perishes, and that Babylon, Damascus, Tyre, and others about which I spoke, are destroyed? Behold, now I see the consummation of the whole earth." For the Lord, who established heaven and earth, consuming all things by fire, empties and devastates the earth with all its furnishings. And so he afflicts and twists, as a towel is usually twisted or as some herb from which juice and liquid are squeezed. For the earth, too, will have nothing attractive until it is cleansed. You have this devastation of the earth in . . . , "The heavens and the earth that now exist are stored up for fire, until the day of judgment." . . . "In the beginning, you, Lord, laid the foundation of the earth, and the heavens are the works of your hands. They will perish, but you remain." Commentary on Isaiah 24:1.[3]

A Far Greater Plague. Thomas Cooper: The prophet sets forth this plague of God's heavy judgment on the Jews in the form of a waste or desolation made in war. For while the Jews, after they were rejected, indeed were brought to miserable waste and desolation by war under Vespasian and Titus, yet this passage is not to be understood only to be about that. But it should also and especially be understood to be about their spiritual calamity of being utterly refused as the people of God and turned away from all the heavenly riches, glory, blessing, and comfort that they had previously through the law, the promise, and the covenant almighty God gave to them. This was a far more grievous plague than the spoiling of their country and the subversion of their city. Second Sunday in Advent at Evening Prayer.[4]

Equal Judgment but Not Equal Punishments. Heinrich Bullinger: Further in this judgment by God, the prophet affirms that no human is going to be spared, in kind, order, or age, but each and every one will be punished according to their merits. Therefore he enumerates various states of humans and always brings them together as equal, such as priests and people, lords and servants. . . . The apostle teaches the same when he says to the Colossians, "The one who sinned will carry his sin," and, "he is not a respecter of persons." In the Law and the Prophets throughout, judgments are presented as an example of the ultimate judgment, and they are ordered not to show favoritism in judgment. So then, corrupt leaders will be spared no less in the judgment of God than

[2]Schnepff, *In Esaiae*, 358.

[3]Oecolampadius, *In Iesaiam*, 150v; citing 2 Pet 3:7; Ps 102:25-26.
[4]Cooper, *Brief Exposition*, 17*.

those who are from the humblest and lowest common people. For the person is not considered, but what he did. . . .

Next, although there is no "respecter of persons" before God, yet it does not follow that the punishments of persons are equal. For the king will be punished as a king, just as wisdom likewise attests, "The powerful will be punished powerfully or severely." And the servant who knows the Lord's will and does not do it will be beaten with many blows. And it will be more tolerable for Sodom on the day of judgment than for any of the cities rejecting the gospel. Therefore let us fear God. Sermons on Isaiah 24:1-3.[5]

Just Judgment Again. Konrad Pellikan: That land, where these things go unpunished, will be devastated wretchedly on some occasion when the judgment of God comes, and everything that had been swept together by unjust claim will be plundered. For so the Lord swore; so he decreed by his immutable will, "The earth will be oppressed by an invincible tyranny and will fall into the hands of cruel lords. The harshness of heaven will sterilize it, and what springs forth from the earth will wither away." And those who were the first and best among men will die. And in their place will be substituted hypocrites, fools, the inconsiderate, the ambitious, and the wicked. For it is most just that those who contradict the wishes and laws of God and oppose his works, that earth and heaven respond to them against their wishes, that creation is armed for the vindication of the Creator, and that human disobedience be worthily punished by the Lord. Commentary on Isaiah 24:3-4.[6]

Kinds of Laws. John Trapp: "For they have transgressed the laws," natural and moral, those bounds and banks set to keep people within the compass of obedience. "But the unjust knows no shame." . . . He is lawless, yokeless, untamable, intractable, like the wild colt of a donkey, as a horse and mule. . . . Here, some understand by "laws" the judicial laws; by "statutes," the ceremonial; and by "everlasting covenant," the Decalogue. Others understand by "laws" the municipal laws of the commonwealth; by "statutes," the laws of nations, such as not violating an ambassador and so on; and by "everlasting covenant," the law of nature, which is that "light that comes into the world that enlightens every person." Exposition on Isaiah 24:5.[7]

The Everlasting Covenant as the Law of Nature. Ulrich Zwingli: By "everlasting covenant" we do not take it so much to be what God agreed with Noah, Abraham, Moses, and David, but what is written on our hearts, namely, the law of nature, from which all laws and codes descend. Annotations on Isaiah 24:5.[8]

The Law of Nature Needs Renewing. Johannes Oecolampadius: Here he does not speak about human statutes and traditions, for they are not so great that they are unable to vary by some urgent occasion or usefulness or public necessity. No, as long as they are laws, and not beyond, is how long they are established for use. It remains that we are speaking about the law of nature, which is inscribed in the hearts of people. All other laws are an exposition of this law, whether by Moses or the prophets condemning us because we have squandered the law of nature, which needed to be renewed. Commentary on Isaiah 24:5.[9]

The Eternal Covenant Renewed. Heinrich Bullinger: And he says they have "broken the everlasting covenant." Some explain this everlasting covenant as the bond of charity and the duties of humanity. But the meaning is not at all obscure, because it is the eternal covenant made between God and people from the beginning of the world and often renewed, as with Noah,

[5]Bullinger, *Isaias*, 112v-113r; citing Col 3:25; Rom 2:11.
[6]Pellikan, *Commentaria Bibliorum*, 3:29r.
[7]Trapp, *Commentary or Exposition*, 87-88*; citing Zeph 3:5; Jn 1:9.
[8]CR 101:267.5-10.
[9]Oecolampadius, *In Iesaiam*, 150r.

Abraham, Moses, and all the people, and under Christ our Lord and Savior. It was made because God wanted to be our God, to be adored, called on, and worshiped alone, since he is God alone and all-sufficient; because he wanted us to be reconciled to him through the Son and by him to save or restore us; because we must cling to him in true faith and walk in his ways and commands, that is, to arrange everything in our life according to his will.

But from the very beginning God expelled all who violated this covenant. And so, neglect of the covenant is an entirely just reason for all the evils that are in the world. And from that, now likewise spills over the manifold evils of our time, which will not be removed except by proper repentance and diligent keeping of the eternal covenant. Commentary on Isaiah 24:5.[10]

The Sum of Israel's Religion. Wolfgang Musculus: This is why it is necessary that we refer these things to the people of Israel who, with astonishing wickedness, transgressed, perverted, and squandered the laws, the statutes, and the covenant of God. I understand the interpretive philosophy for applying these to all nations. But it is more appropriate to rest in the simplicity of Sacred Scripture and not invert the expressions that have been specifically and repeatedly applied to God's people, and twist them from the sense in which they were given to a foreign one. . . . The prophet adds, "They change the statutes," that is, whatever is decreed by the Lord, they recklessly corrupt, change, and pervert. The statutes are the ceremonies prescribed in the law, such as those concerning the established sacrifices, days, and rituals. The covenant is that agreement that was undertaken between God and Abraham and all his descendants, which we read about. . . . By these three, the prophet summed up the whole religion that was divinely delivered to the people of Israel. Commentary on Isaiah 24:4-5.[11]

A Curse on the Earth. Johannes Oecolampadius: "Therefore a curse devours the earth." According to the thought of the apostle in Romans, by despising the law of nature, the Gentiles were deservedly handed over to a reprobate sense, and sin became their punishment for their sins. When Adam first transgressed the commandment of God, the earth was cursed. . . . But when the sons added sins upon sins, the curse devoured the earth. And it is not absurd to understand "by earth" in this passage, people. For the earth, our flesh, is cursed because of Adam's sin so that it produces thorns and thistles. Commentary on Isaiah 24:6.[12]

24:7-13 *Desolation in the City*

Joy Allowed by the Lord. Konrad Pellikan: The Lord does not refuse the honest joy of humans, if they do not cross the line, if people join together with thanksgiving for God's kindness, if righteous people rejoice with one another, if music refreshes their souls—not driving them to madness, not being aroused to lust, not drawing them toward forbidden desires, but with guarded discipline, youthfulness is also ruled with righteous control, so that nothing in these things is tempting too much or too little, and the fear of God is guarded in the heart always, even if the soul is physically expressing a joy that is not harmful. Commentary on Isaiah 24:7.[13]

A Twofold Problem Regarding Wine. Wolfgang Musculus: The prophet does not look back here to what precedes about the scarcity of wine but to what follows, where he prophesies about the destruction of the city. He predicts that it will be so bad that even for those who were going to have something to drink, they are not even going to enjoy a fermented cider because of the sad desolation of the city and the bitter sense of the present evils. This was going to make their hearts and palates embittered as wormwood.

[10]Bullinger, *Isaias*, 114v.
[11]Musculus, *In Esaiam*, 379; citing Gen 17.
[12]Oecolampadius, *In Iesaiam*, 150r-v; citing Romans 1:21-25; Gen 3.
[13]Pellikan, *Commentaria Bibliorum*, 3:30v.

Therefore the Lord was about to strike this people with a twofold problem regarding their use of wine. Some would be afflicted by the scarcity of wine, but others would be so unhappy that the wine that they did have they could not drink at all without it becoming bitter. COMMENTARY ON ISAIAH 24:7-9.[14]

THE EMPTY CITY IS THE WHOLE EARTH. JOHANNES OECOLAMPADIUS: "The wasted is broken down." Understand this as the world, in which is nothing but emptiness, as what is in Ecclesiastes, "Vanity of vanities. All is vanity." Moreover, the world will be vain, that is, empty, and destitute of worshiping him, until it is renewed more blessed. . . . For although now the city of the world appears glorious, yet the thing itself is like a bubble, which, when it is spent, he declares that it will be nothing. And that this is so, clearly shows both the death of each one and the consummation of the age. COMMENTARY ON ISAIAH 24:10.[15]

THE DEVASTATED CITY IS FUTURE BABYLON. MARTIN BORRHAUS: This spiritual city of Babylon is the seat of the antichrist, the confounder of all. This interpretation agrees with the words of John, where in Revelation, he describes the fall of the city of Babylon. It appears that our prophet foreshadowed that in this oracle. If it seems to anyone that the city is to be taken collectively for the states, it is permissible to me to interpret it this way. But a more superior interpretation seems rather that this pertains to extending the adornment of the city of Jerusalem descending from heaven. The city is called *tōhû* [emptiness] at the end of the world, because it is going to be devastated, reduced to all disfigurement. For so John: "Fallen is Babylon the great city. She has become a dwelling place for demons." ORACLES IN ISAIAH ON 24:12.[16]

ALL PEOPLE IN DANGER OF MISERY. DIETRICH SCHNEPFF: Finally, he prophesies about the destruction of the city as well: "Desolation is left in the city; the gate is beaten into ruins." Previously this was a very large place for considering and executing judgment, from which we can conjecture that the other places with smaller populations of people were likewise devastated. Therefore in the way he described the disaster of the Jewish people to this point, all people in general are endangered: Judea was plundered and deprived of all goods. Few from that disaster survived and remained unharmed. Everything that could bring happiness was taken away. There was an uprising in the city itself. Finally, the city was conquered such that in the middle of the market there was great loneliness. All the remaining evils can be summed up in two categories, which are contained in the statement above: there is going to be a miserable condition for the citizens and all the property of the Hebrews. SCHOLIA ON ISAIAH 24:12-13.[17]

NO LONGER THE PEOPLE OF GOD. JOHANNES BRENZ: The prophet explained in the earlier part of his speech the blindness, devastation, and dejection of the Jews, which happened so that the Jews, after they rejected Christ, were no longer the people and the church of God. Therefore you will say, "If the Jews were rejected to not be the church of God, where do the divine promises remain that were spoken to this people? And where is the church of God, if it is no longer among the Jews?"

About this matter, now, Isaiah addresses and teaches that even if the multitude of the Jewish people are blind and rejected, nevertheless a remnant will be saved. . . . † "Thus it shall be," it says, "in the midst of the earth among the nations." That is, I said now the Jews are going to be rejected and devastated; that is not to be understood that absolutely none of the Jews are going to obtain salvation, since in the midst of the earth among those Jews, the same thing will happen that happens when olives are to be skinned and grape harvest is to be collected. For when olives are skinned, some remnants remain, and when grape

[14]Musculus, *In Esaiam*, 381.

[15]Oecolampadius, *In Iesaiam*, 151v.

[16]Borrhaus, *In Iesaiae Prophetae Oracula*, 226; citing Rev 18:2.

[17]Schnepff, *In Esaiae*, 360.

harvest is collected, a few grapes remain from that, which the poor obtain for themselves. So it will happen with the rejection of the Jews—even if a multitude perish, nevertheless a remnant will be saved. Commentary on Isaiah 24:13.[18]

24:14-16 *Responses to the Lord's Judgment*

The God of Israel Glorified by Other Peoples. Heinrich Bullinger: So the prophet emphatically expresses that God alone must be glorified, and not just any god but the God of Israel, and certainly not any foreign god. He included among those who do this all the worshipers of God throughout the world. For by naming the valleys and the islands of the sea, he means all the parts of the inhabited world. Further, he imagines that he now hears from afar and from the edge, that is, from the most remote parts of the earth, singing praise with psalms or hymns to the Lord, glorifying his righteousness in punishing the wicked and preserving the faithful. Therefore, we also have evidence of thanksgiving—and add our praying. But here we are slow, deserving to be rebuked by this word and stirred up to right diligence. Sermons on Isaiah 24:14-15.[19]

Refusing the Messiah. Thomas Cooper: Here the prophet breaks out in sorrowful lamentation that his people and countrymen are rejected from the favor of God because of their obstinate transgression. It is as if he had said, "Woe is me, for with sorrow and heaviness of heart, I foresee that at the revealing of the gospel by the Messiah, while many other nations will embrace him, few of my countrymen will receive the sweet comfort thereof. For they shall heinously and grievously transgress in condemning and refusing Christ the Messiah and Savior. And therefore God shall, by his just wrath, refuse and cast them out from the number of his people." Second Sunday in Advent.[20]

Exiting the Sea When the Lord Comes in Glory. Johannes Oecolampadius: "Over the majesty of the Lord." This is when the Lord will come in his glory. The saints will go marching in and will be caught up in the air. They will shout joyfully by the sea, having obtained the transportation of sailors. For this life is compared to the sea, because it is dangerous, so the saints rejoice that they are going to exit from it to the port of eternal happiness. Commentary on Isaiah 24:14.[21]

The Glory of Christ the Righteous. Rudolf Gwalther: Moreover, because Isaiah was foreseeing the glory of Christ in the Spirit, he responds to himself when he says, "From the ends of the earth we hear praise, glory to the Righteous One." It is as if he were saying, "This exhortation of mine will not be in vain. In fact, I now seem to hear from the ends of the earth those who sing praises to God and give glory to the Righteous One." By the name "Righteous One," he means Christ, whom the prophets and the apostles often name this way, not only because he is righteous but also because he declares righteous those who believe in him and even was made our righteousness by the Father. And he makes this point later . . . where it says, "By his knowledge shall the Righteous One, my servant, make many to be accounted righteous. . . ."

But in this passage, he speaks about the conversion of the Gentiles to Christ, which was not without the public rejoicing of believers, as is seen in the examples of the Samaritans and the Philippian jailer. . . . However many have clung to Christ by faith cannot but rejoice about the grace of God and be certain of their own salvation. Sermons on Isaiah 24:15-16.[22]

The Depravity of the World. Konrad Pellikan: "But oh my," the prophet says, "I waste away. Oh my, the meagerness," that is, "Oh, the misery; oh, my anguish; oh, the scarcity of the elect

[18]Brenz, *Esaias*, 311-12. †Brenz draws the parallel to Paul in Rom 9.
[19]Bullinger, *Isaias*, 115v.
[20]Cooper, *Brief Exposition*, 18-19*.
[21]Oecolampadius, *In Iesaiam*, 151r.
[22]Gwalther, *Isaias*, 135v (135r, misnumbered 134); citing Is 53:11; Acts 8; 16.

and the depravity of this world." How difficult it is to go the narrow way; how wide is the way many walk, which leads to destruction. Woe to the maliciousness of this world and the depravity of this life. Alas, I see everything is filled with liars; the whole world resides in malice. The majority of them are those who violate the work given to them, who rejoice in the worst things, who do not fear the judgment of the Lord, because they do not believe in God, nor his righteousness. By necessity, a pit, a snare, and the harsh sentence of the judge remains on these. He does not permit any iniquity at the throne of his glory. He does not allow those who despise him to go unpunished. He powerfully opposes and pursues the wicked. Those who are unafraid to betray his prophets and he himself, he does not let them escape. Commentary on Isaiah 24:16.[23]

Persistent Sin. Heinrich Bullinger: And still more clearly, "Woe, miserable me!" For what do I say is going to be for many ungrateful people? Truly, "The traitors have betrayed." With a repetition of the phrase,† he repeats it again for the sake of emphasis and adds, "With betrayal, the traitors have betrayed!" In other words, they have not just sinned out of ignorance or human weakness but with eagerness, rebellion, and premeditated malice. For although they see and hear, they do not want to see or hear but persist in their unbelief. Sermons on Isaiah 24:16.[24]

Sorrow Until Judgment Day. Johannes Oecolampadius: Moreover these words ["I waste away"] have this sense: although we have discovered that on that day of judgment there is going to be great glory and joy for the righteous ones—who are here in this song called the "glory of the righteous"—yet we still have a continuous sorrow over the scarcity of those who could have been saved with the others except here they ruined themselves in their laziness. Isaiah calls that scarcity "his meagerness,"† where the Vulgate reads "my secret from me." Commentary on Isaiah 24:16.[25]

24:17-23 *The Lord's Punishment and Reign*

A Pit and Snare. John Trapp: This is a metaphor from hunters, elegantly expressed in the original by words of a similar sound. God has a variety of plagues at his command. His quiver is full of shafts, and he cannot possibly lack a weapon to defeat those who rebel against him. If the Amorites escape the sword, they are then pelted with hailstones. . . . If the Syrians flee into a walled city, there they are then killed by the fall of a wall on them. Exposition on Isaiah 24:17-18.[26]

God's Wrath Poured Out like a Flood. Johannes Oecolampadius: "For the windows on high." The windows of heaven are opened when the wrath of God is clearly and obviously poured out, as if the rains flow down with a certain vigor, like at the time of the flood . . . where the floodgates are said to have opened. We can also draw from this a proverbial saying and use it whenever the wrath of God is on us. . . . The bowls of God's wrath are poured out. . . . "The anger of his wrath is poured out." And the foundations of the earth tremble, that is, the earth will be agitated from its foundations so that nothing is so firm that it will not be shaken. Commentary on Isaiah 24:18.[27]

After the Millennium. Martin Borrhaus: "And after many days they will be punished." Similarly John, interpreter of the prophets . . . , "And when the thousand years are ended, Satan will be released from this prison and will come out to deceive the nations that are at the four corners of

[23]Pellikan, *Commentaria Bibliorum*, 3:30v; citing Mt 7:13.

[24]Bullinger, *Isaias*, 115v. †The technical term Bullinger uses for the repetition of a phrase is *anadiplosis*.

[25]Oecolampadius, *In Iesaiam*, 152v. †Oecolampadius translates *rāzî* as *macilentiam* instead of the Vulgate's *secretum*.

[26]Trapp, *Commentary or Exposition*, 89*; citing Josh 10:11; 1 Kings 20:30.

[27]Oecolampadius, *In Iesaiam*, 152r; citing Gen 7; Rev 16; Nahum 1:6.

the earth, Gog and Magog." Ezekiel also prophesies similarly to John and the prophet Isaiah. . . . We will comment on that mystical interpretation in another place. Oracles in Isaiah on 24:21-22.[28]

Liberation by the Medes and Persians. Wolfgang Musculus: "And after many days they will be visited." This is, they will be liberated. He speaks about another kind of visitation, in which they are visited for liberating the afflicted and the captive. This was going to happen by the Medes and the Persians, whose work the Lord was using to overthrow the Babylonian monarchy and liberate the captive peoples. These things are clearly said with the same sense that was in the previous chapter, "And it will be after seventy years, the Lord will visit Tyre and return to her." Commentary on Isaiah 24:22.[29]

Many for All. Ulrich Zwingli: Let me add that "many" in the Hebrew, as well as in the Greek, is taken as "all," as in, "Many are called." That is, indeed all are called by the preaching of the apostolic word, of course. For in Romans, calling is taken differently, "Those he called, he also justified. . . ." And with "which is poured out for many," that is, for the entire multitude. And with "There is one bread and the many are one body." So also, in this passage, by "many days" they cannot be anything but "all days." Therefore we translate it as "endless days." Annotations on Isaiah 24:22.[30]

Infinite Days of Punishment. Konrad Pellikan: For those gathered together, as in a bundle, will be thrown into eternal fire and will be "visited for a multitude of days," that is, they will be punished for the longest time. The Hebrews explain this to be about the enemies of the Messiah. Some say it is about the Jewish captivity, which they were then in. But it is more surely explained as the infinite and endless days that the wicked will suffer before God and will be thrown into prison, until they stand at the judgment to be damned in body and soul. This is evident from what follows. Commentary on Isaiah 24:22.[31]

The Gospel Outshines the Sun and Moon. Johannes Brenz: "The moon will be confounded and the sun will be ashamed." There will be such brightness of Christ's kingdom that it will obscure and extinguish not only the brightest of monarchies on this earth but even the lights in the sky, the sun and the moon. The sun is the illuminator of the day, the moon of the night. And surely there is nothing in this world brighter and more brilliant than these lights. And yet the light that will shine in the kingdom of Christ will be much brighter and more brilliant. The sun and moon indeed shine on humanity so that they may walk in the earthly way so that the physical foot does not stumble on a stone. And they shine so that you may finish your physical works. But they do not shine so that you may walk without a hurdle to true and eternal happiness.

But the gospel of Christ's kingdom lights the way from sin to righteousness, from death to life, from the darkness of hell to the splendor of heaven. What is brighter than this light? This is why it is rightly said that the light of the sun and the moon is put to shame and obscured before the great brightness of this light that shines through the preaching of the gospel in the church, or the kingdom of Christ. Commentary on Isaiah 24:23.[32]

Glory Greater than the Sun and Moon. Francisco Forerius: And so he metaphorically calls this failure a shaming and an averting of the eyes. Here you have the glory of the gospel, the glory of the kingdom of God, which the apostle Paul often states shines more brightly than the face of Moses. And that glory of the Lord Jesus is

[28]Borrhaus, *In Iesaiae Prophetae Oracula*, 228; citing Rev 20:7-8; Ezek 38.
[29]Musculus, *In Esaiam*, 386, 387; citing Is 23:17.
[30]CR 101:270.28-37; citing Mt 20:16; Rom 8:30; Mt 26:28; 1 Cor 10:17.
[31]Pellikan, *Commentaria Bibliorum*, 3:30r.
[32]Brenz, *Esaias*, 317.

so great that the apostles were beholding his glory like a mirror because of the enormous power and efficacy of his glory in brightness, and they were likewise transformed, and would be the brightest, like the sun, in the world. All other brightness, all other majesty, would surely disappear if compared to his majesty and glory. Because when he was God, "he was manifested in the flesh, vindicated by the Spirit, was seen by angels, proclaimed among the nations, believed on in the world, taken up in glory." Therefore, wanting to signify that there was no other glory comparable to this, the prophet most elegantly signified by the confounding of the moon and the stars that Christ the Lord would shine more brightly than those great lights. Commentary on Isaiah 24:23.[33]

Signs in the Heavens and on the Cross. Johannes Oecolampadius: This corresponds to the saying . . . , "There will be signs in sun and moon. . . ." And where the Evangelist says the Son of Man is going to come on the clouds and in great glory, here the prophet says, "his glorification and kingdom before the elders." The confounding of the moon and the blushing of the sun, some want to be about the excessive brightness at Christ's return, whose immensity is going to obscure the sun and the moon. Indeed, though, the diligent reader should not ignore that Christ also began the judgment on the cross, and a certain consummation of the world happened at that time, and signs in heaven and on earth were not missing. For there also the sun was darkened, the rocks split, and an enormous earthquake occurred, and the supernatural powers were defeated. For the one who trusts him is saved by his death; what is earthly will cease, and the Lord will have his kingdom. Commentary on Isaiah 24:23.[34]

[33]Forerius, *Iesaiae*, 83r; citing 1 Tim 3:16.

[34]Oecolampadius, *In Iesaiam*, 153v; citing Lk 21:25.

25:1-12 Song of Praise

25 *O* Lord, *you are my God;*
I will exalt you; I will praise your name,

for you have done wonderful things,
plans formed of old, faithful and sure.

2 *For you have made the city a heap,*
the fortified city a ruin;

the foreigners' palace is a city no more;
it will never be rebuilt.

3 *Therefore strong peoples will glorify you;*
cities of ruthless nations will fear you.

4 *For you have been a stronghold to the poor,*
a stronghold to the needy in his distress,
a shelter from the storm and a shade from the heat;

for the breath of the ruthless is like a storm against a wall,
5 *like heat in a dry place.*

You subdue the noise of the foreigners;
as heat by the shade of a cloud,
so the song of the ruthless is put down.

6 *On this mountain the* Lord *of hosts will make for all peoples*
a feast of rich food, a feast of well-aged wine,
of rich food full of marrow, of aged wine well refined.

7 *And he will swallow up on this mountain*
the covering that is cast over all peoples,
the veil that is spread over all nations.
8 *He will swallow up death forever;*

and the Lord God *will wipe away tears from all faces,*
and the reproach of his people he will take away from all the earth,
for the Lord *has spoken.*

9 *It will be said on that day,*
"Behold, this is our God; we have waited for him, that he might save us.
This is the Lord*; we have waited for him;*
let us be glad and rejoice in his salvation."

10 *For the hand of the* Lord *will rest on this mountain,*
and Moab shall be trampled down in his place,
as straw is trampled down in a dunghill.[a]

11 *And he will spread out his hands in the midst of it*
as a swimmer spreads his hands out to swim,
but the Lord *will lay low his pompous pride together with the skill*[b] *of his hands.*

12 *And the high fortifications of his walls he will bring down,*
lay low, and cast to the ground, to the dust.

a The Hebrew words for *dunghill* and for the Moabite town *Madmen* (Jeremiah 48:2) sound alike **b** Or *in spite of the skill*

Overview: This chapter offers praise to God for his faithfulness in carrying out his promises. The Reformers comment on the theme of God's eternal plan, which includes the nations turning to the Lord. The feast on the mountain, portrayed in the middle of the song, receives several different interpretations. Some recount a Jewish interpretation that this is drinking God's wrath, while others understand this as the preaching of the gospel or the sacrament of the Lord's Supper. The language about tears and death being wiped away enables several commentators to link this passage with similar New Testament passages. These commentators also emphasize the necessary response of trusting in God.

Praise for Planning Long Ago. Johannes Oecolampadius: As is his custom, the prophet breaks forth into praise and singing when he hears about the glory of the life to come, in which the elders reigning with Christ will glorify God and say on that day, "Lord, you are my God. Idols are nothing to us; whatever is in the world is nothing to us. You are the one and only Lord and God; you are sufficient for us, and nothing is a danger to us, even the destruction of the whole world. Since you delight us, the end of the world does not frighten us. It is enough for us that you, God, are glorified. And so we will exalt you, not ourselves or our works, or any creatures, which we consider all as flax. But we will not only glorify you with our heart, but we will also confess with our mouth and testify to your name, that is, your renown, with our actions and with joyful and perpetual thanksgiving. This is especially because of your power, since you do marvelous things that exceed the capacity of human understanding—and because of your goodness and truth, since nothing of everything predicted through your prophets remains undone." Commentary on Isaiah 25.[1]

Pause to Celebrate. John Trapp: Piscator says these are the words of the subjects of Christ's kingdom, who at the end of the previous chapter are called his "ancients" or "elders." . . . But I like better what Oecolampadius has: "The prophet, as is his custom, breaks forth into a joyful jubilation,"[†] and being ravished and, as it were, rapt beyond himself when considering such marvelous things, first takes a pause or breathing and then sweetly celebrates God's power, truth, justice, and mercy, the naked bowels of which were seen (as it were in the anatomy) in the sending of his Son, and the benefits that came with it, which the apostles later portray more plainly and plentifully when they yet make use of some passages in this chapter, as is to be seen. Exposition on Isaiah 25.[2]

Blessings for the Church at All Times. Dietrich Schnepff: The following two chapters have the same argument, for they contain the thanksgiving that should be applied to the whole church. Because not only does it mention their blessings, which to this point exist in the church as the highest and greatest, but it also mentions the resurrection of the dead. Isaiah prophesies about this very eloquently. So I will skip over other people's interpretations. We understand this chapter to be about the thanksgiving that the righteous have toward Christ the Lord, in view of the enormous blessings that he, the great benefactor of humankind, has shown and offered to all mortals from the first day the world began all the way until the last. . . . Therefore, since this prophecy extends to the last day, we must certainly understand it to be about the church universal, not about Jerusalem, as Jerome thought, or about other peoples, as some supposed. Scholia on Isaiah 25.[3]

25:1-5 *A Song of Praise for Deliverance*

God's Faithfulness to His Promises. Martin Borrhaus: This is praise from a certain and firm faith, whereby the promises formerly made to the ancestors supply firm and consistent faith. Back in paradise, it was promised to Adam himself that the seed of the woman, the Messiah, was going to crush the head of the serpent, Satan. To Abraham after the flood, it was promised that in his seed all the nations would be blessed. That promise is often repeated in later times. And finally the angels surrounding the throne, and the animals, and the elders, and thousands of thousands see this fulfilled in the Messiah and by the Messiah, with a great and clear voice, as in the vision of John. Oracles in Isaiah on 25:1-2.[4]

Eternal Plans. Wolfgang Musculus: "Plans of old," it says. Therefore, the plans of God do not

[1]Oecolampadius, *In Iesaiam*, 153r.

[2]Trapp, *Commentary or Exposition*, 90*; citing Rev 4:4; 1 Cor 15; Rev 7; 21. [†]See Oecolampadius, *In Iesaiam*, 153r.

[3]Schnepff, *In Esaiae*, 373.

[4]Borrhaus, *In Iesaiae Prophetae Oracula*, 229; citing Rev 5.

grow weak at all over time. They do not change; they are not nullified. They are not like our plans, which either change by the hour or disappear. Rather, his plans remain firm until they are truly fulfilled. It should not be attributed to slowness or impotence, just because plans are not fulfilled as soon as they are formed. There is no place for the saying, "Whatever is to be done, decide quickly; when you plan it, do it." They are ancient to us who experience the course of time. To God, nothing is ancient, since in his presence a thousand years are like one day, and in his eyes both the beginning and the end of all things are seen with the same perspective. As for us, we must acknowledge supreme providence, because the things being fulfilled this way have been planned from eternity, so they are ancient plans to us. Let us not suppose with the wicked that all things happen at random and by chance, but rather from eternal plans. Commentary on Isaiah 25:1.[5]

God Alone Overthrows Tyrants. Konrad Pellikan: You are the one who is angry with the cities of wicked people. You reduce them to a heap. You consume and devastate. You overthrow the most fortified states and leave them in ruins because of the iniquity of those who subvert justice, distrusting people, taking offices, advancing their own interests rather than the public good, and tolerating crimes. You also expel from the city the palaces of the wicked, who revere no one out of fear of a foreign god. And you confound them with perpetual and open reproach. For you alone are the one who brings down and judges tyrants, while they do not stop oppressing your righteous ones when they persecute your faithful ones both in their situations and in their bodies. Commentary on Isaiah 25:2.[6]

Glorifying the Lord in Fear. Wolfgang Musculus: The sense from that is, because you are going to put into piles of stone this most terrible city, so extensive, so fortified, so widely dominant, each of the strong peoples and the cities of ruthless nations will fear your name and revere your power, which they were holding most contemptible of all. What is expressed convenes well to this sense, because he does not simply say, "People and cities," but, "Strong people and the cities of ruthless nations will fear you," seeing that no matter how great their power, they should not be presumptuous against you, when not even Babylon could stand against your strength.

But it may seem that these two phrases, "They will glorify" and "They will fear you," do not correspond well with each other, and especially the word *glorifying* is incongruous with this sense. The prophet does not say that the strong people and the cities of ruthless nations will glorify the Lord because of the devastation of Babylon, but rather that they will begin to fear him. For although this kind of fear—of the strong and the mighty—happens to the glory of God's power, yet these people do not fear him for the reason that they return to the glorious and bright one. This is why I consider that the Hebrew word *yĕkabdûāk*,[†] "they will glorify you," should not refer to the affection of the people themselves but rather to the outcome of their fear. And this sense was not used by the prophet inappropriately. Yet, I would not want to contend with anyone if they also suppose the prophet speaks about the affection of glorifying the Lord. Commentary on Isaiah 25:2-3.[7]

Persecutors Will Bow the Knee. Johannes Oecolampadius: "Therefore a people will praise you." That strong people are the tyrants and the wicked who persecute the good ones, or even demons themselves. On the day of judgment, those will glorify the righteous Lord by paying the penalty for their own wickedness. So also the apostle speaks about the dead, that at the name of Jesus every knee is bowed. And in the Gospel, demons glorify Christ—with fear and trembling.

[5]Musculus, *In Esaiam*, 389.
[6]Pellikan, *Commentaria Bibliorum*, 3:30r.
[7]Musculus, *In Esaiam*, 389-90. [†]The spelling of the Hebrew word has been fixed here. The text has the first three letters transposed.

Jerome and the Septuagint understand this to be about the saints, but the Hebrew truth opposes that. COMMENTARY ON ISAIAH 25:3.[8]

JUST REPAYMENT AGAINST THE AFFLICTERS. KONRAD PELLIKAN: Lord, you know to apprehend those who hate you, to afflict most severely those who resist you, to make a fitting repayment to those who caused anguish to your saints. You humiliate the arrogance and uprising of tyrants; you hold in check their incorrigible audacity. You are a cloud that shelters the righteous and those faithful to you when they are tested by the heat. But he will put down the ruthless with all their posterity and afflict them with just judgment. COMMENTARY ON ISAIAH 25:4.[9]

THE RICH CAN BE POOR. MARTIN BORRHAUS: Christ embraces such poor people when he says, "Blessed are the poor in spirit." And so there are those who are poor from the riches of this world but rich in the opinion of human wisdom and integrity. Christ is not acknowledging these. Likewise, there are those who are poor and destitute in integrity of mind and wisdom, who acknowledge that they lack the wisdom and integrity that accord with God and any human power by which the abandoned could free themselves, and have placed their hope solely in God's protection. The Messiah has regard for these kind of poor, and he makes them rich by the wealth of his power, his wisdom, his righteousness, and his life. Counted among the poor of this kind are those who did not lack the riches of this world, but they lacked the desire for them. Abraham and other patriarchs are examples, as well as righteous kings and princes.

There are kings considered among this kind of poor, about which our prophet later says, "And kings will serve you." Therefore, these are the poor that Christ mercifully regards. There are also the poor he rejects. So many of these kind are found in the kingdom of the beast, and even some are found who profess poverty and begging but hope for the riches of kings and hypocritically pretend they have the integrity of angels. So there are also rich people whom the Lord loves and some whom he rejects. ORACLES IN ISAIAH ON 25:4.[10]

A RAGING SEA AGAINST AN UNMOVED CLIFF. DIETRICH SCHNEPFF: To start, if we compare the magnitude of the sea with a cliff, who would not say that the sea is far more powerful than any such rock? So if we look with our eyes around this world and we contrast the scarcity of those who believe and are righteous with the infinite number of those who are wicked, we will immediately start to tremble. For naturally we hear that the many have victory over the few. But there is no ratio of the wicked to the righteous, if you consider the population. Add to this point that the waves of the sea are driven with great force and rage, but the cliff stands there unmoved and does not appear to push back the violence. So also nearly all people rage against the righteous, lay plans, and try all kinds of things. Meanwhile the church possesses her strength in silence and hope. And like a cliff on the ocean breaks the waves of the seas by enduring and standing, so the church conquers through suffering, lives by dying, and is watered when she sheds blood. SCHOLIA ON ISAIAH 25:4-5.[11]

25:6-8 *The Lord on His Mountain*

THE FEAST ON THE MOUNTAIN SIGNIFIES WRATH. JOHANNES OECOLAMPADIUS: The Hebrews explain this to be about Gog and Magog, because they will kill each other with wounds on the holy mountain when they begin to drink the cup of the Lord's wrath. But we reject their fable. A "feast of rich food, and of filtered drink, and meat with marrow" signifies the wrath and indignation of God, as frequently the Scriptures indicate the

[8]Oecolampadius, *In Iesaiam*, 154v; citing Phil 2.
[9]Pellikan, *Commentaria Bibliorum*, 3:31v.
[10]Borrhaus, *In Iesaiae Prophetae Oracula*, 230; citing Mt 5:3; Is 60:10.
[11]Schnepff, *In Esaiae*, 375.

same with the term *cup*. . . . "Behold, I make them a cup of staggering to all the surrounding peoples," that is, the cup of drunkenness. . . . "To you also the cup shall pass, and you shall become drunk." . . . "A golden cup in the Lord's hand."

For just as those who drink the cup of drunkenness begin to act crazy and ruin themselves with strong drink, when they want to offend others, so likewise those who drink the strong drink on this mountain—that is, those who seek to offend the church of God and the spiritual Israelites—invite destruction on themselves. For just as Christ is the stone of offense, so also the people of Christ is the rock of stumbling. Those who intend to offend it hurt themselves, and when they want to devour the bread and chug the drink, they ruin themselves. Moreover, he says this feast is going to be for all peoples, because as the apostle says, "We have become a spectacle to the whole world." The whole world persecutes the church, just as they also persecuted Christ. Mount Zion is a type for the church. Commentary on Isaiah 25:6.[12]

Eating and Drinking at the Lord's Table. Ulrich Zwingli: Here we think Isaiah breaks off the song and returns to the category of prophecy. Moreover, that feast that he promises can be nothing other than what Christ himself established as food of all peoples, which, if we eat truly, we will find rest with him on his holy mountain, eating and drinking at that very table, which he instructed us according to the Father. Annotations on Isaiah 25:6.[13]

The Feast on the Mountain Is the Preaching of the Gospel. Johannes Brenz: But if anyone compares what precedes and what follows in this passage, they will see that it is quite obvious that the prophet is preaching about the gospel banquet, which Christ established first in his preaching, then by sending the Holy Spirit on the day of Pentecost—on Mount Zion, or in Jerusalem. It says, "On this mountain, the Lord of hosts will make for all peoples a feast of rich food, a feast of filtered drink," that is, a feast of sumptuous foods and the purest of wine. This is how the prophet himself interprets it. Here the Lord of hosts is Christ. Moreover, his feast is the preaching of the gospel. It is said that he prepared this feast on Mount Zion for all peoples, because he personally preached his gospel in the city of Jerusalem, where Mount Zion is. And he sent out his apostles from that place on the day of Pentecost into the world, to preach the gospel to all nations. . . . Then also Christ himself calls the preaching of the gospel a feast when he compares the kingdom of heaven with a great wedding banquet. . . . And surely no more lavish feast has ever been prepared on earth than the preaching of the gospel of Christ! Commentary on Isaiah 25:6.[14]

The Veil Removed. Konrad Pellikan: The Lord will throw off, disperse, and also remove the veil over the faces through the mystery of Christ fulfilled on Mount Zion. That veil had covered the conscience of all the Gentiles. It was as much a thick and worldly understanding of Holy Scripture and the divine laws among the Jewish people as it was a darkness of abominable errors and the idolatry of superstitions over the eyes of all the Gentiles. He will remove it so that, by the gospel of Christ, the will of God is clearly recognized, the sacrilegious worship of false gods ceases, and the one true God is worshiped alone by faith alone. Commentary on Isaiah 25:7.[15]

Deliverance by Constantine. John Mayer: Calvin says that some understand that this refers to the calamities of Christ's churches in all places, covering them or overwhelming them, so that the glory could not appear among them. But he and Musculus[†] both rather prefer another

[12]Oecolampadius, *In Iesaiam*, 154r-155v; citing Zech 12:2; Lam 4:21; Jer 51:7; 1 Cor 4:9.
[13]CR 101:272.30-35; citing Mt 8:11.
[14]Brenz, *Esaias*, 323-24; citing Mt 22; Lk 14.
[15]Pellikan, *Commentaria Bibliorum*, 3:31v.

understanding, namely, the covering of ignorance. But in as much as the word translated "will take away" signifies to swallow up, as a variation of the word, and it says, "the reproach of his people," it is not so genuine to understand by this that their ignorance is their outward misery causing tears, because he says these will be wiped away. Therefore, I resolve that the deliverance of the church in the time of Constantine, after long periods of persecutions, is what is prophesied here. They were all at that time "covered," as it were, with sackcloth like the two witnesses in Revelation, and they sowed in tears, and they were told that their God was poor and unable to help them, because they, his servants, were in such want and misery. Commentary on Isaiah 25:7.[16]

The Twofold Veil. Martin Borrhaus: Now he brings to mind the twofold covering that miserably enveloped and covered the human race. One is of sin and death, in which all those born from the first Adam are covered over by original sin. The apostle says it with these words, "Sin came into the world through one man, and death through sin." And so our prophet displays this lethal and deadly covering with these words, "And he will swallow up death." The second covering and veil is the ignorance of God and his Son, Jesus Christ, and is the veil and covering of the mysteries of the kingdom of heaven. This is connected to the first one, as you see from the apostle. . . . Only the Spirit removes and takes away this covering spread over the eyes of our souls, when the Messiah is revealed through the holy gospel. "That same veil remains when they read the old covenant, because only through Christ is it taken away." The foreskin of the flesh prefigured this veil and covering, and the circumcision of the foreskin prefigured its removal by the Spirit of the Messiah. Oracles in Isaiah on 25:7.[17]

Life to the World. Rudolf Gwalther: Our Lord Jesus Christ not only became the sacrificial victim for our sins and gave his own flesh for the life of the world, but he also earned complete and lasting salvation for us when he rose from the dead. The end or goal of this is eternal life, which he sacredly promised to those who believe in him. Isaiah just prophesied about this when he said, "He will swallow up death" in victory, and, " He will wipe away tears from all faces, and the reproach of his people he will take away from the whole earth." Indeed, he indicates that all the disasters of this age will cease, and there will not be anything that impedes the happiness of those who believe. So, these should so strengthen us that we always remember our duty, that is, to offer ourselves willingly to such a great Savior. For if those blessings that are useful to the body alone deserve our thanks, how much more do we owe to the redeemer of our souls and the author of eternal salvation?

Therefore again the prophet adds a doxology that teaches the righteous to give thanks to God their Savior and to sing his praises. . . . Truly we experience that our God is faithful and reliable in his promises. Indeed, we have waited for him just as he commanded, and he has not disappointed us. But now, "Behold," he is already present. Therefore we confess that he is our Lord, and "we exult and rejoice in his salvation," which he certainly earned for us. Sermons on Isaiah 25:8.[18]

A Promise of Tears Wiped Away. Johannes Oecolampadius: Truly by dying, Christ destroyed sin, and the tyranny of the devil, and indeed death itself for all who believe in him, saying, "And he will destroy death forever." Further, on that day of judgment, this will be clear to all, for then, with our hope granted, we will always rejoice and live immortal, impeccable, and secure with Christ, and death and the frightful face of sin will not appear. . . . "The last enemy to be destroyed is death," and "death is swallowed up in

[16]Mayer, *Commentary upon All the Prophets*, 4:157*.
[†]CTS 14:197-198 (CO 36:418); Musculus, *In Esaiam*, 392.
[17]Borrhaus, *In Iesaiae Prophetae Oracula*, 231; citing Rom 1:12; 2 Cor 3:14.

[18]Gwalther, *Isaias*, 140r.

victory." Then we will say, "O death, where is your sting? O hell, where is your victory?" . . . "They shall hunger no more, neither thirst anymore; the sun shall not strike them, nor any scorching heat, for the Lamb in the midst will reign over them and guide them to springs of living water." . . . "God will wipe every tear from their eyes, and death shall be no more." For we are restored to life by Christ, and the faces of sin that had covered everyone are covered over. . . .

And now it says "from all faces," where earlier it said "faces." For just as the wicked, although they appear to be laughing on the outside, yet because of the wickedness dwelling within them, they are restless in heart. It is the opposite for the good ones: although tears appear on the outside, yet they have internal consolation, and eventually the disgrace of the saints who were despised in this world will cease. Commentary on Isaiah 25:8.[19]

The Kisses of Christ Suck Out Death. John Trapp: As fire swallows up fuel, or as Moses' serpent swallowed up the sorcerers' serpents, the kisses of Christ's mouth have sucked out the sting of death from a justified believer so that his soul lives forever. . . . And if so, then in death itself one can, like Cyprian, receive the sentence of death with a "Deo gratias" [thanks be to God], as did Bradford and many more martyrs accounting the days of their death as their birthdays and welcoming it accordingly. . . . Ever since death ran through the veins of Jesus Christ, who is "life essential," it is destroyed or "swallowed up," just like the bee dies when she has left her sting in the wound. Exposition on Isaiah 25:8.[20]

Death Destroyed Forever. Martin Luther: "An hour is coming when all who are in the tombs will hear his voice and come out." Then only the work that he has portrayed in this example will really begin, which he has put off until that time, since he wishes to complete it not only in one or a few but in all at one time, in order to destroy death with one blow, . . . so that no one will forever afterward be overcome or taken captive by it. This will then form a truly joyous and glorious procession, when he will bring together, in a moment of time, all who have died, calling them forth with one word from the earth, dust and ashes, air, water, and all other places, and, as Saint Paul says . . . , will bring with him as the head an innumerable company of all believers, having freed all from death and given them eternal life, and, . . . having "wiped away all tears from their eyes," so that they may forever and without ceasing praise and glorify their Lord, with everlasting joy, praise, and honor. Sermon for Sixteenth Sunday After Trinity.[21]

25:9-12 *The Lord Brings Down the Proud*

Three Holy Acts. Johannes Brenz: Here is included three particular holy acts that people ought to present to Christ their king and Savior. First, is expectation, or faith in Christ. For one ought to believe that he is our true Lord God, our true and only Savior—and that there is not another, whether from the patriarchs or the prophets of old or of other people now, from whom the forgiveness of sins, liberation from death, and eternal life is obtained. For this is what the righteous were always expecting from the foundation of the world and in which they put their entire trust.

The second is the external confession of Christ. For one should not only believe with the heart but also confess with the mouth that the name of Christ may shine before people and knowledge of him be extended among people. It says, "They will say, 'Behold this is our God.' . . . 'We have waited for him,'" or, "'We hope in him that he might save us.'" "This is the Lord . . ." is making confession of faith. "If you confess with your mouth," Paul says, "that Jesus is Lord, and believe in your heart that God

[19] Oecolampadius, *In Iesaiam*, 155v, 155r; citing 1 Cor 15:26, 54; Rev 7:16-17; 21:4.

[20] Trapp, *Commentary or Exposition*, 91; citing Ps 22:6; 1 Cor 15:55-57.

[21] Luther, *Sermons*, 5:132; citing Jn 5:28; Is 25:8; 1 Thess 4:14.

raised him from the dead, you will be saved. For with the heart one believes and is justified, and with the mouth one confesses and is saved." So Peter honored Christ when he said, "You are the Christ, the Son of the Living God." And again, "Let all the house of Israel know for certain that God has made this Jesus whom you crucified both Lord and Christ." And again, "There is no other name under heaven given among people by which we must be saved." And Paul, "He bestowed on him the name that is above every name, so that at the name of Jesus every knee should bow. . . ." This is to say truly, "Behold, this is our God. . . ."

The third is the exultation and joy in our conscience, because of the salvation that is granted in Christ. "Let us exult," it says, "and rejoice in his salvation." This is what Paul says, "Since we have been justified by faith, we have peace with God through our Lord Jesus Christ. . . ." For after we acknowledge and believe through the gospel that our sins are forgiven on account of Christ and that God is going to save us from all evils, then our conscience obtains peace, that is, tranquility, and lives a secure life before God, even if this broken world falls. Commentary on Isaiah 25:9.[22]

Three Sacrifices of Worship. Thomas Cooper: Here the prophet notes the three sacrifices by which the church of Christ and his people worship him: (1) The first is faith and belief of the heart, noted in the phrase "We have waited for him." That is, with constant faith, we have abided his coming, being assured that he would deliver us. (2) The second is confession with the mouth. For we must not only believe in our heart that Christ Jesus is the Savior of the world, but, as Saint Paul says, "We must also confess with our mouth," and therefore the prophet says here, "Behold, this is our God. . . ." (3) The third is triumphant gladness in heart and conscience for the salvation brought about by Christ our Savior, which is uttered in these words, "We will be glad and rejoice in his salvation." Third Sunday in Advent at Morning Prayer.[23]

Hands Stretched Out. John Trapp: He shall destroy them with greatest facility. The motion in swimming is easy, not strong: for strong strokes in the water would rather sink than support. Vatable refers this to Christ stretching out his hands on the cross, whereby he overcame Satan and his imps. Exposition on Isaiah 25:11.[24]

Enemies of the Church Easily Conquered. Dietrich Schnepff: He also augmented this with persons, since he says the Lord is going to subject the Moabites to his church. But this is synecdoche,[†] for by Moabites he means the immortal enemies of the Jewish people, all the enemies of the righteous—indeed some that are external but also those greatest enemies: sin, death, hell, and the devil. He also adds to this by amplifying how the Lord is going to erase those enemies of the church, namely, he is going to trample them. . . . By making this comparison, he wants to express how the Lord is going to trample his enemies. As easy as it is for someone swimming in water to propel by hand through the waves that come, so the Lord conquers his enemies without difficulty. Scholia on Isaiah 25:10-12.[25]

---

[22]Brenz, *Esaias*, 328-29; citing Rom 10:9-10; Mt 16:16; Acts 2:36; 4:12; Phil 2:9-11; Rom 5:1.

[23]Cooper, *Brief Exposition*, 21r-22v*; citing Rom 10:9.

[24]Trapp, *Commentary or Exposition*, 91*. See François Vatable, *Commentarius in Iesaiam*, in *Uratislaviensis Tractationum Theologicarum* (Neustadt, 1589), 2:371.

[25]Schnepff, *In Esaiae*, 379. [†]*Synecdoche* is a figure of speech when a part of something is used to refer to the whole.

26:1-21 A SONG OF TRUST

26 *In that day this song will be sung in the land of Judah:*

"We have a strong city;
he sets up salvation
as walls and bulwarks.

2 *Open the gates,*
that the righteous nation that keeps faith
may enter in.

3 *You keep him in perfect peace*
whose mind is stayed on you,
because he trusts in you.

4 *Trust in the LORD forever,*
for the LORD God is an everlasting rock.

5 *For he has humbled*
the inhabitants of the height,
the lofty city.

He lays it low, lays it low to the ground,
casts it to the dust.

6 *The foot tramples it,*
the feet of the poor,
the steps of the needy."

7 *The path of the righteous is level;*
you make level the way of the righteous.

8 *In the path of your judgments,*
O LORD, we wait for you;

your name and remembrance
are the desire of our soul.

9 *My soul yearns for you in the night;*
my spirit within me earnestly seeks you.

For when your judgments are in the earth,
the inhabitants of the world learn
righteousness.

10 *If favor is shown to the wicked,*
he does not learn righteousness;
in the land of uprightness he deals corruptly
and does not see the majesty of the LORD.

11 *O LORD, your hand is lifted up,*
but they do not see it.

Let them see your zeal for your people, and be
ashamed.
Let the fire for your adversaries consume
them.

12 *O LORD, you will ordain peace for us,*
for you have indeed done for us all our
works.

13 *O LORD our God,*
other lords besides you have ruled over us,
but your name alone we bring to
remembrance.

14 *They are dead, they will not live;*
they are shades, they will not arise;

to that end you have visited them with
destruction
and wiped out all remembrance of them.

15 *But you have increased the nation, O LORD,*
you have increased the nation; you are
glorified;
you have enlarged all the borders of the land.

16 *O LORD, in distress they sought you;*
they poured out a whispered prayer
when your discipline was upon them.

17 *Like a pregnant woman*
who writhes and cries out in her pangs
when she is near to giving birth,

so were we because of you, O LORD;
18 *we were pregnant, we writhed,*
but we have given birth to wind.

We have accomplished no deliverance in the
earth,

and the inhabitants of the world have not
fallen.

19 *Your dead shall live; their bodies shall rise.*
You who dwell in the dust, awake and sing
for joy!

For your dew is a dew of light,
and the earth will give birth to the dead.

20 *Come, my people, enter your chambers,*
and shut your doors behind you;
hide yourselves for a little while
until the fury has passed by.

21 *For behold, the Lord is coming out from his*
place
to punish the inhabitants of the earth for
their iniquity,

and the earth will disclose the blood shed on it,
and will no more cover its slain.

Overview: This chapter is another song celebrating the salvation brought about by God. Some interpreters read this as directly referring to the time of Christ, while others see it as for the people in Isaiah's time. The song brings up themes of righteousness, peace, and resurrection, which the Reformers then apply to people in their own day. There is considerable debate about whether the concept of free will can be refuted from this passage because of the phrases that indicate that all accomplishments come from God alone. The descriptions regarding death near the end of the song lead the Reformation interpreters to explain the future resurrection and to encourage patience because of the relative brevity of affliction in this life.

Another Song About Punishment and Salvation. Heinrich Bullinger: I have already repeated several times that Isaiah composes a song to describe the judgments of God as he punishes the wicked and saves the righteous in every generation. All of these are actually aimed at this one purpose: that the righteous, in the changing and crushing turbulence of this age, may stand firm in the faith. At the same time, he also describes the pursuits and actions of the righteous, and he exhorts them to do well, just as often happens in the Psalms. Up to this point in chapter 26, we have heard the saints boast that they have a well-fortified and greatly secure city, of which God is the builder and foundation. Its citizens are the righteous and those who keep the truth. God generously bestows on these citizens his perfect peace.

It is not in vain that we often repeat the goal of this prophetic song. For if anyone does not know what relates to them, then he listens or reads these words with no profit. Therefore, I said that the prophet shows that God punishes the wicked in every age, and he preserves and comforts the righteous. He describes their behavior in the church with this goal, that all the righteous of every age follow the example portrayed and always continue in true piety no matter what tribulations against the church arise in the world. And finally, he spoke about the punishment exacted on the enemies of God. Sermons on Isaiah 26.[1]

The Song Is a Parable. Johannes Oecolampadius: In his custom, the prophet supplies a hymn and song after the history. And by the term *canticle*, according to the prophets, we understand a parable. Moreover, he wishes to say that the saints can sing these things with such joy and such security for the future. "In that day," it says, when what was said earlier will come to pass, namely, when at that time we believe that, through the cross of Christ, the devil will truly be conquered, death and condemnation abolished, and sin removed. And especially also at the

[1]Bullinger, *Isaias*, 119v, 120r.

second coming of Christ when death is conquered, we will reign with Christ. Moreover, the righteous will sing spiritual songs, which proceed from the Holy Spirit. And among the fruit of that is joy, because of their trust in God. COMMENTARY ON ISAIAH 26:1.[2]

A SONG WHEN CHRIST COMES. DIETRICH SCHNEPFF: When therefore Christ the Lord will have come, the true Jews are going to compose and recite such a song about his kindnesses. We cannot give thanks enough to God our heavenly Father for the greatest kindnesses that he bestows undeservedly on us. For he transferred us into his kingdom and made us citizens of his heavenly city, which is called the church and is fortified against all the power of both people and devils, with the strongest bulwarks. For Christ, who is salvation itself, presides over it and indeed is the unconquerable foundation, against which the gates of hell does not prevail. PARAPHRASE OF ISAIAH 26:1-2.[3]

26:1-6 *A Song of Confident Praise*

THE TWOFOLD CITY. MARTIN BORRHAUS: In this city, there is going to be no place for the wicked. Regarding this, John says, "Nothing unclean will enter into it, nor anyone who does what is detestable or false, but only those whose names are written in the Lamb's book of life." But what is that righteousness provided for those who enter in this holy city? This righteousness is explained later. . . . But truly there is a twofold meaning for this city of ours. One is portrayed in descending from heaven in the first resurrection and sojourning on the earth, the kind that is described in the prophets and John. The other is portrayed in ascending into heaven with the glorious promise of being conformed to the Messiah in the second resurrection. As I said, the contemplation of Jerusalem is twofold, from the twofold resurrection. So the contemplation of righteousness is adorned with two parts: one that corresponds to those sojourners as the firstfruits of the Spirit; the second, what will happen in the glorified state after the race of the sojourning. About that righteousness, "The righteous will shine like the sun." ORACLES IN ISAIAH ON 26:1-2.[4]

CHRIST THE WALL AND RAMPART. JOHANNES BRENZ: It says, "The city is our strength; the Savior will be set up in it as a wall and rampart." That is, the city is strong for us; we have a strong city, in which he placed salvation itself as a wall and rampart, or in which the Savior himself was placed as a wall and the bulwark of a wall. But the prophet speaks about the heavenly Jerusalem, or the church, by antithesis to the earthly city of Jerusalem. For this earthly Jerusalem not only does not protect us, but it even attacks and massacres us; there is not any city in the land so righteous and so powerful that it either wants or seeks to protect us from dangers. But we have a heavenly city, which is powerful enough, in which the Lord God himself is the Savior, wall, and bulwark, and in that alone, we will be protected against all the assaults of our enemies. . . . This city is the church of Christ, the city that was founded on Christ himself and his teaching. He says, "On this rock I will build it."

Similarly, the wall and its rampart is Christ, our true salvation. For nothing is more secure, nothing is stronger, than Christ the Son of God. . . . The only church of Christ is that city, in which the residents are protected from Satan and death, and also saved in the way of death, because the wall of this city and the bulwark is the Son of God, who is one with the Father in majesty and omnipotence. Therefore, where will we find the gates of this city so that we also may enter into it; and who or what kind of residents and citizens does this city accept? It follows, "Open the gates that the righteous nation that keeps faith may enter." The gates of this city are not in one part of the earth, but they are wherever the gospel of

[2]Oecolampadius, *In Iesaiam*, 156v.
[3]Scnhepff, *In Esaiae*, 398.
[4]Borrhaus, *In Iesaiae Prophetae Oracula*, 237; citing Rev 21:27; Is 53: Mt 13:43.

Christ is preached, clearly, in all the whole world. Commentary on Isaiah 26:1-2.[5]

The Glistening Sin of Civil Righteousness. John Trapp: "The righteous nation that keeps truth." And here we have a true definition of a right church member. Civil righteousness is but a beautiful abomination. If people do not lay faith as a foundation to their virtue . . . , then it is no better than a glistening sin. Exposition on Isaiah 26:2.[6]

The New People of God. Francisco Forerius: With this side comment, Isaiah reveals his emotion because of the multitude of the new people of God hurrying themselves to the church and the holy city. There is no doubt that this is an allusion to the psalm of David where he says: "Open the gates of righteousness; I will confess to the Lord when I enter through them. This is the gate of the Lord; the righteous shall enter through it." For this is also a word about the church and the holy city. "The righteous nation." Insult and implicit blame belong to those who had entered to this point. The kingdom of God was going to be taken from them and given to others who would produce its fruit. . . . This nation is most perverse; sons in whom there is no *ʾēmūn*, "faith," which is a phrase Paul imitated when he calls them sons of distrust, faithlessness, and disobedience. The righteous nation is the opposite of them, keeping faithfulness, that is, very trustworthy and of faith with the most steadfast obedience. These are epithets of the new people, which the apostle calls a "holy nation." Commentary on Isaiah 26:2.[7]

Continue to Hope in the Creator. Johannes Oecolampadius: "Trust in the Lord." He speaks to the church as if he were saying, "You act rightly as the righteous nation to whom the gates are opened, because you place your hope in the Lord. Now continue that and place your hope in him perpetually. For you rightly lean on God who is a rock—indeed, the Creator of everything, because by all things were built and remain." And see again how he calls you to faith, not to works. Commentary on Isaiah 26:3-4.[8]

Grace to the Humble. Heinrich Bullinger: The prophet adds the reason why each of us believe in the Lord: because it is in him, the rock of ages, who is no doubt the true and eternal God, the strength of all the faithful, their power, salvation, and refuge. Faithful worshipers of God have fled to him in all generations and have been saved. He also adds another reason: because he humbles "the inhabitants of a lofty place." For as Peter said, "God opposes the proud but gives grace to the humble." . . . He then attaches to this something more: "Those laid low will be trampled by the feet of the needy," that is, the feet of the faithful in Christ, who are both poor in spirit and insignificant in this world, but according to God, rich and powerful. This indeed happens daily when the faithful spiritually triumph over the wicked, but most clearly of all will happen on the day of judgment. Besides, we know what the apostle says, "The God of peace will soon crush Satan under your feet." Sermons on Isaiah 26:4.[9]

The Rock of All Ages. Wolfgang Musculus: This is the reason God keeps his people in peace: certainly because they depend on him with firm confidence which one cannot despise and confuse. Above in the preceding chapter, the prophet used the verb "expecting"; in this passage here, he utilizes the word "trusting," as the root of expectations and hope. We are admonished that our trust be fixed on the Lord for true and solid peace. . . . Moreover, when he says, "in the Lord, the rock of ages," understand that as during every time of all ages of mortals. From the beginning of the world to the end, there was not, there is not, nor

[5]Brenz, *Esaias*, 332-33 (misnumbered 323); citing Zech 2; Rev 21–22.
[6]Trapp, *Commentary or Exposition*, 92*; citing 2 Pet 1:5.
[7]Forerius, *Iesaiae*, 87v; citing Ps 118:19-20; 1 Pet 2:9.
[8]Oecolampadius, *In Iesaiam*, 156r.
[9]Bullinger, *Isaias*, 119v; citing 1 Pet 5:5; Rom 16:20.

will there be another God who is the rock and the preserver of mortals than this God, the Lord. Therefore, the one who builds all things, he is also the rock of all things. Therefore, the one who alone is the rock of all ages, he alone is also the one to be worshiped and called upon in every age. We do not have, we do not call on, and we do not worship any God other than the one who is the Alpha and Omega, the beginning and the end of all things. Commentary on Isaiah 26:4.[10]

Trust in the Lord Forever. Martin Luther: If you love peace and wish to have a quiet heart, "trust in the Lord," because there is no other way to genuine peace than to trust in the Lord, to hear the word from which hope and faith arise. "Forever." Do not leave but trust always in all afflictions and trials. If he wanted me to be poor and hungry forever, I would not want to leave faith. "For the Lord is an everlasting rock." Hope should be eternal, because the foundation is eternal, since our God does not ever grow weary of helping, and so we should also not stop hoping. . . . The Christian is daily attacked by Satan and therefore must keep hoping forever. Since the battle and struggle to keep faith is very great, Satan is so evil that he plots how to weary to exhaustion the one who stands on the word. Satan devises this plan in order to tire those who endure in the word. So Cyprian describes his wickedness in that some martyrs who were willing to die most gladly, he did not want to be killed before he had wearied them for a long time. Therefore we must keep hoping, not for one hour but always, from the morning watch all the way to the night. Lectures on Isaiah 26:4-5.[11]

26:7-15 *The Path of Righteousness in God's Judgments*

The Righteous Walk with Freedom and Delight. Heinrich Bullinger: Further he shows that the way of God is unhindered for the righteous in the church. This verse is read and explained variously. According to the word, it expresses, "The way for the righteous is straight," or, "The righteous walk on the right way," or, "The way of God is level and right for the righteous." Of all these, this seems to be the most simple sense. For the wicked, the way of God seems to be entangled, difficult, and uncertain, but for the righteous it is unhindered, straight, easy, and delightful. . . . So then, it is that the way of God, or the rule of living by God, handed down to us, is unhindered for the righteous. For God makes it level for the righteous by his Spirit he gave. The wicked suppose that they do what they want, or refrain from what they say they do not know, since they indeed pretend that Scripture is obscure, difficult, doubtful, and not absolute. The righteous think differently. Sermons on Isaiah 26:7-8.[12]

The Righteous Way Made by God's Judgments. Johannes Oecolampadius: "The way of the righteous is straight." The words of the church should attribute everything to God. So also this passage disparages free will to an extent. . . . "I know, O Lord, that the way of man is not in himself, that it is not in man to direct his steps." . . . "The heart of man plans his way, but the Lord directs his steps." Therefore he says, "O God, you are right; you will show the way to the righteous, and you will 'smooth it out,' that is, you will 'direct,' so that the righteous one works nothing less or more than necessary, nor are they too hot or too cold, and the courageous do not become rash, or the prudent cowardly. They do not turn to the right or to the left, but proceed in the royal way." And so God makes a prosperous path for those he saved. . . .

So he also says here, "We waited, we endured, we hoped in you, not only to be affected by kindnesses from you but also in the way of your judgments," that is, the afflicted and chastised. For affliction and the cross is the way of God's

[10]Musculus, *In Esaiam*, 397.

[11]LW 16:201* (WA 31.2:141-42); possibly referring to Pseudo-Cyprian, *De duplici matyrio* (PL 4:979-82).

[12]Bullinger, *Isaias*, 119r.

judgments, which turn us away from sins. And here it is evident that God is loved more by the righteous in adversity than by the wicked in prosperity. For the righteous think they are unworthy to be visited with so much kindness from the Father. This is what the prophet himself makes clear when he says, "Your name and your remembrance are the desire of our soul," that is, the soul is delighted greatly in the memory of your name. When it is chastened, it is content. Only let your name be hallowed, no matter what happens. You can also understand, by the "way of God's judgments," those profound judgments of predestination and justification of God by faith alone. Those who are good do not murmur about these judgments, as is the custom of the wicked and blasphemers. Commentary on Isaiah 26:7-8.[13]

Three Works of the Holy Spirit. Wolfgang Musculus: "In the way of your judgments, O Lord, we wait for you. . . ." The prophet recounts three things the Holy Spirit works in righteous people. The first is that they walk uprightly in the ways of God. Isaiah sang about this in the preceding verse. The second is that they wait patiently on the Lord, that is, on his goodwill, grace, and help. The third is that they yearn with desire to glorify and praise God's name. The prophet speaks about the latter two in this verse. Commentary on Isaiah 26:8.[14]

The Difference Between Soul and Spirit. Johannes Oecolampadius: But "my soul yearns for you," and not only my soul but also my spirit. There is a difference between soul and spirit, because there are things of the soul that pertain to nature, but the things that are of the spirit are beyond nature. Commentary on Isaiah 26:9.[15]

Learning Righteousness. Johannes Brenz: "For when your judgments are in the earth, the inhabitants of the world learn righteousness." The judgments of the Lord, about which the prophet here speaks, are not the law or afflictions but are that path and that way about which was said before, namely, the gospel of our Lord Jesus Christ. And similarly, the "name and remembrance" of God in this passage are the preaching of the gospel, by which God is recognized and celebrated. Therefore the faithful say, "O Lord, since the rightness of your judgments, or of your gospel, is so great that it leads us straight to righteousness and heavenly happiness, what else is left but to receive it and believe it, and hope for what he promises with sure and firm confidence." But we must do this not sleepily or lazily but with the desire of all our hearts. And not only once per year but by day and by night. For then people can obtain true righteousness, "When your judgments are in the earth," that is, when the gospel of Christ is preached sincerely and purely on the earth. Commentary on Isaiah 26:9.[16]

The Best Schoolmasters. John Trapp: God's judgments are the best schoolmasters. Queen Elizabeth learned much from Mr. Ascham, but more from her affliction. Our Savior himself learned something by the things that he suffered . . . , and so do all his members. Exposition on Isaiah 26:9.[17]

Learning and Not Learning Righteousness. Wolfgang Musculus: The sense is, since we have settled throughout the whole entire earth such that wherever we are chastised by "your judgments in the earth," we are instructed to "learn righteousness." This is confirmed in us, he says. The chastising and flogging, you push us to learn righteousness. The passage is about the usefulness of the cross, tribulation, and affliction. . . . "When favor is shown to the wicked, that one does not learn righteousness." That is, when one is not afflicted for what he deserves but thinks these are

[13]Oecolampadius, *In Iesaiam*, 157v; citing Jer 10:23; Prov 16:9.
[14]Musculus, *In Esaiam*, 399.
[15]Oecolampadius, *In Iesaiam*, 157r.
[16]Brenz, *Esaias*, 336-37.
[17]Trapp, *Commentary or Exposition*, 93*; citing Heb 5:8; Ezek 20:37.

good days, does not fear the Lord, is not urged to pursue righteousness, and does not learn, instead he persists and proceeds in his wickedness. Here we are admonished how foolish and harmful mercy is, that either we spare those wicked and sinful people, or when they are chastised, we think the wicked are going be spared. . . .

But it is apparent that this is said not about just any wicked people but about those who are mixed in among the people of God, including the notables and the nobles who were among them. Those people prove continuously to be wicked, such that they could not be influenced even by the kindness of God's grace to learn righteousness. God acted with his goodness toward them and was most merciful. In fact, when they experienced more grace, they departed further from the pursuit of righteousness. This is why they are finally exterminated. And so the sentence could be read to say it all this way, "When the people of the wicked were spared and were blessed, they did not learn righteousness; in the land of those who are right, that is, those acting rightly, they act unjustly, they do not see the magnificence of the Lord." Commentary on Isaiah 26:10.[18]

Peace and the Providence of God. Johannes Oecolampadius: God certainly destroys the wicked, but there will be peace for us. And while the hypocrites have momentary peace now that does not last, the righteous have truly eternal peace, which Christ also promises, saying, "My peace I give to you. . . ." Here the hypocrites always tremble, while we ourselves are certain and we trust in divine mercy that our peace will never be lacking. "Since in this age, there is so much evidence of your benevolence, O God, we indeed confess that you made all our works, you created us, you redeemed, you supplied the strength; whatever good we ever did, we did by your authorship and your work; we ourselves are nothing except organs and instruments of the greatest worker." Therefore we ascribe to providence and not to our fortitude, nor our strength, whatever is good or evil, whether prosperous or hostile. . . . "In him, we live and move and we exist." Commentary on Isaiah 26:11-12.[19]

God Does All the Work in Us. John Mayer: To this effect Calvin and Musculus reject applying this verse against the papists to prove that we have no strength of free will to attain grace but that is solely God's work in us. For they say we have enough clear passages to prove this, and if we should insist on this interpretation, it would easily be eluded. But if we deduce from this peace in heaven forever and the perfecting of the good work begun in us, as Musculus does, I can see no reason why we should not take it as meant by this phrase "all our works" the grace wrought in us, as well as any other favor we receive in this world. On the contrary, because he spoke last about the uprightness of the way of the righteous, it then comes to this conclusion. And it is a true position that God works all the works of grace by his Spirit, whereby we become acceptable to him, for the bringing of us to his special favor here and to the life hereafter, since our weakness is such that we can do nothing in ourselves. Yet to show that he does not work in us as in dead images, he bids us turn and reproves those who will not, thus implying a will concurring with his grace in the act of turning. Commentary on Isaiah 26:12.[20]

Responding to Objections. Dietrich Schnepff: These are the praises in the chapter, but the remaining part of the song is spent on the solution to implicit objections. The first one is: If Christ teaches righteousness to all, then why are there so many wicked people? He responds, Indeed, that kindness of true righteousness is offered to all, but not all accept it. The second objection is, When the church is oppressed with tyranny and affliction, how can we attribute peace to it? He responds that this is indeed true, but when the righteous call on the Lord, the wicked are punished,

[18]Musculus, *In Esaiam*, 400.

[19]Oecolampadius, *In Iesaiam*, 158v; citing Jn 14:27; Acts 17:28.

[20]Mayer, *Commentary upon All the Prophets*, 4:163*.

and in contrast persecutions serve the enlargement of the church. Second, afflictions sharpen the faith and praying among the righteous. The third response is that death itself is not a nuisance (1) since the dead are going to be raised, (2) because the resurrected are joyful, (3) because graves are chambers in which the righteous rest until the wrath of the Lord comes, and (4) the Lord is not going to forget his own who were killed unjustly but is going to reveal their blood. Scholia on Isaiah 26:10-14.[21]

Blinded Eyes. John Trapp: Mrs. Hutchinson, that Jezebel of New England, as she had vented about thirty misshapen opinions there, so she brought forth about thirty deformed monsters. After this (because they would not be reclaimed but rejected admonition, saying, "This is for you, you legalists, that your eyes might be further blinded by God's hand upon us, in your legalistic ways . . ."), she and her family were slain (some say burned) by the Indians, who never used to exercise such an outrage on anyone. Exposition on Isaiah 26:14.[22]

Spirits Do Not Rise. Heinrich Bullinger: And now, the specific goal of this canticle is going to be repeated again as he clearly mentions the penalty of the ungodly. "Your dead," he says, "will not live." He calls the tyrants and persecutors "the dead." One is called such, as the Lord said, "Let the dead bury their dead." And Paul, "The widow who is self-indulgent is dead while she lives." Now, there are such dead in this life, because they lack faith and life in God. Therefore they will not live but will perish perpetually in death, according to the statement of the Savior, "Unless you believe that I am, you will die in your sins." And certainly toward this, "Truly, truly I say to you," he says, "if anyone keeps my word, that one will never see death."

He adds to these another reason to be explained when he said, "And the Rephaim will not rise." In fact, now he calls those whom he had termed the dead the Rephaim, that is, the tyrants and giants. And because he had said, "They will not live," now he explains, "They will not rise." Although it is not that simple: For all people, whether good or bad, are going to be resurrected for judgment, as is testified throughout Scripture. Therefore, those ones "will not rise" to glory and to heavenly joy but to disgrace and the eternal underworld of sorrow and everlasting fire. Truly by antonomasia† and according to metonymy,† he expresses as giants all the persecutors and wicked, alluding to those who were rebelling against God at the time of the flood. . . .

By "dead," therefore, he understands the bodies of the dead. For the soul does not die. The bodies die, with the souls then transported. Moreover, they are blessed who die in the Lord. Hence, "Your," it says, "dead will live," of course, to eternal life. But this is the antithesis to the earlier statement, "Your dead will not live, and the Rephaim will not rise." And to express the truth of the bodily resurrection of the dead more significantly, he adds, "And they will rise with my body." Others read, "And as my corpse they will rise." Sermons on Isaiah 26:14.[23]

Increasing the Nation. Wolfgang Musculus: He continues the direct address to God he had begun. To "increase the nation" is to either add to its number or pile blessings on it. Jerome expressed the latter sense when he translated it, "You have shown favor, O Lord, to the nation." And we say in German, "Gott gibt all tag zum, Gott hat weidlich zum geben" [God gives every day; God has plenty to give], when we speak about the blessings of his grace. But God has bestowed both on the Jewish nation, his people. So the prophet says about them, "He has multiplied his nation,

[21]Schnepff, *In Esaiae*, 382.

[22]Trapp, *Commentary or Exposition*, 94; citing Thomas Welde, preface to "A Short Story of the rise, reign, and ruin of the Antinomians, Familists & Libertines, that infected the churches of New England," by John Winthrop (London, 1644).

[23]Bullinger, *Isaias*, 121v, 122v; citing Lk 9:60; 1 Tim 5:6; Jn 8:24, 51; Is 29:16. †*Antonomasia* is a figure of speech in which some defining word or phrase is substituted for a person's proper name or a group of people. *Metonymy* is when a closely related term or attribute is used to refer to something or someone else.

and piled on it innumerable blessings," when he says, "You have increased the nation, O Lord, you have increased the nation." The sense seems to be, "You have blessed our nation, Lord; you have multiplied and enriched it." But the latter part of this verse is more difficult and so is explained in various ways. . . . Now if this sense is acceptable, the rest of it is going to be read more easily. "You will add to the nation, O Lord, you will add to the nation; you will be glorified when you expand it to the ends of the earth." So this is a prophecy about Christ's kingdom, which will extend through all the nations of the entire world. Commentary on Isaiah 26:15.[24]

26:16-21 *Lament in Helplessness and Hope in Resurrection*

The Father's Comforting Mercy. Hans Has von Hallstatt: Behold, what joy overflowing with grace there might be to a believing, troubled person when one notices and acknowledges the paternal mercy the eternal Father has for one. One takes note of and recognizes this most clearly, however, when one is in fear, need, and tribulation; there one learns best what the eternal providence of God is, what good it is, how comforting it is. Otherwise one cannot lay hold of and experience it without danger, regardless of how attractively or beautifully one may debate the issue. All this can obviously be received and acknowledged only through the living Spirit. Here one learns with the heart that all our deeds and salvation arise from no other power than God's might. Concerning the Comfort of Christians.[25]

The Parable of the Pregnant Woman. Johannes Oecolampadius: "Like a pregnant woman." With another parable here they show the various sufferings that the righteous bear. They are compared to the sufferings of labor, and without fruit. The Lord used this same parable. . . . Now he wishes to say, "We have carried so much suffering in the presence of God, who chastises us as a pregnant woman in the presence of a midwife. And although we have suffered to such an extent, we did not murmur at God in the way one does to a midwife or doctor. On the contrary, we loved him more in gratitude, and our sufferings increased, because we did not give birth to a child, that is, salvation. For the tribulation is not yet over; we have given birth to spirit and wind, that is, we have carried these sufferings in vain." And what follows indicates that this is the mind of the prophet. For he says that salvations that happen in the earth and those exalted inhabitants of the world are not yet humbled, nor have they fallen. Commentary on Isaiah 26:17-18.[26]

Every Work of Liberation from God. Wolfgang Musculus: "We have accomplished no deliverance in the earth, and the inhabitants of the world have not fallen." When it says, "We have given birth to wind," it means "they open." They were pregnant with the salvation and restoration of their land, from which they were cast out, and the fall of the inhabitants of the world, namely, the Babylonian nations. But they were not giving birth to what they had carried in the womb. They were not at all powerful to cause the land to be restored to them and the Babylonians to be knocked down. These are both in the hand of God, who alone fulfills both in his own time. They remember this helplessness of theirs, so they convey that the entire work of their liberation is credited to God. Commentary on Isaiah 26:18.[27]

The Resurrected Bodies of Your People. Johannes Brenz: These also pertain to another part of the antithesis about the righteous. But these things clearly preach not only about the resurrection of the righteous but also about their eternal joy. Earlier he said about the wicked, "They

[24]Musculus, *In Esaiam*, 403.
[25]CRR 12:452.
[26]Oecolampadius, *In Iesaiam*, 159v; citing Jn 16.
[27]Musculus, *In Esaiam*, 404.

will die; they will not live." But now he says the opposite about the righteous, "Your dead will live; my slain ones will rise." You see that a change in the personal pronoun happened. The prophet says, "Your dead will live." Either Christ immediately takes up his speech and speaks himself, "My slain," he says, "will rise, so that you recognize this entire speech is not a human dream, but the voice of the Son of God." Or the righteous are called "the dead" or "the slain in Christ" (since the emphasis of this speech is placed on these pronouns, *your* and *my*). And either they die in Christ or they are killed on account of Christ.

And so this is the meaning. The wicked, even if they are happy for a long time in this age, nevertheless they will not have a happy life in the resurrection of the dead, but rather they must perish and suffer perpetually. But for the righteous, although in this age they were afflicted all the way to death, yet they will be preserved in death and they will be raised to eternal joy. . . . It is evident that this passage is about the resurrection of the righteous to eternal happiness. First, indeed, the godly are not simply called the dead and the slain but the dead and the slain of Christ. "*Your* dead," it says, "will live," and, "*My* slain will rise." That is why just as Christ, who is head of the church, did not perish in his body in death but rose from the dead and sat down at the right hand of God, so also the righteous who die in Christ do not perish in death but will be raised from death to the kingdom of heavenly joy, so that with Christ they may enjoy all the divine benefits. Commentary on Isaiah 26:19.[28]

Resurrection as Certainty of Promises. John Trapp: God can as easily raise the dead as refresh the herbs of the earth with a reviving dew, even when they have been scorched to death with the heat of the sun. Do we not see a yearly resurrection of grass, grain, flowers, fruits every spring? And surely if nature can produce out of a small seed a great tree, or a butterfly out of a worm, or the beautiful feathered peacock out of a misshapen egg, cannot the Almighty raise our bodies out of dust, who first made them out of dust? Or can the condition of any people or person be so desperate that he is not able to help them out? The assurance of God's power, which shall show itself in the raising of the dead, is a most excellent argument to assure us of the certainty of God's promises, even if they ever seem so incredible to flesh and blood. Exposition on Isaiah 26:19.[29]

The Brevity of Affliction. Johannes Oecolampadius: "Come, my people." Again the prophet comforts the people based on the brevity of time, and by this influences them toward patience. And so frequently this is often the way Scripture consoles. . . . "The sufferings of this present time are not worth comparing to the glory that is to be revealed." . . . "Our light, momentary affliction is preparing for us an eternal weight of glory beyond all comparison." Moreover, he wants to say, "No one should be bothered that the body is afflicted here for a time and lies in dust. For the time is brief and momentary when compared to eternity. However much other afflictions are, let us take even more comfort here." So also . . . it is responded to the souls under the altar who had been slain that they are "to rest a little longer." Commentary on Isaiah 26:20.[30]

Memorable Exhortation. Johannes Brenz: This is a memorable exhortation. "Enter your chambers" . . . is a form of expression that seems to be taken from Genesis 43 when Joseph entered his chamber to cry. And . . . when the Israelites were commanded by God to stay in their homes with no one coming out the door of their house until the Lord had passed through Egypt to strike down the firstborn. And from . . . when Micaiah says to Zedekiah that he would go from chamber to chamber to hide because of his shame. But Christ

[28]Brenz, *Esaias*, 342-43; citing Is 26:14.

[29]Trapp, *Commentary or Exposition*, 95-96*.

[30]Oecolampadius, *In Iesaiam*, 159r; citing Rom 8:18; 2 Cor 4:17; Rev 6:9-11.

also admonishes when praying. "Go," he says, "into your room and shut the door and pray to your Father who is in secret." Let us therefore be stirred up by this exhortation not to lose heart in adversity and fail in courage, as if God himself in heaven were dead and had perished. But let us know that this is strength for the righteous to suffer affliction in this world, and let us enter into our chambers. Commentary on Isaiah 26:20.[31]

The Place of Heaven. Heinrich Bullinger: Behold, you will find that what you have heard so far about the coming of the Lord in judgment is true, and the wicked will feel what they never imagined or expected would happen. For the Lord God will come out from his place to judge or to punish the wicked. The place of God (although his essence is confined to no place) is properly heaven, as the prophet says: "The Lord has established his tabernacle in the heavens, and his kingdom rules over all." And Christ, the Son of God, who took on flesh, ascended into heaven. Of course, from this, by "from his place," I say, "from heaven," according to the rule of faith, "he will come to judge the living and the dead." The clear testimonies of Scripture confirm this when they attest that Christ the Lord is going to descend from heaven in judgment. . . .

About these certain teachings full of consolation, these new Pyrrhonian skeptics of ours dispute, asserting that it is possible to teach what it is not and where heaven is not, but not likewise what it is or where it is. And they oppose those who teach that heaven is a certain place above us in the highest realms. For they deny that heaven is a place because they claim that it is everywhere the Lord wants it to be. Obviously this is a strange teaching and is to be considered by all the righteous as worthy to be mocked and rejected. Sermons on Isaiah 26:21.[32]

[31]Brenz, *Esaias*, 344-45; citing Gen 43; Ex 12; 1 Kings 22:25; Mt 6:6.

[32]Bullinger, *Isaias*, 123v; citing Ps 103:19; Mt 24; Acts 1; Phil 3; 1 Thess 4; 2 Thess 1.

27:1-13 SONG OF THE VINEYARD

27 In that day the LORD with his hard and great and strong sword will punish Leviathan the fleeing serpent, Leviathan the twisting serpent, and he will slay the dragon that is in the sea.

2In that day,
"A pleasant vineyard,[a] sing of it!
3I, the LORD, am its keeper;
every moment I water it.
Lest anyone punish it,

I keep it night and day;
4I have no wrath.

Would that I had thorns and briers to battle!
I would march against them,
I would burn them up together.

5Or let them lay hold of my protection,
let them make peace with me,
let them make peace with me."

6In days to come[b] Jacob shall take root,
Israel shall blossom and put forth shoots
and fill the whole world with fruit.

7Has he struck them as he struck those who struck them?
Or have they been slain as their slayers were slain?

8Measure by measure,[c] by exile you contended with them;
he removed them with his fierce breath[d] in the day of the east wind.

9Therefore by this the guilt of Jacob will be atoned for,
and this will be the full fruit of the removal of his sin:[e]

when he makes all the stones of the altars
like chalkstones crushed to pieces,
no Asherim or incense altars will remain standing.

10For the fortified city is solitary,
a habitation deserted and forsaken, like the wilderness;

there the calf grazes;
there it lies down and strips its branches.

11When its boughs are dry, they are broken;
women come and make a fire of them.

For this is a people without discernment;
therefore he who made them will not have compassion on them;
he who formed them will show them no favor.

12In that day from the river Euphrates[f] to the
Brook of Egypt the LORD will thresh out the grain,
and you will be gleaned one by one, O people of Israel.
13And in that day a great trumpet will be blown, and
those who were lost in the land of Assyria and those who were driven out to the land of Egypt will come and worship the LORD on the holy mountain at Jerusalem.

a Many Hebrew manuscripts *A vineyard of wine* b Hebrew *In those to come* c Or *By driving her away*; the meaning of the Hebrew word is uncertain d Or *wind* e Septuagint *and this is the blessing when I take away his sin* f Hebrew *from the River*

OVERVIEW: In this chapter, Isaiah gives us a prophetic song about the Lord's work to care for his vineyard and make it fruitful. The Leviathan mentioned in the first verse receives a great deal of discussion, since it was variously understood as a reference to the human kings in Isaiah's time, to

Satan, to devilish empires in general, and even to specific rulers in each commentators' own day. The Reformation interpreters then explain the allegory of the vineyard, often connecting the promises with the true church and the pronouncements of judgment to the Jews or the practices in the church they rejected. This is particularly evident in how some of them address the atonement for sins mentioned in the song. They insist from this passage that God rejects the abominable ceremonies in the church and that sins can only be atoned by the death of Christ, not through deeds of satisfaction or human afflictions.

27:1 *The Punishment of Leviathan*

Leviathan Represents the Kings. Wolfgang Musculus: This verse is explained variously. Rabbi Kimchi explains it to be about the overthrow of God and Magog.[†] Our ancients, which a few more recent ones follow, explain it to be about the destruction of the kingdom of Satan done by Christ. There are some who suppose the prophecy is directed against Egypt, Assyria, and Judah, who were going to be destroyed by the Romans. They perhaps are moved to this because they discern the prophet sees a threefold division when he preaches, "The Lord will punish with a hard, great, and strong sword," when it says about Leviathan the serpent, which is the image conveyed, "Leviathan the twisting serpent, and he will slay the dragon that is in the sea."

In my judgment, it would not be absurd to explain that the dragon is the king of Babylon, just as the same dragon is in the sea, which is the serpent Leviathan, similarly conveyed as the twisting serpent. . . . Yet I am unwilling to contend with anyone if it seems the prophet is not exclusively prophesying about the overthrow of only one, but of three kinds to be ruined, because of the coupled *vav*, that is, "and," which is repeated a second time. In that sense, by "Leviathan," which he says is the image conveyed, is meant the king of Assyria, by "Leviathan the twisting serpent" is meant the king of Babylon, and by the "dragon in the sea" is meant the king of Egypt. I prefer this view over others who apply this to the Egyptians, the Assyrians, and the Jews. There were three such kings, Assyria, Babylon, and Egypt, who were the most powerful enemies of the people of God, the same as whales, Leviathan, and the dragon in the sea rule over the sea. And the Lord was going to visit and extinguish them, by which he would rescue his people and the remaining nations with them by their necks. Commentary on Isaiah 27:1.[1]

Leviathan as Satan. Ulrich Zwingli: Indeed, I judge that in this case why we treat this passage so obscurely is that in the Septuagint translation, they consistently render *Leviathan* as "Satan," who is the "dragon." We proceeded to understand that it is not even the king of Babylon. Yet then I easily allow him to become a demon through our allegory, though not of the prophet. Now it appears (as above)[†] that when Babylon was called Lucifer, we are keeping in this passage what was the common meaning according to the Hebrews in the case of Lucifer, even though from the sacred writings nothing else is clearly signified about him than this: he fell and was bound with ropes, he is a being clothed as a serpent, he seduced the first parents and now lies in ambush no differently than from the beginning. But from this the catagogies[‡] were obtained by godly men that if the most prideful adversary was going to be brought down, that is, descended, they already attributed that it would be Lucifer by catagogy, such that all the things above attributed to the king of Babylon correspond to Lucifer. So also in this passage, it seems that strength is allegorized by catagogy when the name Leviathan is also used as a paraphrase for the Babylonian. Annotations on Isaiah 27:1.[2]

[1]Musculus, *In Esaiam*, 406; citing Ps 74:13-14. [†]Kimchi, *Commentary on Isaiah*, 153.

[2]CR 101:278.32–279.11. [†]The reference to what Zwingli had addressed earlier is 234.1-7 on Is 14:12. [‡]*Catagogy* derives from the Greek word *katagogia* and refers to an interpretive method that "brings something down." In comparison to an anagogical

The Metaphor of Leviathan. Adam Sasbout: "In that day the Lord will visit. . . ." That is, at the consummation of the age, God will particularly treat Leviathan not in the way he treats the rest but with his hard, great, and strong sword. Now, if the prophet had said, "In that day the Lord will visit the devil," this would have been a very easy passage, and it would have been obvious to anyone. But now there is a difficulty because of the word *Leviathan,* which he wanted to signify the devil. This is certain because all Jews and Christians alike agree on this interpretation. But this word (Leviathan) naturally signifies a specific kind of fish, vast and enormous, as according to us, an expression for a large sea animal or whale. Although there are those who do not want this to signify a certain kind of fish but any kind of vast and large thing found in the sea, such as, among the Latins, a sea monster. But whether there is a certain kind of fish is not evident from the Scriptures. . . .

The name Leviathan itself is not used anywhere else more naturally than . . . , "Can you draw out Leviathan with a fishhook?" Because Job had spoken something more arrogantly, his arrogance is suppressed, and it is proposed to him that his strength is nothing by two things that are superior to his strength, the second of which is to draw out a Leviathan with a fishhook. On that passage, Gregory understands the Leviathan to be the devil. The same word is found in the Psalms, "The sea is great and wide with creatures," that is, bending with winding, "there are innumerable reptiles." Such a serpent you formed to mock them.

What Job did . . . , David did this in that psalm, namely, he relates the magnificence of God from two things: He first enumerates the wonderful works of God that may be seen on the earth and concluded that with the saying, "O Lord, how great are your works. In wisdom you have made them all; the earth is full of your possession." Then he added the things that are to be admired in the sea—"I spoke about the earth, let the spacious sea with its creatures be considered," that is, bending with much winding and roundabout ways. There you will see no less miraculous things. There the serpent that was formed to mock them, that is, "You formed among the other aquatic animals also Leviathan to play in the sea." For where we have *serpent,* Jerome reads *Leviathan,* and that is what the Hebrews have. But that it is said "to mock them," in the Greek is said "to play in it," that is, the sea. This seems to be the first and most genuine sense.

Yet the commentaries generally explain it figuratively in this way: Among the rest of the creatures of this world (for they understand by the sea, the world), you have formed the devil to play games with us. From this it should be asked whether such is interpreted by a metaphor, and if by a metaphor, from where that is derived. With it derived from the nature of the thing, what property does it have that corresponds to the devil? Or if by an allegory of things they understand the devil by the name Leviathan, from where do they get this, when that is usually asked about things done and not about the nature of things? Where can it be taught from Scripture that the Lord wanted that fish to be a type of the devil? . . . It is certain that this word was not simply put in this passage, since the Lord will not simply deal with fish but with people and demons. Therefore it is necessary to recognize the metaphor by which the devil is signified, or his servants, his people. And it corresponds more to understand the devil because of the powers of Leviathan, which require a hard, great, and strong sword to overcome.

So the sense of this passage is this: you, my chosen ones, who in this world experience how difficult it is to overcome the devil and to avoid his deceptions and temptations, behold, at the end of the world I will destroy him and everything that belongs to him once and for all. Commentary on Isaiah 27:1.[3]

interpretation that "brings up" to a higher (typically heavenly) point, a catagogical interpretation leads to a lower point.

[3]Sasbout, *In Esaiam,* 185; citing Job 41:1; Ps 104:26, 24.

Devilish Empires Swallowing Up. John Trapp: By Leviathan here, Oecolampadius understands the devil, who is elsewhere also called the serpent and the great dragon. . . . But they do better, in my judgment, who by Leviathan here understand some great tyrant, acted on by the devil against the church: such as was Pharaoh . . . , Sennacherib . . . , or Nebuchadnezzar, . . . and in this day the Grand Signior, who has swallowed up countries as the Leviathan or the whale does to fishes. For by the greatness of his empire is swallowed up both the name and empire of the Saracens, the most glorious empire of the Greeks, the empire of Trapezonum, the renowned kingdoms of Macedonia, Peloponnesus, Epirus, Bulgaria, Serbia, Bosnia, Armenia, Cyprus, Syria, Egypt, Judea, Tunis, Argeirs, Media, Mesopotamia, a great part of Hungary, and also the Persian kingdom.

His territories do somewhat resemble a long and winding serpent, as some learned men have observed: and for the slights and might that he uses against Christians still, who does not know them from the Turkish story? God therefore will shortly take him to task, happily sharpening the swords of men (as he has lately and marvelously done to the Venetians) as instruments to destroy this vast empire, which labors with nothing more than the weightiness of itself. Exposition on Isaiah 27:1.[4]

27:2-6 *The Fruitful Vineyard of the Lord*

Multiple Meanings of That Day. Johannes Oecolampadius: "In that day." And this pertains to the day of judgment, not only to when Christ hung on the cross but also to when he is going to come in majesty. For in both not only are sinners condemned but so is the devil himself, who is called Leviathan, the serpent, and dragon. Commentary on Isaiah 27:2.[5]

[4]Trapp, *Commentary or Exposition*, 96-97*; citing Rev 12:9; 20:2; Ezek 29:3; Is 8:7; Jer 51:13,

[5]Oecolampadius, *In Iesaiam*, 160v; citing Rev 12; 1 Cor 15; John 16:11.

Two Different Vineyards. Konrad Pellikan: It says that "a pleasant vineyard" will answer him, namely, the church, not God, for this is sung alternately to the former and latter vineyard. For this vineyard of the new people, "I, the Lord, am its keeper," that it may bring forth the best fruits of faith and that it may never fall away from faith in the true God. But the previous deprived vineyard was deprived of a hedge because of the wild vines, and its wall was trampled by beasts exposing it. For this one, every moment the grace of the divine Spirit from on high irrigates and makes it fertile, but that one has been condemned to perpetual dryness and barrenness by the rains and dew denied it. Commentary on Isaiah 27:2-3.[6]

The Planter and Keeper of the Vineyard. Heinrich Bullinger: God himself preaches (for he is introduced by the prophet as the speaker) that he is the planter and keeper of his vineyard. For this vineyard requires two things, that it has a planter and a keeper. All the cultivation is expressed by irrigation, and when he affirms that he "waters it every moment," it certainly signifies the most meticulous care and cultivation. Further, God waters the church by his Spirit and with life-giving drink, as he himself explains. . . . But also he waters by the ministry of his word and renders his vineyard fruit-bearing, as is testified by the apostle. . . . He likewise shows that he is the most vigilant keeper by far when he says he keeps his vineyard day and night.

And at the end is added about the keeping, "Lest anyone punish it," without doubt meaning that enemies may not invade it and plunder it and devastate it. For there are many enemies of the church, not only invisible but also visible, malignant spirits, and depraved people, heretics, persecutors, and others like that. One cannot preach enough the immeasurable kindness of God toward the church, when each moment proves that God is the most vigilant and best keeper against every danger and all evils. Sermons on Isaiah 27:3.[7]

[6]Pellikan, *Commentaria Bibliorum*, 3:33v.

[7]Bullinger, *Isaias*, 124v; citing Jn 15; 1 Cor 3.

Restrained Wrath Because of Election. Martin Borrhaus: "There is no wrath in me." Among the different interpretations offered, it seems the simplest one to explain the thought of our prophet is as follows: "I do not harbor wrath toward my vineyard. For if I did harbor it, obviously I would angrily burn down what produces for me thorns and briers instead of grapes—unless my strength was restrained such that I would raze less in my wrath." But how is divine wrath contained so that the vineyard of the church is razed less? It is restrained by the faith of the covenant and promised salvation. So even if the Lord especially desired to remain angry forever, he cannot, because by election he loves his own from eternity. So then, having been conquered by the weapons of faith, the vineyard is convinced of what comes next: "He will make peace with me," by reconciling himself to me through the Spirit of the Messiah, my husband. This is the Spirit of divine grace against the law of sin and death; through the blood of the Messiah, the Spirit is the reconciler and guarantor against all the power of the enemy. Oracles in Isaiah on 27:4.[8]

Thorns and Briers from God. Johannes Oecolampadius: Yet a more hidden sense lies here, namely, that Christ is ours, whom God the Father gives briers and thorns and who makes peace. For to some he is the resurrection; to others he is their downfall, as if he were saying, "Although I am God most merciful, nevertheless if anyone will strike against the Son, he makes me a thorn and brier, a warrior and fire. But if he loved my Son, he will find me to be a peaceful Father in all things. Therefore Christ is our one mediator between God and humanity." . . . He specifies that God is a thorn and brier if you strike against him, and he brings peace if you believe. He will also remove all the fruit of sin from Jacob, that is, of his elect. Commentary on Isaiah 27:4.[9]

[8]Borrhaus, *In Iesaiae Prophetae Oracula*, 248.
[9]Oecolampadius, *In Iesaiam*, 160r.

War Against Thorns and Briers. Johannes Brenz: "Who will give me a brier and thorn to battle?" I will trample it (the thorn) and set it on fire at the same time. Or one can be captured by the hand or with my strength, and he will make peace with me. "Peace," I say, "he will make with me." That is, although I allow my vine to be ravaged by boars and lions, and if I turn a blind eye at it, my church is afflicted by the wicked, I do not do this out of indignation and furor against the church. I do not intend to desert, ruin, and crush the church, but rather I do this out of favor and love, so that the church may be preserved more marvelously and receive greater benefits from God.

I do not wage war against the good and fertile vines in my vineyard but against the thorns and briers, which are impediments to the vines. And I indeed accept that the vines must be pruned and cleansed so that they will bear more abundant fruit. I accept that thorns either must be eradicated entirely, trampled underfoot, and cast into the fire, or, if perhaps I did not eradicate a thorn, I still "lay hold of my protection," and I force it to have peace with me. "Let them make," I say, "peace with me," that is, let them be made subject to me, serve me willingly, and either be a peg to which vines are tied or a hedge by which vines are protected. And so I make a distinction between the thorns: some I pull out and cast into the fire; others I use for hedges to keep out the beasts. But I only plant and keep vines so that they bear fruit in their season. Commentary on Isaiah 27:4-5.[10]

Fruit of the Promised Land. Ulrich Zwingli: "To fill the whole world with its fruit." What further fruit is this, if Christ is not the Savior of the world? For in this passage it does not specify *land* as the word that Jews could use for their cause that the Promised Land would be filled with the seed he promises here, but it is *world*. Therefore he promises there will be so much lacking that Jacob is totally abandoned and that he

[10]Brenz, *Esaias*, 348.

is going to claim the world for himself. This is what happens then, when we rightly claim his name and that of Israel by the faith received. Annotations on Isaiah 27:6.[11]

The Allegory of the Vineyard Explained. Dietrich Schnepff: Everyone understands these are allegorical. So the prophet himself briefly explains what he had said about the Lord's vineyard. Moreover, he teaches the vineyard is clearly Jacob or Israel, that is, the church assembled from Hebrews and Gentiles. For all who believe are Israelites. But the church, gathered from both peoples, has grown so much in the whole world that its boundaries even are the whole world. Now Isaiah interprets himself what he says about these things when he says, "The days are coming when Jacob shall take root, Israel shall sprout and blossom, and the surfaces of the world will be filled with fruit." The prophet used two terms in this passage, namely, Jacob and Israel, to show eloquently that when he speaks about the vineyard, he wants us to understand the church, as in their custom the prophets call it Israel and Jacob. . . .

But now that Isaiah added, "The surfaces of the earth will be filled with fruit," he wanted to explain what he understood by "red wine," when he commends the vine. By "red wine" he means the fruit that the Israelites carried into the whole world. Christ preached about this fruit. . . . "Every branch in me that does not bear fruit he takes away, and every branch that does bear fruit he prunes, that it may bear much fruit." And again, "Whoever abides in me and I in him, this one bears much fruit." And in the same passage, "By this my Father is glorified, that you bear much fruit." Paul also prays for the Philippians . . . that they be "filled with the fruit of righteous that comes through Jesus Christ." And he likewise says . . . , "The gospel is bearing fruit in the whole world." But the fruit of that gospel and of the righteous are the true knowledge of God, calling on him, and true worship, which is only in the church of Christ. The fruit of the righteous are also good works. Scholia on Isaiah 27:6.[12]

27:7-13 *Purifying and Enlarging the Vineyard*

The Branch as the Elect. Martin Borrhaus: Other interpretations are also offered, but this one I suggest seems to be simple enough and according to the thought of the prophet. This is the interpretation that the apostle used when he said that the branches of the shoot of Israel were broken off due to unfaithfulness: "For if God did not spare the natural branches, see that it does not happen that he will not spare you." But the times of antichrist[†] are evidence that this has happened. So we recognize that in general, what is described about the church of the elect from among Israelites and Gentiles is what we read here, "He prunes his branches moderately."

Further, by "the east wind," a "northerner," a more harsh and rough kind is signified. It blows from that region that lies between the north and the east. Some interpret this as Eurus, the wind that blows from the east at the returning or the solstice of the winter sun, which the Romans called *vulturnus*. Oracles in Isaiah on 27:8.[13]

Human Afflictions Do Not Expiate Sins. Johannes Brenz: So this should not be understood [as saying] that human afflictions are expiations of sins before God. By the affliction of the Son of God alone, by the death of Christ alone, he expiates our sin before God. But our afflictions are not of such significance that they expiate sins in the judgment of God and placate his wrath. So therefore our sins are said to be expiated because they lead to the recognition of sin, they arouse us to seek the forgiveness of sin, and they invite us to flee from sins to Christ and avoid them, that we maintain obedience in our duty. Here God

[11]CR 101:280.7-13.

[12]Schnepff, *In Esaiae*, 404; citing Jn 15:2, 5, 8; Phil 1:11; Col 1:5-6.

[13]Borrhaus, *In Iesaiae Prophetae Oracula*, 249; citing Rom 11[:21].

[†]By "the times of antichrist," he likely means the papacy in his day.

considers that when he hurls afflictions at his people, certainly he does not want to ruin them but to help and to save them so they do not perish. Commentary on Isaiah 27:9.[14]

How Chastisement Removes Sin. Wolfgang Musculus: Now, there is an emphasis in what he says, "By this," and what he adds, "this will be the full fruit," that is, the usefulness of correction. Now, in the time of peace, Jacob continues to act unjustly against the Lord, and he cannot be brought to repentance by any laws or prophetic warnings so that their iniquities could be atoned. But "by this will he be atoned," and "this will be the full fruit where his sin is removed, and he placed all the stones of the altars. . . ." But we must be careful that we do not understand by the word *atoned* the satisfaction for sins. . . . Even when our sins are atoned for after scourging, they are not atoned on account of our satisfaction or sufficient suffering, but on account of the merciful atonement of God. This is so because it cannot have a place among the untroubled and unrepentant. Yet without the scourge we do not repent; it needs chastisement so that we are humbled and moved to repentance.

Therefore, to the extent he employs the scourge of chastisement to repentance (without which sins are not forgiven) to that extent the prophet here says it will be that the iniquities of Jacob are atoned. "Where he removed," it says, "his sin." By sin, I understand in this place the external idolatry of the Jewish people, the altars, certainly the sacred groves, the shrines, the idols, and the worship of foreign gods. He says the Lord is going to remove this sin, and so he explains what follows. Commentary on Isaiah 27:9.[15]

The Fruit of Repentance. Francisco Forerius: Therefore the prophet responds on account of this that he groans and suffers so much that his iniquities are atoned; indeed, this is the fruit of all. With that rebuke, God wanted nothing other than to remove his error. He was not striking to strike as enemies do, but he was striking to remove sin by bringing Israel to repentance. They would prove this to be true by one thing—reducing the stones of the altars that had been erected in honor of false gods to dust, like chalkstones. And hereafter groves or statues should not be raised or stand. And I think this is the genuine exposition of this passage. Commentary on Isaiah 27:9.[16]

Atonement in Christ on the Cross. Heinrich Bullinger: Now he uses two terms, what I mean is, *atoning* and *removing*, and in turn *guilt* and *sin*. Some understand this to mean the fruit of sin, and so they read it, "And he will remove all the fruit of the nation's sin." By fruit of sin, they understand the death, condemnation, and all the other things that come from sin. But whatever the case may be, the prophet is very obviously showing that sin itself and whatever is understood by the term *sin* is fully pardoned or remitted by the grace of God through Christ, both with respect to its guilt and its punishment. Incidentally, he also signifies when this will be: at the time when the altar is reduced to ashes, that is, when the Jewish sacrifices in the temple of Jerusalem were abolished. This, of course, happened when Christ offered himself to God the Father on the cross. By his one sacrifice, he abolished all others and perfected for all time the holy ones, as Scripture testifies elsewhere. . . .

And so, by the death of Christ all sacrifices were abolished and removed. As confirmation of this fact, the Lord cried out as he was breathing his last, "It is finished." And the veil of the temple was torn in two. . . . So then, let us cling to the immense love of God toward his church, which Christ showed us, and in which we have the forgiveness of all sins and freedom from both Judaism and paganism. Christ gained this freedom for us by his death, and it was indeed efficacious for the salvation of all believers in all generations, even though it was finally completed under Pontius Pilate, the governor of

[14]Brenz, *Esaias*, 353.
[15]Musculus, *In Esaiam*, 409-10.
[16]Forerius, *Iesaiae*, 92v.

the Romans, who were then ruled by the emperor, Tiberius Caesar. So we see that everywhere, or whenever a suitable opportunity arose, Isaiah prophesied about Christ, the Savior of all the elect, just as he did here. Sermons on Isaiah 27:9.[17]

Abominable Ceremonies in the Church. Konrad Pellikan: In the same way that he has spoken about how the congregations of the faithful church are, so also does one read about the companies of idolaters, cities, villages, shrines, and monasteries—the many kinds of things found extensively among the heathens. He says that all these profane sacrileges and their worshipers, as equally as Jerusalem and the ancient ceremonial worship of God through Christ, will likewise perish—but not for the same reason. They will be forsaken, abandoned, devastated, and horrid as the wilderness, such that there is going to be in that place a pasture for calves—such that no remnants of heathens remain. But if some of the holy fathers had taken more diligent care of this, the church would not have had so many abominable ceremonies in the meantime. But with good intentions, they changed what seemed to be evil for the better, which in time degenerated into intolerable abuses and sacrileges, as these days teach us. Commentary on Isaiah 27:10.[18]

The Destruction of the Jerusalem Temple. Johannes Oecolampadius: "When the fortified city." These things will happen at the time when the complete deprivation of the city of Jerusalem is at hand, so that where there were buildings there will be pastures. So he returns to the earlier similitude. For since he had compared the people to a vineyard, he calls the vine branches useless, which the enemies graze. For because of the death of Christ, the sanctuary and Jerusalem were destroyed. And the sanctuary is called a beautiful "habitation deserted and forsaken," because according to the Lord's prophecy, "There will not be left one stone upon another." And the useless branches will dry out and be consumed with fire. Commentary on Isaiah 27:10.[19]

The Rejection of the Hebrews and Calling of the Gentiles. Dietrich Schnepff: "For the fortified city will be solitary." We should understand the remarks that follow as concerning Jerusalem and the rejection of the Jewish people. Because he eloquently says that the people do not understand, that is, they are blind and rebellious. And when the prophet promises knowledge of the true God to other nations, such as the Egyptians, but denies mercy to those to whom he is speaking, there is no doubt that what is said in this passage is to be understood as referring to the ungodly Hebrews. Finally, because the next comments have to be taken as referring to the calling of the Gentiles, and because the prophets routinely connect the rejection of the Hebrews and the adoption of the Gentiles into the kingdom of Christ, there is no doubt that what is said here about the fortified city is to be taken as Jerusalem. . . . These comments regarding the prophet's intention should be enough.

Now, in order to explain the more difficult statements, we will briefly describe the rejection of the Hebrews and the calling of the Gentiles. The prophet speaks of the devastation of Jerusalem in these words: "For the fortified city will be solitary." He employs antithesis, stating that the very well-fortified city of Jerusalem, which was then very populous and admired by all, would now become so empty that flocks would pasture there. And to develop the comparison further, he says that they would graze on shoots, that is, that a foreign enemy would deprive them of all good things. Scholia on Isaiah 27:10.[20]

Humiliating Judgment on the Land. John Calvin: I do not translate it, "When the

[17]Bullinger, *Isaias*, 125v; citing Zech 3; Heb 10:9-10.
[18]Pellikan, *Commentaria Bibliorum*, 3:33v-r.
[19]Oecolampadius, *In Iesaiam*, 162v; citing Is 6; Mt 24:2.
[20]Schnepff, *In Esaiae*, 407.

harvest shall be withered," but, "When the harvest shall wither." In this passage *wither* means nothing other than to approach to maturity. Before the harvest of the land is ripe, it shall be cut down. It is as if he had said, "The Lord will take away from you the produce, even that which was already prepared for you and was in your hand." "The women coming shall burn it." When he says that "women shall come," he means that God will have no need of robust soldiers to execute his judgment and that he will make use only of the agency of women. This exhibits in a still stronger light the disgracefulness of the punishment, for he threatens that the calamity shall also be accompanied by disgrace, because it is more shameful and humiliating to be plundered by women, who are unused to war, than by men. Commentary on Isaiah 27:11.[21]

External Harms for Our Good. Johannes Brenz: Moreover, you see the external harms did not overwhelm but increased the glory of the Lord and the church. Examples of this are the persecution of Israel in Egypt, the captivity of the ark by the Philistines under Eli the priest, the devastation of the city of Jerusalem by the Babylonians, and similarly their later devastation by the Romans. But what is said about the church of God must also be understood about each individual who is a member of the church. There are many tribulations for the righteous, many harms and heavy burdens that happen to them. But all these things are more for helping them for the good than for the detriment. How great the glory that came from Joseph in captivity, the exile of David, the pit of Daniel, the cross of Christ himself? For although freedom may not happen in this world, yet eternal and heavenly freedom does happen. This is why we do not fear the harms of this age, but we only care to remain in the church of Christ, and all the remnant will be saved. Commentary on Isaiah 27:12-13.[22]

The Gathering of the Church. Johannes Oecolampadius: But he will gather the humble, those deprived of the pleasures of the age, and those who are going to believe in him, but he leaves behind the carnal, the drunkards, and those who despise the word of the Lord. And it is evident that this meaning also corresponds to the sequence of the prophecy. So he says, "In that day," by which Christ reigns from the cross, the Lord will shake, thresh, and cleanse the people. He has a winnowing shovel in his hand to gather them as wheat into a storehouse. . . .

"And in that day will be blown." The great trumpet is the apostolic preaching by which the church is summoned as one, some who are from the circumcision and those from among the Gentiles. For . . . Jesus was going to die not only for the nation but also to gather the sons of God who had perished and were either in the place of Assyria or in Egypt. Further, the nations in particular are named here where they were captives. In any case, the Assyrians and Egyptians signify to us the worldly and the carnal, which are all abandoned to follow Christ and come to the heavenly Jerusalem. So this prophecy pertains to Christ and the church. What the Jews promise themselves here are dreams. Commentary on Isaiah 27:13.[23]

The Great Trumpet of King Cyrus. Wolfgang Musculus: With this simile the prophet signifies that the remnant of Israel are going to flock to Mount Zion in the same way as if they were summoned by a great trumpet as a military signal. Now, if anyone thinks that the "great trumpet" should be understood as the edict of King Cyrus that made it so whoever from the Israelites was free to go up to Jerusalem when they wanted, in my judgment one has not deviated at all. For that edict was proclaimed with the sound of a herald, which a great royal trumpet usually accompanied, or from the fact that in the last chapter of 2 Chronicles is read, "In the first year of

[21]CTS 14:263 (CO 36:458).

[22]Brenz, *Esaias*, 354.

[23]Oecolampadius, *In Iesaiam*, 162v-r; citing Jn 16.

Cyrus king of Persia . . . the Lord stirred up the spirit of Cyrus king of Persia, who ordered it to be proclaimed throughout all his kingdom and also put it in writing, 'Thus says Cyrus king of Persia, "The Lord, the God of heaven, has given me all the kingdoms of the earth, and he has charged me to build him a house in Jerusalem, which is in Judah. Whoever is among you of all his people, may the Lord his God be with him. Let him go up."' . . ." And then after the return from Babylon and Egypt, they worshiped the Lord their God. This was going to be the end of their exile. Commentary on Isaiah 27:13.[24]

The Calling and Flourishing of the Gentiles. Dietrich Schnepff: But believe me, at the same time as the purging and rejection of those people, I will work to increase my vineyard so that what until now flourished in Judea will now be seen among the Gentiles, from the uttermost boundaries of Chaldea and Egypt, where those great rivers are, the Euphrates and the Nile. I will gather from those people my elect, who I have set apart from the filth of the world with my winnowing fork. So they will come to the fellowship of faith and confession with the believing Hebrews and be gathered into one sheepfold. Then with the trumpet blast of the gospel, echoing throughout the whole world, I will call my lambs who seemed lost, the Assyrians, the Egyptians, and many more others. So in that deadly punishment of the Hebrews, I will not forget my vineyard, but I will keep it more pruned and enlarged to the end of the world. Paraphrase of Isaiah 27:12-13.[25]

[24]Musculus, *In Esaiam*, 411-12; citing 2 Chron 36:22.

[25]Schnepff, *In Esaiae*, 410.

28:1–29:24 Judgment Against the Leaders

28 *Ah, the proud crown of the drunkards of Ephraim,*
and the fading flower of its glorious beauty,
which is on the head of the rich valley of those overcome with wine!

2 *Behold, the Lord has one who is mighty and strong;*
like a storm of hail, a destroying tempest,

like a storm of mighty, overflowing waters,
he casts down to the earth with his hand.

3 *The proud crown of the drunkards of Ephraim*
will be trodden underfoot;

4 *and the fading flower of its glorious beauty,*
which is on the head of the rich valley,

will be like a first-ripe fig[a] *before the summer:*
when someone sees it, he swallows it
as soon as it is in his hand.

5 *In that day the* Lord *of hosts will be a crown of glory,*[b]
and a diadem of beauty, to the remnant of his people,

6 *and a spirit of justice to him who sits in judgment,*
and strength to those who turn back the battle at the gate.

7 *These also reel with wine*
and stagger with strong drink;

the priest and the prophet reel with strong drink,
they are swallowed by[c] *wine,*
they stagger with strong drink,

they reel in vision,
they stumble in giving judgment.

8 *For all tables are full of filthy vomit,*
with no space left.

9 *"To whom will he teach knowledge,*
and to whom will he explain the message?

Those who are weaned from the milk,
those taken from the breast?

10 *For it is precept upon precept, precept upon precept,*
line upon line, line upon line,
here a little, there a little."

11 *For by people of strange lips*
and with a foreign tongue

the Lord *will speak to this people,*
12 *to whom he has said,*

"This is rest;
give rest to the weary;

and this is repose";
yet they would not hear.

13 *And the word of the* Lord *will be to them*

precept upon precept, precept upon precept,
line upon line, line upon line,

here a little, there a little,

that they may go, and fall backward,
and be broken, and snared, and taken.

14 *Therefore hear the word of the* Lord, *you scoffers,*
who rule this people in Jerusalem!

15 *Because you have said, "We have made a covenant with death,*
and with Sheol we have an agreement,

when the overwhelming whip passes through
it will not come to us,

for we have made lies our refuge,
and in falsehood we have taken shelter";

16 therefore thus says the Lord GOD,
"Behold, I am the one who has laid[d] as a foundation in Zion,
a stone, a tested stone,

a precious cornerstone, of a sure foundation:
'Whoever believes will not be in haste.'

17 And I will make justice the line,
and righteousness the plumb line;

and hail will sweep away the refuge of lies,
and waters will overwhelm the shelter."

18 Then your covenant with death will be annulled,
and your agreement with Sheol will not stand;

when the overwhelming scourge passes through,
you will be beaten down by it.

19 As often as it passes through it will take you;
for morning by morning it will pass through,
by day and by night;

and it will be sheer terror to understand the message.

20 For the bed is too short to stretch oneself on,
and the covering too narrow to wrap oneself in.

21 For the LORD will rise up as on Mount Perazim;
as in the Valley of Gibeon he will be roused;

to do his deed—strange is his deed!
and to work his work—alien is his work!

22 Now therefore do not scoff,
lest your bonds be made strong;

for I have heard a decree of destruction
from the Lord GOD of hosts against the whole land.

23 Give ear, and hear my voice;
give attention, and hear my speech.

24 Does he who plows for sowing plow continually?
Does he continually open and harrow his ground?

25 When he has leveled its surface,
does he not scatter dill, sow cumin,

and put in wheat in rows
and barley in its proper place,
and emmer[e] as the border?

26 For he is rightly instructed;
his God teaches him.

27 Dill is not threshed with a threshing sledge,
nor is a cart wheel rolled over cumin,

but dill is beaten out with a stick,
and cumin with a rod.

28 Does one crush grain for bread?
No, he does not thresh it forever;[f]

when he drives his cart wheel over it
with his horses, he does not crush it.

29 This also comes from the LORD of hosts;
he is wonderful in counsel
and excellent in wisdom.

29 *Ah, Ariel, Ariel,*
the city where David encamped!

Add year to year;
let the feasts run their round.

2 Yet I will distress Ariel,
and there shall be moaning and lamentation,

and she shall be to me like an Ariel.[g]

3 And I will encamp against you all around,
and will besiege you with towers
and I will raise siegeworks against you.

4 And you will be brought low; from the earth you shall speak,
and from the dust your speech will be bowed down;

your voice shall come from the ground like the voice of a ghost,
and from the dust your speech shall whisper.

5 *But the multitude of your foreign foes shall be like small dust,*
and the multitude of the ruthless like passing chaff.

And in an instant, suddenly,
6 *you will be visited by the LORD of hosts*

with thunder and with earthquake and great noise,
with whirlwind and tempest, and the flame of a devouring fire.

7 *And the multitude of all the nations that fight against Ariel,*
all that fight against her and her stronghold and distress her,

shall be like a dream, a vision of the night.

8 *As when a hungry man dreams, and behold, he is eating,*
and awakes with his hunger not satisfied,

or as when a thirsty man dreams, and behold, he is drinking,
and awakes faint, with his thirst not quenched,

so shall the multitude of all the nations be that fight against Mount Zion.

9 *Astonish yourselves*[h] *and be astonished;*
blind yourselves and be blind!

Be drunk,[i] *but not with wine;*
stagger,[j] *but not with strong drink!*

10 *For the LORD has poured out upon you a spirit of deep sleep,*

and has closed your eyes (the prophets),
and covered your heads (the seers).

11 *And the vision of all this has become to you like*
the words of a book that is sealed. When men give it
to one who can read, saying, "Read this," he says, "I
cannot, for it is sealed." 12 *And when they give the*
book to one who cannot read, saying, "Read this," he
says, "I cannot read."

13 *And the Lord said:*
"Because this people draw near with their mouth
and honor me with their lips,
while their hearts are far from me,

and their fear of me is a commandment taught by men,

14 *therefore, behold, I will again*
do wonderful things with this people,
with wonder upon wonder;

and the wisdom of their wise men shall perish,
and the discernment of their discerning men shall be hidden."

15 *Ah, you who hide deep from the LORD your counsel,*
whose deeds are in the dark,
and who say, "Who sees us? Who knows us?"

16 *You turn things upside down!*

Shall the potter be regarded as the clay,

that the thing made should say of its maker,
"He did not make me";

or the thing formed say of him who formed it,
"He has no understanding"?

17 *Is it not yet a very little while*
until Lebanon shall be turned into a fruitful field,
and the fruitful field shall be regarded as a forest?

18 *In that day the deaf shall hear*
the words of a book,

and out of their gloom and darkness
the eyes of the blind shall see.

19 *The meek shall obtain fresh joy in the LORD,*
and the poor among mankind shall exult in the Holy One of Israel.

20 *For the ruthless shall come to nothing*
and the scoffer cease,
and all who watch to do evil shall be cut off,

[21]*who by a word make a man out to be an*
offender,
and lay a snare for him who reproves in the
gate,
and with an empty plea turn aside him who
is in the right.

[22]*Therefore thus says the* Lord, *who redeemed Abraham, concerning the house of Jacob:*

"Jacob shall no more be ashamed,
no more shall his face grow pale.

[23]*For when he sees his children,*
the work of my hands, in his midst,
they will sanctify my name;

they will sanctify the Holy One of Jacob
and will stand in awe of the God of Israel.

[24]*And those who go astray in spirit will come to*
understanding,
and those who murmur will accept
instruction."

a Or *fruit* **b** The Hebrew words for *glory* and *hosts* sound alike **c** Or *confused by* **d** Dead Sea Scroll *I am laying* **e** A type of wheat **f** Or *Grain is crushed for bread; he will surely thresh it, but not forever* **g** *Ariel* could mean *lion of God*, or *hero* (2 Samuel 23:20), or *altar hearth* (Ezekiel 43:15–16) **h** Or *Linger awhile* **i** Or *They are drunk* **j** Or *they stagger*

Overview: This passage is composed of two chapters that are directed at foolish leaders portrayed as drunk. The first part of Isaiah 28 addresses the Northern Kingdom of Israel, referring to them as drunken Ephraim whose beauty has been marred. The second part of Isaiah 28 and much of Isaiah 29 charges the Southern Kingdom of Judah with forgetting God's kindness, seeking false security in their practices and mocking God's word. Isaiah's metaphors and illustrations prompt application by Reformation interpreters to actual drunkenness in their own day and abuses they saw in the Roman Catholic Church. The verses that speak about the people being unable to read and engaging in false worship are especially directed at what they perceived as problems in their time. These interpreters emphasize at the end of this passage that since Christ is the promised Rock, the true church will endure, and the time will come when the previously deaf and erring will believe and return to the Lord.

Four Parts to the Oracle. Dietrich Schnepff: There are four parts to this chapter. In the first, he accuses the Israelites, that is, the ten tribes, of arrogance, with the term *drunkenness*, and he adds the penalties too. The second part is the consolation that the Lord is going to preserve his church in the kingdom of Judah. The third part has the accusation against the kingdom of Judah that those who forget God's kindnesses with drunkenness, contempt of the word, and carelessness sin in a greater way. To this he adds the penalties that the Lord himself decreed. But since they were more arrogant about the name of the temple and their lineage than is proper, he shows that in the last times, when Christ is going to come, he is also going to bring his spiritual benefits and true righteousness. When the Hebrews are not going to acknowledge those kindnesses, the Lord is going to decree on them *panolethriam* [utter destruction]. And so when all the people, the city, and the temple are removed and finally cast down, those who were living then ought not to hope that their safety is because of the temple. The fourth part has the solution to the objection of how the church is going to remain while the Hebrew people are cast out. Scholia on Isaiah 28.[1]

Arrogance and Ignorance of God. Rudolf Gwalther: Now, the primary point of this chapter, as we learn, is the nature of those sins that greatly inflame God's wrath and that ruined whole nations. These are arrogance and drunkenness,

[1]Schnepff, *In Esaiae*, 413.

which contain within them every abuse of God's gifts. The source and origin of both of these is ignorance of God. For those who did not recognize him are the same ones who did not understand that he is the generous giver of all good things. This is the reason that those elevated by his gifts are arrogant. But arrogance is the beginning of sin, and those who yield to it do everything for their own lust. And, with immense contempt for others, they abuse God's gifts to satisfy their own luxury and appetite. Finally, the more they receive God's many blessings, the more wicked they become. Sermons on Isaiah 28.[2]

28:1-13 *Judgment on Ephraim's Leaders*

The Proud Crown of Drunkards. Konrad Pellikan: The prophecy is difficult enough to understand. It is first against the kingdom of Israel, then against Judah. The kingdom of Israel was addressed because of its fertility, wealth, and the multitude of arrogant people devoted to luxury and the gluttony that comes from those—but especially in the royal city of Samaria, which was positioned on the mountain in the tribe of Ephraim. It has valleys most pleasant and fertile, most favorably disposed to planting for luxury and pleasure, to drunkenness. And it was not only its citizens and leaders but also the priests and prophets who were without the fear of God and the keeping of the law. In fact they were also worshiping idols and Baals, feeding many priests in this. Here the prophet speaks against all those: "Woe to the proud crown of the drunkards" in Samaria. Woe to the blooming city at the top of the mountain, soon to be cast down, because he can no longer stand for the excessive luxury and drunkenness. Commentary on Isaiah 28:1.[3]

Stained and Beautiful Crowns. Johannes Oecolampadius: He wishes to say: "O Ephraim and sons of this age, you will not be among those who will be selected. For your crown will be like a ruined flower, and whatever is of joy in this age will be trampled underfoot. For the great day of the Lord and the end of luxury is coming. . . ." Indeed, he falls with a serious lapse and stains the crown so that it is useless to him and is as abominable in his crimes and fall as it once appeared beautiful, crowned with flowers of prosperity. . . .

The Jews explain this to be about those who were with Ezekiel in Jerusalem. We explain it to be about the apostles who, when others were ruined by pleasures, boasting in human wisdom and despising the law of God, humbly and truly were following Christ. They were not obtaining a perishable crown but the Lord himself. Nor were they redeemed with gold or flower garlands but were boasting in the Lord, as Paul also says . . . , "in the hope of the glory of God." Likewise they are sitting on the seat, judging the twelve tribes of Israel. For they received the Holy Spirit and the spirit of judgment, so that whoever's sins they forgive are forgiven, and whatever they bind is bound. In addition, they have the mind of Christ spiritually judging, judgeable by no one. Commentary on Isaiah 28:3-4.[4]

A New Covenant Crown of Beauty. Konrad Pellikan: When the kingdom of Israel will be destroyed for their sins and they will be carried away into exile in Assyria and the land fiercely devastated, which had been most opulent, and all because of their sins against the Lord their God, then it will be the sixth year of the holy king Hezekiah in the kingdom of Judah and Benjamin, under whom the Lord Almighty will shine. And as "a crown of glory" he will glorify the remnant of his people in the kingdom of Judah who listen to the Lord and the prophets. And in return, he will be glorified by his people, having entered into a new covenant and restored divine worship, when the Assyrians are cut down by the angel in that glorious miracle. These things will indeed happen in Jerusalem at that time, when Samaria will be

[2]Gwalther, *Isaias*, 156v.

[3]Pellikan, *Commentaria Bibliorum*, 3:33r.

[4]Oecolampadius, *In Iesaiam*, 163v, 163r; citing Rom 5:2; 1 Cor 2.

squalored in its ruins and deprivation. Commentary on Isaiah 28:5.[5]

The Crime of Drunkenness. Martin Borrhaus: Drunkenness is seriously blamed as a crime in the rebel nation. By this, the drunk Ephraimites, deprived of the divine spirit, were sure of the judgment of God the defender against the wicked, while they were prone to charge into all kinds of crimes. As it is usual for drunkenness to blur the human mind and to bring it down from a position of piety, the sacred covenant is neglected. That covenant requires the heart to be cut off from luxury, debauchery, drunkenness, and the lust that drunkenness breeds. . . . It is also drunkenness that creates human wisdom and the doctrine of false prophets. So earlier the drunkenness of the Egyptians was refuted. This was a cup of the wisdom of Egypt mingled with a spirit of confusion from the Lord that produced empty vessels.

Similarly, this drunkenness in the following chapter is blamed: "They are blinded and they blind others; they are drunk and not from wine." Both types of drunkenness declare clearly enough that the age of the antichrist has miserably profaned the place of the church. You could say that this blaming of the Ephraimites truly fits. This drunkenness is seen in the Apocalypse of John, "I will show you the judgment of the great prostitute, who is seated on many waters, with whom the kings of the earth prostituted themselves and with the wine of whose sexual immorality the dwellers on earth have become drunk." Oracles in Isaiah on 28:7.[6]

The German Habit of Drunkenness. Johannes Brenz: And are not these the habits of our Germany, which even one unfortunately hears by this name from foreign nations, because it indulges more excessively in drunkenness? And are not the tables of the Germans full of vomit and filth at their drinking parties? And is there not also among us so great a stupor from wine, equally among men and women, to acknowledge the pious doctrine of the gospel, such that if you want to assemble the church, you must gather more from those weaned and plucked from breasts, that is, from children and adolescents, than you do from older people? Although there are also the habits that even children begin to indulge on wine and get drunk. Therefore, it remains that unless we repent, the judgment of drunkards will also come on us, which is sudden and unexpected destruction. Commentary on Isaiah 28:8.[7]

Drunk Priests like Foolish Children. Heinrich Bullinger: Further, I say it is going to be taught that he shows more clearly that the drunk priests are not able to discharge their duty properly. The minister of the church, it says, who is given to wine, "To whom will he teach? To whom will he explain the message?" that is, the preaching of the word of God. And he responds by suggesting, "They are like weaned children and even infants taken from their mother's breasts." For just as infants cannot teach—indeed, they cannot even speak—so drunken priests and prophets cannot teach, and if they do teach, they still teach with no authority. For because of their drunkenness they are despised, and even if their teaching is good, it is still disdained and considered as silly and for children. The poets imagined Bacchus at a childish age because drunkards are portrayed as very foolish children. Sermons on Isaiah 28:7-9.[8]

Knowledge Needs an Audience. John Trapp: Isaiah had no lack of knowledge, since he was apt and able to teach, but he wanted a fit audience, since he had to deal with a sort of drunken sots that were unteachable and incapable. So . . . when the waters of the sanctuary flowed, the miry places could not be healed. Think the same also of those that are drunk with pride . . .

[5]Pellikan, *Commentaria Bibliorum*, 3:34r.
[6]Borrhaus, *In Iesaiae Prophetae Oracula*, 252; citing Is 19:12-15; 29:9; Rev 17:1-2.
[7]Brenz, *Esaias*, 364.
[8]Bullinger, *Isaias*, 128r.

and self-conceitedness, who make divinity only a matter of discourse, or who come to sit as judges or critics on their ministers' gifts. . . . It will be long enough before such will be taught anything. Exposition on Isaiah 28:9.[9]

Incapable Infants. John Mayer: The Hebrews, as Sasbout shows, do not take this as an answer to the question raised here but as a continuation that shows it is impossible that any of them should become good from teaching, since they are like infants with respect to knowledge.[†] And since they have as little capacity to make good use of it, the interrogation therefore continues to the end of the verse. Musculus also agrees, rejecting what some understand by infants as those spiritually newborns. . . . And the view that refers this to the apostles seems not to agree much better, because though comparatively they were babes, yet he seems here to speak of no one being capable of teaching, for they are all reproved and threatened. . . . And so Junius also understands it. . . . It appears that you all are as incapable as sucking children or those just weaned, because those taught a little now and a little then learn something, but you all learn nothing. Commentary on Isaiah 28:9-13.[10]

Enjoying the Lusty Life. Menno Simons: They boast that they are called in accordance with Scriptures, as you may hear, even though it is obvious and palpable that they lead a life as the one portrayed by Peter and Jude. Many of them are so fallen in the fullness of Bacchus that they, alas, live night and day as swine in full rest. Their tables are full of vomit and filthiness, so that there is no place clean, as the prophet says. . . . They fearlessly walk after their own lusts, as Jude says. And they esteem as joy the temporal, lusty life, says Peter. They are spots and blemishes, sporting themselves with their own deceptions while they feast with you.

Some of them also are open fornicators and adulterers. How their wives, as a general thing, conform themselves to Scriptures, may be educed from their fruits. Others are so greedy that they have become open usurers. They are so intent on perishable lucre, money, and possessions that I dare truthfully say that they, through the easy doctrine of their gospel, have become lords on earth. Yet, most of them are loved by the world and highly esteemed by the ignorant. Their pomp, laziness, ease seeking, vanity, light-mindedness, pride, and so on baffle all description, to say nothing of their tyranny, lying, brawling, slandering, betraying, and uproaring against all who seek and fear the Lord. Reply to Gellius Faber.[11]

Clear Teaching Heard as a Foreign Language. Johannes Brenz: This is the meaning of these words: The older ones were given a dull disposition from drunkenness, so that even though you recite the precepts and promises of God that command us to expect God's help, and you repeated and impressed them, and you related the specific rules of life to them, and you explained all the fragments or compendia, and certain brief pericopes from various passages of Sacred Scripture most clearly to them, they still do not understand them, but they seem to be uncivilized, strange, and entirely foreign, as if you were speaking, as they say, the Calicut language[†] to them. Commentary on Isaiah 28:10-11.[12]

Faith, Faith, Faith. Dietrich Schnepff: And he adds, "For it is precept upon precept. . . ." Some understand these words to mean that he gives precepts to those stupid people, but they still understand nothing, and it is just as if he were speaking to them in a foreign and stammering language (as the prophet later says). I do not condemn that explanation, since what follows

[9]Trapp, *Commentary or Exposition*, 100*; citing Ezek 47:11; Is 28:1.
[10]Mayer, *Commentary upon All the Prophets*, 4:173*; citing 1 Pet 2:1. [†]See Sasbout, *In Esaiam*, 199-200; Musculus, *In Esaiam*, 417.

[11]Simons, *Complete Works* 2:20.
[12]Brenz, *Esaias*, 358. [†]Brenz seems to be referring to the language spoken by the people of Kozhikode, also called Calicut, in southwestern India. This city was discovered by Vasco da Gama in 1498 and became a trading post in 1511.

(where the same things are repeated) shows that it is said with irony and mockery in the Hebrew. However, the prophet afterward writes, "And the word of the Lord will be to them precept upon precept. . . ." That is, when the Lord speaks to his people, they raise jeers, and the very words of the Lord are despised by them, and in what follows he calls them mockers.[†]

But since those words are ecliptic irony,[†] let us explain what they intend. *Ṣāw* signifies "precept" and is repeated falsely, "precept upon precept." So the prophet wants to imitate the mockery of the wicked who often ridicule the law and the repeated reminders of the prophets, saying, "They rattle nothing besides law, law." In the same way, the word *qāw* is repeated, which signifies "line," or the measuring line that stonemasons follow until they complete walls, and so we take this metaphorically to signify the rule for spiritual things. . . . When, therefore, the prophets were saying that everything is to be weighed according to the norm and the prescribed words, and they were condemning the worship with nothing but contrived words, they were ridiculed by the blind Hebrews, who were saying, "They convey nothing in the midst other than their norm or rule." So today the Romans clamor that we echo nothing other than, "Faith, faith, faith." Scholia on Isaiah 28:10, 13.[13]

God Accommodates with Lisping Language. Johannes Oecolampadius: "While on strange lips." He was saying to anyone, "Those doctrines are so lofty that our weakness is unable to grasp them." But Christ himself, accommodating our smallness, took parables from ordinary life, as if he were speaking with lisping speech, imitating nurses with stuttering children. So also in the Scriptures a remarkable clarity appears on those things that are necessary for our salvation. But he also speaks of other languages given and the gift of languages, so that everyone is without excuse. . . . The people say, "We hear them speaking about the mighty deeds in our own languages." Christ likewise commands things that are easy for the godly. And the burden of the yoke is light and pleasant. For the command of Christ is to love one another and to foster compassion, which here he calls "to give rest to the weary; and this will be repose." But the Pharisees do not preach the gospel and rest but rather impose heavy burdens.

The apostle . . . suitably uses this testimony against those who speak in the church but not for edification, where it says, "Why would you speak words in church which are not understood, when God himself accommodates us with lisping speech and other languages? And when the excellent gift of the Holy Spirit is to recognize languages, what usefulness is your speech that no one understands?" Commentary on Isaiah 28:11.[14]

A New Hebrew Popery. John Trapp: We read of John Elmar, bishop of London in Queen Elizabeth's reign, that on a time when he saw his listeners grow dull in their attention to his sermon, he presently read to them many verses out of the Hebrew text: to which they all stared, admiring what use he meant to make of them. Then he showed them their folly that whereas they neglected English, by which they might be edified, they listened to Hebrew, of which they did not understood a word. And how justly God might bring in popery again (with Latin service, blind obedience, and dumb offices) for their contempt of the gospel. Exposition on Isaiah 28:11-13.[15]

28:14-22 *Covenant with Death*

Scoffers Make a Covenant with Death. Martin Borrhaus: "We have made a covenant with death." The people are charged for their security in the midst of their crimes by this representation of the ungodly regarding divine judgment. They are not concerned about the

[13]Schnepff, *In Esaiae*, 420. [†]See also his paraphase on 432. An ecliptic statement is one that gets repeated or circles back around like an eclipse.

[14]Oecolampadius, *In Iesaiam*, 164r; citing Acts 2:11; 1 Cor 14.

[15]Trapp, *Commentary or Exposition*, 101*.

goodness of God calling them back to a better harvest, nor threats intended for rebellion, saying those who have entered into a covenant with death are not going to perish. This form of speaking with mockery by true prophets is displayed. Above he mentioned drunkenness, but here he addresses the false sense of security that arises from drunkenness. Let us notice the miserable state of the church during our generation. It is obvious enough she is ruled by those who have no concern for divine judgment and that those who are so governed are oblivious as well. Each day some disaster is announced that would certainly destroy us unless we repent. It is a story told to the deaf. These men mock the word of the true prophets when with the Jews they dare to say, "We have struck a covenant with death, and with Sheol we have made an agreement." Oracles in Isaiah on 28:14-15.[16]

Shameful Teaching. Menno Simons: How truly are you associates of those of whom it stands written that they say, "We have made a covenant with death, and with Sheol we have an agreement; when the overwhelming scourge passes through, it will not come to us; for we have made lies our refuge, and in falsehood we have taken shelter." . . . Again, "Woe to those who call evil good and good evil; who put darkness for light and light for darkness." . . . However, I am not much astonished that such persons teach such shameful doctrine, since they have known neither Christ nor his word, but they hold and teach all things as they were taught from youth up, out of the old usages and the papistical laws. The Doctrine of Preachers.[17]

The Cornerstone Connects the Church. Konrad Pellikan: Zion and Jerusalem will have and hold onto their everlasting glory, as I promised the throne of David, with a splendor worthy of the sun and moon. For I will connect the foundation in Zion and the church of the faithful with a huge stone, cut from the mountain without hands, Christ the Lord. As the cornerstone, he will make the two one, an exceedingly precious and only foundation, firm for the church. On this foundation, the church can stand against the power and force of all waves and temptation. If anyone trusts in this rock, they will not stumble, nor be overwhelmed by the hardships of misfortune to the point of loss. But they will stand unconquered through everything, if they yet persevere patiently and do not waver at all. Commentary on Isaiah 28:16.[18]

Christ as the Rock of the Church. Martin Borrhaus: "As a foundation in Zion," not in Samaria; it is founded in the house of David, not of Jeroboam, much less in Damascus and Babylon. This foundation of the church of the elect is Jesus Christ, about whom the apostle says, "For no one can lay any foundation other than that which is laid, which is Jesus Christ." The stone speaks about himself with these words, "And on this rock I will build my church." He does not say, "I will build my church on Moses, on Elijah, on some angel, on the strength of innate free will (that is contrived since one is a slave to sin), or partly on those things and partly on Christ." Oracles in Isaiah on 28:16.[19]

Faithfully Wait for That Day. Johannes Oecolampadius: By faith in Christ, salvation is indeed certain, yet it should not be cold and false but great and long-suffering, questioning nothing that he promises is going to happen. For it will happen that he saves the faithful, and the wicked and unfaithful are going to perish. The impatient ones cry out with faithlessness, "Is that day coming?" as if it were not going to come and they should be dismayed if they wait and hope. Habakkuk: "If it seems slow, wait for it, and it will surely

[16]Borrhaus, *In Iesaiae Prophetae Oracula*, 255 (misnumbered 257), 258.

[17]Simons, *Complete Works*, 1:58; citing Is 5:20.

[18]Pellikan, *Commentaria Bibliorum*, 3:34r; citing Dan 2:45.

[19]Borrhaus, *In Iesaiae Prophetae Oracula*, 256; citing 1 Cor 3:11; Mt 16:18.

come and will not delay." Our prophet says, "Whoever believes will not be in haste," that is, one will be long-suffering and certain. One will not be dismayed, as the apostles render this following the Septuagint . . . , "one will not be ashamed." Commentary on Isaiah 28:16.[20]

The Foundation Stone. Dietrich Schnepff: But I will lay as a foundation in Zion that foundation stone, Jesus Christ, my Son. The Hebrews are going to reject and condemn him as a criminal and not at all suitable for building my spiritual temple. But I will test him in every way so as to make him not only the foundation but also the precious cornerstone. He will gather to himself a church from the Hebrews and the Gentiles into his most welcoming and saving embrace in order to enlarge the spiritual Jerusalem. He will be that firm foundation. Those who rely on it, the covenant with death and all the sorrows that can happen to people should be considered done. For through that mediator, my Son, the most perfect righteousness will be brought forth according to my most exacting standard, as if weighed against norm and balance.

Those who are made participants in him will not experience the harm of death nor any disasters—in fact, not even hell itself. For what sorrows may come to others, they will be to these reinforcement and support for salvation. Even against death and hell, Christ the mediator will be a firm protection for them. He is the rock against whom the gates of hell will not prevail. He will ensure that they are not moved or cast down from their secure position. Paraphrase of Isaiah 28:16-18.[21]

The Mystical History of the Hailstorm. Martin Borrhaus: "And hail will sweep away the hope of lies." He colors the oracle with another similitude, taken from a hailstorm. If one follows the thread of the mystical history, the Assyrian enemy is denoted, who was about to overthrow the fortress of deceit among the Jews. We read above that this hailstorm was also sent on the Ephraimites. But if you consider what is figured in this history, the times that are signified have been indicated several times above. The origin and nature of a hailstorm and its harmful effects must be known from physics, so that the metaphor can be better understood and explained. Oracles in Isaiah on 28:17.[22]

Christ's Kingdom Remains and Advances. Johannes Brenz: This, therefore, is the meaning of Isaiah: just as David twice overthrew the Philistines, who were preventing him from being able to reign in Israel twice, once on Mount Perizim and again in the valley of Gibeon, so he remarkably scattered and routed them that they flowed and dissolved like water, so also Christ will rout and cast aside the wicked Jews, who will endeavor with all their strength to prevent him from advancing his kingdom. It is well-known how much effort the Jews invested in this that they immediately oppressed Christ from the very beginning of his preaching, and did not stop until they had forced him to the cross, and even afterward they persecuted him in the apostles. And yet the kingdom of Christ was spread more broadly by that. But they themselves were oppressed so that not only were they expelled from their region, but they were also disinherited so that they were no longer the people of God. . . .

Afterward, when Isaiah mentions the two victories that David reported about his enemies the Philistines, on Mount Perizim and in the valley of Gibeon, he indeed prophesies that the Jews, as the enemies of Christ, will be rejected and oppressed, just as David oppressed his enemies. But this very fact teaches that the kingdom of Christ will remain most firm, even though it has many enemies. The church, which is the kingdom of Christ, even in the midst of enemies in this world, has its progress. "Rule," it says, "in the midst of your enemies." It does

[20]Oecolampadius, *In Iesaiam*, 166v; citing Hab 2:3; Rom 9:33; 1 Pet 2:6.
[21]Schnepff, *In Esaiae*, 432-33.
[22]Borrhaus, *In Iesaiae Prophetae Oracula*, 258; citing Is 28:2.

not say, "in the midst of friends," since Christ finds few friends among people of this time but has as many enemies as the ungodly, which is the largest part of humanity. And among these he not only gathers but also preserves and enlarges his church. This is therefore placed before us to consider that it is of concern to us, since we ourselves are members of the church, or the kingdom of Christ. Commentary on Isaiah 28:21-22.[23]

28:23-29 *The Lord's Plan Not to Punish Forever*

Different Responses to Judgments. Rudolf Gwalther: Further, when the prophets said these things, the judgments of people are heard as various and very different from one another. For there are some who say that God should have stretched out his hand long ago, before the audacity of the wicked had progressed so much. Others complain about the harshness of him who afflicts the righteous along with the wicked, and issues the same judgment even on those who have already been grieved enough by the ungodly and repented of their known delusions. But most of them murmur because of the present and future fortune of the righteous, who even now labor under the cross and will someday suffer more grievously than these. And, of course, it sometimes happens that the best ones are struck severely, and there are examples of prophets who bitterly complained that the wicked behave more happily and the righteous are treated more harshly. Therefore, for Isaiah to remove these stumbling blocks, he concludes this sermon with an elegant admonition in which he teaches that God does all things according to his certain plan and righteous judgment. Sermons on Isaiah 28:23.[24]

The Providence of God as like Eating Bread. Konrad Pellikan: Finally, when bread is to be baked, both the threshers and the carting cease at that time, since they cannot crush grain into flour. So, the providence of God does not plow all the time by administering afflictions. It does not always sow by instilling in their hearts more sacred practices, nor by crushing the hard clods of hinderances and idle thoughts. Now, after the humbling and contrition of the heart provided by the Lord, he introduces the various seeds of holy pursuits, according to the capacity and nature of each. For he sows each one in its place and does not grant everyone the ability to do all things. He is the giver of all good gifts, and from him all good things descend from above on them. Grain is crushed for bread. So the righteous are refined by grinding and squeezing to become suitable stones for establishing a heavenly building. And the grain of God is gathered into the storehouse and is ground by the millstones of persecution so that, in Christ, it may be made into pure bread, to be eaten with enjoyment. But this does not happen by the pursuit of hard human works but by divine grace and favor. Commentary on Isaiah 28:24-28.[25]

Almighty in Wisdom and Counsel. Johannes Oecolampadius: Truly the counsel and mystery is hidden from the ages—the mystery of the cross is utterly remarkable, because the wise of this age cannot grasp either that Christ suffered for us or that God tests his elect in this way. So then, no one who sees the righteous afflicted here is offended and blasphemes, as if God permits some kind of injustice. For although it is a remarkable thing, yet all the earth is full of the righteousness of God. Those he condemns forever, he justly condemns; and no less does he justly rebuke someone more and another less among those who he also mercifully crowns as sons. Commentary on Isaiah 28:29.[26]

[23]Brenz, *Esaias*, 368, 370-71; citing Ps 110:2.
[24]Gwalther, *Isaias*, 164r.
[25]Pellikan, *Commentaria Bibliorum*, 3:35v.
[26]Oecolampadius, *In Iesaiam*, 167r.

29:1-8 *Ariel's Lament*

The City of David. Dietrich Schnepff: "Woe, Ariel, Ariel." In the same way that prophets generally signify by the term *burden* that they wish to bring a sad prophecy, so also with the interjection *woe* they announce threats. But Isaiah also quickly teaches to whom the disasters and adversities are threatened, namely, Ariel. Now, by Ariel he means the city of David. For he immediately adds, "the city where David encamped." Now, we know that David adorned Jerusalem with buildings, and especially the tower, so it is called the city of David. . . . And Ariel, if we translate it from the Hebrew, means, "the lion of the Lord."

Ezekiel . . . does not obscurely signify that the altar [*ʾăram*] of the temple is called that so that by the altar, this city is understood. But why they wanted to use this term for "altar" is uncertain. I follow the thought of those who believe that it was called this because of the frequent slaughterings, for in the evening and morning the lamb was offered on it.† But the lion is a most ravenous and voracious animal. And later Isaiah will teach why he calls the city Ariel, clearly because there are many around it who will be slaughtered—and this is indeed about the term and intention of the prophet. Scholia on Isaiah 29:1-2.[27]

A Type of History. Johannes Oecolampadius: For again let us weave together the historical events as a type. Although they heard that they would be delivered at the time of Hezekiah, yet many still did not truly hope in the Lord but rather trusted more in the help of Egypt than in God. That is what he delivers in the next two chapters. But let us rather follow the reality, understanding that such things are fulfilled in Christ, who, when we were humiliated by the law and surrounded by enemies on every side, was revealed by his gospel to the simple and little children and was hidden from the wise. He taught us to preach, and he freed his own through the cross. For the humble take refuge in Christ, but the proud seek help in the flesh. Commentary on Isaiah 29:1.[28]

The Lion and the Altar. Dietrich Schnepff: Woe to you, Jerusalem, with the famous name of David, who increased you with buildings and fortifications and wanted the seat of his kingdom to be there and the most distinguished altar in the temple of the Lord. On account of the multitude of slaughtered sacrifices, the place of this altar is called in our language Ariel, that is, the lion of the Lord. Indeed, like that most ferocious animal, the lion, scatters and tears to pieces all the beasts in its way, so will be the innumerable victims of Jerusalem. And indeed the Hebrews trusted in these things so much that they thought they were surrounded by certain protections, as if those saved them from being victims. But although you observe those feast days year by year and you offer daily sacrifices of lambs, yet I will drive you, the lion of the Lord, into the greatest distress so that you are filled with grief and sorrow and may actually be Ariel. For I will allow you to be encircled with a wall and for siegeworks to be raised against you. And besides that, the citizens will be attacked such that the number of the slain around you is as great as the number of sacrifices on the altar of Ariel in Jerusalem. Paraphrase of Isaiah 29:1-3.[29]

False Hope in the Promises of God. Johannes Brenz: This chapter should be commended to us for many reasons, but especially because both Christ and Paul select from this chapter testimonies for their sermons, as we will show in their respective places. And the prophet issues this sermon against the city of Jerusalem and prophesies that it would be destroyed and the Jews be blinded. At the same time, though, he comforts the righteous, teaching that the church will always

[27]Schnepff, *In Esaiae*, 437; citing 2 Sam 5; Ex 29; Ezek 43.
†Oecolampadius includes Ezek 34; 43; Jer 33; Hos 3 (*In Iesaiam*, 168r).

[28]Oecolampadius, *In Iesaiam*, 168r.
[29]Schnepff, *In Esaiae*, 453.

be preserved, but the wicked persecutors of the church will perish eternally. Further, not only Isaiah but also other prophets have many and plentiful pronouncements about the desolation of the city of Jerusalem and the extermination of the nation of Judah.

The first is that the Lord spares, as Scripture says, "his people and his dwelling place"; therefore he was sending to them by the hand of his messengers what rises in the night and reminders every day. Then, because they held to a false understanding of God's promises and to empty hope in the temple and its ceremonies, they did not repent truly and from the heart. For they boasted only in words regarding the law, the temple, the divinely instituted ceremonies, and the promises of God about the preservation of Abraham's seed and the perpetual dwelling of God on Mount Zion. But at the same time, they did not rightly understand these promises, nor did they change their lives for the better by faith, but they persisted in their wickedness and crimes. This is why it was necessary that the prophets, by the call of God placed heavily on them, also pronounced the wrath of God on them, so that perhaps they would repent and obtain salvation. Commentary on Isaiah 29:1-3.[30]

The Law as the Mystical Sense. Johannes Oecolampadius: "And I will distress Ariel." As far as the history is concerned, Sennacherib besieged Jerusalem so that the Jews could not escape. And although God did this through the enemies, as instruments, he still speaks as if he had done it himself. And the rest that follows, where he speaks about the land and similar things, signifies the utmost humility and anxiety. Additionally, in a mystical sense, see how we are humbled and crushed by the law, since the law tells us what to do and what not to do, but we lack the strength to fulfill what is commanded. From this our flesh, too, is inclined to evil and, having hatred for the word of God, incites more, and the enemy prepares many traps and openly attacks the ramparts of earthly activities so that we do not escape his snares. Commentary on Isaiah 29:2.[31]

Two Comforts. Martin Borrhaus: Let us be comforted by two things here. One is that if we are distressed, we are distressed by God. And so the affliction should not be considered as from an enemy but from the kind will of God, who afflicts us not with the purpose of destroying but to save the afflicted. For we read, "I will besiege Ariel." The other is that the enemies of the church should not be thought of as anything other than dust of the earth and chaff, which is easily blown by any wind. So as chaff and dust were Pharoah, the Canaanite kings, the Assyrians, the Babylonians, the Greeks, and the Romans. And so as chaff is the antichrist with the kings of the earth, on whom the stronger breath of the Messiah blows, and they are immediately scattered like the dust of the earth. Oracles in Isaiah on 29:2-3.[32]

God Overthrows His Enemies Without Trouble. Heinrich Bullinger: Then he mentions the extraordinary works of God, by which he makes it clear that God is able to destroy his enemies suddenly, whenever he pleases. And he mentions thunder, lightning, earthquake, a whirlwind, and tempest. . . . God often declared these things, and he still declares his power. He often overthrew and punished his enemies with these. Therefore, he will be able to even now, when he chooses, scatter the Assyrians before the walls of Jerusalem, as we will also hear . . . that he routed and crushed them. Sermons on Isaiah 29:5.[33]

Like the Emptiness of a Dream. Rudolf Gwalther: An elegant simile follows as confirmation in this passage, in which he depicts the frustrated efforts of the enemy, saying, "There will be a multitude of all the nations fighting against Ariel" (I would say a militant army), "and all that

[30]Brenz, *Esaias*, 374.

[31]Oecolampadius, *In Iesaiam*, 169v.

[32]Borrhaus, *In Iesaiae Prophetae Oracula*, 263.

[33]Bullinger, *Isaias*, 135v; citing Is 36.

fight against her and her stronghold, and distress her," or restrict her, "will be like a dream, a vision of the night." He again mentions the "multitude of the nations," that is, the various nations that fought under the Assyrians. And he mentions the "stronghold" where the besieged city would be surrounded and pursued on all sides. But all these things are compared to a dream in the night. There is hardly anything more empty and void than when people in general imagine their own dreams, as the poet said about lovers. Sermons on Isaiah 29:5-7.[34]

Dream and Reality. Johannes Brenz: Meanwhile, how many infants, virgins, and girls do you think perished? Nebuchadnezzar, the enemy of God's people, returned to his own country with great glory, and the people of God lay oppressed by all kinds of disasters. Were these not reality, were their not vigils but only a dream? Antiochus Epiphanes took possession of the city of Jerusalem, set up an idol, burned the law of the Lord, slaughtered the women who circumcised their boys, and most cruelly killed many more who professed and defended the law of the Lord. This is not merely a mockery of a dream, is it? Is it not reality?

I will come to the enemies of the church and the saints after the gospel of Christ was revealed. Herod captured John the Baptist and killed him in prison. And so Herod leads a happy life while John perishes unhappily. Should we say that these things did not really happen but are only a vision of a dream? The council of the Jews roars against Stephen, and Stephen is stoned. Jews and Gentiles arose against the apostles and martyrs and most brutally killed them. What? Are these occasions of happiness for the wicked and unhappiness for the righteous' just dreams, and not reality itself?

Let us therefore consider that the similitude that the prophet employs in this passage is not a human figment but is the word of God. And the word of God cannot be empty or false. Therefore, when this word calls the happiness of the wicked and the unhappiness of the righteous a dream, it certainly is necessary that the reality itself is also so. . . . "As when a hungry man dreams," says Isaiah, "and is eating, but when he awakes, his soul is empty." Here he implicitly reminds us of the resurrection to eternal life. Commentary on Isaiah 29:7-8.[35]

29:9-14 *The Blindness of Empty Religion*

Human Sin Hardens the Heart. Heinrich Bullinger: I truly do not think that the blindness of humans is assigned to God completely such that we make God the author of our sin. Indeed, it is the evil from us and the corruption that is in us that we are charged with sin. Moreover, God hardens Pharaoh and all those hardened when he withdraws grace (which he had given) in his just judgment on a person, or when he does not soften the human heart, but he leaves or allows one to oneself. Sermons on Isaiah 29:9-19.[36]

Enlightenment from the Seven Spirits. Martin Borrhaus: The Chaldean Paraphrases explain these words about the obstruction of the eyes, "The Lord will stir up in you a spirit of error, and the prophets, the scribes, and the teachers who taught you the doctrine will be hidden from you, and he will hide the law." Then he mentions two things by which the eyes of the mind are darkened so that they do not see the glory of the grace of God. One is the spirit of error, keeping one in error. This is the spirit of Satan, about which the apostle speaks with these words, "following the principality of the spirit of the air that is at work in the disobedient." The other is to rob the prophets and teachers of the truth. When their light is absent, darkness covers their hearts and blocks their eyes so that they cannot see the brightness of salvation shining in the Messiah. . . .

Therefore, just as mistrust and unbelief closes the Books of the Prophets and the Gospels, so

[34]Gwalther, *Isaias*, 167v.

[35]Brenz, *Esaias*, 378-79.

[36]Bullinger, *Isaias*, 135r.

holding to the faith opens them. John speaks about this in the Apocalypse with these words: "Behold, the lion of the tribe of Judah, the Root of David, has conquered, so that he can open the scroll and its seven seals." But with what key does he open the book and its seals? John continues, "And behold, I saw between the throne and the four living creatures and among the elders a lamb standing, as though it had been slain, with seven horns, which are the seven spirits of God sent out into all the earth." So, it is these seven spirits sent into the earth that open the book and its seals. For these seven spirits contain all the enlightenment that enlightens the souls of the saints so they understand the oracles of divine wisdom. This is what the apostle says: "The Spirit searches everything, even the depths of God." But to receive the sevenfold spirit of the Messiah for the minds of the elect to be enlightened, mention was made about that in the eleventh chapter. Oracles in Isaiah on 29:10-11.[37]

Some Ignore the Spirit. Leonhard Schiemer: [Some people] are indolent toward the light. They do not exactly bind up the beak of Peter's rooster but also do not really like to leave it free. But when their conscience judges them for sin, they are alarmed and fix a hood over the rooster's head, which means that they generously allow it to crow but pay no attention to it. The Scripture says people like that are overcome by a drowsy spirit. Elsewhere they are called lukewarm. . . . They go their way, halfheartedly fearing God; they are very self-confident but fear the opinion of others. Human knowledge, understanding, good advice, strength, and skill are highly prized by them. They are very inquisitive, ask many questions, and want to experience everything. These people are very beguiling, for they often appear as angels of light. Concerning the Grace of God.[38]

Need for Illumination. Dietrich Schnepff: Let us also learn that the true interpretation of Scripture is a unique gift of God. For the Scriptures are understood to the extent that the Lord has opened their eyes and understanding of them. How rudimentary were the apostles themselves at the beginning? How little were they understanding the sacred things? But when Christ the Lord opened the Scriptures to them, they advanced in such a way that they enlightened the whole world with evangelical teaching. Let us therefore pray to the Lord to illuminate our eyes so that we do not fall asleep in death but are directed toward true piety and knowledge of God. What could further be said about the blindness, and why the Lord sends a spirit of deep sleep that is said to harden, we have treated above. Scholia on Isaiah 29:11.[39]

The Spirit's Light Illuminates the Scriptures. Margaret Fell: Turn to the light, and there you will come to see; and learning there, in the light, you will come to see and know the mysteries of God, which to the world are parables and to all you who deny the light shall be shut for evermore. Though you may get all the words of the whole Scriptures in your brains and comprehension, so long as you deny the light, and turn your minds from the light, and seek to know these things without you, you shall never know them, but they shall be as a book sealed to you; the depth of the mysteries of them you shall never understand. To All the Professors of the World.[40]

How to Read Scripture. Johannes Oecolampadius: Christ tells us to read the Scriptures. Again, if at any time they seem to disagree, we must not produce a gloss from our heads but rather let the more obscure passages be illuminated by the clearer ones, consult characteristics of the languages in which they were first written, pay attention to what precedes and what follows and to

[37]Borrhaus, *In Iesaiae Prophetae Oracula*, 264; citing Eph 2:2; Rev 5:6.
[38]CRR 12:214-15; citing Rev 3:15; 2 Cor 11:14.
[39]Schnepff, *In Esaiae*, 441-42; citing Is 6.
[40]Fell, *Women's Speaking Justified and Other Pamphlets*, 72*.

the very context of the words. And finally, with a faithful and fearful mind, seek the glory of the Father and of Christ and not our own. And the Father of mercies will open the secrets to those who ask with such diligence.

Today many argue that the Scriptures are ambiguous, when more accurately it is that those would address their laziness and sleepiness, or more correctly, their malice, to establish ungodly dogmas that either make them do nothing or avoid suffering. To have the key of knowledge and refuse to open the book, what is that but a decision of sheer perversity? A truly unfaithful servant, not managing the measure of one's time. Commentary on Isaiah 29:11-12.[41]

Why Rabbis Cannot Understand. John Mayer: "And the vision has become to you like a sealed book. . . ." That is, the prophecies of your destruction, which the learned among you cannot read because it is sealed, nor the unlearned, even if it were open, because they depend entirely on their rabbis. But the rabbis are opposed to this notion that the time of the Messiah's coming is long ago past; indeed, they set the times themselves. And according to the word of shutting here used, Rabbi Solomon confesses in his comments on Daniel that their modern rabbis say that the reason why they have been deceived in the time is that the sayings about this in the prophets are shut. Commentary on Isaiah 29:11-12.[42]

Pursue Christ and the Things of Christ. Johannes Oecolampadius: Our Isaiah also treats those things . . . when he says to those whose heart is far from God and their fear of God is a commandment taught by people that there will be a mixed spirit of sleep from the Lord, and their eyes will be so closed that all their vision is like the words in a sealed book.[†] So when some people give letters to the knowledgeable and say, "Read it," he will respond, "I cannot, for it is sealed." And when letters are given to the unlearned, he also says, "I do not know how to read." God also threatens them through the prophet, "Behold, I will again do a great and astonishing miracle with this people: I will ruin the wisdom of their wise, and the discernment of their discerning ones shall be hidden." Do you see what closed the book to them and their eyes, namely, that their hearts were far from the Lord and they were following human commands and teachings? But let us not become like them, but rather, once we have said goodbye to worldly things, let us pursue Christ himself and the things of Christ, and let us ask for wisdom from the Lord, and I dare to promise that Christ in his mercy will deny nothing to such righteous vows. Preface to Commentary on Isaiah.[43]

Hypocrisy and the True Church. Johannes Brenz: These are memorable sayings that ought to be preserved with the most careful diligence. For where he says, "This people draw near with their mouth and honor me with their lips . . .", he overturns and condemns all hypocrisy not only of the Jewish priests, the sacrificing priests, the Pharisees and the scribes, but also the papistic priests, monks, nuns, and mothers. But so that we may understand this more rightly, we must go through each part of the saying that describes the characteristics and manners of the hypocrites. . . . Since, then, the Israelites neither had true faith nor had obeyed the call of God, as follows later, their boasting was most empty.

So also the papists, pontiffs, bishops, priests, and monks boast that they are the true church of God, because they are the successors of those to whom Christ says, "I chose you and appointed you that you should go and bear fruit, and that your fruit should abide," and again, "I will be with you always, to the end of the age." And indeed these things were said to the apostles and about the true church of Christ, in which the apostolic teaching and the pure gospel of Christ resound. But where there is conflict with the apostolic

[41]Oecolampadius, *In Iesaiam*, 170r.
[42]Mayer, *Commentary upon All the Prophets*, 4:182*.
[43]Oecolampadius, *In Iesaiam*, 2r. [†]See also 171v-r.

teaching and human ordinances are taught in place of the gospel of Christ, which is what usually happens in the papistic meetings, there is not the true church of Christ. Commentary on Isaiah 29:13-14.[44]

How the Roman Church Sins. Dietrich Schnepff: This is the way the Romans sin today. They profess to worship God with all their earnest care and diligence, but at the same time they diligently do everything to suppress the evangelical teaching. There are also among us many such people who conduct themselves with piety and innocence of life, but in their innermost hearts they have nothing besides the filth of barbarous sins. They feign peace, and their hearts speak war. They profess chastity and abstinence while their hearts still burn with impure lusts and flames. Such people attempt to impose themselves on God, as if he were only a spectator of external works and not also of the heart. This is to mock God. But the Lord is not mocked. Rather, he punishes that outrageous behavior of people with more severe penalties.

But then he also specifies another sin of theirs, namely, worship of a counterfeit human character. He says, "Their fear of me is a commandment taught by people." Christ cites these words . . . , "In vain do they worship me, teaching as doctrines human commandments." The Lord interpreted what had been said by our prophet somewhat more succinctly. Those things that are established outside the word by human counsel are proven not to be among the sacred things by the Lord. For when the Hebrews were being rebuked by the prophets and the entire institution of the Pharisees was being condemned by Christ and the apostles, they immediately shouted many and various ways they worship the Lord. All those boastings Christ overturned with one word. Not only are they not approved by the Lord, but they are even more displeasing, because God wants to be worshiped in the ways prescribed by him; all other worship is condemned and detested as foreign. Scholia on Isaiah 29:13-14.[45]

The Twofold Perishing of Wisdom. Johannes Oecolampadius: "And wisdom will perish." This is explained twofold. For "wisdom will perish" is either that none of your wisdom other than what you have from the Scriptures will help you, and any other gifts entrusted to you will be of no benefit—even wisdom that seems true. Or the wisdom that seems to be wisdom is not; that is, the wisdom of this world, or fleshly wisdom, will perish, being conquered by the foolishness of preaching. . . . And it is necessary for that kind of wisdom to perish among those who are being saved, so that even its reason or mind is crucified and subjected to the obedience of faith, because it is not capable of divine things. Commentary on Isaiah 29:14.[46]

The Destruction of Human Wisdom. Andreas Bodenstein von Karlstadt: Through this ordinance God clearly shows for all time that all the learned, the princes, and the masses can err and stumble. Therefore God alone has also let it be proclaimed in general and in particular that each one should hasten to righteousness for oneself, . . . and that no one must follow the masses in deviating from what is right.

God also calls it prostitution and whoring eyes when people look at things other than his rule of conduct—that is, God's Word. God has forbidden us to follow our own thoughts. All our good opinions have been chopped down and altogether eradicated: acting or speaking as other people act or speak, or as we believe to be good. . . . "The wisdom of all the wise must be destroyed" to its foundations if divine wisdom is to arise. Not only your own wisdom, dear brother, must become nothing but foolishness, but also the wisdom of all other people. This must happen so that you do not

[44]Brenz, *Esaias*, 382; citing Jn 15:16; Mt 28:20.

[45]Schnepff, *In Esaiae*, 442; citing Mt 15:9.

[46]Oecolampadius, *In Iesaiam*, 171r; citing 1 Cor 1.

let yourself be moved by either learned or unlearned people, and so that without mediation you hit on the naked truth, which frees you and will not let you be harmed for eternity. Whether One Should Proceed Slowly.[47]

29:15-24 *The Foolishness of Secret Plans*

Unable to Hide from the Lord. Menno Simons: And with Isaiah, "Woe to those who seek deep to hide their counsel from the Lord, whose deeds are in the dark, and who say, 'Who sees us? And who knows us?'" . . . Observe this denunciation, "Woe to them." . . . Chosen brethren, take heed; none under the canopy of heaven can so conceal oneself that one cannot be seen by the flaming eyes of the Lord, or not be found by the avenging hand of his wrath in his wickedness. Indeed, the least thought is not concealed in our hearts that is not open to the eyes of the Lord. I therefore warn all in general, that you with all your powers watch against sin, whether secret or open; if sin is not sincerely repented of, your portion will be eternal death. Let all the impenitent and heedless sinners reflect on this. Explanation of the True Apostolic Separation, or Excommunication.[48]

Clay and Potter. Wolfgang Musculus: What they were saying is, "Who sees us? Who knows us?" It is the same, he says, as if "the thing made should say to its maker, 'You did not make me,' and the invention about its inventor, 'He has no understanding.'" They did not say these things with words, but when they honored God with their mouths and lips and they were echoing every day. But they thought that their wickedness and malice were beautifully covered up in the sight of God by that false appearance of piety, as if everything hidden, both in thought and deed, is not manifest to the eyes of God's majesty. And finally that was the most wicked denial of the maker. Commentary on Isaiah 29:15-16.[49]

Carmel and Lebanon Producing Together. Johannes Brenz: Lebanon, the mountain with the highest cedars are the nobles, and Carmel, the mountain with fruitful wine, are the famous people. Therefore, at the time when Christ comes, Lebanon will be converted into Carmel, and Carmel in turn to Lebanon, that is, all will be cultivated into the kingdom of Christ, fertile and blessed. Lebanon indeed has cedars suitable for building, but they lack grape vines and olives. Carmel has many vines and olives but lacks cedars. Therefore, when Christ receives his kingdom, there will be such blessings that Lebanon produces vines together with cedars, and Carmel produces cedars together with vines. Commentary on Isaiah 29:17.[50]

Understanding the Words of the Book. Martin Borrhaus: "And in that day, the deaf will hear the words of a book." He proceeds to be comforted by the ability to hear and understand the words of the book that had been closed. The times of Hezekiah are known, that those among them who were deaf before the destruction of the Assyrians began to understand the words of the book of the oracles issued by the prophet Isaiah when those were conquered. But the priests and false prophets, who thought they themselves were wise and strong in hearing, were not understanding. Now, in the time of the heavenly Hezekiah, our Lord Messiah himself indicates in the Gospel that those suffering both physical and mental deafness and blindness began to hear and see. Oracles in Isaiah on 29:18-19.[51]

Eyes Closed to Prophecies. Wolfgang Musculus: So it happens that the visions of the prophets remain closed and sealed to them until the time of their fulfillment comes, so that they

[47]Karlstadt, *Whether One Should Proceed Slowly*, 50; citing Ex 23:2; Lk 15; Mt 16; Deut 12:8.
[48]Simons, *Complete Works*, 1:254.
[49]Musculus, *In Esaiam*, 433.
[50]Brenz, *Esaias*, 389.
[51]Borrhaus, *In Iesaiae Prophetae Oracula*, 267.

may experience for themselves what they previously refused to believe, and what they could not understand they may perceive with the senses of their own eyes and ears, appalled and anxious. And today we see the same thing happening with all the prophecies and heavenly visions. The eyes of the mind have been closed in this present age, and the ears completely stopped. Commentary on Isaiah 29:18-21.[52]

The True Redemption of the Sons. Dietrich Schnepff: Now, by the redemption of Abraham, he means that great kindness that the Lord granted to this patriarch. For he guarded him among the greatest hardships when he brought him out of Mesopotamia; he was mercifully protected among the nations and the enemies, and he did not suffer shame when his wife was endangered with King Abimelech. And with the most brilliant promises and signs he set forth true redemption, which is in Christ the Lord, when he promised a blessing to all peoples through the seed of Abraham. . . .

Therefore, the things said in this passage about the house of Jacob are to be understood to be about the members of the true church. For not all who are from Israel are Israel, and just because they are the seed of Abraham does not mean they are all sons. But those who are sons of the promises are counted among the seed, and those who are of faith are the sons of Abraham. Therefore Isaiah speaks about the sons of Jacob and properly of Abraham, that is, believers, of whom certainly neither Jacob nor others ought to be ashamed. For they are, as Isaiah testifies in this passage, not so much of Jacob as they are sons of his Lord who are born not from the bloodline, nor by human will, but of God; indeed, they are truly born again of water and spirit. Scholia on Isaiah 29:22-23.[53]

When the Gentiles Will Believe. Konrad Pellikan: This prophecy is most clearly about the calling of the Gentiles and the true glory of the holy patriarchs. For although Judah and the temple with the ark was going to cease, and the wicked Jews relegated into exile, yet because of this Jacob will not be ashamed. On the contrary, then he will be more glorified, and his merits before God will shine more clearly throughout the world. . . . The Gentiles, who were formerly sinning through innumerable errors of idolatry, are going to be enlightened by the Holy Spirit. They will learn understanding. They will be taught by God. And they will know the difference between true and false piety. And those who had always been unbelieving and ignorant of religion and heavenly discipline, they will learn the law of God, embrace the old and sacred literature. And they will understand, believe, teach, and spread among all the nations. Commentary on Isaiah 29:22-24.[54]

[52]Musculus, *In Esaiam*, 435.

[53]Schnepff, *In Esaiae*, 447-48.

[54]Pellikan, *Commentaria Bibliorum*, 3:36r.

30:1–31:9 DEPENDING ON EGYPT

30 *"Ah, stubborn children," declares the LORD,*
"who carry out a plan, but not mine,

and who make an alliance,[a] but not of my Spirit,
that they may add sin to sin;

2who set out to go down to Egypt,
without asking for my direction,

to take refuge in the protection of Pharaoh
and to seek shelter in the shadow of Egypt!

3Therefore shall the protection of Pharaoh turn to your shame,
and the shelter in the shadow of Egypt to your humiliation.

4For though his officials are at Zoan
and his envoys reach Hanes,

5everyone comes to shame
through a people that cannot profit them,

that brings neither help nor profit,
but shame and disgrace."

6An oracle on the beasts of the Negeb.

Through a land of trouble and anguish,
from where come the lioness and the lion,
the adder and the flying fiery serpent,

they carry their riches on the backs of donkeys,
and their treasures on the humps of camels,
to a people that cannot profit them.

7Egypt's help is worthless and empty;
therefore I have called her
"Rahab who sits still."

8And now, go, write it before them on a tablet
and inscribe it in a book,

that it may be for the time to come
as a witness forever.[b]

9For they are a rebellious people,
lying children,

children unwilling to hear
the instruction of the LORD;

10who say to the seers, "Do not see,"
and to the prophets, "Do not prophesy to us what is right;

speak to us smooth things,
prophesy illusions,

11leave the way, turn aside from the path,
let us hear no more about the Holy One of Israel."

12Therefore thus says the Holy One of Israel,

"Because you despise this word
and trust in oppression and perverseness
and rely on them,

13therefore this iniquity shall be to you
like a breach in a high wall, bulging out and about to collapse,
whose breaking comes suddenly, in an instant;

14and its breaking is like that of a potter's vessel
that is smashed so ruthlessly

that among its fragments not a shard is found
with which to take fire from the hearth,
or to dip up water out of the cistern."

15For thus said the Lord GOD, the Holy One of Israel,

"In returning[c] and rest you shall be saved;
in quietness and in trust shall be your strength."

But you were unwilling, 16and you said,

"No! We will flee upon horses";
therefore you shall flee away;

and, "We will ride upon swift steeds";
therefore your pursuers shall be swift.

17 A thousand shall flee at the threat of one;
at the threat of five you shall flee,

till you are left
like a flagstaff on the top of a mountain,
like a signal on a hill.

18 Therefore the Lord waits to be gracious to you,
and therefore he exalts himself to show mercy to you.

For the Lord is a God of justice;
blessed are all those who wait for him.

19 For a people shall dwell in Zion, in Jerusalem; you
shall weep no more. He will surely be gracious to you at
the sound of your cry. As soon as he hears it, he
answers you. 20 And though the Lord give you the bread
of adversity and the water of affliction, yet your Teacher
will not hide himself anymore, but your eyes shall see
your Teacher. 21 And your ears shall hear a word behind
you, saying, "This is the way, walk in it," when you
turn to the right or when you turn to the left. 22 Then
you will defile your carved idols overlaid with silver and
your gold-plated metal images. You will scatter them as
unclean things. You will say to them, "Be gone!"

23 And he will give rain for the seed with which you
sow the ground, and bread, the produce of the ground,
which will be rich and plenteous. In that day your
livestock will graze in large pastures, 24 and the oxen
and the donkeys that work the ground will eat
seasoned fodder, which has been winnowed with
shovel and fork. 25 And on every lofty mountain and
every high hill there will be brooks running with
water, in the day of the great slaughter, when the
towers fall. 26 Moreover, the light of the moon will be
as the light of the sun, and the light of the sun will be
sevenfold, as the light of seven days, in the day when
the Lord binds up the brokenness of his people, and
heals the wounds inflicted by his blow.

27 Behold, the name of the Lord comes from afar,
burning with his anger, and in thick rising smoke;[d]

his lips are full of fury,
and his tongue is like a devouring fire;

28 his breath is like an overflowing stream
that reaches up to the neck;

to sift the nations with the sieve of destruction,
and to place on the jaws of the peoples a bridle that leads astray.

29 You shall have a song as in the night when a holy
feast is kept, and gladness of heart, as when one sets
out to the sound of the flute to go to the mountain of
the Lord, to the Rock of Israel. 30 And the Lord will
cause his majestic voice to be heard and the descend-
ing blow of his arm to be seen, in furious anger and a
flame of devouring fire, with a cloudburst and storm
and hailstones. 31 The Assyrians will be terror-stricken
at the voice of the Lord, when he strikes with his rod.
32 And every stroke of the appointed staff that the
Lord lays on them will be to the sound of tambou-
rines and lyres. Battling with brandished arm, he will
fight with them. 33 For a burning place[e] has long been
prepared; indeed, for the king it is made ready, its
pyre made deep and wide, with fire and wood in
abundance; the breath of the Lord, like a stream of
sulfur, kindles it.

31 Woe[f] to those who go down to Egypt for help
and rely on horses,

who trust in chariots because they are many
and in horsemen because they are very strong,

but do not look to the Holy One of Israel
or consult the Lord!

2 And yet he is wise and brings disaster;
he does not call back his words,

but will arise against the house of the evildoers
and against the helpers of those who work iniquity.

3 The Egyptians are man, and not God,
and their horses are flesh, and not spirit.

When the LORD stretches out his hand,
the helper will stumble, and he who is helped will fall,
and they will all perish together.

4*For thus the LORD said to me,*
"As a lion or a young lion growls over his prey,
and when a band of shepherds is called out against him
he is not terrified by their shouting
or daunted at their noise,
so the LORD of hosts will come down
to fight[g] *on Mount Zion and on its hill.*
5*Like birds hovering, so the LORD of hosts*
will protect Jerusalem;
he will protect and deliver it;
he will spare and rescue it."

6*Turn to him from whom people*[h] *have deeply*
revolted, O children of Israel. 7*For in that day*
everyone shall cast away his idols of silver and his
idols of gold, which your hands have sinfully made
for you.

8*"And the Assyrian shall fall by a sword, not of man;*
and a sword, not of man, shall devour him;
and he shall flee from the sword,
and his young men shall be put to forced labor.
9*His rock shall pass away in terror,*
and his officers desert the standard in panic,"
declares the LORD, whose fire is in Zion,
and whose furnace is in Jerusalem.

a Hebrew *who weave a web* **b** Some Hebrew manuscripts, Syriac, Targum, Vulgate, and Greek versions; Masoretic Text *forever and ever* **c** Or *repentance* **d** Hebrew *in weight of uplifted clouds* **e** Or *For Topheth* **f** Or *Ah,* **g** The Hebrew words for *hosts* and *to fight* sound alike **h** Hebrew *they*

OVERVIEW: These two chapters address the unreliability of Egypt and the disappointment that will result for those who depend on them. Isaiah rebukes God's people for being stubborn and rebellious. Many Reformation interpreters identify that the core sins in this passage are putting confidence in the flesh, not consulting God, making sinful alliances, and rejecting the proper teaching of God's Word. Some give specific examples in their own day, such as praying to saints, engaging in war, and refusing to listen to good preaching. Portions of these chapters also provide the opportunity for some to teach about the inspiration of Scripture and heaven and hell. The conclusion, where Isaiah prophesies about the fall of Assyria, demonstrates again the power and sovereignty of God over all.

30:1-7 *Futile Trust in Egypt*

REBEL SONS. HEINRICH BULLINGER: Now he shows the nature of their sin. For he names them "renegade sons." Some read this as "deserters." The Septuagint has "apostate." Others have "obstinate." Indeed, the Jews were sons of God, as we are, by the gracious adoption of God. And consequently we owe obedience to God our Father, and we are not permitted to institute anything on our own accord and for our own will without consulting God our Father. Further, if we do not do this, we are rightly called renegades, rebels, obstinate, or, if you prefer, deserters. . . . Why he named them "renegade sons," he illustrates in the following words: "who dare to carry out a plan, but not mine." For it is the duty of sons to obey their parents (as has already been said) and to institute nothing without consulting them. SERMONS ON ISAIAH 30:1.[1]

ACCUMULATING SIN. KONRAD PELLIKAN: He calls them apostates, deserters, and degenerates

[1]Bullinger, *Isaias*, 141v.

who place their confidence in people, who enter into an alliance with the unfaithful, and who refuse to yield to the words of the prophets. It is said to happen by the counsel of the Lord, because the exhortation from the prophets is that the counsel of the Lord should be sought by them. Those who spurn them spurn the Lord. The one who does not listen to the word of the Lord, who spurns the prophets, and who begs for help from the wicked accumulates sin upon sin. Commentary on Isaiah 30:1.[2]

Counsel Without God. Argula von Grumbach: And neither the pope, with his decretals, nor Aristotle, who has never been a Christian, nor you yourselves can manage it. You imagine that you can defy God, cast down his prophets and apostles from heaven, and banish them from the world. This shall not happen. . . . God will surely preserve his holy and blessed Word. As he has hitherto declared, has done in the Old and New Testaments, still does, and will continue to do. God will fall on you, as the prophet says. . . . "They puffed up their hearts and forgot me. I will be to them as a lion in their path. And will fall upon them like a bear who sees her young being stolen." . . . "I smote them with the words of my mouth." "Woe to you! For you carry out a plan, but not mine." . . . "Woe to the fools, to those who prophesy according to their own conceits! They see useless things and teach lies." To the University of Ingolstadt.[3]

Apostasy in Matters of the Soul. Johannes Oecolampadius: So let the bishops see that they are composing new laws rashly. Where the matter of souls is concerned, what do they do? They prove monastic vows from here, imploring the patronage of the saints and many other things that are not prescribed in the sacred writings. And at the same time they dare to call the canonical writings a source of heresies. They are truly thieves and apostate sons. For it is not a small sin to question the mouth of the Lord in matters of the soul. So here it is called apostasy and a heaping up of sin upon sin. And justifiably such people are disappointed in the human help where they had placed their hope. Commentary on Isaiah 30:1.[4]

Examples of Sinful Associations. John Trapp: They were flatly forbidden to do this [go down to Egypt]. But state policy sometimes carries with it things that go against express Scripture, for formalizing and enervating the power of truth, until at length they have left us a heartless and sapless religion, as one well observes. This is certainly no thriving course. Here we have a dreadful woe hung on the heels of it. The Grecian churches first called in the Turks to help them, who distressed them. And then, through fear of the Turks in the year 1438, they sent for and subjected themselves to the bishop of Rome to get help from the Latin churches. But shortly after that, they were destroyed, their empire subdued, and so on, teaching all others by their example not to trust in worldly alliances and not to seek the association of others in a sinful way. Exposition on Isaiah 30:2.[5]

Seeking Help from Egypt. Martin Borrhaus: The mystical word from "going down" here should not be neglected. If anyone inquires here about what time and under which king these Egyptian protections were sought, the sacred narrative does not clearly indicate. Neither Ahaz nor Hezekiah sent ambassadors to Egypt during their reign to request its help against Assyria. This is why there are those who wish to say it is about the time when Zedekiah ruled, who raised his mind for help from the Egyptians. But what follows does not correspond to the times of Zedekiah but to the age of the prophet Isaiah.

[2]Pellikan, *Commentaria Bibliorum*, 3:36r.
[3]Von Grumbach, *Argula von Grumbach: A Woman's Voice*, 77-78; citing Hos 13:8; 6:5; Is 30:1; Ezek 13:2.
[4]Oecolampadius, *In Iesaiam*, 172v-173r.
[5]Trapp, *Commentary or Exposition*, 108*.

Accordingly, although the narrative does not clearly portray that at the time of Ahaz or Hezekiah help from the Egyptians was implored, yet we may learn from earlier passages and from the speech of the ambassadors of the Assyrian king that the Jews turned their mind to protection from Egypt. So later we read that the ambassador of the Assyrians says, "In whom do you now trust, that you have rebelled against me? You are trusting in Egypt, that broken reed of a staff, which will pierce the hand of anyone who leans on it. Such is Pharaoh king of Egypt to all who trust in him." And we read above, "And they shall be ashamed because of Cush and of Egypt, in whom they boasted." The argument is that the defeats that Judea suffered under the Assyrians, a good part of the tribes of Judah and Benjamin trusted in the Egyptians. Mention was made earlier about this disaster, "And he will go through Judah, flooding it, and he will come, passing through it all the way to the mountains." Oracles in Isaiah on 30:1-5.[6]

True Weapons. Menno Simons: O, beloved reader, our weapons are not swords and spears but patience, silence and hope, and the Word of God. With these we must maintain our cause and defend it. Paul says, "The weapons of our warfare are not carnal but mighty through God." With these we intend and desire to resist the kingdom of the devil; and not with swords, spears, cannons, and coats of mail. . . . According to the declaration of the prophet, they have beaten their swords into plowshares and their spears into pruning hooks. They shall sit every man under his vine and under his fig tree, Christ; neither shall they learn war any more. A Humble and Christian Defense.[7]

Beasts Carrying Treasures to Egypt. Wolfgang Musculus: "A burden," it says, "on the beasts of the south." By "beasts of the south," understand those beasts on which they placed their treasures as gifts to be carried to the king of Egypt. Truly the oracle is against those sent by the leaders into Egypt along with the people, that is, future disaster is threatened. He calls them beasts of the south because they were bringing wealth and treasures to Egypt, situated in the south. Commentary on Isaiah 30:6.[8]

30:8-18 *The Foolishness of Failing to Trust the Lord*

Written Scripture. Heinrich Bullinger: We gather from this passage that the holy prophets of God wrote books, which we receive as if by hand from our fathers, not by their own decision or will but by the compulsion and command of God. Evidence of this fact can be sought from other passages of Scripture. . . . There is no doubt that even the Gospel writers and apostles wrote what they wrote for the salvation of the church at God's order or command. So then, those are wicked who, using sacrilegious words, disparaging the Scriptures, clamor, "Who ordered them to write these? Who handed down the writings to us? How can we be certain they wrote by the Spirit of God? Why then should I believe the Scriptures are without contradiction?" These are wicked, sacrilegious, and blasphemous voices, which, if the holy magistrates do not restrain severely, will not be restrained. Yet God is awfully truthful, who never allowed his name to be blasphemed without punishment. Sermons on Isaiah 30:8.[9]

Forgive Those Who Shut Out God's Word. Argula von Grumbach: It is a joy to me to be reviled for the sake of the holy gospel. God forgive them, they know not what they do. I pray with all my heart that God may enlighten them, and beg you also to pray for them and for all whose hearts are hardened. Hear the Lord. . . . This people moves God to anger, for they "shut

[6]Borrhaus, *In Iesaiae Prophetae Oracula*, 270-71; citing Is 36:5-6; 20:5.
[7]Simons, *Complete Works*, 2:307; citing Eph 6:17; Heb 4:12; 2 Cor 10:4-5; Job 41:27; Mt 10:21; Lk 12:53; Is 2:4; Mic 4:3.
[8]Musculus, *In Esaiam*, 440.
[9]Bullinger, *Isaias*, 143v; citing Deut 3.

their ears to the word of God and say to the seers, 'Do not see.'" To the Honorable, Wise Council of the Town Ingolstadt.[10]

Don't Teach Us. Johannes Oecolampadius: But this one expressly says, "Do not speak to us." For they want to spare themselves, not even caring if others are accused. But as charity sustains all things, so the spirit of zeal spares no one, and least of all those who scarcely bear to be reviled. Further, when he says, "Prophesy what is right, smooth, and absurd," he says that according to his own opinion. For the wise ones do not want their worldly business to be called absurd and errors. Commentary on Isaiah 30:10-11.[11]

Preach God's Holy Word. Argula von Grumbach:

His sole command is that we preach
And bring his Holy Word to speech.
In Deuteronomy, chapter 4,
And chapter 12, you'll find what's more,
How earnestly God, each one forbids
to tear his Sacred Word to bits.
Add nothing to, nor take away.
Decretal, then, how can you stay?
Or Scotus with his subtlety?
Not much of God's Word there we see!
Even the greatly learned master
produces garrulous palaver
Which God for certain has forbidden;
In Isaiah 30, it is written:
"Woe to you, who fail to note
the counsel of the mouth of God."
Christ says all worship in vain
Which human precept sets in train.
And this same chapter further states,
What God hasn't put in place,
Must be uprooted from the earth.

Johannes of Lanzhut: Attack and Response.[12]

Not a Calling to Laziness. Johannes Brenz: Then it is specified to us in this speech of Isaiah, a memorable saying that is to be stored up in the mind and to be applied for use in all our business. "In rest," it says, "and in quietness, you shall be saved. In silence, or calmness, and trust shall be your strength." This statement does not command us to be idle and lazy in our calling and expect help to come from heaven while we are sleeping. But first of all, he forbids us to be troubled in our affairs about the foreign help, and commands us to serve in our calling with a calm mind, and to do those things that are our legitimate duty with a quiet mind. Then he commands us to hope and wait on only God for help and salvation with a firm faith. Commentary on Isaiah 30:15.[13]

Repentance and Rest Required. Johannes Oecolampadius: "For thus said the Lord." He still is treating human wisdom, which rejected hope in God and leans on the flesh and one's own works. And first he calls them to repentance and rest and true Sabbath. For so we attain salvation. . . . He names that sitting, "quiet and silence." Then he adds, "and trust." In that "shall be your strength." Further, the wicked and foolish flesh always seeks help from somewhere else and sends messengers to Egypt. Therefore we should have nothing to do with consulting those who have abandoned the faith. Because whatever they do will be sin. Commentary on Isaiah 30:15.[14]

Christians Are Not Instruments of Judgment. Menno Simons: This parable [of the servants] some adulterate and say, "The enemies of God must be destroyed before the coming of Christ, and therefore we will be the instruments to do." But they must come to shame, [those who say], "'No, we will flee upon horses,' therefore you shall flee away, and, 'We will ride on

[10]Von Grumbach, *Argula von Grumbach: A Woman's Voice*, 119.
[11]Oecolampadius, *In Iesaiam*, 174r.
[12]Von Grumbach, *Argula von Grumbach: A Woman's Voice*, 180.
[13]Brenz, *Esaias*, 401.
[14]Oecolampadius, *In Iesaiam*, 174v-175r.

swift steeds,' therefore your pursuers shall be swift." Oh, that the advocates of the Word would observe these words! Yea, those who would be angels to root up the tares while Christ told the parable with a different understanding. . . . Since the Christians are the good seed, how then can they be the angels or reapers; or if they are the reapers, how can they be the seed? These two are quite different things, the seed and the reapers; its plainness is incontrovertible. TESTIMONY AGAINST JOHN VAN LEYDEN.[15]

THE BLESSEDNESS OF HOPE IN THE LORD. MARTIN BORRHAUS: A summary of what is read here is: blessed are all those who hope in him in contrast, that is in opposition, to those who were blamed earlier. Since you trust in slander and depravity, "Woe to the rebellious sons," who persist in going down to Egypt, hoping in the shadow of Egypt. If those who trust in the Lord are happy that what they possess is enough for them, abounding in an abundance of good things, that is to be blessed. On the other hand, those are unhappy who, lacking the greatest good from God, trust in creatures. In all of them there belongs a native emptiness flowing down from nothing. For it is certain, "Cursed is the one who makes flesh his strength." ORACLES IN ISAIAH ON 30:15.[16]

VICTORY IN GOD'S WORD. ARGULA VON GRUMBACH: If your Princely Grace saw to it that the gospel were preached to the poor, the land would be blessed with happiness and victory, as David says . . . , "I will not be afraid of a thousand." . . . "A thousand shall flee at the hand of one." Wherever the Word of God is exalted, victory will follow; conversely, whoever oppresses God's Word will be beset by every manner of plague. . . . But I know for sure that they cannot harm me unless the power to do so has been given them by God. He will keep me safe for his name's sake. Paul says . . . , "We suffer all things without complaint for the Lord's name." [And Isaiah,] "I will not fear a thousand." . . . "One person will make a thousand tremble." Hear what the Lord says . . . , "Do not be afraid of them, for I am with you and without me there is no salvation." . . . God says, "I myself will comfort you. Who are you, then, to fear mortals who are like grass . . . ?" TO DUKE WILHELM.[17]

GOD SUSPENDS HIS HAND FROM STRIKING. JOHANNES OECOLAMPADIUS: "And therefore he will wait." The prophet wishes to say, "God promised salvation to you, commanding you to rest and hope in him. And although your sins deserved a heavy punishment, yet he was patient and waited for you to repent. And because you refuse to hear him, you are without doubt justly ruined." But in the same sentence he says two things. For here it is the same God who is exalted and who waits. For with this imagery he imagines that it is as if he is lifting up his hand and brings it back to strike them, and suspends it as he is about to strike, so that at the same time we are humbled and escape his wrath. So you see here where all these threats aim, even if they frighten greatly, namely that we be converted and trust in God. COMMENTARY ON ISAIAH 30:18.[18]

TWO WAYS GOD DEALS WITH SIN. MARTIN BORRHAUS: Here is where God shows the affection of a father, when in chastising his children he does not aim to destroy the persons, whom he loves, but their sins, which he hates. Hence, "Blessed are those whom God disciplines." Consequently, sins are handled in two ways. One way is according to its nature: how they are horribly shameful and filthy and separating us from friendship with God. In this way, when the law accuses, they get the severe justice of being condemned and destroyed, in which God is

[15]Simons, *Complete Works* 2:438; citing Mt 12:36.
[16]Borrhaus, *In Iesaiae Prophetae Oracula*, 275; citing Jer 17:5.
[17]Von Grumbach, *Argula von Grumbach: A Woman's Voice*, 109, 121; citing Ps 3:6; 2 Cor 4; Is 43; 51:12.
[18]Oecolampadius, *In Iesaiam*, 175r-v.

experienced justly, not as a father disciplining in love but as a judge condemning severely.

The other way sins are handled is how he atones for and covers them to be transferred to himself, who is the blessed Messiah. So, when sins are weighed in a state of repentance, afflictions may arise for a time, to open the way to him. This is what the prophet speaks about when he says, "Therefore, the Lord makes himself wait for you to show mercy to you." Clearly, he takes on the person of father and sets aside that of judge. Oracles in Isaiah on 30:18.[19]

30:19-33 *A Time of Healing and Restoration*

The Double Meaning of Fruitfulness. Johannes Oecolampadius: Now, where we hear the gospel with our consciences gladdened, we obtain the fruitfulness of all things, and there is no longer a "bronze heaven and an iron earth" . . . to prevent rain. And this is what the Lord says, "Blessed are those who mourn, for they shall be comforted." No more will he give the rain wings to fly away. It seems that the prophet clearly speaks of a twofold rain, namely, the temporal one for crops and the spiritual one for the cultivation of souls. For the word according to the Hebrew, *mōwrēh*, is ambiguous, signifying "rain" and "teacher." . . . For among the blessings he recounts for the righteous is to have a faithful teacher, who will teach them the royal way they are to go. Now, the royal way is what has been handed down in the sacred writings, from which one must not deviate, either to the right or to the left. That is, nothing should be added to them, nor anything taken away from them. Commentary on Isaiah 30:19-20.[20]

Seek the Teacher Diligently. Margaret Fell: As all of you continually desire to know the mysteries of God, which are hidden from all the world and the world's profession, though never so high, turn to the light, wait in the light, keep your minds within the light, and walk in the light. It checks you and convinces you of sin and evil, discerns the thoughts of your hearts, and lets you see the out-goings of your mind. It discerns every sinful lust, both what appears and what rises to it. This is what the Lord God teaches in his day: the teacher is never put in the corner by those who listen attentively and turn their minds to it. A Testimony of the Touchstone for All Professions.[21]

Teachers Hidden No More. Wolfgang Musculus: The sense is that you will no longer contradict those who have been sent by the Lord to teach you. It does not simply say, "Your teacher will be prevented," but, "Your teacher will be prevented anymore." It is as if he were saying, "In the same way, he is already prevented by the stubborn and rebellious leaders who say to the seers, 'Do not see,' and to the foreseers, 'Do not prophesy to us what is right; speak to us smooth things.' . . ." So now, when you eat and drink "the bread of adversity and the water of affliction," you will no longer resist your teachers, but your eyes will be fixed on them. Commentary on Isaiah 30:20.[22]

A Memorable Comparison for Idolatry. Martin Borrhaus: "Like the uncleanness of a menstrual rag." This is a memorable comparison. Formerly it was custom that a menstruating woman be separated from her husband on account of the poisonous impurity of her menstruation. So an idol must be separated from the temple, which is consecrated to God, who dwells in it. After the veil was removed, this temple happens to be the mystical temple about which the apostle speaks, "You yourselves are the temple of God," where nothing else is permitted to dwell besides God, because he is worshiped and adored by faith. But if anything else is worshiped that would not otherwise be

[19]Borrhaus, *In Iesaiae Prophetae Oracula*, 275; citing Job 5:17.
[20]Oecolampadius, *In Iesaiam*, 177v; citing Deut 28:23.
[21]Fell, *Women's Speaking Justified and Other Pamphlets*, 89*; citing 1 Jn 1:7.
[22]Musculus, *In Esaiam*, 447; citing Is 30:10-11.

considered unclean, it is now considered a menstrual rag. Oracles in Isaiah on 30:22.[23]

An Allegory for Teachers and Learners. Johannes Oecolampadius: But the allegory here must not be detested.† For by "bulls and donkeys," we understand teachers, whose purpose is to take care of the land with their learning, as Paul says . . . where he quotes the passage from Deuteronomy, "You shall not muzzle an ox when it treads out the grain," and asks, "Is it for oxen that God is concerned?" But we understand the livestock to be the simpler listeners, whom the Lord often calls sheep. But there is one kind of food for the learned and another for the simpler. . . . Bulls and teachers have seasoned fodder. By "seasoned" it signifies authority, as Moses commanded that animals that chew the cud and divide their hoofs should be the only ones for food, so the authority that is found in the Scriptures means that the profane and the sacred should not be mixed. Commentary on Isaiah 30:23-24.[24]

The Hyperbole of Brighter Days. Wolfgang Musculus: There is truly no necessity that we are compelled to scurry from the simplicity of this prophecy to the end of the world.† With hyperbolic language, the seer expresses the magnificence and glory of God's help. Because it is such a great and magnificent future, it is as if the two luminaries of the world, the moon and the sun, were congratulating the people liberated at that time for what will be a more cheerful and brilliant future than usual. Certainly no light was going to come near them besides the usual. But just as when one is disposed to anguish, the sun itself is darkened at noon, so it seems that when prosperous things unexpectedly happen to us, it seems to be brighter than usual.

That not only the sun but especially the moon is mentioned was because the deliverance of the people was going to happen at night. And when he says, "The light of the sun will be sevenfold, as the light of seven days," it is does not refer precisely to the number seven but should be explained according to the custom of Scripture, where this number is usually used for the increase of grace. Commentary on Isaiah 30:26.[25]

The Brightest Light. Dietrich Schnepff: Jerome understands that the "seven days" is about the seven days when the world was created. But the context itself shows that this is epexegetical.† For before he said, "The light of the sun will be sevenfold." This is now interpreted, "They will be as seven days," that is, seven days will not have as much splendor as day one is going to have. As we have said, this should be understood as the greatest joy, which the Hebrews are going to have when they see their enemy defeated.

It is easy to draw theological topics from these. For if these are taken as the kingdom of Christ, we see that the prophet wanted to describe that brightest light of the knowledge of God, which is in the New Testament, and also at the same time to set before our eyes that greatest fruit of consolation, which believers behold in the gospel. For when we progress in it, our minds conceive the certain hope of his eternal life. But if another meaning is preferable, from the same passage we see that the Lord is an artist, such that he can suddenly move people from the greatest difficulties into the brightest light. Scholia on Isaiah 30:26.[26]

Spiritual Success. Thomas Cooper: God shall pour on his people such great joy and gladness that the sun and moon shall seem to them to be far brighter than they were before. For to those who are in danger and heaviness, the sun and

[23]Borrhaus, *In Iesaiae Prophetae Oracula*, 277; citing 1 Cor 3:16.
[24]Oecolampadius, *In Iesaiam*, 177r. †See also Pellikan, *Commentaria Bibliorum*, 3:38v; citing 1 Cor 9:9; Deut 25:4.
[25]Musculus, *In Esaiam*, 450. †He rejects Jerome's interpretation that this refers to the end of the world with the arrival of the new heavens and new earth.
[26]Schnepff, *In Esaiae*, 468. †An *epexegetical* statement is a word or phrase joined to a pervious word or sentence for further clarification or explanation.

moon seem dark and dim, and when they have been delivered, because of their joy, all things seem brighter and more comfortable. And because in the prophets these particular deliverances of the Jews from their enemies are often figures of the great deliverance of the people of God from their spiritual enemies by Christ Jesus, this whole passage may well be interpreted as the happy and spiritual success that will come to the faithful by Christ, and the great brightness of his Holy Spirit, who then should shine far more plentifully than he ever did before. The Fourth Sunday in Advent at Morning Prayer.[27]

God the Consuming Fire. Martin Borrhaus: "Burning with his anger." The appearance of an angry person is applied to God, whose face burns with wrath, whose "lips are full of fury, and tongue is like a devouring fire, and breath is like an overflowing stream." This appearance is attributed to the Messiah in the Apocalypse of John, which is going to be displayed at that time when he will take vengeance on the antichrist. For John says it this way, "His eyes were like a flame of fire, his feet like burnished bronze, refined in a furnace, and his voice was like the roar of many waters." . . .

The same is read in the Apocalypse about the adversary of the heavenly Jerusalem who is going to be destroyed by the fire of divine fury: "For this reason, her plagues will come in a single day, death and mourning and famine, and she will be burned up with fire." . . . God the judge is a consuming fire. So the fire affects the righteous one way, the wicked another way. Some are delighted by its brightness, and it makes happy those whom it undoubtedly illuminates by its light of life and glory; others it condemns to darkness and gloom. Oracles in Isaiah on 30:27-28.[28]

Keeping the Feast Day. Johannes Oecolampadius: Furthermore, the prophet wants to teach from this that salvation does not come from our labors, nor by our wisdom, but to those who rest and at the same time "keep the feast day" in the Lord, it comes by divine power and mercy. And so gratitude is commended. For God wants blessings to be obtained from prayers, but obtained with thanksgiving that is preserved and multiplied. And so the spiritual Assyrian will be cut off from those who are keeping the Lord's feast. Commentary on Isaiah 30:29.[29]

When to Sing with Praise. John Mayer: When the Assyrians would be destroyed, . . . then the people of God would have joy, leading them to sing and to play music with pipes and other instruments in a way to praise him, as at times they did, like Miriam, . . . and the godly are exhorted to do. . . . Neither is it unlawful for the faithful now to do thus. But it is, "as in the night when a holy feast is kept," done in a godly way, as they did of old the evening before their solemnity or festival day, for their Sabbaths began in the evening. So there is nothing here to countenance vain songs and pipings but to stir us to solemn praising of God and keeping a day to do so, he takes our part when fighting against our enemies. And to show where this should be done he says, "as one sets out with a flute to the mountain of the Lord," that is, the temple, which stood upon a mountain, now in every house of God. Commentary on Isaiah 30:29.[30]

The Eternal Fire of Hell. Johannes Oecolampadius: "For it has been prepared from yesterday." He says here that not only are the Assyrians going to be slain, but that there is also another excruciating perpetual punishment of fire. For here Gehenna is called Tophteh, and I do not know where else you will find it so clearly described, with agreement from our Hebrew expositors.

Now, first it says it was "prepared from yesterday," that is, from the beginning of the world. For

[27]Cooper, *Brief Exposition*, 31r-32v*.

[28]Borrhaus, *In Iesaiae Prophetae Oracula*, 278-79, 282; citing Rev 1:14-15.

[29]Oecolampadius, *In Iesaiam*, 178r.

[30]Mayer, *Commentary upon All the Prophets*, 4:194*; citing Is 39; 10; 16; 18; Ex 15; Ps 92.

this is what yesterday signifies. . . . "Depart into the eternal fire prepared for the devil and his servants." So the Hebrew in the preceding prophets relates that hell was already prepared beforehand, even though he has not perished with his host.

Second is the depth and width of hell, where you will recognize the multitude of the damned.

Third is its fiery habitation with the fuel of firewood, so you understand its most severe torture. For the abominations and burning lusts of the soul, which are not purged by faith here, will be the kindling for the eternal fire and will turn into firewood and coals, such that the conscience itself will torment the wicked like fire.

The fourth point from this is the eternity of hell, because the Spirit of the Lord, that is, the will and "breath of the Lord, like a bellows of sulfur," supplies a perpetual and inextinguishable power for the fire. Commentary on Isaiah 30:33.[31]

31:1-3 *Disappointment from Egypt*

Another Sermon on Egypt. Johannes Brenz: Since Isaiah is not content with one sermon, he adds another that calls back his fellow citizens from trusting in Egyptian help but to trust in heavenly and divine help. "Woe," he says, "to all those who send ambassadors to Egypt to request human help" in these most difficult times of our republic. For although God has promised us that in this present disaster he is going to come and save us in a wonderful way, yet these people do not respect the holy God, who wonderfully helps his church, nor do they consult with the will and the word of the Lord on any concern, but they seek their help in horses, which abound in Egypt, and they trust more in chariots of war and Egyptians horses, which they judge to be the strongest of all, than they do in the divine promise. Commentary on Isaiah 31:1.[32]

Do Not Fear and Trust in Humans. Katharina Schütz Zell: As God says many times in the prophet Isaiah, "Fear not, I am with you," and says again, "Why do you fear a mortal man? And the son of man, who withers like the grass, and has forgotten your Creator, who is strong?" He does not want us to fear human beings. . . . Equally little does he want us to trust in human beings and their help. So he cries out in the prophet Isaiah . . . , "Woe to those who trust in the great number and strength of human beings and not in the Holy One of Israel, and who do not seek God." And he tells how he intends to send evil on them and not allow his word to be overcome, and that he will rise up against the wicked and their help. We have consolations enough in all Scripture, which we should always have before the eyes of our hearts. Apologia for Master Matthew Zell, Her Husband.[33]

Duplicated Impiety in Going to Egypt. Dietrich Schnepff: And this wickedness is duplicated when a specific command of God occurs. For the Hebrews, as was said in the previous chapter, were commanded to wait for divine help, because the Lord was going to deliver them from the power of that tyrant. There was also another general command not to enter into covenants with the nations. But after all this had happened, the Hebrews called on the Egyptians for an alliance of war, as if it were a thoughtless trifle. With all the miracles for reassuring the soul, they were still always preferring humans, and even those who had been enemies to their ancestors. Scholia on Isaiah 31:1.[34]

God the Wise. Wolfgang Musculus: Since it does not simply say, "Yet he is wise," but says, "Yet he is also wise," the prophet insinuates that those who went down to Egypt to seek the favor of help wanted this plan of theirs to be considered as great wisdom, and in contrast the prophet's teaching on trusting in God was being treated as stupidity to be mocked. These were not common people but

[31]Oecolampadius, *In Iesaiam*, 179v; citing Mt 25:41.
[32]Brenz, *Esaias*, 412; citing Mt 10:26, 28; Lk 12:4.
[33]Zell, *Katharina Schütz Zell, Church Mother*, 80.
[34]Schnepff, *In Esaiae*, 476.

chiefs and princes, and what they presumed against the word of the Lord they attributed to their own special wisdom and prudence. So they wanted their devised plan to appear very wise, because they were trying to obtain Pharaoh's help against the power of the Assyrians. Commentary on Isaiah 31:2.[35]

Trusting in Flesh. Johannes Oecolampadius: For what is Egypt other than flesh and something weak? So then, that help is empty and fleshly help. What is it for Egypt to boast of so many thousands of horses and four-horse chariots? For you remember they are nothing but flesh. And now those who want to be delivered from spiritual enemies, if they seek refuge in anything other than Christ, are they not fleeing to flesh? And if Christ was only human and not God, how will he also save us? And since anyone who puts their hope in the flesh is accursed, it is therefore necessary that Christ is the Son of God. The Egyptian horses, that is, whatever strength is in Egypt, is flesh and not spirit. That is, it will be feeble. Likewise, too, the letter on which most people rely is useless flesh. But the words that Christ speaks to the hearts of his own are life and spirit, and salvation comes through them. Commentary on Isaiah 31:3.[36]

31:4-9 *Return to the Lord the Defender*

Comfort from the Lord's Rule. Martin Borrhaus: "A band of shepherds." The lion, restrained by the hand of whatever shepherd, "is not terrified." So also the Lord is not moved by the power and multitude of the enemy. How little it is for the Lord of hosts, who rules over all things in heaven and hell, to free his city, Jerusalem. As it follows, "So the Lord of hosts will protect Jerusalem." This argument brought by the most powerful Lord in the universe about his rule has the greatest weight to comfort in all afflictions. Oracles in Isaiah on 31:4.[37]

God as Both Lion and Bird. Johannes Oecolampadius: Now he compares God to two animals: a lion and its cub devouring its prey, and a bird hovering over its young to protect them. He is compared to a lion because of his strength and unconquerable courage. So Christ is called a lion's cub. . . . "The Lion of the tribe of Judah has conquered." For disregarding and making nothing of all his enemies, he is not frightened by many or by few. But he is compared to birds because of his concern and affection and remarkable love toward us. . . . "How often would I have gathered you together as a hen gathers her chicks." . . . "Like an eagle that stirs up its chicks to fly and flutters over them, spreading out its wings." These two images are joined together well, for neither would comfort us without the other. Commentary on Isaiah 31:4-5.[38]

God as an Eagle. John Trapp: This is the second similitude: the eagle, when she flies highest of all from the nest and seems to set herself among the clouds, still keeps her eye on her nest, so that if any come near her young ones to disturb them, she makes all possible speed for their defense. Such an eagle is Almighty God . . . such a hen is Jesus Christ. . . . The church is God's nest; who dare meddle with it? Exposition on Isaiah 31:5.[39]

Turning to God in Repentance. Heinrich Bullinger: Because the prophet of God declared to the Jews that they sin against God gravely because they placed their trust in that covenant with Egypt and turned their souls away from the Lord God, who alone is able and wants to rescue them from whatever tribulations and dangers, he consequently exhorts them to repentance where they readily return to the Lord their God. For it is not enough to hear the word of God that refutes our sins, unless we also recognize and confess to God the sins we have

[35]Musculus, *In Esaiam*, 454.
[36]Oecolampadius, *In Iesaiam*, 179r.
[37]Borrhaus, *In Iesaiae Prophetae Oracula*, 285.
[38]Oecolampadius, *In Iesaiam*, 180v; citing Gen 49; Rev 5:5; Mt 23:37; Deut 32:11.
[39]Trapp, *Commentary or Exposition*, 114*; citing Deut 32:11; Mt 23:37; Ps 91:1-2.

committed, and indeed turn to God in true faith and correct those things by which we offend the Lord. Sermons on Isaiah 31:6-7.[40]

Images Are Not Books. Andreas Bodenstein von Karlstadt: God does not want us to call on him by looking at images; he wants us to hate and run away from those. On the day when the Lord will be lifted up, people will cast away and flee their images. From this we conclude that images are not ever books from which we can learn. Scripture likens images and idols to knaves, in several places referring to the godless court images as whorish court knaves. I am forced to sound coarse and uncouth, but I am not ashamed to speak as Scripture speaks. On the Removal of Images.[41]

A Sword Not Human. Wolfgang Musculus: "And the Assyrian shall fall," it says, "by a sword, not of man; and a sword, not of man, shall devour him." It was not with human weapons that Assyria would be brought down but with the sword of an angel, as is clear from the history. The prophet predicts the future with this, for the sake of strengthening the hearts of the righteous so they would not lose heart. And at the same time, he belittles the foolish exhaustion of the leaders, who were going down to Egypt in vain to find refuge in the horses, chariots, and swords of Pharoah to be protected against Assyria. You have in this passage an image of the antichrist, whom the Lord will slay with a sword not of humankind but "with the breath of his mouth and by the appearance of his coming." This is to be understood about that kingdom of the antichrist. Additionally, in the meantime, the right of the sword is not taken away from the governing authorities for the purpose of punishing those reprobate people who belong to the antichrist. Commentary on Isaiah 31:8-9.[42]

The Defeat of Sennacherib. Konrad Pellikan: The prophet especially seems to prophesy more often about the defeat of Sennacherib, because they were vigorously fearing his coming and the people were barely clinging to the Lord with restrained faith. No matter how much they had a holy king in Zedekiah (whose father and son were both wicked on account of the wickedness of the people), the leaders and the false prophets who were reporting that the Assyrian king was coming were persuading one another to surrender themselves to him so that what happened to Samaria would not happen to them. The prophet earnestly cries out against them to cast down their idols and not fear humans, if they are going to have the Lord be favorable to them. For Assyria will fall by the sword of the angel and be devoured with its army, so that there will be few remaining, and even those are going to flee and be put into forced labor by their enemies. Commentary on Isaiah 31:8-9.[43]

Tested by Fire. Johannes Oecolampadius: But this part of the verse is variously explained. For some say that God has fire in Zion and Jerusalem because of the altar and the sacrifices that were burned on it. Others explain that this is about vindication against the adversaries of the church, because none who injure the sons of God will go unpunished, since he is a fire to them, that is, he will carry out vengeance against those in Jerusalem as in an oven. And that explanation is not displeasing. But I do not reject the third, which is that all the elect of God are proven by the fire of trials, as gold is tested, so that it may be seen whether what each has built on the rock is gold, which fire does not consume, like Hezekiah, Isaiah, and the other righteous ones; or whether it is wood, which perishes in the fire, like Shebna and the others who fled into Egypt. For also above . . . , it said that he is going to burn away the dross and remove all that stood in Jerusalem. Commentary on Isaiah 31:9.[44]

[40]Bullinger, *Isaias*, 151r.
[41]CRR 8:155; citing Is 2:17; Mic 5:12; Ezek 6:8; 16:11-17.
[42]Musculus, *In Esaiam*, 457; citing 2 Thess 2:8.
[43]Pellikan, *Commentaria Bibliorum*, 3:39v-r.
[44]Oecolampadius, *In Iesaiam*, 181v; citing Is 1.

32:1–33:24 THE KINGDOM OF RIGHTEOUSNESS

32 *Behold, a king will reign in righteousness,*
and princes will rule in justice.

2 *Each will be like a hiding place from the wind,*
a shelter from the storm,

like streams of water in a dry place,
like the shade of a great rock in a weary land.

3 *Then the eyes of those who see will not be closed,*
and the ears of those who hear will give attention.

4 *The heart of the hasty will understand and know,*
and the tongue of the stammerers will hasten to speak distinctly.

5 *The fool will no more be called noble,*
nor the scoundrel said to be honorable.

6 *For the fool speaks folly,*
and his heart is busy with iniquity,

to practice ungodliness,
to utter error concerning the LORD,

to leave the craving of the hungry unsatisfied,
and to deprive the thirsty of drink.

7 *As for the scoundrel—his devices are evil;*
he plans wicked schemes

to ruin the poor with lying words,
even when the plea of the needy is right.

8 *But he who is noble plans noble things,*
and on noble things he stands.

9 *Rise up, you women who are at ease, hear my voice;*
you complacent daughters, give ear to my speech.

10 *In little more than a year*
you will shudder, you complacent women;

for the grape harvest fails,
the fruit harvest will not come.

11 *Tremble, you women who are at ease,*
shudder, you complacent ones;

strip, and make yourselves bare,
and tie sackcloth around your waist.

12 *Beat your breasts for the pleasant fields,*
for the fruitful vine,

13 *for the soil of my people*
growing up in thorns and briers,

yes, for all the joyous houses
in the exultant city.

14 *For the palace is forsaken,*
the populous city deserted;

the hill and the watchtower
will become dens forever,

a joy of wild donkeys,
a pasture of flocks;

15 *until the Spirit is poured upon us from on high,*
and the wilderness becomes a fruitful field,

and the fruitful field is deemed a forest.

16 *Then justice will dwell in the wilderness,*
and righteousness abide in the fruitful field.

17 *And the effect of righteousness will be peace,*
and the result of righteousness, quietness and trust[a] *forever.*

18 *My people will abide in a peaceful habitation,*
in secure dwellings, and in quiet resting places.

19 *And it will hail when the forest falls down,*
and the city will be utterly laid low.

20 *Happy are you who sow beside all waters,*
who let the feet of the ox and the donkey range free.

33 *Ah, you destroyer,*
who yourself have not been destroyed,

you traitor,
whom none has betrayed!

When you have ceased to destroy,
you will be destroyed;

and when you have finished betraying,
they will betray you.

2 *O* LORD, *be gracious to us; we wait for you.*
Be our arm every morning,
our salvation in the time of trouble.

3 *At the tumultuous noise peoples flee;*
when you lift yourself up, nations are scattered,

4 *and your spoil is gathered as the caterpillar gathers;*
as locusts leap, it is leapt upon.

5 *The* LORD *is exalted, for he dwells on high;*
he will fill Zion with justice and righteousness,

6 *and he will be the stability of your times,*
abundance of salvation, wisdom, and knowledge;
the fear of the LORD *is Zion's*[b] *treasure.*

7 *Behold, their heroes cry in the streets;*
the envoys of peace weep bitterly.

8 *The highways lie waste;*
the traveler ceases.

Covenants are broken;
cities[c] *are despised;*
there is no regard for man.

9 *The land mourns and languishes;*
Lebanon is confounded and withers away;

Sharon is like a desert,
and Bashan and Carmel shake off their leaves.

10 *"Now I will arise," says the* LORD,
"now I will lift myself up;
now I will be exalted.

11 *You conceive chaff; you give birth to stubble;*
your breath is a fire that will consume you.

12 *And the peoples will be as if burned to lime,*
like thorns cut down, that are burned in the fire."

13 *Hear, you who are far off, what I have done;*
and you who are near, acknowledge my might.

14 *The sinners in Zion are afraid;*
trembling has seized the godless:

"Who among us can dwell with the consuming fire?
Who among us can dwell with everlasting burnings?"

15 *He who walks righteously and speaks uprightly,*
who despises the gain of oppressions,

who shakes his hands, lest they hold a bribe,
who stops his ears from hearing of bloodshed
and shuts his eyes from looking on evil,

16 *he will dwell on the heights;*
his place of defense will be the fortresses of rocks;
his bread will be given him; his water will be sure.

17 *Your eyes will behold the king in his beauty;*
they will see a land that stretches afar.

18 *Your heart will muse on the terror:*
"Where is he who counted, where is he who weighed the tribute?

Where is he who counted the towers?"

19 *You will see no more the insolent people,*
the people of an obscure speech that you cannot comprehend,

stammering in a tongue that you cannot understand.

[20]*Behold Zion, the city of our appointed feasts!*
Your eyes will see Jerusalem,
an untroubled habitation, an immovable tent,

whose stakes will never be plucked up,
nor will any of its cords be broken.

[21]*But there the LORD in majesty will be for us*
a place of broad rivers and streams,

where no galley with oars can go,
nor majestic ship can pass.

[22]*For the LORD is our judge; the LORD is our lawgiver;*
the LORD is our king; he will save us.

[23]*Your cords hang loose;*
they cannot hold the mast firm in its place
or keep the sail spread out.

Then prey and spoil in abundance will be divided;
even the lame will take the prey.

[24]*And no inhabitant will say, "I am sick";*
the people who dwell there will be forgiven their iniquity.

a Or *security* **b** Hebrew *his* **c** Masoretic Text; Dead Sea Scroll *witnesses*

Overview: Most of the Reformation commentators identify this passage as almost entirely about Christ as the righteous King and his kingdom. They explain the references to shelter, refuge, the stream, the rock, the pouring out of the Spirit, and even bread and water as corresponding to the time of Jesus and his kingdom. These two chapters provide the solution to the foolish ways of the people by portraying the promised righteous king. Some interpreters use this passage to argue for the need of righteous leaders in their own day. They also provide examples of broken treaties like those about which Isaiah warns. The passage concludes with a celebration of the victory achieved by the Lord and the forgiveness of sins brought by the righteous king.

32:1-8 *The Righteous King and Leaders*

Christ as King of Righteousness. Johannes Oecolampadius: "Behold, he will reign in righteousness." The Hebrews connect this chapter to the previous ones, attributing the praises listed here to the righteous king Hezekiah, because the Jews lived peacefully after the army of Sennacherib, the leader himself, was defeated, and they listened to the law of the Lord. But to us this is a shadow, because what the Hebrews rejoice about does not go far enough. For if you stick to the letter, it is apparent that this was not fulfilled under Hezekiah unless you explain it hyperbolically as a parable. For what is the justice, the peace, the truth of Hezekiah compared to the justice and peace of Christ, who reigns in the hearts of his people and restores consciences to tranquility?

Let us therefore learn from this passage what kind of kingdom is Christ's, and at the same time the conditions of a kingdom that is established well. First of all, the king is just himself and a lover of justice, and so he reigns in righteousness. And our Christ is not only just and without iniquity but is righteousness itself and the just one who renders others righteous by his own righteousness. Commentary on Isaiah 32:1.[1]

Good Leaders Have the Spirit. Martin Borrhaus: In the leaders whom Hezekiah used in governing his kingdom, a slight shadow is observed. Truly these are those who regulate the office of the kingdom of the heavenly Hezekiah,

[1]Oecolampadius, *In Iesaiam*, 181r; citing Jer 23; 1 Cor 2.

the Messiah, whom the apostle describes with these words, "And he gave some to be apostles, some true prophets, some evangelists, and some to be pastors and teachers." But for what use did he give them? It follows in that passage, "For the renewal of the saints and the building up of the body of Christ." The Messiah, the King of kings and Prince of princes, appoints such princes to judge rightly and to govern his republic with a heavenly spirit and lift from them an earthly spirit. And being appointed in this way, he puts them in charge over his state with these words: "Receive the Holy Spirit." But for what use does he breathe on them his divine Spirit? It follows in John, "Whoever's sins you forgive, they are forgiven; whoever's sins you retain, they are retained." Therefore, those lacking his Spirit should depart from the kingdom of this king Hezekiah. Those endowed with it, of course, conduct themselves as good leaders. Those lacking it do not. Oracles in Isaiah on 32:2.[2]

Four Qualities of a Good Magistrate. Heinrich Bullinger: Consequently he explains how much fruit sprouts from it if the king or the magistrate is good, righteous, and diligent. He relates four parables or comparisons: (1) The king is faithful to his people, "like a hiding place from the wind." (2) The same is true for "a shelter from the storm." (3) And "like streams of water in a dry place" are irrigated, so a good leader influences the people entrusted to him with many benefits. Otherwise they would be miserable. (4) Finally, just like "the shade of a great rock in a weary" and fabled land cools those who are gripped with heat and struggle in the sand, so a good magistrate preserves and protects the afflicted. Sermons on Isaiah 32:1-2.[3]

King of the Earth and the Church. Menno Simons: The house of Jacob is the believing church, as is generally understood. Of this, Christ is king, as the angel clearly testified and as Jeremiah says concerning Christ, that he would be a king who should reign and prosper. . . . Isaiah also says, "Behold, a king will reign in righteousness and princes will rule in justice." . . . As Christ is king, both over all the earth and of his believing church, as we have shown by the plain Scriptures, according to the grace received of God, how can John Van Leyden now call himself a joyous king of all, who has become the joy of the miserable? If he would be our king, our Lord, then Paul and Isaiah must stand back. Paul says, "For although there may be so-called gods in heaven or on earth (as indeed there are many gods and many lords), but for us there is one God, the Father, from whom are all things and we in him, and one Lord, Jesus Christ, by whom are all things and we by him." . . . Isaiah says, "The Lord is our judge; the Lord is our lawgiver; the Lord is our king." Testimony Against John Van Leyden.[4]

The Shade of the Rock. Wolfgang Musculus: But it is not without reason that he specified the "shade of a great rock," that is, of a large and thick rock. And "streams of water" is not simply water. He wanted to express the extensive, abundant, and solid justice of this king. The shade of the rock is large, solid, and cool. The streams of water are abundant to quench even though the thirst is great and the land dry. So, he says, the righteousness of this king will be abundant and manifest to all. The shade will be for the weary, the stream of water for the thirsty, hiding them from the face of the windy storm. In contrast, the tyrant himself is a most impetuous storm and dries everything up with heat. God appointed a just king over the afflicted and humiliated people, but a tyrant over the proud and rebellious. One we owe to grace, the other to his wrath. Commentary on Isaiah 32:2.[5]

[2]Borrhaus, *In Iesaiae Prophetae Oracula*, 287-88; citing Eph 4:11; Jn 20:22-23.
[3]Bullinger, *Isaias*, 153r.
[4]Simons, *Complete Works* 2:429; Jer 23:5; Is 32:1; 1 Cor 8:5; Is 33:22.
[5]Musculus, *In Esaiam*, 460.

Eyes to See and Ears to Hear. Wolfgang Musculus: "And the eyes of those who see," it says, "will not be closed." It is as if he were saying what was said previously. . . . But now they will see and understand the judgments and the works of the Lord, and "the ears of those who hear" will not be stopped but will listen and "give attention" to learn the word of the Lord. But this does not happen without reason, because it does not simply say, "Your eyes will see, and your ears will listen," but it says, "The eyes of those who see will not be closed, and the ears of those who hear will give attention." By "those who see" and "those who hear," he means those who were going to have eyes to see and ears to hear. The eyes of these, it says, will not be closed, nor will their ears be stopped, which is exactly what happens with the just judgment of God: those who see do not see, and those who hear do not hear, and therefore they do not understand with their hearts. Commentary on Isaiah 32:3.[6]

Faithful Leaders. Konrad Pellikan: Now, the kind and faithful leaders are made to prosper in all things, always meditating on what is just and beneficial to the many, whose entire will is in the law of the Lord and in love for neighbor. This way they benefit many, they burden none, and in everything that happens to everyone, all may gain, with none thinking too highly but being in harmony with the lowly. How much less they seek praise and glory among people, that much more they are lifted up by God and the righteous and will shine in this present age and in the one to come. Commentary on Isaiah 32:3-4.[7]

Fools Made Wise. Johannes Brenz: In the kingdom of Christ, the hearts of the foolish understand knowledge. Something much different happens in kingdoms of this world. For in those kingdoms, the one who is foolish is not rendered wise but is provoked repeatedly to become even more foolish. But in the kingdom of Christ, the foolish become wise. That is what Christ said. . . . "I thank you, Father, Lord of heaven and earth, that you have hidden these things from the wise and understanding and have revealed them to little children," or foolish ones. Such little children, or foolish ones, were the apostles, who, when considered from the perspective of the people at that time, were foolish and insane, yet they were more understanding and wiser than all the kings and leaders. Commentary on Isaiah 32:4-6.[8]

Those Who Stand and Fall. Wolfgang Musculus: "And that one will stand on noble things." That is, he will prosper and will stand immovable because he is kind and behaves this way in all things. The spirit of the prophet does not only make this promise about prosperity to those who are just. But at the same time he threatens the downfall and destruction of the foolish, the greedy, and the unjust. For when he says, "And he will stand on noble things," it also includes the opposite for unjust and unfair judges. It is as if he says, "But a fool and a greedy person will not stand because of their unjust pursuits." Commentary on Isaiah 32:8.[9]

32:9-14 *Judgment on Complacency*

Not Even Women and Daughters Spared. John Mayer: Calvin says some think this is the beginning of a new sermon or prophecy addressing judgments to come afterward, but it is the manner of the prophet that when he has spoken comfort, as he has done in this chapter so far, suddenly to turn to threatening judgments, that all might not think that the previously mentioned comforts belong to them. But hearing of judgments, which are the portion of the wicked, they would be moved to repent and fear. But when this judgment should come he does not say "but women are spoken to" because that sex is often spared in time of war, but rather he speaks to arouse them to

[6]Musculus, *In Esaiam*, 460; citing Is 6.
[7]Pellikan, *Commentaria Bibliorum*, 3:40v.
[8]Brenz, *Esaias*, 420; citing Mt 11:25.
[9]Musculus, *In Esaiam*, 462.

show what a bloody time is to come, when no sex or age shall be spared. Therefore he names women and daughters, though some by "women" understand, as the Hebrews, greater cities, and by "daughters," little villages, basing that on Joshua, where a city and her daughters are often spoken of. COMMENTARY ON ISAIAH 32:9.[10]

JEWS AS EXAMPLES. JOHANNES OECOLAMPADIUS: And he address the citizens of Judah as rich women, because they were very affluent at the time. And it is fine if you also say that the synagogues and congregations of the Jews were trusting in the riches of their works of the law in the same allegorical way that gospel riches, which were clothing them daily in purple and linen, are an example of the Jewish people. Therefore he bids them, "Rise up," to hear more attentively. For we hear better when we are standing but are sleepier when we are sitting. COMMENTARY ON ISAIAH 32:9.[11]

CONFIDENT WOMEN ARE ARROGANT MEN. WILLIAM DAY: He applies this to the time of Zedekiah, when Jerusalem was destroyed by Nebuchadnezzar, saying that the men are here spoken to by the name of women for their faintheartedness. And their confidence, whereby they are upbraided, was the trust that they had in their strong walls. EXPOSITION OF ISAIAH 32:9-11.[12]

STRIPPING AS A PARABLE. JOHANNES OECOLAMPADIUS: "Strip and be naked." These things are said with shouting, and understand: they are imminent to you. The stripping of all clothes and jewels that women wear more rarely and the captivity are signified by the girding of loins. But the nakedness of modest women is the most disturbing, even though it is said here as a parable. COMMENTARY ON ISAIAH 32:11-14.[13]

32:15-20 *Justice After Desolation*

UNTIL THE DAY OF PENTECOST. DIETRICH SCHNEPFF: The adverb *until* does not disturb us, for it ought to be noted how it is used in Hebrew. For it does not signify the end and conclusion but consummation and perfection. So in this place the prophet wants to say, "The Lord is going to eradicate the kingdom of the Hebrews and is going to extend that bright kingdom of his Son by the Holy Spirit sent on the day of Pentecost." SCHOLIA ON ISAIAH 32:15.[14]

THE SPIRIT POURED ON A REMNANT. JOHANNES OECOLAMPADIUS: Many theologians suppose that at the end of the world all the Jews are going to be converted, and they can obtain that by using this testimony. But I do not dare to promise salvation to all the Jewish people but to a certain remnant and seed, in the same way that today, too, nothing prohibits some of the Jews from being added to our religion. It is certain that, on the day of Pentecost, the Spirit was "poured out from on high" on the apostles, a great renewing of things happened, and the "wilderness," that is, the people of the Gentiles, "became a fruitful field," but the fruitful field of the Jews became a wilderness. . . . But it is exceedingly pleasing that he says, "These things are not going to happen until the Spirit is sent from heaven," for then the end of ceremonies and Jewish rituals will be, and the fullness of the Gentiles will enter in. COMMENTARY ON ISAIAH 32:15.[15]

THE SPIRIT BRINGS PEACE AND QUIET. MARGARET FELL: If you look for the promise of the Lord to be fulfilled, you must look for the Spirit; for the promise of God is the Spirit, until the Spirit be poured out on us from on high, and the wilderness be a fruitful field, and the fruitful field be counted for a forest. Mark, here your fruitful field must be counted for a forest, when the

[10]Mayer, *Commentary upon All the Prophets*, 4:201*.
[11]Oecolampadius, *In Iesaiam*, 183v.
[12]Day, *Exposition*, 200*.
[13]Oecolampadius, *In Iesaiam*, 183v.

[14]Schnepff, *In Esaiae*, 486.
[15]Oecolampadius, *In Iesaiam*, 183r.

Spirit is poured from on high, and that which has been the wilderness must be the fruitful field; then will judgment dwell in the wilderness and righteousness remain in the fruitful field. The work of righteousness will be peace, and the effect of righteousness quietness and assurance forever. And my people shall dwell in a peaceable habitation and in sure dwellings and quiet resting places. A LOVING SALUTATION TO THE SEED OF ABRAHAM AMONG THE JEWS.[16]

WHEN RIGHTEOUSNESS AND JUSTICE WILL DWELL. SEBASTIAN CASTELLIO: He speaks about the devastation of Judah that is going to begin by Sennacherib and be completed at the time of Christ. Although Sennacherib did not take the city, he did ravage Judea and start that disaster, which was followed by other disasters until finally in the time of Christ the Jewish race was demolished. For Sennacherib was followed by the Babylonian captivity, and calamity continued to inflict those who returned from it. So the city was taken by Ptolemy son of Lagus, then devastated by Antiochus, then by Pompey, then by Herod and Sosius, and last it was completely overthrown and leveled by Titus.

And yet when Christ came, who breathed the Holy Spirit from above on his own, he also turned the uncultivated place into Carmel† and vice versa. This refers to the foreigners who were uncultivated and outsiders to the true religion, who honored the gospel. But the Jews, who were Carmel, that is, they worshiped according to the oracles and teachings (for Carmel was a place of worship), he "deemed a forest" when he transferred the kingdom from them to a nation that would eat the fruit. And so justice dwells both in the uncultivated and the cultivated place. That is, whether a barbarian or Jew, access to Christ is open, so that one may become righteous and innocent by faith and happy again. ANNOTATION ON ISAIAH 32:15-16.[17]

[16]Fell, *Women's Speaking Justified and Other Pamphlets*, 115.
[17]Castellio, *Adnotationes*, 70. †The Hebrew translated in the ESV as "fruitful field" is *lākārmēl*, which is why Castellio translates it as the place Carmel.

JUSTICE AND RIGHTEOUSNESS SHOULD FLOURISH. JOHN CALVIN: The prophet teaches what is the actual condition of the church, that is, when righteousness and justice take place. For people should not to be like cattle, which seek nothing but plenty of food and abundance of outward things. And so, it is sufficiently apparent that in the teaching of the law, the Jews were not confined to transitory enjoyments, so as to have their hope fixed exclusively on earthly blessings, as some fanatics imagine. For they were specifically commanded to attend to what makes righteousness and justice flourish; and undoubtedly they knew that true happiness consists in this. It is therefore our duty to look chiefly to this, that we should not, like hogs in a sty, measure the happiness of life by the abundance of bread and wine. For this is the end of all the blessings that the Lord bestows on us, this is the object of our deliverance, as Zechariah says, "that we should serve him in holiness and righteousness." . . .

By the terms *justice* and *righteousness*, as we have already seen, he includes all that belongs to uprightness; for although these two words relate strictly to that equity that ought to be mutually cultivated among us, yet, since it is customary to describe the observation of the whole law by the duties of the second table [of the Decalogue], here the prophet, by a figure of speech in which a part is taken for the whole, embraces also godliness and the worship of God. The prophets usually point out the chief duties of love and what pertains to the second table, because by these, more than by any others, we manifest the real state of our feelings toward God. COMMENTARY ON ISAIAH 32:16.[18]

PEACE AS THE FRUIT OF RIGHTEOUSNESS. JOHANNES BRENZ: Let us hear, then, what is the effect or what is the fruit that is the result and the usefulness of this righteous. First, the effect, or fruit, of the righteousness of Christ is peace. So, since in this passage it is not an earthy kingdom

[18]CTS 14:421-22* (CO 36:552-53); citing Lk 1:74-75.

being addressed but the kingdom of Christ, it should also not be understand to be an earthly peace but the peace that corresponds to the spiritual kingdom of Christ, which is the peace of consciences before God. About this peace, Christ himself speaks, "Peace I leave with you; my peace I give to you. Not as the world gives do I give to you." And Paul says, "Since we have been justified by God, we have peace with God through our Lord Jesus Christ."

And so this peace contains within it that the conscience is cleared by the gospel with God appeased because of Christ, the righteousness of Christ given to us, no longer doubting the favor of God, not hating the judgments of God, not murmuring against God, not fleeing from the face of God, but receiving all the kindness of God promised to us and confidently approaching his throne of mercy and calling up him as Father without any hesitation or fear. This is the fruit of Christ's righteousness given to us by faith. Commentary on Isaiah 32:17.[19]

Faith Incarnate. John Trapp: In this and the next verse, he sets forth the sweet effects of God's Spirit in the saints, and in hypocrites, once they come to be converted. These are righteousness, peace, and joy in the Holy Ghost. . . . By "righteousness and judgment," there is to be understood the righteousness of faith, together with all those good works that are the fruits of it. I mean obedience, which Luther had the habit of calling *fidem incarnatam*, "faith incarnate." Exposition on Isaiah 32:17.[20]

Enjoying Perpetual Peace and Rest. Konrad Pellikan: This is like a repetition of the same sentence. The one who is truly the people of the Lord, whose God is the Lord, the bride being held by the beloved, enraptured with excessive love for the creatures and the goodness of God rightly recognized as given by Christ, this one abides in the enjoyment of perpetual peace and in "secure dwellings," that is, the firm possession of his grace, of which the one who has tasted the delights of the Spirit cannot despair, and is rich in rest. For a believer can easily reject and neglect nearly everything, who has at one time experienced the riches of God's goodness in sincere faith. And whatever people, city, or righteous person has repelled the slavery of guilt, they will produce the fruits of honesty and innocence, will live a quieter, sweeter, and more pleasant life, and will enjoy a more enjoyable peace. Commentary on Isaiah 32:18.[21]

Beautiful Mansions. Martin Borrhaus: "In the beauty of peace." The holy people are going to dwell in a beautiful and pleasant habitation. This is without doubt in heaven, to enjoy the divine splendor and eternal life, full of glory. It is not in this transient and fickle world and in the rite of the stormy sea. Our Lord says about this heavenly mansion, "In my Father's house are many mansions," which are distinguished according to the various offices of the Holy Spirit and the distinction of the members in the body of Christ, that is, the church of the elect. Oracles in Isaiah on 32:18.[22]

Titles of Ministers. Philipp Heilbrunner: Topic 20. On Church Ministry. What are the titles and epithets of church ministers?

1. Farmer. . . . "Happy are you who sow beside all waters, who let the feet of the ox and the donkey range free."
2. Keepers or watchers. . . . "On your walls, O Jerusalem, I have set watchmen; all the day and all the night they shall never be silent."
3. Teachers and instructors. . . . "And he will not make your teacher vanish anymore, but your eyes shall see your instructor."
4. Levite. . . . "And some of them also I will take for priests and for Levites, says the Lord."

[19]Brenz, *Esaias*, 428; citing Jn 14:27; Rom 5:1.
[20]Trapp, *Commentary or Exposition*, 117*; citing Rom 14:17.
[21]Pellikan, *Commentaria Bibliorum*, 3:40r; citing Jn 14:2.
[22]Borrhaus, *In Iesaiae Prophetae Oracula*, 296.

5. Messenger of God. . . . "Who is blind but my servant, or deaf as my messenger whom I send?" . . . "Who confirms the word of his servant and fulfills the counsel of his messengers." . . . "How beautiful upon the mountains are the feet of him who brings good news, who publishes peace, who brings good news of happiness, who publishes salvation, who says to Zion, 'Your God reigns.'"
6. Shepherds. . . . "But they are shepherds who have no understanding."
7. Princes, as the apostles are titled. . . . "Behold, a king will reign in righteousness, and princes will rule in justice."
8. Prophets. . . . "Priest and prophet are ignorant because of strong drink." . . . "He will close your eyes, prophets, and your princes who see visions, he will cover."
9. Priests. . . . "And it shall be, as with the people, so with the priest." . . . "Priest and prophet are ignorant because of strong drink." . . . "And some of them also I will take for priests and for Levites, says the Lord."
10. Servant of God. . . . "Then the Lord said, 'As my servant Isaiah has walked naked and barefoot.'" . . . "Who confirms the word of his servant." . . . "Who among you fears the Lord and obeys the voice of his servant?"
11. Watchmen. . . . "The voice of your watchmen—they lift up their voice." . . . "His watchmen are blind."
12. Seers. . . . "Who say to the seers, 'Do not see,' and to the prophets, 'Do not prophesy to us what is right; speak to us smooth things, see deceptions for us.'" . . . "Then the eyes of those who see will not be closed, and the ears of those who hear will give attention."

Theological Topics Arranged from the Prophecy of Isaiah.[23]

God Causes Growth. Johannes Oecolampadius: Additionally, as much as it pertains to the Spirit that consciences were quieted and the peace of Christ was obtained, so much also they will succeed as they sow, and they will obtain a great amount of fruit among others. But when they "sow beside waters," the grace of God is accompanying them. For "neither the one who plants nor the one who waters is anything, but only God, who gives the growth." There are those who explain that those "who sow beside the waters" are the apostles, that is, they are going to preach the gospel to all nations, such that you should understand "the waters" as the peoples. Commentary on Isaiah 32:20.[24]

33:1-4 *Threats and Promises*

Destruction of the Destroyer. Wolfgang Musculus: The argument of this chapter is diverse. The prophet threatens the destruction of the destroyer Sennacherib, he prays to the Lord, he prophesies as much against the enemy as on behalf of the people of God, he preaches and teaches, and he promises prosperous things for the city of Jerusalem. Commentary on Isaiah 33:1.[25]

The Example of Assyria. Johannes Brenz: But again the ruin of this king and his kingdom is not hidden. For not only was it necessary that the great defeat when he fled disgracefully from Judea be addressed, but also that he would be cruelly killed by his own sons and his kingdom transferred to the Babylonians. About the devastation of the city of Nineveh, which was the major city of the kingdom of the Assyrians, you have the prophet Nahum and Tobit. . . . And although Isaiah saw the future by a special revelation of the Spirit that Sennacherib, the destroyer of so many kingdoms, would soon perish, nevertheless he uses this in a general sense, in which it is divinely brought

[23]Heilbrunner, *Esaiae Prophetae Vaticinia*, 417-20; citing Is 32:20; 62:6; 30:20; 66:21; 42:19; 44:16; 52:7; 56:11; 32:1; 28:7; 29:10; 24:2; 28:7; 66:21; 20:3; 44:26; 50:10; 52:8; 46:10; 30:10; 32:3.

[24]Oecolampadius, *In Iesaiam*, 184v; citing 1 Cor 3:7.

[25]Musculus, *In Esaiam*, 467.

against all violent predators and destroyers. Commentary on Isaiah 33:1.[26]

The Law of Retaliation. Wolfgang Musculus: "And will you not suffer as prey?" It is as if he says, "You are more liable to the judgment of God who preys on others. And how do you think it will not happen that you also suffer being preyed on?" This is the law of retaliation, approved by the common sense of all, that what each one plans against others, that is the same as what he will suffer from others. You prey on others, so others will prey on you in turn. Others explain it this way: "You have not suffered as prey," that is, "You preyed on others unjustly when you never sustained the power of anyone. You inflicted on others, but no one inflicted on you. You, who have not been wounded, wound." This view argues that the person is extremely evil who delights to inflict more on an earlier injury and who does not hestiate to afflict those who have already suffered evil from him. . . . Observe what he says in the second line, "When you have ceased, you will cease." Let us be reminded that for every tryant, there is a fixed amount of tyranny for them when he will be subjected to the complete judgment of God. Commentary on Isaiah 33:1.[27]

External and Internal Enemies. Johannes Oecolampadius: In this verse he insults the enemy, who is no doubt Sennacherib and the antichrist, whom he prefigures. Therefore he says, "Woe, cruel one. No one has harmed you with damage, and you, who destroyed, act according to the just judgment of God. When you bring an end to your tyranny, you will be destroyed so that God may pay you back with the same measure that you dispensed upon others. And as wisdom says, 'Since you did not listen to the cry of the poor, you will cry out and not be answered.'" Now, the second part against the traitor seems to be said against Shebna and other internal enemies who behaved with fraud and deceit in Jerusalem against Hezekiah, not keeping faith. And it is said to those that no faith will be kept for them. Commentary on Isaiah 33:1.[28]

A Formula for Prayer. Dietrich Schnepff: "Lord, have mercy on us. . . ." We see a formula for prayer proposed by the prophet, but these things are said for that purpose, to understand how so great an enemy should be repelled, namely, by righteous prayer. . . . The statement is, "Lord, have mercy on us." The first reason is "because we have relied on you." For as the psalm testifies, "All who wait on you, their faces will not be put to shame." Then another reason is added when he says, "Be our arm every morning." For the most powerful Lord has promised not only help but also readiness. . . . Now, the formula of the prophet that prescribes the true gifts of prayer should not be disregarded sluggishly, so that we may take refuge in the Lord by true faith when facing afflictions and disturbances, and have no doubt that certain hope is prepared for us by him. But the reason for praying is said abundantly elsewhere. Scholia on Isaiah 33:2.[29]

Gathered like Locusts. Wolfgang Musculus: Now, as he signifies that there would be a great overthrow of them, he does not simply say, "You are struck and you will flee," but, "Your spoil is gathered as the caterpillar gathers," in the usual way that an innumerable multitude of caterpillars and locusts is gathered and exterminated. When everything is filled with caterpillars and locusts by divine intervention, it is the custom in those regions that they burst forth into all fields, gardens, vineyards, and meadows for the gathering of them. They run, gather, pile up, and either consign them to fire or throw them in ditches. In the same way, he says, that will happen to our enemies. They are going to occupy our lands like caterpillars and locusts. "You will be scattered and

[26]Brenz, *Esaias*, 430; citing Tobit 14.
[27]Musculus, *In Esaiam*, 468-69.
[28]Oecolampadius, *In Iesaiam*, 184v-r; citing Prov 21:13.
[29]Schnepff, *In Esaiae*, 492-93; citing Ps 9; 30; 50; 92; 25:3.

disperesed, and your spoils will be gathered in the way that caterpillars are gathered up. And those who gather them will run among them like those who gather locusts run." Commentary on Isaiah 33:4.[30]

Rushing Locusts. Francisco Forerius: Now, the Hebrew term for "locust" identifies the species. . . . For they are gathered in a pile, and they are killed either in a pit or in water, the same way whether in the East and in Africa as in Spain. But if you pay attention to how the term is derived, it is said from "absuming."

"When the trenches were full." The Vulgate attends to the sense, not the words. For it should be translated according to the word, as you see in our version. Now, he calls the locusts themselves "rushing, ravaging, or advancing." Therefore the sense here can be that the Assyrians and their spoils are compared to those locusts at the time of gathering, when they have been stirred up from here and there and chased to gather in one place. And this second part explains the first. As it says, rushing locusts rush into that gathering, that is, as a swarm of locusts at that time when they are gathered, they rush and are expelled into a heap at some singular place.

There can also be another sense, that the gatherers of the spoil are compared here to the gatherers of locusts. As it says, "the rushing of locusts," that is, "among the locusts," that is, as those running among the locusts make them run at the time of gathering or to the gathering itself. So the citizens of Jerusalem will hasten to plunder the spoils with great pursuit and zeal without anyone resisting. Commentary on Isaiah 33:4.[31]

33:5-16 *The Lord Exalted*

The Key to the Treasure. Johannes Oecolampadius: Again he foretells the kingdom of Christ, to whom these things especially correspond. For only a shadow of those things were under Hezekiah. And what is mentioned here was also said earlier . . . about the gifts of the Spirit. For in the times of Christ, truth, fortitude, wisdom, knowledge, and fear reign. And here he teaches that the fullness of the gifts of the Holy Spirit are going to be poured out.

Observe in this passage that fear is preferred to knowledge and wisdom, but the fear here is pure and endures forever. It is not the fear of punishment, which is cast out by love. Rather, it is a certain reverance for the divine majesty, from which even the angels reverently shrink back when they show their faces. And so, this particular degree of love is called a treasure, by which we fear so that we do not love less than we should. Fear is praised, because it is the guardian and preserver of the other virtues. Commentary on Isaiah 33:5-6.[32]

For Your Times About Christ. Johannes Brenz: With these words ("your times"), the prophet is not considering Hezekiah, about whom he had previously made no mention, but he is considering Christ, in whose times these things recounted here were fulfilled and are always being fulfilled in the church, the kingdom of Christ. Now, whom the prophet addresses here in the second person he had just said a little earlier in the third person, "The Lord will be exalted, for he dwells on high; he will fill Zion with justice and righteousness." Therefore, he is calling Christ, Lord Jehovah, that is, the true God. So this is the thought of the prophet.

Sennacherib's blasphemy charges the God of Zion with being weaker than one who can help and defend his people. But, you citizens, be well assured; do not be frightened by these blasphemies and do not abandon the Lord. For the Lord, who now appears to the enemies to be very weak, will be exalted in his times, when he clothes himself with humanity, so that his majesty may become known to the whole world. Then he bestows all

[30]Musculus, *In Esaiam*, 470.

[31]Forerius, *Iesaiae*, 117r; citing 1 Kings 8; Ps 78.

[32]Oecolampadius, *In Iesaiam*, 185v; citing Is 11.

kinds of blessings on Zion. Commentary on Isaiah 33:6.[33]

What the Messengers Cry. Wolfgang Musculus: "Behold, their messengers cry outside." In these three verses . . . he describes with a few words the tribulation that was going to come from the Assyrians, which he mentions earlier in the second verse when he says while praying, "And be our salvation in the time of trouble." And he describes this not as it were actually going to happen but as it was going to be perceived from the crying and weeping of the messengers. Commentary on Isaiah 33:7-9.[34]

Announcing Despair. Martin Borrhaus: Accordingly, it is not surprising that such a disaster should be announced—a kind that is explained mystically here by the seer. If you require examples from our times, consider what happened to Germany in the previous years with the Interim.[†] We do not hear the ambassadors here comforting the citizens of Jerusalem and raising their hope of acquiring salvation from God, who is more powerful to save than the enemy is to destroy. Rather, we read the opposite things magnified by them to cast down the hope of the afflicted. It is obvious that they foreshadowed the kinds of ambassadors in the times of the antichrist, who amplify the power of the antichrist, the spiritual Assyrian enemies, and diminish the powers of the Messiah, the heavenly Hezekiah. Oracles in Isaiah on 33:7-9.[35]

Broken Covenants. John Mayer: For it is not probable that Hezekiah would send [the Assyrian king] so great a sum of money unless there was this kind of a covenant. And therefore the papists are most wicked, like Sennacherib, and void of all fear of God, because they hold it as a maxim that faith is not to be kept toward heretics. On these grounds, King Vladislaus [III of Hungary], after ten years, had made peace with Amurath [Murad II] the great Turk.[†] Then, at the pope's persuasion, he broke the peace and received a mighty great defeat at his hands. Likewise, Henry III of England broke his covenant with the barons, often confirmed by the pope's dispensation since they were still of one religion, and it cost him dearly. Commentary on Isaiah 33:8.[36]

The Lord Rises. Martin Borrhaus: Consequently, when the Lord is viewed this way by his enemies, and the righteous do not recognize his help, he says, "I will arise." From this we learn that God has fixed times in the tables of his providential decrees in which he permits the pleasure of his enemies to trouble his own. And he likewise has that for when he boldly sets free his own who were severely troubled, who seemed destitute of all human and divine aid. When he does this, he declares his goodness and his brilliant power, and the constant faith of his promises toward those who pray with these words, "Have mercy on us." When this prayer is heard, he says, "I will arise"—the one who the enemies thought was asleep, not weighing carefully that "he who keeps Israel will neither slumber nor sleep." And Israel is the elect in the Messiah, the church. Therefore, in the last days, the antichrist fears for himself at the sound, "Now I will arise; now I will lift myself up; now I will be exalted." The antichrist, who already for many ages confidently ravages everything in the church, thinking that the Messiah is sleeping, when he arises will experience what follows in this mystical oracle. Oracles in Isaiah on 33:10.[37]

[33]Brenz, *Esaias*, 434-35.

[34]Musculus, *In Esaiam*, 472.

[35]Borrhaus, *In Iesaiae Prophetae Oracula*, 300. [†]Borrhaus most likely refers to the Augsburg Interim (1548), which sought doctrinal agreement between German Catholics and Protestants at the insistence of Charles V, the Holy Roman Emperor.

[36]Mayer, *Commentary upon All the Prophets*, 4:205*. [†]Mayer most likely refers to the Peace of Szeged (1444), which ended a crusade against the Ottomans. Within a month of the end, Vladislaus broke his oath at the urging of the papacy and resumed the crusade. He was later killed at the Battle of Varna (November 1444) when the crusaders were defeated.

[37]Borrhaus, *In Iesaiae Prophetae Oracula*, 301; citing Is 33:2; Ps 121:4.

People Set Ablaze with Consuming Fire. Wolfgang Musculus: "And the people will be as if burned to lime, like thorns cut down, which are burned in the fire." He compares the coming plague to fire because of its consuming power. But he compares it not to just any fire but to a very serious one. It is the kind that burns stones, however hard they are, into lime. At the same time, he compares the people of the enemy to stones and thorns cut down to be burned. By "stones" is noted fierce hardness; by "thorns," malice that sprouts forth to prick and wound. It is as if the army of the Assyrians were tossed like a stone into the furnace until it perished in the heat of God's vengeance.† It was made to resemble cut-off thorns when it became ripe for the completed action of desolation for punishment. This passage admonishes us to think about when we experience the inflexible and fierce hardness of the wicked and thorny malice. We should think about the fire of revenge that burns these same stones into lime, and eventually, when the thorns are cut off, their trouble is reduced to ash easily. Commentary on Isaiah 33:12.[38]

Walking in Righteousness. Francisco Forerius: He teaches that their fear is in vain and that it is nothing but a pretense for ungodliness. For God is only a consuming fire to the ungodly and the wicked. With these words, he seems to be alluding to the words of Moses. . . . "Your God is a consuming fire." And in the following verse you will see with what names the prophet labels those who were saying they dwell with the devouring fire—that they are ungodly hypocrites. "In righteousness." The word for "walking" or "going" in Hebrew sometimes directs the accusative, as in this passage. And it is to "walk about," that is, to exercise every kind of righteousness. . . .

"Who shakes his hands." When we do not want any dust on our hands, or anything else, we clap our hands together and shake them palm by palm. So this is a symbol of hatred, by which we will not be in business with a person, or of disgust, by which we signify that we will have nothing to do with that, so we wash our hands of it. Commentary on Isaiah 33:14-15.[39]

Every Part of the Body. Johannes Brenz: Observe, I ask you, that his right duty demands something from nearly every member, that is to say, we do not supply ourselves with weapons of injustice. About the feet he says, "who walks righteously." For we walk with our feet. About the tongue and the whole face he says, "who speaks uprightly and despises the gain of oppressions." For we speak with the tongue, and we turn our face away to despise what we condemn. About the hands, "who shakes his hands away from every bribe." About the ears, "who stops his ears from hearing of bloodshed." About the eyes, "who shuts his eyes from looking on evil." Although these things seem ordinary and can easily be applied, if you consider them properly they encompass a summary of all the duties of a righteous person. Commentary on Isaiah 33:15.[40]

Christ Gives Bread and Water. Johannes Oecolampadius: "He gives his bread." Here the king is generous and grants the gifts of his spirit. Christ gives himself to us as the bread of life and his faithful waters, that is, the perpetual and never-ceasing fount of salvation, from which those who drink will never thirst. But that parable is likewise marked with the highest abundance. Commentary on Isaiah 33:16.[41]

33:17-24 *The King of Beauty Protecting the Land*

The Beauty of a Happy Magistrate and People. Heinrich Bullinger: They will see their king in glory. The happiness and beauty of a magistrate is connected with the happiness and

[38]Musculus, *In Esaiam*, 473-74. †See also Oecolampadius, *In Iesaiam*, 187v.

[39]Forerius, *Iesaiae*, 118r-v; citing Deut 4:24.

[40]Brenz, *Esaias*, 441-42.

[41]Oecolampadius, *In Iesaiam*, 187r.

glory of the people. For if a magistrate is unhappy and miserable, the people can only be very miserable. So Jeremiah commands the people of God to pray for the king of Babylon and their Babylonian masters. The prophet therefore signifies that the kingdom is going to enjoy abundant happiness and glory, if it perseveres in the friendship of God. What is it that the saints will see in heaven? Christ their King in glory, and by him they will be glorified.

Additionally, "they will see a land that streches far," or one not beseiged by enemies but purged of them and already, as it were, widened or enlarged with the addition of foreigners to the kingdom of the righteous. The saints will likewise see the land that is furthest from us—a beautiful homeland, I say, large enough to receive all the righteous. Sermons on Isaiah 33:17.[42]

Christ the King Dresses Us Like Himself. Pilgram Marpeck: Lovely garments, which are the virtues of the Holy Spirit, remain eternally unspotted, untorn, and undamaged. Only love wears the virtues unspotted; for her honor, they were prepared and made in eternity. Whoever does not contemplate or know love in her finery and adornment neither knows nor loves oneself. She is the daughter who has left her father's house and who has been brought to see the king in her embroidered dress. Whoever wishes to see her form should behold her in the adornment of her king. Her Christ and king, who is himself thus dressed and adorned, has dressed her. Whoever, even once, truly sees this loveliest of all brides in her adornment and form will praise her in wonderment. The Christian and Hagarite Churches.[43]

An Army of Many Languages. Heinrich Bullinger: In addition to all these things, he recounts another benefit, "and the insolent people," and the rest. Now he calls the people "insolent"—a cruel, harsh, shameless soldier. Soldiers are gathered from several kingdoms, and indeed, it will not be the best but rather the worst who will assemble for war. And they do not all use the same language but very different ones among them. One speaks German or Turkish, this one Scythian, yet another Greek, or Italian, or Spanish, or French. But the citizens to whom the foreign-speaking soldiers are coming do not understand those languages. And it is most troublesome to cherish in your homes what you do not understand. To hear them croaking and shouting with the most displeasing voices is received very poorly. Sermons on Isaiah 33:19.[44]

What Is Foreshadowed Endures. Martin Borrhaus: What is read here is that the mansion and tabernacle of Jerusalem will be firm. This is fulfilled in the heavenly Jerusalem, which the earthly one foreshadowed to us. Similar things are read about the kingdom of David, the priesthood of Aaron, and the figures in the Old Testament. Everything foreshadowed in these things is considered firm. When the shadows disappear, the body and the things they foreshadowed are enduring. What endures are the kingdom of the Messiah for all eternity, the heavenly Jerusalem and the temple built from the elect, the anointing of the Holy Spirit and the covenant started by him, the heavenly inheritance foreshadowed by the earthly, the fire burning above in heavenly love and divine light, and if there is anything else like these. Oracles in Isaiah on 33:20-21.[45]

The Lord's Protection as Unpassable Waters. Wolfgang Musculus: "But there the Lord, the mighty one, is for us." It is as if he says, "What shall I say about the tabernacle of the Lord? Indeed, the Lord is mighty and powerful here with us." He is a place for us, or if you prefer, "a place of broad rivers and streams," where no ships of the enemy can go; whether large or small, they will not

[42]Bullinger, *Isaias*, 161v; citing 1 Jn 2; Phil 3; citing Jer 29.
[43]CRR 12:551; citing Ps 45:10, 14; 1 Chron 16:24; Ps 96:3.
[44]Bullinger, *Isaias*, 161r.
[45]Borrhaus, *In Iesaiae Prophetae Oracula*, 306.

be able to pass. So, he compares the protection of God to the broadest rivers, and Jerusalem to a city surrounded by waters all around such that it is inaccessible to an enemy. Jerusalem possessed none of this. And for this reason, the wicked Shebna was trembling so much, because he thought the city was weaker than what could withstand the power of the Assyrians. But the prophet shows that it was sufficiently secured and surrounded by insurmountable waters in that the Lord of hosts was in their midst, the mighty and invincible protector of his people. But Shebna† could not see these streams of divine protection because he was wicked and lacking the eyes of faith. Commentary on Isaiah 33:20-21.[46]

The Lord Is Judge, Lawgiver, and King. Johannes Oecolampadius: He is our judge, not only because he recognizes the iniquity of our enemies but also because he rescues. He is our lawgiver, who writes his law on our hearts. And he is our king, who takes care of everything for us to save us. From him we await the reward and praise of our work. Isaiah himself teaches sufficiently that he is not speaking about King Hezekiah but about our Savior, the Lord Christ. Commentary on Isaiah 33:22.[47]

Happiness and Forgiveness. Johannes Brenz: And where these troubles are not, there is the highest happiness. But where there is no remission of sins, there is no wealth, no power, no human life, no majesty that can bring any advantage before God. Among the Turks, there is no remission of sins. That is why true happiness cannot exist among them, even if they delight in all the good things of this world. Among the Jews of today, there is no remission of sins. Therefore, there is no happiness among them, even if they seem to have some tranquility. Among the papists, there is no remission of sins, because they seek it not in Christ alone by faith but in the merits of their own works. Therefore, there is no happiness among them, even if they obtain all the power and majesty of this age. In the true church alone, in which the gospel of Christ is purely preached and received by faith, is the remission of sins. That is why in the true church alone is happiness, even if it is afflicted with the highest dangers. Commentary on Isaiah 33:24.[48]

Sins Forgiven. Johannes Oecolampadius: "The people who dwell there." With this epiphonema† many things are said, namely, what was the cause of sin, why the Jews were afflicted, and why we are all afflicted. We also learn that this prophecy properly pertains to Christ, who alone takes away the sin of the world. We learn in the end that our happiness and our salvation are from the forgiveness of sin. Moreover, to forgive sin is by divine mercy alone, because the people dwelling in Jerusalem are not forgiven in a temporal or earthly way but a heavenly one, where our citizenship is also. Amen. Commentary on Isaiah 33:24.[49]

[46]Musculus, *In Esaiam*, 479. †On Shebna, see Is 22:15-25.
[47]Oecolampadius, *In Iesaiam*, 188r.
[48]Brenz, *Esaias*, 455.
[49]Oecolampadius, *In Iesaiam*, 189v. †An *epiphonema* is a summarizing statement of exclamation.

34:1–35:10 Judgment Against the Nations

34 *Draw near, O nations, to hear,*
and give attention, O peoples!

Let the earth hear, and all that fills it;
the world, and all that comes from it.

2 *For the LORD is enraged against all the nations,*
and furious against all their host;
he has devoted them to destruction,[a] *has given them over for slaughter.*

3 *Their slain shall be cast out,*
and the stench of their corpses shall rise;
the mountains shall flow with their blood.

4 *All the host of heaven shall rot away,*
and the skies roll up like a scroll.

All their host shall fall,
as leaves fall from the vine,
like leaves falling from the fig tree.

5 *For my sword has drunk its fill in the heavens;*
behold, it descends for judgment upon Edom,
upon the people I have devoted to destruction.

6 *The LORD has a sword; it is sated with blood;*
it is gorged with fat,
with the blood of lambs and goats,
with the fat of the kidneys of rams.

For the LORD has a sacrifice in Bozrah,
a great slaughter in the land of Edom.

7 *Wild oxen shall fall with them,*
and young steers with the mighty bulls.

Their land shall drink its fill of blood,
and their soil shall be gorged with fat.

8 *For the LORD has a day of vengeance,*
a year of recompense for the cause of Zion.

9 *And the streams of Edom*[b] *shall be turned into pitch,*
and her soil into sulfur;
her land shall become burning pitch.

10 *Night and day it shall not be quenched;*
its smoke shall go up forever.

From generation to generation it shall lie waste;
none shall pass through it forever and ever.

11 *But the hawk and the porcupine*[c] *shall possess it,*
the owl and the raven shall dwell in it.

He shall stretch the line of confusion[d] *over it,*
and the plumb line of emptiness.

12 *Its nobles—there is no one there to call it a kingdom,*
and all its princes shall be nothing.

13 *Thorns shall grow over its strongholds,*
nettles and thistles in its fortresses.

It shall be the haunt of jackals,
an abode for ostriches.[e]

14 *And wild animals shall meet with hyenas;*
the wild goat shall cry to his fellow;

indeed, there the night bird[f] *settles*
and finds for herself a resting place.

15 *There the owl nests and lays*
and hatches and gathers her young in her shadow;

indeed, there the hawks are gathered,
each one with her mate.

16 *Seek and read from the book of the LORD:*
Not one of these shall be missing;
none shall be without her mate.

For the mouth of the LORD has commanded,
and his Spirit has gathered them.

17 He has cast the lot for them;
his hand has portioned it out to them with the line;
they shall possess it forever;
from generation to generation they shall dwell in it.

35 The wilderness and the dry land shall be glad;
the desert shall rejoice and blossom like the crocus;
2 it shall blossom abundantly
and rejoice with joy and singing.
The glory of Lebanon shall be given to it,
the majesty of Carmel and Sharon.
They shall see the glory of the Lord,
the majesty of our God.

3 Strengthen the weak hands,
and make firm the feeble knees.
4 Say to those who have an anxious heart,
"Be strong; fear not!
Behold, your God
will come with vengeance,
with the recompense of God.
He will come and save you."

5 Then the eyes of the blind shall be opened,
and the ears of the deaf unstopped;
6 then shall the lame man leap like a deer,
and the tongue of the mute sing for joy.
For waters break forth in the wilderness,
and streams in the desert;
7 the burning sand shall become a pool,
and the thirsty ground springs of water;
in the haunt of jackals, where they lie down,
the grass shall become reeds and rushes.

8 And a highway shall be there,
and it shall be called the Way of Holiness;
the unclean shall not pass over it.
It shall belong to those who walk on the way;
even if they are fools, they shall not go astray.[g]
9 No lion shall be there,
nor shall any ravenous beast come up on it;
they shall not be found there,
but the redeemed shall walk there.
10 And the ransomed of the Lord shall return
and come to Zion with singing;
everlasting joy shall be upon their heads;
they shall obtain gladness and joy,
and sorrow and sighing shall flee away.

a That is, set apart (devoted) as an offering to the Lord (for destruction); also verse 5 **b** Hebrew *her streams* **c** The identity of the animals rendered *hawk* and *porcupine* is uncertain **d** Hebrew *formlessness* **e** Or *owls* **f** Identity uncertain **g** Or *if they are fools, they shall not wander in it*

Overview: The two chapters that form this passage portray strong images of God's judgment against the nations. The Reformers debated, along with the Jewish rabbis, whether this passage referred to the end of the world. Many of the Reformation interpreters affirm that this describes when Christ will come to judge the living and the dead. They identify the reference to Edom as merely an example of the enemies of the church. Several comment on the difficulties related to identifying the various animals named in this passage. In fact, a few deal with the word previously translated as "unicorns." Some commentators note the repetition of two main themes in Isaiah, namely, the fairness of God's just judgment against all people and the unmerited provision of healing and deliverance for a few. They note that this prophecy should give consolation to those who trust in the Lord and his Word.

Possibly the End of the World. John Trapp: Eusebius, along with many other ancients, will have this chapter to be understood as the end of the world and the Last Judgment. He further says that Plato has taken this passage from the prophet Isaiah into his writings and made it his own. But Scultetus says this cannot be the literal sense of the text.[†] The Jewish doctors will need to understand these two chapters as a prophecy of their return to the holy land once Idumaea will be destroyed, and they contend for this from Lamentations . . . , which still does not prove it. Exposition on Isaiah 34.[1]

34:1-4 *Judgment on the World*

Judgment on All Enemies of the Church. Johannes Brenz: This chapter is rightly separated from the previous one. For although this chapter refers to the same end as the prior speech, namely that the enemies of the church of God must perish miserably while the people itself is preserved forever, yet another speech is delivered in this chapter. There is no doubt that the prophet preaches against Edom. For so it follows, "Behold, it descends upon Edom." And then soon, "a sacrifice in Bozrah, a great slaughter in the land of Edom." But some interpreters feel that by "Edom," all the ungodly Israelites and the synagogue of the Jews are signified, and think that what is preached here is about the rejection and blindness of the Jews, and the destruction of them that happened by the Romans after Christ was revealed. This is a good thought. But I think that the sermon is more general than something said to the Jews alone. For by the name "Edomites" is included all the enemies and persecutors of the true church of God in the world, whether Gentiles or Jews. Commentary on Isaiah 34.[2]

Eternal Devastation. Konrad Pellikan: The difficulty of this chapter is known to all, no matter how the Jews explain it or our own interpreters, who themselves follow various views. If one does not see here more reliable things, it seems that the prophet is describing the eternal devastation of the Jews and of Zion. They are those who descended from Jacob who would not even hardly bear the severity of his judgment, and the rest of the nations, too, that would not mock the misery of the Jews. He foresees, in nearly the same context, the devastation of all nations, which happened after the time of Isaiah, but naming them Edomites, who are brothers of the Israelites from Isaac, having descended from Esau. It is as if he says, "The judgment is heavy on the Edomites, because they most seriously threaten the children of Israel and indeed even Zion itself." Commentary on Isaiah 34.[3]

Hyperbole of the Light Darkened. Martin Borrhaus: "Mountains will dissolve." He amplifies the disaster with exaggeration. A kind of hyperbole is discerned in this, "All the host of heaven will dissolve." What contains the starry host in the sky marches with its leader, the sun. The term *mountains* figuratively indicates the powers of tyrants in the world. These will be defeated to decay by the Messiah: "He is going to rule them with a rod of iron." . . . "The skies will be rolled up like a scroll." The heavens, about which David sings, "are stretched out like a tent." The prophet here prophesies that they will be rolled up. The sky, which is stretched out over the earth, provides light by its luminaries, giving life and cheer to everything. Now rolled up in the Lord's anger, the light of the earth is going to be withdrawn. All these natural things will be hostile to the wicked. They are going to suppose that the mountains are falling, the skies are being rolled up like a scroll, and the darkened stars are falling from the sky. Oracles in Isaiah on 34:3.[4]

Christ Will Come to Judge the Living and the Dead. Heinrich Bullinger: With

[1]Trapp, *Commentary or Exposition*, 122*; citing Lam 4:22. [†]See Scultetus, *Idea Concionum*, 290-94.
[2]Brenz, *Esaias*, 456; citing Is 34:5, 6.
[3]Pellikan, *Commentaria Bibliorum*, 3:42v.
[4]Borrhaus, *In Iesaiae Prophetae Oracula*, 309; citing Ps 2:9; 104:2.

God, he is always the same and like himself. Therefore, this prophetic teaching must be accommodated to each and every time, even ours in which we live today. We should not suppose that those ancient examples and grave warnings of the prophets have nothing that pertains to us. It is remarkable ungodliness and prodigious ingratitude when faithful and necessary doctrines of this kind are despised and rejected as if they have nothing that pertains to them. For this teaching universally pertains to making clear the righteousness of God against crimes and criminals, and finally for us to declare that article of faith, "I believe Christ will come to judge the living and the dead."

And one should know that Scripture mentions a twofold judgment of God. For God's judgment is specific, I say, whenever God punishes sin through pestilence, famine, and war. On the other hand, there is a universal judgment, in which the Son of God is going to come in the flesh and on the clouds of heaven to judge the living and the dead. So also there are two "last days." Each person has their own last day when they pass on from this age by death, and that last day at the end of the age for the whole of creation. So likewise the end is considered twofold: particularly, in the death of each person, and universally, at the end of the age. Sermons on Isaiah 34:1-4.[5]

34:5-12 *Judgment on Edom*

Jews Without God's Word. Johannes Oecolampadius: But by Edom, which he distinguishes from the nations, I said it should be understood as a Jew. And they are like the churches of Judea, destitute of God's word, among whom Christ does not reign, but foreigners like Herod and the Idumaeans who lead the people away from the true worship of God with their systems. As much as the wrath of God raged against the Gentiles on earth, against the Jews and those in whom the law had worked, that wrath also increased in heaven. . . . But Edom is a people of indignation. Like a servant who knows the will of his master is less excusable, he deserves to be beaten with many stripes. This also corresponds to our Pharisees who know the law and daily ask that those blind to Christ among his members be blinded and experience a more severe wrath when they are handed over, in the reprobate sense. Commentary on Isaiah 34:5-6.[6]

A Prophecy of Bloodshed. Wolfgang Musculus: Observe: The sword of the Lord descends from heaven intoxicated, not to randomly prowl but to take up punishments against the reprobate with just judgment. However much the wrath of God is exaggerated in these prophecies, the fairness of his just judgment is constantly imparted. "The sword of the Lord is filled with blood. . . ." That is, the vengeance of the Lord will be full of blood, in the way that it will be bloodthirsty. It especially signifies that it will be the slaughter of the Edomites. "It will be gorged with fat," it says, as if "with the blood of lambs." He compares the future slaughter with the sacrifices of lambs, goats, and rams, in which the knife of sacrificing is saturated with blood and fat. And he understands by "lamb," the common person; by "goats and rams," the wealthier and more powerful. He signifies that no one, whether the more feeble or the more powerful, will be spared. Commentary on Isaiah 34:6.[7]

An Amplified Personification of Judgment. Dietrich Schnepff: "Since it has drunk." He used a twin personification. In order to illustrate and augment the activity, he compares the Lord to a butcher, and his knife or sword to drunkenness. With this kind of speech he grabbed hold of an implicit amplification when he says that the knife was not only wet with blood but also was stained with fat. . . . The Lord says, "My sword descending from heaven will rage against the Edomites and those like them, who are subject to

[5]Bullinger, *Isaias*, 163v.

[6]Oecolampadius, *In Iesaiam*, 190r-v.

[7]Musculus, *In Esaiam*, 483.

my wrath and condemnation, and will be stained with the blood and fat of the wicked, whom I am going to slaughter, a great number of victims. And in this example of my wrath and indignation, no wicked will be spared. For in Bozrah, the city of the Edomites, and in all the world where the wicked are, I will exercise that judgment of mine. Then, not only the lambs, that is, the common people, but the unicorns and bulls, that is, the most powerful, are also given the punishments for the persecution that they have inflicted on my church in every time." SCHOLIA ON ISAIAH 34:5-7.[8]

UNICORNS OR RHINOCEROS. JOHANNES OECOLAMPADIUS: "And unicorns will fall with them." His strength upholds none, for along with the nations that will fall to destruction, so will unicorns, about which the psalmist has the same, "and my humility from the horns of unicorns."[†] As Job says, this animal is powerfully ferocious and untamable, although there we read "rhinoceros." Now, the Hebrews use *rĕʾēm* and *rêm* for the same thing, and it would be expedient to translate them equally. For there is no difference between a one-horned animal, that is, a unicorn, and a rhinoceros, for one has a horn on its forehead, the other on the nose. COMMENTARY ON ISAIAH 34:7.[9]

STRONG AND CRUEL BEASTS. FRANCISCO FORERIUS: "Unicorns." This is from the verb *rāʾam*, which is read only once, . . . that is, "lifted up." It is said that the animal rhinoceros is *rĕʾēm* because it has a horn that is lifted up high or because it raises its horn. . . . It is a ferocious animal and a beast of immense strength, whose strength is compared to the strength of the Israelites. . . . Joseph's posterity is also compared in strength to this animal. . . . Its cruelty is noted. . . . Further, a rhinoceros and a monoceros are not the same animal, since the first is said from one horn, and the second is from a horn on the nose, which has been raised up.

We saw the Lusitani rhinoceros brought from India in 1515. The elephant feared its strength. Martial of Rome saw this animal fighting with a bear, who had conquered a bull.[†] But the rhinoceros threw the bear, like a ball, into the air. He attributed to this animal a twin horn. For besides the horn on its nose, it has another small one above its forehead. Therefore he says that it lifted up the heavy bear with its twin horns and flung it like a ball to the bull portrayed in the stars. And again, how terribly prone to anger it was; how great was the horn that made the bull seem like just a ball. Some were deceived there because they did not think they had seen the rhinoceros with one horn. But Pausanias also mentions the other little [horn]. Therefore, in my judgment, in all the passages I have raised, this animal should be understood. But I do not think there is only one species of a one-horned animal. And that is why there arose so much diversity in those who write about it. . . .

Indeed, I have read nothing more ancient than Philostratus in *The Life of Apollonius*, where the words . . . are, "They say that many wild donkeys are captured in the neighboring marshes," that is, the River Hyphasis, "and beasts of this kind have a horn on the forehead, with which they fight most nobly like a bull, and the Indians make cups from those horns, and they declare that no one would be afflicted with diseases on the day on which they would drink from such a cup, nor would anyone suffer if they have been wounded, and they would also be able to come out of a fire unscathed, and would not be harmed by any poison whatsoever that is given to harm them when drank. . . ." I have complete doubt about these animals, whether Sacred Scripture mentions them anywhere. This is why I gladly translate it as "rhinoceros" everywhere. COMMENTARY ON ISAIAH 34:7.[10]

[8]Schnepff, *In Esaiae*, 509, 513 (misnumbered 493).
[9]Oecolampadius, *In Iesaiam*, 191v. [†]In the Vulgate, Ps 21:22 [22:21] reads, "et de cornibus unicornium exaudi me." See also Job 39:9-10 for the translation of "unicorn." In the Vulgate, Ps 28:6 [29:6] is translated as *rinocerotis* and Ps 91:11 [92:10] as *monocerotis*.
[10]Forerius, Iesaiae, 122r; citing Zech 14:10; Num 23; Deut 33; Ps 22; Job 29. [†]See Martial, *Epigrams* 15-16; Philostratus, *The Life of Apollonius of Tyana* (LCL 16:236-37).

General and Specific Days of Vengeance. Wolfgang Musculus: Now, the disposition of the times is twofold, general and special. The general is what carries on in a sure direction from the beginning of the world all the way to the end, which is seen . . . where we read, "In all the days of the earth, seedtime and harvest, cold and heat, summer and winter, day and night, shall not cease." The special is what is dispensed either by the grace of God to the righteous and those who fear God, or when wrath, vengeance, and judgments are exercised on the ungodly and the obstinate. Commentary on Isaiah 34:8.[11]

Differences of the Fire of Hell. Johannes Brenz: By its nature, the fire in this world shines. And yet Christ calls hell an outer darkness where there is weeping and gnashing of teeth. Peter calls it "chains of night," and "gloomy darkness." This is why it can be easily conjectured that the fire of hell differs with great distinction from our physical fire. Then consider that this fire of hell does not last only for a time but is eternal. "Night and day," the prophet says, "it shall not be quenched." The apostolic writings, which we mentioned a while ago, also testify to the same thing. But some wonder how it is fair that an eternal punishment is inflicted for a temporary sin. Commentary on Isaiah 34:9.[12]

A Plumb Line of Desolation. Martin Borrhaus: "And he shall stretch over it." A line and the standard of emptiness and devastation is going to be stretched over the earth. This elegant figure of speech, borrowed from a builder, describes the devastation of the earth. The expressions that Moses used when he was describing the empty and formless earth, here the prophet used, signifying that because of the immortality of its inhabitants, the earth will be reduced to utter desolation by the Lord, the avenger and vindicator of immorality. He is going to employ a straight edge and a plumb line to devastate the earth. With the same diligence that he used, as it were, to build the earth and adorn it with all kinds of trees and animals and numerous people in their various cities and states, so is he going to use that to devastate it, using a rule for destroying, not for building. Oracles in Isaiah on 34:11.[13]

34:13-17 *Wild Animals Take Over*

The Unfortunate Animals Are the Ungodly. Johannes Brenz: Those who understand in this speech that the name "Edom" is the synagogue of the Jews interpret the "streams of perpetually burning pitch" as the final rejection and devastation of the Jews when they were so oppressed by the Romans that they could never recover the former state of their kingdom or politics. Now, by "thorns, nettles, and thistles," and "pelicans, birds, owls," and the other unfortunate animals, they understand the wicked Pharisaical and Talmudic doctrine, which the Jews, after their rejection, were so drunk with and fascinated by that they had before them absolutely no reasoning for righteous, prophetic, and apostolic doctrine. But we generally understand by "the Edomites" all the ungodly adversaries and enemies of Christ and his church—whether the hypocrites among the Jews, or the tyrants among the Gentiles, or any other persecutors of faithful teaching. When Christ came into the world, these are who he went to war with and gloriously defeated, as we have shown earlier. Commentary on Isaiah 34:13-14.[14]

Unknown Animals. John Trapp: The Hebrews themselves do not agree what these creatures are mentioned here. They are so far from the knowledge of the Scripture. Their tale about Lilith† (once Adam's first wife but now a screech owl or an evil spirit) is not worthy of mentioning. Exposition on Isaiah 34:13-15.[15]

---

[11]Musculus, *In Esaiam*, 484; citing Gen 8:22.

[12]Brenz, *Esaias*, 464; citing Mt 24:32; 2 Pet 2:4.

[13]Borrhaus, *In Iesaiae Prophetae Oracula*, 311.

[14]Brenz, *Esaias*, 461, 462; citing Is 34:9.

[15]Trapp, *Commentary or Exposition*, 123*. †The idea that Lilith was Adam's first wife seems to appear first in the satirical *Alphabet of*

The Book of the Law and a Full Land. William Day: Calvin says this is best explained as the Book of the Law and the diverse sorts of warnings against the wicked contained in it. . . . For whatever God threatens against his own people when they sin, their enemies must expect that much more should come on them. Then, proceeding to speak about the owls and vultures that should dwell there, males and females, as he had said . . . , he says, none shall be lacking a mate (in Hebrew, "his female"), implying that the land should be full of them, and that not just for a long time but forever and ever. . . . It is necessary that hyperbole must be acknowledged. Exposition of Isaiah 34:16.[16]

Infallible Written Prophecy. Wolfgang Musculus: For this appears to be the sense: You who will be alive at that time in the future when these things will be fulfilled, "seek and read this book" of the Lord's oracle. You will find that what I have already said is so infallibly true that not one of these beasts is missing and not a single one is without its mate. That is, you will see the desolation of Edom happen in such a way that I predict that is certainly going to be the future.[†] These parts belong to the verification of this prophecy, to which he invites the posterity. Of course, with great faith, they could benefit from examining these writings of the prophets and gather from them what was happening. For in this way, the truth itself from the oracles of God was allowed to be known. And by this plan the Holy Spirit wanted the prophecies not only to be uttered by the mouth of the prophets but also to be commanded to be read in letters by future generations. Commentary on Isaiah 34:16.[17]

The Mystery of the Trinity. Johannes Oecolampadius: "Because his mouth has commanded." Deduce from these words the mystery of the Trinity. For the Father is signified when it says "his," the Son truly by "mouth," and the Holy Spirit by "the spirit." . . . "By the word of the Lord the heavens were made, and by the spirit of his mouth all their host." Where we read "his" according to the Hebrew is *hûʾ*. That is what the kabbalists contend to be the most excellent name of God, by which his most perfect incommunicable substance is signified, and all other excellence, and everything happening within himself and abiding equally in himself. And finally it is said, "his Spirit," the one who proceeds from the Father and the Son. He does not proceed as from two but as from one, proceeding from both in the beginning. Commentary on Isaiah 34:16.[18]

Possession Forever. Wolfgang Musculus: In the same way he said . . . above, "From generation to generation it shall lie waste; none shall pass through it forever and ever," so at the end of this prophecy he is going to express the same perpetuity of desolation when he affirms that the beasts "shall possess it forever." Why? Because they were receiving their possession that the Lord had assigned to them. "The earth is the Lord's and all the fullness of it." He has free power over all things, and he uses his right when, after expelling the reprobates, he gives the land to be inhabited by those whom he wishes. Commentary on Isaiah 34:17.[19]

All Need This Prophecy. Johannes Oecolampadius: This chapter concludes with a certain enigma that all are under sin so that God may have mercy on all. So also Isaiah turns his sermon toward the people. And he wants nothing in the whole world, no matter how small it may be, to disregard this prophecy, for it pertains to all. And he wants one not only to hear but also to properly draw near and diligently perceive with this heart. Commentary on Isaiah 34:17.[20]

Sirach (c. AD 700–1000), and then was developed extensively during the Middle Ages in Jewish mysticism.

[16]Day, *Exposition*, 210-11*; citing Lev 26; Deut 28; 32.

[17]Musculus, *In Esaiam*, 488. [†]See also Pellikan, *Commentaria Bibliorum*, 3:43v.

[18]Oecolampadius, *In Iesaiam*, 191v-192r; citing Ps 33:6.

[19]Musculus, *In Esaiam*, 488; citing Is 34:10.

[20]Oecolampadius, *In Iesaiam*, 190v.

35:1-4 *Divine Retribution Will Come*

Part of the Previous Speech. Johannes Brenz: This is the second part of the same speech that began in chapter 34. And just as the prophet previously expresses by the name "Edomites" all the wicked and the enemies of the people and the church of Christ, whether Jews or Gentiles or hypocrites or tyrants, so now by the name "desert, dry land, and wilderness," he understands the church of Christ. And surely if you consider the outward appearance of the church of Christ in this age, the surname of "desert" and "wilderness" would be assigned most fittingly, when meanwhile the field of the wicked seems most flowering and the farm most fertile. Commentary on Isaiah 35:1.[21]

I Believe in Eternal Life. Heinrich Bullinger: Isaiah demonstrated with the first part of this speech that God is just and therefore can punish the crimes of humanity in any time but especially at the final judgment. In the latter part he places opposite the antithesis—the consolation to the righteous in this age. He shows that the same God in whatever age, and especially in his final judgment, floods his worshipers with good things of every kind. This treatment illustrates the article of faith, "I believe in eternal life." Sermons on Isaiah 35.[22]

Blessings on the Land. David Joris: Blessed are you, O you of the earth; rejoice in the heavens, which pour out their riches and fullness on you, to the help and trust, to the glory and joy, of the burdened who dwell therein. For they who have lain alone in the long desert will appear pleasant, verdant, and joyful. The field will blossom just like a lily and open like a rose. And it will smell of the sweetness of pleasant-smelling herbs and overflowing blossoms, just like the powder of an apothecary's fire. The mandrake and all the good, holy fruits will grow to overflowing and increase on the earth, which will be renewed and refreshed in mercy. This is what the earnest love, truth, and righteousness of God will do. He will certainly dwell therein and remain eternally unchanged. Pay attention; the mouth of the Lord has spoken it. A Blessed Instruction for Hungering, Burdened Souls.[23]

Restored Glory. Martin Borrhaus: "The glory of Lebanon." These are the famous cedars from which Solomon's temple was built with great splendor. But since this was destroyed by the Babylonians, it was restored with great glory by Zerubbabel. So the temple of the Messiah, which the antichrist destroyed, will be restored to glory in these last days from the lofty heavenly cedars of Lebanon, that is, from what is written in the book of life. What follows is about this. Oracles in Isaiah on 35:2.[24]

Ministers Should Strengthen the Weak. Rudolf Gwalther: First, ministers ought to strengthen by their example and their teaching so that they are not mercenaries that flee if they see a wolf and allow it a place. And second, they should not cast aside those considered as unworthy for some reason but strengthen, reinforce, and build them up. And they should imitate the example of Christ, the chief shepherd, who is gentle and meek, and does not quench a burning wick, nor break a bruised reed. Sermons on Isaiah 35:3.[25]

Christ Is the God Who Comes. Heinrich Bullinger: Christ is God from the beginning, and indeed "your God," it says. Therefore Christ is not a foreign or new god but the same true God, with the Father, whom the ancestors in the Old Testament worshiped. In fact, it follows, "God himself will come." Therefore the one who comes in the flesh, the Son of God, is certainly God his very own self. But our Lord came in the flesh, as

[21]Brenz, *Esaias*, 465.
[22]Bullinger, *Isaias*, 166v.
[23]CRR 7:252; citing Song 7:12-13.
[24]Borrhaus, *In Iesaiae Prophetae Oracula*, 313.
[25]Gwalther, *Isaias*, 210r; citing Jn 10; Ezek 34; Mt 11; 12; Is 42; 2 Tim 2.

John says, "Every spirit that confesses that Jesus Christ has come in the flesh is from God." . . . So let no one listen to the Jews and Muhammadans, and those worse than these, the Arians and the Servetans, who deny the true divine nature of the Son of God, who is coequal and consubstantial with the Father. Here we clearly hear that Christ is our God, the true God, God his very own self. Sermons on Isaiah 35:4.[26]

Certain Comfort. Dietrich Schnepff: Now, this word of comfort is also repeated several times: "Take courage, be strong, be encouraged, do not fear." But the fullest reason for this consolation is provided: because God himself will come. And with the coming of such a helper, he exhorts us to be of great spirit. For since he is omnipotent, victory is certain. Then he "will come with vengeance, with recompense." And that vengeance is to be understood according to the reasoning of Christ's kingdom. The one who conquered sin, death, and hell will finally avenge all the enemies of his church. Scholia on Isaiah 35:4.[27]

35:5-10 *The Way of Holiness*

The Miracle of the Gospel. William Day: Luther says here that miracles confirm that the gospel is of God, against those who deride his ministers, saying they cannot make so much as a lame horse sound. For all those in whose hearts it takes effect are the blind made to see, the deaf made to hear, the lame to walk, and the dumb to speak. Exposition of Isaiah 35:5-6.[28]

Waiting for the Second Coming. Johannes Oecolampadius: By "blind," "deaf," "lame," and "mute" is designated humankind, because it was blind and did not recognize Christ. It was deaf to hearing the heavenly speech, mute to praising God, lame to serving neighbor and preaching the gospel. These are all vices Christ healed in his coming. Further, we wait for the greater glory in his second coming, when those who lie in dust will lift their hands to everlasting glory, when we will see not in a mirror or an enigma but face to face, when we will hear that ineffable mystery, when finally we will praise God with the angels for eternity. Commentary on Isaiah 35:5-6.[29]

The Ears of the Predestined Are Opened. Martin Borrhaus: "And the ears of the deaf will be unstopped." This is by the Spirit of faith. Those who are among that number have the Spirit of the Messiah, who opens the ears of the deaf: "My sheep hear my voice." Therefore, they are the deaf whose ears are immediately opened to hear the heavenly teaching as they were called to listen. The apostle says about this, "Those whom he predestined, he also called; those he called, he justified." Those predestined are clearly called to listen to the gospel fruitfully and so the called are justified—that is, given the Holy Spirit. By his power, those who believe in him have their sins forgiven and the righteousness they had lost and life restored. The ears of such deaf people will be opened—those whose deafness the grace of divine election in Jesus Christ preceded. The benefits of calling and justification flow from this. Regarding this kindness is said, "Whoever is of God hears the words of God." And regarding those who are "of God" is said, "As many as were appointed to life believed." Oracles in Isaiah on 35:5.[30]

Spiritual and Physical Healing Evidence of Christ's Arrival. Johannes Brenz: The following clearly testifies that these things are said about the coming of Christ, our true Lord and God, in the flesh. "Then the eyes of the blind shall be opened," it says, "and the ears of the deaf unstopped. Then shall the lame man leap like a

[26]Bullinger, *Isaias*, 166r; citing 1 Jn 4:2; 1; 3; 5-6; 8-10; 14; 17 and many other places as testimony to Christ's divinity.

[27]Schnepff, *In Esaiae*, 516.

[28]Day, *Exposition*, 212-13*.

[29]Oecolampadius, *In Iesaiam*, 193r.

[30]Borrhaus, *In Iesaiae Prophetae Oracula*, 315; citing Jn 10:27; Rom 8:30; Jn 8:47; Acts 13:48.

deer, and the tongue of the mute will be free." For although these miracles are always being fulfilled spiritually in the church of Christ through the gospel when people are truly healed of all their infirmities, yet Christ himself teaches that these outward miracles, by which he opens the eyes of the blind and the ears of the death, and makes the lame walk with ease, are testimonies that he has arrived in their presence to fulfill the prophecies in the prophets about him.

For according to Matthew and Luke, when John the Baptist was interrogated by the disciples whether he truly was the Christ or they should be expecting another, Christ preferred to answer with what was done rather than just words, "Go and report to John what you hear and see: the blind receive their sight, and the lame walk, lepers are cleansed and the deaf hear, the dead are raised up, and the poor hear the gospel." And this is the view of Christ. Isaiah . . . foretold what would be when Christ came: "the eyes of the blind shall be opened and the ears of the deaf unstopped," and . . . "the poor will hear the gospel." Commentary on Isaiah 35:5-6.[31]

Christ Is the Holy Way. Rudolf Gwalther: The sense is that the roads will be opened again so that all may safely travel wherever they want through the land that the Assyrians had occupied a short time earlier. Now first he speaks about the way leading to Jerusalem, which at that time they were going to take in order to give thanks to God for such great kindness. But this should also be explained in a deeper sense about Christ, who said to his disciples, "I am the way, the truth, and the life. No one comes to the Father except through me." Indeed, he is that ladder of Jacob, which rises from earth all the way to heaven.

And in him the Father (as Paul writes) "was pleased to have all the fullness dwell, and through him to reconcile to himself all things, whether on earth or in heaven, making peace by the blood of his cross." . . . First he calls the way "holy," no doubt because of Christ, who is himself holy and is holiness itself. And he not only sanctifies those who believe in him but also makes everything that they use in this age holy for them. This is what the apostle considers when he says, "To the pure all things are pure." This way is also holy because it is open to no others but the saints. Sermons on Isaiah 35:8.[32]

The Church Is the Way. Francisco Forerius: "There." Throughout these places, which were dry and only fodder for snakes and a den for beasts, there will be a way, a well-trodden way, or public and royal. But in the church is Christ the Lord, who is the way. There is the faith, and the sacraments, and the teaching of most holy conduct by which one is taken into heaven. Therefore it is "the way of holiness," or the sanctified, not only because of the boundary but also because of who passes through it, who are full of holiness. Indeed, the church itself is the house of God, but at the same time it is the way and the gate to heaven. Commentary on Isaiah 35:8.[33]

The Redeemed Walk on the Way of Holiness. Johannes Oecolampadius: "Those who walk on the way." It is certain that those who are led by the Spirit of God to the extent they are ruled by the word of God, and they continue in this way, will not go astray. For they have a teacher, the Holy Spirit, whom Christ promised them. But in those things that do not pertain to salvation, it is not surprising that, when left to themselves, if they go astray and even fall seven times a day, they get back up. It is sufficient for them that they do not go astray on the way where blessedness is obtained or that they rightly discern those who go astray in the end, at the point of death.

But having said this, those who do not have the Spirit of Christ or who reject the word of God, they cannot boast. By "walking on the way"

[31]Brenz, *Esaias*, 469-70; citing Mt 11:4-5; Lk 7:22; Is 61:1.

[32]Gwalther, *Isaias*, 211r; citing Jn 14:6; Col 1:19-20; Titus 1:15; Gen 28.

[33]Forerius, *Iesaiae*, 124v.

understand the one who is an expert on the journey, that is to say, a teacher. And by "fools" understand the rest who are not experts on the journey. For Christ accommodates himself to all and rejects neither the little ones nor the publicans. Only remain in Christ, and there will be no danger of you going astray. Commentary on Isaiah 35:8.[34]

Satan Replaced. Martin Borrhaus: The dominion of Satan is rightly signified, which thrives when the antichrist is sitting in the holy place. In the last times it will be overthrown by the Lord through the gospel reigning in his elect. For this is how John speaks about Satan, the seducing dragon: "And that great dragon was thrown down, that ancient serpent, who is called the devil and Satan, who seduces the whole world." And this is what we read here, "in the dens where dragons were formerly dwelling." But what will dwell in such places and dens? It follows, "the grass shall become reeds and rushes." He had recalled the waters and the rivers; now he recalls the reeds and rushes springing from the wetlands. Observe from the divine waters of heavenly speech in this passage that the saints, produced from the life-giving liquid of the holy gospel, are going to dwell where previously Satan the dragon dwelt in the wilderness and desert. . . .

"And no lion shall be there." The lion is to be taken figuratively, as Peter recalls, "Your adversary the devil prowls around like a roaring lion, seeking someone to devour." The power of Satan the lion to seduce the world, and those to whom he gives it, will be subverted by the Savior, Messiah. The prophet speaks about him here, "He will save you." Oracles in Isaiah on 35:9.[35]

No More Weeping and Crying. Johannes Brenz: "The sound of weeping and the sound of crying shall no longer be heard in it." This is the happiness that Christ brings to his church. But you may say, how does the church have perpetual joy when there is yet nothing in this age facing more misery than her, and because of the persecutions and various troubles that befall it, it nearly always marches in sadness?

I respond: This happiness, which Isaiah promises to the church on account of Christ, is not to be relegated only to the future age but even in this present age is to be understood in its own way. For although the church is most gravely afflicted and trampled in this world, it still does not lack true and heavenly joy. For great is the misery of the person—not just to be poor or sick or undistinguished, or even to die in one's body, but to be subject to sins, subject to Satan, eternal death, and the fire of hell, and to be deprived of the most pleasing and happiest appearance of God and the heavenly kingdom. Commentary on Isaiah 35:10.[36]

Oracles for the Present and Future. Konrad Pellikan: The holy prophet, instructed by the divine Spirit, wanted to foretell equally the imminent grace of God in his time with the great miracle of divine omnipotence against Sennacherib, and at the same time to foretell with all the prophets the most notable grace to be displayed to the world in the time of the Messiah. That is, glory for all those faithful to God and the exultation of the Gentile and Israelite saints. As all those ancient oracles served things for those present at the time and signified a type of far better and greater things to come, so light is better than shadow and is signified by a type. Commentary on Isaiah 35:8-10.[37]

Not Judaizing the Chapter. Wolfgang Musculus: Up to this point in the thirty-fifth chapter we have explained plainly with a simple, historical sense that is consistent with the preceding prophecies. We see the expositions of others greatly varying among them. And we are not

[34]Oecolampadius, *In Iesaiam*, 194v.

[35]Borrhaus, *In Iesaiae Prophetae Oracula*, 316-17; citing Rev 12:9; 1 Pet 5:8.

[36]Brenz, *Esaias*, 472.

[37]Pellikan, *Commentaria Bibliorum*, 3:43r.

deterred by the judgment of some that we have not sufficiently inspected the text, which seems to be about Judaism when not everything is drawn directly to the mysteries of Christ, with disregard for the historical sense. Although their pursuit itself should by no means be blamed, yet it pours much darkness into the historical simplicity and opens the floodgates to transform the sense of the Scriptures into a thousand forms based on anyone's sharp cleverness. This seems to be a game in human hearts rather than the right and sincere exposition of the Scriptures. Many err in this because they think that, by this method, the mysteries of Christ the Savior are explained and his kingdom is illuminated. Yet in this way, when they transform everything subtly, they raise doubts on every exposition of the Scriptures from the sharp cleverness of the scholastics and philosophers, and they do not consider the consciences of the readers in any way. Commentary on Isaiah 35.[38]

[38]Musculus, *In Esaiam*, 493.

36:1-20 THE THREAT OF ASSYRIA

36 In the fourteenth year of King Hezekiah, Sennacherib king of Assyria came up against all the fortified cities of Judah and took them. [2]And the king of Assyria sent the Rabshakeh[a] from Lachish to King Hezekiah at Jerusalem, with a great army. And he stood by the conduit of the upper pool on the highway to the Washer's Field. [3]And there came out to him Eliakim the son of Hilkiah, who was over the household, and Shebna the secretary, and Joah the son of Asaph, the recorder.

[4]And the Rabshakeh said to them, "Say to Hezekiah, 'Thus says the great king, the king of Assyria: On what do you rest this trust of yours? [5]Do you think that mere words are strategy and power for war? In whom do you now trust, that you have rebelled against me? [6]Behold, you are trusting in Egypt, that broken reed of a staff, which will pierce the hand of any man who leans on it. Such is Pharaoh king of Egypt to all who trust in him. [7]But if you say to me, "We trust in the LORD our God," is it not he whose high places and altars Hezekiah has removed, saying to Judah and to Jerusalem, "You shall worship before this altar"? [8]Come now, make a wager with my master the king of Assyria: I will give you two thousand horses, if you are able on your part to set riders on them. [9]How then can you repulse a single captain among the least of my master's servants, when you trust in Egypt for chariots and for horsemen? [10]Moreover, is it without the LORD that I have come up against this land to destroy it? The LORD said to me, "Go up against this land and destroy it."'"

[11]Then Eliakim, Shebna, and Joah said to the Rabshakeh, "Please speak to your servants in Aramaic, for we understand it. Do not speak to us in the language of Judah within the hearing of the people who are on the wall." [12]But the Rabshakeh said, "Has my master sent me to speak these words to your master and to you, and not to the men sitting on the wall, who are doomed with you to eat their own dung and drink their own urine?"

[13]Then the Rabshakeh stood and called out in a loud voice in the language of Judah: "Hear the words of the great king, the king of Assyria! [14]Thus says the king: 'Do not let Hezekiah deceive you, for he will not be able to deliver you. [15]Do not let Hezekiah make you trust in the LORD by saying, "The LORD will surely deliver us. This city will not be given into the hand of the king of Assyria." [16]Do not listen to Hezekiah. For thus says the king of Assyria: Make your peace with me[b] and come out to me. Then each one of you will eat of his own vine, and each one of his own fig tree, and each one of you will drink the water of his own cistern, [17]until I come and take you away to a land like your own land, a land of grain and wine, a land of bread and vineyards. [18]Beware lest Hezekiah mislead you by saying, "The LORD will deliver us." Has any of the gods of the nations delivered his land out of the hand of the king of Assyria? [19]Where are the gods of Hamath and Arpad? Where are the gods of Sepharvaim? Have they delivered Samaria out of my hand? [20]Who among all the gods of these lands have delivered their lands out of my hand, that the LORD should deliver Jerusalem out of my hand?'"

a *Rabshakeh* is the title of a high-ranking Assyrian military officer b Hebrew *Make a blessing with me*

OVERVIEW: The style of the book shifts at Isaiah 36 to narrate the historical events regarding Sennacherib's invasion of Judah. The Reformation commentators frequently note that this demonstrates the fulfillment of many of the previous oracles, and they refer to the parallel passages in Kings and Chronicles that describe the same events. Some also include other historical references. A few of the interpreters, in addition to describing the history of Hezekiah, also relate how this speaks about Christ and the ways of Satan and the antichrist. This especially comes from their explanations about the speech by the Rabshakeh, because while he speaks some things that are true, he twists the words of the Lord. They also address when it is permissible to be silent in the face of blasphemy, how Hezekiah is an example of public repentance and trust in the Lord, and how the high places are like the imaginary sacraments and false practices in their own day.

The Smallest of Previous Prophecies Confirmed. Wolfgang Musculus: What up to this point was predicted about the siege and liberation of Jerusalem, with several prophecies and figurative speeches before they happened, now in this and the following chapter the historical narration of how they were fulfilled is explained. Whether the prophet himself related this history with his prophecies or it was done by others who arranged his prophecies in this order, it was not done with useless intention. For from this a great deal of light is conveyed in the foregoing prophecies. So it is certainly surprising how some could pour so much obscurity over them by not explaining them but by entangling them.

Next, the truth of the prophetic spirit is also confirmed, which very few recognized during the prophesying. For the prophet seemed to utter constantly incredible things. Consequently, even now, for this same reason, these prophecies relate the history of the people about whom all these things were so often foretold. But as often as it was being read by the Jews, so often it was charging them with unbelief. Commentary on Isaiah 36.[1]

The History of Hezekiah and the Mystery of Christ. Johannes Oecolampadius: What earlier was obscured with many figures and covers of prophecies is now explained in these two chapters. Now we have a remarkable example of faith, by which we can be comforted in all adversities. Divine help is not going to abandon us as long as saving faith remains. There was no more need to present so many figures and to commemorate the miracle with such careful exposition. And although the history is not narrated clearly, it is still pregnant with the greatest type of those mysteries. In the same way that the history of the bronze serpent that Moses lifted up is true and we cannot deny that it was also nevertheless a figure of Christ, so too here, we have become the citizens of our Jerusalem, the true church of God, through true faith in Christ.

You should also understand that it also has its own Sennacherib and its own Rabshakeh, the antichrist who attends to the business of his ruler. For they endeavor to assault the church in various ways, and they attempt to reduce us under their slavery away from the true worship of God, which is by faith. But God, through his "angel" Jesus Christ, crushed the adversarial powers without anything from us by the power of his own death on the cross. What remains is for us to have faith in Christ, and he will triumph in us over demons and their servants. He is going to triumph fully when he has abolished death and all things have been made subject to him. Commentary on Isaiah 36.[2]

As Useful an Account as the Exodus. Heinrich Bullinger: The description of the same things with nearly the same words as Isaiah exists in 2 Kings 18 and 19, and 2 Chronicles 32. Just as the history of the deliverance of the children of Israel from Egypt is treated with great care by sacred writers because of its multifaceted usefulness, so also this deliverance of the city of Jerusalem is presented to us to contemplate with no less care. As a matter of fact, he graphically describes the nature of God for us, I would say, the truth that he keeps his promises and likewise fulfills what he threatened. . . . And so this very history teaches us to believe in God with firm confidence.

[1]Musculus, *In Esaiam*, 494.

[2]Oecolampadius, *In Iesaiam*, 194r.

An example of this will be exhibited to us, in both King Hezekiah and the prophet Isaiah, and finally in the Jewish people themselves. . . . How King Hezekiah behaved at the beginning of this Assyrian war is carefully recorded in 2 Kings 18, and especially 2 Chronicles 32. For he first attempts to turn the enemy away from the necks of the people with money, and indeed the greatest amount or abundance of it. But that money proved empty, and since the Lord was going to strike, it did not keep away the unrepentant people. Sermons on Isaiah 36.[3]

36:1-3 *Sennacherib's Invasion of Judah*

The Spirit of Tyranny Did Not End. Wolfgang Musculus: "Sennacherib, king of Assyria, came up," it says, "against all the fortified cities of Judah and took them." The three kings of the Assyrians who preceded Sennacherib, Pul, Tiglath-pileser, and Shalmaneser, had overthrown the kingdom of the ten tribes and led that people into captivity. Following these, desiring to enlarge the limits of his monarchy and to increase the glory of his name, Sennacherib had the thought that he should bring the kingdom of Judah, which still remained, under his control. For this purpose he came up against all the fortified cities of Judah. So the spirit of tyranny was not dead with the death of the tyrants who preceded him but was poured into their successor until the time of his punishment would come. Commentary on Isaiah 36:1.[4]

The Fulfillment of Previous Preaching. Johannes Oecolampadius: Isaiah preached about this earlier where he and the Assyrians are called . . . the "bees resting in the valleys," . . . "the waters of the river," . . . "the rod of anger," . . . "the thunder of many peoples," . . . "Sargon, the capturer of Ashdod," . . . "the covering that is cast,"[†] and . . . "the destroyer who destroys." Now he captures and conquers all the cities of Judah except Jerusalem, that is, the true church of God, those trusting in the Word of God alone. Further, when it says, "He ascends," it partly refers to the location of the place and partly indicates his confidence in conquering, as the spiritual Sennacherib said, "I will ascend to heaven; above the stars of God I will set my throne on high." Commentary on Isaiah 36:1.[5]

The Identity of Rabshakeh. Dietrich Schnepff: Here too is mentioned the ambassador, Rabshakeh, which the Jewish interpreters suppose was the son of Isaiah who defected to the Assyrians. Yet they are swayed by the thin reason that he knew Hebrew. But who does not see how uncertain those things are? The deserter could have been someone other than the son of Isaiah, and there is no doubt that the Assyrians had their own interpreters who had learned Hebrew. From the etymology it seems possible to deduce that Rabshakeh was not a proper term but the name of an office. For *rab-šāḵēh* signifies "chief of drinking." Perhaps he was the king's taste tester. Ceratinly we see that he was special in the royal court and in addition that he was eloquent and diligent. The king entrusted many things to him. Scholia on Isaiah 36:2.[6]

Where Isaiah Previously Prophesied. Wolfgang Musculus: "And he stood by the conduit of the upper pool on the highway to the Washer's Field." About this place, see what was said earlier. . . . It is not stated why the Rabshakeh stood at this aqueduct. Josephus says that he was encamped at the very walls of the city.[†] Clearly there was such presumption against the God of Israel. And that upper pool was not far from the walls and was probably the place for public exhibition, which the enemy determined to be a

[3]Bullinger, *Isaias*, 168r, 169v.
[4]Musculus, *In Esaiam*, 494-95.

[5]Oecolampadius, *In Iesaiam*, 195v; citing Is 7:18; 8:7; 10:5; 17:12; 20:1; 25:7; 33:1; 14:13. [†]In the Vulgate, Is 25:7 reads *faciem vinculi conligati* (the face bound with a chain).
[6]Schnepff, *In Esaiae*, 524.

convenient place for his purpose to compress and oppress the city. Commentary on Isaiah 36:2.[7]

Eliakim, Shebna, And Joah. Konrad Pellikan: Bringing together what was said earlier with the present passage, it seems that Shebna was removed from being governor of the royal house to become the king's secretary. But Eliakim the son of Hilkiah was praised in the earlier passages and was predestined by the Lord to the office of governor. Let the Jews respond to how he could be commended to this office, or Shebna to that of a scribe, when he was deprived of the governorship because of his treason and treachery, and the greatest honesty is required for notaries and scribes of the cities. They do the worst harm if they are malicious. But they are most useful to the republic if they demonstrate honesty. And in the commentaries, Joah is called what now princes call chancellors. Commentary on Isaiah 36:3.[8]

36:4-10 *The Speech of the Chief Adviser*

Empty Words about Undependable Egypt. Johannes Oecolampadius: Moreover, as we read here, the Rabshakeh says, "I said, and those with me, how do you think you are going to be liberated by prayers and that they are your strategy and power? But you are deceived; you will need some other protection." Now pay careful attention to what the antichristian rhetorician proposes in his speech. For he introduces three things in his attempt to persuade us not to put hope in something, mixing truth with falsehood. And the first two he says are true. For we must not trust in ourselves, nor in any creature, but in God. But what the enemy especially intends is to cut off hope in God. . . .

The second he also says rightly that when we are in danger, our hope should not be placed in externals, that is, in people or any other creature. For "all mankind are liars," as the psalm says. Therefore those who trust in pleas to the saints forsake Christ and act foolishly. Commentary on Isaiah 36:4.[9]

Truth Spoken with Insincerity. Heinrich Bullinger: Actually to trust in the strength and help of people is nothing other than to have one's hope disappointed and to throw oneself into a certain crisis. This is what the prophet explains elsewhere in the same form of speech: "But it is good to trust in the Lord and to hope in his mercy." He does this by his power so that even human help is effective. Blessed Isaiah shows this very clearly and abundantly in his speeches. And this teaching should not be despised because it was conveyed in their midst by an uncivilized and Gentile person. Although he may have brought it with an insincere mind, nevertheless what he said is true. Sermons on Isaiah 36:4-6.[10]

The Abuse of Images and Sacraments. Johannes Oecolampadius: "But if you say to me." Here the tricks of the enemy appear. For he makes danger where there is no danger and turns the highest righteousness into unrighteousness. Because what is more admirable than the zeal of Hezekiah to remove the high places and break the bronze serpent in pieces? And see here, the enemy is especially attempting to bring down hope. So he clearly wants to bring them to desperation by portraying Hezekiah as if he were such a sinner who is unworthy to be heard and to present him before the people as wicked. And indeed, there were high places erected in honor of God but not at his command, and for that reason they were abominable before his eyes, even though they were most pleasing to the people and viewed as worthy of the highest honor. None of the kings before could remove them, even those who were most righteous, as Asa, Jehoshaphat, Joash, Amaziah, Jotham. But only Hezekiah destroyed the high

[7]Musculus, *In Esaiam*, 495; citing Is 7:3. †See Josephus, *Antiquities of the Jews* 10.1.
[8]Pellikan, *Commentaria Bibliorum*, 3:44v.

[9]Oecolampadius, *In Iesaiam*, 196v; citing Ps 116:11.
[10]Bullinger, *Isaias*, 169r-v.

places, smashed the statues, cut down the sacred groves, and broke the bronze serpent in pieces, to which the children of Israel had begun offering incense, against God's command.

So Rabshakeh says here, "What hope will you place in God, when your king has destroyed the altars that were erected in honor of God? Why would he help you who are demolishing his altars?" But the vile enemy objected to things that had been constructed without the decree of God and had not been approved by God. Today we hear of similar things happening—in sacraments, images, and other things that until now were viewed by the common people as beautiful to their eyes. But those very things should be considered dangerous because of their abuse. So while those things are being corrected according to the Word of God, the enemies of piety say, "What hope do you have when you demolish the things that were instituted in honor of God?" Commentary on Isaiah 36:7.[11]

Removing Superstitions and Idols. Rudolf Gwalther: But let us observe in these things how Satan is always similar when the churches of the Sophists have had superstitions and idols removed and have been reformed according to the command of the gospel by his servants. They reproach us today. They claim that we destroy the faith of the ancient fathers, abolish the true worship of God, profane the sacraments, are insulting the saints and their images, are ruining the sacrilegious audacity of convents and monasteries (which people are in the habit of calling houses of God), and remove from their entire midst fasting, prayers, almsgiving, and all good works. From all this they ultimately conclude that we are deservedly hated by people, angels, and even God, and that we should not hope for anything happy and fortunate. But if we each examine God's Word, it will be clear that no less wrong has been done by us and our leaders than was once done by King Hezekiah. Sermons on Isaiah 36:7.[12]

[11]Oecolampadius, *In Iesaiam*, 196r.

[12]Gwalther, *Isaias*, 215r.

The Temptation of Scarcity. Heinrich Bullinger: They were lacking soldiers, and so they were not equipped with horses or riders. From this he concludes, "But if I, who am a servant of my king, give you horses to fight with me, but you do not have riders to put on them, it is certainly unlikely that you will be able to repulse my king when you cannot even join with the least servant of my king. Therefore you would be most wise if you surrender."

The righteous are tempted, and have always been tempted, by the objection of scarcity—that they have no strength, but that of their adversaries are visible and powerful. But they can be refuted with the single statement from John, "He who is in us is greater than he who is in the world." And also, faith does not look to the multitude but to the promise of God. Therefore, when the antichrist boasts that he has many councils, many kingdoms, and the rule for a long time, with a plurality of universities and teachers, the faithful look to the Word of God and rest in this alone. And indeed the Rabshakeh here carries a type of the antichrist. Sermons on Isaiah 36:8-9.[13]

Temptation to Claim the Lord's Will. Johannes Brenz: Did the king of Assyria undertake this war by divine command? I believe that the Assyrians received the report that the prophets in the kingdom of Judah had prophesied disaster and devastation to its kingdoms, as Amos prophesied . . . and Micah. . . . Or perhaps, he argues from the result, "So far I have waged war against the kingdom of Judah very successfully, and I have taken all its fortified cities, which I certainly could not have done without the special favor and help of God. Therefore, it is evident that I wage war by the divine will."

This is a very significant temptation, but it is easy to go against this and refute it by looking into the Word of God and rightly understanding it. The prophets indeed threatened the kingdom of Judah with disaster, but at the same time they also

[13]Bullinger, *Isaias*, 169v-170r; citing 1 Jn 4:4.

promised deliverance, especially to those who repented and trusted in the Lord's mercy. And God indeed willed that the kingdom of Judah should be afflicted, but he did not will that it should be destroyed at this time by the Assyrians. Commentary on Isaiah 36:7-9.[14]

Abusing the Providence of God. Rudolf Gwalther: The purpose of his argument is to show that the Jews would be taking up war with God if they continued to resist the king of the Assyrians. There is no doubt that he took this from the words of the prophets, who had foretold many things about the coming of the Assyrians and had the habit of naming Sennacherib "the rod of fury in the hand of God."

For the wicked have their own Coryciana,[†] through which they ascertain whatever is said and done. And of course, it was true that he did not provoke this war without the will and agreement of the Lord. But he abuses the decree of God and errs in that because he does not look at the whole picture. For the prophets had not foretold to Sennacherib the manner of his coming to the kingdom of Judah, but they had warned that God was not going to permit him to overthrow that kingdom by capturing the city. Rather, he was going to impart severe punishments for his wickedness, where God had used their actions to chastise his people. Therefore, Hezekiah is not sinning when he resists him and teaches the people to trust in God. But the Rabshakeh wickedly abuses the providence and decree of God. Today people sin in abusing the providence of God with a similar error when they excuse their crimes or establish public impunity for crimes. Sermons on Isaiah 36:10.[15]

The Imitation of Satan. Martin Borrhaus: Without a doubt he knew that uttered oracle of the prophet Isaiah about Assyria: "The Lord will bring against you the king of the Assyrians." But the one who attempts to deceive is deceived. For the false speaker omitted the second part of the oracle, which was given for Hezekiah and for Jerusalem that, by faith in him, they would be secure as he brought all the power of the adversary to nothing. But what is that second part, which the untrustworthy ambassador omitted? It is this: prepare yourselves, and you will be conquered. Similarly, "O my people who dwell in Zion, be not afraid of the rod." Therefore, the Rabshakeh imitates his master and teacher, Satan, who, when he was tempting the heavenly Hezekiah, Christ Jesus, quoted part of the sacred Scriptures and left out part. This is clear from the Gospel writer. Oracles in Isaiah on 36:10.[16]

36:11-20 *Request of the Jewish Leaders and Response of the Chief Adviser*

The Antichrist from Among Us. Johannes Oecolampadius: It may appear that the Rabshakeh was from the deserters of the Judeans and the friends of Shebna because he knew the prophecies and because he had spoken Jewishly. But this is a weak conjecture. Yet, the antichrist who goes out from us and is not of us is not ignorant of similar tricks, which he learned from his father, the devil, who first used this to seduce Eve as the more vulnerable one. Commentary on Isaiah 36:11.[17]

Poisoned Abuse of Language. Heinrich Bullinger: Knowledge of languages has many uses in human affairs, and indeed abuse. Here the Rabshakeh abuses the holy language to deceive the Jewish people. So today many learn the sacred language not to sincerely teach piety in the church but to maintain devised errors. These ones

[14]Brenz, *Esaias*, 479-80; citing Amos 2; Mic 1.

[15]Gwalther, *Isaias*, 216v. [†]In Greek mythology, Corycia was a female nymph who inspired poetry. Here Gwalther most likely refers to a collection of poems published in 1524, titled *Coryciana*, by Roman humanist Johannes Guritz, nicknamed Corycius. This collection includes poems on statues, frescoes, and sculptures, including Raphael's *Isaiah*. See Julia H. Gaisser, "The Rise and Fall of Goritz's Feasts," *Renaissance Quarterly* 48 (1995): 41-48.

[16]Borrhaus, *In Iesaiae Prophetae Oracula*, 319; citing Mt 4; Is 10:24.

[17]Oecolampadius, *In Iesaiam*, 197r.

therefore turn all that they can offer from the languages into sophistry. But languages must be learned and used for the expansion of piety and pure simplicity. If the knowledge and learning of language falls on a depraved person, that one's knowledge and learning is destructive. In this way, all the studies and expertise in languages by the Rabshakeh were infected with poison. Sermons on Isaiah 36:11.[18]

Eat Filth and Drink Urine. Johannes Brenz: At the beginning, he provokes a hatred toward Hezekiah, as if he were the author of the disaster on the people and as if the Assyrian were grieving for the plight of the people. "Has not my king," he says, "instead sent me to the men sitting on the wall, doomed to eat their own dung and drink their own urine?" He wants to say this: "My king Sennacherib desires more to be kind to this people than to harm them. He will pity their disaster that has to happen if the siege lasts a little longer, because their destitution means they eat their own dung and drink their own urine, that is, the dirtiest and foulest of all. They are thrust into this need not by my king but by that king of yours, Hezekiah, who by maintaining his tyranny and oppressing the people for his own lust is the author of this disaster." You have a fabricator stirring up sedition against their legitimate government. Commentary on Isaiah 36:12.[19]

Speaking the Language of Judah. Wolfgang Musculus: "And called out in a loud voice in the language of Judah." He had also spoken in Hebrew before, and in such a loud voice that the ambassadors of Hezekiah were afraid that since he was speaking to the ears of the people he might persuade them to surrender. But now he does not simply speak but "calls out in a loud voice," in as fluent Hebrew as he is able, so that those who are on the wall understand everything exactly. Commentary on Isaiah 36:13.[20]

A Wolf Speech. Heinrich Bullinger: Moreover, this is actually a wolf speech, where the wolf persuades the sheep to leave their shepherd and yield to the wolf, that is to say, to security and enjoyment. Of course, Satan certainly never ceases to drop in his temptations in the exact same way, so that we separate ourselves from Christ, the true shepherd, and the antichristians call the teachers of the truth, heretics, empty, liars, and deceivers. Therefore, may the faithful ones withdraw from them and their teaching about grace and the bosom of the mother church, which is not catholic but Roman, and its supreme pontiff. So also the corrupters of citizens, the senators, disparage all the men holding to righteousness and desiring sound discipline, and they strive to push them away from obedience. But the faithful servants of God despise these kind of suggestions and do not retreat from the good and holy obedience of God. Sermons on Isaiah 36:11-20.[21]

A Cunning, Persuasive Argument. Dietrich Schnepff: Now he composed his arguments cunningly to persuade them. The first argument is what he had stated earlier, that the divine help that Hezekiah promised should not be expected, since the Lord himself wished to punish the wickedness of the king of the Hebrews. The second way he aims to persuade is by specifying the advantages they are going to have if they would yield to the king of Assyria. For they are either going to be left in their homeland to enjoy their fields and farms, or they are certainly going to be transported to a better land. But this sharply contrasts with the hardships of the siege, which he said earlier was going to endanger them with hunger and thirst.

The last argument is joined with the highest blasphemy. That is, "The Lord, the God of Israel—even if he wanted—is not able to save Jerusalem." Now it seems he wants to prove this from the mightier ones: "There was no region whose gods were able to resist me; how then could

[18]Bullinger, *Isaias*, 171v.

[19]Brenz, *Esaias*, 481.

[20]Musculus, *In Esaiam*, 502.

[21]Bullinger, *Isaias*, 171r.

the God of Israel be the only one to deliver his people from my hand and power?" Scholia on Isaiah 36:15-20.[22]

Temptation to Compare the Lord to Other Gods. Johannes Brenz: How will your God be able to deliver you from my hands? For the fact itself also declares that he is too weak to be able to help you. See Samaria. Did not the Israelites who lived in Samaria worship the same God whom your worship? But he could not save the inhabitants of Samaria, so how can he save you? This is a terrible blasphemy that also leads God to hasten the destruction he is going to bring on the king of the Assyrians and his army. But since Hezekiah and Isaiah clearly criticize and refute this blasphemy a little later, we will hold off on explanation of this until we get to their prayers.

But we must consider that Satan also tempts us in a similar way and spews out similar blasphemies against our Lord Jesus Christ. If any is oppressed with poverty, he promises great riches. . . . Out of necessity, he says, you will have to die of hunger unless you are willing to eat your own dung and drink your own urine. But why would you throw yourself into such dangers when you could have obtained many riches, if you just surrendered yourself to me and obeyed my commands? Commentary on Isaiah 36:18-19.[23]

The Turks Object to God. Dietrich Schnepff: There is truly such confidence in his spirit that he dares to bring even God himself into contempt. That sufficiently shows that the highest blasphemy is from that instrument, the Rabshakeh, when he attempts to cast down the true God below all the idols. He says that it would never be possible for the God of Israel alone to protect his people when the gods of so many peoples and nations could not save their own. So today, the Turks, puffed up by their perpetual victories, object to Christians that their god cannot save them. All the wicked in general object to the saints, "Where is your God?" Scholia on Isaiah 36:20.[24]

[22]Schnepff, *In Esaiae*, 527.

[23]Brenz, *Esaias*, 483.

[24]Schnepff, *In Esaiae*, 532.

36:21–37:38 Response to Sennacherib's Invasion

21 But they were silent and answered him not a word,
for the king's command was, "Do not answer him."
22 Then Eliakim the son of Hilkiah, who was over the
household, and Shebna the secretary, and Joah the
son of Asaph, the recorder, came to Hezekiah with
their clothes torn, and told him the words of the
Rabshakeh.
37 As soon as King Hezekiah heard it, he tore
his clothes and covered himself with sackcloth
and went into the house of the Lord. 2 And he sent
Eliakim, who was over the household, and Shebna the
secretary, and the senior priests, covered with
sackcloth, to the prophet Isaiah the son of Amoz.
3 They said to him, "Thus says Hezekiah, 'This day is
a day of distress, of rebuke, and of disgrace; children
have come to the point of birth, and there is no
strength to bring them forth. 4 It may be that the
Lord your God will hear the words of the Rabshakeh,
whom his master the king of Assyria has sent to mock
the living God, and will rebuke the words that the
Lord your God has heard; therefore lift up your
prayer for the remnant that is left.'"
5 When the servants of King Hezekiah came to
Isaiah, 6 Isaiah said to them, "Say to your master,
'Thus says the Lord: Do not be afraid because of the
words that you have heard, with which the young
men of the king of Assyria have reviled me. 7 Behold, I
will put a spirit in him, so that he shall hear a rumor
and return to his own land, and I will make him fall
by the sword in his own land.'"
8 The Rabshakeh returned, and found the king of
Assyria fighting against Libnah, for he had heard that
the king had left Lachish. 9 Now the king heard
concerning Tirhakah king of Cush,[a] "He has set out to
fight against you." And when he heard it, he sent
messengers to Hezekiah, saying, 10 "Thus shall you
speak to Hezekiah king of Judah: 'Do not let your God
in whom you trust deceive you by promising that
Jerusalem will not be given into the hand of the king of
Assyria. 11 Behold, you have heard what the kings of
Assyria have done to all lands, devoting them to
destruction. And shall you be delivered? 12 Have the
gods of the nations delivered them, the nations that my
fathers destroyed, Gozan, Haran, Rezeph, and the
people of Eden who were in Telassar? 13 Where is the
king of Hamath, the king of Arpad, the king of the city
of Sepharvaim, the king of Hena, or the king of Ivvah?'"
14 Hezekiah received the letter from the hand of the
messengers, and read it; and Hezekiah went up to the
house of the Lord, and spread it before the Lord.
15 And Hezekiah prayed to the Lord: 16 "O Lord of
hosts, God of Israel, enthroned above the cherubim,
you are the God, you alone, of all the kingdoms of the
earth; you have made heaven and earth. 17 Incline
your ear, O Lord, and hear; open your eyes, O
Lord, and see; and hear all the words of Sennacherib,
which he has sent to mock the living God. 18 Truly, O
Lord, the kings of Assyria have laid waste all the
nations and their lands, 19 and have cast their gods
into the fire. For they were no gods, but the work of
men's hands, wood and stone. Therefore they were
destroyed. 20 So now, O Lord our God, save us from
his hand, that all the kingdoms of the earth may
know that you alone are the Lord."
21 Then Isaiah the son of Amoz sent to Hezekiah,
saying, "Thus says the Lord, the God of Israel:
Because you have prayed to me concerning Sennach-
erib king of Assyria, 22 this is the word that the Lord
has spoken concerning him:

"She despises you, she scorns you—
the virgin daughter of Zion;

she wags her head behind you—
the daughter of Jerusalem.

23 "Whom have you mocked and reviled?
Against whom have you raised your voice

and lifted your eyes to the heights?
Against the Holy One of Israel!

24 By your servants you have mocked the Lord,
and you have said, With my many chariots

I have gone up the heights of the mountains,
to the far recesses of Lebanon,

to cut down its tallest cedars,
its choicest cypresses,

to come to its remotest height,
its most fruitful forest.

25 I dug wells
and drank waters,

to dry up with the sole of my foot
all the streams of Egypt.

26 "Have you not heard
that I determined it long ago?

I planned from days of old
what now I bring to pass,

that you should make fortified cities
crash into heaps of ruins,

27 while their inhabitants, shorn of strength,
are dismayed and confounded,

and have become like plants of the field
and like tender grass,

like grass on the housetops,
blighted[b] before it is grown.

28 "I know your sitting down
and your going out and coming in,
and your raging against me.

29 Because you have raged against me
and your complacency has come to my ears,

I will put my hook in your nose
and my bit in your mouth,

and I will turn you back on the way
by which you came.

30 "And this shall be the sign for you: this year
you shall eat what grows of itself, and in the second
year what springs from that. Then in the third year
sow and reap, and plant vineyards, and eat their
fruit. 31 And the surviving remnant of the house of
Judah shall again take root downward and bear
fruit upward. 32 For out of Jerusalem shall go a
remnant, and out of Mount Zion a band of
survivors. The zeal of the Lord of hosts will
do this.

33 "Therefore thus says the Lord concerning the
king of Assyria: He shall not come into this city or
shoot an arrow there or come before it with a shield
or cast up a siege mound against it. 34 By the way
that he came, by the same he shall return, and he
shall not come into this city, declares the Lord.
35 For I will defend this city to save it, for my own
sake and for the sake of my servant David."

36 And the angel of the Lord went out and
struck down 185,000 in the camp of the Assyrians.
And when people arose early in the morning, behold,
these were all dead bodies. 37 Then Sennacherib king
of Assyria departed and returned home and lived
at Nineveh. 38 And as he was worshiping in the
house of Nisroch his god, Adrammelech and
Sharezer, his sons, struck him down with the sword.
And after they escaped into the land of Ararat,
Esarhaddon his son reigned in his place.

a Probably *Nubia* **b** Some Hebrew manuscripts and 2 Kings 19:26; most Hebrew manuscripts a *field*

Overview: Inserted into the historical account of Sennacherib's invasion on Judah is one of Hezekiah's recorded prayers and God's answer through Isaiah and the angel of the Lord. The Reformers note the piety of Hezekiah and draw out many examples to apply his actions of turning to prayer, going to the temple, and praying for God's glory and not his own. They often contrast the behavior of Hezekiah with the enemies of Judah who were boasting and blaspheming. They also frequently point out the various places throughout Scripture and the book of Isaiah where the events recounted in this chapter are also portrayed. The theme of God's providence and protection is prominent in these chapters, not only in the prayers but in the description of how God used the angel of the Lord to defeat the Assyrians.

The Harmony of Scripture Accounts. Heinrich Bullinger: This memorable history of the besieged city of Jerusalem, of the great difficulties pressed on it, and finally its deliverance, is carefully explained in three passages of Scripture: 2 Chronicles 32; 2 Kings 19; and this present chapter of Isaiah. Now, the descriptions of these last two agree with each other, and [2 Chronicles 32] does not differ from them, except that it is more succinct. The history would not have been described with such diligence unless it was of the greatest importance and produced the most abundant fruit among the faithful. Sermons on Isaiah 37.[1]

The Perpetually Militant Church. Rudolf Gwalther: Just as, in all this history, we have identified Sennacherib as a type of the tyrants who attack Christ and his church, so also in the example of Hezekiah, the Holy Spirit teaches what the righteous should do if they are ever endangered. Sennacherib is proud in his own confidence, boasts of his victories, threatens, and there is nothing he does not promise himself from his strength. But in this insolence of his he perishes miserably. But Hezekiah, along with his people, trusts in the one and only God, turns to him, engages in repentance and public prayers, and is preserved by God, along with the city. This is the perpetual state of the church militant on earth under the head of Christ. Sermons on Isaiah 37.[2]

36:21–37:4 *Hezekiah's Response*

Silence by the King's Command. Wolfgang Musculus: Now it is explained what those who were on the wall did about these things. "And they were silent," it says, "and answered him not a word." I understand that this is not about the ambassadors sent outside the walls to the Rabshakeh but about the people who were on the wall. However, I do not wish to dispute if someone refers these things also to the ambassadors, as some do. It could have been that Hezekiah himself was on the wall and carefully ordered that no one should respond with any word to the blasphemies of the wicked and proud man. And it was not a matter of little importance to be concerned anxiously in such a crisis. So nothing should be presumed rashly or imprudently by those who were on the wall. . . .

Some raise the question here of whether this silence can be excused. For it seems not to be a righteous person to maintain silence at such horrendous blasphemy of God's name, and not to be a faithful people at the denigration of their king. In my judgment, the answer is easy. The silence of the people is excused by the command of the king. And it seems Scripture presents this reason to excuse their silence: "because the king's command was, 'Do not answer him.'" But why Hezekiah did not want them to answer anything, I judge that to be given to his prudence, because there is no doubt about his faith and piety toward God, since there are clear evidences of it expressed throughout this history. Commentary on Isaiah 36:21.[3]

Proper Praying and Fasting. Johannes Oecolampadius: The godliness of the king also does not appear small. And learn that although we have the most certain promises of God, and we are well aware of ourselves, yet it is not proper for us to be lazy and content in those things, especially when in danger. But rather, one should act with repentance and disturb God with prayers. Hezekiah was just, and he had heard may promises, yet he did not consider it opposed to the dignity of his reign to put on a goat-hair garment and to be an example of humility and frugality to others. He not only clothed himself in sackcloth, but he also did

[1] Bullinger, *Isaias*, 174r; citing 2 Chron 32; 2 Kings 19.
[2] Gwalther, *Isaias*, 222r.
[3] Musculus, *In Esaiam*, 505.

not want anyone to see him covered this way, evidently fulfilling with sackcloth what Christ commanded when fasting to anoint our faces with oil. But by the term *sackcloth*, also understand fasting and other things that pertain to the chastising of the body. Similarly also, prayer too is necessary for us in temptations. . . .

"And he sent Eliakim." It did not seem enough to the righteous king to pray by himself, so he also sends for Isaiah to intercede, either because the prayers of the many are more readily heard or because the prophet prays with greater trust. You have here the example of asking for the intercession of the saints living in this life, but we do not have the same in Scripture to appeal to the saints who have departed from this life. Additionally, in order for the intercession of others to benefit us, we should also pray together, following the example of Hezekiah. Moreover, see how great was the holiness of our prophet, in whose prayers alone the salvation of the city seems to be. See also how much was contained in that dignity, since he also carries a figure of Christ, as his name indicates. For we offer our prayers to the Father through Christ, who is our sole mediator, advocate, and high priest before God. Commentary on Isaiah 37:1.[4]

Priests Sent to the Prophet for Prayer. Heinrich Bullinger: Now he does not send for the priests, but he sends the priests to the prophet. And this is a kind of royal commission that explains how much they are enveloped with dangers and covered with all kinds of evils, especially how grievously God was provoked by the blasphemy of the Assyrians. And they inquire from the prophet whether God heard such terrible things and that they have no strength to give birth. They inquire what the prophet perceives about whether God is going to deliver them. But for God to do this, they ask for the prayers of the prophet when he says, "This day is a day of distress, of rebuke, and of blasphemy." He feels that the present is a most disastrous time because they have been reduced to extreme anguish by that siege and because the wicked denounce and blaspheme God. Sermons on Isaiah 37:2-3.[5]

The Small Remnant Repeated. Johannes Oecolampadius: "For the remnant that is left." He says that the people of God have been reduced to a small number such that God may be more provoked to mercy. But the small number of people was predicted in many passages: . . . a seed remains; . . . the children are "signs and portents"; . . . "a people more rare than gold"; . . . the consummation happens on earth; . . . the cluster and the shaking of the oil; . . . an island; and . . . "a flagstaff on the top of a mountain." Commentary on Isaiah 37:4.[6]

37:5-13 *Responses to Hezekiah*

Revelation from the Holy Spirit. Johannes Brenz: What Isaiah reports to Hezekiah is not taken from the general promise that God guarantees he is going to defend his people and punish blasphemers. But this was revealed to Isaiah alone by the gift of the Holy Spirit. For the prophet not only announces the destruction of the king of the Assyrians in general—which would not have been hidden from any righteous person, since it is easy to know from the general promises and threats of God that the wicked cannot be eternally happy against the people of God. But he also adds the specific circumstances, namely, the manner and the location, where the wicked Assyrian is going to perish. . . . You see the circumstances of the way and place where the king of the Assyrians will perish. And what Isaiah prophesies here, the history testifies is fulfilled this way, as follows afterward. This is a remarkable and clear prophecy by which God comforts the most miserable and afflicted King Hezekiah through Isaiah. Commentary on Isaiah 37:5-7.[7]

[4]Oecolampadius, *In Iesaiam*, 199v.

[5]Bullinger, *Isaias*, 173r.

[6]Oecolampadius, *In Iesaiam*, 199r; citing Is 8:18; 13:12; 18; 17; 20; 30:17.

[7]Brenz, *Esaias*, 491-92.

A Spirit That Moves the Wicked. Martin Borrhaus: "I will put a spirit" that moves him instead, as the wind moves the dust of the earth. The movement and stimulation of God is noted by the term *spirit*, by which he moves and stirs all things by his command and will. Therefore he moves the wicked with one spirit, the righteous with another—these with a pleasant and sweet spirit, by which they are saved; those with an angry and vengeful spirit, by which they perish. Oracles in Isaiah on 37:7.[8]

Sennacherib Blasphemes the Lord Again. Johannes Brenz: Now, even though it is reported to Assyria that the king of Cush has set out to fight against him, yet the Assyrians are not even frightened nor eased by this report, such that he rises up more fiercely against Hezekiah than against the Lord his God. For what he delivered before by his ambassadors, he now does in the letter he sends to Hezekiah, full of horrible blasphemies against God. "Do not let," it says, "your God in whom you trust deceive you." Commentary on Isaiah 37:8-10.[9]

The Same Blasphemy. Dietrich Schnepff: That letter of the king contains the same blasphemy that earlier the Rabshakeh spewed out against the Lord: The one God of Israel cannot be sufficient to repel the Assyrians when all the cities and empires with their own gods were forced to yield to the power of that king. Scholia on Isaiah 37:10-13.[10]

Double the Affliction for Greater Glory. Thomas Cooper: Here we have to learn that God oftentimes, after giving a promise and comfort of deliverance, increases and, as it were, doubles the affliction of his people for a time. This is what he does here with Hezekiah and his subjects by this second message, which is indeed more terrible and blasphemous than the former. And yet he does not do this with the intent to break his promise or to forsake his people, but for the purpose of exercising and testing their faith, and to stir them up to more earnest prayer and calling on his name. He intends that in the end their deliverance may be both more pleasant to his people, to himself more glorious, and to the adversaries the greater confusion. First Sunday After Christmas at Morning Prayer.[11]

37:14-20 *Hezekiah's Prayer*

Spreading the Letter Before the Lord. Johannes Brenz: So when the righteous Hezekiah receives the letters of the Assyrians full of horrible blasphemies against God, and he sees that the dangers are greater than can be handled with human counsel, he does not murmur against God or his word but brings himself again to the temple and to prayer, his ancient refuge in every adversity. And he spreads the blasphemous letters before the Lord his God, to whom he obediently entrusts whatever is before him with righteous prayers. Commentary on Isaiah 37:14.[12]

Addressing God in Prayer. Konrad Pellikan: He calls on the Lord of hosts, whom he believes has the strength of angels and men in his hand, and gives victory. He is also "the God of Israel," the friend of their forefathers, who was always present with special favor in the temple between the cherubim at the mercy seat, giving clear answers to the faithful, appearing in mystery—the one and only God, omnipotent and merciful to his worshipers, the Lord of lords, on whose will all things depend, the Creator of all things. These are the true epithets of the Almighty and true God. He loves to be addressed by these names in faith. Commentary on Isaiah 37:15.[13]

[8]Borrhaus, *In Iesaiae Prophetae Oracula*, 322.
[9]Brenz, *Esaias*, 492.
[10]Schnepff, *In Esaiae*, 540.
[11]Cooper, *Brief Exposition*, 38v*.
[12]Brenz, *Esaias*, 493-94.
[13]Pellikan, *Commentaria Bibliorum*, 3:45r.

The Power of Prayer. Viktorin Strigel: Hezekiah set forth the subject of his prayer and explained the reason why he was praying for the liberation of his city and himself: "May you, O Lord, bring us aid and salvation, so that this liberation might be a witness to your presence among your church, which is fighting blasphemous enemies. By this, may many nations be invited into the fellowship of your church." We ought to consider such things, praying to God for the liberation or mitigation of public and private punishments. Book of Kings.[14]

The Ineffable Covenant Name. Johannes Oecolampadius: You have here a form of holy and righteous prayer, since there are many words included here for strengthening our faith. First, the prayer begins with the ineffable name, the tetragrammaton, which we utter as Adonai. The Hebrew is written with the four letters *yhwh*, in which many mysteries are that we must now pass over. Nevertheless, it is most pleasing that God wanted that name to be familiar to the Jewish people, and he gave it to them in the covenant. So then, they were accustomed to calling up to him in this particular way, just as we also address God as Father in learning the Lord's Prayer, which is a name commemorating no small covenant. Commentary on Isaiah 37:16.[15]

Three Epithets for God. Johannes Brenz: You have here three epithets by which the true God is portrayed. One is that he made heaven and earth. The second is that he establishes and governs all kingdoms of the earth. The third is that he sits above the cherubim at the mercy seat. These reveal that he promises to give the seed of Abraham, atonement for our sins, and the manifestation of divine decision. Commentary on Isaiah 37:16.[16]

The Cherubim as Certainty of Promises. Dietrich Schnepff: "Who sits above the cherubim": this is a paraphrase for the ark on which the cherubim were, and there the Lord promised that he would hear the Hebrews. Therefore by the term *cherubim* was included those most certain promises that the Lord made to the Hebrews in this sacred place. But these are implicitly opposed to the blasphemies of the king who had written to Hezekiah, "Do not let your God deceive you." For in this way Hezekiah strengthened himself that none of these promises, which truth itself had given, would be void, and this was displayed by the symbol of the ark and the mercy seat. Scholia on Isaiah 37:16.[17]

Creator of All Kingdoms. Martin Borrhaus: "You have made heaven and earth," it was not the gods of the Assyrians. Based on that ability, the one who is the founder of all things can deliver his people and overthrow the proud enemy. This is why it follows, "Incline your ear, O Lord"—the ear of mercy and goodness that listens to your prayers against the gashing tyranny mocking your name. The righteous king knew that promise: "Call on me in the day of trouble, and I will deliver you and you shall glorify my name." The king prayed, depending on faith in this promise, and he obtained what he prayed for. Oracles in Isaiah on 37:16.[18]

Calling on the True God. Johannes Brenz: "I admit," he says, "that the Assyrians have laid waste to many kingdoms of the nations and cast their gods into the fire. But these were not truly gods but the works of human hands, wood and stone. But you are the true and living God, who not only created all things but also promised to hear us and deliver us in all our afflictions." Observe, then, how the true God is distinguished from the fictitious gods. The nations do not call on the true God, even if they claim to call on him. . . .

The Muhammadan does not call on the true God, because even if one claims that one calls on the one God, the Creator of heaven and earth, yet

---

[14]Strigel, *Libri Samuelis, Regum et Paralipomenon*, 388.
[15]Oecolampadius, *In Iesaiam*, 201v.
[16]Brenz, *Esaias*, 495.
[17]Schnepff, *In Esaiae*, 540.
[18]Borrhaus, *In Iesaiae Prophetae Oracula*, 324; citing Ps 50:15.

because one does not call on God the Father of our Lord Jesus Christ, foreshadowed by the mercy seat, one does not call on the true God. The Jew living now does not call on the true God, because even if one uses the words "who sits above the cherubim," yet one denies the one whom the Spirit signifies with these words, namely, the Father of our Lord Jesus Christ. The monk does not call on the true God, because he claims these words, "The Father of our Lord Jesus Christ"—like the Jews use the words "who sits above the cherubim"—yet he does not mean that Christ is the true place of atonement but rather attributes atonement and expiation to the merits of his own works. Commentary on Isaiah 37:18-20.[19]

Our Conception of God in Prayer. Rudolf Gwalther: By his example, Hezekiah reminds us what kind of God we, too, should conceive in our minds when we pray. He is of course the Lord of hosts, that is, the almighty Creator and ruler of heaven and earth, and for that reason he is able to rescue us. He is also our God and Father and therefore wants to be near us. This is what Christ teaches when he commands us to begin our prayers, "Our Father who is in heaven." Sermons on Isaiah 37:20.[20]

37:21-35 *God's Answer to Prayer Through Isaiah*

What God Permits Against His Daughter. Johannes Oecolampadius: Now he addresses his people with the terms "Zion and Jerusalem," like a young boy and a delicate daughter, whom the father does not want to be mistreated. It is as if he says, "I consider well how the enemy has inflicted harm on you, my beloved and gentle daughter. I only allowed him to scorn and mock." Meanwhile, understand by the term "Zion and Jerusalem" also the church. Commentary on Isaiah 37:21-22.[21]

The Boasting of Assyria. Konrad Pellikan: He turns the discussion to Assyria. It seems too little to you to have taunted and cursed both the people of God and God himself. For you are accustomed to doing harm to all and therefore you consider even to curse as nothing. You dare to boast of your strength and triumphs, especially the victories over many gods. You boast of the greatest abundance of armies and proclaim yourself to be the most invincible, and even have no fear to spew blasphemies against the God of Israel. You boast that you laid waste to the whole land of Israel, from Lebanon to Carmel, and that you removed whatever you found that was distinguished and high, cutting down the cedars and cypresses and all that was beautiful. And there is no end to your boasting, because nothing has escaped your sword. Commentary on Isaiah 37:23-25.[22]

Using Gifts for the Glory of God. Johannes Brenz: Observe also in this passage how much the wicked defile the most beautiful gifts of God with their wickedness. For the victories over all the kingdoms Sennacherib had reported to this point were remarkable gifts of God. But Sennacherib so pollutes them with his wickedness and blasphemy that the whole kingdom of the Assyrians begins to be defiled before God and to fall into destruction. In such a way, the nations had the most excellent gifts of industry, wisdom, courage, civil justice, and many other virtues, but since they did not recognize God in these, nor did they glorify him as God, they were therefore abominable before God, along with all their great deeds.

Therefore, let us learn from this the fear of God. If any remarkable gifts have been conferred upon us, let us recognize the mercy of God in them, use them for the glory of God's name, and serve our neighbor through them. Commentary on Isaiah 37:24-25.[23]

Providence Against Free Will. Martin Borrhaus: We are reminded in this passage that

[19]Brenz, *Esaias*, 495.
[20]Gwalther, *Isaias*, 224r (misnumbered 225), 225r.
[21]Oecolampadius, *In Iesaiam*, 203r.
[22]Pellikan, *Commentaria Bibliorum*, 3:46v.
[23]Brenz, *Esaias*, 503.

everything that happens, whether prosperity or adversity, results now from what was long ago destined and decided by God from eternity, so that no one can boast that anything can be done by oneself other than as an instrument of divine power. Nor does anything happen differently than is foreseen in God's providence. This meaning was stated earlier by Isaiah with these words: "Shall the axe boast over him who hews with it, or the saw magnify itself against the one who wields it?" So it is accomplished, not because Assyria was going to lay waste to the fortified cities of the people and so God foresaw that this was going to happen to them. But rather it should be concluded that because God decreed from eternity to plague the nations through Assyria, he foresees that they were infested with war and subjected to his rule. . . .

It is therefore an absurd error of those who, in order to support "free will," make divine foreknowledge subject to human plans and actions—both good and evil. They affirm that it is not because God foreknows what we will or do not will that we will or do not will it, but rather, because we want to do whatever or something else, for that reason God foreknows what we will or do not will. This is contrary to what the sacred letters teach and the faith of the saints knows and experiences in severe trials. Armed with the providence of God like a bulwark against the storm of afflictions, one acknowledges that all things must be subject to the decrees and plans of divine foreknowledge. That one confesses that foreknowledge is the infallible and certain cause of things present and future, and the human will depends on it. . . .

So likewise it is not a minor error for those who in the explanation and treatment of "free will" allege that divine providence and predestination should not be mentioned. Nothing more strongly overturns the errors that the opponents point out in the defense of free will than a correct exposition of divine providence and predestination. And no teaching has greater importance and weight to comfort us against the temptations of sin and death, and in other afflictions, than what Christ reminds us, "Rejoice that your names are written in heaven," and the apostle asks, "Who will bring charges against the elect?" Oracles in Isaiah on 37:26.[24]

The Lord Knows All. Heinrich Bullinger: These words first commend to us the omniscience of God. For he knows all, even the smallest things done by humans, and he sees them that he may punish them. Then they commend to us the power of God, who subdues the cruelest tyrants with much less difficulty than some beggar bringing out a bear to dance for the people. Let us not be anxious, then, and not let our soul despair if we see that the strength of persecutors is great and their insolence is most insurmountable and intolerable. The omniscient and omnipotent God will repress these at his time. Commentary on Isaiah 37:28.[25]

A Three-Year Sign for Hezekiah. Johannes Brenz: "For you," he says, "this shall be the sign," that is, "I do not want you to think that your deliverance will be delayed for a thousand or two thousand years, but in these next few years you will be wonderfully delivered from this enemy. With this sign, I will display the certainty of the matter and the arrangement of this deliverance. For this war and this disaster on the city of Jerusalem will still continue up to a third year." . . . It is another miracle that Isaiah not only foretells in general terms the deliverance of the city of Jerusalem and the destruction of Assyria, but he also explains the specific circumstances of these events, namely, at what time and in what manner these things are going to happen. This could not be gathered from human reason or from the general promises of God, but a singular revelation by the Holy Spirit was necessary. Commentary on Isaiah 37:30-32.[26]

The Three Years a Sign of Christ's Life. Johannes Oecolampadius: And this sign was

[24]Borrhaus, *In Iesaiae Prophetae Oracula*, 326-27; Is 10:15; Lk 10:20; Rom 8:33.
[25]Bullinger, *Isaias*, 178r.
[26]Brenz, *Esaias*, 504.

indeed given to them, but no less to us, of course, in Christ himself, if indeed we would believe. For since he satisfies us more happily with his own flesh than the manna that previously fed those who were in the wilderness, surely also he will keep us more safe for the future life by feeding us than what fed the once fallen and renewed people of Jerusalem. The "third year" also carries with it the mystery of the resurrection, which bears with it the fullness of peace and the abundance of all fruit. Commentary on Isaiah 37:30.[27]

Always a Remnant. Konrad Pellikan: For always in Jerusalem and Zion a remnant is found, and all the way to the birth of Christ, the seed of David, too, could not cease; through him the elect from every nation are continually made sons of David as much as sons of Abraham. "The zeal of the Lord of hosts will do this." It is as much the love for his faithful ones, the king and the prophet, as the wrath of God against blasphemers that he brings about this glorious victory. Consequently, those actions are clearly narrated. Commentary on Isaiah 37:31-32.[28]

The Lord Hears Prayers. Dietrich Schnepff: At the beginning we see that the Lord answered Hezekiah, calling on him the second time through Isaiah. Therefore, let us not doubt that the Lord hears the prayers of the righteous. For this is what he promised to those who believe: "Call on me in the day of trouble; I will deliver you, and you will glorify me," and likewise, "Ask, and you shall receive." While the Lord does not send us special messengers every day, still his heart toward us should by no means be doubted. For he has spoken to us in these last days by a messenger more excellent than all the patriarchs and prophets, our Lord and Savior Jesus Christ, who sent his ambassadors into the whole world so that they would make us more certain about his mercy and merit shown to us. And since he promises to us that while heaven and earth will perish, his word will not perish, we should not look for new revelations but let us rest in his promises, which have unshakable and perpetual certainty. Scholia on Isaiah 37:30-32.[29]

For the Lord's Glory. Dietrich Schnepff: The last consolation is that the king of Assyria will not be able to create any trouble for the people of Jerusalem: "He will not shoot a weapon in the city; he will not build a siege mound. . . ." In sum, the Lord will save that city against the fury of that tyrant. But there are two reasons for this last consolation added to this. The first is that the Lord is going to do this not because of the dignity and merits of the people but because of the glory of his name. The second is "for the sake of David," to whom he made those greatest promises about a perpetual kingdom and the Messiah. Scholia on Isaiah 37:33-35.[30]

My Servant David. Martin Borrhaus: "For the sake of my servant David." With the shadow of the mystical David removed, it comes to mind, "And they shall be my people, and I will be their God. My servant David shall be king over them." And that David is the King Messiah, in whom and through whom and for whose sake God the Father delivers his people and overthrows his enemies. Oracles in Isaiah on 37:35.[31]

37:36-38 *The Defeat and Death of Sennacherib*

Like the Passover Death. Heinrich Bullinger: The manner and method by which they perished, whether by sudden death, or by punishment, or by some other fate, is not expressed. Briefly, the Lord struck them down, perhaps like the firstborns in Egypt. . . . But however it happened, it is soon added that horror

[27]Oecolampadius, *In Iesaiam*, 203r.

[28]Pellikan, *Commentaria Bibliorum*, 3:46r.

[29]Schnepff, *In Esaiae*, 545; citing Ps 50:15.

[30]Schnepff, *In Esaiae*, 545.

[31]Borrhaus, *In Iesaiae Prophetae Oracula*, 329; citing Ezek 37:23-24.

strikes again and shows the power of God, and human frailty, weakness, and misery. Surely it would be horrendous to behold the overthrow of all those many and great princes to be devoured in one night and as if in one hour, and the plains and mountains around Jerusalem covered with dead bodies. This is the hand of the Lord outstretched even today against all his enemies. Therefore let us fear God and offer ourselves in obedience to him so that he does not rise up against us in a similar way. And let us hope greatly for the same if we see today the enemies of God being fierce and insolent. Sermons on Isaiah 37:36.[32]

A Perplexed King Spared for a Time. Konrad Pellikan: With divine strength, the angel sent by God suddenly struck down an infinite army in the night such that the very few who remained with the perplexed king all withdrew. But it can be understood that those who "arose in the morning and saw these were all dead bodies" are the citizens of Jerusalem and King Sennacherib himself. Along with a few others, he was saved for a time by divine providence in order that they would see and marvel at the power of the living God, and be astounded at whom they had blasphemed. Commentary on Isaiah 37:36-37.[33]

Blasphemous Rabshakeh Perished. Heinrich Bullinger: 185,000. . . . We read that the angel struck down "all the mighty warriors and commanders and officers" of the army. Therefore in this mob of powerful people, the Rabshakeh, that blasphemous scoundrel, also perished. And all the most excellent in the army perished together with the largest part of the army. A band of soldiers, perhaps small and miserable, and maybe less depraved, escaped. Sermons on Isaiah 37:36.[34]

The Miracle Prophesied Earlier. Johannes Oecolampadius: This remarkable miracle of the deliverance of Jerusalem from the most cruel enemies is the one that is mentioned up and down in this book. It was not by a human but the divine hand. . . . "The rod of the oppressor has been broken as on the day of Midian." . . . It is "a whip as when he struck Midian, and a staff over the sea," and that same one "a flask to be broken" in terror. . . . Its end is dust and misery its finish. . . . It is "like chaff on the mountains before the wind, and whirling dust before the storm. This is the portion of those who plunder us." . . . The Lord is "a stronghold to the poor, a shelter from the storm, a shade from the heat," and he holds "a feast of rich food." . . . "The Lord will rise up as on Mount Perazim, as in the valley of Gibeon." . . . "The multitude shall be like small dust, passing chaff" to you, and that same one "will be visited with thunder and earthquake." . . . "The Lord will fight on Mount Zion as a lion." . . . The one who preys will be prey, and the one who devastates is devastated. Commentary on Isaiah 37:36.[35]

The Defeat of Sennacherib. John Calvin: Where that slaughter was carried into effect by the angel is not very evident. The opinion generally entertained is that it happened at the siege of Jerusalem; but it is also possible that it may have happened during the march of Sennacherib's army, that is, while he was coming to besiege the city. I leave that matter uncertain, because it is of little importance. From the context, certainly, we may clearly learn that the tyrant did not approach so closely that he was able to throw a dare into the city.

We must indeed reject that invention by which Satan, through profane historians, has attempted to obscure this extraordinary judgment of God, that, in consequence of a part of the army having been destroyed by a plague during the war in Egypt, Sennacherib returned into his own dominions. So great a number of persons dying in one night cannot be attributed to a plague; and the father of lies, with his deceitful cunning, has

[32]Bullinger, *Isaias*, 180r.

[33]Pellikan, *Commentaria Bibliorum*, 3:46r.

[34]Bullinger, *Isaias*, 180r; citing 2 Chron 32:21.

[35]Oecolampadius, *In Iesaiam*, 204v-205r; citing Is 9:4; 10:26-27; 17:13-14; 25:4-5; 28:21; 29:5-6; 31:4.

turned aside into Egypt the blessing that God bestowed on his church. The event itself cries aloud that Jerusalem was miraculously rescued, as it were, out of the midst of destruction; especially since Isaiah had already delivered that message by which God testified, in a manner that could not be mistaken, that God would bestow this deliverance on the Jews and not on the Egyptians. COMMENTARY ON ISAIAH 37:36.[36]

KILLED BY HIS OWN SONS. WOLFGANG MUSCULUS: This retribution was both unique and shameful, and very fitting for a tyrant. First, immense pain of heart was inflicted on him because his plan was hindered. Then came the disgrace of fleeing, and third the greatest contempt in that he became detested by his own people. Fourth, he was going to be slain by his own sons, because that kind of death with a double name is fitting for tyrants. For since they are enemies of humankind, it is most fitting that they should either kill their own, as Herod did, or be killed by their own, as is mentioned in what happened here to Sennacherib. Such a father is worthy of such offspring. And he is deservedly not safe from his own sons, who allowed no one to be safe.

Fifth, he was not at home in his kingdom but was in the temple of his god among the worshipers when he was killed. This is to the disgrace of his god Nisroch, whom he truly preferred to God even after he had experienced the emptiness of his god and the power of God in his greatest disaster. It is a worthy death for the tyrant who blasphemes the true God and worships a false one to perish in the very temple of that false god and be killed by his own sons while worshiping it. While we are considering these matters, it is quite evident that it was not without reason that Sennacherib was not slain by the hand of the angel with the others in the mountains around Zion but was allowed to flee with a band of his soldiers and return to Nineveh. COMMENTARY ON ISAIAH 37:38.[37]

[36]CTS 15:145* (CO 36:641-42).

[37]Musculus, *In Esaiam*, 528.

38:1-22 HEZEKIAH'S SICKNESS AND PRAYER FOR RECOVERY

*38 In those days Hezekiah became sick and was
at the point of death. And Isaiah the prophet
the son of Amoz came to him, and said to him, "Thus
says the LORD: Set your house in order, for you shall
die, you shall not recover."[a] 2 Then Hezekiah turned
his face to the wall and prayed to the LORD, 3 and said,
"Please, O LORD, remember how I have walked before
you in faithfulness and with a whole heart, and have
done what is good in your sight." And Hezekiah wept
bitterly.*

*4 Then the word of the LORD came to Isaiah: 5 "Go
and say to Hezekiah, Thus says the LORD, the God
of David your father: I have heard your prayer; I
have seen your tears. Behold, I will add fifteen years
to your life.[b] 6 I will deliver you and this city out of the
hand of the king of Assyria, and will defend this city.*

*7 "This shall be the sign to you from the LORD,
that the LORD will do this thing that he has promised:
8 Behold, I will make the shadow cast by the declining
sun on the dial of Ahaz turn back ten steps." So the
sun turned back on the dial the ten steps by which it
had declined.[c]*

*9 A writing of Hezekiah king of Judah, after he
had been sick and had recovered from his sickness:*

*10 I said, In the middle[d] of my days
I must depart;*

*I am consigned to the gates of Sheol
for the rest of my years.*

*11 I said, I shall not see the LORD,
the LORD in the land of the living;*

*I shall look on man no more
among the inhabitants of the world.*

*12 My dwelling is plucked up and removed
from me
like a shepherd's tent;*

*like a weaver I have rolled up my life;
he cuts me off from the loom;*

*from day to night you bring me to an end;
13 I calmed myself[e] until morning;*

*like a lion he breaks all my bones;
from day to night you bring me to an end.*

*14 Like a swallow or a crane I chirp;
I moan like a dove.*

*My eyes are weary with looking upward.
O Lord, I am oppressed; be my pledge of
safety!*

*15 What shall I say? For he has spoken to me,
and he himself has done it.*

*I walk slowly all my years
because of the bitterness of my soul.*

*16 O Lord, by these things men live,
and in all these is the life of my spirit.
Oh restore me to health and make me live!*

*17 Behold, it was for my welfare
that I had great bitterness;*

*but in love you have delivered my life
from the pit of destruction,*

*for you have cast all my sins
behind your back.*

*18 For Sheol does not thank you;
death does not praise you;*

*those who go down to the pit do not hope
for your faithfulness.*

*19 The living, the living, he thanks you,
as I do this day;*

*the father makes known to the children
your faithfulness.*

[20]*The Lord will save me,*
and we will play my music on stringed instruments
all the days of our lives,
at the house of the Lord.

[21]*Now Isaiah had said, "Let them take a cake of figs and apply it to the boil, that he may recover."* [22]*Hezekiah also had said, "What is the sign that I shall go up to the house of the Lord?"*

a Or *live;* also verses 9, 21 **b** Hebrew *to your days* **c** The meaning of the Hebrew verse is uncertain **d** Or *In the quiet* **e** Or (with Targum) *I cried for help*

Overview: Similar to the previous chapter, the Reformers find in this chapter opportunity to explain various aspects of prayer and prophecy. In particular, they remark on what appears to be God changing his mind in response to Hezekiah's prayer and how God's threat could still be true when it did not actually come to pass. Several offer explanations about different kinds of prophecies. They also seem to be compelled to clarify some of Hezekiah's words in his prayers, particularly what appears to be a claim of his own merit. In applying these texts to their own time, they identify right ways that signs and miracles can be received to strengthen one's faith, and they point out the legitimate use of medicine for God to cure and heal people. The Reformation interpreters also address life after death based on some of the phrases in Hezekiah's prayers.

38:1-8 *Prophecy About Hezekiah's Sickness*

The Example of Hezekiah. Heinrich Bullinger: And so this chapter is summed up in two parts. For in the beginning the king's sickness and what happened with that is explained. Then how he behaved when he was healed and gave thanks to God. This history is not only pleasant to hear but also very useful; in fact, it is always necessary for each of us. For since we are all mortal and wait for hours to be called by God from this life, and since we, too, are subject to many various diseases and are already caught by these and others, what, I ask, is more useful and necessary for us than to have a certain instruction and a living example where we learn exactly how to prepare ourselves for death or how to conduct ourselves when facing our sicknesses? This is what we learn in the beautiful example of Hezekiah. Sermons on Isaiah 38:1-8.[1]

Conditional Prophecy. Martin Borrhaus: Finally, we learn that not all divine sentences and threats are immutable and infallible, as the threats issued to the Ninevites and to Hezekiah teach clearly enough about their lives being ended. This does not mean that God is mutable, if things he announces by his prophets are not fulfilled. For there is a difference among the prophetic statements of God. Some are pronounced simply, without any qualification or condition, such as the statements about the Canaanites being destroyed; about the changing of kingdoms in this world, and the reign and rule over all things being given to the Messiah; about the kingdom of the antichrist being abolished; about the liberating of the elect by the seed of the woman, the Messiah; about writing a new law in the hearts of those who are written in the book of life; about the renewal of the world and the resurrection of the dead; about the judgment of the living and the dead according to the book of the gospel. All these sentences are pronounced without qualification.

Then there are divine sentences that are given with conditions, such as the sentence that was issued concerning the destruction of the people of Nineveh, "unless they repented." This is likewise the kind of threatening given to Hezekiah, "You shall die," which had the implicit qualification,

[1]Bullinger, *Isaias,* 181r.

"Unless you are granted an answer to your prayers and weeping so that you will not die." Oracles in Isaiah on 38:1.[2]

Two Kinds of Prophecy. Johannes Brenz: But some wonder what is intended by this, because the prophet says by the word of God that Hezekiah is going to die from this sickness, and yet later this sentence of God is retracted. God is not changeable, is he? The prophets do not predict changeable and uncertain things, do they? But it is said most truly in other passages, "I am God, and I do not change." And again, "The victor of Israel will not spare words and will not be moved to repentance. For he is not a man that he should repent."

Since this is so, the Jews say there are two kinds of prophecies. For one is to predict adversity. They say that this kind is changed if the people are changed and respond. This was the kind of prophecy Jonah made about the destruction of Nineveh. But the other is to prophesy prosperity. Accordingly, if a prophet foretells prosperity to anyone and that does not come to pass, they say that he is a false prophet. Commentary on Isaiah 38:1.[3]

The Reason for Hezekiah's Illness. Johannes Oecolampadius: Some say that the reason for his illness was that he delayed to take a wife, but that is not evident, for the law does not prescribe within how many years one ought to take a wife. Hence I think the illness was sent by God for testing and strengthening Hezekiah as well as the faith of others. And see how there are many things with which the righteous king is burdened at the same time. Commentary on Isaiah 38:1.[4]

Visiting the Sick. Abraham Scultetus: Question: But are we truly bound to perform the same duty of visitation when the plague is raging? Response: This is a matter of great debate among most people. But love does not dispute many things; instead it provides many things, though not without prudence. For as alms are given but the distributions depend on the circumstances—how much, when, and who is to be blessed—so also one visits the diseased at the most necessary time. Let it be the rule, then, that no one rushes to those whom the plague has infected with a kind of impudent confidence or rashness, but if necessity requires it, everyone is bound to do what is charitable. If the sheep desires comfort, the shepherd will not run away. If the patient implores the doctor for help, the doctor will provide it. A household will do the same. The same for whoever else.

For if you knew someone lies ill at home, seized by a contagious disease, deserted by all, truly these and other things would help you—what if you were able to help the person? Perhaps that person could be restored. Unless you do what the soul says, you sin entirely. The early Christians received this praise from their enemies, because in the time of the plague, they performed services of charity not only for themselves but also for the Gentiles. See Eusebius.[†]

Objection: But everyone is closer to themselves, and love begins with oneself. Response: This is the way the scholastics argue with reason. Scripture is different. "By this we know the love of God, that he laid down his life for us. Therefore, we ought to lay down our lives for our brothers." . . .

But death is to be feared. Response: Although Christ knew that he was going on his final journey to his impending death, yet he went there for our sake. We must do the same. Edit: However, the sick and Christians themselves should have consideration toward the healthy so that if some are a little more timid or if they have numerous young children, they can be spared so much—and the same for ministers of the church, especially if there are few in any one place. But this does not require many details of rules. For where true love binding people together is found, one's conscience will dictate to each one what needs to be done. On Visitation. Sermon Ideas on Isaiah 38:1.[5]

[2]Borrhaus, *In Iesaiae Prophetae Oracula*, 331.
[3]Brenz, *Esaias*, 510; citing Mal 3:6; 1 Sam 15:29 from the Vulgate.
[4]Oecolampadius, *In Iesaiam*, 204v.

[5]Scultetus, *Idea Concionum*, 496; citing 1 Jn 3:16. [†]Eusebius, *Ecclesiastical History* 7.22.6-10 (*NPNF*[2] 1: 306-307).

Endurance Through Continuous Afflictions. John Calvin: So it appears that not long after the fourteenth year, Hezekiah suffered from this disease. It is only doubtful whether he fell ill at the same time as the siege. It seems to me, at least, a more probable conjecture that he fell into the disease when he was released from the siege. . . . In doubtful matters, therefore, let us follow what is more probable, namely that the godly king, having been delivered from the enemy, is attacked by disease and is in great danger. Yet it is not without reason that our attention is also directed to an almost uninterrupted succession of events, that we may know that he scarcely had space to breathe but, after having scarcely reached the shore from one shipwreck, suddenly fell into another equally dangerous.

Let us therefore remember that believers must endure various temptations, so that they are assailed sometimes by wars, sometimes by diseases, sometimes by other calamities, and sometimes one calamity follows another in unbroken succession, and they are laid under the necessity of maintaining uninterrupted warfare during their whole life; so that, when they have escaped from one danger, they are on the eve of enduring another. They ought to be prepared in such a manner, that when the Lord shall be pleased to add sorrow to sorrow, they may bear it patiently and may not be discouraged by any calamity. If any respite be allowed, let them know that this is granted for their weakness, but let not a short truce lead them to form a false imagination of a lengthened peace; let them make additional exertions until, having finished the course of their earthly life, they arrive at the peaceful harbor. Commentary on Isaiah 38:1.[6]

Not Appealing to His Own Righteousness. Johannes Oecolampadius: The Pelagians twist this passage that he is trusting in works and so teaches that another part of hope is our works, to which we should look so we do not despair. But this is deception. For if we go before the Lord in judgment, who will stand? Who will boast that one's heart is free from sins? Surely our hope must be placed in the Lord alone, who is our righteousness and redemption. So the sense of these words is, "O Lord, because you have granted me to live before you righteously, if I die now, will not some of your glory diminish, and will you not be blasphemed by the wicked because you are cruel to your own and there are no rewards for righteousness?" . . .

But God hears prayers and sees tears. Notice that he does not say, "I have seen your works and how you walk," but rather prayer and tears. So let us not trust in our own works and our own righteousness but in divine mercy. For when it says he is heard because of prayers and tears, they are heard not because of his merit but because of divine mercy. Commentary on Isaiah 38:3.[7]

Years and Numbers. Martin Borrhaus: "Behold, I will add fifteen years to your days." But to what days? To the days that the disease would have finished him based on the disposition of causes found in nature—not to the days that the divine mind had appointed from eternity for how long Hezekiah would live. Therefore, these fifteen years complete the number of years already recorded in the journals of God's decrees before the creation of the world and this nature. If you look at our Hezekiah, the blessed Messiah, we are reminded here that his everlasting life, which he would have through his resurrection from the dead on the third day, is signified by seven plus eight. The first of these numbers [seven] is set apart as referring to rest, the second to immovable and stable perfection, since it is a cubic number that is produced by two times two times two. Oracles in Isaiah on 38:5-6.[8]

The Time of the Prophecy. Heinrich Bullinger: The time designated when the king was caught with this destructive disease is, as I said,

[6]CTS 15:151-52* (CO 36:645-46).

[7]Oecolampadius, *In Iesaiam*, 205r.

[8]Borrhaus, *In Iesaiae Prophetae Oracula*, 332.

in those days of the Assyrian war. I see that the views of interpreters vary here, but the matter itself seems to be expressed sufficiently in the Scriptures. In fact, it is plain that Hezekiah reigned for twenty-nine years. It is also clearly handed down that the Assyrian war broke out during Hezekiah's fourteenth year. And it is no less plain that the fifteen years added to the king's life from the time of this disease would leave fourteen years remaining if you take that from the total of Hezekiah's twenty-nine-year reign. Therefore, in the fourteenth year of the king, the king was sick around the time the Assyrian war began. What does the Lord say among the other words spoken? "And I will deliver you and this city out of the hand of the king of Assyria." So it is consistent that the disease impaired this king at the beginning of the war and not after the war. Sermons on Isaiah 38:4-6.[9]

The Age of Hezekiah. Dietrich Schnepff: For naturally the life of Hezekiah ought to be prolonged for many years. In fact, from the sacred history we can make the conjecture that Hezekiah, when he was being disciplined with this illness, was in the thirty-ninth year of his life. For he began to reign in the twenty-fifth year of his life, as is written . . . , and he reigned twenty-nine years, as the same book includes. He became sick in the fourteenth year of his rule, which added to twenty-five makes thirty-nine years, which is nearly in the middle part of a human life, if the sum of the time of life is calculated to eighty years, as is according to the psalm. Scholia on Isaiah 38:5.[10]

Correcting Errors About Death. Adam Sasbout: From this passage the error of Origen is refuted, who said that souls were detained in the body on account of sins committed in another life. For if to live in the body is condemnation, how (says Jerome) does the Lord give as a kindness to one who would have been released fifteen more years living in a prison? At the same time, the question of fate is solved, and the bounds and causes of necessity, because a day of death is by no means fixed for each person, but by the will of God and by causes unknown to mortals either a person lives or dies, especially since the necessity of a stated death is now postponed. . . .

"On the dial of Ahaz." Kings usually have their own dials. The interpreters, however, think variously about this dial. For some think that the lines were so distinct that the shadow of the sun touching the line would make only a half-hour. So then, according to these days, it was not prolonged for more than ten hours, namely, five when sun was retreating toward the east, and five when the sun returned to that point from which it had begun to retreat. But others are of the opinion that it did not make a half but a full hour. According to them, that day was prolonged by twenty hours. And this is the opinion of Dionysius the Areopagite,[†] chief of the theologians, in his letter to Polycarp, who should be believed in this matter, as one who was instructed by the apostle Paul. Commentary on Isaiah 38:5-8.[11]

Signs Can Strengthen Faith. Rudolf Gwalther: In fact, as the ungodly and reprobate ask for signs out of distrust in order to tempt God (which we read that the Pharisees did more than once to Christ), or even when God freely offers them those signs, they wickedly reject them (which Ahaz once did), so the elect, aware of their own weakness, sometimes ask for signs to be given them to be strengthened in their faith. Examples of this are found in Gideon and Moses, whom Hezekiah righteously imitates at this time. And this was not displeasing to the Lord, as is evident from the words of Isaiah, who said to him, "This shall be the sign to you from the Lord, that the Lord will do this thing that he has promised: behold, I will

[9]Bullinger, *Isaias*, 181r-v.

[10]Schnepff, *In Esaiae*, 562; citing 2 Chron 29; Ps 90:10.

[11]Sasbout, *In Esaiam*, 276. [†]See "Letter VII," in *The Works of Dionysius the Areopagite*, trans. John Parker (London, 1897), 147-48. Pseudo-Dionysius lived in the late fifth and early sixth century, but his works were written as if they were composed by Dionysius from the first century.

make the shadow cast by the declining sun on the dial of Ahaz turn back ten steps." SERMONS ON ISAIAH 38:7.[12]

FAITH SEES THE ILLOGICAL MADE POSSIBLE. CATHARINA REGINA VON GREIFFENBERG: Oh, blessed is the one who, at the instigation of God, believed things most derided by the world, things that appeared to be nonsensical foolishness, and blessed is the one who suffered all manner of scorn and reproach for it, one who finally triumphs with success and sees all derision prostrated. The greatest bliss on earth that could be thought up by all wise people, indeed, by those very angels, is to gain through faith a victory thought impossible by all the world; the unnatural rock basin supplies the sweetest nectar of victory; the Israelite walls of the Red Sea please me more than all seven wonders of the world because they are the triumphant proof of possible impossibility. The course of the sun, which renews and rejoices the world, is never so pleasant to me as its standing still, halted by Joshua's faith, and its resuming its course upon Hezekiah's demand. The most pleasant things are those impossibilities achieved through faith. MEDITATIONS ON THE INCARNATION OF JESUS CHRIST.[13]

THE SIGN OF THE SHADOW. JOHANNES BRENZ: Therefore Hezekiah chooses that the shadow should turn back ten steps, or lines, on the dial of Ahaz. Now, it is apparent that the dial was a mural, as they call it, erected vertically, not horizontally. But interpreters dispute what kind of miracle this was. Did the sun itself go back ten hours? If that had happened, they doubt how the methods and tables of astronomers would not be confused by this miracle, when it is evident from their experiment that it remains firm and fixed. Or was this miracle exhibited not in the physical sun itself, but only in the shadow that was projected on to the lines of Ahaz's dial?

There is certainly nothing that God's omnipotence cannot accomplish. And if the sun stood still by divine power under Joshua for a day, that same divine power could also have it go back ten hours under Hezekiah and at the same time have the rule of heavenly motion preserved, or soon restored. But if only the shadow was reversed, that is also a great miracle, sufficient enough to strengthen Hezekiah's faith. But we do not want to be too stubborn in declaring things that Scripture does not clearly teach. COMMENTARY ON ISAIAH 38:7-8.[14]

THE MEANING OF THE MIRACLE. JOHANNES OECOLAMPADIUS: The miracle by itself is great, even if it happened for only a small part of the day. Nevertheless, the sign is fitting, for by "the heat of the sun" we can understand adversities. By these he wishes to signify that as much adversity as there had been so far, so much is going to go backward, that is, it is all going to be removed. Further, it is significant that he says "on the dial of Ahaz," that is, what was indebted to the judgment brought on by the sins of Ahaz.

Finally, this entire history prefigures the mystery of the cross and resurrection of Christ. For Christ is the righteous king who became sick for us and received the judgment of death on the cross. But according to his prayer, it was added to him—and through him to us—fifteen years, that is, all longevity. For he, as the firstborn of the dead, now lives by the seven of this age and will live by the eight of the future age. And the sign was given to Christ and to us, that the adversity brought on us by the first Adam stops and goes backward by this one Jesus Christ. COMMENTARY ON ISAIAH 38:8[15]

THE PRAYER AND THE SONG. TILEMANN HESSHUSIUS: This chapter has two parts. The first is the narration about the most serious sickness of Hezekiah, in which the prophet Isaiah is sent to the king to indicate to him that his

[12]Gwalther, *Isaias*, 233r; citing Mt 12; 16; Is 7; Jude 6; Ex 4.
[13]Greiffenberg, *Meditations*, 214; citing Josh 10:12-14; 2 Kings 20:8-11.
[14]Brenz, *Esaias*, 514.
[15]Oecolampadius, *In Iesaiam*, 206r.

sickness will result in death. But when Hezekiah prays fervently to the Lord and pours out his tears, Isaiah is sent back to him by the command of God to inform him that God is going to add fifteen years to his life. And so that he has a visible sign of this, at the prayer of Isaiah, the sun turns back ten steps, and King Hezekiah is restored to his former health.

The second part is a song of celebration for the wonder of God freeing him from death. Three things happen in this: (1) It commemorates how much anguish clung to him and how close he was to death. (2) It explains what a great kindness the Lord bestowed on him that he was brought back from death itself and God restored him when he was beyond all hope of life. It teaches that he was made alive by the word of God, that nothing is obtained by his merit, but rather the Lord bestowed all things on him out of immense love, and that God even forgave all his sins. (3) It teaches the purpose for which he was preserved by God in life and by what duty he wants to declare his gratitude to such a merciful God. It was not for the purpose of living in safety, flowing in leisure, and indulging in pleasures that he was brought back from death, but rather that he celebrate the name of God, that is, his mercy, compassion, righteousness, power, wisdom, truth, and that he help build up the church, teach heavenly doctrine to children, and extend it to future generations. Commentary on Isaiah 38.[16]

38:9-22 *Hezekiah's Song of Response*

The Spirit-Inspired Hezekiah. Heinrich Bullinger: The title is written first, indicating the author of what follows and the connecting argument. "A writing of King Hezekiah." Therefore the author of this is King Hezekiah, inspired by the Holy Spirit of God. He not only gives thanks to God with words, but he transmits to posterity in writing what was commanded. Moreover, it is shown that he composed this at the time he had been sick and was restored to health again. Accordingly, this is a psalm of rejoicing or a song of thanksgiving, in which he explains how much he was afflicted with diseases, how much danger he was in, how much he was enveloped with calamities, and how the goodness of the Lord delivered him from all those things. It is in his name that Hezekiah rightly gives and wants to give the greatest perpetual thanks. That is the reason for this song. Sermons on Isaiah 38:9.[17]

Pray for Physical Things Too. Johannes Brenz: Then you have an example in these prayers that it is allowed for us to call on God not only for spiritual and heavenly goods but also for physical and earthly goods. For there are many who are so superstitious that they dare not ask God for even moderate provisions—and in the Lord's Prayer, by the phrase "daily bread," they do not understand physical bread but heavenly bread. But the example of Hezekiah refutes their superstition. Commentary on Isaiah 38.[18]

The Gates of the Dead. Wolfgang Musculus: "I walk to the gates of the grave." I consider that after he received the sentence of death, he turned to the wall and prayed to the Lord between tears and weeping; he muttered out of the swelling of his heart within him and said, "Do I therefore walk to the gates of the grave?" That is, "Am I then dying, to be taken from this life and forced to migrate to the underworld?" He refers to the gates as a tomb by which one descended to the underworld, that is, to the state and fate of the dead, as regards the body. For the grave is not a gate for the spirit, by which it returns to the one from whom it was given. The Hebrews, whom those among us also follow, identify two realms of the dead, that is, two receptacles for souls after this life: the upper realm of the dead, where the righteous are, and the lower, where the souls of the wicked and reprobate

[16]Hesshusius, *In Prophetam Jesaiam*, 322.

[17]Bullinger, *Isaias*, 184r.

[18]Brenz, *Esaias*, 514-15.

are. So what is said here about Hezekiah refers to the upper realm. . . .

We think it is simpler that, since Hezekiah does not speak about the gates of limbo where souls are kept, but "of the grave" where bodies are buried, we should assign these words to the grave. Then the sense is, "I, therefore, walk and approach the grave, of whose gates I have now become a neighbor. I am dying and I will soon be buried." So he protests that he is already near death and the grave—in fact, he is walking and the direction is to the grave. But it is not without reason that "the gates of the grave" are ascribed. A metaphorical saying is recorded for the multitude of those dying, which the grave receives through its many and wide gates every day throughout the world. COMMENTARY ON ISAIAH 38:10.[19]

TEARS ACCOMPANY PRAYERS OF THE STRONG. HEINRICH BULLINGER: Weeping, and even the most intense weeping, accompanied Hezekiah's prayers; in fact, he poured out his prayer with weeping. The Psalms and some passages of the Prophets also declare that the weeping poured out from a faithful, concerned, and contrite heart is acceptable to God. Tears are not unsuitable for a good and strong man. On the contrary, it is customary to say that good men are easy to tears. How often do we read that David, the strongest and bravest man in Israel, wept? Indeed, more than once we read that Christ himself, the Lord of the universe, wept. Yet let our tears be the blood of a conquered and wounded soul, and even pricked by the Spirit of God, but let them not be the tears of crocodiles. SERMONS ON ISAIAH 38:3, 13-14.[20]

TWO WAYS OF BEHOLDING DEATH. THOMAS COOPER: By these words it may appear in what way Hezekiah beheld death and why he showed himself so pensive about it—namely, because he thought he was out of favor with God and therefore in the danger of hellfire. For death indeed is terrible to those who consider themselves to be in such a situation. But to those who in strength of faith behold it joined with the favor of God, it is very pleasant, and therefore Paul said, "I desire to depart and to be with Christ." FIRST SUNDAY AFTER CHRISTMAS AT EVENING PRAYER.[21]

GOD HAS SPOKEN TO ME. JOHANNES BRENZ: And interpreters explain variously what follows: "Lord, if one lives this way, and in all these is the life of my spirit." Indeed, even a moderate learner of Hebrew recognizes the terms in the sayings, but the arrangement of the phrase is not known to anyone, especially to those educated in a foreign language. We will therefore divine it ourselves and follow to some extent the interpretation of our teacher, Doctor Martin Luther.

Hezekiah already sang about the years added to his life. He therefore continues to speak of these things. "Lord," he says, "these," namely, the years, "will be lived," that is, the days of my life will be. And according to all that has happened between them is "the life of my spirit," that is, the fifteen years promised to me by the word of the Lord. "I therefore believe that it will be certain that my life will last that long, and so all the other things that have been done in this matter—clearly, the miracle and other kindnesses of God—truly refresh my soul and restore my spirit. Before my spirit had almost completely failed, but now it has been restored to me by all those kindnesses which God has granted to me in this matter." And he adds, "You will lay hold of me and make me live," which is what was translated from, "You made my dreams reality and made me live," that is, "Although you instilled in me a most grievous dream, clearly, that I thought I was going to die and pretty much perish forever, yet you revived me and restore me again." COMMENTARY ON ISAIAH 38:16.[22]

LIFE FROM GOD'S WORD. HEINRICH BULLINGER: Next he proclaims the power of the

[19]Musculus, *In Esaiam*, 537.
[20]Bullinger, *Isaias*, 183v.
[21]Cooper, *Brief Exposition*, 43v*; citing Phil 1:21.
[22]Brenz, *Esaias*, 521-22.

divine word. My Lord, it says, "By these is one alive, and in all these is the life of my spirit," that is, from these your most truthful promises does one live, and my spirit received life from all your words. Therefore he says that he believed the word of God and in that, or by that, he lived again. For God, who is our life, makes us alive, and by his word he offers himself to us in such a way that if we receive him by true faith, we will live. Others interpret this passage differently. He adds above, "You are the one who consigned me to sickness and healed me from that sickness again. By you, therefore, I live." Sermon on Isaiah 38:16.[23]

Favor and Forgiveness. Dietrich Schnepff: Now Hezekiah conveys another praise to the Lord, because he turned what was most bitter into peace, that is, to a sweet life. For when it is recorded that the Lord brought him up from the grave, he became more certain of God's will and mercy, with the greatest sweetness of mind. For this miracle was the greatest sign of the Lord's favor. Another point is added to this written praise (*encomium*) because he now feels consolation in his heart and conscience: the Lord forgave his sins. And he speaks this with an anthropopathism,† "The Lord cast sins behind his back," for this is a human gesture to throw away in the back what you wish to forget. Many things are very usefully learned from these matters: that the afflictions of the righteous also work together for good, and that we ask the Lord for tangible joy from adverse and sad situations. Then we see that saints are also sinners, because in this passage Hezekiah openly admits that he is a sinner. Scholia on Isaiah 38:17.[24]

Body and Soul Celebrate the Lord. Martin Borrhaus: You might say that the soul of the one who glorifies the Lord outlives the body in the grave. That one indeed glorifies, but not as a whole person praising the Lord in the church "in the land of the living." And Hezekiah is speaking about the whole person, not just a part. Yet it is not the soul alone that composes a person, but body and soul. For that is what we read in the book on the origin of the world, "Let us make humanity in our image, after our likeness." There he is not speaking about the soul as what is created in the image of God, nor about the body; but about the nature that is forged from body and soul, as we have demonstrated in the published commentaries on Moses. That nature was composed in such a way that not only the soul should become a partaker in the glory of the heavenly kingdom, but also the body, by raising it from the dust of the earth and conforming it to the glorious body of Christ. He is the image of God the Father, after whom a person is fashioned, restoring it in body, feeling, mind, and sacred spirit. Oracles in Isaiah on 38:10-11, 18.[25]

A Different Kind of Purgatory. Johannes Brenz: Indeed, this is rightly said about purgatory, if one understands that it is not about the papal purgatory that the pontiffs pretend to be a satisfactory punishment for sins after this life. Rather, this is about the pains of hell that commonly affect the righteous in this life. For it should be realized that while only the wicked and those rejected by God are cast into the perpetual fire of suffering after this life, yet in this physical life, it is often common that not only the wicked but also the righteous are cast before the horrors of perpetual death and the pains of hell.

But there is a great difference—of course, not in the sense of suffering, which is most grave to both, but in the manner of bearing it and in its end. For the wicked are so chastised by the horrors of death and hell that they also give up on salvation and remain perpetually liable to those things. And these horrors are truly called the flames of the fire of hell. . . . And these horrors among the righteous are also the flames of the fire of hell, but because

[23]Bullinger, *Isaias*, 185r.

[24]Schnepff, *In Esaiae*, 565. †*Anthropopathism* is a figure of speech that refers to the attribution or ascription of human emotions or feelings to a non-human being, such as God.

[25]Borrhaus, *In Iesaiae Prophetae Oracula*, 337-38; citing Gen 1:26.

their hope is in salvation and future liberation, these fires are rightly called a purgatory. Examples are Job, David, Jonah, Hezekiah, and Christ the Son of God himself. Therefore, today let us hear Hezekiah sing to us about the flames of the fire of his hell, or rather his purgatory. COMMENTARY ON ISAIAH 38:17-18.[26]

NO PLACE FOR REPENTANCE AFTER DEATH. JOHANNES OECOLAMPADIUS: A person is made to praise God; and what praise is there to God if that person is buried? For hell is also sometimes called "a pit" and "the grave." I will praise God much more by being alive. Truly, since he said before, "You have cast all my sins behind your back," it corresponds that we explain this to be about repentance. We confess and repent while we still live in our bodies. For here is the place of repentance and the purification of souls, and not the place where either rest is promised or eternal punishment.

So afterward, "death will not praise you"—not because souls do not praise the Lord after death but because repentance is over after death. Also consider here why saints are so passionate about this life—of course, so that they may glorify God more. And they not only glorify God, but they also teach others the truth, and not just for one day but continually for all the days of their lives. But in the house of the Lord is that place where the Lord wants to be praised, that is, according to the command and will of the Lord, not as we see fit. COMMENTARY ON ISAIAH 38:17-19.[27]

THE DEAD AND THE LIVING. HECTOR PINTO: "Because hell will not confess you." That is, those who are tormented in hell. So it says in the psalm, "Because in death there is no remembrance of you. And in hell, who will confess you?" And in another psalm, "The dead do not praise you Lord, nor all who descend into hell." By "death" also understand as the same as hell. For death is Tartarus, and those who dwell in there for eternal punishment are called "the dead." Hell is also referred to as "the pit," to where the wicked descend, where they expect no blessing from God because there is no redemption in hell. "The living, the living, confesses you." A dead person does not praise you, Lord, in this life, but the one who lives raises praises to you, and if you give one children, one instructs them, teaching them your law, so that they observe it and pursue you with singular love. COMMENTARY ON ISAIAH 38:18.[28]

THE DIAL DOES NOT MOVE. JOHN TRAPP: Those who live a natural life, if they live with all the life of grace, then they are living alive and not dead while they live. For the wicked cannot praise God. They can say thanks to God, and that is all. But as it is with the hands on a clock when the finger of the dial stands at twelve and the minute hand has not moved one minute, so although their tongues issue forth praises, yet their hearts stand still. What they do this way is but dead work. EXPOSITION ON ISAIAH 38:19.[29]

THREE DESCRIPTIONS OF THE SAME ACTION. SEBASTIAN CASTELLIO: "The buried do not preach faithfulness." It seems that the letters written have been transposed, *yśbrw* for *ybśrw*,[†] so that here there are three words with the same idea: give thanks, praise, and preach faithfulness. And they likewise correspond to the three stated terms on the same matter, which are "Sheol," "the dead," and "the buried." ANNOTATIONS ON ISAIAH 38:18.[30]

THE PROPHET GIVES THE MEDICINE. MARTIN BORRHAUS: In the history of Kings, it is included, "And Isaiah said, 'Bring a cake of figs,'" which when they had brought it, they put it on the boil, and he was cured. This indicates that God in treating Hezekiah's boil did not disregard medicine, which

[26]Brenz, *Esaias*, 517.
[27]Oecolampadius, *In Iesaiam*, 207v-208r.
[28]Pinto, *In Esaiam*, 319; citing Ps 6:5; 115:17 (113 in the Vulgate).
[29]Trapp, *Commentary or Exposition*, 127*.
[30]Castellio, *Adnotationes*, 71. [†]The first spelling translates to "wait or hope," as most English translations today have; the second would translate to "bring good news or preach," as Castellio suggests here.

was made from figs, and that Isaiah supplied the medicine. For it is probable that the priests and prophets were trained and educated in the knowledge that is sought from what is hidden and concealed in nature. For they were teachers of the law of Moses, part of which deals with ceremonies that determine the treatment of needs in this visible world. These include metals, salts, gems, herbs, plants, trees and their fruits, and various kinds of living things that are contained on the land, in the water, and in the air. Oracles in Isaiah on 38:21.[31]

God the Physician Uses Medicine. Heinrich Bullinger: First, Isaiah had commanded them to bring medicine to the sick king. This was a bandage composed of crushed figs, and they put it on the boil. Medicine is commended to us in this matter, which no one should reject as the care and help of God, as we hear from some who boast rashly, "I do not want physicians or surgeons to come near me when I am sick. For I do not need them because I acknowledge God as my physician. And if he does not heal me, then the medics labored in vain." Surely God alone does heal us, but he uses means in healing our diseases, just as he does in feeding and clothing our bodies.

Yet in the same way that too much should not be attributed to the means and the glory due God be transferred to them, so the ordination of God and the course of nature should not be despised, nor the Lord be tempted. But rather, it must be recognized that God, to whom all glory is due, works through those means. If he did not want us to be restored to health, he would remove medicine. Sermons on Isaiah 38:21.[32]

The Placement of the Last Verses. Dietrich Schnepff: I believe that these words were annotated in the margins from the books of Kings. For they were omitted above in the recitation of the history, and so perhaps they were designated to be inserted into the history, which otherwise would seem mutilated unless they were added. That chronological order was not heeded in this commemoration is certain from this chapter, since this is said by Isaiah after Hezekiah sang this song about being restored to health. He orders a cake of figs to be applied, because they say that figs are useful for hastening sores. Or at least they point a finger toward the histories that exist in Kings and Chronicles. Scholia on Isaiah 38:21-22.[33]

[31]Borrhaus, *In Iesaiae Prophetae Oracula*, 339; citing 2 Kings 20:7.

[32]Bullinger, *Isaias*, 186v.

[33]Schnepff, *In Esaiae*, 566.

39:1-8 Envoys from Babylon

39 At that time Merodach-baladan the son of
Baladan, king of Babylon, sent envoys with
letters and a present to Hezekiah, for he heard that he
had been sick and had recovered. 2*And Hezekiah*
welcomed them gladly. And he showed them his
treasure house, the silver, the gold, the spices, the
precious oil, his whole armory, all that was found in
his storehouses. There was nothing in his house or in
all his realm that Hezekiah did not show them. 3*Then*
Isaiah the prophet came to King Hezekiah, and said
to him, "What did these men say? And from where
did they come to you?" Hezekiah said, "They have
come to me from a far country, from Babylon." 4*He*
said, "What have they seen in your house?" Hezekiah
answered, "They have seen all that is in my house.
There is nothing in my storehouses that I did not
show them."
5*Then Isaiah said to Hezekiah, "Hear the word of*
the LORD of hosts: 6*Behold, the days are coming,*
when all that is in your house, and that which your
fathers have stored up till this day, shall be carried to
Babylon. Nothing shall be left, says the LORD. 7*And*
some of your own sons, who will come from you,
whom you will father, shall be taken away, and they
shall be eunuchs in the palace of the king of Babylon."
8*Then Hezekiah said to Isaiah, "The word of the*
LORD that you have spoken is good." For he thought,
"There will be peace and security in my days."

Overview: This brief chapter concludes the account of Hezekiah with the visit from the messengers of Babylon. The Reformers again emphasize the godly example of Hezekiah and that Isaiah the prophet was sent to preach a difficult word. Some of them acknowledge Hezekiah's failure and articulate why Scripture includes stories of failure such as this one. But they also identify Hezekiah as one who repents, sometimes comparing him with King David after being confronted by the prophet Nathan. A few interpreters draw broader application from this passage that it is more difficult to remain faithful to God during times of prosperity. This passage also concludes one of the major divisions of the entire book, no matter how a certain interpreter had organized and divided the book of Isaiah.

Continuing the Account. Dietrich Schnepff: This chapter deals with the next affairs of this king, just as was said before about his adversities in the previous chapter. First, therefore, by the kindness of the Lord, he enjoyed good and even certain health at that time, because his life was extended fifteen years. Second, he was very wealthy. For it is said that he revealed his treasures to the Babylonian ambassadors, which he certainly would not have done unless he thought they were the greatest. But how much were his riches is written at length [elsewhere]. For the sake of brevity I will not transcribe that passage here. Also his fame and celebrity are described. For the fame of his miracle spread all the way to Chaldea, as is testified [there] such that the ambassadors were sent to inquire about that great miracle. Scholia on Isaiah 39.[1]

39:1-4 *Hezekiah Displays His Treasures*

The Agenda of the Babylonian Envoy. Rudolf Gwalther: When they had learned what had happened because of Hezekiah, whose fame was most distinguished on account of the recent defeat of the Assyrians, Merodach "sent envoys with letters and a present" to congratulate him on his restored health and to ask him about the sign. The history in Chronicles records this reason for that delegation. But there is no doubt that under this pretext, Babylon also sought something else at the

[1]Schnepff, *In Esaiae*, 571; citing 2 Chron 32.

same time. They wanted to solicit a friendship or a treaty with Hezekiah. They knew he would be afraid of the Assyrians himself and that by an alliance he could solidify his kingdom with the Babylonians. This was the occasion of the history when several things happened. These should not be observed sleepily. Sermons on Isaiah 39:1.[2]

The Reason for Hezekiah's Gladness. Wolfgang Musculus: Now, why Hezekiah is glad about them is not expressed in this passage. There is no doubt that he was glad because of the gifts they had brought. Otherwise, he would not have showed his wealth to them and he would have been a greedy person. And he was not glad for the reason offered to glorify the name of God. For that would have driven him to commemorate and extol the works of God more than to show off his riches. It remains, then, that he was glad because of the celebrity of his own name, which he was seeing made known throughout all the lands. And this is what is read. . . . "But he did not make return according to the benefit done to him, for his heart was raised. . . ." Moreover, he was excessively delighting too much in the friendship of strangers, as if he could be made more secure against Assyria by them in the future. Commentary on Isaiah 39:2.[3]

Why Scripture Includes the Failures. Rudolf Gwalther: Holy Scripture not only preaches the virtues and excellences done by the saints but also describes their failures and vices—not to diminish their reputation but so that we may recognize in them the common viciousness of human nature. Then, by being warned by their examples, we also guard ourselves from falling when we seem to be standing. And here we also use the present history of Hezekiah, who, when he was in the midst of the most serious danger of war oppressing the whole kingdom and having a deadly sickness, he was faithful to God and the people of his country at the same time. Then, as soon as he was rescued from them, he abounded in peace and leisure, as if forgetting what happened to him. And he began to accumulate vices upon vices. Sermons on Isaiah 39:1-4.[4]

The Besetting Sin of Pride. Martin Luther: The prophet has sufficiently described this memorable story, namely that the king was struck with an illness so that his presumption might be cast out. What is there to say? If our life had no reason for desiring death, because of this monster of pride and presumption our life would be detested. For we are all proud and are elevated by the remembrance of a life well lived. This makes us happy, and we rejoice in prosperous and favorable things. That is the highest idolatry. So here the king is extremely lifted up in his boasting and having established a good government. He recalled the memory of the defeated king of Assyria, and there again came this monster of pride, which was suppressed by his sickness.

Third, this monster is not yet dead but is again inflated by the envoys and the gifts from the king of Babylon. What else is there to say? Ambition, presumption, boasting, and *philautia* [self-love] are a great monster in this life, which is a plague cultivated in every person's life, and especially old people. Lust ravages young people. Greed inflames the old. Beyond this comes the perpetual passion of ambition, in which our entire life is beset. What shall I say? All periods of our life are beset by the most ungodly sins. Therefore it is not evil for us to be oppressed by countless dangers and afflictions. I have asked God daily to free me from this ambition. I shall not avoid it as long as I live. So in this king, this sin could not be overcome, no matter how much it was suppressed by worries. . . .

This king could not be cleansed of the disease by these two extreme trials, and no one has ever been able to surpass him. Therefore we must despair of ourselves and run to Christ and beg him to be gracious. This is a dreadful and accursed sin,

[2]Gwalther, *Isaias*, 240v.
[3]Musculus, *In Esaiam*, 545; citing 2 Chron 32:25.
[4]Gwalther, *Isaias*, 241v.

on account of which death would be desired, so that we might return to ashes as quickly as possible, because here a most godly king could not be cleansed with three cleansings. Lectures on Isaiah 39:1.[5]

Isaiah Sent by God. Heinrich Bullinger: And further it follows after this sin and the occasion of the sin by King Hezekiah how the Lord brought back the erring king through his prophet, and the means by which we can be brought back from the way of sinners to the way of righteousness. Clearly, when our merciful Lord sends us prophets, that is, his servants, who place our sin before our eyes by the preaching of God's Word and faithfully inspire us to true repentance, we recognize our sin, willingly surrender ourselves into the hands of God, and pray the petitions that he would forgive us our sins and preserve us by his grace. For the prophet Isaiah is sent by God to King Hezekiah. He rebukes the king here and pronounces a serious punishment for his sin. For the prophet does not go to the king out of some curiosity, but he comes sent by God, just as Nathan was sent by God to David. Sermons on Isaiah 39:3.[6]

39:5-8 *Isaiah's Prophecy*

Intervening Pride. Konrad Pellikan: Isaiah issues the sentence of God. It is not so much about what he did as about the future state of the kingdom that would not happen for a long time. The judgments of God are much different from those of people. Hezekiah wanted to treat his guests kindly, but a certain pride intervened, like with Moses and the rock. Even the saints pray to God for their ignorance. There is no perfect security for us from our consciences. Since it is good to be fearful of our own works apart from God's mercy, what should be judged about works that are obviously bad? Commentary on Isaiah 38:5.[7]

When the Prophecy Will Be Fulfilled. Johannes Brenz: What Isaiah prophesied here was going to happen after a hundred years and be fulfilled under Jeconiah and Zedekiah. Amos, Micah, and the other prophets contemporaneous with Isaiah also agree with this prophecy. This is why from that time it was publicly well-known by the kingdom of Judah that they were also going to be devastated by the Babylonians in the same way that Samaria was devastated by the Assyrians. The main cause of this devastation was idolatry and contempt for the word of God. They were mocking, Scripture says, the messengers of God and paying no attention to their words, and they were ridiculing the prophets. But in this passage, Isaiah also commemorates another reason, namely that God punishes the exhibition of riches, treasures, and human magnificence with a plundering enemy. So observe that God most seriously punishes the arrogance and exhibition of proud people. Commentary on Isaiah 39:6-7.[8]

Why Nothing Is Said About the Temple. Wolfgang Musculus: Now, the question arises here why the prophet made no mention in this prophecy about the vessels of the Lord's temple, since they, too, were to be transferred to Babylon. It can be answered that either King Hezekiah did not show them to the Babylonians, since the prophet only asked him what the Babylonians saw in his house and the king only answered about his vessels and treasures, and consequently that is the extent of what is foretold in this prophecy about would be taken away to Babylon, or that the vessels of the Lord's temple were to be restored by Cyrus, but the vessels of the royal house would not at all. For there is no mention of them later, when it is recounted that the vessels of the Lord's temple were restored by Cyrus. Commentary on Isaiah 38:6-7.[9]

The Consequences on Posterity. Dietrich Schnepff: Now, because the punishment that

[5]LW 16:346-47* (WA 31.2:258).
[6]Bullinger, *Isaias*, 187r.
[7]Pellikan, *Commentaria Bibliorum*, 3:48r.
[8]Brenz, *Esaias*, 531.
[9]Musculus, *In Esaiam*, 547; citing 1 Esdras 1; 6.

Hezekiah deserved is diverted to his posterity, it should not be understood that they were innocent but being punished for this, because they provoked the divine wrath on themselves with greater sins, such as Manasseh the son of Hezekiah, Jehoachin, Jehoachim, and Zedekiah, who were nearly infamous, some for their cruelty and some for their idolatry. Scholia on Isaiah 39:7.[10]

True Repentance and Trust. Johannes Oecolampadius: These are entirely righteous words. Hezekiah is truly repentant and prepared for the flogging of the divine will. This is why you should not listen to those who argue from this passage that Hezekiah should have followed Moses or Paul and chose to become accursed for the people. For the Lord did not say in this passage that he was going to destroy the people but that the treasures were going to be transferred and the children carried into captivity. For he was trusting that these adversities would be useful to the people, for their life to be saved, since he had already discovered in himself how little it profited a sinful man to chase everything in this life. For how much more holy did he live when he was oppressed by a siege, when he was sick, when he was seeing everything disturbed, than now, when he was reigning in peace, having defeated his enemies and recovered his health? Commentary on Isaiah 39:8.[11]

Hezekiah Receives God's Just Punishment. Johannes Brenz: "Only let there be peace and truth in my days," that is, "I acknowledge that I have sinned grievously. That is why the judgment of the Lord that he brought against me and my descendants is good, right, and just. God is truthful; I am a liar. God is just; I am unjust and deserving of far greater punishments than what I am now getting. And although I desire to appease the wrath of God in whatever way possible in order to spare my posterity also, yet since that cannot happen, I give the greatest thanks to God that when he promised me that he would defend me and the city of Jerusalem where I live, he constantly keeps this promise to me, and grants us public peace and tranquility, all the days of my life." This is an example of repentance that, even if the entire physical punishment to be inflicted is not removed in this age on account of the covenant, yet it is mitigated and made tolerable in the present. Commentary on Isaiah 39:8.[12]

Hezekiah Repents. Dietrich Schnepff: The last part of the chapter, although it is short and concise, has the most beautiful praises of Hezekiah. First, he does not receive the words of the prophet in a tyrannical way, but he reveres him as an ambassador of the Lord. For he does not say, "What you have said is good," but rather, "The word of the Lord is good." Then he humbly submits himself to divine chastisement and acknowledges it as just and good. Finally, even in the punishment itself, he acknowledges the mercy of the Lord, because he wishes to suspend the punishment for another time, for the prophet said that the Babylonians would take away his sons. Hezekiah made a conjecture from this that those threats belonged to his posterity, so he says, "May the peace and truth of the Lord be in my days." By "truth," he understands the truthfulness of the promise, which was hidden in the threat itself. Luther thinks that he pleaded for pardon from the punishment during his own time. Scholia on Isaiah 39:8.[13]

Hezekiah's Example About the Future. John Calvin: But it may be thought that Hezekiah was cruel in not caring about his posterity and not giving himself much trouble about what should happen afterward. Such sayings as, "When I am dead, let the earth be committed to the flames," that is, "When I am dead, all are dead," and other sayings of the same kind, which are now

[10]Schnepff, *In Esaiae*, 574.
[11]Oecolampadius, *In Iesaiam*, 210v.
[12]Brenz, *Esaias*, 531-32.
[13]Schnepff, *In Esaiae*, 573.

in the mouths of many swine and Epicureans, are profane and shocking. But Hezekiah's meaning was quite different. For while he wished well to those who should live after him, yet it would have been undutiful to disregard that token of forbearance that God gave by delaying his vengeance. For he might have been led by it to hope that this mercy would in some degree be extended to his posterity.

Some reply that he rejoiced at the delay, because "We ought not to be anxious about tomorrow, since sufficient for the day is its own affliction." But this does not apply to the present passage. For Hezekiah does not disregard his posterity, but, perceiving that God moderates the punishment by forbearance, he gives thanks to God, as we have already said. And although this punishment awaited a future age, still it was his duty to acknowledge the present favor. And indeed we ought to labor most for our own time and to pay our chief regard to it. The future ought not to be overlooked, but what is present and immediate has stronger claim on our services. For we who live at the same time are bound by God with a stronger tie, in order that, by mutual relationship, we may assist each other as far as it is in our power.

It ought likewise to be observed that, while the Lord had formerly promised a lengthened life to Hezekiah, when he was very near death, there was now strong reason to fear that he would again cut short his life on account of that sin. When he is informed that the promise is ratified, he gives thanks to God and bears more patiently the calamity that was to come, though he felt it to be grievous and distressing. Commentary on Isaiah 39:8.[14]

[14]CTS 15:193-94* (CO 36:671-72); citing Mt 6:34.

Map of Europe at the Time of the Reformation

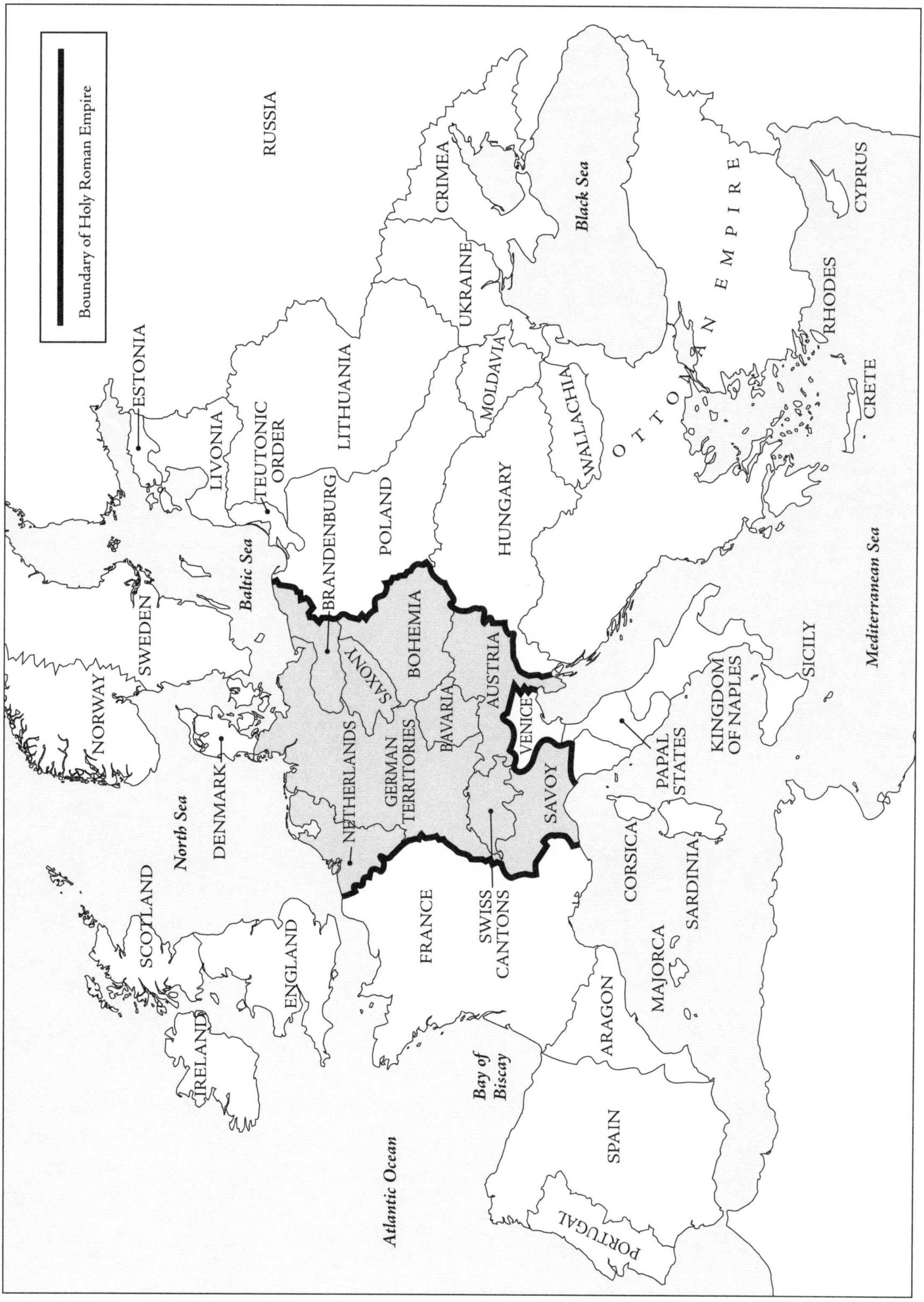

Timeline of the Reformation

	German Territories	France	Spain	Italy	Switzerland	Netherlands	British Isles
1309–1377		Babylonian Captivity of the Papacy					
1337–1453		d. Nicholas of Lyra Hundred Years' War	b. Paul of Burgos (Solomon ha-Levi)(d. 1435) Alonso Tostado (1400–1455)				Hundred Years' War
1378–1415		Western Schism (Avignon Papacy)		Western Schism			
1384							d. John Wycliffe
1414–1418					Council of Basel (1431–1437)		
1415				Council of Constance; d. Jan Hus; Martin V (r. 1417–1431); Council of Florence (1438–1445)			
1450	Invention of printing press						
1452				b. Leonardo da Vinci (d. 1519)			
1453				Fall of Constantinople			
1455–1485	b. Johannes Reuchlin (d. 1522)						War of Roses; rise of House of Tudor
1456	Gutenberg Bible						
1460				Pope Pius II issued *Execrabilis*			
1466		b. Jacques Lefèvre d'Étaples (d. 1536)					
1467						b. Desiderius Erasmus (d. 1536)	b. John Colet (d. 1519)
1469	b. Antoius Broickwy von Königstein (d. 541)						
1470				b. Santes Pagninus (d. 1541)			b. John (Mair) Major (d. 1550)
1475				b. Michelangelo (d. 1564)			
1478	b. Wolfgang Capito (d. 1541)		Ferdinand and Isabella	b. Jacopo Sadoleto (d. 1547)			b. Thomas More (d. 1535)

	German Territories	France	Spain	Italy	Switzerland	Netherlands	British Isles
1480	b. Balthasar Hubmaier (d. 1528); b. Andreas Bodenstein von Karlstadt (d. 1541)						
1481–1530			Spanish Inquisition				
1482					b. Johannes Oecolampadius (d. 1531)		
1483	b. Martin Luther (d. 1546)						
1484	b. Johann Spangenberg (d. 1550)				b. Huldrych Zwingli (d. 1531)		
1485	b. Johannes Bugenhagen (d. 1554)						b. Hugh Latimer (d. 1555)
1486	r. Frederick the Wise, Elector (d. 1525); b. Johann Eck (d. 1543)						
1488	b. Otto Brunfels (d. 1534)						b. Miles Coverdale (d. 1568)
1489	b. Thomas Müntzer (d. 1525); b. Kaspar von Schwenckfeld (d. 1561)						b. Thomas Cranmer (d. 1556)
1491	b. Martin Bucer (d. 1551)		b. Ignatius Loyola (d. 1556)				
1492			Defeat of Moors in Grenada; Columbus discovers America; expulsion of Jews from Spain	Alexander VI (r. 1492–1503)			
1493	b. Justus Jonas (d. 1555)						
1494							b. William Tyndale (d. 1536)
1496	b. Andreas Osiander (d. 1552)					b. Menno Simons (d. 1561)	
1497	b. Philipp Melanchthon (d. 1560); b. Wolfgang Musculus (d. 1563) b. Johannes (Ferus) Wild (d. 1554)						

	German Territories	France	Spain	Italy	Switzerland	Netherlands	British Isles
1498				d. Girolamo Savonarola	b. Conrad Grebel (d. 1526)		
1499	b. Johannes Brenz (d. 1570) b. Justus Menius (d. 1558)			b. Peter Martyr Vermigli (d. 1562)			
1500			b. Charles V (–1558)				
1501	b. Erasmus Sarcerius (d. 1559)						
1502	Founding of University of Wittenberg			Julius II (r. 1503–1513)		b. Frans Titelmans (d. 1537)	
1504					b. Heinrich Bullinger (d. 1575)		
1505	Luther joins Augustinian Order			b. Benedict Aretius (d. 1574)			
1506		b. Augustin Marlorat (d. 1562)		Restoration of St. Peter's begins			
1507				Sale of indulgences approved to fund building			
1508	b. Lucas Lossius (d. 1582)						
1509		b. John Calvin (d. 1564)					r. Henry VIII (–1547)
1510	Luther moves to Rome			b. Immanuel Tremellius (d. 1580)			b. Nicholas Ridley (d. 1555)
1511	Luther moves to Wittenberg						
1512				Sistine Chapel completed			
1512–1517				Fifth Lateran Council; rejection of conciliarism			
1513	Luther lectures on Psalms			r. Pope Leo X (–1521)			b. John Knox (d. 1572)
1515	Luther lectures on Romans	r. Francis I (–1547); b. Peter Ramus (d. 1572)					
1516		Est. French National Church (via Concordat of Bologna)		Concordat of Bologna		Publication of Erasmus's Greek New Testament	
1517	Tetzel sells indulgences in Saxony; Luther's Ninety-five Theses						

	German Territories	France	Spain	Italy	Switzerland	Netherlands	British Isles
1518	Heidelberg Disputation; Luther examined by Cajetan at Diet of Augsburg			Diet of Augsburg			
1519	Leipzig Disputation	b. Theodore Beza (d. 1605)	Cortés conquers Aztecs; Portuguese sailor Magellan circumnavigates the globe		Zwingli appointed pastor of Grossmünster in Zurich; b. Rudolf Gwalther (d. 1586)		
1520	Publication of Luther's "Three Treatises"; burning of papal bull in Wittenberg		Coronation of Charles V	Papal Bull v. Luther: *Exsurge Domine*			
1521	Luther excommunicated; Diet/Edict of Worms—Luther condemned; Luther in hiding; Melanchthon's *Loci communes*	French-Spanish War (–1526)	French-Spanish War; Loyola converts	Papal excommunication of Luther			Henry VIII publishes *Affirmation of the Seven Sacraments* against Luther; awarded title "Defender of the Faith" by Pope
1521–1522	Disorder in Wittenberg; Luther translates New Testament						
1521–1525		First and Second Habsburg–Valois War					
1522	Luther returns to Wittenberg; Luther's NT published; criticizes Zwickau prophets; b. Martin Chemnitz (d. 1586)		Publication of Complutensian Polyglot Bible under Cisneros		Sausage Affair and reform begins in Zurich under Zwingli		b. John Jewel (d. 1571)
1523	Knight's Revolt	Bucer begins ministry in Strasbourg	Loyola writes Spiritual Exercises	r. Pope Clement VII (–1534)	Iconoclasm in Zurich		
1524	Luther criticizes peasants; d. Johann von Staupitz					Erasmus's disputation on free will	
1524–1526	Peasants' War						
1525	Luther marries; execution of Thomas Müntzer; publication of Luther's *Bondage of the Will*				Abolition of mass in Zurich; disputation on baptism; first believers' baptism performed in Zurich		

	German Territories	France	Spain	Italy	Switzerland	Netherlands	British Isles
1526					Zurich council mandates capital punishment of Anabaptists	Publication of Tyndale's English translation of NT	
1527	d. Hans Denck (b. c. 1500) d. Hans Hut (b. 1490) b. Tilemann Hesshus (d. 1588)			Sack of Rome by mutinous troops of Charles V	First Anabaptist executed in Zurich; drafting of Schleitheim Confession		
1528	Execution of Hubmaier						
1529	Second Diet of Speyer; evangelical "protest"; publication of Luther's catechisms; Marburg Colloquy; siege of Vienna by Turkish forces	Abolition of mass in Strasbourg			d. Georg Blaurock (b. 1492)		Thomas More appointed chancellor to Henry VIII
1530	Diet of Augsburg; Confession of Augsburg	d. Francois Lambert (Lambert of Avignon) (b. 1487)	Charles V crowned Holy Roman Emperor				
1531	Formation of Schmalkaldic League				d. H. Zwingli; succeeded by H. Bullinger		
1532		Publication of Calvin's commentary on Seneca; conversion of Calvin	b. Francisco de Toledo (d. 1596)				
1533	b. Valentein Weigel (d. 1588)	Nicholas Cop addresses University of Paris; Cop and Calvin implicated as "Lutheran" sympathizers	b. Juan de Maldonado (d. 1583)				Thomas Cranmer appointed as Archbishop of Canterbury; Henry VIII divorces
1534	First edition of Luther's Bible published	Affair of the Placards; Calvin flees d. Guillame Briçonnet (b. 1470)		Jesuits founded; d. Cardinal Cajetan (Thomas de Vio) (b. 1469)			Act of Supremacy; English church breaks with Rome
1535	Bohemian Confession of 1535; Anabaptist theocracy at Münster collapses after eighteen months				b. Lambert Daneau (d. 1595)		d. Thomas More; d. John Fisher

	German Territories	France	Spain	Italy	Switzerland	Netherlands	British Isles
1536	Wittenberg Concord; b. Kaspar Olevianus (d. 1587)				First edition of Calvin's *Institutes* published; Calvin arrives in Geneva (–1538); First Helvetic Confession	Publication of Tyndale's translation of NT; d. W. Tyndale	d. A. Boleyn; Henry VIII dissolves monasteries (–1541)
1537					Calvin presents ecclesiastical ordinances to Genevan Council		
1538					Calvin exiled from Geneva; arrives in Strasbourg (–1541)		
1539		Calvin publishes second edition of *Institutes* in Strasbourg		d. Felix Pratensis			Statute of Six Articles; publication of Coverdale's Great Bible
1540				Papal approval of Jesuit order			d. Thomas Cromwell
1541	Colloquy of Regensburg	French translation of Calvin's *Institutes* published	d. Juan de Valdés (b. 1500/1510)		d. A. Karlstadt; Calvin returns to Geneva (–1564)		
1542	d. Sebastian Franck (b. 1499)			Institution of Roman Inquisition			War between England and Scotland; James V of Scotland defeated; Ireland declared sovereign kingdom
1543	Copernicus publishes *On the Revolutions of the Heavenly Spheres*; d. Johann Eck (Johann Maier of Eck) (b. 1486)						
1545–1547	Schmalkaldic Wars; d. Martin Luther			First session of Council of Trent			b. Richard Bancroft (d. 1610)
1546	b. Johannes Piscator (d. 1625)						
1547	Defeat of Protestants at Mühlberg	d. Francis I; r. Henri II (–1559)					d. Henry VIII; r. Edward VI (–1553)
1548	Augsburg Interim (–1552) d. Caspar Cruciger (b. 1504) b. David Pareus (d. 1622)						

	German Territories	France	Spain	Italy	Switzerland	Netherlands	British Isles
1549	d. Paul Fagius (b. 1504)	d. Marguerite d'Angoulême (b. 1492)			Consensus Tigurinus between Calvin and Bullinger		First Book of Common Prayer published
1550	b. Aegidius Hunnius (d. 1603)						
1551–1552				Second session of Council of Trent			
1552	d. Sebastian Münster (b. 1488) d. Friedrich Nausea (b. c. 1496)						Book of Common Prayer revised
1553	d. Johannes Aepinus (b. 1449)				Michael Servetus executed in Geneva		Cranmer's Forty-Two Articles; d. Edward VI; r. Mary I (d. 1558)
1554							Richard Hooker (d. 1600)
1555	Diet of Augsburg; Peace of Augsburg establishes legal territorial existence of Lutheranism and Catholicism b. Johann Arndt (d. 1621)	First mission of French pastors trained in Geneva				b. Sibbrandus Lubbertus (d. 1625)	b. Lancelot Andrewes (d. 1626) b. Robert Rollock (d. 1599); d. Hugh Latimer; d. Nicholas Ridley d. John Hooper
1556	d. Pilgram Marpeck (b. 1495) d. Konrad Pellikan (b. 1478) d. Peter Riedemann (b. 1506)		Charles V resigns			d. David Joris (b. c. 1501)	d. Thomas Cranmer
1557							Alliance with Spain in war against France
1558			d. Charles V				b. William Perkins (d. 1602); d. Mary I; r. Elizabeth I (–1603)
1559		d. Henry II; r. Francis II (–1560); first national synod of French reformed churches (1559) in Paris; Gallic Confession		First index of prohibited books issued	Final edition of Calvin's *Institutes*; founding of Genevan Academy	b. Jacobus Arminius (d. 1609)	Elizabethan Settlement

	German Territories	France	Spain	Italy	Switzerland	Netherlands	British Isles
1560	d. P. Melanchthon	d. Francis II; r. Charles IX (1574); Edict of Toleration created peace with Huguenots	d. Domingo de Soto (b. 1494)		Geneva Bible		Kirk of Scotland established; Scottish Confession
1561-1563				Third session of Council of Trent			
1561						Belgic Confession	
1562	d. Katharina Schütz Zell (b. 1497/98)	Massacre of Huguenots begins French Wars of Religion (–1598)					The Articles of Religion—in Elizabethan "final" form (1562/71); publication of Latin edition of Jewel's *Apology*
1563	Heidelberg Catechism						
1564				b. Galileo (d. 1642)	d. J. Calvin		b. William Shakespeare (d. 1616); publication of Lady Ann Bacon's English translation of Jewel's *Apology*
1566	d. Johann Agricola (b. 1494)			Roman Catechism	Second Helvetic Confession		
1567						Spanish occupation	Abdication of Scottish throne by Mary Stuart; r. James VI (1603–1625)
1568						d. Dirk Phillips (b. 1504) Dutch movement for liberation (–1645)	*Bishops' Bible*
1570		d. Johannes Mercerus (Jean Mercier)		Papal Bull *Regnans in Excelsis* excommunicates Elizabeth I			Elizabeth I excommunicated
1571	b. Johannes Kepler (d. 1630)		Spain defeats Ottoman navy at Battle of Lepanto				b. John Downame (d. 1652)
1572		Massacre of Huguenots on St. Bartholomew's Day		r. Pope Gregory XIII (1583–1585)		William of Orange invades	b. John Donne (d. 1631)
1574		d. Charles IX; r. Henri III (d. 1589)					

	German Territories	France	Spain	Italy	Switzerland	Netherlands	British Isles
1575	d. Georg Major (b. 1502); Bohemian Confession of 1575						
1576		Declaration of Toleration; formation of Catholic League		b. Giovanni Diodati (d. 1649)		Sack of Antwerp; Pacification of Ghent	
1577	Lutheran Formula of Concord						England allies with Netherlands against Spain
1578	Swiss Brethren Confession of Hesse d. Peter Walpot		Truce with Ottomans				Sir Francis Drake circumnavigates the globe
1579			Expeditions to Ireland			Division of Dutch provinces	
1580	Lutheran Book of Concord						
1581			d. Teresa of Avila				Anti-Catholic statutes passed
1582				Gregorian Reform of calendar			
1583							b. David Dickson (d. 1663)
1584		Treaty of Joinville with Spain	Treaty of Joinville; Spain inducted into Catholic League; defeats Dutch at Antwerp			Fall of Antwerp; d. William of Orange	
1585	d. Josua Opitz (b. c. 1542)	Henri of Navarre excommunicated		r. Pope Sixtus V (–1590)			
1586							Sir Francis Drake's expedition to West Indies; Sir Walter Raleigh in Roanoke
1587	d. Johann Wigand (b. 1523)	Henri of Navarre defeats royal army					d. Mary Stuart of Scotland
1588		Henri of Navarre drives Henri III from Paris; assassination of Catholic League Leaders	Armada destroyed				English Navy defeats Spanish Armada
1589		d. Henri III; r. Henri (of Navarre) IV (–1610)	Victory over England at Lisbon				Defeated by Spain in Lisbon
1590		Henri IV's siege of Paris		d. Girolamo Zanchi (b. 1516)			Alliance with Henri IV

	German Territories	France	Spain	Italy	Switzerland	Netherlands	British Isles
1592	d. Nikolaus Selnecker (b. 1530)						
1593		Henri IV converts to Catholicism					Books I-IV of Hooker's *Laws of Ecclesiastical Polity* published
1594		Henri grants toleration to Huguenots					
1595		Henri IV declares war on Spain; received into Catholic Church		Pope Sixtus accepts Henri IV into Church			Alliance with France
1596		b. René Descartes (d. 1650) b. Moïse Amyraut (d. 1664)					
1597							Book V of Hooker's *Laws of Ecclesiastical Polity* published
1598		Edict of Nantes; toleration of Huguenots; peace with Spain	Treaty of Vervins; peace with France				
1600	d. David Chytraeus (b. 1531)						
1601							b. John Trapp (d. 1669)
1602					d. Daniel Toussain (b. 1541)		
1603							d. Elizabeth I; r. James I (James VI of Scotland) (–1625)
1604	d. Cyriacus Spangenberg (b. 1528)						d. John Whitgift (b. 1530)
1605						b. Rembrandt (d. 1669)	Guy Fawkes and gunpowder plot
1606							Jamestown Settlement
1607							b. John Milton (d. 1674)
1608							
1610		d. Henri IV; r. Louis XIII (–1643)	d. Benedict Pererius (b. 1535)			The Remonstrance; Short Confession	

	German Territories	France	Spain	Italy	Switzerland	Netherlands	British Isles
1611							Publication of Authorized English Translation of Bible (AV/KJV); George Abbot becomes Archbishop of Canterbury (–1633)
1612							b. Richard Crashaw (d. 1649)
1616							b. John Owen (d. 1683)
1617							b. Ralph Cudworth (d. 1689)
1618–1619						Synod of Dordrecht	
1618–1648	Thirty Years' War						
1620							English Sepratists land in Plymouth, Massachusetts
1621							d. Andrew Willet (b. 1562)
1628							Puritans establish Massachusetts Bay colony
1633	d. Christoph Pelargus (b. 1565)						Laud becomes Archbishop of Canterbury
1637	d. Johann Gerhard (b. 1582)					*Statenvertaling*	
1638							d. Joseph Mede (b. 1638)
1640				Diodati's Italian translation of Bible published			
1642–1649							English civil wars; d. Charles I; r. Oliver Cromwell (1660)
1643		d. Louis XIII; r. Louis XIV (–1715)					
1643–1649							Westminster Assembly
1645							d. William Laud (b. 1573)

	German Territories	France	Spain	Italy	Switzerland	Netherlands	British Isles
1648		Treaty of Westphalia ends Thirty Years' War					Books VI and VIII of Hooker's *Laws of Ecclesiastical Polity* posthumously published
1656	d. Georg Calixtus (b. 1586)						
1658							d. Oliver Cromwell
1659							Richard Cromwell resigns
1660							English Restoration; r. Charles II (–1685)
1662							Act of Uniformity; Book VII of Hooker's *Laws of Ecclesiastical Polity* posthumously published
1664						d. Thieleman Jans van Braght (b. 1625)	d. John Mayer (b. 1583)
1671							d. William Greenhill (b. 1591)
1677							d. Thomas Manton (b. 1620)
1678						d. Anna Maria von Schurman (b. 1607)	
1688							Glorious Revolution; r. William and Mary (-1702); d. John Bunyan (b. 1628)
1691							d. Richard Baxter (b. 1615)

BIOGRAPHICAL SKETCHES OF REFORMATION-ERA FIGURES AND WORKS

This list is cumulative, including all the authors cited in the Reformation Commentary on Scripture to date as well as other people relevant to the Reformation and Reformation-era exegesis. For works consulted, see "Sources for Biographical Sketches," p. 435.

Cornelius À Lapide (1567–1637). Flemish Catholic biblical exegete. A Jesuit, Lapide served as professor of Holy Scripture and Hebrew at Louvain for twenty years before taking a similar role in Rome, where he taught until his death. He is best known for his extensive commentaries on the Scriptures. Encompassing all books of the Bible except Job and the Psalms, his work employs a fourfold hermeneutic and draws heavily on the work of patristic and medieval exegetes.

Thomas Adams (1583–1653). Anglican minister and author. He attended the University of Cambridge where he received his BA in 1601 and his MA in 1606. Following his ordination in 1604, Adams served as curate at Northill in Bedfordshire. In 1611, he became vicar of Willmington. Three years later he served the parish of Wingrave, Buckinghamshire, where he remained until 1618. From 1618 to 1623 Adams was preacher at St. Gregory by St. Paul's. He also served as chaplain to Henry Montague, First Earl of Manchester, and Lord Chief Justice of England. Among his most important works are the *Happiness of the Church* (1618) and an extensive commentary on 2 Peter (1638).

Johannes Aepinus (1499–1553). German Lutheran preacher and theologian. Aepinus studied under Martin Luther,* Philipp Melanchthon* and Johannes Bugenhagen* in Wittenberg. Because of his Lutheran beliefs, Aepinus lost his first teaching position in Brandenburg. He fled north to Stralsund and became a preacher and superintendent at Saint Peter's Church in Hamburg. In 1534, he made a diplomatic visit to England but could not convince Henry VIII* to embrace the Augsburg Confession.* His works include sermons and theological writings. Aepinus became best known as leader of the Infernalists, who believed that Christ underwent torment in hell after his crucifixion.

Johann Agricola (c. 1494–1566). German Lutheran pastor and theologian. An early student of Martin Luther,* Agricola eventually began a controversy over the role of the law, first with Melanchthon* and then with Luther himself. Agricola claimed to defend Luther's true position, asserting that only the gospel of the crucified Christ calls Christians to truly good works, not the fear of the law. After this first controversy, Agricola seems to have radicalized his views to the point that he eliminated Luther's *simul iustus et peccator* ("at the same time righteous and sinful") paradox of the Christian life, emphasizing instead that believers have no need for the law once they are united with Christ through faith. Luther responded by writing anonymous pamphlets against antinomianism. Agricola later published a recantation of his views, hoping to assuage relations with Luther, although they were never personally reconciled. He published a commentary on Luke, a series of sermons on Colossians, and a massive collection of German proverbs.

Henry Ainsworth (1571–1622/1623). English Puritan Hebraist. In 1593, under threat of persecution, Ainsworth relocated to Amsterdam, where he served as a teacher in an English congregation. He composed a confession of faith for the community and a number of polemical and exegetical works, including annotations on the Pentateuch, the Psalms and Song of Songs.

Henry Airay (c. 1560–1616). English Puritan professor and pastor. He was especially noted for his preaching, a blend of hostility toward Catholicism and articulate exposition of English Calvinism. He was promoted to provost of Queen's College Oxford (1598) and then to vice chancellor of the university in 1606. He disputed with William Laud* concerning Laud's putative Catholicization of the Church of England, particularly over the practice of genuflection, which Airay vehemently opposed. He also opposed fellow Puritans who wished to separate from the Church of England. His lectures on Philippians were his only work published during his lifetime.

Albert the Great (1201–1280). German theologian, philosopher, scientist, and ecclesiastic. Albert was born in Lauingen, located in the Bavarian-Swabian region. After completing his studies at Padua, Albert joined the Dominicans in 1220s. Upon finishing further theological studies at Cologne, Albert became a conventual lecturer during the 1230s at Hildesheim, Freiberg (Saxony), Regensburg, and Strasbourg. In the early 1240s, Albert was sent to Paris where he became a master of theology, and regent of the university in 1245. He served as regent until 1248. While at Paris, Albert commenced his paraphrases of Aristotle's works. Furthermore, Albert authored a systematic theology, and lectured on the four Gospels and nine books of the Old Testament. Albert is best known for having taught Thomas Aquinas,* who, as his assistant, transcribed his course on the works of Dionysius and Aristotle's *Nicomachean Ethics*.

Alexander (Ales) Alesius (1500–1565). Scottish Lutheran theologian. Following the martyrdom of his theological adversary Patrick Hamilton (c. 1504–1528), Alesius converted to the Reformation and fled to Germany. In 1535 Martin Luther* and Philipp Melanchthon* sent him as an emissary to Henry VIII* and Thomas Cranmer.* He taught briefly at Cambridge, but after the Act of Six Articles reasserted Catholic sacramental theology he returned to Germany, where he lectured at Frankfurt an der Oder and Leipzig. Alesius composed many exegetical, theological and polemical works, including commentaries on John, Romans, 1–2 Timothy, Titus and the Psalms.

Robert Allen (fl. 1596–1612). English Protestant clergyman and writer. Allen is known only by his writings, which reveal few biographical details except that he was a minister and he wrote from London and Suffolk. His works include a theological summary of Proverbs and Ecclesiastes, an exposition of the Gospel, and a catechism.

Andreas Althamer (c. 1500–1539). German Lutheran humanist and pastor. Forced from the chaplaincy at Schwäbisch-Gmünd for teaching evangelical ideas, Althamer studied theology at Wittenberg before serving as a pastor in Eltersdorf, Nuremberg, and Ansbach. A staunch Lutheran, he contended against Reformed theologians at the 1528 disputation at Bern and delivered numerous polemics against Anabaptism. He also composed an early Lutheran catechism, published at Nuremberg in 1528.

William Ames (1576–1633). English Puritan theologian. Heavily influenced by William Perkins* while at Cambridge, Ames was unable to find employment in the English church due to his Puritan commitments. Most of his life was spent in exile in the Netherlands, where he served as chaplain to English forces at The Hague and was the pastor of a small congregation. Best known as a controversialist during his early career, Ames was the theological advisor to the president of the Synod of Dort (1618–1619) and was later installed as chair of theology at the University of Franeker in Friesland. *The Marrow of Theology* (1627) is viewed as a model of seventeenth-century Puritan theology.

Moïse Amyraut (1596–1664). French Reformed pastor and professor. Originally intending to be a lawyer, Amyraut turned to theology after an encounter with several Huguenot pastors and having read Calvin's* *Institutes*. After a brief stint as a parish pastor, Amyraut spent the majority of his career at the Saumur Academy. He was well known for his irenicism and ecumenicism (for example, in advocating intercommunion with Lutherans). Certain aspects of his writings on justification, faith, the covenants and especially predestination proved controversial among the Reformed. His doctrine of election is often called hypothetical universalism or Amyraldianism, stating that Christ's atoning work was intended by God for all human beings indiscriminately, although its effectiveness for salvation depends on faith, which is a free gift of God given only to those whom God has chosen from eternity. Amyraut was charged with grave doctrinal error three times before the National Synod but was acquitted each time. Aside from his theological treatises, Amyraut published paraphrases of almost the entire New Testament and the Psalms, as well as many sermons.

Anabaptists of Trieste (1539). Following a meeting between Swiss Brethren and the Hutterites at Steinabrunn on December 6, 1536, around 140 radicals were arrested and imprisoned in Falkenstein Castle. After six weeks in captivity, the ninety men of the group were forced to march to Trieste to be sold as galley slaves. Twelve days after arrival, all but twelve prisoners managed to escape and return to Moravia, where they published a confession of their beliefs.

Jakob Andreae (1528–1590). German Lutheran theologian. Andreae studied at the University of

Tübingen before being called to the diaconate in Stuttgart in 1546. He was appointed ecclesiastical superintendent of Göppingen in 1553 and supported Johannes Brenz's* proposal to place the church under civil administrative control. An ecclesial diplomat for the duke of Württemberg, Andreae debated eucharistic theology, the use of images, and predestination with Theodore Beza* at the Colloquy of Montbéliard (1586) to determine whether French Reformed exiles would be required to submit to the Formula of Concord.* Andreae coauthored the Formula of Concord. He and his wife had eighteen children.

Lancelot Andrewes (1555–1626). Anglican bishop. A scholar, pastor and preacher, Andrews prominently shaped a distinctly Anglican identity between the poles of Puritanism and Catholicism. He oversaw the translation of Genesis to 2 Kings for the Authorized Version.* His eight-volume collected works—primarily devotional tracts and sermons—are marked by his fluency in Scripture, the Christian tradition and classical literature.

Thomas Aquinas (1225–1274). Dominican medieval theologian. Thomas Aquinas was born into a noble family in Rocasecca, Italy. In 1230 Thomas's father sent him to the abbey at Monte Casino as a child oblate. When, at age fourteen, Thomas was given the choice between taking his final vows and leaving, he chose to go to Naples to study at the school recently founded by the Holy Roman Emperor. While studying at Naples, Thomas came into contact with the Dominicans, and joined this order in 1244. Although his family objected to his decision at first, to the point of actually imprisoning Thomas, they came to accept his decision the following year. Afterwards, Aquinas traveled to Paris where he began his formal studies under Albert the Great (1200–1280). Aquinas followed his teacher to Cologne in 1248 where he was ordained a priest, and completed his course in theology. Four years later, he was appointed a bachelor in the Dominican convent in Paris where he lectured on Peter Lombard's (1096–1160)* *Sentences*. In 1256, Thomas was incepted as a master of the sacred page, and he taught in Paris until 1259. In 1261, he was appointed lecturer at a school in Orvieto. Four years later, Aquinas was transferred to Rome, and in 1268 returned to Paris. In 1272, the Dominican order appointed Aquinas to start a new school in Naples. A mystical experience reportedly caused Aquinas to abruptly cease his writing. Aquinas died at a monastery in Fossanova. In addition to his major works, *Summa Theologia* and *Summa Contra Gentiles,* Aquinas's voluminous corpus includes extensive commentaries on Jeremiah, Lamentations, Isaiah, Job, and an incomplete one on the Psalms. Aquinas also wrote commentaries on the Gospels of Matthew and John as well as the Pauline Epistles. Furthermore, at the request of the pope, Aquinas produced the *Catena Aurea*, a commentary on the four Gospels consisting of exegetical statements by the Latin and Greek fathers. One of the most significant features of Aquinas's biblical commentaries is his emphasis on the literal meaning of a Scriptural text. As a representation of medieval Catholic theology, Aquinas's theology was regularly challenged by the Protestant reformers.

Benedict Aretius (d. 1574). Swiss Reformed professor. Trained at the universities of Bern, Strasbourg and Marburg, Aretius taught logic and philosophy as well as the biblical languages and theology. He advocated for stronger unity and peace between the Lutheran and Reformed churches. Aretius joined others in denouncing the antitrinitarian Giovanni Valentino Gentile (d. 1566). He published commentaries on the New Testament, as well as various works on astronomy, botany and medicine.

Aristotle (388–322 BC). Ancient Greek philosopher and scientist. Aristotle was born in Stagira, Chalkdice, northern Greece. He is considered the "Father of Western Philosophy" along with his teacher, Plato, because his teaching produced the bases for almost every discipline studied in the Western world. After his father's death while he was still a child, Aristotle was raised by his guardian, Proxenus of Atarneus. At the age of about eighteen, Aristotle joined Plato's Academy in Athens, where he remained until his was thirty-seven. Aristotle's writings cover a wide range of subjects: physics, biology, zoology, metaphysics, logic, ethics, aesthetics, poetry, theater, music, rhetoric, psychology, linguistics, and politics. Shortly after Plato's death, King Philip II of Macedonia requested his services as a tutor to his son, Alexander the Great. Aristotle began tutoring the young prince in 343 BC. While teaching Alexander, Aristotle was able to acquire hundreds of books for the library of what would become his Lyceum. Aristotle's work profoundly shaped scholarship during the Middle Ages and early modern period as his logic was employed in the exegesis of Scripture and formation of theology. Among the major theologians who incorporated Aristotle's methods into their theological systems was Thomas Aquinas.* Aristotle's methods and categories would also be utilized by many Protestant theologians throughout the sixteenth and seventeenth centuries.

Jacobus Arminius (1559–1609). Dutch Remonstrant pastor and theologian. Arminius was a vocal critic of high

Calvinist scholasticism, whose views were repudiated by the Synod of Dordrecht. Arminius was a student of Theodore Beza* at the academy of Geneva. He served as a pastor in Amsterdam and later joined the faculty of theology at the university in Leiden, where his lectures on predestination were popular and controversial. Predestination, as Arminius understood it, was the decree of God determined on the basis of divine foreknowledge of faith or rejection by humans who are the recipients of prevenient, but resistible, grace.

Johann Arndt (1555–1621). German Lutheran pastor and theologian. After a brief time teaching, Arndt pastored in Badeborn (Anhalt) until 1590, when Prince Johann Georg von Anhalt (1567–1618) began introducing Reformed ecclesial policies. Arndt ministered in Quedlinberg, Brunswick, Eisleben and Celle. Heavily influenced by medieval mysticism, Arndt centered his theology on Christ's mystical union with the believer, out of which flows love of God and neighbor. He is best known for his *True Christianity* (1605–1609), which greatly influenced Philipp Jakob Spener (1635–1705) and later Pietists.

John Arrowsmith (1602–1659). English Puritan theologian. Arrowsmith participated in the Westminster Assembly, and later taught at Cambridge. His works, all published posthumously, include three sermons preached to Parliament and an unfinished catechism.

Articles of Religion (1562; revised 1571). The Articles underwent a long editorial process that drew from the influence of Continental confessions in England, resulting in a uniquely Anglican blend of Protestantism and Catholicism. In their final form, they were reduced from Thomas Cranmer's* Forty-two Articles (1539) to the Elizabethan Thirty-Nine Articles (1571), excising polemical articles against the Anabaptists and Millenarians as well as adding articles on the Holy Spirit, good works and Communion. Originating in a 1535 meeting with Lutherans, the Articles retained a minor influence from the Augsburg Confession* and Württemberg Confession (1552), but showed significant revision in accordance with Genevan theology, as well as the Second Helvetic Confession.*

Anne Askew (1521–1546). English Protestant martyr. Askew was forced to marry her deceased sister's intended husband, who later expelled Askew from his house—after the birth of two children—on account of her religious views. After unsuccessfully seeking a divorce in Lincoln, Askew moved to London, where she met other Protestants and began to preach. In 1546, she was arrested, imprisoned and convicted of heresy for denying the doctrine of transubstantiation. Under torture in the Tower of London she refused to name any other Protestants. On July 16, 1546, she was burned at the stake. Askew is best known through her accounts of her arrests and examinations. John Bale (1495–1563), a bishop, historian and playwright, published these manuscripts. Later John Foxe (1516–1587) included them in his *Acts and Monuments*, presenting her as a role model for other pious Protestant women.

Mary Astell (1666–1731). English writer and philosopher. Astell received an informal education from her uncle, a clergyman. Left almost penniless after the death of her parents, she settled in London, where she made her career as a writer. She is best known for her proto-feminist works, including *A Serious Proposal to the Ladies* (1694, 1697), *Some Reflections on Marriage* (1700), and *The Christian Religion, as Professed by a Daughter of the Church of England* (1705). In these works she argues for the moral and intellectual equality of the sexes and the need for women to receive a similar education to men so that they can navigate the world by themselves. Retiring from writing, Astell spent her final decades organizing a charity school for girls in Chelsea backed by the Society for the Propagation of Christian Knowledge.

Augsburg Confession (1530). In the wake of Luther's* stand against ecclesial authorities at the Diet of Worms (1521), the Holy Roman Empire splintered along theological lines. Emperor Charles V sought to ameliorate this—while also hoping to secure a united European front against Turkish invasion—by calling together another imperial diet in Augsburg in 1530. The Evangelical party was cast in a strongly heretical light at the diet by Johann Eck.* For this reason, Philipp Melanchthon* and Justus Jonas* thought it best to strike a conciliatory tone (Luther, as an official outlaw, did not attend), submitting a confession rather than a defense. The resulting Augsburg Confession was approved by many of the rulers of the northeastern Empire; however, due to differences in eucharistic theology, Martin Bucer* and the representatives of Strasbourg, Constance, Lindau and Memmingen drafted a separate confession (the Tetrapolitan Confession). Charles V accepted neither confession, demanding that the Evangelicals accept the Catholic rebuttal instead. In 1531, along with the publication of the Augsburg Confession itself, Melanchthon released a defense of the confession that responded to the Catholic confutation and expanded on the original articles. Most subsequent Protestant confessions followed the general structure of the Augsburg Confession.

Augustine of Hippo (354–430 AD). North African bishop and theologian. Augustine was born in Thagaste

(Ahras, Algeria), a small town in the Roman province to Numidia, the son of a Christian mother, Monica, and a non-Christian father, Patricius, a local official of modest means. Enabled by local patronage, Augustine received a classical education, which afforded him the opportunity to pursue advanced training in rhetoric at Carthage. Upon completing his education at Carthage, Augustine taught rhetoric there as well as in Rome and Milan, where he was appointed official rhetorician of that city. Inspired by his reading of Cicero's *Hortensius*, Augustine embarked upon a quest for wisdom. While in Carthage, Augustine was repulsed by the seemingly simplistic Christianity he encountered, and therefore joined the Manicheans. Having become disillusioned by the Manichaeans' failure to lead him to the wisdom they promised, Augustine was eventually drawn to orthodox Christianity by the preaching of Ambrose (340–397) and his reading of the Neo-Platonist philosopher Plotinus (204–270). As a result of his conversion in 386, Augustine abandoned his secular ambitions in favor of a celibate life fully committed to intellectual and spiritual devotion to God. Towards this end, Augustine returned to north Africa to establish a semi–monastic community. However, in 391, while visiting Hippo Regius, he was forcibly ordained into the priesthood, and made bishop of that church in 396. In addition to his many duties as a bishop, Augustine engaged in controversies against the Manicheans, Donatists, and Pelagians, which took up the remainder of his life and career. He died in 430 while the Vandals besieged Hippo. Among his many works, Augustine devoted several to exegesis. He outlines exegetical principles in his *De Doctrina Christiana* ("On Christian Doctrine"), and he authored extensive series of homilies on most of the books of the New Testament as well as the Old Testament books of Psalms and Genesis (incomplete). During the Reformation era, both Catholic and Protestant theologians appealed to and engaged with Augustine's theology, especially his emphases upon original sin and humanity's need for God's grace.

Authorized Version (1611). In 1604 King James I* commissioned this new translation—popularly remembered as the King James Version—for uniform use in the public worship of the Church of England. The Bible and the Apocrypha was divided into six portions and assigned to six companies of nine scholars—both Anglicans and Puritans—centered at Cambridge, Oxford and Westminster. Richard Bancroft, the general editor of the Authorized Version, composed fifteen rules to guide the translators and to guard against overly partisan decisions. Rather than offer an entirely fresh English translation, the companies were to follow the Bishops' Bible* as closely as possible. "Truly (good Christian Reader)," the preface states, "we neuer thought from the beginning that we should need to make a new Translation, nor yet to make of a bad one a good one . . . but make a good one better, or out of many good ones, one principall good one, not iustly to be excepted against: that hath bene our endeauour, that our mark." Other rules standardized spelling, dictated traditional ecclesial terms (e.g., *church, baptize* and *bishop*), and allowed only for linguistic marginal notes and cross-references. Each book of the Bible went through a rigorous revision process: first, each person in a company made an initial draft, then the company put together a composite draft, then a supercommittee composed of representatives from each company reviewed these drafts, and finally two bishops and Bancroft scrutinized the final edits. The text and translation process of the Authorized Version have widely influenced biblical translations ever since.

Gervase Babington (1549/1550–1610). English Anglican bishop. Born into an influential family, Babington studied at Cambridge and spent time as a preacher at the university and as prebendary of Hereford Cathedral before serving, in turn, as bishop of Llandaff, Exeter, and Worcester. He published a number of sermons, expositions of the Ten Commandments and Lord's Prayer, and notes on Genesis, Exodus, and Leviticus.

Robert Bagnall (b. 1559 or 1560). English Protestant minister. Bagnall authored *The Steward's Last Account* (1622), a collection of five sermons on Luke 16.

Friedrich Balduin (1575–1627). German Lutheran theologian. After spending time in the pastorate at Freiberg and Oelsnitz, Balduin was appointed professor of theology at Wittenberg in 1604, where he remained until the end of his life. He also served as head of the theology faculty, superintendent of churches, and assessor of the consistory. Known for his commitment to Lutheran orthodoxy, Balduin's major works include a commentary on the Pauline letters and writings on exegesis, homiletics, and casuistry.

John Ball (1585–1640). English Puritan theologian. Ball was a respected educator. He briefly held a church office until he was removed on account of his Puritanism. He composed popular catechisms and tracts on faith, the church and the covenant of grace.

John Barlow (1580/1581?–1629/1630). English Protestant minister. Educated at Oxford, Barlow ministered in Plymouth, Halifax, and Chester. A number of his sermons have been preserved, including his teachings on 2 Timothy 1 and 1 Thessalonians 4:18.

Thomas Bastard (c. 1565–1618). English Protestant minister and poet. Educated at Winchester and New College, Oxford, Bastard published numerous works, including collections of poems and sermons; his most famous title is *Chrestoleros* (1598), a collection of epigrams. Bastard was alleged to be the author of an anonymous work, *An Admonition to the City of Oxford*, which revealed the carnal vices of many clergy and scholars in Oxford; despite denying authorship, he was dismissed from Oxford in 1591. Bastard was recognized as a skilled classical scholar and preacher. He died impoverished in a debtor's prison in Dorchester.

Jeremias Bastingius (1551–1595). Dutch Reformed theologian. Educated in Heidelberg and Geneva, Bastingius pastored the Reformed church in Antwerp for nearly a decade until the Spanish overran the city in 1585; he later settled in Dordrecht. He spent the last few years of his life in Leiden on the university's board of regents. He wrote an influential commentary on the Heidelberg Catechism that was translated into English, Dutch, German and Flemish.

Johann (Pomarius) Baumgart (1514–1578). Lutheran pastor and amateur playwright. Baumgart studied under Georg Major,* Martin Luther* and Philipp Melanchthon* at the University of Wittenberg. Before becoming pastor of the Church of the Holy Spirit in 1540, Baumgart taught secondary school. He authored catechetical and polemical works, a postil for the Gospel readings throughout the church year, numerous hymns and a didactic play (*Juditium Salomonis*).

Richard Baxter (1615–1691). English Puritan minister. Baxter was a leading Puritan pastor, evangelist and theologian, known throughout England for his landmark ministry in Kidderminster and a prodigious literary output, producing 135 books in just over forty years. Baxter came to faith through reading William Perkins,* Richard Sibbes* and other early Puritan writers and was the first cleric to decline the terms of ministry in the national English church imposed by the 1662 Act of Uniformity; Baxter wrote on behalf of the more than 1700 who shared ejection from the national church. He hoped for restoration to national church ministry, or toleration, that would allow lawful preaching and pastoring. Baxter sought unity in theological, ecclesiastical, sociopolitical and personal terms and is regarded as a forerunner of Noncomformist ecumenicity, though he was defeated in his efforts at the 1661 Savoy Conference to take seriously Puritan objections to the revision of the 1604 Prayer Book. Baxter's views on church ministry were considerably hybrid: he was a paedo-baptist, Nonconformist minister who approved of synodical Episcopal government and fixed liturgy. He is most known for his classic writings on the Christian life, such as *The Saints' Everlasting Rest* and *A Christian Directory*, and pastoral ministry, such as *The Reformed Pastor*. He also produced *Catholick Theology*, a large volume squaring current Reformed, Lutheran, Arminian and Roman Catholic systems with each other.

Thomas Becon (1511/1512–1567). English Puritan preacher. Becon was a friend of Hugh Latimer,* and for several years chaplain to Archbishop Thomas Cranmer.* Becon was sent to the Tower of London by Mary I and then exiled for his controversial preaching at the English royal court. He returned to England upon Elizabeth I's* accession. Becon was one of the most widely read popular preachers in England during the Reformation. He published many of his sermons, including a postil, or collection of sermon helps for undertrained or inexperienced preachers.

Belgic Confession (1561). Written by Guy de Brès (1523–1567), this statement of Dutch Reformed faith was heavily reliant on the Gallic Confession,* although more detailed, especially in how strongly it distances the Reformed from Roman Catholics and Anabaptists. The Confession first appeared in French in 1561 and was translated to Dutch in 1562. It was presented to Philip II (1527–1598) in the hope that he would grant toleration to the Reformed, to no avail. At the Synod of Dordrecht* the Confession was revised, clarifying and strengthening the article on election as well as sharpening the distinctives of Reformed theology against the Anabaptists, thus situating the Dutch Reformed more closely to the international Calvinist movement. The Belgic Confession in conjunction with the Heidelberg Catechism* and the Canons of Dordrecht were granted official status as the confessional standards (the Three Forms of Unity) of the Dutch Reformed Church.

Robert Bellarmine (1542–1621). Italian Catholic cardinal. A Jesuit, Bellarmine first taught at Louvain before being appointed chair of polemical theology at the Roman College. Much of Bellarmine's career was devoted to the refutation of Protestant teachings, and his three volume work, the *Controversies* (1586–93), was widely disseminated in the post-Tridentine era as the foremost refutation of the evangelical message. He was influential in the official revision of the Vulgate* text during the reign of Pope Clement VIII (1536–1605), with the resulting version, the Sixto-Clementine Vulgate, providing the basic biblical text for Catholics until Vatican II. Bellarmine is also a controversial figure in the history of science. Appointed to the Holy Office, also known as the

Inquisition, by Pope Paul V (1550–1621), it was he who examined Galileo Galilei (1564–1642) and ordered him to treat heliocentrism as a hypothesis rather than a reality, believing the evidentiary threshold had not yet been met. Later in his career, Bellarmine's attention turned to works on devotion and piety, and include his extensive commentary on the Psalms (1611).

Bernard of Clairvaux (1090–1153). French abbot and theologian. Born the son of a Bugundian knight, Bernard became interested in the new reforming movement at Citeaux, and thus abandoned his preparation for a secular career in favor of monastic life there. Towards this end, Bernard persuaded thirty-one of his friends and relatives to follow him to Citeaux, and join the Cistercian order. Among this group were four of Bernard's brothers. In 1115, Bernard went with others of his order to found a Cistercian monastery at Claivaux. Bernard's austere approach to the monastic life attracted many followers to the point that by the time of his death there were sixty-eight Cistercian houses. Throughout his career, Bernard preached, mediated theological disputes, and advised. Bernard is best known for having preached the Second Crusade (1147–1150) as well as advising his former student, Pope Eugenius III (r. 1145–1153), and engaging in theological controversies with Peter Abelard (1079–1142) and Gilbert of Poitiers (1085–1154). One of the distinguishing characteristics of Bernard's theology is his Christocentric mysticism. Among Bernard's most important works are his treatises *On Consideration* and *On Loving God* along with his *Sermons on the Song of Songs* as well as many other sermons on the liturgical year and other subject. Many of the reformers in the sixteenth century cited Bernard extensively, especially Martin Luther* and John Calvin*.

Richard Bernard (1568–1641). English Puritan minister. A moderate Puritan, Bernard eschewed separation from the Church of England, spending the majority of his career in parish ministry at Batcombe, Somerset. Many of his works, including a handbook for pastors and a household catechism, were well received and printed numerous times during his lifetime.

Theodore Beza (1519–1605). French Reformed pastor and professor. Beza was compatriot and successor to John Calvin* as moderator of the Company of Pastors in Geneva during the second half of the sixteenth century. He was a noteworthy New Testament scholar whose *Codex Bezae* formed the basis of the New Testament section of later English translations. A leader in the academy and the church, Beza served as professor of Greek at the Lausanne Academy until 1558, at which time he moved to Geneva to become the rector of the newly founded Genevan Academy. He enjoyed an international reputation through his correspondence with key European leaders. Beza developed and extended Calvin's doctrinal thought on several important themes such as the nature of predestination and the real spiritual presence of Christ in the Eucharist.

Theodor Bibliander (1504?–1564). Swiss Reformed Hebraist and theologian. Professor of Old Testament at the Zurich Academy from 1531, Bibliander published two Hebrew grammars, a collection of letters by Zwingli* and Oecolampadius*, commentaries on Isaiah, Ezekiel, and Nahum, a Latin translation of the Qur'an, and a tract warning Christians against the threat of Islam. He taught a universalist view of predestination, arguing that God saved all people unless they rejected divine grace. Following a dispute with double-predestinarian Peter Martyr Vermigli*, he was forced into retirement in 1560.

Thomas Bilson (1546/1547?–1616). English Anglican Bishop and theologian. A celebrated preacher and theologian, Bilson served as canon of Winchester Cathedral and warden of Winchester College before becoming bishop of Worcester. He held this position for only one year, however, before his appointment to the wealthier see of Winchester. As an advisor to King James I,* he preached at his coronation, and he was involved with the publication of the 1611 Authorized Version,* being part of the Cambridge company responsible for translating the Apocrypha, the author of part of the front matter, and one of the text's final editors. His extant writings defend the episcopacy against Erastianism, condemn rebellion, and argue for a literal understanding of Christ's descent into hell.

Hugh Binning (1627–1653). Scottish Presbyterian theologian. At the age of eighteen, Binning became a professor of philosophy at the University of Glasgow. In his early twenties he left this post for parish ministry, and died of consumption a few years later. His commentary on the Westminster Confession and a selection of his sermons were published after his death.

Samuel Bird (d. 1604). Anglican minister and author. A native of Essex, Bird matriculated at Queen's College, Cambridge, where he received his BA in 1570 and his MA in 1573, at which time he was also elected a fellow of Corpus Christi College, Cambridge. For reasons unknown, Bird resigned his fellowship sometime in 1576. He spent nearly the entirety of his post-university career as rector of St. Peter's in Ipswich until his death in 1604. Among Bird's major works are *A Friendlie Communication or Dialogue Betweene Paule and Demas, wherein is Disputed*

How We are to Use the Pleasures of This Life (1580), *Lectures upon the 11. Chapter of Hebrews and upon the 38. Psalme* (1598), and *Lectures upon the 8 and 9 Chapters of the Second Epistle to the Corinthians* (1598).

Bishops' Bible (1568). Anglicans were polarized by the two most recent English translations of the Bible: the Great Bible (1539) relied too heavily on the Vulgate* and was thus perceived as too Catholic, while the Geneva Bible's* marginal notes were too Calvinist for many Anglicans. So Archbishop Matthew Parker (1504–1575) commissioned a new translation of Scripture from the original languages with marginal annotations (many of which, ironically, were from the Geneva Bible). Published under royal warrant, the Bishops' Bible became the official translation for the Church of England. The 1602 edition provided the basis for the King James Bible (1611).

Christopher Blackwood (1607/1608–1670). English Baptist pastor. Initially an Anglican priest, Blackwood served at the parishes of Stockbury and Rye until Puritan sympathies led him to migrate to New England. Returning to England, he pastored briefly at Cranbrook until Baptist preaching caused him to leave the established church, be rebaptized, and serve as a pastor of a General Baptist congregation in Staplehurst. Joining the Parliamentary Army in their goal to evangelize Ireland, he helped plant a number of Baptist churches and pastored at Wexford, Kilkenny, and Dublin. His numerous writings include treatises on baptism and repentance, a catechism, and a commentary on the first ten chapters of Matthew.

Georg Blaurock (1492–1529). Swiss Anabaptist. Blaurock (a nickname meaning "blue coat," because of his preference for this garment) was one of the first leaders of Switzerland's radical reform movement. In the first public disputations on baptism in Zurich, he argued for believer's baptism and was the first person to receive adult believers' baptism there, having been baptized by Conrad Grebel* in 1525. Blaurock was arrested several times for performing mass adult baptisms and engaging in social disobedience by disrupting worship services. He was eventually expelled from Zurich but continued preaching and baptizing in various Swiss cantons until his execution.

Bohemian Confession (1535). Bohemian Christianity was subdivided between traditional Catholics, Utraquists (who demanded Communion in both kinds) and the *Unitas Fratrum*, who were not Protestants but whose theology bore strong affinities to the Waldensians and the Reformed. The 1535 Latin edition of this confession—an earlier Czech edition had already been drafted—was an attempt to clarify and redefine the beliefs of the *Unitas Fratrum*. This confession purged all earlier openness to rebaptism and inched toward Luther's* eucharistic theology. Jan Augusta (c. 1500–1572) and Jan Roh (also Johannes Horn; c. 1490–1547) presented the confession to King Ferdinand I (1503–1564) in Vienna, but the king would not print it. The *Unitas Fratrum* sought, and with slight amendments eventually obtained, Luther's advocacy of the confession. It generally follows the structure of the Augsburg Confession.*

Bohemian Confession (1575). This confession was an attempt to shield Bohemian Christian minorities—the Utraquists and the *Unitas Fratrum*—from the Counter-Reformation and Habsburg insistence on uniformity. The hope was that this umbrella consensus would ensure peace in the midst of Christian diversity; anyone who affirmed the 1575 Confession, passed by the Bohemian legislature, would be tolerated. This confession was, like the Bohemian Confession of 1535, patterned after the Augsburg Confession.* It emphasizes both justification by faith alone and good works as the fruit of salvation. Baptism and the Eucharist are the focus of the sacramental section, although the five traditional Catholic sacraments are also listed for the Utraquists. Though it was eventually accepted in 1609 by Rudolf II (1552–1612), the Thirty Years' War (1618–1648) rendered the confession moot.

Samuel Bolton (1606–1654). English Anglican minister. Bolton served a number of parishes in London before being elected to the Westminster Assembly. He spent the remainder of his career as master of Christ's College, Cambridge. A number of his writings were published, including works on sin, the sacraments, and Christian freedom.

Book of Common Prayer (1549; 1552). After the Church of England's break with Rome, it needed a liturgical manual to distinguish its theology and practice from that of Catholicism. Thomas Cranmer* drafted the Book of Common Prayer based on the medieval Roman Missal, under the dual influence of the revised Lutheran Mass and the reforms of the Spanish Cardinal Quiñones. This manual details the eucharistic service, as well as services for rites such as baptism, confirmation, marriage and funerals. It includes a matrix of the epistle and Gospel readings and the appropriate collect for each Sunday and feast day of the church year. The 1548 Act of Uniformity established the Book of Common Prayer as *the* authoritative liturgical manual for the Church of England, to be implemented everywhere by Pentecost 1549. After its 1552 revision, Queen Mary I banned it; Elizabeth I* reestablished it in 1559, although it was rejected by Puritans and Catholics alike.

The Book of Homilies (1547; 1563; 1570). This collection of approved sermons, published in three parts during the reigns of Edward VI and Elizabeth I,* was intended to inculcate Anglican theological distinctives and mitigate the problems raised by the lack of educated preachers. Addressing doctrinal and practical topics, Thomas Cranmer* likely wrote the majority of the first twelve sermons, published in 1547; John Jewel* added another twenty sermons in 1563. A final sermon, *A Homily Against Disobedience*, was appended to the canon in 1570. Reprinted regularly, the *Book of Homilies* was an important resource in Anglican preaching until at least the end of the seventeenth century.

Martin (Cellarius) Borrhaus (1499–1564). German Reformed theologian. After a dispute with his mentor Johann Eck,* Borrhaus settled in Wittenberg, where he was influenced by the radical Zwickau Prophets. He travelled extensively, and finally settled in Basel to teach philosophy and Old Testament. Despite his objections, many accused Borrhaus of Anabaptism; he argued that baptism was a matter of conscience. On account of his association with Sebastian Castellio (1515–1563) and Michael Servetus (1511–1553), some scholars posit that Borrhaus was an antitrinitarian. His writings include a treatise on the Trinity and commentaries on the Torah, historical books, Ecclesiastes and Isaiah.

Sigmund Bosch (unknown). German Anabaptist hymn writer. An elder in the Swiss and South German Anabaptist churches, Bosch collaborated with Pilgram Marpeck* in his ministry. He is known to have composed three hymns and a letter on the end times, which he addressed to the congregation in Austerlitz.

John Bourchier (d. 1660). English Puritan parliamentarian. Bourchier served as a justice of the peace in Yorkshire until imprisoned at the outbreak of the English Civil War. After his release, he was elected as the member of parliament for Ripon, and in this capacity he served as a judge at the trial of Charles I and signed the king's death warrant. Deemed too ill for trial with the other regicides, he died soon after the Restoration of the monarchy under Charles II.

John Bowle (d. 1637). Anglican pastor. After matriculating from Cambridge, Bowle was household pastor to Sir Robert Cecil (1563–1612) and held a pastorate at Tilehurst in Berkshire. He was appointed dean of Salisbury in 1620 and bishop of Rochester in 1629.

John Boys (1571–1625). Anglican priest and theologian. Before doctoral work at Cambridge, Boys pastored several parishes in Kent; after completing his studies he was appointed to more prominent positions, culminating in his 1619 appointment as the Dean of Canterbury by James I.* Boys published a popular four-volume postil of the Gospel and epistle readings for the church year, as well as a companion volume for the Psalms.

John Bradford (1510–1555). English Reformer, prebendary of St. Paul's, and martyr. Bradford was born in Blackley, Manchester, to an affluent family. After grammar school, Bradford at first began legal studies at the Inner Temple in London. However, while there, he heard the preaching of a fellow student, and thus converted to an evangelical faith. This conversion caused Bradford to abandon his study of law and enroll at St. Catherine's Hall, Cambridge, to study theology. He completed his MA in 1549, and in the same year, received an appointment of fellow at Pembroke Hall, Cambridge. In August, 1550, Bishop Nicholas Ridley ordained Bradford a deacon, and appointed him his personal chaplain. Bradford's exceptional preaching moved King Edward VI to select him as his chaplain and prebendary at St. Paul's Cathedral. After Mary Tudor succeeded her half-brother to throne, Bradford was tried and convicted of heresy on January 31, 1555. He was executed at the stake on July 1 of the same year.

Anne Bradstreet (1612–1672). English-American Puritan poet. Born in Northampton, Bradstreet married at sixteen and emigrated to the Massachusetts Bay Colony, of which both her father and husband would serve as governors. Mother to eight children, Bradstreet also wrote poetry. Much of her verse reflects on marriage, children, and her Puritan faith. While her writing received a mixed reception from contemporaries, many of whom viewed poetry as outside a woman's purview, she is today celebrated as the most significant early English poet in North America.

Thieleman Jans van Braght (1625–1664). Dutch Radical preacher. After demonstrating great ability with languages, this cloth merchant was made preacher in his hometown of Dordrecht in 1648. He served in this office for the next sixteen years, until his death. This celebrated preacher had a reputation for engaging in debate wherever an opportunity presented itself, particularly concerning infant baptism. The publication of his book of martyrs, *Het Bloedigh Tooneel of Martelaersspiegel* (1660; *Martyrs' Mirror*), proved to be his lasting contribution to the Mennonite tradition. *Martyrs' Mirror* is heavily indebted to the earlier martyr book *Offer des Heeren* (1562), to which Braght added many early church martyrs who rejected infant baptism, as well as over 800 contemporary martyrs.

David Bramley (unknown). English lay preacher. Two works by Bramley survive, an exposition of Matthew 11:25 and a treatise arguing for the acceptance of lay preachers without university training like himself. On both tracts, he is identified simply as a "Preacher of the Gospel."

Johannes Brenz (1499–1570). German Lutheran theologian and pastor. Brenz was converted to the reformation cause after hearing Martin Luther* speak; later, Brenz became a student of Johannes Oecolampadius.* His central achievement lay in his talent for organization. As city preacher in Schwäbisch-Hall and afterward in Württemberg and Tübingen, he oversaw the introduction of reform measures and doctrines and new governing structures for ecclesial and educational communities. Brenz also helped establish Lutheran orthodoxy through treatises, commentaries and catechisms. He defended Luther's position on eucharistic presence against Huldrych Zwingli* and opposed the death penalty for religious dissenters.

Guillaume Briçonnet (1470–1534). French Catholic abbot and bishop. Briçonnet created a short-lived circle of reformist-minded humanists in his diocese under the sponsorship of Marguerite d'Angoulême. His desire for ecclesial reform developed throughout his prestigious career (including positions as royal chaplain to the queen, abbot at Saint-Germain-des-Prés and bishop of Meaux), influenced by Jacques Lefèvre d'Étaples.* Briçonnet encouraged reform through ministerial visitation, Scripture and preaching in the vernacular and active study of the Bible. When this triggered the ire of the theology faculty at the Sorbonne in Paris, Briçonnet quelled the activity and departed, envisioning an ecclesial reform that proceeded hierarchically.

William Bridge (1600?–1670). English Puritan minister. Bridge ministered in Norfolk and Essex until excommunicated as a Nonconformist and exiled, leading him to Rotterdam, where he copastored a church with Jeremiah Burroughs.* Returning to England, he was a member of the Westminster Assembly and pastored at Great Yarmouth until ejected from the ministry by the Act of Uniformity (1662). Many of Bridge's sermons were published during his life, and he also composed a number of works designed to encourage struggling believers.

Walter Bridges (unknown). English Anglican minister. Three works are attributed to Bridges. Two were published anonymously, a sermon on Joab before the House of Commons and a catechism for those taking the Eucharist, while a third, a sermon on unity given before the Lord Mayor and Aldermen of London, names him and his position as preacher at St. Dunstans-in-the-East, London.

Thomas Brightman (1562–1607). English Puritan pastor and exegete. Under alleged divine inspiration, Brightman wrote a well known commentary on Revelation, influenced by Joachim of Fiore (d. 1202). In contrast to the putatively true churches of Geneva and Scotland, he depicted the Church of England as a type of the lukewarm Laodicean church. He believed that the Reformation would result in the defeat of the Vatican and the Ottoman Empire and that all humanity would be regenerated through the spread of the gospel before Christ's final return and judgment.

Hugh Broughton (1549–1612). English Puritan Hebraist and theologian. Following his time as a student and fellow at Cambridge, Broughton established himself as a scholar and preacher in London. His first work, *A Concent of Scripture* (1588), an attempt to harmonize the chronology of Scripture, caused significant controversy and led him to spend much of the next two decades traveling throughout Europe. On the Continent, he built a reputation in disputes with numerous Jewish, Catholic, and Protestant scholars and helped to plant an English Reformed church in Amsterdam, a congregation he may also have pastored for a time. Broughton's extensive writings include comments on numerous aspects of the Old Testament and New Testaments, a genealogy of Christ, and an explication of Christ's descent into hell.

Robert Browne (c. 1550–1633). English Nonconformist minister. While drawn to Puritan teachings, Browne began his career within the Church of England, ministering in London and Cambridge. Convinced that more radical reformation was needed outside the constraints of the state, Browne is recognized as the first to found a separatist church, establishing a congregation in Norwich, with those who followed him becoming known as Brownists. After a brief imprisonment, he left for Middelburg in the Netherlands, gathering a church based on the principles he espoused in his two most important works, *A Treatise of Reformation Without Tarrying* (1582) and *The Life and Manners of All True Christians* (1582), which set forth the foundations of congregationalist church government. Browne did not remain a separatist, however, and after a few years returned to England and reentered the Church of England, serving as a school headmaster and pastoring in Northamptonshire.

Antonio Brucioli (c. 1498–1566). Italian Protestant humanist and translator. Born in Florence, Brucioli and other humanists fled to Lyon after implication in a conspiracy to assassinate Guilio de' Medici (1478–1534, later Pope Clement VII r. 1523–1534). After publishing a series of philosophical dialogues, he returned to Florence, only to be expelled for involvement in further political intrigues, anticlerical writings, and suspected Lutheranism. Settling in Venice, Brucioli established a publishing house and began a prodigious printing program. Best known for rendering the first translation of the Scriptures into Italian directly from Hebrew and Greek, he also composed introductions and commentaries on the books of the Bible and published translations of philosophers such as Cicero, Pliny, and Aristotle. His writings on Scripture were scrutinized for their Protestant teachings, particularly with regard to the sacraments, and he was called before the Inquisition three times. The first time, Brucioli was fined and exiled from Venice; the second, his writings were banned and burned; and the third, he was imprisoned and left to die penniless upon release.

Otto Brunfels (c. 1488–1534). German Lutheran botanist, teacher and physician. Brunfels joined the Carthusian order, where he developed interests in the natural sciences and became involved with a humanist circle associated with Ulrich von Hutten and Wolfgang Capito.* In 1521, after coming into contact with Luther's* teaching, Brunfels abandoned the monastic life, traveling and spending time in botanical research and pastoral care. He received a medical degree in Basel and was appointed city physician of Bern in 1534. Brunfels penned defenses of Luther and Hutten, devotional biographies of biblical figures, a prayer book, and annotations on the Gospels and the Acts of the Apostles. His most influential contribution, however, is as a Renaissance botanist.

Martin Bucer (1491–1551). German Reformed theologian and pastor. A Dominican friar, Bucer was influenced by Desiderius Erasmus* during his doctoral studies at the University of Heidelberg, where he began corresponding with Martin Luther.* After advocating reform in Alsace, Bucer was excommunicated and fled to Strasbourg, where he became a leader in the city's Reformed ecclesial and educational communities. Bucer sought concord between Lutherans and Zwinglians and Protestants and Catholics. He emigrated to England, becoming a professor at Cambridge. Bucer's greatest theological concern was the centrality of Christ's sacrificial death, which achieved justification and sanctification and orients Christian community.

Johannes Bugenhagen (1485–1558). German Lutheran pastor and professor. Bugenhagen, a priest and lecturer at a Premonstratensian monastery, became a city preacher in Wittenberg during the reform efforts of Martin Luther* and Philipp Melanchthon.* Initially influenced by his reading of Desiderius Erasmus,* Bugenhagen grew in evangelical orientation through Luther's works; later, he studied under Melanchthon at the University of Wittenberg, eventually serving as rector and faculty member there. Bugenhagen was a versatile commentator, exegete and lecturer on Scripture. Through these roles and his development of lectionary and devotional material, Bugenhagen facilitated rapid establishment of church order throughout many German provinces.

Henry Bull (d. 1575?). English Protestant theologian and martyrologist. Little is known about Bull's circumstances after he was expelled from Magdalen College, Oxford, for snatching the censer from the hand of a priest officiating Mass. A committed reformer, he edited, translated, compiled, and published a number of Protestant works, including a book of prayers and meditations and writings by John Hooper* and Martin Luther.* He also worked alongside John Foxe* in the compilation of *Acts and Monuments*, while Miles Coverdale's* *The Letters of the Martyrs* is largely Bull's work.

Heinrich Bullinger (1504–1575). Swiss Reformed pastor and theologian. Bullinger succeeded Huldrych Zwingli* as minister and leader in Zurich. The primary author of the First and Second Helvetic Confessions,* Bullinger was drawn toward reform through the works of Martin Luther* and Philipp Melanchthon.* After Zwingli died, Bullinger was vital in maintaining adherence to the cause of reform; he oversaw the expansion of the Zurich synodal system while preaching, teaching and writing extensively. One of Bullinger's lasting legacies was the development of a federal view of the divine covenant with humanity, making baptism and the Eucharist covenantal signs.

Heinrich Bünting (1545–1606). Lutheran theologian and pastor. Bünting was born in Hanover, Germany, and studied theology at the University of Wittenberg, where he graduated in 1569. Upon finishing his studies at Wittenberg, Bünting became a pastor at Lemgo, where he was dismissed in 1575. Afterward he moved to Gronau an der Leine, where he served until his appointment as superintendent in Goslar. However, due to controversy over some of his teachings, Bünting was relieved of his position in 1600, retiring thereafter to Hanover, where he lived the remainder of his life. Bünting's most notable work is his *Itinerarium Sacrae Scripturae* (1581), a summary of biblical geography. Throughout this treatise, Bünting follows the travels of various major biblical figures, highlighting their theological as well as exegetical importance. When published, the *Itinerarium Sacrae Scripturae* was the most complete summary of biblical geography. Among the work's distinctive features is its collection of maps.

John Bunyan (1628–1688). English Puritan preacher and writer. His *Pilgrim's Progress* is one of the best-selling English-language titles in history. Born to a working-class family, Bunyan was largely unschooled, gaining literacy (and entering the faith) through reading the Bible and such early Puritan devotional works as *The Plain Man's Pathway to Heaven* and *The Practice of Piety*. Following a short stint in Oliver Cromwell's parliamentary army, in which Bunyan narrowly escaped death in combat, he turned to a preaching ministry, succeeding John Gifford as pastor at the Congregational church in Bedford. A noted preacher, Bunyan drew large crowds in itinerant appearances and it was in the sermonic form that Bunyan developed his theological outlook, which was an Augustinian-inflected Calvinism. Bunyan's opposition to the Book of Common Prayer and refusal of official ecclesiastical licensure led to multiple imprisonments, where he wrote many of his famous allegorical works, including *Pilgrim's Progress, The Holy City, Prison Meditations* and *Holy War*.

Michelangelo Buonarroti (1475–1564). Italian Catholic artist and poet. Michelangelo was born in Florence but spent the majority of his career in Rome, completing artworks commissioned by the popes of the early sixteenth century. One of the most recognized artists of all time, his artworks include the *Pietà* (1499), *David* (1501–1504), the ceiling of the Sistine Chapel (1508–1512), *Moses* (1515), and the *Last Judgment* (1536–1541), which remain famous and have done much to shape Western aesthetics. Toward the end of his life, his interests shifted toward architecture, culminating with his contributions to the designs of St. Peter's Basilica in Rome. Michelangelo is thought to have been devoutly Catholic throughout his life, but recent scholarship has considered the complexity of his relationship with the Catholic Reformation and the Protestant movement.

Jeremiah Burroughs (c. 1600–1646). English Puritan pastor and delegate to the Westminster Assembly. Burroughs left Cambridge, as well as a rectorate in Norfolk, because of his nonconformity. After returning to England from pastoring an English congregation in Rotterdam for several years (1637–1641), he became one of only a few dissenters from the official presbyterianism of the Assembly in favor of a congregationalist polity. Nevertheless, he was well known and respected by presbyterian colleagues such as Richard Baxter* for his irenic tone and conciliatory manner. The vast majority of Burroughs's corpus was published posthumously, although during his lifetime he published annotations on Hosea and several polemical works.

William Burton (d. 1616). English Puritan minister. Burton first ministered in Norwich, where he was present for the burning of Francis Kett (d. 1589) for Arianism. He later pastored in Bristol, Reading, and London. Throughout his life, he published a number of his sermons and treatises as well as a brief catechism.

Anthony Cade (d. 1641). Anglican pastor. Cade served as tutor and chaplain to George Villiers, First Duke of Buckingham (1592–1628), a close confidante of King James I* before holding a number of pastoral positions in Leicestershire and Northamptonshire.

Cardinal Cajetan (Thomas de Vio) (1469–1534). Italian Catholic cardinal, professor, theologian and biblical exegete. This Dominican monk was the leading Thomist theologian and one of the most important Catholic exegetes of the sixteenth century. Cajetan is best-known for his interview with Martin Luther* at the Diet of Augsburg (1518). Among his many works are polemical treatises, extensive biblical commentaries and most importantly a four-volume commentary (1508–1523) on the *Summa Theologiae* of Thomas Aquinas.*

Georg Calixtus (1586–1656). German Lutheran theologian. Calixtus studied at the University of Helmstedt where he developed regard for Philipp Melanchthon.* Between his time as a student and later as a professor at Helmstedt, Calixtus traveled through Europe seeking a way to unite and reconcile Lutherans, Calvinists and Catholics. He attempted to fuse these denominations through use of the Scriptures, the Apostles' Creed, and the first five centuries, interpreted by the Vincentian canon. Calixtus's position was stamped as syncretist and yielded further debate even after his death.

John Calvin (1509–1564). French Reformed pastor and theologian. John Calvin was born in Noyon, France. After receiving his primary education in the aristocratic family of Charles de Hangest, he attended the University of Paris to prepare for further study of theology. However, after completing his BA degree, as per his father's instructions, Calvin proceeded to the study of the law at Orleans of Bourges. While at Orleans, Calvin's interests in Greek and Latin literature were reawakened. Upon his father's death, Calvin resumed his study of classical literature at the newly founded College of Royal Readers in Paris under the direction of Guillaume Bude. The product of these studies was his commentary on Seneca's *De Clementia* (1532). Sometime between 1533 and 1534 Calvin experienced a "sudden conversion" due largely to the influence to Martin Luther's 1520 treatises. Calvin's embracing of an evangelical faith forced him to flee France. From there he went to Basel, where he wrote the first edition of his *Institutes of the Christian Religion* in 1536. The *Institutes* became a theological dogmatics for the Reformed churches. Calvin spent most of his career in Geneva (excepting a three-year ministry in Strasbourg with Martin Bucer*). In Geneva, Calvin reorganized the structure and governance of the church and established an academy that became an international center for theological education. He was a tireless writer, revising his *Institutes* several times, and authoring theological treatises as well as biblical commentaries. Calvin is also known for his debates with his contemporaries, including Michael Servetus, whose anti-Trinitarian views led to his execution in Geneva in 1553. Calvin also maintained friendly correspondence with many reformers, including Melanchthon* and Bullinger*, the latter of whom he was able to come to an agreement with regarding the presence of Christ in the Lord's Supper with the signing of the *Consensus Tigurinus* in 1551, which brought a degree of unity between Geneva and Zurich and to the Reformed tradition. One of the foremost figures during the Reformation period, Calvin has an extensive exegetical and theological legacy.

Wolfgang Capito (1478?–1541). German Reformed humanist and theologian. Capito, a Hebrew scholar, produced a Hebrew grammar and published several Latin commentaries on books of the Hebrew Scriptures. He corresponded with Desiderius Erasmus* and fellow humanists. Capito translated Martin Luther's* early works into Latin for the printer Johann Froben. On meeting Luther, Capito was converted to Luther's vision, left Mainz and settled in Strasbourg, where he lectured on Luther's theology to the city clergy. With Martin Bucer,* Capito reformed liturgy, ecclesial life and teachings, education, welfare, and government. Capito worked for the theological unification of the Swiss cantons with Strasbourg.

Pietro Carnesecchi (1508–1567). Italian humanist. Carnesecchi rose in the papal bureaucracy under Medici patronage, but after the death of Clement VII* he began to deviate from Catholic orthodoxy, aligning himself with Juan de Valdés.* While he retained relations with the established church, he also read Protestant works by theologians such as Luther,* Calvin,* and Bucer,* and his only extant doctrinal writing defends Bucer's view of the Eucharist over that of Zwingli.* Carnesecchi was able to avoid arrest by the Inquisition for a time, and his condemnation to death in absentia was pardoned under Pope Pius IV (1499–1565). However, Pius V (1504–1572) was a longtime opponent of Carnesecchi, and upon his election to the papal office, reopened the case and those of a number of others suspected of Protestant leanings. While seeking refuge in Florence, Carnesecchi was betrayed to the Inquisition by Cosimo I de' Medici, and following trial he was beheaded.

François Carrière (d. 1665). French Catholic theologian. A Franciscan doctor of theology, Carrière composed a commentary on the whole Bible, a summary of Catholic doctrine, and a history of the papacy.

John Carter (1554–1635). English Puritan minister. After graduating from Cambridge, Carter served as vicar at Bramford, Suffolk, until disputes over his Puritanism within the congregation led him to be moved to the nearby parish of Belstead.

Denis the Carthusian (1402/1403–1471). Belgian Catholic theologian and mystic. Denis studied philosophy and theology at the University of Cologne before entering the Carthusian monastery at Roermond, where he spent most of his career in strict seclusion. A prodigious writer, his work spanned diverse genres, including popular devotional works, scholastic summaries of Lombard* and Aquinas,* and dogmatic works on numerous topics, including Mary, ecclesiology, and morality. Denis also produced commentaries on every book of the Bible.

Thomas Cartwright (1535–1606). English Puritan preacher and professor. Cartwright was educated at St. John's College, Cambridge, although as an influential leader of the Presbyterian party in the Church of England he was continually at odds with the Anglican party, especially John Whitgift.* Cartwright spent some time as an exile in Geneva and Heidelberg as well as in Antwerp, where he pastored an English church. In 1585, Cartwright was arrested and eventually jailed for trying to return to England despite Elizabeth I's* refusal of his request. Many acknowledged him to be learned but also quite cantankerous. His publications include commentaries on Colossians, Ecclesiastes, Proverbs and the Gospels, as well as a dispute against Whitgift on church discipline.

Sébastien Castellion (1515-1563) French Reformed humanist, pastor, and theologian. Born a peasant, Castellion converted to the evangelical faith while studying at Lyon. He initially aligned himself with John Calvin*, studying with him in Strasbourg and serving with him in Geneva as principal of the Latin school. Theological differences and financial concerns brought Castellion and Calvin into conflict, however, leading to Castellion's dismissal from Geneva. Impoverished and with a large family, he eventually resettled in Basel, where he worked as an editor and published translations of the Bible into Latin (1551) and French (1555). Appointed professor of Greek at the University of Basel, Castellion became a leading advocate for religious toleration, and after condemning the Genevans for executing Michael Servetus in *Concerning Heretics and Whether They Are to be Persecuted* (1554), he built a network of supporters calling for religious toleration, voluntary piety, and an end to religiously-motivated violence.

Mathew Caylie (unknown). English Protestant minister. Caylie authored *The Cleansing of the Ten Lepers* (1623), an exposition of Luke 17:14-18.

Jan Cents (Unknown). Dutch Anabaptist. Believed to be a leader of the Anabaptist congregation in Amsterdam, Cents was the first signer and possibly author of a confession intended to unite Frisian and High German Mennonites.

John Chardon (d. 1601). Irish Anglican bishop. Chardon was educated at Oxford. He advocated Reformed doctrine in his preaching, yet opposed those Puritans who rejected Anglican church order. He published several sermons.

Christian Chemnitz (1615–1666). German Lutheran theologian. Grandnephew of Martin Chemnitz,* Christian Chemnitz was principal at the high school in Jena before serving the church as a deacon and archdeacon in Weimer and Braunschweig then as superintendent in Eisenach. Returning to Jena, he received his doctorate and replaced John Major as professor of theology, also serving as dean of the theology faculty and rector of the university. He wrote on numerous biblical, pastoral, and controversial topics, with his works including a defense of Lutheranism, instructions for young ministers, and a series of sermons on judgement.

Martin Chemnitz (1522–1586). German Lutheran theologian. A leading figure in establishing Lutheran orthodoxy, Chemnitz studied theology and patristics at the University of Wittenburg, later becoming a defender of Philipp Melanchthon's* interpretation of the doctrine of justification. Chemnitz drafted a compendium of doctrine and reorganized the structure of the church in Wolfenbüttel; later, he led efforts to reconcile divisions within Lutheranism, culminating in the Formula of Concord*. One of his chief theological accomplishments was a modification of the christological doctrine of the *communicatio idiomatium*, which provided a Lutheran platform for understanding the sacramental presence of Christ's humanity in the Eucharist.

David Chytraeus (1531–1600). German Lutheran professor, theologian and biblical exegete. At the age of eight Chytraeus was admitted to the University of Tübingen. There he studied law, philology, philosophy, and theology, finally receiving his master's degree in 1546. Chytraeus befriended Philipp Melanchthon* while sojourning in Wittenberg, where he taught the *Loci communes*. While teaching exegesis at the University of Rostock Chytraeus became acquainted with Tilemann Heshusius,* who strongly influenced Chytraeus away from Philippist theology. As a defender of Gnesio-Lutheran theology Chytraeus helped organize churches throughout Austria in accordance with the Augsburg Confession.* Chytraeus coauthored the Formula of Concord* with Martin Chemnitz,* Andreas Musculus (1514–1581), Nikolaus Selnecker* and Jakob Andreae.* He wrote commentaries on most of the Bible, as well as a devotional work titled *Regula vitae* (1555) that described the Christian virtues.

Isidorus Clarius (1495–1555). Italian Catholic humanist, biblical scholar, and bishop. As a leading Benedictine monk, Clarius sought reform the Roman Catholic Church from within. He participated in the commission that composed the *Consilium de Emendanda Ecclesia* (1536), and as bishop of Foligno, he sought to put many of its recommendations into action, demanding moral reform and consistent preaching from the clergy while reorganizing the charitable work of his diocese. Clarius was also open to rapprochement with Protestants. In 1540, he published *Adhortatio ad Concordiam* seeking compromise with the Lutherans, and his annotated revision of the Vulgate text (1542) interacted with Lutheran and Reformed scholars. This confessional openness was scrutinized after Clarius's death, and his edition of the Vulgate was included in the *Index Librorum Prohibitorum* (1557). For his work on the text of Scripture, however, he is recognized by name in the introduction to the 1611 King James Bible.

David Clarkson (1622–1686). English Puritan theologian. After his dismissal from the pastorate on account of the Act of Uniformity (1662), little is known about Clarkson. At the end of his life he ministered with John Owen* in London.

Robert Cleaver (1571–1613). English Puritan pastor. Cleaver served as rector at Drayton in Oxfordshire until silenced by Archbishop Richard Bancroft for advocating Nonconformity. Despite opposition from ecclesiastical authorities, Cleaver enjoyed a reputation as an excellent preacher. His published works include sermons on Hebrews 4 and Song of Songs 2 as well as one on the last chapter of Proverbs. Cleaver also authored *The Parsimony of Christian Children*, which contained a defense of infant baptism against Baptist criticisms.

George Close (unknown). English Protestant preacher. A series of Close's sermons on Matthew 16 were copied and published while he served as a reader at St. Antholin, London.

Michael Cobabus (d. 1686). German Lutheran theologian and mathematician. Trained in philosophy, mathematics, and theology at the University of Rostock, Cobabus remained in the city, serving as rector of the city school until appointed professor of mathematics at the university. He later received a doctorate in theology from the University of Griefswald and exchanged his position in the Rostock mathematics faculty for a professorship in theology.

Johannes Cocceius (1603–1669). German Reformed theologian. Cocceius first served as professor of biblical philology in his hometown of Bremen before moving to Franeker, where he taught Hebrew and theology, and finally to Leiden, where he spent the majority of his career as professor of theology. Cocceius is perhaps best remembered for his exposition of Reformed federal theology, defining the relationship between humanity and God in terms of progressive covenants. His critics, chief among them Gisbertus Voetius (1589–1676), argued that Cocceius's view of salvation history ignored the unity of the Scriptures and spiritualized the Old Testament. His other writings are extensive, including commentaries on all the books of the Bible, an influential Hebrew and Aramaic lexicon, and numerous works on theology, ethics, and philology.

John Colet (1467–1519). English Catholic priest, preacher and educator. Colet, appointed dean of Saint Paul's Cathedral by Henry VII, was a friend of Desiderius Erasmus,* on whose classical ideals Colet reconstructed the curriculum of Saint Paul's school. Colet was convinced that the foundation of moral reform lay in the education of children. Though an ardent advocate of reform, Colet, like Erasmus, remained loyal to the Catholic Church throughout his life. Colet's agenda of reform was oriented around spiritual and ethical themes, demonstrated in his commentaries on select books of the New Testament and the writings of Pseudo-Dionysius the Areopagite.

Vittoria Colonna (1490–1547). Italian Renaissance poet. Born into a noble family, Colonna was betrothed at three years of age to Fernando d'Ávalos (1489–1525), and they married in 1509. D'Ávalos was largely absent on military campaigns during their marriage, while she exercised his governorship of Benvenuto and became involved in the literary circles of Rome and Naples. One of the most important writers of her age, her friends included Pietro Bembo (1470–1547), Marguerite de Navarre,* and Michelangelo Buonarroti.* Writing primarily in the Petrarchan style, Colonna's reputation as a poet grew after the death of her husband, and much of her poetry was dedicated to his memory. Spiritual concerns form a major element of Colonna's writings, promoting contemplation and the ascetic life. While denied her desire to take holy orders in widowhood, Colonna spent much of her life residing in religious communities, and she was actively involved in movements seeking their improvement, collaborating with reformers such as Reginald Pole,* Juan de Valdés,* and Bernardo Ochino.*

Gasparo Contarini (1483–1542). Italian statesman, theologian and reform-minded cardinal. Contarini was an able negotiator and graceful compromiser. Charles V requested Contarini as the papal legate for the Colloquy of Regensburg (1541), where Contarini reached agreement with Melanchthon* on the doctrine of justification (although neither the pope nor Luther* ratified the agreement). He had come to a similar belief in the priority of faith in the work of Christ rather than works as the basis for Christian life in 1511, though unlike Luther, he never left the papal church over the issue; instead he remainied within it to try to seek gentle reform, and he adhered to papal sacramental teaching. Contarini was an important voice for reform within the Catholic Church, always seeking reconciliation rather than confrontation with Protestant reformers. He wrote many works, including a treatise detailing the ideal bishop, a manual for lay church leaders, a political text on right governance and brief commentaries on the Pauline letters.

Thomas Cooper (1517?-1594) English Anglican Bishop and scholar. Prior to ordination, Cooper taught at Magdalen College School and worked as a physician. Entering the service of the church in about 1559, he served as dean of Christ Church and Gloucester until becoming Bishop of Lincoln and later Bishop of Winchester. A defender of the Elizabethan church order against Catholics and Puritans, Cooper is best remembered as a lexicographer, with his *Thesaurus Linguae Romanae et Britannicae* (1565) published in multiple editions.

Michel Cop (c. 1501–1566). Swiss Protestant pastor. Son of the physician to Francis I* and childhood friend of John Calvin,* Cop was a cathedral canon until fleeing France after his brother Nicholas's (c. 1501–1566) inaugural sermon as rector of the University of Paris was declared heretical for its Lutheran themes. Cop spent some time in Basel before settling in Geneva, where he served as a pastor, taught Calvin Hebrew, and published a sermon series on Proverbs and Ecclesiastes.

Christoph Corner (1518–1594). German Lutheran theologian. Professor of philosophy, rhetoric, and theology at the University of Frankfurt, Corner participated in the drafting of the Formula of Concord.* He also served as superintendent of churches in Mark Brandenberg.

Antonio del Corro (1527–1591). Spanish Reformed pastor and theologian. After encountering the ideas of Martin Luther* and other reformers, Corro abandoned the Hieronymite order. Leaving Spain to avoid charges of heresy, he traveled through Europe, spending time in Geneva and Lausanne before pastoring churches in France and the Low Countries. The arrival of Spanish armies in the Netherlands saw Corro and his family relocate to England, where he pastored a church of Spanish exiles in London and taught at Temple Church and Oxford. Corro courted controversy throughout his career, entering into debates with a wide array of Protestant theologians. In England, he was suspended from his pastorate for slander and examined a number of times for heresy, with some finding suggestions of Arianism in his Christology. Although these charges were never upheld, they clouded his later career and legacy.

Antonius Corvinus (1501–1553). German Lutheran theologian and administrator. After meeting Luther* and Melanchthon,* Corvinus left the humanist circle of Erasmus* to serve as a pastor in cities including Goslar, Witzenhausen, and Pattensen. A signatory of the Schmalkald Articles,* much of his career was devoted to constructing the organizational apparatus of the Lutheran church, and he established disciplinary procedures and church orders for numerous cities in northern Germany. His expository postils on the Gospels, Epistles, Psalms, and Genesis were also distributed widely in order to aid preachers of the region.

John Cosin (1594–1672). Anglican preacher and bishop. Early in his career Cosin was the vice chancellor of Cambridge and canon at the Durham cathedral. But as a friend of William Laud* and an advocate for "Laudian" changes, he was suspected of being a crypto-Catholic. In 1640 during the Long Parliament a Puritan lodged a complaint with the House of Commons concerning Cosin's "popish innovations." Cosin was promptly removed from office. During the turmoil of the English Civil Wars, Cosin sojourned in Paris among English nobility but struggled financially. Cosin returned to England after the Restoration in 1660 to be consecrated as the bishop of Durham. He published annotations on the Book of Common Prayer* and a history of the canon.

John Cotton (1584–1652). New England Puritan minister. Cotton was born to Puritan parents in Derby, England. He entered Trinity College, Cambridge, graduating with his bachelor's degree in 1603. Afterward, Cotton became a fellow at Emmanuel College, Cambridge, which at the time was heavily influenced by Puritanism. There, Cotton finished his master's degree in 1606. Cotton then served as head lecturer, dean, and catechist for the college. It was in this period that he heard the preaching of Richard Sibbes,* which proved instrumental in Cotton's personal conversion. Cotton received a bachelor of divinity in 1610 from Cambridge and was shortly thereafter ordained into the priesthood of the Church of England. However, Cotton's increasing nonconformity brought him into conflict with episcopal authorities, which prompted him to move to the colony of Massachusetts in July 1633. Upon his arrival, he immediately assumed a position of leadership as the teacher of the First Church of Boston. Throughout his tenure, Cotton exerted significant influence in the civic and ecclesiastical affairs of the colony. He continued in his ministry at First Church until his death on December 23, 1652. Over the course of his ministry, Cotton wrote nearly forty works. Among these were the *Keys of the Kingdom of Heaven, and the Power Thereof* (1644) and *Exposition upon the Thirteenth Chapter of Revelation* (1655).

Council of Constance (1414–1418). Convened to resolve the Western Schism, root out heresy and reform the church in head and members, the council asserted in *Sacrosancta* (1415) the immediate authority of ecumenical councils assembled in the Holy Spirit under Christ—even over the pope. Martin V was elected pope in 1417 after the three papal claimants were deposed; thus, the council ended the schism. The council condemned Jan Hus,* Jerome of Prague (c. 1365–1416) and, posthumously, John Wycliffe. Hus and Jerome, despite letters of safe conduct, were burned at the stake. Their deaths ignited the Hussite Wars, which ended as a result of the Council of Basel's concessions to the Bohemian church. The council fathers sought to reform the church through the regular convocation of councils (*Frequens*; 1417). Martin V begrudgingly complied by calling the required councils, then immediately disbanding them. Pius II (r. 1458–1464) reasserted papal dominance through *Execrabilis* (1460), which condemned any appeal to a future council apart from the pope's authority.

Council of Trent (1545–1563) Convoked by Pope Paul III (r. 1534–1549) with the support of Charles V*, the nineteenth ecumenical council was convened in the northern Italian city of Trent. Attended primarily by Italian clerics, it met in three distinct phases. Beginning in December 1545, during its first eight sessions, the council issued doctrinal decrees, asserting the authority of tradition alongside Scripture, the authenticity of the Vulgate, the prerogative of the church in interpretation, and the necessity of human cooperation in the work of salvation. Ecclesial abuses were also addressed, as attempts were made to eliminate absenteeism and pluralism and devolve power from Rome to bishoprics and parishes. The council was suspended following the outbreak of the plague in Trent in March 1547. A number of Protestant delegates were present during the second phase of the council, which met between May 1551 and April 1552 under the supervision of Pope Julius III (r. 1550–1555). The primary achievement of this period of the council was the clarification of teachings on the seven sacraments, with transubstantiation, the objective efficacy of the Eucharist, and the necessity of auricular confession confirmed as dogma. Reconvened by Pope Pius IV (r. 1559–1565) in 1561, the third phase of the council addressed the relationship between bishops and Rome, resulting in affirmations of the divine appointment of the church hierarchy and the obligation of bishops to reside in their dioceses. Clerical education, the regulation of marriage, and teachings on purgatory, indulgences, the use of images, and the saints were also addressed.

Miles Coverdale (1488–1568). Anglican bishop. Coverdale is known for his translations of the Bible into English, completing William Tyndale's* efforts and later producing the Great Bible commissioned by Henry VIII* (1539). A former friar, Coverdale was among the Cambridge scholars who met at the White Horse Tavern to discuss Martin Luther's* ideas. During Coverdale's three terms of exile in Europe, he undertook various translations, including the Geneva Bible*. He was appointed bishop of Exeter by Thomas Cranmer* and served as chaplain to Edward VI. Coverdale contributed to Cranmer's first edition of the Book of Common Prayer.*

William Cowper (Couper) (1568–1619). Scottish Puritan bishop. After graduating from the University of St. Andrews, Cowper worked in parish ministry for twenty-five years before becoming bishop. As a zealous Puritan and advocate of regular preaching and rigorous discipline, Cowper championed Presbyterian polity and lay participation in church government. Cowper published devotional works, sermon collections and a commentary on Revelation.

Benjamin Coxe (fl. 1646). English Baptist minister. Coxe began his career in the Church of England, ministering at parishes in Devonshire, Bedford, and Coventry. After preaching against infant baptism, he was challenged to a public debate by Richard Baxter.* Coxe lost and was briefly arrested after refusing to leave the city. Following his release, he joined a congregation of Anabaptists in London.

Walter Cradock (1606–1659). Welsh Anglican minister. Cradock was born in Llangwm, Monmouthshire, Wales. After completing his education at the University of Oxford, Cradock assumed his first position as curate at Peterson-super-Ely, Glamorgan. In 1633, Cradock, along with some other Welsh ministers, was reported to Archbishop William Laud* and the Court of High Commission for preaching nonconformity and for refusing the *Book of Sports*. In 1634 Cradock traveled throughout Wexham and Herefordshire encouraging the establishment of Welsh Nonconformist congregations. Cradock later became pastor of an Independent congregation at Llanfair Waterdine in 1639. When the English Civil War began, Cradock and his conventicle moved to Bristol, but when Royalist forces came to occupy the city, he and some of his group departed for All-Hallows-the-Great, where he preached regularly with Henry Jessey (1603–1663). In 1641, Cradock was among the group of preachers for Wales commissioned by the Long Parliament. Later, he served as regular preacher for the Barebones Parliament. Throughout this period, Cradock was an ardent supporter of Oliver Cromwell. Cradock lived the remainder of his life quietly while ministering to a congregation at Llangwm. Throughout his career, Cradock authored a number of devotional works, among which were *Gospel Liberty* (1648) and *Gospel Holiness* (1655).

Thomas Cranmer (1489–1556). Anglican archbishop and theologian. Cranmer supervised church reform and produced the first two editions of the Book of Common Prayer.* As a doctoral student at Cambridge, he was involved in the discussions at the White Horse Tavern. Cranmer contributed to a religious defense of Henry VIII's* divorce; Henry then appointed him Archbishop of Canterbury. Cranmer cautiously steered the course of reform, accelerating under Edward VI. After supporting the attempted coup to prevent Mary's assuming the throne, Cranmer was convicted of treason and burned at the stake. Cranmer's legacy is the splendid English of his liturgy and prayer books.

Richard Crashaw (1612–1649). English Catholic poet. Educated at Cambridge, Crashaw was fluent in Hebrew, Greek and Latin. His first volume of poetry was *Epigrammatum sacrorum liber* (1634). Despite being born into a Puritan family, Crashaw was attracted to Catholicism, finally converting in 1644 after he was forced to resign his fellowship for not signing the Solemn League and

Covenant (1643). In 1649, he was made a subcanon of Our Lady of Loretto by Cardinal Palotta.

Herbert Croft (1603–1691). Anglican bishop. As a boy Croft converted to Catholicism; he returned to the Church of England during his studies at Oxford. Before the English Civil Wars, he served as chaplain to Charles I. After the Restoration, Charles II appointed him as bishop. Croft ardently opposed Catholicism in his later years.

John Crompe (d. 1661). Anglican priest. Educated at Cambridge, Crompe published a commentary on the Apostles' Creed, a sermon on Psalm 21:3 and an exposition of Christ's passion.

Oliver Cromwell (1599–1658). Commander of the Parliamentary forces during the English Civil War. Lord Protector of the Commonwealth of England, Scotland, and Ireland. Cromwell was born in Huntingdon, East Anglia, the only surviving son of Robert Cromwell. In 1616, he enrolled at the University of Cambridge as a fellow commoner. However, he withdrew from the university the following year due to his father's death. He represented Huntingdon in Parliament in 1628, and later Cambridge in the Short and Long Parliaments. During the Civil War, he commanded the Parliamentary forces, which he led to victory at the Battles of Marston Moor (1644) and Naseby (1645). After the execution of King Charles I in 1649, he became a member of the Council of State. It was at this time that the monarchy was abolished. In 1653, he was elevated to the position of Lord Protector of the Commonwealth. He declined the crown, though it was offered him in 1657. As Lord Protector, he endeavored to lead the postwar recovery, suppress military resistance, and advance British influence throughout Europe and the world. Moreover, he promoted a limited religious toleration in the kingdoms of England, Scotland, and Ireland. After his death in 1658, his son Richard (1626–1712) succeeded him as Lord Protector. However, due to incompetence, Richard was forced to resign, which paved the way for the Restoration of the monarchy in 1660 with the ascension of Charles II (1630–1685) to the throne. One year after the Restoration, Oliver Cromwell's body was disinterred from Westminster Abbey, hung on the gallows at Tyburn, and cast into an unmarked grave.

Caspar Cruciger (1504–1548). German Lutheran theologian. Recognized for his alignment with the theological views of Philipp Melanchthon,* Cruciger was a scholar respected among both Protestants and Catholics. In 1521, Cruciger came Wittenberg to study Hebrew and remained there most of his life. He became a valuable partner for Martin Luther* in translating the Old Testament and served as teacher, delegate to major theological colloquies and rector. Cruciger was an agent of reform in his birthplace of Leipzig, where at the age of fifteen he had observed the disputation between Luther and Johann Eck.*

Elisabeth Cruciger (c. 1500–1535). German Lutheran hymnist. Following her conversion to Lutheranism, Cruciger left the Praemonstratensian order and relocated to Wittenberg, where she married Caspar Cruciger.* While her authorship has been contested, recent scholarship has assigned Cruciger the place of the first female Lutheran hymnist for her composition of "Lord Christ is the Only Son of God" (Herr Christ der einig Gotts Sohn) (1524).

Ralph Cudworth (d. 1624) English Protestant minister. Father of noted Cambridge Platonist Ralph Cudworth (1617–1688), the elder Cudworth was a fellow of Emanuel College, Cambridge and rector of Aller in Somersetshire.

Marguerite d'Angoulême (1492–1549). French Catholic noblewoman. The elder sister of King Francis I of France, Marguerite was the Queen of Navarre and Duchess of Alençon and Berry. She was a poet and author of the French Renaissance. She composed *The Mirror of a Sinful Soul* (1531)—condemned by the theologians of the Sorbonne for containing Lutheran ideas—and an unfinished collection of short stories, the Heptaméron (1558). A leading figure in the French Reformation, Marguerite was at the center of a network of reform-minded individuals that included Guillame Briçonnet,* Jacques Lefèvre d'Etaples,* Gérard Roussel (1500–1550) and Guillame Farel (1489–1565).

Jakob Dachser (1486–1567). German Anabaptist theologian and hymnist. Dachser served as a Catholic priest in Vienna until he was imprisoned and then exiled for defending the Lutheran understanding of the Mass and fasting. Hans Hut* rebaptized him in Augsburg, where Dachser was appointed as a leader of the Anabaptist congregation. Lutheran authorities imprisoned him for nearly four years. In 1531 he recanted his Radical beliefs and began to catechize children with the permission of the city council. Dachser was expelled from Augsburg as a possible insurrectionist in 1552 and relocated to Pfalz-Neuberg. He published a number of poems, hymns and mystical works, and he versified several psalms.

Jean Daillé (1594–1670). French Reformed pastor. Born into a devout Reformed family, Daillé studied theology and philosophy at Saumur under the most influential contemporary lay leader in French Protestantism, Philippe Duplessis-Mornay (1549–1623). Daillé held to

Amyraldianism—the belief that Christ died for all humanity inclusively, not particularly for the elect who would inherit salvation (though only the elect are in fact saved). He wrote a controversial treatise on the church fathers that aggravated many Catholic and Anglican scholars because of Daillé's apparent demotion of patristic authority in matters of faith.

Lambert Daneau (1530?–1595). French Reformed pastor and theologian. After a decade of pastoring in France, following the St. Bartholomew's Day Massacre, Daneau fled to Geneva to teach theology at the Academy. He later taught in the Low Countries, finishing his career in southern France. Daneau's diverse works include tracts on science, ethics and morality as well as numerous theological and exegetical works.

John Davenant (1576–1641). Anglican bishop and professor. Davenant attended Queen's College, Cambridge, where he received his doctorate and was appointed professor of divinity. During the Remonstrant controversy, James I* sent Davenant as one of the four representatives for the Church of England to the Synod of Dordrecht.* Following James's instructions, Davenant advocated a *via media* between the Calvinists and the Remonstrants, although in later years he defended against the rise of Arminianism in England. In 1621, Davenant was promoted to the bishopric of Salisbury, where he was generally receptive to Laudian reforms. Davenant's lectures on Colossians are his best-known work.

William Day (1605–1684). Anglican theologian. Born and raised in Windsor, Berkshire, Day received his early education from Eton College. Afterward, he matriculated at King's College, Cambridge, where he was elected a fellow in 1624. Day received his BA in 1629, and MA in 1632. In 1635, Day was incorporated MA at Oxford and in 1637 became vicar of Mapledurham, Oxfordshire. Throughout his long career, Day conformed to all the ecclesiastical changes dictated by the government through the Restoration, during which he retained his vicarage. Finally, Day was made divinity reader at the King's Chapel, Windsor Chapel. He published two commentaries, *An Exposition of the Book of the Prophet Isaiah* (1654) and *A Paraphrase and Commentary upon the Epistle of St. Paul to the Romans* (1666).

Defense of the Augsburg Confession (1531). See *Augsburg Confession.*

Hans Denck (c. 1500–1527). German Radical theologian. Denck, a crucial early figure of the German Anabaptist movement, combined medieval German mysticism with the radical sacramental theology of Andreas Bodenstein von Karlstadt* and Thomas Müntzer.* Denck argued that the exterior forms of Scripture and sacrament are symbolic witnesses secondary to the internally revealed truth of the Sprit in the human soul. This view led to his expulsion from Nuremberg in 1525; he spent the next two years in various centers of reform in the German territories. At the time of his death, violent persecution against Anabaptists was on the rise throughout northern Europe.

Stephen Denison (unknown). English Puritan pastor. Denison received the post of curate at St. Katherine Cree in London sometime in the 1610s, where he ministered until his ejection from office in 1635. During his career at St. Katherine Cree, Denison waded into controversy with both Puritans (over the doctrine of predestination) and Anglicans (over concerns about liturgical ceremonies). He approached both altercations with rancor and rigidity, although he seems to have been quite popular and beloved by most of his congregation. In 1631, William Laud* consecrated the newly renovated St. Katherine Cree, and as part of the festivities Denison offered a sermon on Luke 19:27 in which he publicly rebuked Laud for fashioning the Lord's house into a "den of robbers." Aside from the record of his quarrels, very little is known about Denison. In addition to *The White Wolf* (a 1627 sermon against another opponent), he published a catechism for children (1621), a treatise on the sacraments (1621) and a commentary on 2 Peter 1 (1622).

Arthur Dent (d. 1607). English Puritan preacher. Ordained in the Church of England, Dent ministered in Essex, where he made his Puritan sympathies clear and was disciplined for refusing to wear a surplice and make the sign of the cross. He published a number of works, including an exposition of the Articles of Faith and an exposition of Revelation targeted against the Roman Catholic Church.

Marie Dentière (1495–1561). Belgian Reformed theologian. Dentière relinquished her monastic vows and married Simon Robert (d.1533), a former priest, in Strasbourg. After Robert died, she married Antoine Froment (1508–1581), a reformer in Geneva, and became involved in the reform of that city. Her best-known writings are a tract addressed to Marguerite d'Angoulême,* the *Very Useful Epistle* (1539), in which she espoused the evangelical faith and the right of women to interpret and teach scripture, and a preface to Calvin's sermon on 1 Timothy 2:8-12. Dentière is the only woman to have her name inscribed on the International Monument to the Reformation in Geneva.

Edward Dering (c. 1540–1576). English Puritan preacher. An early Puritan, Dering's prospects of advancement in the Elizabethan church were effectively ended after a sermon in front of the Queen in which he described her as an "untamed and unruly heifer" while criticizing the state of the church and clergy. While continuing with intemperate and critical attacks throughout his career, Dering established himself as a preacher at St. Paul's Cathedral in London, where he became known for his pastoral concern and desire to teach the assurance of salvation.

Jean D'Espagne (1591–1659). French Independent pastor. After leading churches at Orange and the Hague, D'Espagne departed under accusations of immorality and settled in London, where he pastored a French congregation. A fractious figure, he led a group that separated from the established French congregation and entered into numerous controversies. Many of his extant writings are targeted toward errors he perceived in the theology and practice of others.

David Dickson (1583?–1663). Scottish Reformed pastor, preacher, professor and theologian. Dickson defended the Presbyterian form of ecclesial reformation in Scotland and was recognized for his iteration of Calvinist federal theology and expository biblical commentaries. Dickson served for over twenty years as professor of philosophy at the University of Glasgow before being appointed professor of divinity. He opposed the imposition of Episcopalian measures on the church in Scotland and was active in political and ecclesial venues to protest and prohibit such influences. Dickson was removed from his academic post following his refusal of the oath of supremacy during the Restoration era.

Veit Dietrich (1506–1549). German Lutheran preacher and theologian. Dietrich intended to study medicine at the University of Wittenberg, but Martin Luther* and Philipp Melanchthon* convinced him to study theology instead. Dietrich developed a strong relationship with Luther, accompanying him to the Marburg Colloquy (1529) and to Coburg Castle during the Diet of Augsburg (1530). After graduating, Dietrich taught on the arts faculty, eventually becoming dean. In 1535 he returned to his hometown, Nuremberg, to pastor. Later in life, Dietrich worked with Melanchthon to reform the church in Regensburg. In 1547, when Charles V arrived in Nuremberg, Dietrich was suspended from the pastorate; he resisted the imposition of the Augsburg Interim to no avail. In addition to transcribing some of Luther's lectures, portions of the Table Talk and the very popular *Hauspostille* (1544), Dietrich published his own sermons for children, a manual for pastors and a summary of the Bible.

Louis de Dieu (1590–1642). Dutch Reformed pastor and linguist. Committed to his pastoral and teaching ministry in Leiden, Dieu turned down the opportunity to teach theology and Old Testament at the University of Utrecht. He published grammars of Hebrew (1626) and Persian (1639); a comparative grammar of Hebrew, Aramaic, and Syriac (1628); and a collection of writings on the New Testament text.

Giovanni Diodati (1576–1649). Italian Reformed theologian. Diodati was from an Italian banking family who fled for religious reasons to Geneva. There he trained under Theodore Beza;* on completion of his doctoral degree, Diodati became professor of Hebrew at the academy. He was an ecclesiastical representative of the church in Geneva (for whom he was a delegate at the Synod of Dordrecht*) and an advocate for reform in Venice. Diodati's chief contribution to the Italian reform movement was a translation of the Bible into Italian (1640–1641), which remains the standard translation in Italian Protestantism.

John Dod (c. 1549–1645). English Puritan pastor. Over the course of his lengthy pastoral career (spanning roughly sixty years), Dod was twice suspended for nonconformity and twice reinstated. A popular preacher, he published many sermons as well as commentaries on the Ten Commandments and the Lord's Prayer; collections of his sayings and anecdotes were compiled after his death.

John Donne (1572–1631). Anglican poet and preacher. Donne was born into a strong Catholic family. However, sometime between his brother's death from the plague while in prison in 1593 and the publication of his *Pseudo-Martyr* in 1610, Donne joined the Church of England. Ordained to the Anglican priesthood in 1615 and already widely recognized for his verse, Donne quickly rose to prominence as a preacher—some have deemed him the best of his era. His textual corpus is an amalgam of erotic *and* divine poetry (e.g., "Batter My Heart"), as well as a great number of sermons.

Dordrecht Confession (1632). Dutch Mennonite confession. Adriaan Cornelisz (1581–1632) wrote the Dordrecht Confession to unify Dutch Mennonites. This basic statement of Mennonite belief and practice affirms distinctive doctrines such as nonresistance, shunning, footwashing, and the refusal to swear oaths. Most continental Mennonites subscribed to this confession during the second half of the seventeenth century.

Johann George Dorsche (1597–1659). German Lutheran theologian. Dorsche pastored briefly at Entzheim before being called to Strasbourg, where he earned his doctorate, was appointed professor of theology, and served as a preacher at the cathedral. He spent the last five years of his life as professor of theology at the University of Rostock. Dorsche published a number of theological works as well as commentaries on the Gospels and Hebrews.

John Downame (c. 1571–1652). English Puritan pastor and theologian. See *English Annotations*.

Charles Drelincourt (1595–1669). French Reformed pastor, theologian and controversialist. After studying at Saumur Academy, Drelincourt pastored the Reformed Church in Paris for nearly fifty years. He was well known for his ministry to the sick. In addition to polemical works against Catholicism, he published numerous pastoral resources: catechisms, three volumes of sermons and a five-volume series on consolation for the suffering.

The Dutch Annotations (1657). See *Statenvertaling*.

Daniel Dyke (d. 1614). English Puritan preacher. Born of nonconformist stock, Dyke championed a more thorough reformation of church practice in England. After the promulgation of John Whitgift's* articles in 1583, Dyke refused to accept what he saw as remnants of Catholicism, bringing him into conflict with the bishop of London. Despite the petitions of his congregation and some politicians, the bishop of London suspended Dyke from his ministry for refusing priestly ordination and conformity to the Book of Common Prayer.* All of his work was published posthumously; it is mostly focused on biblical interpretation.

John Eachard (unknown). English Anglican minister. After graduating with his master of arts from Trinity College, Cambridge, Eachard was the vicar at Darsham in Suffolk. At least two of his sermons, one on Matthew 3:10 and another on Revelation 12:11, were published in his lifetime.

Johann Eck (Johann Maier of Eck) (1486–1543). German Catholic theologian. Though Eck was not an antagonist of Martin Luther* until the dispute over indulgences, Luther's Ninety-five Theses (1517) sealed the two as adversaries. After their debate at the Leipzig Disputation (1519), Eck participated in the writing of the papal bull that led to Luther's excommunication. Much of Eck's work was written to oppose Protestantism or to defend Catholic doctrine and the papacy; his *Enchiridion* was a manual written to counter Protestant doctrine. However, Eck was also deeply invested in the status of parish preaching, publishing a five-volume set of postils. He participated in the assemblies at Regensburg and Augsburg and led the Catholics in their rejection of the Augsburg Confession.

Edward VI of England (1537–1553). English monarch. Son of Henry VIII* and Jane Seymour (1508–1537), Edward ascended to the throne as a minor, leaving the practical power of the monarchy in the hands of those appointed by the Regency council as Lord Protector of the Realm, first, his uncle, Edward Seymour, duke of Somerset (1500–1552), and afterwards, John Dudley, duke of Northumberland (1504–1553). Under Somerset and Northumberland, and with Thomas Cranmer* installed as Archbishop of Canterbury, the eclectic reforms made during the reign of Henry VIII were drawn into the service of a thoroughly Protestant transformation. During the reign of Edward, communion in two kinds was instituted, all services were held in the vernacular, and a series of ecclesiastical visitations oversaw the suppression of Catholic religion. Alongside the flood of Protestant refugees from the continent that sheltered in the kingdom, the publication of the revised Book of Common Prayer*, the Book of Homilies* and the Forty–Two Articles (1553) helped establish the future direction of Anglicanism.

Elizabeth I of England (1533–1603) English monarch. The daughter of Henry VIII* (r. 1509–1547) and Anne Boleyn (c. 1501–1536), Elizabeth outwardly conformed to Catholicism during the reign of her sister Mary I (r. 1553–1558), but her Protestant upbringing encouraged the hopes of many reformers upon her accession in 1558. With the 1559 Elizabethan Settlement, Elizabeth redefined England as a Protestant country, with the Act of Supremacy asserting the monarch as the head of the English church, and the Act of Uniformity establishing the 1559 *Book of Common Prayer** as the valid order of service within the realm. However, Elizabeth resisted the aggressive persecution of Catholics for political reasons, while also allowing some traditional vestments, furniture and ceremonies to be retained. Her moderate and pragmatic reforms frustrated many who wished for more thorough change and led to the emergence of the Puritan movement. Elizabeth faced numerous threats during her reign, including the machinations of Scottish Catholics and claims to the throne of Mary Stuart (1542–1547), leading to her rival's imprisonment and execution in 1587; the attempted invasion of England by Spain, which culminated in the celebrated defeat of the Spanish Armada in 1588; and a Catholic rebellion in Ireland that was suppressed during the Nine Years War (1594–1603). Elizabeth never married, and was succeeded on the throne by James I* following her death in 1603.

Edward Elton (1569–1624). Puritan minister. Elton served as pastor of St. Mary Magdalen's Church in Bermondsey, Surrey. Richard Baxter* praised him for his exegetical works, among which were *Three Excellent Pious Treatises in Sundry Sermons upon the Whole Seventh,*

Eighth, and Ninth Chapters of the Epistle to the Romans and *An Exposition of the Epistle of St. Paul to the Colossians.*

English Annotations (1645; 1651; 1657). Under a commission from the Westminster Assembly, the editors of the English Annotations—John Downame* along with unnamed colleagues—translated, collated and digested in a compact and accessible format several significant Continental biblical resources, including Calvin's* commentaries, Beza's* *Annotationes majores* and Diodati's* *Annotations.*

Desiderius Erasmus (1466–1536). Dutch Catholic humanist and pedagogue. Erasmus, a celebrated humanist scholar, was recognized for translations of ancient texts, reform of education according to classical studies, moral and spiritual writings and the first printed edition of the Greek New Testament. A former Augustinian who never left the Catholic Church, Erasmus addressed deficiencies he saw in the church and society, challenging numerous prevailing doctrines but advocating reform. He envisioned a simple, spiritual Christian life shaped by the teachings of Jesus and ancient wisdom. He was often accused of collusion with Martin Luther* on account of some resonance of their ideas but hotly debated Luther on human will.

George Estey (c. 1560–1601). English Anglican priest. After graduating from Cambridge, Estey was ordained in the Church of England and served as vicar of St. Mary in Bury St. Edmunds, Suffolk.

Paul Fagius (1504–1549). German Reformed Hebraist and pastor. After studying at the University of Heidelberg, Fagius went to Strasbourg where he perfected his Hebrew under Wolfgang Capito.* In Isny im Allgäu (Baden-Württemberg) he met the great Jewish grammarian Elias Levita (1469–1549), with whom he established a Hebrew printing press. In 1544 Fagius returned to Strasbourg, succeeding Capito as preacher and Old Testament lecturer. During the Augsburg Interim, Fagius (with Martin Bucer*) accepted Thomas Cranmer's* invitation to translate and interpret the Bible at Cambridge. However, Fagius died before he could begin any of the work. Fagius wrote commentaries on the first four chapters of Genesis and the deutero-canonical books of Sirach and Tobit.

Guillaume Farel (1489–1565) French Reformed preacher and theologian. At the vanguard of the French Reformation, Farel was a student of Jacques Lefèvre d'Étaples* and member of Archbishop Briçonnet's* circle in Meaux until his desire for more rapid change saw him depart in 1523 to preach the Protestant message in Basel, Montbéliard, Strasbourg, Bern, and Aigle. During this period of his ministry, he composed the first French Protestant book, an evangelical commentary on the Lord's Prayer and the Apostle's Creed, as well as the first French Confession of Faith. A catalyst in Geneva's acceptance of the Reformation in 1536, it was Farel who persuaded Calvin* to settle in the city. After he and Calvin were banished from Geneva in 1538, Farel accepted the pastorate in Neuchâtel, a position he held until his death while continuing to travel and support the Reformation in the French-speaking lands.

John Fary (unknown). English Puritan pastor. Fary authored *God's Severity on Man's Sterility* (1645), a sermon on the fruitless fig tree in Luke 13:6-9.

Margaret Fell (1614–1702). English Quaker. Known as the "Mother of Quakerism," Fell was born at Dalton-in-Furness in northern England. The daughter of a local judge, she married Thomas Fell, who was a judge as well as a member of Parliament, representing Lancashire. In 1652, under the preaching of George Fox (1624–1691), Fell and her daughters became members of the Society of Friends (the Quakers). From that time onward, she became a pivotal figure in the subsequent development of the Quaker movement. Throughout her extensive correspondence to powerful members of the nobility, including King Charles II (r. 1660–1685), she pleaded for the release of imprisoned Quakers. Fell was arrested in 1664 for leading Quaker meetings and for her refusal to swear the Oath of Obedience, and she was sentenced to four and a half years imprisonment. After her release, she married George Fox in 1669, her first husband having died eleven years earlier. In addition to her advocacy for incarcerated Quakers, Fell enhanced the work of the Quaker Women's Meeting, which consisted of caring for the sick and elderly as well as orphans and prisoners. Her exegetical works include *For Mannaseth Ben Israel* and *A Loving Salutation to the Seed of Abraham,* both published in 1656, and translated into Hebrew (the latter believed to have been translated by the Jewish philosopher Benedict Spinoza). Moreover during her imprisonment, she authored her most famous treatise, *Women's Speaking Justified, Proved and Allowed of by the Scriptures.*

Dudley Fenner (1558?–1587). English Puritan minister. Fenner ministered briefly in Kent before following his mentor Thomas Cartwright* to Antwerp, where he was ordained in the Reformed church. After pastoring the English congregation alongside Cartwright, Fenner returned to his previous congregation in Kent, but he was soon suspended and arrested for refusing to conform to the Book of Common Prayer* and Thirty-Nine Articles.*

Once released, he returned to the Low Countries, spending the remainder of his career leading an English congregation in Middelburg. He composed devotional and polemical writings as well as commentaries on Song of Songs and Philemon.

William Fenner (1600–1640). English Puritan pastor. After studying at Cambridge and Oxford, Fenner ministered at Sedgley and Rochford. Fenner's extant writings, which primarily deal with practical and devotional topics, demonstrate a zealous Puritan piety and a keen interest in Scripture and theology.

Charles Ferme (1566–1617). Scottish Reformed pastor and educator. After studying and teaching at the University of Edinburgh, Ferme pastored in Philorth, where he later served as the principal of a newly chartered university. The reconstitution of the episcopacy brought challenges for Ferme, and his resistance saw him imprisoned a number of times, including a three-year incarceration on the Isle of Bute. His only extant writing is a logical analysis of Romans.

Henry Ferne (1602–1662). English Protestant minister. Ferne ministered at a number of parishes in the north of England before serving as an extraordinary chaplain to Charles I* after earning his doctorate of divinity. A committed Royalist, he left official ministry during the Civil War (1642–1651), though he often preached, wrote a number of theological treatises against the Roman Catholics, and accompanied the king on a number of occasions. After the Restoration, Ferne served as master at Trinity College, Cambridge, and dean of Ely Cathedral before becoming bishop of Chester.

Richard Ferrers (Unknown). English poet. Ferrers is remembered for his poem *The Worth of Woman* (1622), defending the equality and value of women.

First Helvetic Confession (1536). Anticipating the planned church council at Mantua (1537, but delayed until 1545 at Trent), Reformed theologians of the Swiss cantons drafted a confession to distinguish themselves from both Catholics and the churches of the Augsburg Confession.* Heinrich Bullinger* led the discussion and wrote the confession itself; Leo Jud, Oswald Myconius, Simon Grynaeus and others were part of the assembly. Martin Bucer* and Wolfgang Capito* had desired to draw the Lutheran and Reformed communions closer together through this document, but Luther* proved unwilling after Bullinger refused to accept the Wittenberg Concord (1536). This confession was largely eclipsed by Bullinger's Second Helvetic Confession.*

John Fisher (1469–1535). English Catholic bishop and theologian. This reputed preacher defended Catholic orthodoxy and strove to reform abuses in the church. In 1521 Henry VIII* honored Fisher with the title *Fidei Defensor* ("defender of the faith"). Nevertheless, Fisher opposed the king's divorce of Catherine of Aragon (1485–1536) and the independent establishment of the Church of England; he was convicted for treason and executed. Most of Fisher's works are polemical and occasional (e.g., on transubstantiation, against Martin Luther*); however, he also published a series of sermons on the seven penitential psalms. In addition to his episcopal duties, Fisher was the chancellor of Cambridge from 1504 until his death.

Matthias Flacius (1520–1575). Lutheran theologian. A native of Croatia, Matthias Flacius commenced his studies at the University of Tubingen, and completed them at Wittenberg, where through Luther's influence, he embraced the university's evangelical theology. Flacius began his career as instructor of Hebrew at the University of Wittenberg in 1544, and remained in this post until 1549. As a devoted follower of Luther's teachings, Flacius sought to defend them in their purity which drove him and Nikolaus von Amsdorf as leaders of the Gnesio-Lutherans to oppose the more moderate positions of Philipp Melanchthon and his sympathizers, the Philippists, in several controversies concerning the role of free will and good works in justification as well as relations with Calvinism. After serving as a professor at the University of Jena (1557–1561), Flacius spent the remainder of his life as an independent scholar, frequently moving from one city to another to escape persecution. Flacius died in Frankfurt am Main in 1575. His important exegetical works are *De vocabula Dei* (1549), *Clavis Scripturae Sacrae* (1567), and *Glossa Novi Testamenti* (1570). Flacius also published two historical works, *Catalogus Testium Veritatis* (1556) and the *Magdeburg Centuries*.

Marcantonio Flaminio (1498–1550). Italian humanist and poet. Flaminio was dependent on patronage, and he spent much of his life in the houses of noble benefactors in Bologna, Genoa, and Verona. While he never left the Roman church, he was drawn to intellectual currents that sought reform. In Naples, he participated in an intellectual circle that included Juan de Valdés* and Pietro Carnesecchi* before joining the house of Cardinal Pole* in Viterbo. Alongside his poetry and humanistic writings, Flaminio also edited one of the most significant Italian texts of the Reformation, Benedetto de Mantova's* *The Benefit of Christ* (1543).

John Flavel (c. 1630–1691). English Puritan pastor. Trained at Oxford, Flavel ministered in southwest England from 1650 until the Act of Uniformity in 1662, which reaffirmed the compulsory use of the Book of Common Prayer. Flavel preached unofficially for many years, until his congregation was eventually allowed to build a meeting place in 1687. His works were numerous, varied and popular.

Giovanni Battista Folengo (1490–1559). Italian Catholic exegete. In 1528 Folengo left the Benedictine order, questioning the validity of monastic vows; he returned to the monastic life in 1534. During this hiatus Folengo came into contact with the Neapolitan reform-minded circle founded by Juan de Valdés.* Folengo published commentaries on the Psalms, John, 1–2 Peter and James. Augustin Marlorat* included Folengo's comment in his anthology of exegesis on the Psalms. In 1580 Folengo's Psalms commentary was added to the Index of Prohibited Books.

John Forbes (1568?–1634). Scottish Reformed pastor. While minister at Alford in Aberdeenshire, Forbes was appointed moderator of the Presbyterian Aberdeen Assembly, which met against the orders of King James I.* Refusing to accept the monarch's jurisdiction, he was exiled to the Continent and settled in the Netherlands, where he pastored English congregations at Middleburg and Delft until forced out under the reforms of Archbishop Laud.*

Francisco Forerius (1523-1581) Portuguese Catholic theologian. A Dominican monk, Forerius was a preacher to the Portuguese court. He represented the king to the Council of Trent*, where he worked on the *Index Librorum Phohibitorum*, helped revise the missal and breviary, and contributed to the composition of the catechism. After returning to Portugal, Forerius served as prior of the Dominican convent in Lisbon.

Formula of Concord (1577). After Luther's* death, intra-Lutheran controversies between the Gnesio-Lutherans (partisans of Luther) and the Philippists (partisans of Melanchthon*) threatened to cause a split among those who had subscribed to the Augsburg Confession.* In 1576, Jakob Andreae,* Martin Chemnitz,* Nikolaus Selnecker,* David Chytraeus* and Andreas Musculus (1514–1581) met with the intent of resolving the controversies, which mainly regarded the relationship between good works and salvation, the third use of the law, and the role of the human will in accepting God's grace. In 1580, celebrating the fiftieth anniversary of the presentation of the Augsburg Confession to Charles V (1500–1558), the *Book of Concord* was printed as the authoritative interpretation of the Augsburg Confession; it included the three ancient creeds, the Augsburg Confession, its Apology (1531), the Schmalkald Articles,* Luther's *Treatise on the Power and Primacy of the Pope* (1537) and both his Small and Large Catechisms (1529).

John Foxe (1516–1587). English Protestant martryrologist, historian. John Foxe was born in Boston, Lincolnshire. After completing his early education, Foxe became a fellow at Magdalen College, Oxford, where he completed his BA degree in 1537, and MA in 1543. Also he was lecturer in logic from 1539 to 1540. However, in 1545, Foxe was forced to resign from Magdalen because he had adopted Protestant beliefs. After leaving Oxford, Foxe became tutor to the children of the Earl of Surrey. During this time Foxe made the acquaintance of John Bale (1495–1562) who fostered his interest in history. When Mary Tudor ascended the throne of England in 1553, Foxe fled to the continent. While there, Foxe traveled to Frankfurt, where in 1555 he met Edmund Grindal (1519–1583), who had been composing accounts of Protestant martyrs. Foxe later joined Grindal in Basel, where he translated his narratives into Latin. Foxe published the book resulting from his labors in Basel in 1559. After Elizabeth I* succeeded to the throne in the same year, Foxe returned to England. Upon his return he began working with the printer, John Day, who published the first English edition of Foxe's work. This voluminous work, *The Acts and Monuments*, underwent four editions during the remainder of the author's lifetime. *The Acts and Monuments* contributed significantly to the development of the national identity and piety of Elizabethan England. Shorter versions of this work are known simply as *Foxe's Book of Martyrs*.

Francis I of France (1494–1547). French monarch. Francis ascended to the French throne following the death of Louis XII (1462–1515), who was both his cousin and father-in-law. Much of Francis's reign was dominated by warfare. In Italy, victory over the Swiss allowed him to assert his dynastic claim to the Duchy of Milan, and extract liberties for the French church from Pope Leo X* through the Concordat of Bologna. His campaign against Charles V* was less successful, however, as Milan was lost and following defeat at the Battle of Pavia, Francis was taken prisoner. His release was negotiated by his sister, Marguerite d'Angouleme*, though he reneged in its terms once reaching safety, ensuring continued conflict with the Holy Roman Emperor throughout his reign. Francis fostered humanistic learning within his kingdom, and while he resisted Lutheran and other evangelical thought, he gave some space for its expression, giving protection to scholars such as those gathered around his sister and Bishop Guillaume Briçonnet* at Meaux. His desire for social order saw him take increasingly strident steps against the Reformation, however, particularly after his bedchamber was pamphleted during the Affair of the Placards, and the final years of his reign saw a significant increase in attempts to reassert Catholic doctrine and stamp out Protestantism with persecution.

Sebastian Franck (1499–1542). German Radical theologian. Franck became a Lutheran in 1525, but by 1529 he began to develop ideas that distanced him from Protestants and Catholics. Expelled from Strasbourg and later Ulm due to his controversial writings, Franck spent the end of his life in Basel. Franck emphasized God's word as a divine internal spark that cannot be adequately expressed in outward forms. Thus he criticized religious institutions and dogmas. His work consists mostly of commentaries, compilations and translations. In his sweeping historical *Chronica* (1531), Franck supported numerous heretics condemned by the Catholic Church and criticized political and church authorities.

Leonhard Frick (d. 1528). Austrian Radical martyr. See *Kunstbuch*.

John Frith (1503–1533). English reformer, author, and martyr. Frith was born in Westerham, Kent. He was the son of Richard Frith, the innkeeper of the White Horse Inn. After receiving his earlier education at Sevenoaks Grammar School and Eton College, Frith matriculated at Queen's College, Cambridge, where Stephen Gardiner (1497–1555), future bishop of Winchester, and opponent of the English Reformation, was his tutor. Frith graduated with his BA degree in 1525, having obtained proficiency in Latin and mathematics. While still a student, Frith met Thomas Bilney (1495–1531), who most likely introduced him to evangelical faith. After graduating, Frith became a junior canon at Christ Church, Oxford. However, while at Oxford, Frith along with nine others was imprisoned in a fish cellar for possessing what ecclesiastical authorities considered "heretical books." Upon his release, Frith traveled to the Continent, where he assisted William Tyndale* with his translation work. Also while on the Continent, Frith translated some antipapal polemical works, and authored *A Disputation of Purgatory*. Upon Frith's return to England in 1532, he was arrested and imprisoned several times for publicly preaching against transubstantiation and purgatory. Eventually, Frith was imprisoned in the Tower of London, and later transferred to Newgate Prison. He was burned at the stake on July 4, 1533.

Libert Froidmont (1587–1653). Belgian philosopher, scientist, and theologian. A childhood friend of Cornelius Jansen (1585–1638), Froidmont entered the Society of Jesus and his early career was focused on philosophy and the sciences, teaching at Antwerp, Saint-Michel, and Louvain. Drawn to the rigorous but controversial Augustinianism of Jansen, Froidmont earned his doctorate in theology in 1628 and succeeded Jansen as chair of theology at Louvain. While publishing a number of theological and exegetical works, including a commentary on Paul's letters, Froidmont was also active in the scientific and philosophical debates of his era. He published against Nicolas Copernicus (1473–1543) and Galileo Galilei (1564–1642), whom he argued were wrong but not heretical, and was one of the first to engage with the thought of René Descartes (1596–1650).

William Fulke (1538–1589). English Protestant theologian. Responsible for preaching and lecturing on Old Testament and other subjects, William Fulke courted controversy during his tenure as fellow at Cambridge. He was briefly expelled for his advocacy of Vestarians and later resigned until acquitted of being in an incestuous marriage. He left Cambridge to serve as chaplain to Robert Dudley, Earl of Leicester (1532–1588), returning almost a decade later as master of Pembroke College. He is best remembered as a controversialist and was the author of numerous anti-Catholic tracts.

Thomas Fuller (1608–1661). English Protestant minister. Fuller, the son of a minister, graduated from Cambridge, and his early career was overseen by his uncle John Davenant,* who secured his nephew a number of pastoral positions. Known for his wit and moderation, Fuller was a chaplain in the Royal army during the Civil War (1642–1651), and he served as an extraordinary chaplain to King Charles II (1630–1685) after the Restoration. He composed a number of exegetical and pastoral works, but he is primarily remembered for his historical writings. These include histories of the Crusades and the church in England as well as a biographical dictionary, the *History of the Worthies of England* (1622).

Gallic Confession (1559). This confession was accepted at the first National Synod of the Reformed Churches of France (1559). It was intended to be a touchstone of Reformed faith but also to show to the people of France that the Huguenots—who faced persecution—were not seditious. The French Reformed Church presented this confession to Francis II (1544–1560) in 1560, and to his successor, Charles IX (1550–1574), in 1561. The later Genevan draft, likely written by Calvin,* Beza* and Pierre Viret (1511–1571), was received as the true

Reformed confession at the seventh National Synod in La Rochelle (1571).

Geneva Bible (originally printed 1560). During Mary I's reign many English Protestants sought safety abroad in Reformed territories of the Empire and the Swiss Cantons, especially in Calvin's* Geneva. A team of English exiles in Geneva led by William Whittingham (c. 1524–1579) brought this complete translation to press in the course of two years. Notable for several innovations—Roman type, verse numbers, italics indicating English idiom and not literal phrasing of the original languages, even variant readings in the Gospels and Acts—this translation is most well known for its marginal notes, which reflect a strongly Calvinist theology. The notes explained Scripture in an accessible way for the laity, also giving unlearned clergy a new sermon resource. Although controversial because of its implicit critique of royal power, this translation was wildly popular; even after the publication of the Authorized Version (1611) and James I's* 1616 ban on its printing, the Geneva Bible continued to be the most popular English translation until after the English Civil Wars.

Johann Gerhard (1582–1637). German Lutheran theologian, professor and superintendent. Gerhard is considered one of the most eminent Lutheran theologians, after Martin Luther* and Martin Chemnitz.* After studying patristics and Hebrew at Wittenberg, Jena and Marburg, Gerhard was appointed superintendent at the age of twenty-four. In 1616 he was appointed to a post at the University of Jena, where he reintroduced Aristotelian metaphysics to theology and gained widespread fame. His most important work was the nine-volume *Loci Theologici* (1610–1625). He also expanded Chemnitz's harmony of the Gospels *(Harmonia Evangelicae)*, which was finally published by Polykarp Leyser (1552–1610) in 1593. Gerhard was well-known for an irenic spirit and an ability to communicate clearly.

George Gifford (c. 1548–1600). English Puritan pastor. Gifford was suspended for nonconformity in 1584. With private support, however, he was able to continue his ministry. Through his published works he wanted to help develop lay piety and biblical literacy.

George Gifford (d. 1620). English Puritan minister. A celebrated preacher in Maldon, Essex, Gifford was removed from the pulpit when he refused to subscribe to Articles of Conformity drawn up by Archbishop John Whitgift.* Allowed to continue ministry in the office of lecturer, he also served as a representative for Essex at Puritan synods. He published numerous works, including a primer for common Christians, a dialogue between a Catholic and a Protestant, and two works on witchcraft.

Anthony Gilby (c. 1510–1585). English Puritan translator. During Mary I's reign, Gilby fled to Geneva, where he assisted William Whittingham (c. 1524–1579) with the Geneva Bible.* He returned to England to pastor after Elizabeth I's* accession. In addition to translating numerous continental Reformed works into English—especially those of John Calvin* and Theodore Beza*—Gilby also wrote commentaries on Micah and Malachi.

Bernard Gilpin (1517–1583). Anglican theologian and priest. In public disputations, Gilpin defended Roman Catholic theology against John Hooper (c. 1495–1555) and Peter Martyr Vermigli.* These debates caused Gilpin to reexamine his faith. Upon Mary I's accession, Gilpin resigned his benefice. He sojourned in Belgium and France, returning to pastoral ministry in England in 1556. Gilpin dedicated himself to a preaching circuit in northern England, thus earning the moniker "the Apostle to the North." His zealous preaching and almsgiving roused royal opposition and a warrant for his arrest. On his way to the queen's commission, Gilpin fractured his leg, delaying his arrival in London until after Mary's death and thus likely saving his life. His only extant writing is a sermon on Luke 2 confronting clerical abuses.

Paul Glock (c. 1530–1585). German Radical preacher. A teenage convert to Hutterite Anabaptism, Glock spent nineteen years imprisoned at Hohenwittlingen, unwilling to recant. While incarcerated, he wrote hymns, a confession and defense of his beliefs, and numerous letters that proved influential in the development of Anabaptist thought. After helping extinguish a fire at the prison in 1576, Glock was freed and settled with the Brethren in Moravia.

***Glossa ordinaria*.** This standard collection of biblical commentaries consists of interlinear and marginal notes drawn from patristic and Carolingian exegesis appended to the Vulgate*; later editions also include Nicholas of Lyra's* *Postilla*. The *Glossa ordinaria* and the *Sentences* of Peter Lombard (c. 1100–1160) were essential resources for all late medieval and early modern commentators.

Franciscus Gomarus (1563–1641). Dutch Reformed theologian and pastor. A religious refugee at an early age, Gomarus's family was forced to leave Bruges for the Palatinate, with Gomarus receiving a Reformed education at Strasbourg, Neustadt, Oxford, Cambridge, and Heidelberg. He pastored at Frankfurt am Main until becoming professor of theology at the University of Leiden, where he came into extended conflict with colleague Jacobus Arminius* over predestination. Gomarus left Leiden in protest when Conradus Vorstius,* a follower of Arminius with Socinian tendencies, was appointed over his objections. Gomarus then pastored briefly at Middelburg before teaching at the Reformed academy at Saumur and the University of Groningen. Representing the university at the Synod of Dordrecht,* Gomarus was a leading opponent of Remonstrant theology and a key figure in ensuring their censure.

Robert Gomersall (1602–1646?). English Protestant minister and dramatist. Little is known of Gomersall's life beyond his graduation from Oxford and entrance into the ministry. He published a number of poetic and dramatic works, including a tragedy on the life of Italian prince Ludovicio Sforza (1452–1508) and a poetic meditation on Judges 19–20.

Thomas Goodwin (1600–1679). Puritan minister. Goodwin was born October 5, 1600, in Norfolk. After receiving his early education from local schools, Goodwin matriculated at Christ College, Cambridge, which was a prime center of Puritan influence. He graduated with the BA degree in 1616 and MA in 1620. Upon receiving his MA, Goodwin became a fellow and lecturer at the university. In October 1620, Goodwin experienced a profound conversion on his twentieth birthday. After his conversion, Goodwin joined the Puritan party at Cambridge. He was licensed to preach in the Church of England in 1625. Three years later, Goodwin became lecturer at Trinity Church. He served as vicar of this church from 1632 to 1634. Unwilling to comply with Archbishop William Laud's* directives for conformity, Goodwin was forced to resign all of his ecclesiastical and academic positions, and leave Cambridge. During the remainder of the 1630s, due to John Cotton's* influence, Goodwin came to adopt the principles of Independency. In 1639, in order to escape the increasing restrictions of unauthorized preachers, Goodwin fled to the Netherlands, where he worked with other English Independent exiles. In 1641, Goodwin returned to England per Parliament's request, and preached before it on April 27, 1642. Goodwin was later appointed a delegate to the Westminster Assembly. In the Assembly, Goodwin proved himself to be one of the foremost advocates of Independency. After the Westminster Assembly adjourned, Goodwin was appointed a lecturer at Oxford, and a year later became president of Magdalen College. Furthermore, Goodwin served as an advisor to Oliver Cromwell (1599–1658) and as the Lord Protector's Oxford commissioner. Goodwin also tended to Cromwell on his deathbed. In addition to his university and advisory duties, Goodwin pastored an Independent church at Oxford. Notably, Goodwin was one of the primary authors of the Savoy Declaration of Faith (1658), which served as the confession of faith for the Independent/Congregational churches. When Charles II ascended to the throne of England in 1660, Goodwin withdrew from Oxford to London, where he pastored an Independent congregation until his death at the age of eighty. Throughout his career, Goodwin produced an enormous literary corpus, which includes many exegetical works. Best known among these are his expositions of Ephesians and Revelation.

Marie le Jars de Gournay (1565–1645). French Catholic writer and editor. Born into the minor nobility, the early death of Gournay's father led her family to relocate to their estate in Picardy, where she taught herself Latin and Greek. After reading the *Essais* (1580) of Michel de Montaigne (1533–1592), she committed herself to a life of literature and became active in the intellectual circles of Paris. While she translated many classical writings, she is best known for her editorial work on Montaigne's essays and her advocacy for the rights of women, laid out in a number of writings including *The Equality of Men and Women* (1622) and *The Ladies' Grievance* (1626).

Simon Goulart (1543–1628) French Reformed pastor, translator, and theologian. Goulart spent most of his career as a pastor in Geneva and its surrounds, particularly at the city parish of St. Gervais, and was the leader of the Company of Pastors during the last decades of his life. A prolific translator, he published numerous French editions of classical, patristic, and contemporary works from diverse authors including Plutarch, Seneca, Chrysostom, Cyprian, Tertullian, Beza*, Perkins* and Vermigli*. He also composed numerous devotional writings, important histories of early French Protestantism, and polemical treatises supporting the Huguenot cause.

Thomas Granger (1578–1627). English Protestant pastor. After completing his studies at Cambridge, Granger ministered to congregations at Butterwick and Horbling in Lincolnshire.

Conrad Grebel (c. 1498–1526). Swiss Radical theologian. Grebel, considered the father of the Anabaptist movement, was one of the first defenders and performers of believers' baptism, for which he was eventually imprisoned in Zurich. One of Huldrych Zwingli's* early compatriots, Grebel advocated rapid, radical reform, clashing publicly with the civil authorities and Zwingli. Grebel's views, particularly on baptism, were influenced by Andreas Bodenstein von Karlstadt* and Thomas

Müntzer.* Grebel advocated elimination of magisterial involvement in governing the church; instead, he envisioned the church as lay Christians determining their own affairs with strict adherence to the biblical text, and unified in volitional baptism.

William Greenhill (1591–1671). English Puritan pastor. Greenhill attended and worked at Magdalen College. He ministered in the diocese of Norwich but soon left for London, where he preached at Stepney. Greenhill was a member of the Westminster Assembly of Divines and was appointed the parliament chaplain by the children of Charles I. Oliver Cromwell included him among the preachers who helped draw up the Savoy Declaration. Greenhill was evicted from his post following the Restoration, after which he pastored independently. Among Greenhill's most significant contributions to church history was his *Exposition of the Prophet of Ezekiel*.

Catharina Regina von Greiffenberg (1633–1694). Austrian Lutheran poet. Upon her adulthood her guardian (and half uncle) sought to marry her; despite her protests of their consanguinity and her desire to remain celibate, she relented in 1664. After the deaths of her mother and husband, Greiffenberg abandoned her home to debtors and joined her friends Susanne Popp (d. 1683) and Sigmund von Birken (1626–1681) in Nuremberg. During her final years she dedicated herself to studying the biblical languages and to writing meditations on Jesus' death and resurrection, which she never completed. One of the most important and learned Austrian poets of the Baroque period, Greiffenberg published a collection of sonnets, songs and poems (1662) as well as three sets of mystical meditations on Jesus' life, suffering and death (1672; 1683; 1693). She participated in a society of poets called the Ister Gesellschaft.

Lady Jane Grey (1537–1554). English Protestant monarch, sometimes known as "the Nine Days Queen." The eldest daughter of Henry Grey and Frances Brandon, the daughter of Henry VIII's* younger sister Mary, Jane received an extensive Protestant and humanist education. She married Lord Guildford Dudley (c. 1535–1554), son of Edward VI's* chief minister John Dudley, Duke of Northumberland (1504–1553). Seeking to avoid succession by Edward's Catholic half-sister Mary I, Edward and Northumberland conspired to alter the order of succession, naming Jane as heir in the king's will. Following Edward's death, Jane reluctantly took the crown on July 9, 1553, but Northumberland and other Protestants were unable to raise adequate support for her claim and the Privy Council proclaimed Mary queen on July 19. Upon Mary's accession, Jane was imprisoned in the Tower of London and after trial was executed alongside her husband for treason. A handful of her writings exist demonstrating her religious affections, while the story of her martyrdom is prominent in John Foxe's *Acts and Monuments*.

Edmund Grindal (c. 1519–1583). English Anglican archbishop. Grindal began his career in the church as chaplain to Nicholas Ridley* and King Edward VI* until forced to exile in Strasbourg during the reign of Mary I.* Returning to England upon the accession of Elizabeth I,* Grindal helped set the direction for the Church of England, participating in the 1559 Westminster Conference and serving as a member of the committee revising the liturgy. A moderate reformer, he reluctantly became bishop of London despite concerns over continuing Roman practices such as the wearing of vestments and the use of wafer bread for communion. His tenure as archbishop of York was marked by disputes with Presbyterians who wished to abolish the episcopacy and prayer book. Grindal was appointed Archbishop of Canterbury in 1575, but a conflict with Queen Elizabeth I hampered his ability to make change. He refused her request to suppress the "prophesyings" of Puritan clergy and meetings for theological discussion and sermon preparation. After addressing a remonstrance to the queen, he refused to resign, and he was stripped of the administrative power of his position until his death.

Hugo Grotius (1583–1645). Dutch lawyer, statesman, and humanist. Grotius began practicing law at The Hague in 1599, was appointed Advocate-General of the Fisc for the provinces of Holland, Zeeland, and West Friesland in 1607 and in 1613 became pensionary of Rotterdam. As debates between Calvinists and Arminians came to national significance, Grotius sided with the Remonstrants, especially in his rejection of Reformed arguments for the independence of the church, defending the right of the state to appoint ministers and adjudicate over matters of doctrine. Following the victory of Maurice of Orange (1567–1635) over Grotius's patron Johan van Oldenbarnevelt (1547–1619) and the condemnation of Arminianism at the Synod of Dordrecht* (1618–1619), Grotius was imprisoned, though only briefly, as he escaped in a book chest and fled to Paris. Unable to secure return from exile, Grotius became a Swedish ambassador to France while seeking religious toleration and the establishment of a Christian republic. A number of his works from this period, in particular *De Jure Belli ac Pacis* (On the law of war and peace, 1625) made a significant contribution to the establishment of international law.

Argula von Grumbach (c. 1490–c. 1564) German Lutheran noblewoman. Grumbach, an attendant of Queen Kunigunde of Austria (1465–1520), was one of the first women to publish in support of the Reformation. She is best known for letters from 1523 and 1524 written in defense of Arsacius Seehofer (1503–1545), a lecturer at the university of Ingolstadt accused of Lutheranism. For unknown reasons, Grumberg ceased to publish after 1524, although her private correspondence after this time demonstrates a continued effort to support evangelical reform.

Johann Jacob Grynaeus (1540–1617). Swiss Reformed theologian. Raised Lutheran, Grynaeus replaced his father as pastor at Rotelen. After becoming professor of Old Testament at Basel, however, Grynaeus caused conflict by embracing Reformed theology. He avoided controversy by spending two years at the University of Heidelberg. Upon his return to Basel, his opponents had largely died, and he was made superintendent of the church in the city and professor of New Testament. Grynaeus aligned the Basel church with his Reformed convictions and reorganized the city's educational system while preaching regularly and composing numerous theological, exegetical, and practical works.

William Guild (1586–1657). Scottish Reformed minister and theologian. Guild was born in Aberdeen and educated at Marischal College. He was licensed to preach in 1605 and ordained to serve as minister of the parish of King Edward in 1608. In 1617, Guild joined the protest for the liberties of the Scottish national church. While in Edinburgh, Guild met the acquaintance of Bishop Lancelot Andrewes,* who was accompanying King James VI/I* on his royal visit to the city. Moreover, Guild dedicated his best-known work, *Moses Unveiled* (1620), to both Andrewes and the king. He was later appointed chaplain to Charles I, and shortly thereafter received the degree of doctor of divinity. In 1631, Guild was given his second charge in Aberdeen. When he assumed this charge, Guild expressed his support for episcopacy. He signed the National Covenant in 1638 with some conditions. However, when in 1640 an army came to Aberdeen to enforce full subscription to the Covenant, Guild fled to the Netherlands. After returning to Scotland later that year, he was appointed Guild Principal for King's College Aberdeen, but was deprived of this post by Oliver Cromwell's (1599–1658) military commissioners in 1651. Following his deprivation, Guild lived in retirement until his death in Aberdeen.

Rudolf Gwalther (1519–1586). Swiss Reformed preacher. Gwalther was a consummate servant of the Reformed church in Zurich, its chief religious officer and preacher, a responsibility fulfilled previously by Huldrych Zwingli* and Heinrich Bullinger.* Gwalther provided sermons and commentaries and translated the works of Zwingli into Latin. He worked for many years alongside Bullinger in structuring and governing the church in Zurich. Gwalther also strove to strengthen the connections to the Reformed churches on the Continent and England: he was a participant in the Colloquy of Regensburg (1541) and an opponent of the Formula of Concord.*

Matthias Hafenreffer (1561–1619). German Lutheran theologian. After holding pastoral positions in Herenberg, Ehingen, and Stuttgart, Hafenreffer was appointed professor of theology at Tübingen, a position he held for more than twenty-five years. He composed exegetical works on Nahum, Habakkuk, and Ezekiel, a number of polemical works, and a theological *loci communes* that served as a common textbook within the Lutheran churches for much of the seventeenth century.

Henry Hall (unknown). English Protestant preacher. A fellow of Trinity College, Cambridge, Hall preached and published a sermon given before the House of Commons in 1644 on Matthew 11:12.

Joseph Hall (1574–1656). English Anglican bishop and controversialist. After studying at Cambridge, Hall courted controversy with a series of satires before entering the ministry of the Church of England. As a pastor, Hall served parishes in Suffolk and Essex and was chosen by James I* as an English delegate at the Synod of Dordrecht.* Upon his return, Hall was appointed bishop of Exeter and later transferred to the see of Norwich, where, despite his low-church preferences, his defense of the episcopacy saw him convicted of praemunire by the Puritan parliament and imprisoned in the Tower of London for a short time with a number of other bishops. Hall's literary output was extensive and included controversial tracts against the Brownists and Arminians, treatises on virtue and union with Christ, and numerous devotional works.

Hans Has von Hallstatt (d. 1527). Austrian Reformed pastor. See *Kunstbuch.*

Henry Hammond (1605–1660). Anglican priest. After completing his studies at Oxford, Hammond was ordained in 1629. A Royalist, Hammond helped recruit soldiers for the king; he was chaplain to Charles I. During the king's captivity, Hammond was imprisoned for not submitting to Parliament. Later he was allowed to pastor again, until his death. Hammond published a catechism, numerous polemical sermons and treatises as well as his *Paraphrase and Annotations on the New Testament* (1653).

Jörg Haug (Unknown) German Anabaptist leader. Haug was a radical preacher during the 1525 Peasant's Revolt and composed a tract entitled *A Christian Order of a True Christian* (1524) enumerating seven degrees of faith reached by Christians.

Peter Hausted (d. 1645). Anglican priest and playwright. Educated at Cambridge and Oxford, Hausted ministered in a number of parishes and preached adamantly and vehemently against Puritanism. He is best known for his play *The Rival Friends*, which is filled with invective against the Puritans; during a performance before the king and queen, a riot nearly broke out. Haustead died during the siege of Banbury Castle.

Erhart Hegenwald (Unknown). Swiss Protestant teacher and doctor. A teacher at the Pfäffen Monastery in St. Gallen and at the Schola Carolina in Zurich, Hegenwald recorded the minutes of Zwingli's* First Zurich Disputation in 1523. Correspondence demonstrates he remained in contact with the Zurich reformers while he studied medicine at Wittenberg, and after graduating in 1526, he may have practiced as a physician in Frankfurt.

Heidelberg Catechism (1563). This German Reformed catechism was commissioned by the elector of the Palatinate, Frederick III (1515–1576) for pastors and teachers in his territories to use in instructing children and new believers in the faith. It was written by theologian Zacharias Ursinus (1534–1583) in consultation with Frederick's court preacher Kaspar Olevianus* and the entire theology faculty at the University of Heidelberg. The Heidelberg Catechism was accepted as one of the Dutch Reformed Church's Three Forms of Unity—along with the Belgic Confession* and the Canons of Dordrecht—at the Synod of Dordrecht,* and became widely popular among other Reformed confessional traditions throughout Europe.

Philipp Heilbrunner (1546-1616) German Lutheran pastor and theologian. Heilbrunner pastored churches at Lustnau, Bernhausen, and Lauingen, where he also taught theology. He was involved in establishing the Formula of Concord* and was a disputant at the Regensburg Colloquy (1601).

Ursula Hellrigel (b. c. 1521). Austrian Anabaptist. Imprisoned for her heterodox beliefs at 17, authorities sought Hellrigel's recantation, but she refused to acquiesce. After five years she was released from prison and exiled from the Tyrol. The thirty-sixth hymn in the first known Anabaptist hymnal, the *Ausbund* (1654), is commonly attributed to her.

Niels Hemmingsen (1513–1600). Danish Lutheran theologian. Hemmingsen studied at the University of Wittenberg, where he befriended Philipp Melanchthon.* In 1542, Hemmingsen returned to Denmark to pastor and to teach Greek, dialectics and theology at the University of Copenhagen. Foremost of the Danish theologians, Hemmingsen oversaw the preparation and publication of the first Danish Bible (1550). Later in his career he became embroiled in controversies because of his Philippist theology, especially regarding the Eucharist. Due to rising tensions with Lutheran nobles outside of Denmark, King Frederick II (1534–1588) dismissed Hemmingsen from his university post in 1579, transferring him to a prominent but less internationally visible Cathedral outside of Copenhagen. Hemmingsen was a prolific author, writing commentaries on the New Testament and Psalms, sermon collections and several methodological, theological and pastoral handbooks.

Henry IV of France (1553–1610). French monarch. Son of Jeanne of Navarre* and Antoine de Bourbon (1518–1562), Henry's religious loyalties wavered throughout his life. Raised Protestant at the behest of his mother, he practiced Catholicism while attending the Valois court. After his mother's death in 1572, Henry succeeded her as King of Navarre and soon afterwards married Margaret of Valois (1553–1615), the daughter of Henry II of France (1519–1559) and Catherine de' Medici (1519–1589). Their wedding provided the occasion for the St. Bartholomew's Day Massacre, when Catholic forces seized the opportunity to decimate the Huguenot leadership gathered to celebrate the nuptials in Paris, leading to an outbreak of mob violence that devastated the Huguenot movement. A great proportion of the Protestants in France were killed in the weeks that followed the wedding, while many others, including Henry, reconverted to Catholicism. In 1576, Henry escaped the influence of the Valois court, returned his allegiance to Protestantism and took a leadership role amongst the Huguenots. Following the assassination of Henry III of France (1551–1589), Henry was the presumptive heir, but French Catholics were unwilling to accept his rule and Henry was unable to assert his prerogative outside Huguenot strongholds. In 1593, therefore, Henry converted again to Catholicism, with legend claiming he justified his decision with the phrase "Paris is worth a mass." Over the following years, Henry established his authority throughout his kingdom, and while remaining Catholic, provided some relief to Protestants, particularly through the Edict of Nantes (1598), essentially ending the Religious Wars. Henry's pragmatic reign ended with his assassination by a Radical Catholic in 1610.

King Henry VIII of England (1491–1547). English monarch. The second son of Henry VII (r. 1485–1509) and Elizabeth of York (1466–1503), Henry VIII succeeded his father to the English throne, his elder brother Edward having died in 1502. Soon after accession, he married his brother's widow, Catherine of Aragon (1485–1536). Following several stillbirths and the birth of a daughter, Mary, Henry, who was desperate for a male heir to head off dynastic challenges, wished separation from Catherine in order to marry Anne Boleyn (c. 1501–1536). Believing his marriage cursed as it transgressed the commands in Leviticus against marrying a brother's widow, Henry sought dispensation from the church for his annulment and remarriage. While the case was first heard by a papal legate in England, it was transferred to Rome upon the order of Pope Clement VII*, who wished to placate Charles V, Catherine's nephew, whose troops had recently sacked Rome and held the pope under house arrest. Henry asserted praemunire, arguing that as king, he was supreme in his own kingdom. With the formation of the Reformation Parliament in 1529, the legislative process to disentangle the English Church from the Roman was begun. The issue of Henry's divorce was finalized in 1533, after Thomas Cranmer* became Archbishop of Canterbury and declared his marriage to Catherine invalid. While Henry's divorce, assertion of royal supremacy, and subversion of Catholic institutions gave impetus to English Protestantism, Henry's beliefs remained essentially Catholic, and these continued to be enforced by law. He ultimately married six times, and was succeeded by Edward VI*, his son by his third wife, Jane Seymour (1508–1537). Elizabeth I*, Henry's daughter by Anne Boleyn, later became Queen and with the Elizabethan Settlement in 1559, redefined England as a Protestant country.

George Herbert (1593–1633). Anglican minister, theologian, and poet. Herbert was born in Montgomery Powys, Wales, on April 3, 1593, to a noble family. After completing his early education at Westminster School, Herbert matriculated at Trinity College, Cambridge, in 1609. He graduated with both his bachelor's and master's degrees. Shortly thereafter Herbert was elected a fellow of the college, and then became Reader of Rhetoric. From 1620 to 1627, Herbert was Public Orator for the University of Cambridge. In 1624, Herbert was elected to Parliament. However, after the death of King James I,* and of his other major patrons, Herbert withdrew from politics to pursue a career in the church. Toward this end, Herbert was ordained to the priesthood of the Church of England in 1630, and appointed rector of Fugglestone St. Peter and later Bemerton St. Andrews in Wiltshire near Salisbury. While at St. Andrews, Herbert composed his collection of poems titled *The Temple* and his guide for rural ministers, *A Priest to the Temple, or The Country Parson: His Character and Rule of Holy Life.* Twice a week Herbert traveled to Salisbury, where he attended services at Salisbury Cathedral. Following the services, Herbert would compose music with the cathedral musicians. Herbert died of consumption in 1633.

Tilemann Hesshus (1527–1588). German Lutheran theologian and pastor. Hesshus studied under Philipp Melanchthon* but was a staunch Gnesio-Lutheran. With great hesitation—and later regret—he affirmed the Formula of Concord.* Heshuss ardently advocated for church discipline, considering obedience a mark of the church. Unwilling to compromise his strong convictions, especially regarding matters of discipline, Hesshus was regularly embroiled in controversy. He was expelled or pressed to leave Goslar, Rostock, Heidelberg, Bremen, Magdeburg, Wesel, Königsberg and Samland before settling in Helmstedt, where he remained until his death. He wrote numerous polemical tracts concerning ecclesiology, justification, the sacraments and original sin, as well as commentaries on Psalms, Romans, 1–2 Corinthians, Galatians, Colossians and 1–2 Timothy, and a postil collection.

Edo Hilderich (1533–1599). German Lutheran historian and theologian. Hilderich (also named Hildericus) was born to a noble family in Frisia. After attending a local school, Hilderich went on to the University of Wittenberg, where he received the degree of master of philosophy in 1556. Among his teachers was Philipp Melanchthon.* In 1559, Hilderich was appointed to the Faculty of Arts at Wittenberg. He also served as professor of mathematics at the University of Jena from 1564 until 1567, when he resigned the post in order to return to the arts faculty at Wittenberg, of which he became dean in 1570. Three years later he became rector of the academy in Magdeburg, and went from there to the University of Frankfurt in 1575. In 1577, Hilderich became professor of history and Hebrew at Frankfurt. Following the expulsion of the Reformed theologians from the University of Heidelberg in 1578, he went there to be the second professor of theology and Hebrew language. He received his doctorate at Heidelberg a year later. However, Hilderich's refusal to sign the Formula of Concord resulted in removal from his post. On June 3, 1581, he accepted the professorship of theology at the University of Altdorf, where he later became rector in 1582, and professor of Hebrew in 1584. Hilderich's most important exegetical work is his *Oratio de politia et hierarchia populi Iudaici*, published in 1570, in which he traces the history of ancient Israel's government.

Samuel Hieron (1576?–1617). English Puritan minister. After graduating from Cambridge, Hieron became a minister in the Church of England and gained a reputation as a popular preacher in London before becoming the vicar at Modbury in Devonshire. Many of his sermons were published during his lifetime, and he also composed treatises on prayer and the value of Scripture.

Cornelis Hoen (c. 1460–1524). Dutch humanist, jurist, and theologian. A lawyer at the Court of Holland at the Hague, Hoen was prosecuted in 1523 over his sympathy for the evangelical message. He proposed a symbolic interpretation of Christ's presence in the Eucharist justified with reference to Matthew 24:23 in an influential, posthumously-published treatise.

Melchior Hoffman (1495?–1543). German Anabaptist preacher. First appearing as a Lutheran lay preacher in Livonia in 1523, Hoffman's claim to direct revelation, his perfectionist teachings and his announcements that the end of the world would occur in 1533 saw him alienated from both Lutheran and Reformed circles. After converting to Anabaptism in Strasbourg in 1530, a city he claimed would rise as the spiritual Jerusalem, Hoffman escaped brief arrest and fled to the Netherlands, where his preaching made him the first to bring the radical faith to the Low Countries. Believing himself to be Elijah, Hoffman gathered numerous followers, including future Anabaptist leaders Obbe Philips* and Jan Mathijs (d. 1534), until his arrest in Strasbourg in 1533, whereupon he was imprisoned for the final decade of his life. A tendency toward mystical allegory and apocalyptic exegesis supported by direct revelation is found in his writings, which include commentaries on Romans, Revelation, and Daniel 12 alongside numerous tracts, pamphlets, and letters.

Nathaniel Holmes (1599–1678). English Puritan theologian. Educated at Oxford, Holmes was a preacher in the Anglican Church until his millenarian views led him to establish an independent congregation. His publications include defenses of infant baptism and exclusive psalmody; treatises against witchcraft, usury, and astrology; and a commentary on the Song of Solomon.

Christopher Hooke (unknown). English Puritan physician and pastor. Hooke published a treatise promoting the joys and blessings of childbirth (1590) and a sermon on Hebrews 12:11-12. To support the poor, Hooke proposed a bank funded by voluntary investment of wealthy households.

Richard Hooker (c. 1553–1600). Anglican priest. Shortly after graduating from Corpus Christi College Oxford, Hooker took holy orders as a priest in 1581. After his marriage, he struggled to find work and temporarily tended sheep until Archbishop John Whitgift* appointed him to the Temple Church in London. Hooker's primary work is *The Laws of Ecclesiastical Polity* (1593), in which he sought to establish a philosophical and logical foundation for the highly controversial Elizabethan Religious Settlement (1559). The Elizabethan Settlement, through the Act of Supremacy, reasserted the Church of England's independence from the Church of Rome, and, through the Act of Uniformity, constructed a common church structure based on the reinstitution of the Book of Common Prayer.* Hooker's argumentation strongly emphasizes natural law and anticipates the social contract theory of John Locke (1632–1704).

Thomas Hooker (1586–1647). English-American Puritan Preacher. Hooker ministered at churches in Surrey and Essex and established a school to teach pastors until threatened with arrest as Archbishop Laud* worked to suppress Puritanism. Fleeing to Holland and then New England, he pastored a church in New Town (later Cambridge), Massachusetts before playing an important role in the foundation of Hartford, Connecticut and assisting with the composition of the state constitution.

John Hooper (d. 1555). English Protestant bishop and martyr. Impressed by the works of Huldrych Zwingli* and Heinrich Bullinger,* Hooper joined the Protestant movement in England. However, after the Act of Six Articles was passed, he fled to Zurich, where he spent ten years. He returned to England in 1549 and was appointed as a bishop. He stoutly advocated a Zwinglian reform agenda, arguing against the use of vestments and for a less "popish" Book of Common Prayer.* Condemned as a heretic for denying transubstantiation, Hooper was burned at the stake during Mary I's reign.

John Hoskin (unknown). English Protestant preacher. Hoskin published a sermon on Matthew 18:23 in 1610 in which he is identified as a minister of God's Word and student of divinity.

Rudolf Hospinian (Wirth) (1547–1626). Swiss Reformed theologian and minister. After studying theology at Marburg and Heidelberg, Hospinian pastored in rural parishes around Zurich and taught secondary school. In 1588, he transferred to Zurich, ministering at Grossmünster and Fraumünster. A keen student of church history, Hospinian wanted to show the differences between early church doctrine and contemporary Catholic teaching, particularly with regard to sacramental theology. He also criticized Lutheran dogma and the Formula of Concord*. Most of Hospinian's corpus consists of polemical treatises; he also published a series of sermons on the Magnificat.

Hans Hotz (dates unknown). Swiss Anabaptist leader. Born in Grüningen, near Zurich, Hotz was an associate of Georg Blaurock.* He defended Anabaptism as spokesman for the Swiss Brethren at disputations in Zofingen (1532) and Bern (1538).

John Howson (1557?–1632). English Anglican bishop. Howson held a number of pastoral positions in Oxfordshire before becoming vice chancellor of Oxford University. An opponent of Puritanism, he was appointed bishop of Oxford in 1619, and then to the bishopric of Durham in 1628, where he was an advocate for the reform program of Archbishop Laud.*

Caspar Huberinus (1500–1553). German Lutheran theologian and pastor. After studying theology at Wittenberg, Huberinus moved to Augsburg to serve as Urbanus Rhegius's* assistant. Huberinus represented Augsburg at the Bern Disputation (1528) on the Eucharist and images. In 1551, along with the nobility, Huberinus supported the Augsburg Interim, so long as communion of both kinds and regular preaching were allowed. Nevertheless the people viewed him as a traitor because of his official participation in the Interim, nicknaming him "Buberinus" (i.e., scoundrel). He wrote a number of popular devotional works as well as tracts defending Lutheran eucharistic theology against Zwinglian and Anabaptist detractions.

Balthasar Hubmaier (1480/5–1528). German Radical theologian. Hubmaier, a former priest who studied under Johann Eck,* is identified with his leadership in the peasants' uprising at Waldshut. Hubmaier served as the cathedral preacher in Regensberg, where he became involved in a series of anti-Semitic attacks. He was drawn to reform through the early works of Martin Luther*; his contact with Huldrych Zwingli* made Hubmaier a defender of more radical reform, including believers' baptism and a memorialist account of the Eucharist. His involvement in the Peasants' War led to his extradition and execution by the Austrians.

Aegidius Hunnius (1550–1603). German Lutheran theologian and preacher. Educated at Tübingen by Jakob Andreae (1528–1590) and Johannes Brenz,* Hunnius bolstered and advanced early Lutheran orthodoxy. After his crusade to root out all "crypto-Calvinism" divided Hesse into Lutheran and Reformed regions, Hunnius joined the Wittenberg theological faculty, where with Polykarp Leyser (1552–1610) he helped shape the university into an orthodox stronghold. Passionately confessional, Hunnius developed and nuanced the orthodox doctrines of predestination, Scripture, the church and Christology (more explicitly Chalcedonian), reflecting their codification in the Formula of Concord.* He was unafraid to engage in confessional polemics from the pulpit. In addition to his many treatises (most notably *De persona Christi*, in which he defended Christ's ubiquity), Hunnius published commentaries on Matthew, John, Ephesians and Colossians; his notes on Galatians, Philemon and 1 Corinthians were published posthumously.

Jan Hus (d. 1415). Bohemian reformer and martyr. This popular preacher strove for reform in the church, moral improvement in society, and an end to clerical abuses and popular religious superstition. He was branded a heretic for his alleged affinity for John Wycliffe's writings; however, while he agreed that a priest in mortal sin rendered the sacraments inefficacious, he affirmed the doctrine of transubstantiation. The Council of Constance* convicted Hus of heresy, banned his books and teaching, and, despite a letter of safe conduct, burned him at the stake.

Hans Hut (1490–1527). German Radical leader. Hut was an early leader of a mystical, apocalyptic strand of Anabaptist radical reform. His theological views were shaped by Andreas Bodenstein von Karlstadt,* Thomas Müntzer* and Hans Denck,* by whom Hut had been baptized. Hut rejected society and the established church and heralded the imminent end of days, which he perceived in the Peasants' War. Eventually arrested for practicing believers' baptism and participating in the Peasants' War, Hut was tortured and died accidentally in a fire in the Augsburg prison. The next day, the authorities sentenced his corpse to death and burned him.

George Hutcheson (1615–1674). Scottish Puritan pastor. Hutcheson, a pastor in Edinburgh, published commentaries on Job, John and the Minor Prophets, as well as sermons on Psalm 130.

Roger Hutchinson (d. 1555). English reformer. Little is known about Hutchinson except for his controversies. He disputed against the Mass while at Cambridge and debated with Joan Bocher (d. 1550), who affirmed the doctrine of the celestial flesh. During the Marian Restoration he was deprived of his fellowship at Eton because he was married.

Andreas Hyperius (1511–1564). Dutch Protestant theologian. After a peripatetic humanist education that encompassed studies in theology, canon law, and medicine, Hyperius became professor of theology at Marburg in

1541 and held this position until his death. Often viewed as mediating between Lutheran and Reformed thought, Hyperius was particularly concerned with the practical application of theology, demonstrated in his composition of the first Protestant text on homiletic method.

Abraham Ibn Ezra (1089–c. 1167). Spanish Jewish rabbi, exegete and poet. In 1140 Ibn Ezra fled his native Spain to escape persecution by the Almohad Caliphate. He spent the rest of his life as an exile, traveling through Europe, North Africa and the Middle East. His corpus consists of works on poetry, exegesis, grammar, philosophy, mathematics and astrology. In his commentaries on the Old Testament, Ibn Ezra restricts himself to *peshat* (see *quadriga*).

Valentin Ickelshamer (c. 1500–1547). German Radical teacher. After time at Erfurt, he studied under Luther,* Melanchthon,* Bugenhagen* and Karlstadt* in Wittenberg. He sided with Karlstadt against Luther, writing a treatise in Karlstadt's defense. Ickelshamer also represented the Wittenberg guilds in opposition to the city council. This guild committee allied with the peasants in 1525, leading to Ickelshamer's eventual exile. His poem in the Marpeck Circle's *Kunstbuch** is an expansion of a similar poem by Sebastian Franck.*

Arthur Jackson (1593?–1666). English Presbyterian minister. Known for his pastoral concern, Jackson served at a number of parishes in London. Imprisoned briefly for his support of the Royalist cause, after the Restoration, he was ejected from ministry following the 1662 Act of Uniformity. Jackson's primary works are a series of annotations of many books of the Old Testament.

Thomas Jackson (1579–1640). Anglican theologian and priest. Before serving as the president of Corpus Christi College at Oxford for the final decade of his life, Jackson was a parish priest and chaplain to the king. His best known work is a twelve-volume commentary on the Apostles' Creed.

King James I of England (VI of Scotland) (1566–1625). English monarch. The son of Mary, Queen of Scots, James ascended to the Scottish throne in 1567 following his mother's abdication. In the Union of the Crowns (1603), he took the English and Irish thrones after the death of his cousin, Elizabeth I.* James's reign was tumultuous and tense: Parliament and the nobility often opposed him, church factions squabbled over worship forms and ecclesiology, climaxing in the Gunpowder Plot. James wrote treatises on the divine right of kings, law, the evils of smoking tobacco and demonology. His religious writings include a versification of the Psalms, a paraphrase of Revelation and meditations on the Lord's Prayer and passages from Chronicles, Matthew and Revelation. He also sponsored the translation of the Authorized Version*—popularly remembered as the King James Version.

Cornelius Jansen (1585–1638). Dutch Catholic bishop and theologian. Jansen studied and taught in France and Holland, joining the theological faculty of the University of Leuven after receiving his doctorate. He later became bishop of Ypres. An ardent Augustinian, his posthumously published work *Augustinus* (1640) caused great controversy by advocating for the utterly gratuitous character of God's grace in opposition to the teachings of Jesuit Luis de Molina (1536–1609), which put greater emphasis on human choice. Due to its perceived Protestant leanings, *Augustinus* was judged heretical, and Jansen's followers, known as Jansenists, took up his cause in a series of conflicts that carried on into the eighteenth century.

Jeanne of Navarre (1528–1572) French Reformed noblewoman. Daughter of Henry II, King of Navarre (1503–1555) and Marguerite d'Angoulême*, Jeanne was forced into a strategic marriage at age 12 by her uncle, Francis I* to William, Duke of Cleves (1516–1592). Shifting political alignments allowed her an annulment after four years and in 1548 she wed the first Prince of the Blood, Antoine de Bourbon (1518–1562). Jeanne took the throne of her father, and after making a public announcement of her conversion to the evangelical faith, established a Reformed community at Béarn. A regular correspondent of reformers such as Calvin* and Beza* and an advocate for the reformation of her lands, Jeanne nevertheless remained largely neutral and advocated tolerance during the first years of religious war. At the outbreak of the Third War of Religion (1569–1570), however, she recognized her moderate position was untenable, and from the Protestant stronghold of La Rochelle served as political head for the Huguenot cause alongside Gaspard de Coligny (1519–1572), commander of the Huguenot armed forces.

Michael Jermin (1591–1659). English Protestant pastor. Jermin's early career was spent on the Continent, where he served as chaplain for Elizabeth Stuart, queen of Bohemia (1596–1662) and earned a doctorate of divinity from the University of Leiden. Returning to England, he earned a second doctorate at Oxford before becoming chaplain to Charles I* and serving as rector of St. Martin, Ludgate. A Royalist, he was deprived of his living during the English Civil War (1642–1651), and while he continued to preach occasionally, he was forced to survive on charity.

John Jewel (1522–1571). Anglican theologian and bishop. Jewel studied at Oxford where he met Peter Martyr Vermigli.* After graduating in 1552, Jewel was appointed to his first vicarage and became the orator for the university. Upon Mary I's accession, Jewel lost his post as orator because of his Protestant views. After the trials of Thomas Cranmer* and Nicholas Ridley,* Jewel affirmed Catholic teaching to avoid their fate. Still he had to flee to the continent. Confronted by John Knox,* Jewel publicly repented of his cowardice before the English congregation in Frankfurt, then reunited with Vermigli in Strasbourg. After Mary I's death, Jewel returned to England and was consecrated bishop in 1560. He advocated low-church ecclesiology, but supported the Elizabethan Settlement against Catholics and Puritans. In response to the Council of Trent, he published the *Apoligia ecclesiae Anglicanae* (1562), which established him as the apostle for Anglicanism and incited numerous controversies.

St. John of the Cross (Juan de Yepes y Álvarez) (1542–1591). Spanish Catholic mystic. Born into poverty, Álvarez entered the Carmelite order in Medina del Campo, where, after studying theology at Salamanca, he met the famed mystic Teresa of Ávila (1515–1582). Drawn to her vision of the contemplative life, with two others, he established the first house of Discalced (barefoot) Carmelite Friars and became a leader in the Catholic reform movement. An exceptional administrator and spiritual leader, for more than twenty years, John of the Cross sought to return his order to its original vision of asceticism and prayer while establishing many new reformed Carmelite houses. He encountered significant resistance in his work for renewal, however, and spent nine months imprisoned and tortured by his Carmelite superiors. Considered among the foremost poets in Spanish literary history, his poems, including *The Spiritual Canticle*, *Ascent of Mount Carmel*, and *The Dark Night of the Soul* demonstrate his overriding desire for spiritual growth and closeness to God.

Francis Johnson (1562–1618). English Brownist pastor. A popular Puritan preacher at Cambridge, Johnson was arrested for slander and factitiousness after a sermon criticizing the ecclesiastical hierarchy and the comfortable lives of the ministers at the school. Retracting some of his statements, he was released and expelled from Cambridge. While pastoring an English church in the Netherlands, he came across writings from followers of Robert Browne* and became convinced of the need to separate from the established church and commit to congregational church polity, but his attempts to institute these changes in the church led to his firing. Returning to England, Johnson became pastor of the Brownist church in London, for which he was arrested numerous times until he convinced the Privy Council to allow him to found a Brownist church in Newfoundland. The expedition was canceled, however, and he returned to the Netherlands, where he pastored separatist churches, some alongside Henry Ainsworth* and John Smyth,* until his death.

Justus Jonas (1493–1555). German Lutheran theologian, pastor and administrator. Jonas studied law at Erfurt, where he befriended the poet Eobanus Hessus (1488–1540), whom Luther* dubbed "king of the poets"; later, under the influence of the humanist Konrad Muth, Jonas focused on theology. In 1516 he was ordained as a priest, and in 1518 he became a doctor of theology and law. After witnessing the Leipzig Disputation, Jonas was converted to Luther's* cause. While traveling with Luther to the Diet of Worms, Jonas was appointed professor of canon law at Wittenberg. Later he became its dean of theology, lecturing on Romans, Acts and the Psalms. Jonas was also instrumental for reform in Halle. He preached Luther's funeral sermon but had a falling-out with Melanchthon* over the Leipzig Interim. Jonas's most influential contribution was translating Luther's *The Bondage of the Will* and Melanchthon's *Loci communes* into German.

Robert Jones. A pseudonym; see Thomas Lushington.

William Jones (1561–1636). Anglican minister and theologian. After teaching at Cambridge, Jones ministered at East Bergholt in Suffolk for forty-four years, publishing a commentary on Philemon and Hebrews and tracts on suffering, the nativity, and arrangements to be made before one's death.

David Joris (c. 1501–1556). Dutch Radical pastor and hymnist. This former glass painter was one of the leading Dutch Anabaptist leaders after the fall of Münster (1535), although due to his increasingly radical ideas his influence waned in the early 1540s. Joris came to see himself as a "third David," a Spirit-anointed prophet ordained to proclaim the coming third kingdom of God, which would be established in the Netherlands with Dutch as its *lingua franca*. Joris's interpretation of Scripture, with his heavy emphasis on personal mystical experience, led to a very public dispute with Menno Simons* whom Joris considered a teacher of the "dead letter." In 1544 Joris and about one hundred followers moved to Basel, conforming outwardly to the teaching of the Reformed church there. Today 240 of Joris's books are extant, the most important of which is his *Twonder Boek* (1542/43).

Jörg Haugk von Jüchsen (unknown). German Radical preacher. Nothing is known of Haugk's life except that during the 1524–1525 Peasants' War in Thuringia, he was elected as a preacher by the insurrectionists in his district. He composed one extant tract, titled *A Christian Order of a True Christian: Giving an Account of the Origin of His Faith*, published in 1526 but likely written before the Peasants' War. While lacking reference to most distinctive Anabaptist doctrines, this pamphlet became popular among radicals as it set out the stages of Christian growth toward perfection.

Andreas Bodenstein von Karlstadt (Carlstadt) (1486–1541). German Radical theologian. Karlstadt, an early associate of Martin Luther* and Philipp Melanchthon* at the University of Wittenberg, participated alongside Luther in the dispute at Leipzig with Johann Eck.* He also influenced the configuration of the Old Testament canon in Protestantism. During Luther's captivity in Wartburg Castle in Eisenach, Karlstadt oversaw reform in Wittenberg. His acceleration of the pace of reform brought conflict with Luther, so Karlstadt left Wittenberg, eventually settling at the University of Basel as professor of Old Testament (after a sojourn in Zurich with Huldrych Zwingli*). During his time in Switzerland, Karlstadt opposed infant baptism and repudiated Luther's doctrine of Christ's real presence in the Eucharist.

Edward Kellett (d. 1641). Anglican theologian and priest. Kellett published a sermon concerning the reconversion of an Englishman from Islam, a tract on the soul, and a discourse on the Lord's Supper in connection with Passover.

David Kimchi (Radak) (1160–1235). French Jewish rabbi, exegete and philosopher. Kimchi wrote an important Hebrew grammar and dictionary, as well as commentaries on Genesis, 1–2 Chronicles, the Psalms and the Prophets. He focused on *peshat* (see *quadriga*). In his Psalms commentary he attacks Christian interpretation as forced, irrational and inadmissible. While Sebastian Münster* censors and condemns these arguments in his *Miqdaš YHWH* (1534–1535), he and many other Christian commentators valued Kimchi's work as a grammatical resource.

Moses Kimchi (Remak) (1127–1190). French Jewish rabbi and exegete. He was David Kimchi's* brother. He wrote commentaries on Proverbs and Ezra-Nehemiah. Sebastian Münster* translated Kimchi's concise Hebrew grammar into Latin; many sixteenth-century Christian exegetes used this resource.

Andreas Knöpken (c. 1468–1539). German Lutheran pastor. Knöpken worked in Pomerania as assistant to Johannes Bugenhagen* before relocating to Riga. Here he served as pastor of St. Peter's, and after a brief setback that saw him return to his previous position, he returned and won a disputation before the authorities, which allowed him to undertake the evangelical reform of the city. Knöpken oversaw the reorganization of the churches and schools, composed the church order, wrote a commentary on Romans, and arranged a number of hymns based on the Psalms.

John Knox (1513–1572). Scottish Reformed preacher. Knox, a fiery preacher to monarchs and zealous defender of high Calvinism, was a leading figure of reform in Scotland. Following imprisonment in the French galleys, Knox went to England, where he became a royal chaplain to Edward VI. At the accession of Mary, Knox fled to Geneva, studying under John Calvin* and serving as a pastor. Knox returned to Scotland after Mary's death and became a chief architect of the reform of the Scottish church (Presbyterian), serving as one of the authors of the Book of Discipline and writing many pamphlets and sermons.

Antonius Broickwy von Königstein (1470–1541). German Catholic preacher. Very little is known about this important cathedral preacher in Cologne. Strongly opposed to evangelicals, he sought to develop robust resources for Catholic homilies. His postils were bestsellers, and his biblical concordance helped Catholic preachers to construct doctrinal loci from Scripture itself.

Kunstbuch. In 1956, two German students rediscovered this unique collection of Anabaptist works. Four hundred years earlier, a friend of the recently deceased Pilgram Marpeck*—the painter Jörg Probst—had entrusted this collection of letters, tracts and poetry to a Zurich bindery; today only half of it remains. Probst's redaction arranges various compositions from the Marpeck Circle into a devotional anthology focused on the theme of the church as Christ incarnate (cf. Gal 2:20).

Osmund Lake (c. 1543–1621). English Pastor who ministered at Ringwood in Hampshire.

Thomas Lamb (d. 1686). English Nonconformist minister. Lamb earned a living as a soap boiler while serving as a teaching elder and occasional preacher at a congregational church in London. Convicted of the necessity of adult baptism and the invalidity of infant baptism, he formed a Particular Baptist congregation and led this church for four years before rejoining the Church of England as a layman, retracting his former teachings and becoming a vocal opponent of separatism. Toward the end of his life, he turned to philanthropy, seeking to improve the lives of the poor and prisoners and to further the religious education of children.

François Lambert (Lambert of Avignon) (1487–1530). French Reformed theologian. In 1522, after becoming drawn to the writings of Martin Luther* and meeting Huldrych Zwingli,* Lambert left the Franciscan order. He spent time in Wittenberg, Strasbourg, and Hesse, where Lambert took a leading role at the Homberg Synod (1526) and in creating a biblically based plan for church reform. He served as professor of theology at Marburg University from 1527 to his death. After the Marburg Colloquy (1529), Lambert accepted Zwingli's symbolic view of the Eucharist. Lambert produced nineteen books, mostly biblical commentaries that favored spiritual interpretations; his unfinished work of comprehensive theology was published posthumously.

Eitelhans Langenmantel (d. 1528). German Radical writer. The son of the mayor of Augsburg, Langenmantel was converted to Anabaptism and was rebaptized by Hans Hut* in 1527. Arrested for his heterodox views later that year, he was freed after accepting the validity of infant baptism during a debate, but after renouncing his recantation in 1528, he was rearrested and beheaded. Seven tracts he composed during 1526 and 1527 survive, focusing on the Lord's Supper and the moral life.

Emilia Lanier (1569–1645). English poet. The daughter of a musician at the court of Elizabeth I,* she received a humanist education at the home of Susan Bertie, Countess of Kent (b. 1554). Following a long affair with Henry Carey (1526–1596), Lord Chamberlain to the queen, and after conceiving a child, she married a distant cousin, Alfonso Lanier (unknown). She is best known for a book of poetry written in the hope of securing a patron, *Salve Deus Rex Judaeorum* (1611), which contains a number of protofeminist themes. Modern scholars have also suggested she may be the "Dark Lady" who appears in a number of William Shakespeare's (1564–1616) sonnets.

Hugh Latimer (c. 1485–1555). Anglican bishop and preacher. Latimer was celebrated for his sermons critiquing the idolatrous nature of Catholic practices and the social injustices visited on the underclass by the aristocracy and the individualism of Protestant government. After his support for Henry's petition of divorce he served as a court preacher under Henry VIII* and Edward VI. Latimer became a proponent of reform following his education at Cambridge University and received license as a preacher. Following Edward's death, Latimer was tried for heresy, perishing at the stake with Nicholas Ridley* and Thomas Cranmer.*

William Laud (1573–1645). Anglican archbishop, one of the most pivotal and controversial figures in Anglican church history. Early in his career, Laud offended many with his highly traditional, anti-Puritan approach to ecclesial policies. After his election as Archbishop of Canterbury in 1633, Laud continued to strive against the Puritans, demanding the eastward placement of the Communion altar (affirming the religious centrality of the Eucharist), the use of clerical garments, the reintroduction of stained-glass windows, and the uniform use of the Book of Common Prayer.* Laud was accused of being a crypto-Catholic—an ominous accusation during the protracted threat of invasion by the Spanish Armada. In 1640 the Long Parliament met, quickly impeached Laud on charges of treason, and placed him in jail for several years before his execution.

Ludwig Lavater (1527–1586). Swiss Reformed pastor and theologian. Under his father-in-law Heinrich Bullinger,* Lavater became an archdeacon in Zurich. In 1585 he succeeded Rudolf Gwalther* as the city's Antistes. He authored a widely disseminated book on demonology, commentaries on Chronicles, Proverbs, Ecclesiastes, Nehemiah and Ezekiel, theological works, and biographies of Bullinger and Konrad Pellikan.*

Laws and Liberties of the Inhabitants of Massachusetts (1647). North American colonial constitution. The first printed set of laws in the American colonies, the 1647 *Laws and Liberties of the Inhabitants of Massachusetts* was a revision of the *Massachusetts Body of Liberties* (1641), a legal code collected by Puritan minister Nathaniel Ward (1578–1652). The *Laws and Liberties* codified Puritan expectations of doctrine and morality, and included provision for the punishment for heresy, stipulating banishment for Anabaptism. The majority of the document consists of practical clauses addressing general and specific aspects of communal and commercial life.

John Lawson (unknown). Seventeenth-century English Puritan. Lawson wrote *Gleanings and Expositions of Some of Scripture* (1646) and a treatise on the sabbath in the New Testament.

Jacques Lefèvre d'Étaples (Faber Stapulensis) (1460?–1536). French Catholic humanist, publisher and translator. Lefèvre d'Étaples studied classical literature and philosophy, as well as patristic and medieval mysticism. He advocated the principle of *ad fontes*, issuing a full-scale annotation on the corpus of Aristotle, publishing the writings of key Christian mystics, and contributing to efforts at biblical translation and commentary. Although he never broke with the Catholic Church, his views prefigured those of Martin Luther,* for which he was condemned by the University of Sorbonne in Paris. He then found refuge in the court of Marguerite d'Angoulême, where he met John Calvin* and Martin Bucer.*

Edward Leigh (1602–1671). English Puritan biblical critic, historian and politician. Educated at Oxford, Leigh's public career included appointments as a Justice of the Peace, an officer in the parliamentary army during the English Civil Wars and a member of Parliament. Although never ordained, Leigh devoted himself to the study of theology and Scripture; he participated in the Westminster Assembly. Leigh published a diverse corpus, including lexicons of Greek, Hebrew and juristic terms, and histories of Roman, Greek and English rulers. His most important theological work is *A Systeme or Body of Divinity* (1662).

John Lightfoot (1602–1675). Anglican priest and biblical scholar. After graduating from Cambridge, Lightfoot was ordained and pastored at several small parishes. He continued to study classics under the support of the politician Rowland Cotton (1581–1634). Siding with the Parliamentarians during the English Civil Wars, Lightfoot relocated to London in 1643. He was one of the original members of the Westminster Assembly, where he defended a moderate Presbyterianism. His best-known work is the six-volume *Horae Hebraicae et Talmudicae* (1658–1677), a verse-by-verse commentary illumined by Hebrew customs, language and the Jewish interpretive tradition.

Wenceslaus Linck (1482–1547). German Lutheran theologian and preacher. As dean of the theology faculty at the University of Wittenberg and successor to Johannes von Staupitz* as the prior of the Augustinian Monastery, Linck worked closely with Martin Luther* and attended the Heidelberg Disputation with him. He replaced Staupitz as vicar-general of the Augustinian order in 1520 in Germany, a capacity in which he pronounced all members free from their vows before renouncing the order himself. After periods of ministry in Munich and Altenburg, Linck settled in Nuremberg, where he became known as an exemplary preacher and an advisor to cities undertaking Protestant reform. He published a significant number of sermons and practical tracts as well as a paraphrase and annotations on the Old Testament.

Henry Lok (1553?–1608?). English Puritan poet. Patronized by Sir Robert Cecil (1563–1612), Lok served the secretary of state as a foreign agent, working to gather intelligence in Scotland, southern France, and Spain. After falling out of favor, Lok served at least two sentences in debtors' prison and died penniless. He published two works: a collection of devotional sonnets and a paraphrase of Ecclesiastes.

Peter Lombard (1095–1160). Scholastic theologian, bishop of Paris. Though little is known about his life, some records indicate that Lombard came from the region of Novara in Lombardy. Bernard of Clairvaux* patronized his studies at Reims, and later recommended him for further study at St. Victor in Paris. In 1144, Lombard participated in an examination of the writings of Gilbert of Poitiers for heresy. Lombard became a canon at Notre Dame in 1145, and an archdeacon there in 1156. Meanwhile he spent a year and a half in Rome as an assistant to Theobald, bishop of Paris. Lombard was elected bishop of Paris in 1159. He died less than a year later. Lombard's most important work was the *Four Books of the Sentences*, which served as the standard textbook for theology throughout the remainder of the Middle Ages, and at the beginning of the early modern period. Additionally, Lombard produced commentaries on the Psalms and Pauline epistles.

Johannes Lonicer (1499–1569). German Lutheran theologian and linguist. After studying in Erfurt and Wittenberg, Lonicer renounced his Augustinian vows. He briefly taught Hebrew at the University of Freiburg, but controversy saw him flee to Strasburg, where he worked with a printer, translating some early Lutheran vernacular works into Latin. At the opening of the University of Marburg, Lonicer was appointed to teach Greek and Hebrew, and he later also served as professor of theology.

Lucas Lossius (1508–1582). German Lutheran teacher and musician. While a student at Leipzig and Wittenberg, Lossius was deeply influenced by Melanchthon* and Luther,* who found work for him as Urbanus Rhegius's* secretary. Soon after going to work for Rhegius, Lossius began teaching at a local gymnasium (or secondary school), *Das Johanneum*, eventually becoming its headmaster. Lossius remained at *Das Johanneum* until his death, even turning down appointments to university professorships. A man of varied interests, he wrote on dialectics, music and church history, as well as publishing a postil and a five-volume set of annotations on the New Testament.

Sibrandus Lubbertus (c. 1555–1625). Dutch Reformed theologian. Lubbertis, a key figure in the establishment of orthodox Calvinism in Frisia, studied theology at Wittenburg and Geneva (under Theodore Beza*) before his appointment as professor of theology at the University of Franeker. Throughout his career, Lubbertis advocated for high Calvinist theology, defending it in disputes with representatives of Socinianism, Arminianism and Roman Catholicism. Lubbertis criticized the Catholic theologian Robert Bellarmine and fellow Dutch reformer Jacobus Arminius*; the views of the latter he opposed as a prominent participant in the Synod of Dordrecht.*

Thomas Lushington (1590–1661). English Anglican minister. Best known as the tutor of polymath Sir Thomas Browne (1605–1682), Lushington also served as a chaplain to Richard Corbet, bishop of Oxford. Committed to the program of Archbishop Laud,* he lost his position during the English Civil Wars and retired to write. Most of his works were published anonymously or pseudonymously, including a translation of a commentary on Hebrews by Polish theologian Johannes Crellius (1590–1633) as G. W. and a series of sermons given at Oxford as Robert Jones.

Martin Luther (1483–1546). German Lutheran priest, professor, and theologian. Martin Luther was born in Eisleben, Saxony, to an entrepreneurial minor. Upon completing his earlier education at Eisenach, Luther matriculated at the University of Erfurt where he completed his BA in 1502, and MA in 1505. While at Erfurt, Luther studied the philosophy of William of Ockham (1285–1347), and his disciple, Gabriel Biel (1420–1495). After receiving his MA, Luther proceeded to the study of law. However, a number of events culminating in his promise to St. Anne (the patron saint of minors) to become a monk compelled Luther to withdraw from law school and join the Augustinian monastery at Erfurt in 1505. At this monastery, Luther was ordained a priest. Later, the Augustinians sent Luther to the University of Wittenberg to study theology. In 1512, Luther received his doctorate, and took up the post of lecturer in Bible at Wittenberg, a position he would hold the rest of his life. While a professor at this university, Luther reinterpreted the doctrine of justification. Convinced that righteousness comes only from God's grace, he disputed the sale of indulgences with his *Ninety–Five Theses*, which he reportedly posted to the door of All Saints' Church in Wittenberg on October 31, 1517. Luther's positions brought conflict with Rome. He challenged the Mass, transubstantiation, and communion in one kind, and his denial of papal authority led to excommunication. Though Luther was condemned by the Diet of Worms, Frederick III, the Elector of Saxony, provided him safe haven. Luther later returned to Wittenberg with public order collapsing under Andreas Bodenstein von Karlstadt* and steered a more cautious path of reform. Among his most influential works are three treatises published in 1520: *To the Christian Nobility of the German Nation*, *On the Babylonian Captivity of the Church*, and *On the Freedom of a Christian*. His rendering of the Bible and liturgy in the vernacular, as well as his hymns and sermons, proved extensively influential.

Georg Major (1502–1574). German Lutheran theologian. Major was on the theological faculty of the University of Wittenberg, succeeding as dean Johannes Bugenhagen* and Philipp Melanchthon.* One of the chief editors on the Wittenberg edition of Luther's works, Major is most identified with the controversy bearing his name, in which he stated that good works are necessary to salvation. Major qualified his statement, which was in reference to the totality of the Christian life. The Formula of Concord* rejected the statement, ending the controversy. As a theologian, Major further refined Lutheran views of the inspiration of Scripture and the doctrine of the Trinity.

John (Mair) Major (1467–1550). Scottish Catholic philosopher. Major taught logic and theology at the universities of Paris (his alma mater), Glasgow and St Andrews. His broad interests and impressive work drew students from all over Europe. While disapproving of evangelicals (though he did teach John Knox*), Major advocated reform programs for Rome. He supported collegial episcopacy and even challenged the curia's teaching on sexuality. Still he was a nominalist who was critical of humanist approaches to biblical exegesis. His best-known publication is *A History of Greater Britain, Both England and Scotland* (1521), which promoted the union of the kingdoms. He also published a commentary on Peter Lombard's *Sentences* and the Gospel of John.

Juan de Maldonado (1533–1583). Spanish Catholic biblical scholar. A student of Francisco de Toledo,* Maldonado taught philosophy and theology at the universities of Paris and Salamanca. Ordained to the priesthood in Rome, he revised the Septuagint under papal appointment. While Maldonado vehemently criticized Protestants, he asserted that Reformed baptism was valid and that mixed confessional marriages were acceptable. His views on Mary's immaculate conception proved controversial among many Catholics who conflated his statement that it was not an article of faith with its denial. He was intrigued by demonology (blaming demonic influence for the Reformation). All his work was published posthumously; his Gospel commentaries were highly valued and important.

Thomas Manton (1620–1677). English Puritan minister. Manton, educated at Oxford, served for a time as lecturer at Westminster Abbey and rector of St. Paul's, Covent Garden, and was a strong advocate of Presbyterianism. He was known as a rigorous evangelical Calvinist who preached long expository sermons. At different times in his ecclesial career he worked side-by-side with Richard Baxter* and John Owen.* In his later life, Manton's Nonconformist position led to his ejection as a clergyman from the Church of England (1662) and eventual imprisonment (1670). Although a voluminous writer, Manton was best known for his preaching. At his funeral in 1677, he was dubbed "the king of preachers."

Benedetto da Mantova (c. 1495–c. 1556). Italian Catholic monk. Benedetto entered the Benedictine order in Mantua and served as dean at San Giorgio Maggiore in Venice. At San Nicolò l'Arena on Mt. Etna, he became acquainted with Waldensian and Protestant thought, which influenced his composition of *The Benefit of Christ*, one of the most significant Italian writings of the Reformation. Marcantonio Flaminio* was asked to rewrite the text in more elegant prose before its anonymous publication in 1543, and although the work drew the ire of the Inquisition, Benedetto's authorship was not uncovered during his lifetime. His increasingly radical spiritualism saw him arrested in Padua, though nothing of his later life is known.

Felix Mantz (d. 1527). Swiss Anabaptist Leader. An early supporter of Zwingli* in Zurich, Mantz's frustration with the pace of the magisterial Reformation led him to found an independent congregation, the Swiss Brethren, with Conrad Grebel,* Georg Blaurock,* and others. Mantz and Grebel represented the Brethren in two disputations with Zwingli over infant baptism in 1525. Defeated, the Brethren refused to cease meeting and rebaptizing adults, which they considered a first baptism, leading to suppression by the Zurich authorities. Mantz was able to spread his message for a time, traveling through a number of Swiss regions despite several arrests. Imprisoned by the Zurich authorities in March 1526 with Grebel and Blaurock, he briefly escaped, but having returned to his practice of believers' baptism, he was executed by drowning, the punishment for Anabaptism, in January 1527.

Lucrezia Marinella (1571–1653). Venetian poet and writer. While famous for her writings, very little is known of Marinella's personal life. As was expected of a women of her class, she spent most of her life in seclusion, and she did not participate in public life. She married a physician, but the fact that she had two children is only known from her will. Marinella's writings spanned a number of subjects, including, philosophy, religious poetry, and proto-feminist texts on the abilities of women and their place in society. Perhaps her best-known work is *The Nobility and Excellence of Women and the Defects and Vices of Men* (1600), in which she argues for the moral and intellectual superiority of women.

Augustin Marlorat (c. 1506–1562). French Reformed pastor. Committed by his family to a monastery at the age of eight, Marlorat was also ordained into the priesthood at an early age in 1524. He fled to Geneva in 1535, where he pastored until the Genevan Company of Pastors sent him to France to shepherd the nascent evangelical congregations. His petition to the young Charles IX (1550–1574) for the right to public evangelical worship was denied. In response to a massacre of evangelicals in Vassy (over sixty dead, many more wounded), Marlorat's congregation planned to overtake Rouen. After the crown captured Rouen, Marlorat was arrested and executed three days later for treason. His principle published work was an anthology of New Testament comment modeled after Thomas Aquinas's* *Catena aurea in quatuor Evangelia*. Marlorat harmonized Reformed and Lutheran comment with the church fathers, interspersed with his own brief comments. He also wrote such anthologies for Genesis, Job, the Psalms, Song of Songs and Isaiah.

Pilgram Marpeck (c. 1495–1556). Austrian Radical elder and theologian. During a brief sojourn in Strasbourg, Marpeck debated with Martin Bucer* before the city council; Bucer was declared the winner, and Marpeck was asked to leave Strasbourg for his views concerning paedobaptism (which he compared to a sacrifice to Moloch). After his time in Strasbourg, Marpeck traveled throughout southern Germany and western Austria, planting Anabaptist congregations. Marpeck criticized the strict use of the ban, however, particularly among the Swiss brethren. He also engaged in a christological controversy with Kaspar von Schwenckfeld.*

Stephen Marshall (c. 1594–1655). English Presbyterian minister. Known for his Nonconformist preaching, Marshall pastored in Essex before appearing on the national stage prior to the Civil War (1642–1651). An advocate of armed rebellion against a lawful sovereign over religious matters, he preached before Parliament a number of times, was a member of the Westminster Assembly, and served as lecturer at St. Margaret's, Westminster. He also ministered to Archbishop Laud* and Charles I* before their executions.

Gregory Martin (1542?–1582). English Catholic priest and translator. After studying at Oxford, Martin tutored the sons of the Duke of Norfolk until leaving for the college of Douai, where he received his doctorate. He taught for two years at the English college in Rome before returning to the college of Douai, which was temporarily based at Rheims. While he composed a number of polemical writings, he is best known as the primary translator of the Douai-Rheims Bible, an English translation of the Vulgate with commentary and notes intended to provide a Catholic alternative to the influx of Protestant annotated English Bibles. The New Testament was published at Douai in 1582 and the Old Testament at Rheims in 1609–1610.

Mary I of England (1516–1558). English monarch. Daughter of Henry VIII* and his first wife Catherine of Aragon (1509–1553), Mary was raised in the strict Catholicism of her mother. Her succession of Edward VI, her half-brother, was briefly contested by Lady Jane Grey*, daughter of Henry VIII's younger sister, in whom Protestants placed their hopes, but unable to raise adequate support, this challenge was quickly dismissed. Upon her ascent, Mary set about the task of restoring the Catholic religion, a reversal of royal policy that was positively received by much of the populace. While able to reestablish relations with the Pope and reassert the mass and other aspects of Catholicism, the impoverishment of the church following the dissolution of the monasteries and the closure of the chantries was difficult to overcome. Other aspects of popular piety, including the cult of the saints, pilgrimages, and the doctrine of purgatory, were not restored during her reign. Mary looms large in the Protestant imagination, and her persecution of evangelicals led to the moniker "Bloody Mary." The accounts of martyrs such as Thomas Cranmer*, Hugh Latimer*, and Nicholas Ridley* were immortalized in John Foxe's (1516–1587) *Acts and Monuments** and became a mainstay of Protestant propaganda.

Johannes Mathesius (1504–1565). German Lutheran theologian and pastor. After reading Martin Luther's* *On Good Works*, Mathesius left his teaching post in Ingolstadt and traveled to Wittenberg to study theology. Mathesius was an important agent of reform in the Bohemian town of Jáchymov, where he pastored, preached and taught. Over one thousand of Mathesius's sermons are extant, including numerous wedding and funeral sermons as well as a series on Luther's life. Mathesius also transcribed portions of Luther's Table Talk.

Chiara Matraini Contarini (1514–1604). Italian Catholic poet. Widowed at twenty-seven, Matraini became active in the literary circles of Lucca and Pescia. Her early published works were composed on secular topics, and include love poetry, songs, a reflection on warfare, and a translation of Isocrates's (436–338 BC) *Ad Demonicum*. Later in her life, she wrote on spiritual topics, publishing a series of spiritual meditations, reflections on the penitential psalms, and a treatise on Mary.

Anthony Maxey (d. 1618). Anglican minister. Maxey was born in Essex and educated at Westminster School. After completing his early education at Westminster, Maxey matriculated at Trinity College, Cambridge, in 1578. Maxey graduated Cambridge with the BA (1581), MA (1585), BD (1594), and DD (1608) degrees. However, he was unable to obtain a fellowship at Trinity. King James I* appointed Maxey as his chaplain and dean of Windsor on June 21, 1612. Maxey was also inducted into the Order of the Garter. He died on May 3, 1618. Maxey's published works consist of three sermons: *The Churches Sleep*; *The Golden Chain of Man's Salvation*; and *The Fearful Point of Hardening*.

John Mayer (1583–1664). Anglican priest and biblical exegete. Mayer dedicated much of his life to biblical exegesis, writing a seven-volume commentary on the entire Bible (1627–1653). Styled after Philipp Melanchthon's* *locus* method, Mayer's work avoided running commentary, focusing instead on textual and theological problems. He was a parish priest for fifty-five years. In the office of priest Mayer also wrote a popular catechism, *The English Catechisme, or a Commentarie on the Short Catechisme* (1621), which went through twelve editions in his lifetime.

Joseph Mede (1586–1638). Anglican biblical scholar, Hebraist and Greek lecturer. A man of encyclopedic knowledge, Mede was interested in numerous fields, varying from philology and history to mathematics and physics, although millennial thought and apocalyptic prophesy were clearly his chief interests. Mede's most important work was his *Clavis Apocalyptica* (1627, later translated into English as *The Key of the Revelation*). This work examined the structure of Revelation as the key to its interpretation. Mede saw the visions as a connected and chronological sequence hinging around Revelation 17:18. He is remembered as an important figure in the history of millenarian theology. He was respected as a mild-mannered and generous scholar who avoided controversy and debate, but who had many original thoughts.

Philipp Melanchthon (1497–1560). German Lutheran educator, reformer, and theologian. Philipp Melanchthon was born in the Palatinate, the son of an armorer. He attended the Latin school in Pforzheim, where he lived with the sister of Johannes Reuchlin* to whom he was related by marriage. Having completed his early education,

Melanchthon went on to attend the University of Heidelberg, where he received his BA in 1511. Afterwards, he earned his MA from the University of Tubingen in 1514. In 1518, Reuchlin recommended Melanchthon for the new professorship of Greek at the University of Wittenberg, where he remained for the rest of his life. There, Melanchthon taught Greek, rhetoric, and logic. Melanchthon is known as the partner and successor to Martin Luther* in reform in Germany and for his pioneering *Loci Communes*, which served as a theological textbook. Melanchthon participated with Luther in the Leipzig disputation, helped implement reform in Wittenberg, and was a chief architect of the Augsburg Confession.* Later, Melanchthon and Martin Bucer* worked for union between reformed and Catholic churches. On account of Melanchthon's ecumenical disposition and his modification of several of Luther's doctrines, he was held in suspicion by some.

Andrew Melville (1545–1622). Scottish Reformed theologian. Melville was born at Baldovie on August 1, 1545, to an evangelical family. After finishing his early education at Montrose Grammar School, he matriculated at St. Mary's College, St. Andrews, in 1559. Melville graduated St. Andrews in 1564, after which he traveled to Paris, where he studied Greek, Hebrew, mathematics, and other languages. While in Paris, Melville came under the influence of Petrus Ramus,* whose pedagogical methods he would later utilize in Scotland. From there, he proceeded to Poitiers to study law. There, he became regent of the College of St. Marceon. However, when Poitiers came under siege, Melville departed the city for Geneva, where Theodore Beza* warmly received him. Shortly after Melville's arrival in Geneva, he assumed the chair of humanities at the academy. Melville remained in this position at the academy until 1573, when he returned to Scotland. In 1574, Melville was appointed principal of the College of Glasgow. While in this post, Melville led in the reform of the college's curriculum, and engaged in ecclesiastical controversy. He served on the committee that drafted the Second Book of Discipline, and was elected moderator of the General Assembly in 1578. In 1580, Melville became principal of St. Mary's College, St. Andrews, where he initiated the same types of reform as he did at Glasgow. Throughout his career, Melville denounced royal ecclesiastical supremacy, arguing strongly for the autonomy of the national church. For this he was summoned to the Privy Council in Edinburgh in 1584 on the possible charge of treason for his resistance to royal ecclesiastical authority. Though they could not charge Melville with sedition, the Privy Council still determined to consign him to trial, but Melville managed to escape to England. While in England, he visited Puritan leaders at Oxford and Cambridge. He also lectured on Genesis in London. Melville returned to Scotland in 1585, and became rector of the University of St. Andrews in 1590. He was eventually deprived of this rectorship in 1587 for his opposition to episcopacy. In 1606, along with several ministers, he was summoned to appear before Hampton Court, where he gave some uncompromising speeches. These speeches resulted in Melville's imprisonment in several places, including the Tower of London. Melville was released from the Tower on April 19, 1611, and from there traveled to France. Having arrived in France, Melville proceeded through Paris and Rouen to Sedan, where he assumed the chair of theology. He remained in Sedan until his death in 1622. Melville authored an extensive literary corpus, which includes a commentary on Romans.

Justus Menius (1499–1558). German Lutheran pastor and theologian. Menius was a prominent reformer in Thuringia. He participated in the Marburg Colloquy and, with others, helped Martin Luther* compose the Schmalkald Articles.* Throughout his career Menius entered into numerous controversies with Anabaptists and even fellow Lutherans. He rejected Andreas Osiander's (d. 1552) doctrine of justification—that the indwelling of Christ's divine nature justifies, rather than the imputed alien righteousness of Christ's person, declared through God's mercy. Against Nikolaus von Amsdorf (1483–1565) and Matthias Flacius (1520–1575), Menius agreed with Georg Major* that good works are necessary to salvation. Osiander's view of justification was censored in Article 3 of the Formula of Concord*; Menius's understanding of the relationship between good works and salvation was rejected in Article 4. Menius translated many of Luther's Latin works into German. He also composed a handbook for Christian households and an influential commentary on 1 Samuel.

Johannes Mercerus (Jean Mercier) (d. 1570). French Hebraist. Mercerus studied under the first Hebrew chair at the Collège Royal de Paris, François Vatable (d. 1547), whom he succeeded in 1546. John Calvin* tried to recruit Mercerus to the Genevan Academy as professor of Hebrew, once in 1558 and again in 1563; he refused both times. During his lifetime Mercerus published grammatical helps for Hebrew and Chaldean, an aid to the Masoretic symbols in the Hebrew text, and translated the commentaries and grammars of several medieval rabbis. He himself wrote commentaries on Genesis, the wisdom books, and most of the Minor Prophets. These commentaries—most of them only published after his death—were philologically focused and interacted with the work of Jerome, Nicholas of Lyra,* notable rabbis and Johannes Oecolampadius.*

Thomas Mocket (1602–1670?). British Puritan minister. Mocket ministered in Wales and England, publishing numerous works, including a catechism, a tract on the duties of Christians, and an excursus on the celebration of Christmas.

Peter Moffett (d. 1617). English Protestant clergyman. Rector at Fobbing, Essex, Moffett published a commentary on the Song of Solomon and a sermon on 1 Timothy 1:16.

Ambrose Moibanus (1494–1554). German Lutheran bishop and theologian. Moibanus helped reform the church of Breslau (modern Wroclaw, Poland). He revised the Mass, bolstered pastoral care and welfare for the poor, and wrote a new evangelical catechism.

Olympia Morata (1526/27–1555). Italian Protestant humanist and theologian. Daughter of a humanist scholar, her father taught in the court of Ferrara, and she was raised alongside Anna d'Este (1531–1607), daughter of Protestant Renée of France (1510–1574) and later wife of Francis, Duke of Guise (1519–1563), a central antagonist in the St. Bartholomew's Day Massacre. A precocious scholar, Morata's classical, humanist, and biblical studies drew her toward the evangelical currents of the court, but these Protestant leanings also raised the constant suspicion of the Inquisition. In 1550, Morata married Andreas Grundler (unknown), a German Protestant doctor, and moved to his native Schweinfurt, where, facing limited opportunities due to her gender, she continued her studies and privately tutored in Greek and the classics. She developed an extensive correspondence with friends, especially noblewomen she had met at court, and Protestant leaders including Luther*, Melanchthon* and Matthias Flacius (1520–1575), whom she asked to translate some of Luther's work into Italian. Most of Morata's writings were destroyed during the siege of Schweinfurt in 1553–1554, and while she was able to resettle in Frankfurt, she died of tuberculosis soon afterwards. In her writings that survived the siege, her scholarly erudition is clear, and her letters demonstrate a ministerial care for her correspondents and desire for the spread of the Reformation message.

Thomas More (1478–1535). English Catholic lawyer, politician, humanist and martyr. More briefly studied at Oxford, but completed his legal studies in London. After contemplating the priesthood for four years, he opted for politics and was elected a member of Parliament in 1504. A devout Catholic, More worked with church leaders in England to root out heresy while he also confronted Lutheran teachings in writing. After four years as Lord Chancellor, More resigned due to heightened tensions with Henry VIII* over papal supremacy (which More supported and Henry did not). Tensions did not abate. More's steadfast refusal to accept the Act of Supremacy (1534)—which declared the King of England to be the supreme ecclesial primate not the pope—resulted in his arrest and trial for high treason. He was found guilty and beheaded with John Fisher (1469–1535). Friends with John Colet* and Desiderius Erasmus,* More was a widely respected humanist in England as well as on the continent. Well-known for his novel *Utopia* (1516), More also penned several religious treatises on Christ's passion and suffering during his imprisonment in the Tower of London, which were published posthumously.

Henry Morley (d. 1616). English Protestant preacher. Morley published a sermon of the cleansing of the leper given at St. Paul's Cathedral in London during an outbreak of the plague in 1603.

Sebastian Münster (1488–1552). German Reformed Hebraist, exegete, printer, and geographer. After converting to the Reformation in 1524, Münster taught Hebrew at the universities of Heidelberg and Basel. During his lengthy tenure in Basel he published more than seventy books, including Hebrew dictionaries and rabbinic commentaries. He also produced an evangelistic work for Jews titled *Vikuach* (1539). Münster's *Torat ha-Maschiach* (1537), the Gospel of Matthew, was the first published Hebrew translation of any portion of the New Testament. Despite his massive contribution to contemporary understanding of the Hebrew language, Münster was criticized by many of the reformers as a Judaizer.

Thomas Müntzer (c. 1489–1525). German Radical preacher. As a preacher in the town of Zwickau, Müntzer was influenced by German mysticism and, growing convinced that Martin Luther* had not carried through reform properly, sought to restore the pure apostolic church of the New Testament. Müntzer's radical ideas led to expulsions from various cities; he developed a highly apocalyptic theology, in which he heralded the last days that would establish the pure community out of suffering, prompting Müntzer's proactive role in the Peasants' War, which he perceived as a crucial apocalyptic event. Six thousand of Müntzer's followers were annihilated by magisterial troops; Müntzer was executed.

John Murcot (1625–1654). English Puritan pastor. After completing his bachelor's at Oxford in 1647, Murcot was ordained as a pastor, transferring to several parishes until in 1651 he moved to Dublin. All his works were published posthumously.

Simon Musaeus (1521–1582). German Lutheran theologian. After studying at the universities of Frankfurt an der Oder and Wittenberg, Musaeus began teaching Greek at the Cathedral school in Nuremberg and was ordained. Having returned to Wittenberg to complete a doctoral degree, Musaeus spent the rest of his career in numerous ecclesial and academic administrative posts. He opposed Matthias Flacius's (1505–1575) view of original sin—that the formal essence of human beings is marred by original sin—even calling the pro-Flacian faculty at Wittenberg "the devil's latrine." Musaeus published a disputation on original sin and a postil.

Wolfgang Musculus (1497–1563). German Reformed pastor and theologian. Musculus produced translations, biblical commentaries and an influential theological text, *Loci communes Sacrae Theologiae* (*Commonplaces of Sacred Theology*), outlining a Zwinglian theology. Musculus began to study theology while at a Benedictine monastery; he departed in 1527 and became secretary to Martin Bucer* in Strasbourg. He was later installed as a pastor in Augsburg, eventually performing the first evangelical liturgy in the city's cathedral. Displaced by the Augsburg Interim, Musculus ended his career as professor of theology at Bern. Though Musculus was active in the pursuit of the reform agenda, he was also concerned for ecumenism, participating in the Wittenberg Concord (1536) and discussions between Lutherans and Catholics.

Georg Mylius (1548–1607). German Lutheran pastor and theologian. Mylius began his career as a preacher in Augsburg, rising to superintendent of the churches in the city after receiving his doctorate in theology. He was arrested and ejected from the city by the Catholic-dominated council for his opposition to the Gregorian calendar, returning briefly to learn of the death of his pregnant wife and child. After grieving in Ulm, Mylius spend the remainder of his career as a preacher and professor of theology at Wittenberg, with a brief hiatus teaching at Jena.

Hans Nadler (unknown). German Radical layperson. An uneducated and illiterate needle salesman, after receiving baptism from Hans Hut* in 1527, Nadler sought to share the faith with those he met during his extensive travels. He is remembered through the records of his arrest and examination, recorded by a court reporter, which give insight into his beliefs and activities as a committed Anabaptist layperson, whereby he affirmed believer's baptism, the spiritual reception of the Eucharist, and nonresistance.

Friedrich Nausea (c. 1496–1552). German Catholic bishop and preacher. After completing his studies at Leipzig, this famed preacher was appointed priest in Frankfurt but was run out of town by his congregants during his first sermon. He transferred to Mainz as cathedral preacher. Nausea was well connected through the German papal hierarchy and traveled widely to preach to influential ecclesial and secular courts. Court preacher for Ferdinand I (1503–1564), his reform tendencies fit well with royal Austrian theological leanings, and he was enthroned as the bishop of Vienna. Nausea thought that rather than endless colloquies only a council could settle reform. Unfortunately he could not participate in the first session of Trent due to insufficient funding, but he arrived for the second session. Nausea defended the laity's reception of the cup and stressed the importance of promulgating official Catholic teaching in the vernacular.

Melchior Neukirch (1540–1597). German Lutheran pastor and playwright. Neukirch's pastoral career spanned more than thirty years in several northern German parishes. Neukirch published a history of the Braunschweig church since the Reformation and a dramatization of Acts 4–7. He died of the plague.

Nicholas of Lyra (1270–1349). French Catholic biblical exegete. Very little is known about this influential medieval theologian of the Sorbonne aside from the works he published, particularly the *Postilla litteralis super totam Bibliam* (1322–1333). With the advent of the printing press this work was regularly published alongside the Latin Vulgate and the *Glossa ordinaria*. In this running commentary on the Bible Nicholas promoted literal interpretation as the basis for theology. Despite his preference for literal interpretation, Nicholas also published a companion volume, the *Postilla moralis super totam Bibliam* (1339), a commentary on the spiritual meaning of the biblical text. Nicholas was a major conversation partner for many reformers though many of them rejected his exegesis as too literal and too "Jewish" (not concerned enough with the Bible's fulfillment in Jesus Christ).

John Norden (1547–1625). English devotional writer. Norden was born at Somerset, and in 1564 entered Hart Hall, Oxford where he graduated with his BA in 1568, and MA in 1573. Norden spent most of his life Middlesex, moving later to St. Giles in the Fields in 1619, where he remained until his death in 1625. Throughout his life, Norden distinguished himself also as a cartographer, chorographer, and antiquarian. His best known devotional work was his Progress of Piety (1596).

Alexander Nowell (1517–1602). Anglican theologian. Born in Lancashire, Nowell was educated at Brasenose College, Oxford where he shared a room with the future martyrologist John Foxe. Nowell was elected a fellow at the same college, where he spent thirteen years. In 1543, he was appointed master of Westminster School, and in December, 1551, a prebendary of Westminster Abbey. Though elected to the House of Commons in 1553, Nowell was permitted to assume his seat because as a prebendary, he had a seat in Convocation. Because of his evangelical convictions, Nowell lost prebendary in 1554, after which he fled to the Continent, traveling first to Strasbourg, and then to Frankfurt. When Elizabeth I ascended the throne, Nowell returned to England where he afterwards served as chaplain to Edmund Grindal. In 1561 Nowell became Dean of St. Paul's Cathedral, a post which he held until his death. Nowell's best known work was his Catechism originally written in Latin (1563), and translated into English by Thomas Norton in 1570.

Bernardino Ochino (1487–1564). Italian Reformed theologian. After serving as vicar general of the Franciscan order, Ochino left the foundation of the Capuchins, where he assisted in the composition of their constitution and served as vicar general. A famed preacher, his teaching came to the attention of the Inquisition as it began to reflect the thought of Juan de Valdés. Summoned to Rome in 1542, he fled to Geneva with Peter Martyr Vermigli* where his Reformed orthodoxy, tinged with Franciscan mysticism, was brought into the open. Following his flight, Ochino led an unstable life, with brief stays in Basel, Strasbourg, and Augsburg before moving to England with Vermigli in 1548 where he was able to compose a significant treatise against the Roman church. His doctrinal orthodoxy was questioned by the pastor of the Italian congregation in London, but his case left unresolved when he departed for Geneva, then Basel and Zurich, at the accession of Mary*. As pastor of a congregation of Italian refugees in Zurich, Ochino courted considerable controversy. He refused to have his works approved by the city magistrates before publication, and his opponents alleged that his Dialogi XXX (1563) included questionable teachings on the Trinity and divorce while seeming to advocate polygamy. Expelled from Zurich in 1563, he died in Moravia the following year.

Charles Odingsells (d. 1637). English Protestant preacher. Odingsells published two sermons on prophesying and miracles from Matthew 7 given at Langar in Nottinghamshire.

Johannes Oecolampadius (Johannes Huszgen) (1482–1531). Swiss-German Reformed humanist, reformer and theologian. Oecolampadius (an assumed name meaning "house light") assisted with Desiderius Erasmus's* Greek New Testament, lectured on biblical languages and exegesis and completed an influential Greek grammar. After joining the evangelical cause through studying patristics and the work of Martin Luther,* Oecolampadius went to Basel, where he lectured on biblical exegesis and participated in ecclesial reform. On account of Oecolampadius's effort, the city council passed legislation restricting preaching to the gospel and releasing the city from compulsory Mass. Oecolampadius was a chief ally of Huldrych Zwingli,* whom he supported at the Marburg Colloquy (1529).

Kaspar Olevianus (1536–1587). German Reformed theologian. Olevianus is celebrated for composing the Heidelberg Catechism and producing a critical edition of Calvin's *Institutes* in German. Olevianus studied theology with many, including John Calvin,* Theodore Beza,* Heinrich Bullinger* and Peter Martyr Vermigli.* As an advocate of Reformed doctrine, Olevianus oversaw the shift from Lutheranism to Calvinism throughout Heidelberg, organizing the city's churches after Calvin's Geneva. The Calvinist ecclesial vision of Olevianus entangled him in a dispute with another Heidelberg reformer over the rights of ecclesiastical discipline, which Olevianus felt belonged to the council of clergy and elders rather than civil magistrates.

Josua Opitz (c. 1542–1585). German Lutheran pastor. After a brief stint as superintendent in Regensburg, Opitz, a longtime preacher, was dismissed for his support of Matthias Flacius's (1520–1575) view of original sin. (Using Aristotelian categories, Flacius argued that the formal essence of human beings is marred by original sin, forming sinners into the image of Satan; his views were officially rejected in Article 1 of the Formula of Concord.*) Hans Wilhelm Roggendorf (1533–1591) invited Opitz to lower Austria as part of his Lutheranizing program. Unfortunately Roggendorf and Opitz never succeed in getting Lutheranism legal recognition, perhaps in large part due to Opitz's staunch criticism of Catholics, which resulted in his exile. He died of plague.

Lucas Osiander (1534–1604). German Lutheran pastor. For three decades, Osiander—son of the controversial Nuremberg reformer Andreas Osiander (d. 1552)—served as pastor and court preacher in Stuttgart, until he fell out of favor with the duke in 1598. Osiander produced numerous theological and exegetical works, as well as an influential hymnal.

John Owen (1616–1683). English Puritan theologian. Owen trained at Oxford University, where he was later appointed dean of Christ Church and vice chancellor of the university, following his service as chaplain to Oliver Cromwell. Although Owen began his career as a Presbyterian minister, he eventually departed to the party of Independents. Owen composed many sermons, biblical commentaries (including seven volumes on the book of Hebrews), theological treatises and controversial monographs (including disputations with Arminians, Anglicans, Catholics and Socinians).

Ephraim Pagitt (1575–1647). English Protestant minister. Pagitt ministered at St. Edmunds in London until forced into retirement for his Royalist tendencies during the Civil War (1642–1646). Some of his later writings demonstrate sympathy for Presbyterian theology, and he became an opponent of Baptists and other sectarians. His most popular writing was *Heresiography* (1662), in which he set out to catalog the heretics he identified within the church.

Santes Pagninus (c. 1470–1541). Italian Catholic biblical scholar. Pagninus studied under Girolamo Savonarola* and later taught in Rome, Avignon and Lyons. He translated the Old Testament into Latin according to a tight, almost wooden, adherence to the Hebrew. This translation and his Hebrew lexicon *Thesaurus linguae sanctae* (1529) were important resources for translators and commentators.

Johann Pappus (1549–1610). German Lutheran theologian. After a decade as a teacher of Hebrew and professor of theology at the Strasbourg academy, Pappus was appointed president of the city's company of pastors. Despite resistance from the Reformed theologian Johann Sturm (1507–1589), he led the city away from its Swiss Reformed alliances and toward subscription to the Lutheran Formula of Concord. A talented humanist, Pappus published more than thirty works on controversial, theological, historical, and exegetical subjects.

David (Wängler) Pareus (1548–1622). German Reformed pastor and theologian. Born at Frankenstein in Lower Silesia, Pareus studied theology at Heidelberg under Zacharias Ursinus (1534–1583), the principal author of the Heidelberg Catechism.* After reforming several churches, Pareus returned to Heidelberg to teach at the Reformed seminary. He then joined the theological faculty at the University of Heidelberg, first as a professor of Old Testament and later as a professor of New Testament. Pareus edited the *Neustadter Bibel* (1587), a publication of Martin Luther's* German translation with Reformed annotations—which was strongly denounced by Lutherans, especially Jakob Andreae* and Johann Georg Sigwart (1554–1618). In an extended debate, Pareus defended the orthodoxy of Calvin's exegesis against Aegidius Hunnius,* who accused Calvin of "judaizing" by rejecting many traditional Christological interpretations of Old Testament passages. Towards the end of his career, Pareus wrote commentaries on Genesis, Hosea, Matthew, Romans, 1 Corinthians, Galatians, Hebrews and Revelation.

Catherine Parr (1512–1548). The last of King Henry VIII's* six wives, Catherine Parr was Queen Consort to Henry from 1543 until his death in 1547. She enjoyed a close relationship with two of her step children, Elizabeth and Edward (the future Queen Elizabeth I* and King Edward VI), involving herself extensively in their education. Having married three more times after the death of Henry VIII, Catherine died in 1548. Her published works are *Psalms or Prayers* (1543) and a *Lamentation of a Sinner* (1548).

Paul of Burgos (Solomon ha-Levi) (c. 1351–1435). Spanish Catholic archbishop. In 1391 Solomon ha-Levi, a rabbi and Talmudic scholar, converted to Christianity, receiving baptism with his entire family (except for his wife). He changed his name to Paul de Santa Maria. Some have suggested that he converted to avoid persecution; he himself stated that Thomas Aquinas's* work persuaded him of the truth of Christian faith. After studying theology in Paris, he was ordained bishop in 1403. He actively and ardently persecuted Jews, trying to compel them to convert. In order to convince Jews that Christians correctly interpret the Hebrew Scriptures, Paul wrote *Dialogus Pauli et Sauli contra Judaeos, sive Scrutinium Scripturarum* (1434), a book filled with vile language toward the Jews. He also wrote a series of controversial marginal notes and comments on Nicholas of Lyra's* *Postilla*, many of which criticized Nicholas's use of Jewish scholarship.

Christoph Pelargus (1565–1633). German Lutheran pastor, theologian, professor and superintendent. Pelargus studied philosophy and theology at the University of Frankfurt an der Oder, in Brandenburg. This irenic Philippist was appointed as the superintendent of Brandenburg and later became a pastor in Frankfurt, although the local authorities first required him to condemn Calvinist theology, because several years earlier he had been called before the consistory in Berlin under suspicion of being a crypto-Calvinist. Among his most important works were a four-volume commentary on *De orthodoxa fide* by John of Damascus (d. 749), a treatise defending the breaking of the bread during communion, and a volume of funeral sermons. He also published commentaries on the Pentateuch, the Psalms, Matthew, John and Acts.

Konrad Pellikan (1478–1556). German Reformed Hebraist and theologian. Pellikan attended the University of Heidelberg, where he mastered Hebrew under Johannes Reuchlin. In 1504 Pellikan published one of the first Hebrew grammars that was not merely a translation of the work of medieval rabbis. While living in Basel, Pellikan assisted the printer Johannes Amerbach, with whom he published some of Luther's* early writings. He also worked with Sebastian Münster* and Wolfgang Capito* on a Hebrew Psalter (1516). In 1526, after teaching theology for three years at the University of Basel, Huldrych Zwingli* brought Pellikan to Zurich to chair the faculty of Old Testament. Pellikan's magnum opus is a seven-volume commentary on the entire Bible (except Revelation) and the Apocrypha; it is often heavily dependent upon the work of others (esp. Desiderius Erasmus* and Johannes Oecolampadius*).

William Pemble (1591–1623). Puritan theologian and author. Pemble was born in Egerton, Kent. He was educated at Magdalen College, Oxford, where he graduated with his BA degree in 1614. Afterward he moved to Magdalen Hall, where he became a reader and tutor in divinity. He received his MA in 1618. Primarily a Hebrew scholar, Pemble authored commentaries on Ecclesiastes (1629), the first nine chapters of Zechariah (1629), and portions of Ezra, Nehemiah, and Daniel. Pemble also wrote *An Introduction to the Worthy Receiving the Sacrament* (1628), as well as treatises on predestination and justification. He died of a fever on April 14, 1623.

Benedict Pererius (1535–1610). Spanish Catholic theologian, philosopher and exegete. Pererius entered the Society of Jesus in 1552. He taught philosophy, theology, and exegesis at the Roman College of the Jesuits. Early in his career he warned against neo-Platonism and astrology in his *De principiis* (1576). Pererius wrote a lengthy commentary on Daniel, and five volumes of exegetical theses on Exodus, Romans, Revelation and part of the Gospel of John (chs. 1–14). His four-volume commentary on Genesis (1591–1599) was lauded by Protestants and Catholics alike.

William Perkins (1558–1602). English Puritan preacher and theologian. Perkins was a highly regarded Puritan Presbyterian preacher and biblical commentator in the Elizabethan era. He studied at Cambridge University and later became a fellow of Christ's Church college as a preacher and professor, receiving acclaim for his sermons and lectures. Even more, Perkins gained an esteemed reputation for his ardent exposition of Calvinist reformed doctrine in the style of Petrus Ramus,* becoming one of the first English reformed theologians to achieve international recognition. Perkins influenced the federal Calvinist shape of Puritan theology and the vision of logical, practical expository preaching.

François Perrault (1577–1657). French Reformed pastor for over fifty years. His book on demonology was prominent, perhaps because of the intrigue at his home in 1612. According to his account, a poltergeist made a commotion and argued points of theology; a few months later Perrault's parishioners slew a large snake slithering out of his house.

Dirk Philips (1504–1568). Dutch Radical elder and theologian. This former Franciscan monk, known for being severe and obstinate, was a leading theologian of the sixteenth-century Anabaptist movement. Despite the fame of Menno Simons* and his own older brother Obbe, Philips wielded great influence over Anabaptists in the Netherlands and northern Germany where he ministered. As a result of Philips's understanding of the apostolic church as radically separated from the children of the world, he advocated a very strict interpretation of the ban, including formal shunning. His writings were collected and published near the end of his life as *Enchiridion oft Hantboecxken van de Christelijcke Leere* (1564).

Obbe Philips (1500–1568). Dutch radical leader. Trained as a physician, Philips was drawn to mystical Anabaptism, as taught by Melchior Hoffman (1495–1543) in his hometown of Leewarden. After adult rebaptism and ordination, he preached in Amsterdam, Delft, Appingedam, and Grongen, and he ordained other leaders including his brother Dirk Philips*, David Joris*, and Menno Simmons*. Disillusioned with the growth of revolutionary, enthusiastic, and apocalyptic elements within Anabaptism and unable to reconcile any visible church with the church of God, Philips withdrew from the radical movement in 1540, after which nothing is known of his life. His only extant writing, entitled *The Confession of Obbe Philips*, was published after his death and recounts elements of the history of the Anabaptist movement and defends his departure from the movement.

James Pilkington (1520-1576). Protestant bishop of Durham and Elizabethan author. Born in Lancashire, Pilkington received his early education at Manchester Grammar School. Afterwards, he entered Pembroke College, Cambridge, and later transferred to St. John's College, Cambridge, from where he graduated with his

BA degree in 1539, and MA in 1542. Pilkington was appointed vicar of Kendal in 1545, but resigned this position shortly thereafter in order to return to Cambridge. While there, Pilkington was granted a license to preach, and was awarded the degree of Bachelor of Theology in 1551. In this same year, Pilkington became president of the college. When Mary Tudor succeeded her half-brother, Edward VI, in 1553, Pilkington fled to the Continent where he traveled to Zurich, Geneva, Frankfurt, and Strasbourg. He returned to England in 1559 when Elizabeth I ascended the throne of England. After returning to England, Pilkington became Regius Professor of Divinity at Cambridge and after, bishop of Durham in 1560. Pilkington's major work was his voluminous commentary on the Prophet Haggai.

Charles Pinner (Unknown). English Protestant pastor. Pinner studied at New College, Oxford, and served as rector at Wootton Bassett in Wiltshire. His extant writings include two sermons on 1 Timothy and two on 1 Peter.

Hector Pinto (c. 1528–1584). Portuguese Catholic theologian and exegete. A member of the order of Saint Jerome, Pinto taught theology and Scripture at the Universities of Sigüenza and Coimbra. A respected theologian and exegete, he published commentaries on Daniel, Nahum, Jeremiah, and Isaiah and an influential devotional work, *The Image of the Christian Life*.

Caritas Pirckheimer (1466–1532). German Catholic nun. Sister of famed humanist Wilibald Pirckheimer (1470–1530), Caritas received a humanistic education before entering the Franciscan convent at Nuremberg. Extolled by Erasmus* as one of the most learned women in Europe, Pirckheimer served as abbess at the advent of the Reformation, and her experiences are recorded in a journal covering the pivotal years of 1524–1528. While Nuremberg accepted Lutheran theology under the leadership of the city council and preachers such as Andreas Osiander (1498–1552), Pirckheimer defended the right of her order to continue in their vocation. She ultimately won a concession after a visit from Philipp Melanchthon* in 1525, who recommended that the council allow those who wished to remain in the cloister to live out their vows in peace.

Johannes Piscator (1546–1625). German Reformed theologian. Educated at Tübingen (though he wanted to study at Wittenberg), Piscator taught at the universities of Strasbourg and Heidelberg, as well as academies in Neustadt and Herborn. His commentaries on both the Old and New Testaments involve a tripartite analysis of a given passage's argument, of scholia on the text and of doctrinal loci. Some consider Piscator's method to be a full flowering of Beza's* "logical" scriptural analysis, focused on the text's meaning and its relationship to the pericopes around it.

Amandus Polanus von Polansdorf (1561–1610). German Reformed educator and theologian. Polanus spent his career as an educator, serving as a tutor for noble families and a teacher at the Bohemian Brethren school in Moravia before earning his doctorate and becoming professor of Old Testament and later dean of the theological faculty at the University of Basel. His best-known work is the *Syntagma theologiae christianae* (1609), a compendium of Reformed dogmatics.

Constantino Ponce de la Fuente (1502–1559). Spanish Protestant theologian and preacher. A priest in Seville, Ponce de la Fuente was a critic of the established church and associated with the evangelical circle in the city. A popular preacher, he authored a catechism and a number of books on doctrine and the Christian life that focused on the work of Christ. Charged with heresy by the Inquisition, he admitted to the authorship of a number of heretical writings and died in prison awaiting trial while his works were added to the Index of Prohibited Books.

Matthew Poole (1624–1679). English Nonconformist minister. Having made known his preference for simplicity in worship, Matthew Poole was rector of St Michael-le-Querne until the passing of the 1662 Act of Uniformity led him to resign. Living off his inheritance, he preached occasionally and composed some brief tracts but devoted much of his effort to the compilation of Latin biblical commentary in the *Synopsis criticorum* (1669) and the composition of his own annotations on Scripture. He died in Amsterdam, having fled London during the Popish Plot (1678–1681). He believed his life was in danger for his anti-Catholic writings as part of a Catholic conspiracy to kill Charles II, which was ultimately revealed as a fiction concocted by Titus Oates (1649–1705).

Thomas Porter (d. 1667). English Anglican minister. A graduate of Christ's College, Cambridge, Porter ministered in Flintshire in Cheshire and at Whitchurch in Shropshire. Among his published works are a sermon on Matthew 5:13 and a response to antitrinitarian John Knowles (fl. 1646–1668).

Gabriel Powell (1575–1611). Puritan minister. Powell was born at Ruabon in Denbighshire in 1575. Having completed his studies at Jesus College, Oxford, Powell became master of the free-school in Ruthen. During his tenure at Ruthen, Powell closely studied the writings of the church fathers as well as philosophy, and afterward endeavored to publish several works based on this research. Finding his present location to be a hinderance to his literary objectives, Powell relocated to Oxford, entering St. Mary's Hall, where he finished his anticipated projects. Powell is chiefly known for his literary debate with Thomas Bilson (1547–1619) concerning Christ's descent into hell. Later, Richard Vaughan (1550–1607), bishop of London, appointed Powell his domestic chaplain. Powell died on December 31, 1611. In addition to many controversial and polemical works, Powell wrote a commentary on Romans 1.

Vavasor Powell (1617–1670). Welsh Puritan minister and author. Powell was born at Knucklas, Radnorshire, Wales. After completing his education at Jesus College, Oxford, Powell returned to Wales to assume the position of a local schoolmaster. During this time, Powell came under the influence of Walter Cradock's* preaching as well as the writings of Richard Sibbes* and William Perkins,* resulting in his conversion to Puritanism. Soon thereafter he became an itinerant preacher, traveling throughout Wales. He was arrested twice for nonconformity. During the Civil War, Powell first preached in London, and shortly thereafter pastored an Independent congregation in Wales. On December 26, 1641, Royalist forces arrested and imprisoned Powell. In 1646, as victory for the Puritans appeared inevitable, Powell was released, and allowed to return to Wales, having received a letter of endorsement from the Westminster Assembly. Back in Wales, Powell played a prominent role in the Westminster Assembly's 1650 commission for the better propagation of the gospel throughout Wales. In 1653, Powell returned to London, where he preached at St. Ann Blackfriars. It was at this time that Powell denounced Oliver Cromwell (1599–1658) for assuming the position of Lord Protector. For this reason, he was arrested and imprisoned. At the Restoration in 1660, Powell was again arrested and imprisoned for unauthorized preaching for seven years. Though released in 1667, Powell was once more arrested and incarcerated. He remained in custody until his death on October 27, 1660. Powell authored many poems and a concordance to the Bible.

Felix Pratensis (d. 1539). Italian Catholic Hebraist. Pratensis, the son of a rabbi, converted to Christianity and entered the Augustinian Hermits around the turn of the sixteenth century. In 1515, with papal permission, Pratensis published a new translation of the Psalms based on the Hebrew text. His *Biblia Rabbinica* (1517–1518), printed in Jewish and Christian editions, included text-critical notes in the margins as well as the Targum and rabbinic commentaries on each book (e.g., Rashi* on the Pentateuch and David Kimchi* on the Prophets). Many of the reformers consulted this valuable resource as they labored on their own translations and expositions of the Old Testament.

John Preston (1587–1628). Puritan minister and author. Preston was born at Upper Heyford, Northamptonshire, on October 27, 1587. He studied philosophy at King's College and Queen's College, Cambridge, earning his bachelor's degree in 1607. He became a fellow at Queen's in 1609, and a prebendary at Lincoln Cathedral a year later. During this period, Preston studied medicine and astronomy. In 1611, he received the MA degree. Sometime afterward, he experienced a conversion under the preaching of John Cotton.* After his conversion, Preston went on to study theology, concentrating mainly on Thomas Aquinas,* Duns Scotus, and William of Ockham. From there, he proceeded to the reformers, especially John Calvin.* Preston was appointed court chaplain in 1615. In this position he was influential in the promotion of Puritans to high civil office. Preston later assumed the positions of dean and catechist at Queen's College, Cambridge, where he distinguished himself by preaching a series of sermons that formed the basis of his body of divinity. In 1622, he received the degree of bachelor of divinity, becoming thereafter master of Emmanuel College, Cambridge. While at Emmanuel, Preston participated in the conflict between Calvinism and Arminianism. Moreover, in the same year, Preston succeeded John Donne* as preacher at Lincoln's Inn. Two years later, Preston accepted the lectureship at Trinity Church. He died at the age of forty in 1628. Throughout his prodigious career, Preston authored a sizable corpus, which includes published sermons on Romans.

Quadriga. The *quadriga*, or four senses of Scripture, grew out of the exegetical legacy of Paul's dichotomy of letter and spirit (2 Cor 3:6), as well as church fathers like Origen (c. 185–254), Jerome (c. 347–420) and Augustine* (354–430). Advocates for this method—the primary framework for biblical exegesis during the medieval era—assumed the necessity of the gift of faith under the guidance of the Holy Spirit. The literal-historical meaning of the text served as the foundation for the fuller perception of Scripture's meaning in the three spiritual senses, accessible only through faith: the allegorical sense taught what should be believed, the tropological or moral sense taught what should be done, and the anagogical or eschatological sense taught what should be hoped for. Medieval Jewish exegesis also had a fourfold interpretive method—not necessarily related to the *quadriga*—called *pardes* ("grove"): *peshat*, the simple, literal sense of the text according to grammar; *remez*, the allegorical sense; *derash*, the moral sense; and *sod*, the mystic sense related to Kabbalah. Scholars hotly dispute the precise use and meaning of these terms.

Edward Rainbow[e] (1608–1684). Anglican minister, scholar, and bishop. Rainbow was born at Lincolnshire on April 20, 1608. After completing his education, Rainbow matriculated at Corpus Christi College, and later transferred to Magdalene College, Cambridge, where he graduated with the BA (1627), MA (1630), BD (1637), and DD (1643). He was elected a fellow at Magdalene in 1633 and a master there in 1642. In 1630, Rainbow accepted the mastership of the Kirton-in-Lindsey but shortly afterward moved to London. In 1632, Rainbow took holy orders and preached his first sermon in April of that year. His first appointment was that of curate of Savoy Hospital. Rainbow was recalled to Cambridge in 1633 and elected a fellow. Four years later he became dean of Magdalene and master of the same college in 1642. Though dismissed from his mastership by Parliament in 1650, Rainbow was restored to it in the year of the Restoration (1660). At the same time, he was appointed chaplain to the king. In 1661, Rainbow became dean of Peterborough, and appointed vice chancellor of Cambridge a year later. Rainbow was elected bishop of Carlisle in 1664. As bishop, Rainbow led in the systemic reform of his diocese. Rainbow died March 26, 1684. His published works consist of three published sermons and an incomplete treatise, *Verba Christi*.

Petrus Ramus (1515–1572). French Reformed humanist philosopher. Ramus was an influential professor of philosophy and logic at the French royal college in Paris; he converted to Protestantism and left France for Germany, where he came under the influence of Calvinist thought. Ramus was a trenchant critic of Aristotle and noted for his method of classification based on a deductive movement from universals to particulars, the latter becoming branching divisions that provided a visual chart of the parts to the whole. His system profoundly influenced Puritan theology and preaching. After returning to Paris, Ramus died in the Saint Bartholomew's Day Massacre.

Rashi (**Shlomo Yitzchaki**) (1040–1105). French Jewish rabbi and exegete. After completing his studies, Rashi founded a yeshiva in Troyes. He composed the first comprehensive commentary on the Talmud, as well as commentaries on the entire Old Testament except for 1–2 Chronicles. These works remain influential within orthodox Judaism. Late medieval and early modern Christian scholars valued his exegesis, characterized by his preference for peshat (see quadriga).

Reformatio Legum Ecclesiasticarum (1552). Under the leadership of Archbishop of Canterbury Thomas Cranmer,* Edward VI* established a committee of thirty-two bishops, theologians, and lawyers including Nicholas Ridley,* John Hooper,* Peter Martyr Vermigli,* Matthew Parker (1504–1575), and William Cecil (1520–1598) to align the laws of the English church with Reformed theology and English civil law. Completed in 1552, it touched on diverse topics, including church organization, doctrine and heresy, qualifications for ministry, and marriage and divorce. It was brought before Parliament in 1553, where it was blocked by John Dudley, Duke of Northumberland (1504–1553), who wished to decrease church powers, and then dropped upon the accession of Mary I. A manuscript of the proposal revised by John Foxe (1516/1517–1587) was published in 1671, and while some elements of the Reformatio Legum Ecclesiasticarum were adopted under Elizabeth I, thoroughgoing reform of ecclesiastical law was not brought about until the *Book of Canons* (1604).

Remonstrance (1610). See *Synod of Dordrecht*.

Johannes Reuchlin (1455–1522). German Catholic lawyer, humanist and Hebraist. Reuchlin held judicial appointments for the dukes of Württemberg, the Supreme Court in Speyer and the imperial court of the Swabian League. He pioneered the study of Hebrew among Christians in Germany, standing against those who, like Johannes Pfefferkorn (1469–1523), wanted to destroy Jewish literature. Among his many works he published a Latin dictionary, an introductory Greek grammar, the most important early modern Hebrew grammar and dictionary (*De rudimentis hebraicis*; 1506), and a commentary on the penitential psalms.

Edward Reynolds (1599–1676). Anglican bishop. Reynolds succeeded John Donne* as the preacher at Lincoln's Inn before entering parish ministry in Northamptonshire. During the English Civil Wars, he supported the Puritans because of his sympathy toward their simplicity and piety—despite believing that Scripture demanded no particular form of government; later he refused to support the abolition of the monarchy. Until the Restoration he ministered in London; afterward he became the bishop of Norwich. He wrote the general thanksgiving prayer which is part of the morning office in the *Book of Common Prayer*.*

Urbanus Rhegius (1489–1541). German Lutheran pastor. Rhegius, who was likely the son of a priest, studied under the humanists at Freiburg and Ingolstadt. After a brief stint as a foot soldier, he received ordination in 1519 and was made cathedral preacher in Augsburg.

During his time in Augsburg he closely read Luther's* works, becoming an enthusiastic follower. Despite his close friendship with Zwingli* and Oecolampadius,* Rhegius supported Luther in the eucharistic debates, later playing a major role in the Wittenberg Concord (1536). He advocated for peace during the Peasants' War and had extended interactions with the Anabaptists in Augsburg. Later in his career he concerned himself with the training of pastors, writing a pastoral guide and two catechisms. About one hundred of his writings were published posthumously.

Lancelot Ridley (d. 1576). Anglican preacher. Ridley was the first cousin of Nicholas Ridley,* the bishop of London who was martyred during the Marian persecutions. By Cranmer's* recommendation, Ridley became one of the six Canterbury Cathedral preachers. Upon Mary I's accession in 1553, Ridley was defrocked (as a married priest). Ridley returned to Canterbury Cathedral after Mary's death. He wrote commentaries on Jude, Ephesians, Philippians and Colossians.

Nicholas Ridley (c. 1502–1555). Anglican bishop. Ridley was a student and fellow at Cambridge University who was appointed chaplain to Archbishop Thomas Cranmer* and is thought to be partially responsible for Cranmer's shift to a symbolic view of the Eucharist. Cranmer promoted Ridley twice: as bishop of Rochester, where he openly advocated Reformed theological views, and, later, as bishop of London. Ridley assisted Cranmer in the revisions of the Book of Common Prayer.* Ridley's support of Lady Jane Grey against the claims of Mary to the throne led to his arrest; he was tried for heresy and burned at the stake with Hugh Latimer.*

Peter Riedemann (1506–1556). German Radical elder, theologian and hymnist. While traveling as a Silesian cobbler, Riedemann came into contact with Anabaptist teachings and joined a congregation in Linz. In 1529 he was called to be a minister, only to be imprisoned soon after as part of Archduke Ferdinand's efforts to suppress heterodoxy in his realm. Once he was released, he moved to Moravia in 1532 where he was elected as a minister and missionary of the Hutterite community there. His *Account of Our Religion, Doctrine and Faith* (1542), with its more than two thousand biblical references, is Riedemann's most important work and is still used by Hutterites today.

John Robinson (1576–1625). English Puritan pastor. After his suspension for nonconformity, Robinson fled to the Netherlands with his congregation, eventually settling in Leiden in 1609. Robinson entered into controversies over Arminianism, separation and congregationalism. Most of his healthy congregants immigrated to Plymouth in 1620; Robinson remained in Leiden with those unable to travel.

John Rogers (1505–1555). English Protestant Bible translator. Rogers was born in Deritend, Birmingham. After receiving his early education at the Guild School of St. John the Baptist, Rogers matriculated at Pembroke Hall, Cambridge, where he graduated with the BA degree in 1526. He served as rector of Holy Trinity the Less in London from 1532 to 1534, when he left for the Continent to serve as chaplain to the English merchants of the Company of the Merchant Adventurers. It was at this time that he met William Tyndale,* under whose influence he came to embrace an evangelical faith. After Tyndale's death, Rogers completed his late colleague's translation of the Old Testament, which had ended with 2 Chronicles, by adding Miles Coverdale's translation of the remainder, including the Apocrypha. The resulting work, known as the "Matthew Bible" (Rogers published it under the pseudonym "Thomas Matthew") was published in 1537. It has the distinction of being the first complete English Bible translated essentially from the original languages to be printed. "Matthew's Bible" served as the basis for the Great Bible (1540), which in turn was used by those who prepared the Bishops' Bible (1568), on which later the King James Version (1611) was produced. In 1540, Rogers enrolled at the University of Wittenberg, where he became close friends with Philipp Melanchthon.* During his three years at Wittenberg, Rogers was a superintendent of the Lutheran Church in northern Germany. When Rogers returned to England in 1548, he published a translation of Melanchthon's *Considerations of the Augsburg Interim*, and later served in a variety of ecclesiastical roles. Rogers was burned at the stake for heresy during the reign of Mary Tudor on February 4, 1555.

Nehemiah Rogers (1593–1660). Anglican priest. After studying at Cambridge, Rogers ministered at numerous parishes during his more than forty-year career. In 1643, he seems to have been forced out of a parish on account of being a Royalist and friend of William Laud.* Rogers published a number of sermons and tracts, including a series of expositions on Jesus' parables in the Gospels.

Richard Rogers (1550?–1618). English Presbyterian minister. Rogers spent much of his career as lecturer at Wethersfield, Essex, where he was well-known as a Nonconformist. His writings, which include an introduction to the Christian life and a commentary on the book of Judges, demonstrate his Puritan leanings.

Thomas Rogers (d. 1616). Anglican theologian and translator. Rogers attended Christ Church, Oxford, where he completed his BA degree in 1573 and MA in 1576. Later he served as rector of Horrigner in Suffolk, and chaplain to Archbishop of Canterbury, Richard Bancroft. He died at Horringer and was buried in his church. Among his many works were an exposition of the Thirty-Nine Articles as well as a paraphrase of the Psalms and a translation of Niels Hemmingsen's commentary on Psalm 84.

Robert Rollock (c. 1555–1599). Scottish Reformed pastor, educator and theologian. Rollock was deeply influenced by Petrus Ramus's* system of logic, which he implemented as a tutor and (later) principal of Edinburgh University and in his expositions of the Bible. Rollock, as a divinity professor and theologian, was instrumental in diffusing a federalist Calvinism in the Scottish church; he lectured on theology using the texts of Theodore Beza* and articulated a highly covenantal interpretation of the biblical narratives. He was a prolific writer of sermons, expositions, commentaries, lectures and occasional treatises.

David Runge (1564–1604). German Lutheran theologian. First appointed professor of Hebrew at the University of Greifswald, Runge supported and later replaced his father in teaching philosophy and theology. After receiving his doctorate, he was named to the theological faculty at Wittenberg, where he also served as dean and rector of the university.

Johann Rurer (1480–1542). German Lutheran pastor. Rurer was court chaplain to Margrave Casimir of Brandenberg–Kulmbach (1481–1527), and the first Protestant pastor in Ansbach. Conflict over church order and his desire for reform led to his expulsion, but he was recalled after Casimir's death by his successor, George (1484–1543), who sought a throughgoing Lutheran reformation of the town and appointed Rurer preacher at the collegiate church.

Samuel Rutherford (1600–1661). Scottish Reformed theologian. Rutherford was born in Nisbet, Roxburghshire. After completing his early education at Jedborough, Rutherford enrolled at the University of Edinburgh, where he received his MA degree in 1621. In 1623, Rutherford was appointed professor of humanities at Edinburgh. Two years later, he was dismissed from his position on account of misbehavior with the woman who would later be his wife. Sometime after this incident, he underwent a spiritual conversion. In 1625, Rutherford commenced the study of theology at Edinburgh. Upon finishing his studies, Rutherford was called to pastor a church in Antwoth by Solway in Kirkcudbrightshire. Throughout his ministry, Rutherford proved to be an ardent opponent to episcopacy. For this, he was summoned to appear before the Court of High Commission in 1630. Despite the court's warnings to cease and desist, Rutherford continued his nonconformity. Rutherford also participated extensively in the Arminian controversy, writing treatises against Arminius as well as the Jesuits. Since Rutherford's virulent opposition to Arminianism placed him in direct opposition with the English episcopacy, he was once again summoned by the Court of High Commission in 1636. After a three-day trial, Rutherford was deprived of his ministerial office and ordered not to preach anywhere in Scotland. Meanwhile he was confined to Aberdeen. In 1638, when the National Covenant was signed and Presbyterianism restored in Scotland, Rutherford left Aberdeen and assumed the post of professor of theology at St. Mary's College, St. Andrews. Later, Rutherford served as a commissioner to the Westminster Assembly, where he contributed to the discussions related to the Shorter Catechism. In 1647, Rutherford returned to Scotland, where he was appointed principal of St. Mary's College, and rector of the university in 1651. After the monarchy was restored, Rutherford was charged with treason, and deprived of all his ecclesiastical and university positions. He died on March 30, 1661. Throughout his career, Rutherford published many sermons and theological works, most famous of which is *Lex Rex* (The law is king), a treatise arguing against the divine right of kings.

Jacopo Sadoleto (1477–1547). Italian Catholic Cardinal. Sadoleto, attaché to Leo X's court, was appointed bishop in 1517, cardinal in 1536. He participated in the reform commission led by Gasparo Contarini.* However, he tried to reconcile with Protestants apart from the commission, sending several letters to Protestant leaders in addition to his famous letter to the city of Geneva, which John Calvin* pointedly answered. Sadoleto published a commentary on Romans that was censored as semi-Pelagian. His insufficient treatment of prevenient grace left him vulnerable to this charge. Sadoleto emphasized grammar as the rule and norm of exegesis.

Alfonso Salmerón (1515–1585). Spanish Catholic exegete and theologian. While studying at the Sorbonne, Salmerón met Ignatius Loyola (1491–1556) and, with five others, took a vow of poverty and service to church and pope. After ministering in France, the group traveled to Rome, where they were given papal approval to form the Society of Jesus. Salmerón helped write the constitutions of the order, and following the priorities of the Jesuits, spent much of his career focused on education. He lectured throughout Italy, served briefly on the faculty of the University of Ingolstadt, and, in Naples, founded one of the first Jesuit colleges. He also undertook a number of missions as a papal emissary and served as a papal theologian at all three meetings of the Council of Trent. His primary works are his commentaries on the New Testament, which cover the Gospels, Acts, and Paul's letters.

Heinrich Salmuth (1522–1576). German Lutheran theologian. After earning his doctorate from the University of Leipzig, Salmuth served in several coterminous pastoral and academic positions. He was integral to the reorganization of the University of Jena. Except for a few disputations, all of Salmuth's works—mostly sermons—were published posthumously by his son.

Robert Sanderson (1587–1663). Anglican bishop and philosopher. Before his appointment as professor of divinity at Oxford in 1642, Sanderson pastored in several parishes. Because of his loyalty to the Crown during the English Civil Wars, the Parliamentarians stripped Sanderson of his post at Oxford. After the Restoration he was reinstated at Oxford and consecrated bishop. He wrote an influential textbook on logic.

Edwin Sandys (1519–1588). Anglican bishop. During his doctoral studies at Cambridge, Sandys befriended Martin Bucer.* Having supported the Protestant Lady Jane Grey's claim to the throne, Sandys resigned his post at Cambridge upon Mary I's accession. He was then arrested and imprisoned in the Tower of London. Released in 1554, he sojourned on the continent until Mary's death. On his return to England he was appointed to revise the liturgy and was consecrated bishop. Many of his sermons were published, but his most significant literary legacy is his work as a translator of the Bishop's Bible (1568), which served as the foundational English text for the translators of the King James Bible (1611).

Erasmus Sarcerius (1501–1559). German Lutheran superintendent, educator and pastor. Sarcerius served as educational superintendent, court preacher and pastor in Nassau and, later, in Leipzig. The hallmark of Sarcerius's reputation was his ethical emphasis as exercised through ecclesial oversight and family structure; he also drafted disciplinary codes for regional churches in Germany. Sarcerius served with Philipp Melanchthon* as Protestant delegates at the Council of Trent, though both withdrew prior to the dismissal of the session; he eventually became an opponent of Melanchthon, contesting the latter's understanding of the Eucharist at a colloquy in Worms in 1557.

Adam Sasbout (1516-1553) Dutch Catholic monk. A lector at the Franciscan monastery in Louvain, Sasbout authored exegetical works on Leviticus and Isaiah and many of his sermons were published posthumously.

Michael Sattler (c. 1490–1527). Swiss Radical leader. Sattler was a Benedictine monk who abandoned the monastic life during the upheavals of the Peasants' War. He took up the trade of weaving under the guidance of an outspoken Anabaptist. It seems that Sattler did not openly join the Anabaptist movement until after the suppression of the Peasants' War in 1526. Sattler interceded with Martin Bucer* and Wolfgang Capito* for imprisoned Anabaptists in Strasbourg. Shortly before he was convicted of heresy and executed, he wrote the definitive expression of Anabaptist theology, the Schleitheim Articles.*

Girolamo Savonarola (1452–1498). Italian Catholic preacher and martyr. Outraged by clerical corruption and the neglect of the poor, Savonarola traveled to preach against these abuses and to prophesy impending judgment—a mighty king would scourge and reform the church. Savonarola thought that the French invasion of Italy in 1494 confirmed his apocalyptic visions. Thus he pressed to purge Florence of vice and institute public welfare, in order to usher in a new age of Christianity. Florence's refusal to join papal resistance against the French enraged Alexander VI (r. 1492–1503). He blamed Savonarola, promptly excommunicating him and threatening Florence with an interdict. After an ordeal by fire turned into a riot, Savonarola was arrested. Under torture he admitted to charges of conspiracy and false prophecy; he was hanged and burned. In addition to numerous sermons and letters, he wrote meditations on Psalms 31 and 51 as well as *The Triumph of the Cross* (1497).

Leupold Scharnschlager (d. 1563). Austrian Radical elder. See *Kunstbuch*.

Leonhard Schiemer (d. 1528) Austrian radical martyr. Troubled by the hypocrisies he experienced, Scheimer left the Franciscan order and spent a period of time wandering. Attracted to the teachings of Hans Hut* after hearing him debate Balthasar Hubmaier* in Moravia, he was rebaptized and traveled widely throughout Austria and Southern Germany, spreading the Anabaptist message until he was arrested in Rattenberg, where he was condemned to death and beheaded. A number of his essays and hymns survive, dispersed among the *Kunstbuch** and other collections of radical writings.

Hans Schlaffer (c. 1490–1528). Austrian Radical martyr. Drawn by Luther's theology, Schlaffer resigned his priesthood in 1526 only to turn to Anabaptism soon afterward. While contemporaries recognized his ability as a preacher, he never settled in a ministry position. He spent time among Radical congregations in Freistadt, Nicholsburg, Augsburg, Nuremberg, and Regensburg before his arrest in Schatz, where he was executed. Nine writings by Schlaffer remain, most of which were composed during his imprisonment. They include confessions of his beliefs and devotional works, which have been preserved among Hutterite churches.

Schleitheim Articles (1527). After the death of Conrad Grebel* in 1526 and the execution of Felix Manz (born c. 1498) in early 1527, the young Swiss Anabaptist movement was in need of unity and direction. A synod convened at Schleitheim under the chairmanship of Michael Sattler,* which passed seven articles of Anabaptist distinctives—likely defined against both magisterial reformers and other Anabaptists with less orthodox and more militant views (e.g., Balthasar Hubmaier*). Unlike most confessions, these articles do not explicitly address traditional creedal interests; they explicate instead the Anabaptist view of the sacraments, church discipline, separatism, the role of ministers, pacifism and oaths. Throughout the document there is a resolute focus on Christ's example. Also referred to as the Schleitheim Confession and the Schleitheim Brotherly Union, the Schleitheim Articles are considered the definitive statement of Anabaptist theology, particularly regarding separatism.

Schmalkald Articles (1537). In response to Pope Paul III's (1468–1549) 1536 decree ordering a general church council to solve the Protestant crisis, Elector John Frederick (1503–1554) commissioned Martin Luther* to draft the sum of his teaching. Intended by Luther as a last will and testament—and composed with advice from well-known colleagues Justus Jonas,* Johann Bugenhagen,* Caspar Cruciger,* Nikolaus von Amsdorf (1483–1565), Georg Spalatin (1484–1545), Philipp Melanchthon* and Johann Agricola*—these articles provide perhaps the briefest and most systematic summary of Luther's teaching. The document was not adopted formally by the Lutheran Schmalkald League, as was hoped, and the general church council was postponed for several years (until convening at Trent in 1545). Only in 1580 were the articles officially received, by being incorporated into the *Book of Concord* defining orthodox Lutheranism.

Sebastian Schmidt (1617–1696). German Lutheran theologian. After serving as pastor in Entzheim and rector of the high school in Lindau, Schmidt became professor of theology at Strasbourg. His body of writings is extensive and includes commentaries on many of the Pauline letters, Hebrews, John, and Jeremiah.

Dietrich Schnepff (1525–1586). German Lutheran pastor and theologian. Schnepff taught briefly at the city school in Tübingen while working toward his theological doctorate before taking pastorates in Derendingen and Nürtingen. Returning to Tübingen as professor of theology, Schnepff also took on additional roles as rector of the university and pastor of the Collegiate Church.

Anna Maria van Schurman (1607–1678). Dutch Reformed polymath. Van Schurman cultivated talents in art, poetry, botany, linguistics and theology. She mastered most contemporary European languages, in addition to Latin, Greek, Hebrew, Arabic, Farsi and Ethiopian. With the encouragement of leading Reformed theologian Gisbertus Voetius (1589–1676), van Schurman attended lectures at the University of Utrecht—although she was required to sit behind a wooden screen so that the male students could not see her. In 1638 van Schurman published her famous treatise advocating female scholarship, *Amica dissertatio . . . de capacitate ingenii muliebris ad scientias*. In addition to these more polemical works, van Schurman also wrote hymns and poems, including a paraphrase of Genesis 1–3. Later in life she became a devotee of Jean de Labadie (1610–1674), a former Jesuit who was also expelled from the Reformed church for his separatist leanings. Her *Eucleria* (1673) is the most well known defense of Labadie's theology.

Kaspar von Schwenckfeld (1489–1561). German Radical reformer. Schwenckfeld was a Silesian nobleman who encountered Luther's* works in 1521. He traveled to Wittenberg twice: first to meet Luther and Karlstadt,* and a second time to convince Luther of his doctrine of the "internal word"—emphasizing inner revelation so strongly that he did not see church meetings or the sacraments as necessary—after which Luther considered him heterodox. Schwenckfeld won his native territory to the Reformation in 1524 and later lived in Strasbourg for five years until Bucer* sought to purify the city of less traditional theologies. Schwenckfeld wrote numerous polemical and exegetical tracts.

Scots Confession (1560). In 1560, the Scottish Parliament undertook to reform the Church of Scotland and to commission a Reformed confession of faith. In the course of four days, a committee—which included John Knox*—wrote this confession, largely based on Calvin's* work, the Confession of the English Congregation in Geneva (1556) and the Gallic Confession.* The articles were not ratified until 1567 and were displaced by the Westminster Confession (1646), adopted by the Scottish in 1647.

Abraham Scultetus (1566–1625). Silesian Reformed theologian. Scultetus spent the majority of his career in service of the Palatinate, holding a number of pastoral roles before becoming court preacher to Elector Frederic V (1596–1632). Appointed professor of theology at Heidelberg in 1618, he represented the Palatinate at the Synod of Dordrecht* (1618–1619), where he opposed the theology of the Remonstrants. Scultetus is often vilified for encouraging Reformed Frederic V to take the crown of Lutheran Bohemia, an act that led to war and the defeat of Frederic V, but his exegetical, historical, and pastoral teachings nevertheless garnered significant respect from his contemporaries.

Second Helvetic Confession (1566). Believing he would soon die, Heinrich Bullinger* penned a personal statement of his Reformed faith in 1561 as a theological will. In 1563, Bullinger sent a copy of this confession, which blended Zwingli's and Calvin's theology, to the elector of the Palatinate, Frederick III (1515–1576), who had asked for a complete explication of the Reformed faith in order to defend himself against aggressive Lutheran attacks after printing the Heidelberg Confession.* Although not published until 1566, the Second Helvetic Confession became the definitive sixteenth-century Reformed statement of faith. Theodore Beza* used it as the organizing confession for his *Harmonia Confessionum* (1581), which sought to emphasize the unity of the Reformed churches. Bullinger's personal confession was adopted by the Reformed churches of Scotland (1566), Hungary (1567), France (1571) and Poland (1571).

Obadiah Sedgwick (c. 1600–1658). English Puritan minister. Educated at Oxford, Sedgwick pastored in London and participated in the Westminster Assembly. An ardent Puritan, Sedgwick was appointed by Oliver Cromwell (1599–1658) to examine clerical candidates. Sedgwick published a catechism, several sermons and a treatise on how to deal with doubt.

Nikolaus Selnecker (1530–1592). German Lutheran theologian, preacher, pastor and hymnist. Selnecker taught in Wittenberg, Jena and Leipzig, preached in Dresden and Wolfenbüttel, and pastored in Leipzig. He was forced out of his post at Jena because of suspicions that he was a crypto-Calvinist. He sought refuge in Wolfenbüttel, where he met Martin Chemnitz* and Jakob Andreae.* Under their influence Selnecker was drawn away from Philippist theology. Selnecker's shift in theology can be seen in his *Institutio religionis christianae* (1573). Selnecker coauthored the Formula of Concord* with Chemnitz, Andreae, Andreas Musculus (1514–1581), and David Chytraeus.* Selnecker also published lectures on Genesis, the Psalms, and the New Testament epistles, as well as composing over a hundred hymn tunes and texts.

Jean de Serres (1540–1598). French Reformed pastor and historian. Serres fled France under persecution and studied at Lausanne and Geneva before being called to the Genevan parish of Jussy. After publishing a commentary on the French civil wars, he was disciplined and deposed for abandoning his ministry. Relocating to Lausanne, Serres became principal of the college and published a three-volume translation of Plato's works then moved to reform the College of Nimes. He became an advisor to King Henry IV* and was given the title "Historian of France." In this role, he sought resolution of the civil wars and composed a short history of France.

Short Confession (1610). In response to some of William Laud's* reforms in the Church of England—particularly a law stating that ministers who refused to comply with the Book of Common Prayer* would lose their ordination—a group of English Puritans immigrated to the Netherlands in protest, where they eventually embraced the practice of believer's baptism. The resulting Short Confession was an attempt at union between these Puritans and local Dutch Anabaptists ("Waterlanders"). The document highlights the importance of love in the church and reflects optimism regarding the freedom of the will while explicitly rejecting double predestination.

Richard Sibbes (1577–1635). English Puritan preacher. Sibbes was educated at St. John's College, Cambridge, where he was converted to reforming views and became a popular preacher. As a moderate Puritan emphasizing interior piety and brotherly love, Sibbes always remained within the established Church of England, though opposed to some of its liturgical ceremonies. His collected sermons constitute his main literary legacy.

Menno Simons (c. 1496–1561). Dutch Radical leader. Simons led a separatist Anabaptist group in the Netherlands that would later be called Mennonites, known for nonviolence and renunciation of the world. A former priest, Simons rejected Catholicism through the influence of Anabaptist disciples of Melchior Hoffmann and based on his study of Scripture, in which he found no support for transubstantiation or infant baptism. Following the sack of Anabaptists at Münster, Simons committed to a nonviolent way of life. Simons proclaimed a message of radical discipleship of obedience and inner purity, marked by voluntary adult baptism and communal discipline.

Henry Smith (c. 1550–1591). English Puritan minister. Smith stridently opposed the Book of Common Prayer* and refused to subscribe to the Articles of Religion,* thus limiting his pastoral opportunities. Nevertheless he gained a reputation as an eloquent preacher in London. He published sermon collections as well as several treatises.

John Smyth (d. 1612). English Baptist minister. Ordained as an Anglican clergyman, Smyth served as a lecturer in Lincoln, but left the established church for a separatist congregation in Gainsborough. Moving to Amsterdam, he began to follow the teachings of Jacobus Arminius* and led a group to break away from the English Reformed congregation, undertake rebaptism, and form their own church. He soon decided he did not have the authority to establish a church and baptize, but trying to lead his congregation on another course saw him excommunicated with a number of his close followers. This smaller group was rejected when they attempted to join a Mennonite congregation, and so were forced to form another congregation, which dissolved after Smyth's death. Smyth wrote a number of the earliest English treatises expressing Baptist principles including *The Differences of the Churches of the Separation* (1608) and *The Character of the Beast* (1609). He also wrote a reflection on the Lord's Prayer, *A Paterne of True Prayer* (1605).

Domingo de Soto (1494–1560). Spanish Catholic theologian. Soto taught philosophy for four years at the University in Alcalá before entering the Dominican order. In 1532 he became chair of theology at the University of Salamanca; Soto sought to reintroduce Aristotle in the curriculum. He served as confessor and spiritual advisor to Charles V, who enlisted Soto as imperial theologian for the Council of Trent. Alongside commentaries on the works of Aristotle and Peter Lombard (c. 1100–1160), Soto commented on Romans and wrote an influential treatise on nature and grace.

Fausto Sozzini (1539–1604). Italian theologian. Without a formal education, Sozzini used his inherited wealth to travel widely throughout Europe after his family came under the suspicion of the Inquisition for Lutheranism. Spending time in Lyons, Zurich, and Geneva, he published his first work, an explanation of the prologue to John's Gospel, claiming Christ was not divine, but a human worthy of respect due his divinely appointed office. Returning to Italy, Sozzini served at the Florentine court of Isabella de Medici (1542–1576) for more than a decade, departing for Basel, then Transylvania and Poland after her death. His thoroughgoing rationalism saw him elevate human reason over divine revelation and traditional doctrine. He rejected the doctrine of the Trinity and Nicene orthodoxy, instead arguing that Christ was not divine and did not make atonement for humanity, but rather served as a model of victory over death for all people.

Cyriacus Spangenberg (1528–1604). German Lutheran pastor, preacher and theologian. Spangenberg was a staunch, often acerbic, Gnesio-Lutheran. He rejected the Formula of Concord* because of concerns about the princely control of the church, as well as its rejection of Flacian language of original sin (as constituting the "substance" of human nature after the fall). He published many commentaries and sermons, most famously seventy wedding sermons (*Ehespiegel* [1561]), his sermons on Luther* (*Theander Luther* [1562–1571]) and Luther's hymns (*Cithara Lutheri* [1569–1570]). He also published an analysis of the Old Testament (though he only got as far as Job), based on a methodology that anticipated the logical bifurcations of Peter Ramus.*

Johann Spangenberg (1484–1550). German Lutheran pastor and catechist. Spangenberg studied at the University of Erfurt, where he was welcomed into a group of humanists associated with Konrad Muth (1470–1526). There he met the reformer Justus Jonas,* and Eobanus Hessius (1488–1540), whom Luther* dubbed "king of the poets." Spangenberg served at parishes in Stolberg (1520–1524), Nordhausen (1524–1546) and, by Luther's recommendation, Eisleben (1546–1550). Spangenberg published one of the best-selling postils of the sixteenth century, the *Postilla Teütsch*, a six-volume work meant to prepare children to understand the lectionary readings. It borrowed the question-answer form of Luther's *Small Catechism* and was so popular that a monk, Johannes Craendonch, purged overt anti-Catholic statements from it and republished it under his own name. Among Spangenberg's other pastoral works are *ars moriendi* ("the art of dying") booklets, a postil for the Acts of the Apostles and a question-answer version of Luther's *Large Catechism*. In addition to preaching and pastoring, Spangenberg wrote pamphlets on controversial topics such as purgatory, as well as textbooks on music, mathematics and grammar.

John Spilsbury (1593–1668). English Baptist pastor. A cobbler by trade, Spilsbury left congregationalism to found the first Particular Baptist church in London, teaching a theology that attempted to fuse Reformed teachings on the covenant and particular atonement with the Anabaptist demand for adult baptism upon confession of faith. He composed a number of works on baptism and may have been an author of the 1644 London Baptist Confession of Faith.

Georg Spindler (1525–1605). German Reformed theologian and pastor. After studying theology under Caspar Cruciger* and Philipp Melanchthon,* Spindler accepted a pastorate in Bohemia. A well-respected preacher, Spindler published postils in 1576 which some of his peers viewed as crypto-Calvinist. To investigate this allegation Spindler read John Calvin's* *Institutes*, and subsequently converted to the Reformed faith. After years of travel, he settled in the Palatinate and pastored there until his death. In addition to his Lutheran postils, Spindler also published Reformed postils in 1594 as well as several treatises on the Lord's Supper and predestination.

Statenvertaling (1637). The Synod of Dordrecht* commissioned this new Dutch translation of the Bible ("State's Translation"). The six theologians who undertook this translation also wrote prefaces for each biblical book, annotated obscure words and difficult passages, and provided cross-references; they even explained certain significant translation decisions. At the request of the Westminster Assembly, Theodore Haak (1605–1690) translated the *Statenvertaling* into English as *The Dutch Annotations Upon the Whole Bible* (1657).

John Stalham (d. 1681). English Puritan minister. Stalham likely ministered in Edinburgh before becoming vicar of Terling in Essex. An opponent of Quakerism who sought to remove disreputable ministers from their pulpits, Stalham himself lost his position with the 1662 Act of Uniformity, leading him to found a congregational church in the same village.

Johann von Staupitz (d. 1524). German Catholic theologian, professor and preacher. Frederick the Wise summoned this Augustinian monk to serve as professor of Bible and first dean of the theology faculty at the University of Wittenberg. As Vicar-General of the Reformed Augustinian Hermits in Germany, Staupitz sought to reform the order and attempted unsuccessfully to reunite with the conventional Augustinians. While in Wittenberg, Staupitz was Martin Luther's* teacher, confessor and spiritual father. He supported Luther in the early controversies over indulgences, but after releasing Luther from his monastic vows (to protect him), he distanced himself from the conflict. He relocated to Salzburg, where he was court preacher to Cardinal Matthäus Lang von Wellenburg (d. 1540) and abbot of the Benedictine monastery. Staupitz wrote treatises on predestination, faith and the love of God. Many of his sermons were collected and published during his lifetime.

Peter Sterry (d. 1672). English Puritan theologian. Associated with the Cambridge Platonists, Sterry was closely aligned with the Parliamentarians during the English Civil War, serving as chaplain to Robert Greville (1607–1643) and Oliver Cromwell.* After the execution of Charles I, he was appointed preacher to the Council of State and asked to examine its ministers. Cast out from influence after Cromwell's death, Sperry spent the last years of his career writing and tutoring private students.

Petrus Stevartius (1549–1624). German Catholic theologian. A Jesuit, Stevartius spent most of his career as professor of exegesis at the University of Ingolstadt, also serving as rector and procurator. He also established a library for the school and an orphanage in the city. His writings include commentaries on most Pauline letters and James and a defense of the Jesuits.

Michael Stifel (1486–1567). German Lutheran mathematician, theologian and pastor. An Augustinian monk, Stifel's interest in mysticism, apocalypticism and numerology led him to identify Pope Leo X as the antichrist. Stifel soon joined the reform movement, writing a 1522 pamphlet in support of Martin Luther's* theology. After Luther quelled the fallout of Stifel's failed prediction of the Apocalypse—October 19, 1533 at 8 a.m.—Stifel focused more on mathematics and his pastoral duties. He was the first professor of mathematics at the University of Jena. He published several numerological interpretations of texts from the Gospels, Daniel and Revelation. However, Stifel's most important work is his *Arithmetica Integra* (1544), in which he standardized the approach to quadratic equations. He also developed notations for exponents and radicals.

John Stoughton (1593?–1639). English Puritan minister. Stoughton pastored at Aller in Somerset and St. Mary Aldermanbury in the city of London. A Puritan, he was briefly arrested by Archbishop Laud, accused of financially supporting the Puritan cause. A collection of his sermons and other writings was published after his death.

Viktorin Strigel (1524–1569). German Lutheran theologian. Strigel taught at Wittenberg, Erfurt, Jena, Leipzig and Heidelberg. During his time in Jena he disputed with Matthias Flacius (1520–1575) over the human will's autonomy. Following Philipp Melanchthon,* Strigel asserted that in conversion the human will obediently cooperates with the divine will through the Holy Spirit and the Word of God. In the Weimar Disputation (1560), Strigel elicited Flacius's opinion that sin is a substance that mars the formal essence of human beings. Flacius's views were officially rejected in Article 1 of the Formula of Concord*; Strigel's, in Article 2. In 1567 the University of Leipzig suspended Strigel from teaching on account of suspicions that he affirmed Reformed Eucharistic theology; he acknowledged that he did and joined the Reformed confession on the faculty of the University of Heidelberg. In addition to controversial tracts, Strigel published commentaries on the entire Bible (except Lamentations) and the Apocrypha.

William Strode (1602–1645). English Anglican minister, dramatist, and poet. A Royalist and an opponent of Puritanism, Strode spent most of his life around Oxford, where he studied and then served as a public orator and canon of Christ Church. A popular poet, he also preached a number of times before the king and had a number of his plays performed at court.

William Strong (d. 1654). English Independent minister. Forced to leave his ministry in Dorset by Royalists during the Civil War, Strong built a reputation as a preacher in London, ministering to an independent congregation at St. Dunstan's-in-the-West. Many of his sermons were published, as well as treatises on communion with God and the covenants.

Johann Sutell (1504–1575). German Lutheran pastor. After studying at the University of Wittenberg, Sutell received a call to a pastorate in Göttingen, where he eventually became superintendent. He wrote new church orders for Göttingen (1531) and Schweinfurt (1543), and expanded two sermons for publication, *The Dreadful Destruction of Jerusalem* (1539) and *History of Lazarus* (1543).

Swiss Brethren Confession of Hesse (1578). Anabaptist leader Hans Pauly Kuchenbecker penned this confession after a 1577 interrogation by Lutheran authorities. This confession was unusually amenable to Lutheran views—there is no mention of pacifism or rejection of oath taking.

Synod of Dordrecht (1618–1619). This large Dutch Reformed Church council—also attended by English, German and Swiss delegates—met to settle the theological issues raised by the followers of Jacobus Arminius.* Arminius's theological disagreements with mainstream Reformed teaching erupted into open conflict with the publication of the *Remonstrance* (1610). This "protest" was based on five points: that election is based on foreseen faith or unbelief; that Christ died indiscriminately for all people (although only believers receive salvation); that people are thoroughly sinful by nature apart from the prevenient grace of God that enables their free will to embrace or reject the gospel; that humans are able to resist the working of God's grace; and that it is possible for true believers to fall away from faith completely. The Synod ruled in favor of the Contra-Remonstrants, its Canons often remembered with a TULIP acrostic—total depravity, unconditional election, limited atonement, irresistible grace, perseverance of the saints—each letter countering one of the five Remonstrant articles. The Synod also officially accepted the Belgic Confession,* Heidelberg Catechism* and the Canons of Dordrecht as standards of the Dutch Reformed Church.

Arcangela Tarabotti (1604–1652). Italian Catholic nun. At the age of eleven, Tarabotti entered a Benedictine convent as a student-boarder; three years later her father forced her to take monastic vows. The dignity of women and their treatment in the male-controlled institutions of early modern Venice concerned Tarabotti deeply. She protested forced cloistering, the denial of education to women, the exclusion of women from public life and the double standards by which men and women were judged. Tarbotti authored numerous polemical works and an extensive correspondence.

Johannes Tauler (c. 1300–1361). German mystical theologian. A Dominican friar and disciple of Meister Eckhart (c. 1260–c. 1328), Tauler spent most of his career as a mendicant preacher in Strasburg and Basel. Known through a collection of about eighty German sermons, Tauler taught a practical spirituality, accessible to those outside the cloister and intended to draw his audience to deeper contemplation of the divine nature.

Richard Taverner (1505–1575). English Puritan humanist and translator. After graduating from Oxford, Taverner briefly studied abroad. When he returned to England, he joined Thomas Cromwell's (1485–1540) circle. After Cromwell's beheading, Taverner escaped severe punishment and retired from public life during Mary I's reign. Under Elizabeth I,* Taverner served as justice of the peace, sheriff and a licensed lay preacher. Taverner translated many important continental Reformation works into English, most notably the Augsburg Confession* and several of Desiderius Erasmus's* works. Some of these translations—John Calvin's* 1536 catechism, Wolfgang Capito's* work on the Psalms and probably Erasmus Sarcerius's* postils—he presented as his own work. Underwritten by Cromwell, Taverner also published an edited version of the Matthew Bible (1537).

Francis Taylor (1590–1656). English Presbyterian minister. After graduating from Cambridge, Taylor served as vicar of Yalding in Kent and rector of Clapham in Surrey. He was a member of the Westminster Assembly of Divines and was a member of the College of Six Preachers at Canterbury Cathedral.

Jeremy Taylor (1613–1667). Anglican theologian, preacher, and author. Son of a barber, Taylor studied at Cambridge before the patronage of Archbishop Laud* drew him into the work of the English church. After serving as chaplain to Laud and King Charles I (1600–1649), he entered parish ministry. Following the outbreak of the Civil War (1642–51), his commitment to the Royalist cause saw him imprisoned at least three times. Withdrawing to Wales, he ran a school preparing students for university while serving as chaplain to the earl of Carbery. Known for his skill as a writer, it was here that Taylor composed many of his best known works, including his popular devotional manuals, *The Rules and Exercises of Holy Living* (1650), and *The Rules and Exercises of Holy Dying* (1651). After the Restoration, Taylor was made Bishop of Down and Connor in Ireland and served as vice-chancellor of the University of Dublin.

Thomas Taylor (1576–1633). English Puritan pastor. Taylor ministered in Watford and Reading before becoming minister at St. Mary Aldermanbury in the city of London. He wrote more than fifty works on diverse topics, including a commentary on Titus, a response to the Gunpowder Plot, and an explanation of the role of the law under the gospel.

Thomas Taylor (1576–1632). Puritan minister and commentator. Taylor was born in Richmond, Yorkshire. He was educated at Christ's College, Cambridge, where he earned the degrees of Bachelor of Arts (1595) and Master of Arts (1598). Prior to entering pastoral ministry, Taylor served as a fellow and lecturer in Hebrew at the university. Throughout his academic career, Taylor was significantly influenced by the writings of William Perkins.* At the age of twenty-five, Taylor preached a virulent sermon against the papacy before Queen Elizabeth I.* As a Puritan, Taylor denounced the ecclesiastical policies of Archbishop Richard Bancroft.* In 1612, Taylor became minister of a church in Watford, Hertfordshire. While serving this charge, Taylor preached regularly in Berkshire and Reading. Moreover, Taylor formed and led a Puritan seminary, where he personally trained Nonconformist preachers. In the early 1620s, Taylor served as a chaplain to Edward Conway (1564–1631), secretary of state under James VI/I* (1566–1625). In 1625, Taylor was called to be curate and lecturer at St. Aldermanbury, London. While there, he organized and ran another Puritan seminary. Two years later, Taylor joined several other Puritans' efforts to send relief to oppressed Reformed ministers on the Continent. Taylor retired from his labors in 1630 due to ill health. He died of pleurisy in 1632. His main works include *Christ Revealed; or The Old Testament Explained* and *An Exposition of Titus*.

Teresa of Ávila (1515–1582). Spanish monastic reformer and mystical theologian. Born into a wealthy merchant family, Teresa entered the Carmelite order at Ávila in 1535. While Teresa initially enjoyed the lax practices of the convent, reading devotional literature caused her to deepen her spirituality, and in 1555 she began to have visions of God and claimed to have mystical union with him. Convinced the monastic life required complete withdrawal, Teresa could no longer tolerate the practices of her Carmelite cloister and founded the Discalced Carmelites with John of the Cross* (1542–1591) in 1562, which was committed to enclosure and strict asceticism. By her death, she had personally founded fourteen houses for her new order despite significant resistance from Carmelite leaders. She also wrote extensively. Her best-known works are *The Way of Perfection* (1577), a method for the contemplative life, and *The Interior Castle* (1577), a manual for spiritual growth.

Thirty-Nine Articles. See *Articles of Religion*.

Thomas Thorowgood (1595–1669). English Puritan pastor. Thorowgood was a Puritan minister in Norfolk and the chief financier of John Eliot (1604–1690), a Puritan missionary among the Native American tribes in Massachusetts. In 1650, under the title *Jews in America, or, Probabilities that Americans be of that Race*, Thorowgood became one of the first to put forward the thesis that Native Americans were actually the ten lost tribes of Israel.

Thirty-Three Articles (1617). Frisian Anabaptist confession. Also known as the "Confession of Faith According to God's Word," the Thirty-Three Articles was composed by members of the Old Frisians, a Dutch Mennonite sect, at a time when they were coming into conflict with other Anabaptist groups.

John Tillinghast (1604–1655). English Puritan minister. Tillinghast began his ministry in the Church of England, pastoring two congregations in Sussex until he moved to London and became an independent, leading him to pastor Puritan congregations in Suffolk and Norfolk. He was a member of the Fifth Monarchists, a millenarian Puritan sect that believed the political upheaval of their time was ushering in the kingdom of Christ.

Frans Titelmans (1502–1537). Belgian Catholic philosopher. Titelmans studied at the University of Leuven, where he was influenced by Petrus Ramus.* After first joining a Franciscan monastery, Titelmans realigned with the stricter Capuchins and moved to Italy. He is best known for his advocacy for the Vulgate and his debates with Desiderius Erasmus* over Pauline theology (1527–1530)—he was deeply suspicious of the fruits of humanism, especially regarding biblical studies. His work was published posthumously by his brother, Pieter Titelmans (1501–1572).

Francisco de Toledo (1532–1596). Spanish Catholic theologian. This important Jesuit taught philosophy at the universities of Salamanca and Rome. He published works on Aristotelian philosophy and a commentary on Thomas Aquinas's* work, as well as biblical commentaries on John, Romans and the first half of Luke. He was also the general editor for the Clementine Vulgate (1598).

John Tombes (1603–1676). English Baptist pastor. After leaving Oxford, Tombes held many pastoral positions in Anglican churches throughout the Midlands until founding a Baptist church in Bewdley, Worcestershire. He left this congregation following a debate with Richard Baxter,* leading him to take on a number of pastoral positions in Herefordshire while continuing to seek public debates and writing against Quakerism and Roman Catholicism.

Laurence Tomson (1539–1608). English Reformed politician and translator. Tomson was born in Northhamptonshire and educated at Magdalen College, Oxford. He graduated with his BA degree (1559) and MA degree (1564). Tomson was a fellow at Magdalen until he resigned in 1569. Prior to this resignation, Tomson was part of a diplomatic delegation to France. From 1575 to 1587, Tomson served in the House of Commons and attended the royal court at Windsor in 1582. He went on further embassies throughout Europe, where he occasionally lectured on Hebrew. Tomson died on March 29, 1608. Tomson's chief exegetical contribution was his revised text and annotations of the New Testament of the Geneva Bible.

Edward Topsell (d. 1638?). English Protestant minister. Topsell held a number of pastoral posts in Sussex, Dorset, and the Midlands before being appointed perpetual curate of St. Botolph's, Aldersgate, in the city of London. While he composed a number of religious works, including his lectures on Ruth, which were so popular they appeared in three editions, he is primarily remembered for his two illustrated works on natural history, which cataloged four-footed animals and serpents.

Alonso Tostado (1400–1455). Spanish Catholic bishop and exegete. Tostado lectured on theology, law and philosophy at the University of Salamanca, in addition to ministering in a local parish. Tostado entered into disputes over papal supremacy and the date of Christ's birth. Tostado's thirteen-volume collected works include commentaries on the historical books of the Old Testament and the Gospel of Matthew.

Daniel Toussain (1541–1602). Swiss Reformed pastor and professor. Toussain became pastor at Orléans after attending college in Basel. After the third War of Religion, Toussain was exiled, eventually returning to Montbéliard, his birthplace. In 1571, he faced opposition there from the strict Lutheran rulers and was eventually exiled due to his influence over the clergy. He returned to Orléans but fled following the Saint Bartholomew's Day Massacre (1572), eventually becoming pastor in Basel. He relocated to Heidelberg in 1583 as pastor to the new regent, becoming professor of theology at the university, and he remained there until his death.

John Trapp (1601–1669). Anglican biblical exegete. After studying at Oxford, Trapp entered the pastorate in 1636. During the English Civil Wars he sided with Parliament, which later made it difficult for him to collect tithes from a congregation whose royalist pastor had been evicted. Trapp published commentaries on all the books of the Bible from 1646 to 1656.

Immanuel Tremellius (1510–1580). Italian Reformed Hebraist. Around 1540, Tremellius received baptism by Cardinal Reginald Pole (1500–1558) and converted from Judaism to Christianity; he affiliated with evangelicals the next year. On account of the political and religious upheaval, Tremellius relocated often, teaching Hebrew in Lucca; Strasbourg, fleeing the Inquisition; Cambridge, displaced by the Schmalkaldic War; Heidelberg, escaping Mary I's persecutions; and Sedan, expelled by the new Lutheran Elector of the Palatine. Many considered Tremellius's translation of the Old Testament as the most accurate available. He also published a Hebrew grammar and translated John Calvin's* catechism into Hebrew.

Richard Turnbull (d. 1593). English minister. A preacher in London, Richard Turnbull published sermons on James, Jude, and Psalm 15.

William Tyndale (Hychyns) (1494–1536). English reformer, theologian and translator. Tyndale was educated at Oxford University, where he was influenced by the writings of humanist thinkers. Believing that piety is fostered through personal encounter with the Bible, he asked to translate the Bible into English; denied permission, Tyndale left for the Continent to complete the task. His New Testament was the equivalent of a modern-day bestseller in England but was banned and ordered burned. Tyndale's theology was oriented around justification, the authority of Scripture and Christian obedience; Tyndale emphasized the ethical as a concomitant reality of justification. He was martyred in Brussels before completing his English translation of the Old Testament, which Miles Coverdale* finished.

John Udall (1560?–1592). English Puritan pastor. Udall began his pastoral career in the Anglican parish of Kingston-upon-Thames, becoming known for his preaching and Puritan convictions, particularly his rejection of the episcopacy. While facing discipline for his views, he published anonymous and pseudonymous pamphlets critical of the established church alone and with friends, leading to his losing his position in London and relocating to Newcastle, where he continued in ministry and criticism. Udall was arrested under suspicion of complicity in publishing the critical tracts and, unwilling to deny that he wrote them, was convicted and sentenced to death. The death sentence was not carried out, however, and he remained in prison almost two years until pardoned, but died soon after release.

Zacharias Ursinus (1534-1583) German Reformed theologian. Ursinus began his studies at Wittenberg under Melanchthon*, and after teaching briefly in his home city of Breslau, continued his education at many centers of reformation learning, with stops in Strasbourg, Paris, Geneva and Zurich. Called by Elector Frederick III (1515-1576) to teach theology at the *Collegium Sapientiae* in Heidelberg and further reform in the city, Ursinus alongside Kaspar Olevianus*, was a primary author of the *Heidelberg Catechism**. Ejected from his position after the death of the Elector, Ursinus ended his career as chair of theology at the reformed academy in Neustadt.

Guillaume du Vair (1556–1621). French Catholic priest, lawyer, and writer. While du Vair took holy orders in his youth, much of his life was spent serving the state as a counselor of the parliament of Paris, a representative of King Henry IV both in France and abroad, and as Keeper of the Seals, the highest legal office in the country. The last four years of his life were spent as the bishop of Lisieux. His studies on Epictetus and the Stoics, and attempts to relate Stoicism to the Christian faith, were influential in the dissemination of this philosophy during the seventeenth and eighteenth centuries. He also wrote significant works on politics, the moral life, prayer, and the use and abuse of the French language.

Juan de Valdés (1500/10–1541). Spanish Catholic theologian and writer. Although Valdés adopted an evangelical doctrine, had Erasmian affiliations and published works that were listed on the Index of Prohibited Books, Valdés rebuked the reformers for creating disunity and never left the Catholic Church. His writings included translations of the Hebrew Psalter and various biblical books, a work on the Spanish language and several commentaries. Valdés fled to Rome in 1531 to escape the Spanish Inquisition and worked in the court of Clement VII in Bologna until the pope's death in 1534. Valdés subsequently returned to Naples, where he led the reform- and revival-minded Valdesian circle.

Henry Vaughan (1617/1618–1661). English Protestant preacher. Possibly a student at Christ's College, Cambridge, Vaughan published a sermon on Matthew 5:20 given to the House of Commons.

Thomas Venatorius (c. 1490–1551). German Lutheran theologian, mathematician, and humanist. Following a humanistic education, Venatorius spent the majority of his career in Nuremberg, where he advocated for reform as the head of the city's school system and as a preacher and pastor in the city's churches. His theological and pastoral works include one of the first Protestant works on ethics, a short catechism, and a commentary on 1 Timothy. He also edited the first Greek edition of Archimedes's writings and translated Aristophanes's *Plutus*.

Peter Martyr Vermigli (1499–1562). Italian Reformed humanist and theologian. Vermigli was one of the most influential theologians of the era, held in common regard with such figures as Martin Luther* and John Calvin.* In Italy, Vermigli was a distinguished theologian, preacher and advocate for moral reform; however, during the reinstitution of the Roman Inquisition Vermigli fled to Protestant regions in northern Europe. He was eventually appointed professor of divinity at Oxford University, where Vermigli delivered acclaimed disputations on the Eucharist. Vermigli was widely noted for his deeply integrated biblical commentaries and theological treatises.

Matthieu Virel (fl. 1561–1595). French Reformed pastor and theologian. Only two episodes from Virel's life are known: he preached the reformation message at Namur in 1561, and sixteen years later he pastored a French congregation in Basel. He published two known works: an excursus on the calendar and a brief summary of the Christian religion.

Pierre Viret (1511–1571). Swiss Reformed pastor and teacher. Converted to Protestantism at the University of Paris, Viret returned to his hometown, Orbe, where Guillaume Farel* brought him into ministry. Preaching also at Payerne and Neuchâtel, Viret's success in spreading the Reformed faith led to an assassination attempt before he and Farel sought to reform Geneva. Soon after the Genevan Assembly voted to accept the Reformation, Viret relocated to Lausanne, where he established the Reformed faith, served as chief pastor, and founded a Reformed academy. After almost twenty-five years, he was exiled from the city, spending a short time pastoring and teaching in Geneva until establishing himself in southern France, where he brought the evangelical faith to Lyons, pastored, and served as an advisor to Jeanne d'Albret, the queen of Navarre (1528–1572).

Juan Luis Vives (1492?–1540). Spanish Catholic humanist. Born into a Jewish family but baptized Catholic, Vives spent most of his life outside Spain following the persecution of his family by the Inquisition. After studying in Paris, he lived in Bruges, where he became part of the intellectual circle around Erasmus,* and taught at Oxford toward the end of his life. Vives largely avoided entering into religious controversies, and his works received a mixed reception from both Catholics and Protestants. He is best known for his educational and social writings, including an influential Latin primer, works on pedagogy and women's education, and arguments for pacifism and poor relief.

Gisbertus Voetius (1589–1676). Dutch Reformed theologian. Voetius pastored at Vlijmen and Heusden and served as the youngest delegate at the Synod of Dordrecht* before becoming professor of theology and Oriental languages at the University of Utrecht. While Voetius's writings demonstrate concern for missions, practical piety, and personal purity, he also entered into numerous theological controversies during his career. His Reformed commitments led to ongoing conflicts with Arminians and Catholics, and he sought to uphold the importance of the Old Testament against Johannes Cocceius's (1603–1669) formulation of the covenants. He also entered into debate with René Descartes (1596–1650) and his followers, arguing from an Aristotelian perspective that to accept Cartesian skepticism was to reject biblical truth and the Christian tradition.

Conradus Vorstius (1569–1622). Dutch Arminian-Socinian theologian. A student of David Paraeus* and Johannes Piscator,* Vorstius's Socinian tendencies emerged during his tenure as professor of theology at Steinfurt. After an apology and examination, he was allowed to replace Arminius* as professor of theology at Leiden though never permitted to teach, as his questioning of the doctrine of atonement and the eternity, foreknowledge, and omnipresence of God drew wide censure, ultimately from King James I of England.* Exiled to Gouda and deposed at the Synod of Dordrecht,* Vorstius published numerous theological works and a commentary on the Pauline letters.

Vulgate. In 382 Pope Damasus I (c. 300–384) commissioned Jerome (c. 347–420) to translate the four Gospels into Latin based on Old Latin and Greek manuscripts. Jerome completed the translation of the Gospels and the Old Testament around 405. It is widely debated how much of the rest of the New Testament was translated by Jerome. During the Middle Ages, the Vulgate became the Catholic Church's standard Latin translation. The Council of Trent recognized it as the official text of Scripture.

George Walker (1581–1651). Puritan minister. Walker was born at Hawkshead, Lancashire, and educated at St. John's College, Cambridge. After graduating Cambridge, Walker moved to London, where he became rector of St. John the Evangelist on Watling Street in 1614. He served this parish for nearly forty years. Throughout his ministry, Walker showed himself to be an ardent opponent of the papacy and practices within the Church of England that he deemed not sufficiently reformed. Toward this end, Walker engaged numerous disputations and literary debates with both conformists and Catholics. For his sermons that were critical of the Church of England, he was summoned to appear before Archbishop Laud in 1635 and the Star Chamber in 1638, which fined and imprisoned him for twelve weeks. On another occasion, Walker was incarcerated for as long as two years for his nonconformity until released by the Long Parliament. In 1643, Walker was selected to serve in the Westminster Assembly and to participate in the trial of Laud. Walker died in London. Among his many published sermons and polemical works is a treatise on justification.

Thomas Walkington (d. 1621). Anglican minister and author. Born in Lincoln, he was educated at Cambridge, graduating with his BA in 1597 and his MA in 1600. Walkington was elected a fellow at St. John's College, Cambridge, in 1602. Later, he received a BD from Oxford and a DD from Cambridge. He served as rector of parishes in Northamptonshire, Lincolnshire, and Middlesex. A prolific author, Walkington published works on diverse subjects. Among his biblical works are *An Exposition of the First Two Verses of the Sixth Chapter to the Hebrews in form of a Dialogue* (1609) and *Theologicall Rules to Guide Us in the Understanding and Practice of Holy Scripture* (1615).

Peter Walpot (d. 1578). Moravian Radical pastor and bishop. Walpot was a bishop of the Hutterite community after Jakob Hutter, Peter Riedemann* and Leonhard Lanzenstiel. Riedemann's *Confession of Faith* (1545; 1565) became a vital authority for Hutterite exegesis, theology and morals. Walpot added his own *Great Article Book* (1577), which collates primary biblical passages on baptism, communion, the community of goods, the sword and divorce. In keeping with Hutterite theology, Walpot defended the community of goods as a mark of the true church.

Richard Ward (c. 1601–1684). English Anglican pastor. Educated at Cambridge and St. Andrews, Ward pastored in London and Essex. His published writings include a commentary on Matthew and an explanation of the Solemn League and Covenant (1643), which allied Scottish Covenanters and English Parliamentarians during the First English Civil War (1642–1646).

Thomas Watson (d. 1686). English Puritan pastor. After graduating from Cambridge, Watson became pastor of St. Stephen Walbrook in the city of London, a pulpit he served for twenty years, though he was imprisoned for a year for his part in the plot of Christopher Love (1618–

1651) to restore Charles II to the throne. A well-respected preacher, Watson was expelled from official ministry by the 1662 Act of Uniformity, though he continued to preach in private until his retirement. While Watson published many sermons and devotional works, he is perhaps best known for *A Body of Divinity* (1692), a series of sermon on the Westminster Catechism.

Valentin Weigel (1533–1588). German Lutheran pastor. Weigel studied at Leipzig and Wittenberg, entering the pastorate in 1567. Despite a strong anti-institutional bias, he was recognized by the church hierarchy as a talented preacher and compassionate minister of mercy to the poor. Although he signed the Formula of Concord,* Weigel's orthodoxy was questioned so openly that he had to publish a defense. He appears to have tried to synthesize several medieval mystics with the ideas of Sebastian Franck,* Thomas Müntzer* and others. His posthumously published works have led some recent scholars to suggest that Weigel's works may have deeply influenced later Pietism.

Hieronymus Weller von Molsdorf (1499–1572). German Lutheran theologian. Originally intending to study law, Weller devoted himself to theology after hearing one of Martin Luther's* sermons on the catechism. He boarded with Luther and tutored Luther's son. In 1539 he moved to Freiburg, where he lectured on the Bible and held theological disputations at the Latin school. In addition to hymns, works of practical theology and a postil set, Weller published commentaries on Genesis, 1–2 Samuel, 1–2 Kings, Job, the Psalms, Christ's passion, Ephesians, Philippians, 1–2 Thessalonians and 1–2 Peter.

Westminster Assembly (1643–1652). English church council. Called by English Parliament to advise on church reform, the Westminster Assembly was made up of more than 120 clergymen, thirty parliamentary observers, and a delegation from the Church of Scotland. Beginning with a review of the Articles of Religion,* the most heated debates were undertaken over ecclesiology, as factions argued for presbyterianism, congregationalism, Erastianism, and episcopalianism, with the council ultimately recommending presbyterianism to the parliament. Much of the legacy of the assembly is held in the major documents it produced, the *Directory for Public Worship* (1644), *The Form of Presbyterial Church Government* (1645), the *Westminster Confession of Faith* (1646), the *Shorter Catechism* (1647), and the *Larger Catechism* (1648), which became foundational for the English and Scottish churches and many of the Reformed denominations.

William Whitaker (1547/1548–1595). English Puritan theologian. Whitaker spent most of his career at Cambridge, where he served as Regius Professor of Divinity and master of St. John's College. While his tenure was occasionally opposed due to his Puritanism, he was nevertheless widely respected, and he published numerous significant works on topics including the Protestant doctrine of Scripture, original sin, grace, and ecclesiastical authority. He also drafted the Lambeth Articles (1595), a proposed addendum to the Thirty-Nine Articles* endorsing double predestination, but the changes were rejected by Elizabeth I*.

John Whitgift (1530–1604). Anglican archbishop. Though Whitgift shared much theological common ground with Puritans, after his election as Archbishop of Canterbury (1583) he moved decisively to squelch the political and ecclesiastical threat they posed during Elizabeth I's* reign. Whitgift enforced strict compliance to the Book of Common Prayer,* the Act of Uniformity (1559) and the Articles of Religion.* Whitgift's policies led to a large migration of Puritans to Holland. The bulk of Whitgift's published corpus is the fruit of a lengthy public disputation with Thomas Cartwright,* in which Whitgift defines Anglican doctrine against Cartwright's staunch Puritanism.

Johann Wigand (1523–1587). German Lutheran theologian. Wigand is most noted as one of the compilers of the *Magdeburg Centuries*, a German ecclesiastical history of the first thirteen centuries of the church. He was a student of Philipp Melanchthon* at the University of Wittenburg and became a significant figure in the controversies dividing Lutheranism. Strongly opposed to Roman Catholicism, Wigand lobbied against innovations in Lutheran theology that appeared sympathetic to Catholic thought. In the later debates, Wigand's support for Gnesio-Lutheranism established his role in the development of confessional Lutheranism. Wigand was appointed bishop of Pomerania after serving academic posts at the universities in Jena and Königsburg.

Thomas Wilcox (c. 1549–1608). English Puritan theologian. In 1572, Wilcox objected to Parliament against the episcopacy and the Book of Common Prayer,* advocating for presbyterian church governance. He was imprisoned for sedition. After his release, he preached itinerantly. He was brought before the courts twice more for his continued protest against the Church of England's episcopal structure. He translated some of Theodore Beza* and John Calvin's* sermons into English, and he wrote polemical and occasional works as well as commentaries on the Psalms and Song of Songs.

Johann (Ferus) Wild (1495–1554). German Catholic pastor. After studying at Heidelberg and teaching at Tübingen, this Franciscan was appointed as lector in the Mainz cathedral, eventually being promoted to cathedral preacher—a post for which he became widely popular but also controversial. Wild strongly identified as Catholic but was not unwilling to criticize the curia. Known for an irenic spirit—criticized in fact as *too* kind—he was troubled by the polemics between all parties of the Reformation. He preached with great lucidity, integrating the liturgy, Scripture and doctrine to exposit Catholic worship and teaching for common people. His sermons on John were pirated for publication without his knowledge; the Sorbonne banned them as heretical. Despite his popularity among clergy, the majority of his works were on the Roman Index until 1900.

Andrew Willet (1562–1621). Anglican priest, professor, and biblical expositor. Willet was a gifted biblical expositor and powerful preacher. He walked away from a promising university career in 1588 when he was ordained a priest in the Church of England. For the next thirty-three years he served as a parish priest. Willet's commentaries summarized the present state of discussion while also offering practical applications for preachers. They have been cited as some of the most technical commentaries of the early seventeenth century. His most important publication was *Synopsis Papismi, or a General View of Papistrie* (1594), in which he responded to many of Robert Bellarmine's critiques. After years of royal favor, Willet was imprisoned in 1618 for a month after presenting to King James I* his opposition to the "Spanish Match" of Prince Charles to the Infanta Maria. While serving as a parish priest, he wrote forty-two works, most of which were either commentaries on books of the Bible or controversial works against Catholics.

Thomas Wilson (d. 1586). English Anglican priest. A fellow of St John's, Cambridge, Wilson fled to Frankfurt to escape the Marian Persecution. After his return to England, he served as a canon and Dean of Worcester.

George Wither (1588–1667). English poet, satirist, and hymn writer. Wither was born in Bentworth, Hampshire. After finishing his early education under the tutelage of a local minister, Wither continued his studies at Magdalen College, Oxford. Afterward, he studied law at the Inns of Chancery. Wither commenced his literary career with the publication of an elegy on the occasion of the death of Henry Frederick, Prince of Wales (1594–1612). Most of Wither's literary works consist of satirical pamphlets for which he was regularly arrested, imprisoned, and released. He fought in the Parliamentary Army during the Civil War. A conforming Anglican, Wither composed numerous hymns as well as translations of the Psalms. Two of Wither's major works are *Preparation to the Psalter* (1619), in which he explores various literary aspects of the Bible, and *Hymns and Songs of the Church* (1622/1623). He died in London.

John Woolton (c. 1535–1594). Anglican bishop. After graduating from Oxford, Woolton lived in Germany until the accession of Elizabeth I.* He was ordained as a priest in 1560 and as a bishop in 1578. Woolton published many theological, devotional and practical works, including a treatise on the immortality of the soul, a discourse on conscience and a manual for Christian living.

John Wycliffe (c. 1330–1384). English theologian, philosopher, and reformer known as "the Morning Star of the Reformation." While holding benefices from a number of parishes, Wycliffe spent the majority of his career at Oxford, where he studied, taught, and served as head of Balliol College. His early work focused on logic and metaphysics, but after entering into the service of John of Gaunt, Duke of Lancaster (1340–1399) and serving as a royal envoy to discuss taxes with papal representatives, Wycliffe turned his attention to more practical concerns. His criticism of papal power and wealth drew initially civil and ecclesiastical approval, but application of his principle that any headship profiting the governor rather than the governed is illegitimate to the English church brought controversy and censure. This criticism increased as he rejected transubstantiation, criticized monasticism, argued along Augustinian lines that only the invisible body of the elect constituted the true church, that Scripture belongs to the body of the elect rather than the institutional church, and that as many leaders of the visible church were likely reprobate, their offices and sacraments were invalid. While dismissed from Oxford in 1381, powerful defenders protected Wycliffe from further consequences during his lifetime, but he was condemned as a heretic at the Council of Constance (1515), whence he was exhumed and his remains burned. While largely condemned by contemporaries, Wycliffe, and his followers, the Lollards, are often viewed as forerunners of the Reformation who prepared the way for the tumult of the sixteenth century.

Girolamo Zanchi (1516–1590). Italian Reformed theologian and pastor. Zanchi joined an Augustinian monastery at the age of fifteen, where he studied Greek and Latin, the church fathers and the works of Aristotle and Thomas Aquinas.* Under the influence of his prior, Peter Martyr Vermigli,* Zanchi also imbibed the writings of the Swiss and German reformers. To avoid the Inquisition, Zanchi fled to Geneva where he was strongly attracted to the preaching and teaching of John Calvin.* Zanchi taught biblical theology and the *locus* method at academies in Strasbourg, Heidelberg, and Neustadt. He also served as pastor of an Italian refugee congregation. Zanchi's theological works, *De tribus Elohim* (1572) and *De natura Dei* (1577), have received more attention than his commentaries. His commentaries comprise about a quarter of his literary output, however, and display a strong typological and christological interpretation in conversation with the church fathers, medieval exegetes, and other reformers.

Katharina Schütz Zell (1497/98–1562). German Reformed writer. Zell became infamous in Strasbourg and the Empire when in 1523 she married the priest Matthias Zell, and then published an apology defending her husband against charges of impiety and libertinism. Longing for a united church, she called for toleration of Catholics and Anabaptists, famously writing to Martin Luther* after the failed Marburg Colloquy of 1529 to exhort him to check his hostility and to be ruled instead by Christian charity. Much to the chagrin of her contemporaries, Zell published diverse works, ranging from polemical treatises on marriage to letters of consolation, as well as editing a hymnal and penning an exposition of Psalm 51.

Martha Elizabeth Zitter (Unknown). German Catholic nun. Zitter entered the Ursuline convent in Erfurt during her teenage years. Most of what is known about her is drawn from a letter she composed to her mother, explaining her decision to leave the order and become Lutheran, which focuses on aspects of her vows and Roman Catholic piety she believes to be unbiblical. Despite this public departure from the Roman church, however, Zitter returned toward the end of her life.

Ulrich Zwingli (1484–1531). Swiss Reformed humanist, preacher and theologian. Zwingli studied at the University of Vienna, and afterwards the University of Basel, where he received his BA and MA in 1504 and 1506. Ordained in September 1506, Zwingli became priest of the church in Glarus where he taught himself Greek, and read deeply in the church fathers. During this period, Zwingli was also greatly impacted by the writings of Desiderius Erasmus*. In 1516, Zwingli accepted the position of priest at the Benedictine Abbey at Einsiedeln in Schwyz, where he intently studied the Greek New Testament, and learned Hebrew. When he became a preacher in the city cathedral at Zurich, Zwingli enacted reform through sermons, public disputations, and conciliation with the town council, abolishing the Mass and images in the church. Zwingli broke with the lectionary preaching tradition, instead preaching serial expository biblical sermons. He later was embroiled in controversy with Anabaptists over infant baptism and with Martin Luther* at the Marburg Colloquy (1529) over their differing views of the Eucharist. Zwingli, serving as chaplain to Zurich's military, was killed in the Second Battle of Kappel.

SOURCES FOR BIOGRAPHICAL SKETCHES

General Reference Works

Allgemeine Deutsche Biographie. 56 vols. Leipzig: Duncker & Humblot, 1875–1912; reprint, 1967–1971. Accessible online via deutsche-biographie.de/index.html.

Baskin, Judith R., ed. *The Cambridge Dictionary of Judaism and Jewish Culture*. New York: Cambridge University Press, 2011.

Benedetto, Robert, ed. *The New Westminster Dictionary of Church History*. Vol. 1. Louisville: Westminster John Knox Press, 2008.

Bettenson, Henry and Chris Maunder, eds. *Documents of the Christian Church*. 3rd ed. Oxford: Oxford University Press, 1999.

Betz, Hans Dieter, Don Browning, Bernd Janowski and Eberhard Jüngel, eds. *Religion Past & Present: Encyclopedia of Theology and Relgion*. 13 vols. Leiden: Brill, 2007–2013.

Bremer, Francis J. and Tom Webster, eds. *Puritans and Puritanism in Europe and America: A Comprehensive Encyclopedia*. 2 vols. Santa Barbara, CA: ABC-CLIO, 2006.

Ghisalberti, Alberto Maria, ed. *Dizionario Biografico degli Italiani*. 100 vols. Istituto della Enciclopedia italiana, Roma, 1960–2020. Online edition available at treccani.it.

Gritsch, Eric W. *A History of Lutheranism*. Minneapolis: Fortress Press, 2002.

Haag, Eugene and Émile Haag. *La France protestante ou vies des protestants français*. 2nd ed. 6 vols. Paris: Sandoz & Fischbacher, 1877–1888.

Hillerbrand, Hans J., ed. *Oxford Encyclopedia of the Reformation*. 4 vols. New York: Oxford University Press, 1996.

Kolb, Robert, and Timothy J. Wengert, eds. *The Book of Concord: The Confessions of the Evangelical Lutheran Church*. Translated by Charles Arand et al. Minneapolis: Fortress, 2000.

McKim, Donald K., ed. *Dictionary of Major Biblical Interpreters*. Downers Grove, IL: InterVarsity Press, 2007.

Müller, Gerhard, et al., ed. *Theologische Realenzyklopädie*. Berlin: Walter de Gruyter, 1994.

Neue Deutsche Biographie. 28 vols. projected. Berlin: Duncker & Humblot, 1953–. Accessible online via deutsche-biographie.de/index.html.

New Catholic Encyclopedia. 15 vols. New York: McGraw-Hill, 1967; 2nd ed., Detroit: Thomson-Gale, 2002.

Oxford Dictionary of National Biography. 60 vols. Oxford: Oxford University Press, 2004.

Pelikan, Jaroslav. *The Christian Tradition*. 5 vols. Chicago: University of Chicago Press, 1971–1989.

Stephen, Leslie, and Sidney Lee, eds. *Dictionary of National Biography*. 63 vols. London: Smith, Elder and Co., 1885–1900.

Terry, Michael, ed. *Reader's Guide to Judaism*. New York: Routledge, 2000.

Wordsworth, Christopher, ed. *Lives of Eminent Men connected with the History of Religion in England*. 4 vols. London: J. G. & F. Rivington, 1839.

Additional Works for Individual Sketches

Akin, Daniel L. "An Expositional Analysis of the Schleitheim Confession." *Criswell Theological Review* 2 (1988): 345-70.

Astell, Mary. *The Christian Religion, as Professed by a Daughter of the Church of England*. Edited by Jacqueline Broad. Toronto: Iter Inc and the Center for Reformation and Renaissance Studies, 2013.

Bald, R. C. *John Donne: A Life*. Oxford: Oxford University Press, 1970.

Beeke, Joel, and Randall J. Pederson. *Meet the Puritans*. Grand Rapids: Reformation Heritage Books, 2006.

Bireley, Robert, *The Refashioning of Catholicism, 1450–1700*, Washington, DC: Catholic University of America Press, 1999.

Blok, P. J., and P. C. Molhuysen, eds. *Nieuw Nederlandsch Biografisch Woordenboek*. 10 vols.

Brackney, William H. *A Genetic History of Baptist Thought: With Special Reference to Baptists in Britain and North America*. Atlanta: Mercer University Press, 2004.

———. *Historical Dictionary of the Baptists*. 2nd ed. Lanham, MD: Scarecrow, 2009.

Brook, Benjamin. *The Lives of the Puritans*. 3 vols. London: James Black, 1813. Reprint, Pittsburgh, PA: Soli Deo Gloria, 1994.

Brown, Peter. *Augustine of Hippo: A Biography*. Berkeley & Los Angeles, CA: University of California Press, 1967.

Bruening, Michael W. *Refusing to Kiss the Slipper: Opposition to Calvinism in the Francophone Reformation*. Oxford Studies in Historical theology. New York: Oxford University Press, 2021.

Burke, David G. "The Enduring Significance of the KJV." *Word and World* 31, no. 3 (2011): 229-44.

Campbell, Gordon. *Bible: The Story of the King James Version, 1611–2011*. Oxford: Oxford University Press, 2010.

Cathcart, William. *The Baptist Encyclopaedia*. 3 vols. Philadelphia: Louis H. Everts, 1881.

Charles, Amy. *A Life of George Herbert*. Ithaca, NY: Cornell University Press, 1977.

Christian, Jacob. *The Sovereign Map: Theoretical Approaches to Cartography Throughout History*. Chicago: University of Chicago Press, 2006.

Coffey, John. *Politics, Religion, and the British Revolutions: The Thought of Samuel Rutherford*. Cambridge: Cambridge University Press, 1997.

Colish, Marcia. *Peter Lombard*, 2 vols. Leiden, Netherlands: Brill, 1993.

Culpepper, Scott. *Francis Johnson and the English Separatist Influence: The Bishop of Brownism's Life, Writings, and Controversies*. Macon, GA: Mercer University Press, 2011.

Doornkaat Koolman, J ten. "The First Edition of Peter Riedemann's 'Rechenschaft.'" *Mennonite Quarterly Review* 36, no. 2 (1962): 169-70.

Emerson, Everett H. *John Cotton*. New York: Twayne, 1990.

Fischlin, Daniel and Mark Fortier, eds. *Royal Subjects: Essays on the Writings of James VI and I*. Detroit: Wayne State University Press, 2002.

Fishbane, Michael A. "Teacher and the Hermeneutical Task: A Reinterpretation of Medieval Exegesis." *Journal of the American Academy of Religion* 43, no. 4 (1975): 709-21.

Friedmann, Robert. "Second Generation Anabaptism as Illustrated by the Walpot Era of the Hutterites." *Mennonite Quarterly* 44, no. 4 (1970): 390-93.

Frymire, John M. *The Primacy of the Postils: Catholics, Protestants, and the Dissemination of Ideas in Early Modern Germany*. Leiden: Brill, 2010.

Furcha, Edward J. "Key Concepts in Caspar von Schwenckfeld's Thought, Regeneration and the New Life." *Church History* 37, no. 2 (1968): 160-73.

Gerace, Antionio. *Biblical Scholarship in Louvain in the 'Golden' Sixteenth Century*. Göttingen: Vandenhoeck & Ruprecht, 2019.

Gordon, Bruce, *The Swiss Reformation*. Manchester: Manchester University Press, 2002.

Greaves, Richard L. *Society and Religion in Elizabethan England*. Minneapolis: University of Minnesota, 1981.

Greiffenberg, Catharina Regina von. *Meditations on the Incarnation, Passion, and Death of Jesus Christ*. Edited and translated by Lynne Tatlock. The Other Voice in Early Modern Europe. Chicago: University of Chicago Press, 2009.

Grendler, Paul. "Italian biblical humanism and the papacy, 1515-1535." In *Biblical Humanism and Scholasticism in the Age of Erasmus*. Edited by Erika Rummel, 225-76. Leiden: Brill, 2008.

Guggisberg, Hans R. *Sebastian Castellio 1515-1563: Humanist and Defender of Religious Toleration in a Confessional Age*. Translated and Edited by Bruce Gordon. St Andrews Studies in Reformation History. New York: Routledge, 2017.

Haemig, Mary Jane. "Elisabeth Cruciger (1500?–1535): The Case of the Disappearing Hymn Writer." *Sixteenth Century Journal* 32, no. 1 (2001): 21-44.

Harpley, W., ed. *Report and Transactions of the Devonshire Association for the Advancement of Science, Literature and Art* 24 (July 1882). Plymouth: William Brendon and Son, 1892.

Heiden, Albert van der. "Pardes: Methodological Reflections on the Theory of the Four Senses." *Journal of Jewish Studies* 34, no. 2 (1983): 147-59.

Hendrix, Scott H., ed. and trans. *Early Protestant Spirituality*. New York: Paulist Press, 2009.

Hobbs, R. Gerald. "Is Abbot Isidore Also Among the Prophets?": Protestant Influences upon the Annotated Bible of Isidore Clarius." *Renaissance and Reformation*. New series, 17, No. 1 (Winter 1993): 53-71.

Hvolbek, Russell H. "Being and Knowing: Spiritualist Epistelmology and Anthropology from Schwenckfeld to Böhme." *Sixteenth Century Journal* 22, no. 1 (1991): 97-110.

Kahle, Paul. "Felix Pratensis—a Prato, Felix. Der Herausgeber der Ersten Rabbinerbibel, Venedig 1516/7." *Die Welt des Orients* 1, no. 1 (1947): 32-36.

Kelly, Joseph Francis. *The Ecumenical Councils of the Catholic Church: A History*. Collegeville, MN: Liturgical Press, 2009.

Koop, Karl, ed. *Confessions of Faith in the Anabaptist Tradition 1527–1660*. Translated by Cornelius J. Dyck et al. CRR 11. Kitchener, ON: Pandora Press, 2006.

Lake, Peter. *The Boxmaker's Revenge: "Orthodoxy", "Heterodox" and the Politics of the Parish in Early Stuart London*. Stanford, CA: Stanford University Press, 2001.

Lane, Anthony N. S. *Calvin and Bernard of Clairvaux*. Princeton, NJ: Princeton Theological Seminary, 1996.

Lane, Belden C. *Ravished by Beauty: The Surprising Legacy of Reformed Spirituality*. Oxford: Oxford University Press, 2011.

Lee, Jason K. *The Theology of John Smyth* (Macon, GA: Mercer University Press, 2003).

Lockhart, Paul Douglas. *Frederick II and the Protestant Cause: Denmark's Role in the Wars of Religion, 1559–1596*. Leiden: Brill, 2004.

Lubac, Henri de. *Medieval Exegesis: The Four Senses of Scripture*. 3 vols. Translated by Mark Sebanc and E. M. Macierowski. Grand Rapids: Eerdmans, 1998–2009.

Manetsch, Scott, *Calvin's Company of Pastors: Pastoral Care and the Emerging Reformed Church, 1536–1609*. Oxford: Oxford University Press, 2013.

Manschereck, Clyde Leonard. *Melanchthon, the Quiet Reformer*. New York: Abingdon, 1958.

Marinella, Lucrezia. *The Nobility and Excellence of Women and the Defects and Vices of Men*. Edited and translated by Anne Dunhill. Chicago: University of Chicago Press, 1999.

Matheson, Peter, *Argula von Grumbach: A Woman's Voice in the Reformation*. Edinburgh: T&T Clark, 1995.

McGuire, Daniel Patrick. *The Difficult Saint: Bernard of Clairvaux and his Tradition*. Collegeville, MN: Cistercian Publication, 1991.

McKinley, Mary B. "Volume Editor's Introduction." In *Epistle to Marguerite of Navarre and Preface to a Sermon by John Calvin*, edited and translated by Mary B. McKiney. Chicago: University of Chicago Press, 2004.

M'Crie, Thomas. *The Life of Andrew Melville*. 2 vols. Edinburgh: William Blackwood, 1819.

Norton, David. *A Textual History of the King James Bible*. New York: Cambridge University Press, 2005

Nuttall, Geoffrey. *The Welsh Saints, 1640–1660: Walter Cradock, Vavasor Powell, Morgan Llwyd*. Cardiff: University of Wales Press, 1957.

Oberman, Heiko A. *Luther: Man Between God and the Devil*. New York, NY: Doubleday, 1989.

O'Meara, Thomas F. *Albert the Great: Theologian and Scientist*. Chicago: New Priory Press, 2013.

Packull, Werner O. "The Origins of Peter Riedemann's Account of Our Faith." *Sixteenth Century Journal* 30, no. 1 (1999): 61-69.

Papazian, Mary Arshagouni, ed. *John Donne and the Protestant Reformation: New Perspectives*. Detroit: Wayne State University Press, 2003.

Paulicelli, Eugenia. "Sister Arcangela Tarabotti: Hair, Wigs and Other Vices." In *Writing Fashion in Early Modern Italy: From Sprezzatura to Satire*, by idem, 177-204. Farnham, Surrey, UK: Ashgate, 2014.

Pragman, James H. "The Augsburg Confession in the English Reformation: Richard Taverner's Contribution." *Sixteenth Century Journal* 11, no. 3 (1980): 75-85.

Rashi. *Rashi's Commentary on Psalms*. Translated by Mayer I. Gruber. Atlanta: Scholars Press, 1998.

Raynor, Brian. *John Frith: Scholar and Martyr*. Kent, UK: Pond View Books, 2000.

Reid, Jonathan A. *King's Sister—Queen of Dissent: Marguerite of Navarre (1492–1549) and her Evangelical Network*. Leiden: Brill, 2009.

Schmidt, Josef, "Introduction" in Johannes Tauler, *Sermons*. New York: Paulist Press, 1985, 1-34.

Smith, Hannah. "Mary Astell, *A Serious Proposal to the Ladies* (1694), and the Anglican Reformation of Manners in Late-Seventeenth-Century England." In *Mary Astell: Reason, Gender, Faith*, edited by William Kolbrenner and Michal Michelson, 31-48. New York: Routledge, 2007.

Spinka, Matthew. *John Hus: A Biography*. Princeton, NJ: Princeton University Press, 1968.

———. *John Hus at the Council of Constance*. New York: Columbia University Press, 1968.

———. *John Hus and the Czech Reform*. Hamden, CT: Archon Books, 1966.

Steinmetz, David C. *Reformers in the Wings: From Geiler von Kayserberg to Theodore Beza*. Oxford: Oxford University Press, 2000.

———. "The Superiority of Pre-Critical Exegesis." *Theology Today* 37, no. 1 (1980): 27-38.

Stjerna, Kirsi. *Women of the Reformation*. Malden, MA: Blackwell Publishing, 2009.

Synder, C. Arnold. "The Confession of the Swiss Brethren in Hesse, 1578." In *Anabaptism Revisited: Essays on Anabaptist/Mennonite Studies in Honor of C. J. Dyck*. Edited by Walter Klaassen, 29-49. Waterloo, ON; Scottdale, PA: Herald Press, 1992.

———. "The Schleitheim Articles in Light of the Revolution of the Common Man: Continuation or Departure?" *Sixteenth Century Journal* 16, no. 4 (1985): 419-30.

Thornton, Wallace. *John Foxe and His Monument: A Theological-Historical Perspective*. Birmingham, AL: Aldersgate Heritage Press, 2013.

Todd, Margo. "Bishops in the Kirk: William Cowper of Galloway and the Puritan Episcopacy of Scotland." *Scottish Journal of Theology*, 57 (2004): 300-312.

Tschackert, Paul. "Varel, Edo Hilderich of." In *General German Biography* (ADB). Volume 39. Leipzig: Duncker & Humblot, 1895.

Van Liere, Frans. *An Introduction to the Medieval Bible*. New York: Cambridge University Press, 2014.

Voogt, Gerrit. "Remonstrant-Counter-Remonstrant Debates: Crafting a Principled Defense of Toleration after the Synod of Dordrecht (1619–1650)." *Church History and Religious Culture* 89, no. 4 (2009): 489-524.

Wabuda, Susan. "Henry Bull, Miles Coverdale, and the Making of *Foxe's Book of Martyrs*." In *Martyrs and Martyrologies: Papers Read at the 1992 Summer Meeting and the 1993 Winter Meeting of the Ecclesiastical History Society*, edited by Diana Wood, 245-58. Oxford: Blackwell, 1993.

Wallace, Dewey D. Jr. "George Gifford, Puritan Propaganda and Popular Religion in Elizabethan England." *Sixteenth Century Journal* 9, no. 1 (1978): 27-49.

Wawrykow, Joseph P. *The Westminster Handbook to Thomas Aquinas*. Louisville, KY: Westminster John Knox, 2005.

Wendel, Francois. *Calvin: The Origins and Development of His Religious Thought*. New York: Harper & Row, 1963.

Wengert, Timothy J. "'Fear and Love' in the Ten Commandments." *Concordia Journal* 21, no. 1 (1995): 14-27.

Wiesner-Hanks, Merry, ed. *Convents Confront the Reformation: Catholic and Protestant Nuns in Germany*. Translated by Joan Skocir and Merry Wiesner-Hanks. Milwaukee: Marquette University Press, 1996.

———. "Philip Melanchthon and John Calvin against Andreas Osiander: Coming to Terms with Forensic Justification." In *Calvin and Luther: The Continuing Relationship*, edited by R. Ward Holder, 63-87. Göttingen: Vandenhoeck & Ruprecht, 2013.

Wilkinson, Robert J. *Tetragrammaton: Western Christians and the Hebrew Name of God*. Leiden: Brill, 2015.

Yarnell, Malcolm. "Christopher Blackwood: Exemplar of the Seventeenth-Century Particular Baptists." *Southwestern Journal of Theology* 57, no 2 (Spring 2015): 181-205.

BIBLIOGRAPHY

Astell, Mary. *The Christian Religion, as Professed by a Daughter of the Church of England.* Edited by Jacqueline Broad. Toronto: ITER and the Center for Reformation and Renaissance Studies, 2013.

Bibliander, Theodor. *Oratio Theodori Bibliandri ad Enarrationem Esaiae Prophetarum.* Zurich: Christoph Froschauer, 1532. Digital copy online at www.e-rara.ch.

Borrhaus, Martin Cellarius. *In Iesaiae Prophetae oracula, Messiae seruatoris mundi, & Ecclesiae sponsae, atque Aduersarij eorum, mystica descriptione referta.* Basel: Joannem Opporinum, 1561. Digital copy online at books.google.com.

Brenz, Johannes. *Esaias propheta, commentariis explicatus.* Frankfurt: Peter Brubach, 1550. Digital copy online at books.google.com.

Bullinger, Heinrich. *Isaias excellentissimus Dei propheta: cuius testimoniis Christus ipse dominus et eius apostoli creberrime usi leguntur, expositus homiliis CXC, quibus non tam sensus prophetae redditur, quam usus & fructus eius in Ecclesia Christi, ostenditur.* Zurich: Christoph Froschauer, 1567.

Cajetan, Cardinal (Thomas de Vio). *In Psalmos, Parabolas Salomonis, [et] Ecclesiasten, nec non in tria priora Isaiae Capita commentarii: Tomus Tertius.* Lyon: Jean Prost & Pierre Prost, 1639.

Calvin, John. *Commentary on the Book of Isaiah.* 4 vols. Translated and edited by John Pringle. Calvin Translation Society 13-16. Edinburgh: Calvin Translation Society, 1850–1853. Digital copy online at ccel.org.

Castellio, Sebastian. *Adnotationes Bibliorum Sacrorum Interpretationi.* Leipzig: Samuel Benjamin Walther, 1789 [1551]. Digital copy online at books.google.com.

Cooper, Thomas. *A brief exposition of such chapters of the old testament as usually are read in the church at common prayer on the Sundays set forth for the better help and instruction of the unlearned. By Thomas Cooper Bishop of Lincolne.* London: Henri Denham for Rafe Newbery, 1573. Digital copy online at EEBO.

Day, William. *An exposition of the Book of the Prophet Isaiah.* London, 1654. Digital copy online at EEBO.

Dentière, Marie. *Epistle to Marguerite of Navarre and Preface to a Sermon by John Calvin.* Edited and translated by Mary B. McKinley. Chicago: University of Chicago Press, 2004.

Donne, John. *The Works of John Donne.* 6 vols. Edited by Henry Alford. London: John Parker, 1839.

Downame, John, ed. *Annotations upon all the books of the Old and New Testament.* London: John Legatt and John Raworth, 1645. Digital copy online at archive.org.

Fell, Margaret. *Women's Speaking Justified and Other Pamphlets.* Edited by Jane Donawerth and Rebecca M. Lush. Tempe, AZ: Arizona Center for Medieval and Renaissance Studies, 2018.

Forerius, Franciscus. *Iesaiae Prophetae Vetus & Noua Ex Hebraico Uersio cum Commentario.* Zileti: Venice, 1563.

Franck, Sebastian. "Letter to Campanus." In *Spiritual and Anabaptist Writers: Documents Illustrative of the Radical Reformation*, 147-60. Edited by George Hunston Williams. Philadelphia: Westminster, 1957.

Greiffenberg, Catharina Regina von. *Meditations on the Incarnation, Passion, and Death of Jesus Christ.* Edited and translated by Lynne Tatlock. Chicago: University of Chicago Press, 2009.

Grumbach, Argula von. *Argula von Grumbach: A Woman's Voice in the Reformation.* Edited by Peter Matheson. Edinburgh: T&T Clark, 1995.

Gwalther, Rudolf. *Isaias: In Isaiam Prophetam Rodolphi Gualtheri Tigurini Homiliae CCCXXVII*. Zurich: Christoph Froschauer, 1583. Digital copy online at books.google.com.

Heilbrunner, Philipp. *Esaiae Prophetae Vaticinia: In Locos communes Theologicos digesta: & Quaestionibus Methodi illustrata*. Lauingen: Leonard Reinmichel, 1584. Digital copy online at books.google.com.

Hesshusius, Tilemann. *In Prophetam Jesaiam Commentarius Reverendi & Clarißimi Theologi D.D. Tilemanni Heshusii*. Halle: Christoph Bismarck, 1617. Digital copy online at Dilibri Rheinland-Pfalz, www.dilibri.de.

Hickman, Charles. *Fourteen Sermons, Preached at St James in Westminster*. London: James Orme, 1700.

Hoffman, Melchior. *Auslegung der heimlichen Offenbarung Johannis*. France: n.p., 1530.

Karlstadt, Andreas Bodenstein von. *De Legis Litera sive Carne et Spiritu*. Wittenberg: Nikolaus Schirlentz, 1521. Digital copy online at Herzog August Bibliothek, http://diglib.hab.de/edoc/ed000216/start.htm.

———. "On the Removal of Images." In *A Reformation Debate: Karlstadt, Emser, and Eck on Sacred Images; Three Treatises in Translation*, 21-42. 2nd rev. ed. Translated by Bryan D. Mangrum and Giuseppe Scavizzi. Toronto: Centre for Reformation and Renaissance Studies, 1998.

———. "Whether One Should Proceed Slowly." In *The Radical Reformation*, 49-73. Edited by Michael G. Baylor. Cambridge: Cambridge University Press, 1991.

Kimchi, David. *The Commentary of David Kimchi on Isaiah*. Edited by Louis Finkelstein, Reprint, New York: AMS, 1966.

Luther, Martin. *D. Martin Luthers Werke, Kritische Gesamtausgabe [Schriften]*. 73 vols. Weimar: Hermann Böhlaus Nachfolger, 1883–2009. Digital copy online at archive.org.

———. "Jessia, dem Propheten, das gescha (1526)." In *The Handbook to The Lutheran Hymnal*, edited by W. Gustave Polack. St. Louis: Concordia, 1942.

———. *Luther's Correspondence and Other Contemporary Letters*. Vol. 2. Edited by Preserved Smith and Charles M. Jacobs. Philadelphia: The Lutheran Publication Society, 1913.

———. *Luther's Works*. American ed. 82 vols. St. Louis: Concordia; Philadelphia: Fortress, 1955–1986, 2009–.

———. *Sermons of Martin Luther*. Vol. 6. Edited by John Nicholas Lenker. Minneapolis: Luther Press, 1908.

———. *Sermons of Martin Luther: The Church Postils*. 8 vols. Edited by John Nicholas Lenker. Translated by John Nicholas Lenker et al. Reprint, Grand Rapids, MI: Baker Books, 1982, 1995.

Marlorat, Augustin. *Esaiae Prophetia, cum catholica expositione ecclesiastica, quam Augustinus Marloratus verbi dei minister, in sacris literis exercitatissimus, ex theologi omnium huius seculi praestentissimis excerpsit, suumque in eam symbolum contulit.* Geneva: Jean Le Preux, 1610 (1564).

Mayer, John. *A Commentary upon All the Prophets Both Great and Small: Wherein the Divers Translations and Expositions Both Literal and Mystical of All the Most Famous Commentators Both Ancient and Modern Are Propounded, Examined and Censured, for the Singular Benefit of All That Be Studious of the Holy Scriptures*. London: Abraham Miller and Ellen Cotes, 1652. Available online at the Digital Library of Classic Protestant Texts, https://search.alexanderstreet.com/tcpt.

Melanchthon, Philip. *Argumentum in Iesaima Prophetam*. In *Philippi Melanthonis opera quae supersunt omnia*, edited by Carl G. Bretschneider and Heinrich E. Bindseil, CR 13. Halle and Braunschweig, 1834–1860. Digital copy online at books.google.com.

———. *Isaias Propheta Hebraice, graece et latine / addita est autem duplex latina interpretatio, Hieronymi & Munsteri. Accesit & succincta difficiliorum Hebraicorum vocabulorum expositio, collecta per Sebastianum Munsterum ex Davidis Kimchi commentario*. Basel: Heinrich Petri, 1542. Digital copy online at www.e-rara.ch.

Müntzer, Thomas. "A Highly Provoked Defense." In *The Radical Reformation*, edited by Michael G. Baylor, 74-94. Cambridge: Cambridge University Press, 1991.

———. "The Prague Protest." In *The Radical Reformation*, edited by Michael G. Baylor, 1-10. Cambridge: Cambridge University Press, 1991.

Musculus, Wolfgang. *In Esaiam Prophetam Commentarii*. Basel: Johannes Herwagen, 1557. Digital copy online at books.google.com.

Nicholas of Lyra. Bibliorum Sacrorum cum Glossa Ordinaria . . . cum postilla Nicolai Lyrani. 6 vols. Venice, 1603.

Oecolampadius, Johannes. *In Iesaiam prophetam Hypomnematōn, hoc est, Commentariorum, Ioannis Oecolampadii Libri VI*. Basel: Andreas Cratander, 1525. Digital copy online at books.google.com.

Pellikan, Konrad. *Commentaria Bibliorum et Illa Brevia Quidem ac Catholica*. Vol. 1. Zurich: Christoph Froschouer, 1582. Digital copy online at books.google.com.

Pfeiffer, August. *Hermeneutica Sacra*. Leipzig: Brandianis, 1684.

Pinto, Hector. *In Esaiam Prophetam Commentaria*. Lyon: Theobald Paganus, 1572. Digital copy online at books.google.com.

Poole, Matthew. *Annotations Upon the Bible*. Vol 1. London: Printed by Thomas Parkhust, 1683. Digital copy online at EEBO.

Pratensis, Felix. *Biblia Rabbinica*. Venice: Bomberg, 1517.

Sasbout, Adam. *In Esaiam Prophetam Commentaria*. Leuven: Antoine-Marie Bergagne, 1558. Digital copy online at books.google.com.

Schnepff, Dietrich. *In Esaiae Prophetae vaticinia scholae*. Tübingen: George Gruppenbachius, 1575. Digital copy online at books.google.com.

Scultetus, Abraham. *Idea concionum in Jesaiam prophetam, ad populum Haidelbergensem habitarum*. Geneva: Petrus Aubertus, 1618. Digital copy online at books.google.com.

Simons, Menno. *Complete Works*. 2 vols. Elkhart, IN: John F. Funk and Brother, 1871. Digital copy online at ccel.org.

Strigel, Viktorin. *Libri Samuelis, Regum et Paralipomenon*. Leipzig: Ernst Vögelin, 1569. Digital copy online at books.google.com.

———. *Oratio De Propheta Esaia*. Leipzig: Ernst Vögelin, 1564. Digital copy online at books.google.com.

Tarabotti, Arcangela. *Paternal Tyranny*. Edited and translated by Letizia Panizza. Chicago: University of Chicago Press, 2004.

Trapp, John. *A commentary or exposition upon these following books of holy Scripture: Proverbs of Solomon, Ecclesiastes, the Song of Songs, Isaiah, Jeremiah, Lamentations, Ezekiel & Daniel; being a third volume of annotations upon the whole Bible*. London: Robert White for Nevil Simmons, 1660. Digital copy available on EBBO.

Ursinus, Zacharias. *Commentarius in Iesaiam*. In *Uratislaviensis Tractationum Theologicarum*. Vol. 2. Neustadt, 1589. Digital copy available online at Staatsbibliothek zu Berlin, resolver.staatsbibliothek-berlin.de.

Zell, Katharina Schütz. *Katharina Schütz Zell, Church Mother*. Edited and translated by Elise McKee. Chicago: University of Chicago Press, 2006.

Zwingli, Ulrich. *Homilien zum Propheten Jesaja (zweite Parallelüberlieferung): Sermones populares ac vulgares ex propheta Esaia*. CR102 [=ZE 3; = ZSW 15].

———. *Jesaja-Erklärungen: Complanationes Isaiae prophetae foetura prima, cum apologia qur quidque sic versum sit*. CR 101 [=ZE 3; = ZSW 14].

Author and Writings Index

Subject Index

Scripture Index